Monte Carlo Frameworks

*Building customisable high-performance
C++ applications*

Daniel J. Duffy

Jörg Kienitz

A John Wiley and Sons, Ltd., Publication

Registered office
John Wiley & Sons Ltd, The Atrium, Southern Gate, Chichester, West Sussex, PO19 8SQ, United Kingdom

For details of our global editorial offices, for customer services and for information about how to apply for permission to reuse the copyright material in this book please see our website at www.wiley.com.

Library of Congress Cataloging-in-Publication Data

Duffy, Daniel J.
   Monte Carlo frameworks : building customisable high performance C^{++} applications / Daniel J. Duffy, Joerg Kienitz.
     p. cm.
   ISBN 978-0-470-06069-8 (cloth)
   1. Finance–Mathematical models.   2. Monte Carlo method.   3. C^{++} (Computer program language)
I. Kienitz, Joerg. II. Title.
   HG106.D84 2009
   518′.28202855133–dc22

                                                             2009021640

A catalogue record for this book is available from the British Library.

ISBN 978-0-470-06069-8

Typeset in 10/12pt Times by Aptara Inc., New Delhi, India
Printed in Great Britain by Antony Rowe, Chippenhan, Wiltshire

To Brendan and Ilona
Daniel

To Amberley, Beatrice and Benoît
Joerg

Contents

Notation

This section contains a list of the notation used in Chapters 7, 14 to 20, 22, 23, and 26 which are written by Joerg Kienitz. The notation for the remaining chapters, written by Daniel Duffy, is in situ.

$(\cdot)^+$	$\max(\cdot, 0)$
$\{t_1, t_2, \ldots, t_N\}$	A discrete set of time points
α	Parameter
χ^2	χ^2 distribution
ϵ	Small number
$\frac{\partial}{\partial \phi}$	Partial derivative with respect to ϕ
Γ	Gamma distribution, second order Greek
$\hat{C}_t^k(x)$	Expected continuation value estimator
$\hat{Cov}$	Estimator for covariance
$\hat{I}$	Estimator
$\hat{V}$	Estimator of the payoff V
$\hat{V}_{IS}$	Importance sampling estimator
$\hat{V}_C$	Control variate estimator of the payoff V
κ	Mean reversion rate (Heston/Bates model)
λ	Jump intensity
λ_i	Eigenvalue
$\mathbb{C}$	Complex numbers
$\mathbb{E}$	Expectation
$\mathbb{N}$	Positive integers
$\mathbb{P}$	Probability measure
$\mathbb{R}$	Real line
$\mathbb{R}^+$	Positive real line
$\mathbb{V}$	Variance
$\mathcal{F}$	σ algebra
$\mathcal{F}_t$	Filtration
$\mathcal{N}(\mu, \sigma^2)$	Normal distribution with mean μ and variance σ^2
$\mathcal{R}$	Real part of a complex number
$\mathcal{T}$	A discrete set of time points
$\mathcal{T}_{Ex}$	Exercise schedule

μ_J	Mean jump rate for (log)normal jumps
Ω	Probability space
ω	Realisation
ω_{Model}	Martingale correction
$\oplus$	Integer arithmetic $+$
Φ	Long-term variance
ϕ	Characteristic function
π	Transition kernel
ψ_i	Basis function
ρ	Correlation
σ	Volatility
Σ	Correlation matrix
σ_J	Volatility of jumps for (log)normal jumps
τ	Stopping time
ξ	Volatility of variance
$<\cdot,\cdot>$	Scalar product
$1_{\{\ldots\}}$	Indicator function
A^T	Transposed matrix
$C_t^R(x)$	Realised continuation value
Cov	Covariance
d	Dividend
D_∞^*	*-discrepancy
$diag$	Diagonal matrix
dJ	Jump part of stochastic differential equation
dW	White noise
f, g	Functions
H	Barrier level
h	Payoff function
$h(\cdot)$	Payoff function
i	Imaginary number $i = \sqrt{-1}$
K	Strike
K_λ	Bessel function
$L(t)$	Lévy process
$M(t)$	Martingale process
max	Maximum of several variables
min	Minimum of several variables
$N(t)$	Counting process
r	Riskless rate
$r(t)$	Short rate process
R_i	Return relative
RSC	Reverse Swing Cliquet payoff
$S(t)$	Spot price process
$S_{AA}^{\mathcal{T}}$	Arithmetic average with respect to the set $\mathcal{T}$
$S_{GA}^{\mathcal{T}}$	Geometric average with respect to the set $\mathcal{T}$
SC	Swing Cliquet payoff
T	Maturity
t_n	Time point

v_i, m_i	Direction numbers (different representation)
$V_t(\cdot)$	Value of derivative at time t
W	Brownian motion
$X(t)$	Logarithm of the spot price
X, S, Y, Z	Random variable
$Y(t)$	Stochastic process
Z	Gaussian random variable

Executive Overview

WHAT IS THIS BOOK?

The goal of this book is to price one-factor and multi-factor equity options using the Monte Carlo method. In this essentially self-contained book we define the financial models and the underlying mathematical theory for this class of options and we then design the corresponding algorithms using a number of numerical techniques (such as the finite difference method). Having created the algorithms we design the software applications using design and system patterns in C++. Finally, we use the Standard Template Library (STL) and the Boost library suite whenever possible because of their robustness and suitability for applications in computational finance. In short, we have attempted to trace the steps that produce a working software program in C++ from a given financial model.

WHAT'S SPECIAL ABOUT THIS BOOK?

This is the first book in our opinion that discusses the *complete software lifecycle* of the Monte Carlo simulation process for computational finance. In particular, the book introduces the most important issues and topics in Monte Carlo simulation:

- The mathematical theory of stochastic differential equations.
- The Finite Difference Method (FDM) for Monte Carlo.
- One-factor and n-factor option pricing problems.
- Option sensitivities; early exercise features.
- Stochastic volatility and jump models.
- System and design patterns (GOF, POSA).
- Standard libraries (STL, Boost, OpenMP).

Furthermore, we provide working source code for the examples in the book and each chapter has numerous practical exercises and projects that you work on and will be helpful when you wish to extend the software framework. Each exercise is ranked according to its level of difficulty using a 'star system'; simple exercises are denoted as '*' and the most difficult exercises are '*****'. We have attempted to make the book as self-contained as possible by introducing the financial and mathematical underpinnings of the Monte Carlo method. We also give a discussion of advanced C++ and design patterns. This book assumes C++ knowledge to the level discussed in Duffy (2006a), for example.

WHO IS THIS BOOK FOR?

This hands-on book is for those developers, quantitative analysts, designers and modellers who wish to understand the Monte Carlo method, apply it to computational finance and improve their C++ and software design skills. We have written the book in such a way that the reader can learn the material by examining and running test models before moving to more advanced ones. This book is also of interest to those finance professionals who work in model validation and risk management. Finally, we expect the book to be useful to non-financial people such as engineers, mathematical and software developers who wish to gain an understanding of financial models and how to implement them in C++. We assume that the reader has a working knowledge of C++; this is not a book for C++ novices!

THE STRUCTURE OF THIS BOOK

This book contains four major parts and these comprise 27 chapters in total.

Part I deals with the mathematical and numerical background to the Monte Carlo method. We discuss Lebesgue integration, stochastic differential equations, the Finite Difference Method (FDM) as well as specific finance examples such as stochastic volatility models. The added value of Part I is that it contains much of the mathematical foundation needed for an understanding of Monte Carlo simulation.

Part II is devoted to state-of-the-art object-oriented (OOP) and generic (C++ template) programming (GP) techniques, how to use them, how to combine them and how to apply them to computational finance. We show how the appropriate use of OOP and GP can improve the flexibility and robustness of applications. Furthermore, in this part we review the famous GOF and POSA patterns and we show how a subset of these patterns is vital to the creation of a flexible software framework, in particular *Whole-Part*, *Presentation-Abstraction-Control*, *Bridge* and *Adapter*, to name a few. The added value of Part II is that we use advanced C++ programming models and design patterns to produce flexible designs for Monte Carlo applications.

Part III focuses on the application of the Monte Carlo methods to financial applications. We consider path-dependent and multi-asset options. We apply popular stochastic volatility models, models based on exponential Lévy processes and we apply variance reduction techniques to calculate prices of options. Finally, we show how to obtain Greeks and prices for options including early exercise features. The added value of Part III is that it introduces a range of option pricing models and maps them to C++.

Part IV contains background information on a number of topics that are related to the chapters in the first three parts of the book. First, we discuss how to improve the performance of C++ code by avoiding temporary object creation, loop optimisation and by using function objects instead of C-style function pointers. Furthermore, we give an introduction to the design of parallel programs and how to implement them in the OpenMP library, a de facto standard for the creation of multi-threaded applications in shared memory computers. We also devote a chapter to describing how to integrate C++ code with the Excel spreadsheet program using COM and Automation addins. Finally, we devote two chapters to random number generation and other mathematical methods that are needed in this book. The added value of Part IV is the detailed discussion of a number of supporting techniques that add to the robustness, efficiency and flexibility of C++ applications.

HOW CAN I USE THIS BOOK?

After having studied this book, and reviewed and run the code on the CD, you should then have a good understanding of how to create your own Monte Carlo models. There are different ways to achieve this end and seeing that the book consists of 27 chapters we think it is necessary to discuss *how* to read these chapters (and in which order). Some scenarios are:

- Reading the chapters in Parts I, II and III in that order. This is the standard route and it is suitable for those readers who wish to learn the Monte Carlo method in a step-by-step fashion.
- For those readers who wish to start developing their own applications as soon as possible, we advise reading Chapters 4 and 5, moving to the chapters in Part II and then finally examining the code and models for the one-factor and *n*-factor problems in Part III.
- The small software framework in Chapter 0 can be generalised to more complex applications, especially when this process is executed in conjunction with the design and system patterns of Chapters 9, 10, 11 and 12.

Of course, there are many other ways to use the book but the above list may be a useful starting point.

WHAT THIS BOOK IS NOT

This is not a book on how to learn C++. We assume that the reader has a good working knowledge of object-oriented aspects of the language (such as inheritance, composition and polymorphism). We assume some knowledge of STL and template programming to the level that is discussed in Duffy (2004a) and Duffy (2006a). **The code on the CD is not a software package.**

SOURCE CODE, SUPPORT AND CONTACT

You may use the code on the CD for your personal use and in your own applications only. For feedback, (constructive) criticisms and suggestions, please send to **www.datasimfinancial.com** where you can join our forum free of charge. **We have done our utmost to check for typos and errors in the book; if you find any we would be most grateful if you bring them to our attention. We will correct them in the next edition of the book.**

ACKNOWLEDGEMENTS

Daniel Duffy would like to thank all those finance professionals whom he has trained and been in contact with. He thanks Ilona and his son Brendan for their patience during the writing and preparation of this book.

Joerg Kienitz is indebted to his children Amberley and Benoît and his wife Beatrice for their patience and their encouragement. Sometimes it was a burden for them also. He furthermore thanks Daniel Wetterau for fruitful discussions about financial modelling and coding, and finally, Guido Behrendt, Albrecht Flues and Horst Küpker for their (job related) support.

My First Monte Carlo Application
One-Factor Problems

Get it working, then get it right, then get it optimised

0.1 INTRODUCTION AND OBJECTIVES

The goal of this book is to develop algorithms for pricing a range of derivatives products and then mapping these algorithms to C++ code. The technique that we use is the Monte Carlo method. Part I of this book introduces the fundamental mathematical concepts, algorithms and a number of C++ programming techniques that are needed when using the Monte Carlo method.

The main goal in this chapter is to design and implement an initial C++ framework – consisting of a set of loosely coupled classes – that calculate the price of plain one-factor options. The framework has limited functionality and scope but it is structured in such a way that it can be – and will be – extended and generalised to n-factor and path-dependent problems as well as to problems with early exercise features. Some of the features discussed in this chapter are:

- Simple one-dimensional stochastic differential equations (SDE), their formulation and how to find exact and approximate solutions to them.
- Generation of uniform and normal random numbers using random number generators such as Polar Marsaglia and Box-Muller.
- A short introduction to the Monte Carlo method and we apply it to finding the price of a one-factor European option.

In general, we partition the Monte Carlo application into three main subsystems. The core process in the application is to calculate the price of an option by simulation of the path of the underlying variable. We can also develop functionality that displays other relevant information, for example sensitivities or statistics.

This chapter is a self-contained introduction to the Monte Carlo method and its realisation in C++. It can be read by those who are new to the subject as well as by those who have programming experience. You can test your knowledge of C++ by examining and running the corresponding code on the CD. **If the syntax is difficult to understand, then this means that your C++ knowledge needs to be refreshed!**

0.2 DESCRIPTION OF THE PROBLEM

We focus on a linear, constant-coefficient, scalar (one-factor) problem. In particular, we examine the case of a one-factor European call option using the assumptions for the original Black Scholes equation (see Clewlow and Strickland, 1998). We give an overview of the process.

At the expiry date $t = T$ the option price is known as a function of the current stock price and the strike price. The essence of the Monte Carlo method is that we carry out a *simulation experiment* by finding the solution of a *stochastic differential equation* (SDE) from time $t = 0$ to time $t = T$. This process allows us to compute the stock price at $t = T$ and then the option price using the payoff function. We carry out M *simulations* or *draws* by finding the solution of the SDE and we calculate the option price at $t = T$. Finally, we calculate the discounted average of the simulated payoff and we are done.

Summarising, the process is:

1. Construct a simulated path of the underlying stock.
2. Calculate the stock price at $t = T$.
3. Calculate the call price at $t = T$ (use the payoff function).

Execute steps 1–3 M times.

4. Calculate the averaged call price at $t = T$.
5. Discount the price found in step 4 to $t = 0$.

We elaborate this process in the rest of this chapter. We first need to provide some background information.

0.3   ORDINARY DIFFERENTIAL EQUATIONS (ODE)

We examine some simple ODEs. In general, the specification of an initial value problem (IVP) for an ODE is given by

$$\frac{du}{dt} + a(t)u = f(t), \quad 0 < t \leq T$$
$$u(0) = A \tag{0.1}$$

We see that the IVP consists of a linear ODE with a corresponding *initial condition* A. The term $f(t)$ is sometimes called the *inhomogeneous forcing term*. We note that all functions in system (0.1) are deterministic. We can find an exact solution to the system (0.1) by using the *integrating factor method*; in the case when the forcing term is identically zero the solution to (0.1) is given by:

$$u(t) = A \exp\left(-\int_0^t a(s)ds\right) \tag{0.2}$$

ODEs can be used to model simple problems in quantitative finance, for example bond modelling where the interest rate $r(t)$ is a deterministic function of time. If V is the price of the security, then it satisfies the *terminal value problem* (TVP) (Wilmott, Howison and Dewynne, 1995, page 267):

$$\frac{dV}{dt} + K(t) = r(t)V, \quad K(t) = \text{coupon payment}$$
$$V(T) = Z \tag{0.3}$$

We see that the solution is given at $t = T$. This is in contrast to system (0.1) where the value is given at $t = 0$ (we can reduce (0.3) to an initial value problem of the type (0.1) by using a change of variables $\tau = T - t$). We see that the solution of system (0.3) is given by:

$$V(t) = \exp\left(-\int_t^T r(s)ds\right)\left\{Z + \int_t^T K(y)\exp\left(\int_y^T r(s)ds\right)dy\right\} \tag{0.4}$$

If we have a look at system (0.1) again we can see that it is possible to integrate it between times 0 and t:

$$u(t) - u(0) + \int_0^t a(s)u(s)ds = \int_0^t f(s)ds, \quad 0 < t \le T \tag{0.5}$$

This is called a *Volterra integral equation of the second kind* and is given formally as:

$$u(t) + \int_0^t a(s)u(s)ds = F(t) \tag{0.6}$$

$$\text{where } F(t) = \int_0^t f(s)ds + u(0) = \int_0^t f(s)ds + A$$

In this case the function $a = a(s)$ plays the role of the *kernel* and the limit of integration t is variable.

0.4 STOCHASTIC DIFFERENTIAL EQUATIONS (SDE) AND THEIR SOLUTION

We now generalise the deterministic equations that we introduced in section 0.3. In this case we add some random or stochastic terms to the ODE. To this end, we introduce notation that is used in texts on stochastic equations. In general, we denote dependence on time t for a stochastic process X as follows:

$$X_t \equiv X(t) \tag{0.7}$$

Both forms are used in the literature. We must be aware of each form because they are used in many places, including this book. Our first example of an SDE is

$$dX_t = aX_t dt + bX_t W_t \quad a, b \text{ constant}$$
$$W_t = W(t) \text{ (one-dimensional Brownian motion)} \tag{0.8}$$

In this case the equation describes the changes in the stochastic process X_t. The constants a and b are called the *drift* and *diffusion* terms, respectively. Furthermore, we see the presence of the Wiener process W_t. We shall deal with these topics in more detail in later chapters.

A more general SDE is

$$dS_t = \mu(t)S_t dt + \sigma(t)S_t dW_t \tag{0.9}$$

where

$\mu(t)$ is the drift coefficient

$\sigma(t)$ is the diffusion coefficient

This is a model for the evolution of a stock in a certain time interval. Again, we note the presence of a Wiener process in the equation. We usually write the SDE in the 'differential' form (0.9); we can also write the SDE in the integral form:

$$S_t = S_0 + \int_0^t \mu(y)S_y dy + \int_0^t \sigma(y)S_y dW_y \tag{0.10}$$

This equation characterises the behaviour of the continuous time stochastic process S_t as the sum of a Lebesgue integral and an Ito integral. A heuristic explanation of the SDE (0.10) is that the stochastic process S_t changes by an amount that is normally distributed. We say that the stochastic process is a *diffusion process* and is an example of a *Markov process*. When the drift and diffusion terms in system (0.9) are constant we can express the solution in analytic form:

$$S_t = S_0 \exp((\mu - \tfrac{1}{2}\sigma^2)t + \sigma W_t) \tag{0.11}$$

Finally, the values of the stochastic process at two different points are related by

$$S_{t+\Delta t} = S_t \exp((\mu - \tfrac{1}{2}\sigma^2)\Delta t + \sigma(W_{t+\Delta t} - W_t))$$
$$\text{where } \Delta t > 0 \text{ is arbitrary} \tag{0.12}$$

You can check that this result is correct.

0.5   GENERATING UNIFORM AND NORMAL RANDOM NUMBERS

We discuss the generation of random numbers. In particular, we generate random Gaussian numbers for the Wiener process appearing in equations (0.8) and (0.9).

0.5.1   Uniform random number generation

Our starting point is the generation of numbers having a *uniform distribution*. To this end, let us suppose that X is a continuous random variable assuming all values in the closed interval $[a, b]$, where a and b are finite. If the *probability density function* (pdf) of X is given by

$$f(x) = \begin{cases} \frac{1}{b-a}, & a \le x \le b \\ 0, & \text{otherwise} \end{cases} \tag{0.13}$$

then we say that X is *uniformly distributed* over the interval $[a, b]$. A shorthand notation is to say that X is $U(a, b)$. We generate uniformly distributed random numbers by using an algorithm that has been programmed in C or C++.

We now introduce two methods that were popular a number of years ago. We include a discussion of them for historical and pedagogical reasons. We also introduced them in the context of the numerical solution of SDEs in Duffy (2004a).

0.5.2   Polar Marsaglia method

This method uses the fact that if the random variable U is $U(0, 1)$ then the random variable V defined by $V = 2U - 1$ is $U(-1, 1)$. We now choose two variables defined by

$$V_j = 2U_j - 1, \quad U_j \sim U(0, 1), \quad j = 1, 2 \tag{0.14}$$

Then we define

$$W = V_1^2 + V_2^2 \leq 1, \quad W \sim U(0, 1)$$

We keep trying with different values until the above inequality is satisfied. Continuing, we define the intermediate value:

$$Y = \sqrt{-2\log(W)/W}$$

Finally, the pair of values defined by

$$N_j = V_j Y, \quad j = 1, 2$$

constittutes two standard normally (Gaussian) distributed random variables, and we are done.

0.5.3   Box-Muller method

This method is based on the observation that if r and φ are two independent $U(0, 1)$ random variables then the variables

$$N_1 = \sqrt{-2\log r}\cos(2\pi\varphi)$$
$$N_2 = \sqrt{-2\log r}\sin(2\pi\varphi)$$

(0.15)

are two independent standard Gaussian random variables.

0.5.4   C++ code for uniform and normal random variate generation

Central to the accuracy of the Monte Carlo method is the ability to generate normal random variates. In this section we create C++ classes that compute these numbers. In general, we first generate uniform random variates and based on these variates we then generate the corresponding normal variates. We discuss these issues in more detail in Chapter 22. At this stage, however, we just need to use the corresponding generators. Please note that we use the authors' classes for vectors and matrices (as described in Duffy, 2004a; Duffy 2006a).

The abstract base class for uniform generators is

```
class UniformGenerator
{
private:

public:
   UniformGenerator();

   // Initialisation and setting the seed
   virtual void init(long Seed) = 0;

   // Getting random structures (Template Method pattern)
   virtual double getUniform() = 0;// Number in range (0,1), variant
   Vector<double, long> getUniformVector(long N); // Invariant part


};
```

Derived classes must implement the pure virtual functions for defining a seed and a single random number. For example, the generator for uniform random variate generation based on the rand() function is

```
class TerribleRandGenerator : public UniformGenerator
{ // Based on the infamous rand(), that's why it's terrible

private:
    double factor;

public:
    TerribleRandGenerator();

    // Initialise the seed, among others
    void init(long Seed_);

    // Implement (variant) hook function
    double getUniform();
};
```

We have defined other generators and the C++ code can be found on the CD. Continuing, the abstract base class for normal random variate generation is given by

```
class NormalGenerator
{
protected:

    UniformGenerator* ug;       // This is a strategy object

public:
    NormalGenerator(UniformGenerator& uniformGen);

    // Getting random structures (Template Method pattern)
    virtual double getNormal() = 0;    // Get a number in (0,1)

    Vector<double, long> getNormalVector(long N);
    NumericMatrix<double, long> getNormalMatrix(long N, long M);
};
```

The code that generates a vector of normal random variates is

```
// Getting random structures (Template Method Pattern)
Vector<double, long> NormalGenerator::getNormalVector(long N)
{ // Invariant part

    Vector<double, long> vec(N);

    for(long i=vec.MinIndex(); i<=vec.MaxIndex();  ++i)
    {
        vec[i] = getNormal();
    }
    return vec;
}
```

Derived classes must implement the pure virtual function getNormal() for defining a random number. For example, here is the interface for generating standard normal variates based on the Box-Muller method:

```
class BoxMuller : public NormalGenerator
{
private:
    double U1, U2;      // Uniform numbers
    double N1, N2;      // 2 Normal numbers as product of BM

    double W;
    const double tpi;
public:
    BoxMuller(UniformGenerator& uniformGen);

    // Implement (variant) hook function
    double getNormal();
};
```

The code for this generator is based on equation (0.15) and is given by

```
// Implement (variant) hook function
double BoxMuller::getNormal()
{

    U1 = ug->getUniform();
    U2 = ug->getUniform();
    W = sqrt( -2.0 * log(U1));

    N1 = W * cos(tpi * U2);
    N2 = W * sin(tpi * U2);

    return N1;
}
```

We give an example of use. First, we define a uniform random variate and then use this object to generate a normal random variate:

```
    // Based on rand()
    TerribleRandGenerator myTerrible;
    myTerrible.init(0);
    NormalGenerator* myNormal = new BoxMuller(myTerrible);
    Vector<double, long> arr2 = myNormal->getNormalVector(100);

    NumericMatrix<double, long> mat =
        myNormal -> getNormalMatrix(5, 6);

    delete myNormal;
```

Finally, here is an example using a numerical recipes (Press *et al.*, 2002) algorithm:

```
    Ran1 myRan1;              // This is a derived class
    myRan1.init(447);
    Vector<double, long> arrRan1 = myRan1.getUniformVector(20);
```

0.5.5 Other methods

The above methods are somewhat outdated. They have been superseded by other methods such as Mersenne-Twister and lagged Fibonacci generators and by methods for generating random numbers on multi-processor computers. We shall discuss these issues in more detail in later chapters.

0.6   THE MONTE CARLO METHOD

In this section we describe the steps to price a one-factor option using the Monte Carlo method. We have already assembled the building blocks in the previous sections. We describe the algorithm and create working C++ code that computes pricing information for a simple one-factor model. There are several advantages associated with this approach. First, it is a concrete problem that we solve in detail while the simple software framework will be generalised to one based on design and system patterns in later chapters. We recall the SDE that describes the behaviour of a dividend-paying stock. The SDE is given by

$$dS_t = (r - D)S_t dt + \sigma S_t dW_t \tag{0.16}$$

where

$$r = \text{(constant) interest rate}$$
$$D = \text{constant dividend}$$
$$\sigma = \text{constant volatility}$$
$$dW_t = \text{increments of the Wiener process}$$

For the current problem it is possible to transform the SDE to a simpler one. To this end, define the variable:

$$x_t = \log(S_t) \tag{0.17}$$

Then the modified SDE is described as

$$dx_t = vdt + \sigma dW_t, \quad v \equiv r - D - \frac{1}{2}\sigma^2 \tag{0.18}$$

We now discretise this equation by replacing the continuously-defined quantities dx_t, dt and dW_t by their discrete analogues. This gives the following discrete stochastic equation:

$$\Delta x_t = v\Delta t + \sigma \Delta W_t$$

or $\tag{0.19}$

$$x_{t+\Delta t} = x_t + v\Delta t + \sigma(W_{t+\Delta t} - W_t)$$

Since $x_t = \log(S_t)$ we can see that equation (0.19) is equivalent to a discrete equation in the stock price S_t:

$$S_{t+\Delta t} = S_t \exp(v\Delta t + \sigma(W_{t+\Delta t} - W_t)) \tag{0.20}$$

In this case the Wiener increments have distribution

$$N(0, \Delta t) \tag{0.21}$$

Formulae (0.19) and (0.20) constitute the basic *path-generation algorithm*: we calculate the value in equation (0.20) at a set of discrete *mesh points*:

$$0 = t_0 < t_1 < \ldots < t_{N-1} < t_N = T$$
$$t_n = n\Delta t, \quad n = 0, \ldots, N$$
$$\Delta t = N/T$$

Then equation (0.20) takes the more computationally attractive form:

$$x_{t_n} = x_{t_{n-1}} + \nu\Delta t + \sigma\sqrt{\Delta t}\epsilon_n, \quad n = 1, \ldots, N \tag{0.22}$$

where

ϵ_n is a sample from $N(0, 1)$ and $S_{t_n} = \exp(x_{t_n})$

The next step is to run the algorithm in equation (0.22) M times (M is called the number of *simulations* or *draws*); for each price of the stock at $t = T$ we calculate the payoff function for a call option, namely:

$$\text{payoff} = \max(0, S_T - K) \tag{0.23}$$

This formula gives the value of the payoff, and we are done, almost. Finally, we calculate the average call price over all call prices (evaluated at $t = T$) and we take the discounted average of these *simulated paths*. Summarising, the basic algorithm for a call option is given by

$$\begin{array}{c} \text{For each } j = 1, \ldots, M \text{ calculate} \\ C_{T,j} = \max(0, S_{T,j} - K) \end{array} \tag{0.24}$$

and

$$\hat{C} = \exp(-rT)\frac{1}{M}\sum_{j=1}^{M}\max(0, S_{T,j} - K) \tag{0.25}$$

Then $\hat{C}$ is the desired call price.

0.7 CALCULATING SENSITIVITIES

The Monte Carlo method calculates the price of an option for a specific value of the underlying stock. In some applications we wish to calculate the derivative's *hedge sensitivities* (also known as the *Greeks*). These quantities are the partial derivatives of the price with respect to one of the option's parameters. Two of the most important ones are the *delta* and the *gamma*; in order to calculate these quantities we perturb the underlying price by a small amount and use centred finite difference schemes to approximate the derivatives. For example, the formulae for delta and gamma are

$$\delta = \frac{\partial C}{\partial S} \equiv \text{delta} \sim \frac{C(S + \Delta S) - C(S - \Delta S)}{2\Delta S}$$

$$\Gamma = \frac{\partial^2 C}{\partial S^2} = \frac{\partial \delta}{\partial S} = \text{gamma} \sim \frac{\delta(S + \Delta S) - \delta(S - \Delta S)}{2\Delta S} \tag{0.26}$$

In the above examples we have used centred-difference schemes to approximate the derivative. The approximations are second-order accurate if the security is sufficiently smooth.

Failing that, we sometimes take first-order one-sided finite difference approximations (see Duffy, 2006a, for a discussion).

We need values for sensitivities in order to manage risk. This is a major challenge for a Monte Carlo engine, from both a theoretical and a computational point of view. If we use finite difference methods, for example, we tend to get biased estimates (Glasserman, 2004).

We discuss some of the issues when computing sensitivities and we examine how to compute the delta as a representative example. To this end, we deploy the Monte Carlo engine with initial estimates of $S + \Delta S$ and $S - \Delta S$, where ΔS is a small fraction of S. We thus have to run the engine twice and we use the computed values in equation (0.26). On a single-processor CPU we must run the engine twice whereas on multi-processor CPUs we can run the calculations in parallel. Performance is an important issue when developing Monte Carlo code and we shall discuss this topic in more detail in Chapters 24 and 25.

The problems associated with estimating sensitivities in the Monte Carlo method and the associated techniques for approximating them are discussed in Part III.

0.8   THE INITIAL C++ MONTE CARLO FRAMEWORK: HIERARCHY AND PATHS

Since this is a book on the Monte Carlo method, its mathematical foundations and its implementation in C++, we now discuss how to integrate these threads into a working C++ program. In order to reduce the scope we create the code that computes the price of a one-factor plain option. We exclude non-essential details from the discussion and we focus on those issues that will help the reader understand the 'big picture' as it were. To this end, we start with the design of the problem, which we have created using design patterns (we discuss these in more detail in Part II of this book) and documented using a UML (Unified Modeling Language) class diagram, as shown in Figure 0.1. Each box represents a class (this is usually an abstract base class) and it has a clearly defined responsibility; each class is assigned a code for convenience and it corresponds to one of the following activities:

- A1: Defining and initialising the SDE (class B).
- A2: Random number generator (RNG) (class D).
- A3: Approximating the solution of the SDE using finite differences (class C).
- A4: Displaying the results and statistics (in class A).

We have defined a sophisticated factory class E (called a *builder*) that is responsible for the creation of the other objects, inter-object links and data in the application. Each class in Figure 0.1 has services (in the form of member functions) that it offers to other classes (called *clients*) while each class uses the services of other classes (called *servers*).

We describe the process for calculating an option price as follows:

We model a nonlinear one-factor SDE that describes the behaviour of an underlying asset. We approximate its solution by discretising the SDE using a finite-difference scheme (FDM), for example the Euler method. The FDM class uses the services of the RNG class that is an implementation of a random number generator (this is needed for the Wiener increments). The control of the program is the responsibility of the Mediator. Finally, the output is the responsibility of the Datasim Excel visualisation driver.

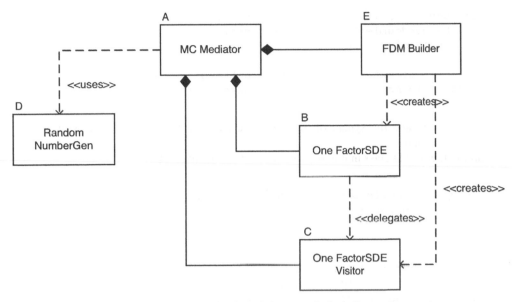

Figure 0.1   Top level class diagram for simple MC framework (including code names)

We now discuss classes B and C. These are the classes that model the various kinds of one-factor SDEs and the finite difference methods that approximate them, respectively. The class hierarchy for SDEs is shown in Figure 0.2; the derived classes are defined in terms of whether the drift and diffusion terms are linear or nonlinear. For example, for type D equations both terms are nonlinear. We mention that there are various ways to create class hierarchies. The interface for the base class SDE is given by

```
class OneFactorSDE
{
private:
    double ic;              // Initial condition
    Range<double> ran;      // Interval where SDE 'lives'
public:
    OneFactorSDE();
    OneFactorSDE(double initialCondition,
                 const Range<double>& interval)
```

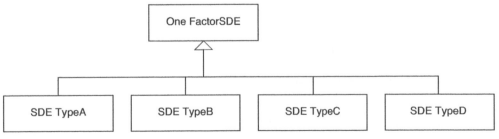

Figure 0.2   SDE hierarchy

```
const double& InitialCondition() const;
const Range<double>& Interval() const;
double getExpiry() const;

// Functional extensions (Visitor pattern, see Part II)
virtual void Accept(OneFactorSDEVisitor& visitor) = 0;
};
```

You should understand the syntax of this code because this book assumes that you are already a C++ developer.

We examine the type D class in this section. Its interface is given by

```
class SDETypeD : public OneFactorSDE
{ // Nonlinear/nonlinear case

private:

    // General function pointers
    double (*drift) (double t, double X);
    double (*diffusion) (double t, double X);

public:
    SDETypeD() : OneFactorSDE();
    SDETypeD(double initialCondition, const Range<double>& interval,
            double (*driftFunction) (double t, double X),
            double (*diffusionFunction) (double t, double X));

    // Selector functions
    double calculateDrift (double t, double X) const;
    double calculateDiffusion (double t, double X) const

    virtual void Accept(OneFactorSDEVisitor& visitor);

};
```

We instantiate this class by defining the initial condition, the interval in which the SDE is defined as well as its drift and diffusion functions. In this chapter we define this information in a namespace defined by

```
namespace ExactSDE
{ // Known solution, dS = aSdt + bSdW

    double a; // Drift
    double b; // Diffusion

    double drift(double t, double X)
    {

        return a*X;

    }
```

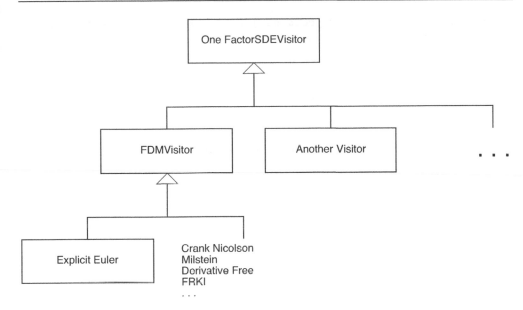

Figure 0.3 FDM hierarchy

```
double diffusion(double t, double X)
{

    return b*X;
}

} // End ExactSDE
```

We shall see how this information is used to instantiate a type D class.

Turning to the finite difference schemes, we show the class hierarchy in Figure 0.3. We have implemented it as a *Visitor* design pattern (GOF, 1995) because this allows us to add new functionality to an SDE in a nonintrusive way. We discuss this pattern in more detail in Part II. The top-level abstract base class in Figure 0.3 has the interface:

```
class OneFactorSDEVisitor
{ // Inline code

private:
public:
    // Constructors and Destructor
    OneFactorSDEVisitor() {}                          // Default constructor
    OneFactorSDEVisitor(const OneFactorSDEVisitor& source) {}
    virtual ~OneFactorSDEVisitor() {}

    // The visit functions
    virtual void Visit(SDETypeA& sde)=0;    // Linear/Linear
    //virtual void Visit(SDETypeB& sde)=0;  // L/NL (for reader)
```

```
    //virtual void Visit(SDETypeC& sde)=0;  // NL/L (for reader)
    virtual void Visit(SDETypeD& sde)=0;    // NL/NL


    // Operators
    OneFactorSDEVisitor& operator =
          (const OneFactorSDEVisitor& source) {}
};
```

The base class for all finite difference schemes has the interface

```
class FDMVisitor : public OneFactorSDEVisitor
{ // Base class for all schemes

//protected:
public: // For convenience, ONLY

    // Initial conditions
    double initVal, VOld;
    // Solution at time level n+1
    double VNew;

    // Mesh data (Vector<T,I> is authors' class)
    Vector<double, long> x;
    double k;                   // Time step
    double sqrk; // Square root of k (for dW stuff)

    // Result path
    Vector<double, long> res;

    // Random numbers
    Vector<double, long> dW;

    // Number of steps
    long N;

public:
    FDMVisitor(long NSteps, const Range<double>& interval,
               double initialValue);
    FDMVisitor(long NSteps, const OneFactorSDE& sde);

    void SetRandomArray(const Vector<double,long>& randomArray);

    virtual Vector<double, long> path() const;

    long getNumberOfSteps() const;
};
```

We can now define (many) specific finite difference schemes to approximate the various SDE types. We examine the explicit Euler scheme for convenience; its interface is defined by

```
class ExplicitEuler : public FDMVisitor
{
public:
     ExplicitEuler(long NSteps, const Range<double> & interval,
                      double initialValue);
     ExplicitEuler(long NSteps, const OneFactorSDE& sde);

     void Visit(SDETypeA& sde);
     void Visit(SDETypeD& sde);
};
```

The corresponding code file is

```
// Euler Method
ExplicitEuler::ExplicitEuler(long NSteps, const Range<double>
 & interval,double initialValue )
                     : FDMVisitor(NSteps, interval, initialValue)
{


}

ExplicitEuler::ExplicitEuler(long NSteps, const OneFactorSDE& sde)
                     : FDMVisitor(NSteps, sde)
{


}

void ExplicitEuler::Visit(SDETypeA& sde)
{
  VOld = initVal;
  res[x.MinIndex()] = VOld;
  for (long index = x.MinIndex()+1; index <= x.MaxIndex(); ++index)
  {
          VNew = VOld *(1.0 + k * sde.calculateDrift(x[index-1])+
             sqrk * sde.calculateDiffusion(x[index-1]) * dW[index-1]);

          res[index] = VNew;
  VOld = VNew;
      }
}

void ExplicitEuler::Visit(SDETypeD& sde)
{
  VOld = initVal;
  res[x.MinIndex()] = VOld;
  for (long index = x.MinIndex()+1; index <= x.MaxIndex(); ++index)
  {
          VNew = VOld  + k * sde.calculateDrift(x[index-1], VOld)+
             sqrk*sde.calculateDiffusion(x[index-1], VOld)*dW[index-1];
```

```
        res[index] = VNew;
        VOld = VNew;
    }
}
```

We now discuss some schemes to calculate the path of the following nonlinear autonomous SDE:

$$
\begin{aligned}
dX(t) &= \mu(X(t))dt + \sigma(X(t))dW(t) \quad 0 < t \leq T \\
X(0) &= A
\end{aligned}
\tag{0.27}
$$

We discretise the interval $[0, T]$ into N subintervals and we adopt the notation

$$
\mu_n \equiv \mu(X_n), \quad \sigma_n = \sigma(X_n) \quad n = 0, \ldots, N, \ \Delta W_n = \sqrt{\Delta t} Z, \ Z \sim N(0, 1)
$$

We have created classes for some other finite difference schemes (from Saito, 1996) and you can find the code on the CD:

- Explicit Euler:

$$
X_{n+1} = X_n + \mu_n \Delta t + \sigma_n \Delta W_n
\tag{0.28}
$$

- Semi-implicit Euler:

$$
X_{n+1} = X_n + [\alpha \mu_{n+1} + (1 - \alpha)\mu_n]\Delta t + \sigma_n \Delta W_n
$$

  with special cases
  $\alpha = \frac{1}{2}$ (Trapezoidal)
  $\alpha = 1$ (Backward Euler)
  $\tag{0.29}$

- Heun:

$$
X_{n+1} = X_n + \frac{1}{2}[F_1 + F_2]\Delta t + \frac{1}{2}[G_1 + G_2]\Delta W_n
$$

  where

$$
\begin{aligned}
F(x) &\equiv \mu(x) - \frac{1}{2}\sigma'(x)\sigma(x) \\
\sigma'(x) &\equiv \frac{d\sigma}{dx} \\
F_1 &= F(X_n), \quad G_1 = \sigma(X_n) \\
F_2 &= F(X_n + F_1\Delta t + G_1\Delta W_n) \\
G_2 &= \sigma(X_n + F_1\Delta t + G_1\Delta W_n)
\end{aligned}
\tag{0.30}
$$

- Milstein:

$$
X_{n+1} = X_n + \mu_n \Delta t + \sigma_n \Delta W_n + \frac{1}{2}[\sigma'\sigma]_n((\Delta W_n)^2 - \Delta t)
\tag{0.31}
$$

- Derivative-free:

$$X_{n+1} = X_n + F_1 \Delta t + G_1 \Delta W_n + [G_2 - G_1] \Delta t^{-1/2} \frac{(\Delta W_n)^2 - \Delta t}{2}$$

where

$$F_1 = \mu(X_n), \quad G_1 = \sigma(X_n)$$
$$G_2 = \sigma(X_n + G_1 \Delta t^{1/2})$$

(0.32)

- First-order Runge Kutta with Ito coefficient (FRKI):

$$X_{n+1} = X_n + F_1 \Delta t + G_2 \Delta W_n + [G_2 - G_1] \Delta t^{1/2}$$

where

$$F_1 = \mu(X_n), \quad G_1 = \sigma(X_n)$$
$$G_2 = \sigma(X_n + \frac{G_1(\Delta W_n \ \Delta t^{1/2})}{2})$$

(0.33)

We now discuss the code for calculating a path of the constant-coefficient SDE:

$$dX(t) = \mu X dt + \sigma X dW(t), \quad 0 \le t \le T$$
$$X(0) = 1$$

(0.34)

whose exact solution is

$$X(t) = \exp \left\{ \left(\mu - \frac{1}{2}\sigma^2 \right) t + \sigma W(t) \right\}$$

(0.35)

In this case we compare the path taken by the exact solution and the solution delivered by the scheme (0.32); we generate normal random variates using classes that we discussed in section 0.5. The code is

```
int main()
{

        // Define the array of random numbers and use this one
        long N = 3000;
        cout << "Give number of paths: "; cin >> N;

        // Create a U(0,1) and N(0,1) array
        MSSecureRandGenerator myUniform;            // .NET generator
        myUniform.init(0);
        NormalGenerator* myNormal = new BoxMuller(myUniform);
        Vector<double, long> dW = myNormal->getNormalVector(N+1);
        delete myNormal;


        // Create the basic SDE (Context class)
        double T = 1.0;
        cout << "Give the value of T:"; cin >> T;

        Range<double> ran (0.0, T);
```

```
Vector<double, long> x = ran.mesh(N);
double ic = 1.0;

// Choose the drift and diffusion functions
// using namespace GenericNLDiffusion;
using namespace ExactSDE;
cout << "Give drift: "; cin >> a;
cout << "Give diffusion: "; cin >> b;

// Create the nonlinear SDE object
SDETypeD sde(ic, ran, drift, diffusion);

// Choose the FDM scheme (Visitor pattern)
DerivativeFree visitor (N, ran, ic);
// or Euler method . . .

// Choose the array of N(0,1) numbers
visitor.SetRandomArray(dW);

// Calculate the FDM 'path'
sde.Accept(visitor);
Vector<double, long> result = visitor.path();

try
{
printOneExcel(x,                        // Abscissa array
    result,
     string("Derivative Free"),    // The title of the chart
     string("time"),               // The title of x axis
     string("Underlying"),         // The title of y axis
     string("Value"));             // Legend describing
                                        the line graph
}
catch(DatasimException& e)
{ // Catch logical errors

     e.print();
}

Vector<double, long> exactSolution =
               GBMRandomWalk(ic, a, b, T, N, dW);

try
{
printOneExcel(x,                          // Abscissa array
     exactSolution,
     string("Exact path solution"),   // The title of the chart
     string("time"),                  // The title of x axis
     string("Underlying"),            // The title of y axis
     string("Value"));                // Legend describing
                                          the line graph
```

```
    }
    catch(DatasimException& e)
    { // Catch logical errors

        e.print();
    }
    return 0;
}
```

You can run this program to see the results. The output is presented in Excel. You can easily adapt the code to test other schemes, for example the Euler method.

0.9 THE INITIAL C++ MONTE CARLO FRAMEWORK: CALCULATING OPTION PRICE

We now extend the results of section 0.8. In particular, we focus on:

- Modelling option data and payoff functions.
- The structure of Monte Carlo algorithm.
- Initialising and creating the object network in Figure 0.1.

First, since we are interested in calculating option prices it is useful to encapsulate all relevant information in a structure. To this end, we define the structure:

```
struct OptionData
{ // Option data + behaviour

    double K;
    double T;
    double r;
    double sig;

    double myPayOffFunction(double S)
    { // Call option


        return max (S - K, 0);
    }
};
```

All data and functions are public (by default). Second, the MCMediator class integrates all control and data flow in the application. Its internal structure and public interface reflect the UML class diagram in Figure 0.1:

```
class MCMediator
{
private:
    FDMTypeDBuilder* bld;    // Creates SDE and FDM objects
    long NSim;               // Number of simulations,for discounting
```

```
      OptionData* opt;

      double (*payoff) (double S);

      OneFactorSDE* sde;
      FDMVisitor* fdm;
public:
      MCMediator(FDMTypeDBuilder& builder, long NSimulations,
                 OptionData& optionData);
      double price() const;
};
```

Here we see that this class has a member function `price()` for calculating the option price. We break the body of this function into logical blocks and we explain each block in turn:

- A: Loop over each iteration.
- B: Find value at $t = T$.
- C: Return the vectors and calculate payoff vectors and average.
- D: Discount the value.

We first need to define arrays, variables and other 'work' data structures:

```
      // The critical variables in the MC process
      double price;      // Option price

      // Create the random numbers
      long N = fdm->getNumberOfSteps();

      // The array of values of the payoff function at t = T
      Vector<double, long > TerminalValue(NSim, 1);

      // The vector of UNDERLYING values at t = T;
      Vector<double, long> result(N+1, 1);

      // Array of normal random numbers
      Vector<double, long> dW(N+1, 1);

      // Create a U(0,1) and N(0,1) array
      MSSecureRandGenerator myUniform;            // .NET generator
      //TerribleRandGenerator myUniform;          // rand()
      // OR YOUR FAVOURITE!
      myUniform.init(0);
      NormalGenerator* myNormal = new BoxMuller(myUniform);

      // Work variables
      double sqrT = sqrt(opt->T);
```

Step A involves calculating the paths based on the SDE and finite difference method that we have already discussed in section 0.8. We produce a vector `TerminalValue` of size `NSim` containing the values of the underlying stock at $t = T$:

```
// A.
for (long i = 1; i <= NSim; ++i)
{ // Calculate a path at each iteration

    if ((i/10000) * 10000 == i)
    {
        cout << i << endl;

    }

    dW = myNormal->getNormalVector(N+1);        // Performance
    fdm ->SetRandomArray(dW);                        bottleneck!

    // Calculate the path by delegation to a visitor
    sde -> Accept(*fdm);
    result = fdm->path(); // Size is N+1

    // Now us this array in the payoff function
    TerminalValue[i] = result[result.MaxIndex()];

}
```

Step B involves the evaluation of the payoff function at $t = T$:

```
//  B. Calculate the payoff function for each asset price
for (long index = TerminalValue.MinIndex();
    index <= TerminalValue.MaxIndex(); ++index )
{
    TerminalValue[index] =
        opt->myPayOffFunction(TerminalValue[index]);

}
```

Step C involves taking the average option price:

```
//  C. Take the average
price = TerminalValue[TerminalValue.MinIndex()];

for (long ii = TerminalValue.MinIndex()+1;
    ii <= TerminalValue.MaxIndex(); ++ii)
{
        price += TerminalValue[ii];

}
```

Finally, step D discounts the option price:

```
price = price / double(NSim);

// D. Finally, discounting the average price
price *= exp(-opt->r * opt->T);
```

```
    // Print out critical values
    cout << "price, after discounting: " << price << endl;;

    // Cleanup; V2 use scoped pointer
    delete myNormal;

    return price;
```

We are now finished because we have described all the steps in the algorithm. Finally, the main program that ties in all the classes in Figure 0.1 is

```cpp
int main()
{
    // Initialise the option data
    OptionData callOption;
    callOption.K = 65.0;
    callOption.T = 0.25;
    callOption.r = 0.08;
    callOption.sig = 0.30; // IC = 60

    // Create the basic SDE (Context class)
    Range<double> range (0.0, callOption.T);
    double initialCondition = 60.0;

    // Discrete stuff

    long N = 100;
    cout << "Number of subintervals: ";
    cin >> N;


    // Tell the Builder what kinds of SDE and FDM Types you want
    // You can use these to test SDE and FDM
    // enum SDEType {A, B, C, D};
    // enum FDMType {Euler, PC, CN, /*MIL*/, SIE,
    // IE, DerivFree, FRKIto, Fit};

    // The builder creates the UML class diagram, chapter 0 of MC book
    FDMTypeDBuilder fdmBuilder(FDMTypeDBuilder::D,
            FDMTypeDBuilder::DerivFree, N, range, initialCondition,
            drift, diffusion);

    // V2 mediator stuff
    long NSimulations = 50000;
    cout << "Number of simulations: ";
    cin >> NSimulations;


    try
    {
        MCMediator mediator(fdmBuilder, NSimulations, callOption);
```

```
        cout << "Final Price: " << mediator.price() << endl;
    }
    catch(string& exception)
    { // CN, IE or IE cannot be used with NL/NL SDEs
        cout << exception << endl;
        cout << "Press any key to stop\n";
        int yy; cin >> yy;
        exit(1);
    }

    return 0;
}
```

You can run this program and test it with your own values. See the CD for more details. The code can be optimised to make it run faster, but this is not a concern in this chapter. We have defined the code so that it can be easily understood and extended.

0.10   THE PREDICTOR-CORRECTOR METHOD: A SCHEME FOR ALL SEASONS?

In this chapter we have introduced a number of schemes for one-factor SDEs and you can experiment with the C++ code to see how well they approximate the solution of linear and nonlinear equations. By experimenting with a range of input parameters you will get a feeling for which schemes are suitable for your situation.

We now discuss a robust scheme that is used for one-factor and multi-factor SDEs in finance. It is called the predictor-corrector method and is a generalisation of a similar scheme that is used to solve ordinary differential equations (Lambert, 1991). In order to apply it to SDEs we examine the nonlinear problem given by equation (0.27). If we discretise this SDE using the trapezoidal rule, for example, we will get a nonlinear system of equations at each time level that we need to solve using Newton's or Steffensen's method:

$$X_{n+1} = X_n + [\alpha\mu(X_{n+1}) + (1 - \alpha)\mu(X_n)]\,\Delta t$$
$$+ \{\beta\sigma(X_{n+1}) + (1 - \beta)\sigma(X_n)\}\Delta W_n, n \geq 0$$

(0.36)

where

$$0 \leq \alpha \leq 1, \quad 0 \leq \beta \leq 1$$

Instead of solving this equation, we attempt to linearise it by replacing the 'offending' unknown solution at time level $n + 1$ with another known quantity (called the *predictor*) that is, we hope, close to it. To this end, we compute the predictor as

$$\tilde{X}_{n+1} = X_n + \mu(X_n)\Delta t + \sigma(X_n)\Delta W_n, \quad n \geq 0$$

(0.37)

that we subsequently use in the corrector equation:

$$X_{n+1} = X_n + \{\alpha\mu(\tilde{X}_{n+1}) + (1 - \alpha)\mu(X_n)\}\Delta t$$
$$+ \{\beta\sigma(\tilde{X}_{n+1}) + (1 - \beta)\sigma(X_n)\}\Delta W_n, \quad n \geq 0$$

(0.38)

However, we modify equation (0.9) by using the so-called *corrector drift function*:

$$\overline{\mu}_\beta(x) = \mu(x) - \beta\sigma(x)\frac{\partial\sigma}{\partial x}(x) \tag{0.39}$$

The new corrector equation is given by

$$X_{n+1} = X_n + \{\alpha\overline{\mu}_\beta(\tilde{X}_{n+1}) + (1-\alpha)\overline{\mu}_\beta(X_n)\}\Delta t$$
$$+\{\beta\sigma(\tilde{X}_{n+1}) + (1-\beta)\sigma(X_n)\}\Delta W_n, n \geq 0 \tag{0.40}$$

The solution of this scheme can be found without the need to use a nonlinear solver. Furthermore, you can customise the scheme to support different levels of implicitness and explicitness in the drift and diffusion terms:

$$\begin{array}{l} \text{A. Fully explicit}(\alpha = \beta = 0) \\ \text{B. Fully implicit}(\alpha = \beta = 1) \\ \text{C. Implicit in drift explicit in diffusion}(\alpha = 1, \beta = 0) \\ \text{D. Symmetric}(\alpha = \beta = 1/2) \end{array} \tag{0.41}$$

We need to determine which combinations of parameters result in stable schemes. We have seen with the schemes in this chapter that reducing the time steps (which is the same as increasing the number of subdivisions of the interval $[0, T]$) does not always increase accuracy and may actually lead to serious inaccuracies. This phenomenon is not common when discretising deterministic equations and can come as a shock if you are not prepared.

We have experimented with a number of test cases and the general conclusion is that the most stable schemes are those that have the same level of implicitness in drift and diffusion, for example the options A, B and D. In particular, the symmetric case D is a good all-rounder in the sense that it gives good results for a range of SDEs. Finally, the predictor-corrector method is popular in interest-rate applications using the Libor Market Model (LMM) (see Gatarek, Bachert and Maksymuk, 2006).

0.11   THE MONTE CARLO APPROACH: CAVEATS AND NASTY SURPRISES

In this section we give a short description of the problems that we encountered when designing and implementing the algorithms related to the Monte Carlo method. In general, some of the obstacles we have encountered are sparsely documented in the literature:

- Many existence and uniqueness results are based on measure theory. Some authors use functional analysis to prove the same results for SDEs. The advantage in the latter case is that these methods allow us to actually construct the solution to such equations. In general, we feel that there is too much emphasis on measure theory in this field.
- The popular numerical schemes (finite difference schemes) for SDEs tend to be extensions of similar numerical schemes for ordinary differential equations (ODEs). This analogy does not always work in practice and we have seen that the most popular schemes fail to realise the levels of robustness and accuracy that they produce in the ODE case.
- Standard numerical schemes break down for stiff SDEs.

- A number of widely-used random number generators (the C function `rand()`, for example) do not work properly. We shall discuss their shortcomings in this book and we provide improved random number generators. In particular, we use the Mersenne Twister random number generator in this book. We advise against using the Box-Muller and Polar Marsaglia methods because their use leads to the so-called Neave effect (Neave, 1973; Chay, Farab and Mazumdar, 1975; Jäckel, 2002). This phenomenon describes the poor agreement between observed and expected frequencies in the tails of the normal distribution when the random normal deviates are generated by a multiplicative congruential scheme. The problem can be resolved by reversing the order of the members of the pairs of successive pseudo-random as in equation (0.15). The discrepancy between observed and expected values in the tails is due to the manner in which the two random numbers in equation (0.15) are generated and the resulting dependency between these two numbers. In short, we interchange the members of the pairs of random numbers generated by multiplicative congruential schemes.

Summarising, we feel that there is more fundamental and applied research to be done in this area.

0.12   SUMMARY AND CONCLUSIONS

We have written this chapter for the benefit of those readers for whom stochastic analysis and the Monte Carlo method are new. Our intention was to describe a simple – but complete – Monte Carlo engine for a one-factor European option. In particular, we developed enough background theory to allow us to code a simple application in C++.

We generalise the results in this chapter to more interesting and complex products as we progress through this book. You should be able to understand the C++ code in this chapter. **If you do not, it will be difficult to continue with the more advanced chapters in this book.**

0.13   EXERCISES AND PROJECTS

1. (*) Prove (by using a change of variables) that the system (0.3) can be posed as an IVP of the form (0.1).
2. (*) Use the integrating factor method to find a closed form solution to system (0.1) (hint: use formula (0.4)).
3. (*) Prove that if the random variable x is $U(0, 1)$ then the random variable y defined by $y = 2x - 1$ is $U(-1, 1)$ (remark: this fact is used in the Polar Marsaglia method).
4. (*) Verify equation (0.18) when using the change of variables (0.17).
5. (***) We have used the same notation (namely the variable x_t) for the solutions of equations (0.18) and (0.19). Mathematically speaking, this is incorrect because these are two different equations; one solution (the *continuous solution*) solves equation (0.18) while the other solution (the *discrete solution*) solves equation (0.19). How can we ensure that the discrete solution is a *good* approximation to the continuous solution (we discuss this topic in Chapter 3)?

6. (***) Determine how to incorporate the following sensitivities into the Monte Carlo engine:

$$vega = \frac{\partial C}{\partial \sigma} \cong \frac{C(\sigma + \Delta\sigma) - C(\sigma - \Delta\sigma)}{2\Delta\sigma}$$

$$theta = \frac{\partial C}{\partial t} \cong \frac{C(t + \Delta t) - C(t)}{\Delta t}$$

$$rho = \frac{\partial C}{\partial r} \cong \frac{C(r + \Delta r) - C(r - \Delta r)}{2\Delta r}$$

7. (**) We consider a formula (it is first-order accurate) for approximating the delta of an option, namely:

$$\delta = \frac{C(S + \Delta S) - C(S)}{\Delta S}$$

Compare this representation with equation (0.26). What are the performance differences?

8. (***) We wish to *stress test* the code in section 0.9 by varying the input parameters. For example, test long-dated options:

```
OptionData callOption;
callOption.K = 100.0;
callOption.T = 30.0;
callOption.r = 0.08;
callOption.sig = 0.3;

double initialCondition = 100.0;
```

Answer the following questions:
– Calculate the call option price using the code on the CD. Compare the answer with the exact solution using the Black-Scholes formula. What do you notice?
– Now compute the put price by modifying the payoff function in `OptionData`. To find the corresponding call price, use the *put-call parity relationship* between the price of a European call option and a European put option having the same strike price K and maturity date T:

$$C + Ke^{-rT} = P + S$$

where C = call price, P = put price and S = stock price at $t = 0$. What do you notice now? Do you get a more accurate answer?

9. (**) An important issue in Monte Carlo simulation is *efficiency*; this refers to the time it takes to compute the option price. Examine the code and determine where performance can be improved (we discuss performance issues in Chapters 21 and 25). In particular, examine how the array of normal random numbers is generated in the code.

10. (***) We wish to modify the code in section 0.9 to support some *path-dependent* options. In this exercise we examine a *down-and-out* call option. This is an option whose value is zero if the underlying stock reaches a *barrier level* H from above. Determine how to modify the code for this case.

Modify the code so that the contribution to the final call price for a given simulation is zero if the simulated stock price is less than or equal to H. Test your code with problems whose solutions you know (Clewlow and Strickland, 1998, page 116; Haug, 2007).

11. (**) This is an exercise for C++ novices and for those who need to refresh their knowledge before continuing with the more advanced topics in later chapters. To this end, consider the four categories of one-factor SDE:

Type A
$$dX = \mu(t)Xdt + \sigma(t)XdW$$

Type B
$$dX - \mu(t)Xdt + \sigma(t, X)dW$$

Type C
$$dX = \mu(t, X)dt + \sigma(t)XdW$$

Type D
$$dX = \mu(t, X)dt + \sigma(t, X)dW$$

We have already written the C++ code for types A and D. The objective of this exercise is to write the code for types B and C as well for the following kinds of SDEs that are used to model the *short rate*:

$$dX = A(B - X)dt + \sigma\sqrt{X}dW$$

where A, B and σ are constants and

$$dX = [\theta(t) - aX]dt + \sigma dW$$

where $\theta(t)$ defines the average direction that X moves at time t.
    Test your software.

12. (***) Optimise the code in section 0.9 so that it runs faster.

Part I
Fundamentals

Mathematical Preparations for the Monte Carlo Method

1.1 INTRODUCTION AND OBJECTIVES

In this chapter we introduce a number of mathematical concepts and techniques. The main goal of this chapter is to motivate and define the *Ito integral*. Having laid this foundation we are then in a position to appreciate what stochastic differential equations (SDEs) are. We also give an introduction to random variables as well as the essentials of a number of concepts associated with stochastic analysis, for example sigma algebras, measure theory and probability spaces.

We assume that the reader has some knowledge of probability, statistics and set theory. For an introduction, see Hsu (1997), for example. This chapter is introductory in nature and is meant to make the book more self-contained than it would otherwise be.

1.2 RANDOM VARIABLES

We define what we mean by a random variable and why it is useful in the current context. Please skip to section 1.5 if you already know this material.

1.2.1 Fundamental concepts

In probability we define an *experiment* as something that refers to any process of observation. The result of the observation is called an *outcome* of the experiment. We speak of a *random experiment* when the outcome cannot be predicted. The set of all possible outcomes is called the *sample space* and an element of the sample space is called a *sample point* or an *elementary event*. An *event* is any subset of the sample space.

It is possible to examine the sample space in more detail. A sample space is called *discrete* if it consists of a finite number of sample points or if it has a *countably infinite* number of sample points (saying that a set is *countable* means that it can be put in one-to-one correspondence with the set of integers). Finally, a sample space is said to be *continuous* if the set of sample points forms a continuum.

Let us take a textbook example. To this end, we consider the random experiment of tossing a coin three times. For each throw of the coin, we know that there are two outcomes, namely heads ('H') or tails ('T'). Then, the sample space is given by the set of elementary events:

HHH, HHT, HTH, THH, HTT, THT, TTH, TTT

where we use the notation 'HHT' to mean a head on the first and second throws and a tail on the third throw. The above set represents the set of outcomes of the experiment. It is also possible to define experiments whose outcome is a subset of the set of all outcomes or even some new set whose elements belong to some given space. Some examples are:

- S1: Observe the number of heads in three tosses.
- S2: Observe the elementary events with an even number of heads.

In the first case, the sample space is the set 0, 1, 2, 3 while in the second case the sample space is the set HHT, HTH and THH.

1.2.2   Relative frequency and the beginnings of probability

We consider the case when a random experiment is repeated n times and when we are interested in determining how often a given event takes place, in some average sense. To be more precise, we let n become very large and we define the probability of event A by the limit:

$$P(A) = \lim_{n \to \infty} \frac{n(A)}{n} \tag{1.1}$$

and we refer to the quantity $n(A)/n$ as the *relative frequency* of event A, where $n(A)$ is the number of times event A occurs. We thus associate a real number with the events in a sample space and this concept is called the *probability measure*.

Since events are sets we can apply set theoretic operations – such as union, intersection and complementation – to them. Furthermore, we need some axiomatic properties of probability P for a finite sample space S:

- Axiom 1: $P(A) \geq 0$ where A is an event.
- Axiom 2: $P(S) = 1$.
- Axiom 3: $P(A \cup B) = P(A) + P(B)$ if $A \cap B = \emptyset$.

In the case of a sample space that is not finite we use:

- Axiom 3: If $A_1, A_2, \ldots$ is an infinite sequence of mutually exclusive events in S, that is $A_i \cap A_j = 0$ for $i \neq j$, then

$$P\left(\bigcup_{j=1}^{\infty} A_j\right) = \sum_{j=1}^{\infty} P(A_j).$$

Finally, we say that two events are *(statistically) independent* if and only if

$$P(A \cap B) = P(A)P(B) \tag{1.2}$$

1.2.3   Random variables

We need a way to compute the probabilities of certain events. To this end, we introduce the notion of a single *random variable*. The name can be confusing because it is not a variable in the strict sense but is rather a real-valued function whose domain is the sample space S and whose range is the real line (see Figure 1.1). In other words, a random variable $X(\zeta)$ (we abbreviate it to *r.v.*) assigns a real number (called the value of $X(\zeta)$) to each point ζ in S. Thus, its range is a subset of the set of all real numbers.

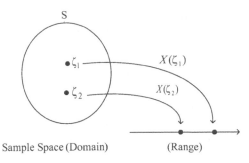

Sample Space (Domain)   (Range)

Figure 1.1 Random variable: domain and range

We note that a *r.v.* is *single-valued* because two range values cannot be assigned to the same sample point. Of course, two sample points might have the same value of $X(\zeta)$.

We can associate events and random variables as follows: let X be a *r.v.* and let x be a fixed real number, then we define the event $(X = x)$ as follows:

$$(X = x) = \{\zeta \in S : X(\zeta) = x\}$$

In the same way we can define events based on other operators, for example:

$$(X \leq x) = \{\zeta : X(\zeta) \leq x\}$$
$$(X > x) = \{\zeta : X(\zeta) > x\}$$
$$(x_1 < X \leq x_2) = \{\zeta : x_1 < X(\zeta) \leq x_2\}$$

The probabilities of these events are

$$P(X = x) = P\{\zeta \in S : X(\zeta) = x\}$$
$$P(X \leq x) = P\{\zeta \in S : X(\zeta) \leq x\}$$
$$P(X > x) = P\{\zeta \in S : X(\zeta) > x\}$$
$$P(x_1 < X \leq x_2) = P\{\zeta \in S : x_1 < X(\zeta) \leq x_2\}$$

We take the example from section 1.2.1 in order to define some random variables. We recall that this is a problem of tossing a coin three times. The complete sample space consists of eight sample points (a set with n elements had 2^n subsets; this is called the *power set*) and we define X to be the *r.v.* that gives two heads returned. First, we define the event A to be $X = 2$. Thus, using our new notation we see that (Hsu, 1997)

$$A = (X = 2) = \{\zeta \in S : X(\zeta) = 2\} = \{HHT, \ HTH, \ THH\}$$

In this case the sample points are equally likely (this means that they all have an equal probability of occurring), from which we can conclude that

$$P(X = 2) = P(A) = \frac{3}{8}$$

Finally, let us consider the event B that is defined by $X < 2$. Then

$$P(X < 2) = \{\zeta \in S : X(\zeta) < 2\} = \{HTT, \ THT, \ TTH, \ TTT\}$$

from which we can deduce that

$$P(X < 2) = \frac{4}{8} = \frac{1}{2}$$

We have now finished the example. An important function in the context of random variables is the *distribution function* (also known as the *cumulative distribution function* or *cdf*) of a *r.v.* defined by

$$F_X(x) = P(X \leq x) \tag{1.3}$$

Much information concerning a random experiment described by a random variable is determined by the behaviour of its cdf. Finally, we can determine probabilities from the cdf, again basing the analysis on equation (1.3). Some examples are

$$
\begin{aligned}
P(a < X \leq b) &= F_X(b) - F_X(a) \\
P(X > a) &= 1 - F_X(a) \\
P(X < b) &= F_X(b^-), \text{ where } b^- = \lim_{0 < \epsilon \to 0} b - \epsilon
\end{aligned}
\tag{1.4}
$$

We now describe two major categories of random variables.

1.3   DISCRETE AND CONTINUOUS RANDOM VARIABLES

We classify random variables based on the degree of continuity of their corresponding cumulative distribution functions. If the distribution function of the *r.v.* X is continuous and has a derivative at all points (with the possible exception of a finite number of points) then we say that X is a *continuous random variable*. However, if the cdf changes values only in jumps and is constant (or undefined) between jumps then we say that X is a *discrete random variable*.

In general, the range of a continuous *r.v.* is a bounded or unbounded interval on the real line, while for a discrete *r.v.* the range contains a finite or countably infinite number of points.

We now discuss two functions that are closely related to distribution functions of continuous and discrete random variables. These are called the *probability density function (pdf)* and *probability mass function (pmf)*, respectively. The pdf is the derivative of the cdf, namely:

$$f_X(x) = \frac{dF_X(x)}{dx} \tag{1.5}$$

Given the analytical form of the pdf, we can construct the cdf by integration, as follows:

$$F_X(x) = P(X \leq x) = \int_{-\infty}^{x} f_X(\xi) d\xi \tag{1.6}$$

Turning now to discrete random variables, let us assume that the cdf of the discrete *r.v.* X occurs at a discrete set of points:

$$x_1, x_2, \ldots, \text{ with } x_i < x_j, \quad i < j$$

(this set may be finite or countable). Then

$$F_X(x_j) - F_X(x_{j-1}) = P(X \leq x_j) - P(X \leq x_{j-1}) = P(X = x_j)$$

We now define the probability mass function (pmf) as

$$p_X(x) = P(X = x) \tag{1.7}$$

Finally, we define the so-called *mean* and *variance* of discrete and continuous random variables by

$$\mu_X \equiv E(X) = \begin{cases} \Sigma_j x_j p_x(x_j), & X \text{ discrete} \\ \int_{-\infty}^{\infty} x f_X(x) dx, & X \text{ continuous} \end{cases} \tag{1.8}$$

and

$$\sigma_X^2 \equiv Var(X) = E\left\{[X - E(X)]^2\right\}$$

and hence:

$$\sigma_X^2 = \begin{cases} \Sigma_j (x_j - \mu_X)^2 p_x(x_j), & X \text{ discrete} \\ \int_{-\infty}^{\infty} (x - \mu_X)^2 f_X(x) dx, & X \text{ continuous} \end{cases} \tag{1.9}$$

We give specific examples of discrete and continuous random variables. First, the *Bernoulli distribution* is a simple discrete distribution having two possible outcomes, namely *success* (with probability p) and *failure* (with probability $1 - p$) where $0 \le p \le 1$. Its pmf is given by

$$p_x(k) = P(X = k) = p^k(1 - p)^{1-k}, \quad k = 0, 1 \tag{1.10}$$

and its cdf is given by

$$F_X(x) = \begin{cases} 0, x < 0 \\ 1 - p, 0 \le x < 1 \\ 1, x \ge 1 \end{cases} \tag{1.11}$$

Finally, the mean and variance are given by

$$\begin{cases} \mu_X = E(x) = p \\ \sigma_X^2 = Var(X) = p(1 - p) \end{cases} \tag{1.12}$$

The Bernoulli distribution is used as a building block for more complicated discrete distributions; for example, individual repetitions of the *binomial distribution* are called *Bernoulli trials*.

Turning our attention to the continuous case, we examine the one-dimensional *uniform distribution* on the interval (a, b) whose pdf is given by

$$f_X(x) = \begin{cases} \frac{1}{b-a}, & a < x < b \\ 0, & \text{otherwise} \end{cases} \tag{1.13}$$

and the corresponding cdf is:

$$F_X(x) = \begin{cases} 0, & x \le a \\ \frac{x-a}{b-a}, & a < x < b \\ 1, & x \ge b \end{cases} \tag{1.14}$$

Finally, the mean and variance are given by

$$\begin{cases} \mu_X = E(x) = (a + b)/2 \\ \sigma_X^2 = Var(X) = (b - a)^2/12 \end{cases} \tag{1.15}$$

We shall encounter the uniform distribution in several places in later chapters of this book because it is used to generate random numbers. In particular, Chapter 22 is devoted to a discussion of discrete and continuous statistical distributions and algorithms for generating random numbers from these distributions. We have provided a C++ class hierarchy for discrete and continuous distributions on the CD.

We conclude this section with the remark that the Boost C++ library has extensive support for about 25 discrete and continuous statistical univariate distributions. A consequence is that developers can use the library in applications without having to create the code themselves. In the later chapters of this book we shall need a number of statistical distributions that the authors developed because the Boost library was not available when they commenced on their projects. We shall discuss Boost distributions in Chapter 3. For now, we give two examples of use to show how easy it is to use the library. We first examine the code in the Boost library that models the Bernoulli distribution. We create an instance of the corresponding class and we calculate some of its essential properties. The code implements the formulae in equations (1.10) and (1.11) and is given by

```cpp
#include <boost/math/distributions/bernoulli.hpp>
//
// Don't forget to tell compiler which namespace
using namespace boost::math;

// Bernoulli distributions
bernoulli_distribution<> myBernoulli(0.4);
cout << "Probability of success: " << myBernoulli.
        success_fraction();

int k = 0;
cout << "pdf of Bernoulli: " << pdf(myBernoulli, k) << endl;
cout << "cdf of Bernoulli : " << cdf(myBernoulli, k) << endl
        << endl;

k = 1;
cout << "pdf of Bernoulli: " << pdf(myBernoulli, k) << endl;
cout << "cdf of Bernoulli : " << cdf(myBernoulli, k) << endl;
```

We now show how the uniform distribution is implemented in C++. In particular, we show the implementation of the formulae in equations (1.13) and (1.14):

```cpp
#include <boost/math/distributions/uniform.hpp>
//

// Don't forget to tell compiler which namespace
using namespace boost::math;
uniform_distribution<> myUniform(0.0, 1.0); // Default type is
                                            'double'
cout << "Lower value: " << myUniform.lower() << ", upper value: "
                        << myUniform.upper() << endl;

// Choose another data type
uniform_distribution<float> myUniform2(0.0, 1.0);
cout << "Lower value: " << myUniform2.lower() << ", upper value: "
                        << myUniform2.upper() << endl;
```

```
// Distributional properties
double x = 0.25;

cout << "pdf of Uniform: " << pdf(myUniform, x) << endl;
cout << "cdf of Uniform: " << cdf(myUniform, x) << endl;
```

This code should give you an idea of how to use Boost for other distributions in your applications. More examples are to be found on the CD.

1.4   MULTIPLE RANDOM VARIABLES

In this section we discuss how to define two or more random variables on the same sample space. We discuss the case in which the range is n-dimensional Euclidean space. Thus, the random variable is a *vector-valued function* (see Figure 1.2). The mapping is formalised as follows:

$$X(\zeta) = (X_1(\zeta), X_2(\zeta), \ldots, X_n(\zeta)), \zeta \in S \tag{1.16}$$

In general terms, we can say that an n-dimensional random variable is an *n-tuple* of one-dimensional random variables. Analogous to the one-dimensional case we now define the generalisations of cdf, pdf and pmf. Let X be an n-variate *r.v.* on a sample space S. Then its *joint cdf* is the generalisation of equation (1.3) and is defined by

$$F_{X_1,\ldots,X_n}(x_1, \ldots, x_n) = P(X_1 \leq x_1, \ldots, X_n \leq x_n) \tag{1.17}$$

The *marginal cdf* is defined by setting one appropriate *r.v.* to ∞ in equation (1.17), for example:

$$F_{X_1,\ldots,X_{n-1}}(x_1, \ldots, x_{n-1}) = F_{X_1,\ldots,X_{n-1}X_n}(x_1, \ldots, x_{n-1}, \infty) \tag{1.18}$$

and

$$F_{X_1 X_2}(x_1, x_2) = F_{X_1,\ldots,X_n}(x_1, x_2, \infty, \ldots, \infty)$$

Thus, a marginal cdf is similar to a slice of the joint cdf in the sense that it results in a lower-dimensional space. A continuous n-variate *r.v.* is described by a joint pdf defined by

$$f_{X_1,\ldots,X_n}(x_1, \ldots, x_n) = \frac{\partial^n F_{X_1,\ldots,X_n}(x_1, \ldots, x_n)}{\partial x_1, \ldots, \partial x_n} \tag{1.19}$$

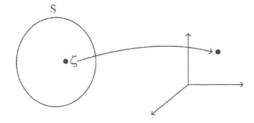

Figure 1.2   Multiple random variables

For a discrete n-variate random variable the joint pmf is given by

$$p_{X_1,\ldots,X_n}(x_1,\ldots,x_n) = P(X_1 = x_1,\ldots,X_n = x_n)$$

This is the n-dimensional generalisation of equation (1.7).

We conclude this section by giving an example of an important random variable. This is the n-variate normal distribution. When $n = 2$ we speak of a *bivariate normal* or *Gaussian r.v.* whose joint pdf is given by

$$f_{XY}(x, y) = \frac{1}{2\pi \sigma_x \sigma_y (1 - \rho^2)^{1/2}} \ \exp(-\frac{1}{2} q\ (x, y))$$

where

$$q(x, y) =$$
$$\frac{1}{1 - \rho^2} \left[\left(\frac{x - \mu_x}{\sigma_x} \right)^2 - 2\rho \left(\frac{x - \mu_x}{\sigma_x} \right) \left(\frac{y - \mu_y}{\sigma_y} \right) + \left(\frac{y - \mu_y}{\sigma_y} \right)^2 \right] \qquad (1.20)$$

and

$\mu_x = $ mean of X
$\mu_y = $ mean of Y
$\sigma_x^2 = $ variance of X
$\sigma_y^2 = $ variance of Y
$\rho = $ correlation coefficient of X and Y

The random variables X and Y are independent when $\rho = 0$.

In Chapter 2 we shall discuss random variables in function space.

1.5   A SHORT HISTORY OF INTEGRATION

The theory of integration began more than 2000 years ago. The invention of the *integral calculus* can be attributed to Archimedes (287–212 BC) who used it to compute the areas under two-dimensional curves. But it was not until the 19th century that a rigorous theory was developed by Cauchy and Riemann. In particular, the *Riemann integral* (this is the integral we study at high school) is used in many applications. However, it does have its limitations and a number of mathematicians (most notably Borel and later Lebesgue) succeeded in defining an integral for a wider class of functions than was possible for the Riemann integral. In particular, Lebesgue introduced the concept of *measure* which is a generalisation of the length concept in classical integration theory (Carter and van Brunt, 2000; Rudin, 1970; Spiegel, 1969). Another generalisation by the Dutch mathematician Stieltjes was how to integrate one function with respect to another function. There are many other kinds of integral types, many of them being named after their inventors. A discussion of these topics is outside the scope of this book.

The above integration theories are not suitable for integrals that arise in connection with stochastic differential equations and a new kind of integral is needed. It was introduced by the Japanese mathematician Kiyoshi Ito (see Ito, 1944) and it is the standard approach to defining stochastic integrals in finance. In this chapter we motivate and define this integral because an understanding of it is important for the results and techniques in this book.

Before we embark on the mathematical details of the Ito integral we give a short description of how it came into existence. For a more detailed discussion we refer the reader to Bharucha-Reid (1972) and Tsokos and Padgett (1974). Norbert Wiener introduced the following integral in 1930:

$$\int_a^b g(t)\, dW(t) \tag{1.21}$$

Here $g(t)$ is a deterministic real-valued function and

$$\{W(\tau);\ \tau \in [a, b]\}$$

is a scalar Brownian motion process. Ito generalised this integral in 1944 (Ito, 1944) to support those cases where the integrand g is also a random function:

$$\int_0^t g(\tau; \omega)\, dW(\tau) \tag{1.22}$$

This is now the so-called Ito *stochastic integral*. In this case ω is a sample point from a given sample space. A more general case is the so-called *stochastic integral equation* defined by

$$x(t; \omega) = c + \int_0^t f(\tau, x(\tau; \omega))\, d\tau + \int_0^t g(\tau, x(\tau; \omega))\, dW(\tau) \tag{1.23}$$

where c is some constant, $t \in [0, 1]$ and $\{W(t); t \in [0, 1]\}$ is a Brownian motion process. Furthermore, the first integral in (1.23) is interpreted as a Lebesgue integral while the second integral is a stochastic integral that we shall presently define. For example, the method of successive approximations can be used to prove the existence and uniqueness of a random solution of equation (1.23), analogous to the way existence and uniqueness of deterministic Fredholm and Volterra integral equations are proved (see Tricomi, 1985). We discuss this topic in more detail in Chapter 2. In much of the literature we see the Ito equation written in differential form:

$$dX(t, \omega) = f(t, X)\, dt + g(t, X)\, dW(t) \tag{1.24}$$

with initial data $X(t_0; \omega) = c$. A remark: some authors denote the Wiener process as depending on two variables, namely time and its sample point dependence:

$$dW(t, \omega) \tag{1.25}$$

We now construct and define the Ito stochastic integral in the following sections. But first, it is necessary to introduce some measure theory and related concepts.

1.6 σ-ALGEBRAS, MEASURABLE SPACES AND MEASURABLE FUNCTIONS

We now introduce several major concepts:

- σ-algebras.
- Measurable space and measurable sets.
- Probability spaces.
- Toplogical spaces and measurable functions.

Let X be a set. Then a collection $\mathcal{F}$ of subsets of X is said to be a σ-algebra if $\mathcal{F}$ has the following properties (Rudin, 1970, page 8):

1. The *empty set* $\emptyset$ is a member of $\mathcal{F}$.
2. If $F \in \mathcal{F}$, then the complement F^c is also in $\mathcal{F}$, $F^c \equiv X - F$.
3. If $A = \cup_{n=1}^{\infty} A_n$ and if $A_n \in \mathcal{F}$, $n = 1, 2, \ldots$, then $A \in \mathcal{F}$.

In other words the σ-algebra is closed under complementation and countable unions of members of the σ-algebra. We note that X is also a member of $\mathcal{F}$ because of 1 and 2. In general, a given set can have many σ-algebras. Let us take a simple example. Define the set $X = \{1, 2, 3, 4\}$; we see that the set $\{\{1, 2\}, \{3, 4\}, \{1, 2, 3, 4\}\}$ is a σ-algebra because:

1. The empty set is a member.
2. The complement of each subset is a member.
3. The union of any number of subsets is a member.

We now discuss the concept of *measure*. In general terms, measure describes the size, area or volume of a set. It is a generalisation of the length of an interval or the area of a closed curve that we are accustomed to in Riemann integration. A measure on a set X is a function that assigns some real number to subsets of X. If $\mathcal{F}$ is a σ-algebra on X then X is called a *measurable space* and the members of $\mathcal{F}$ are called the *measurable sets* in X. We sometimes use the notation $(X, \mathcal{F})$ to denote the measurable space.

We define some specific functions that map measurable sets to the real numbers. An important case is the *probability measure* P defined on the sample space Ω by the mapping:

$$
\begin{aligned}
&P : \mathcal{F} \to [0, 1] \\
&\text{such that} \\
&\text{(i)} \quad P(\emptyset) = 0, \quad P(\Omega) = 1 \\
&\text{(ii)} \quad \text{If } A_1, A_2, \ldots, \in \mathcal{F} \text{ and } A_i \cap A_j = \emptyset \\
&\quad \text{for } i \neq j, \text{ then} \\
&\qquad P\left(\cup_{j=1}^{\infty} A_j\right) = \sum_{j=1}^{\infty} P(A_j) \\
&\text{(iii) } P(A^c) = 1 - P(A), \text{ where } A^c = \Omega - A
\end{aligned}
\tag{1.26}
$$

We call the triple $(\Omega, \mathcal{F}, P)$ a *probability space*.

1.7   PROBABILITY SPACES AND STOCHASTIC PROCESSES

The concept of probability space was introduced by Kolmogorov and it is the foundation for probability theory. In order to align the notation with standard literature on stochastic differential equations we use the symbol Ω instead of the symbol X for a set. In particular, Ω will denote the sample space as already discussed. Then a probability space is a triple consisting of

- A sample space Ω.
- A σ-algebra $\mathcal{F}$ of subsets of Ω.
- A probability measure mapping $\mathcal{F}$ to the real numbers.

This triple is written as $(\Omega, \mathcal{F}, P)$

We now come to the important definition. A *stochastic process* (also called a random process) is a parametrised collection of random variables: $\{X(t); t \in T\}$ defined on a given probability space and indexed by the parameter t in the index set T. We assume that the variable t (sometimes called *time*) is always non-negative. In particular, we shall see in this book that the interval $[a, b]$ in which t is defined has the canonical form $[0, T]$ where the constant $T > 0$ represents the expiry time. Thus, the stochastic process is a function of t on the one hand and it depends on sample space on the other hand. We make this statement precise by noting that, for a fixed value of t we get a *random variable* defined by

$$\omega \rightarrow X_t(\omega), \quad \text{where } \omega \in \Omega \tag{1.27}$$

and then for a fixed $\omega \in \Omega$ is called a *path* of the stochastic process.

Intuitively, we consider t to be 'time' and each sample point ω to be a 'particle' in sample space. Thus, we can view the stochastic process X as a function of two variables:

$$X : [a, b] \times \Omega \rightarrow \mathbb{R}$$

In later chapters we shall encounter a number of examples of stochastic processes.

Finally, we introduce the last topics before we can construct the Ito integral. As before, let us assume that we have a probability space $(\Omega, \mathcal{F}, P)$; then we say that the function

$$f : \Omega \rightarrow \mathbb{R}^n \text{ is } \mathcal{F}\text{-measurable if the set}$$
$$f^{-1}(U) = \{\omega \in \Omega; f(\omega) \in U\} \in \mathcal{F} \text{ for all open sets } U \subset \mathbb{R}^n$$

(an open set U is one where any point x in U can be changed by a small amount in any direction and still be inside U). A random variable X is an $\mathcal{F}$-measurable function $\Omega \rightarrow \mathbb{R}^n$.

Every random variable has a probability measure μ_X on $\mathbb{R}^n$ defined by If $\int_\Omega |X(\omega)| dP(\omega) < \infty$, then the number $E[X] \equiv \int_\Omega X(\omega) dP(\omega) = \int_{\mathbb{R}^n} x d\mu_X(x)$ is called the expectation of X with respect to P.

1.8   THE ITO STOCHASTIC INTEGRAL

We are now in a position to motivate what it means when we speak of an Ito stochastic integral:

$$\int_a^b f(t, \omega) dW_t(\omega) \text{ or, equivalently } \int_a^b f(t, \omega) dW(t, \omega) \tag{1.28}$$

defined on a probability space $(\Omega, \mathcal{F}, P)$ and taking values in $\mathbb{R}^n$. In general, we shall define this integral for a simple class of functions (sometimes called *step functions*) and we define the integral for arbitrary functions that are approximated by these step functions. This is similar to how the Lebesgue integral is motivated and we follow some of the steps from Øksendal (1998). First of all, we define the *indicator function* for a closed interval $[a, b]$ as follows:

$$\chi_{[a,b]}(t) = \begin{cases} 1, & \text{if } t \in [a, b] \\ 0, & \text{if } t \notin [a, b] \end{cases}$$

It is possible to define this function for open and half-open/half-closed intervals in a similar manner as above. We approximate the integral (1.28) by the following discrete sum:

$$I(f)(\omega) \equiv \sum_{n=0}^{N-1} f(t_n^*, \omega) \left\{ W_{t_{n+1}}(\omega) - W_{t_n}(\omega) \right\} \tag{1.29}$$

In contrast to the Riemann integral – where it does not make any difference where we choose the mesh-point argument for the function f – with stochastic integrals the following options have become the most popular:

$$(a)\ t_n^* = t_n \Rightarrow \text{Ito integral}$$
$$(b)\ t_n^* = (t_n + t_{n+1})/2 \Rightarrow \text{Stratonovich integral}$$

(1.30)

We summarise the construction of the integral. We define an elementary function as one that has the representation:

$$\phi(t, \omega) = \sum_{n=0}^{N-1} \alpha_n(\omega) \chi_{[t_n, t_{n+1}]}(t)$$

(1.31)

Then its stochastic integral is defined as follows:

$$\int_a^b \phi(t, \omega) dW = \Sigma_{n \geq 0} \alpha_n(\omega)[W_{t_{n+1}} - W_{t_n}](\omega)$$

(1.32)

where

$$t_n = t_n^{(N)} = \begin{cases} \frac{n}{2^N} \text{ if } a \leq \frac{n}{2^N} \leq b \\ a \text{ if } \frac{k}{2^N} < a \\ b \text{ if } \frac{k}{2^N} > b \end{cases}$$

and

$\{t_0, \dots, t_{N-1}\}$ is a partition of the interval (a, b)

We conclude this section with the definition of the Ito integral and the main result is

Let f be some 'smooth enough' function on $[a, b]$

Then the Ito integral of f on $[a, b]$ is defined by

$$\int_a^b f(t, \omega) dW_t(\omega) = \lim_{n \to \infty} \int_a^b \phi_n(t, \omega) dW_t(\omega)$$

(1.33)

where

$\{\phi_n\}$ is a sequence of elementary functions such that

$$E\left[\int_a^b (f(t, \omega) - \phi_n(t, \omega)^2 dt\right] \to 0 \text{ as } n \to \infty$$

Theorem Let f be defined on $[a, b]$ and let $f_n(t, \omega)$ be a sequence of functions such that

$$E\left[\int_a^b (f_n(t, \omega) - f(t, \omega)^2 dt\right] \to 0 \text{ as } n \to \infty$$

Then

$$\int_a^b f(t, \omega) dW_t(\omega) = \lim_{n \to \infty} \int_a^b f_n(t, \omega) dW_t(\omega) \text{ in the } L^2 \text{ sense}$$

1.9   APPLICATIONS OF THE LEBESGUE THEORY

In this section we discuss a number of theorems and results based on the Lebesgue integration theory. They are important because we can use them in proving existence and uniqueness results for many kinds of equations in particular when we study stochastic equations and their applications to finance. Furthermore, we give some examples on how to apply these results. For an introduction, we refer the reader to Rudin (1964), Rudin (1970) and (the more introductory level) Spiegel (1969).

1.9.1   Convergence theorems

Lemma 1.1 (Fatou's Lemma). Let $\{f_n\}$ be a sequence of non-negative measurable functions defined on a set X and suppose that

$$\lim_{n\to\infty} f_n(x) = f(x) \; \forall \, x \in X$$

Then

$$\liminf_{n\to\infty} \int_X f_n(x)dx \geq \int_X f dx$$

where lim inf of a sequence $\{a_n\}$ is defined as the number a such that infinitely many terms of the sequence are less than $a + \epsilon$ while only a finite number of terms are less than $a - \epsilon$ for $\epsilon > 0$.

We note that this theorem also holds when $\lim_{n\to\infty} f_n(x) = f(x)$ almost everywhere (that is, everywhere except on a set of measure zero).

Theorem 1.1 (Monotone Convergence Theorem, MCT). Let $\{f_n\}$ be a sequence of measurable functions in a set X and suppose that

$$\text{(a) } 0 \leq f_1(x) \leq f_2(x) \leq \ldots \leq \infty \; \forall \, x \in X$$
$$\text{(b) } \lim_{n\to\infty} f_n(x) = f(x), \quad \forall \, x \in X$$

Then f is measurable and we have the following convergence result:

$$\lim_{n\to\infty} \int_X f_n dx = \int_X f dx$$

This is also called the *Beppo Levi theorem*. This result allows us to exchange integration and limits. We now wish to prove similar results under milder and different assumptions concerning the integrands.

Theorem 1.2 (Bounded Convergence). Let $\{f_n\}$ be a sequence of measurable functions on a set X such that $\lim_{n\to\infty} f_n(x) = f(x)$. If the sequence is uniformly bounded, that is

$$\exists \, M > 0 \text{ such that } |f_n(x)| \leq M, \; \forall \, n \geq 0$$

then we have

$$\lim_{n\to\infty} \int_X f_n(x)dx = \int_X \lim_{n\to\infty} f_n(x)dx = \int_X f(x)dx$$

Theorem 1.3 (Dominated Convergence Theorem, DCT). Let $\{f_n\}$ be a sequence of measurable functions on a set X such that

$$\lim_{n \to \infty} f_n(x) = f(x)$$

Then if there exists an integrable function $M(x)$ such that $|f_n(x)| \leq M(x) \; \forall \, n = 0, 1, 2, \ldots$ then we have:

$$\lim_{n \to \infty} \int_X f_n(x)dx = \int_X \lim_{n \to \infty} f_n(x)dx = \int_X f(x)dx$$

We now state the variant of Theorem 3 for series of functions.

Theorem 1.4 (Dominated Convergence for Infinite Series). Let $\{f_n\}$ be a sequence of measurable functions on a set X. If there exists an integrable function $M(x)$ such that $|s_m(x)| \leq M(x)$ where $s_m(x) = \sum_{n=1}^{m} f_n(x)$ and $\lim_{m=\infty} s_m(x) = s(x)$, then

$$\int_X \sum_{n=1}^{\infty} f_n(x)dx = \sum_{n=1}^{\infty} \int_X f_n(x)dx$$

We take an example to show how these theorems can be applied to calculating integrals. The first example will be calculated using the infinite series variant of the Dominated Convergence Theorem. The integral to be computed is

$$I \equiv \int_0^{\infty} \frac{e^{-x}}{1 - e^{-x}} x^{\alpha - 1} dx, \quad \alpha > 1$$

Using the fact that

$$\frac{e^{-x}}{1 - e^{-x}} = \sum_{n=1}^{\infty} e^{-nx}$$

and that each partial sum of this series is bounded we get

$$I = \int_0^{\infty} \sum_{n=1}^{\infty} e^{-nx} x^{\alpha - 1} dx = \sum_{n=1}^{\infty} \int_0^{\infty} e^{-nx} x^{\alpha - 1} dx$$

Now using the change of variables

$$y = nx$$

we get

$$I = \sum_{n=1}^{\infty} \int_0^{\infty} e^{-y} y^{\alpha - 1} n^{-\alpha} dy = \sum_{n=1}^{\infty} n^{-\alpha} \Gamma(\alpha)$$

where we express the integral in terms of the *gamma function*:

$$\Gamma(\alpha) \equiv \int_0^{\infty} e^{-y} y^{\alpha - 1} dy$$

Finally, we can write the integral in the form:

$$I = \Gamma(\alpha) \sum_{n=1}^{\infty} \frac{1}{n^{\alpha}}$$

The second example shows how to use the theorems that exchange integration and limits. Define:

$$f_n(x) = \frac{n}{x+n}, \quad x \in [0,1], \quad n \geq 1$$

We use the following properties of the sequence of functions:

$$0 \leq f_n(x) \leq 1 \, (\text{DCT})$$
$$0 \leq f_n(x) \leq f_{n+1}(x) \, (\text{MCT})$$

Then using either MCT or DCT we can calculate the integral as follows:

$$\lim_{n \to \infty} \int_0^1 f_n(x)dx = \int_0^1 \lim f_n(x)dx = \int_0^1 dx = 1$$

1.9.2 Fubini's theorem

We now discuss the Lebesgue integral in the plane and in particular the *Lebesgue double integral*. The technique is based on *iterated integrals*.

Theorem 1.5 (Fubini's Theorem). Let $f(x,y)$ be a measurable function in the set

$$R = \{(x,y) : a \leq x \leq b, \quad c \leq y \leq d\}$$

Then

$$\int \int_R f(x,y)dxdy = \int_c^d \left\{ \int_a^b f(x,y)dx \right\} dy = \int_a^b \left\{ \int_c^d f(x,y)dy \right\} dx$$

Basically, this theorem allows us to compute a two-dimensional integral by an iteration of two one-dimensional integrals.

Finally, we note that Fubini's theorem can be applied to two-dimensional stochastic integration in which one integral is a Lebesgue integral and the other an Ito integral (for example, Karatzas and Shreve 1991).

1.10   SOME USEFUL INEQUALITIES

We introduce a number of useful results that relate to inequalities between functions. They are useful in many kinds of applications.

The first inequality is named after Gronwall and it is used to prove the stability of solutions to differential, integral and integro-differential equations, for example.

Theorem 1.6 (Gronwall's inequality, continuous case). Let u and β be continuous functions on $[a,b]$ such that $\beta(t) \geq 0 \, \forall \, t \in [a,b]$. Assume the inequality:

$$u(t) \leq K + \int_a^t \beta(s)u(s)ds \text{ where } K \text{ is a constant}$$

Then $u(t) \leq K \exp\left(\int_a^t \beta(s)ds\right), t \in [a, b]$.

The following inequality is the discrete analogue of Theorem 1.6. It is used to prove stability of finite difference schemes and their accuracy.

Theorem 1.7 (Gronwall's inequality, discrete case). Let a_n, $n = 0, \ldots, N$ be a sequence of real numbers such that $|a_n| \leq K + hM \sum_{j=0}^{n-1} |a_n|, n = 1, \ldots, N$ where K and M are positive constants, then $|a_n| \leq (hM|a_0| + K) \exp(Mnh), n = 1, \ldots, N$.

A generalisation of this discrete theorem is

$$\text{Let } |a_n| \leq K + \sum_{r=0}^{n-1} g(r)|a_r| \text{ with } g(r) \geq 0, \text{ then } |a_n| \leq K \exp\left(\sum_{r=0}^{n-1} g(r)\right)$$

We now discuss convex and concave functions. A real function f defined on the interval $[a, b]$ where $-\infty \leq a < b \leq \infty$ is called *convex* if

$$f((1 - \lambda)x + \lambda y) \leq (1 - \lambda)f(x) + \lambda f(y)$$
$$\text{for } x, y \in (a, b) \text{ and } 0 \leq \lambda \leq 1$$

A function f is said to be *concave* if the function $F = -f$ is convex, in other words:

$$f((1 - \lambda)x + \lambda y) \geq (1 - \lambda)f(x) + \lambda f(y)$$

We now introduce Jensen's inequality that relates the integral of a convex function to the convex function of an integral.

Theorem 1.8 (Jensen's Inequality) (Rudin, 1970). Let μ be a positive measure on a σ-algebra in Ω such that $\mu(\Omega) = 1$. If $f \in L^1(\mu)$ and $a < f(x) < b \ \forall x \in \Omega$ then if φ is convex on (a, b), we have the inequality:

$$\varphi\left(\int_\Omega f d\mu\right) \leq \int_\Omega (\varphi \circ f) d\mu$$

Jensen's inequality has the following *finite form*: let $\{a_j\}_{j=1}^n > 0$ and $\{x_j\}_{j=1}^n$ be two sequences and let φ be a real convex function. Then

$$\varphi\left(\frac{\sum_{j=1}^n a_j x_j}{\sum_{j=1}^n a_j}\right) \leq \frac{\sum_{j=1}^n a_j \varphi(x_j)}{\sum_{j=1}^n a_j}$$

1.11   SOME SPECIAL FUNCTIONS

We introduce a class of functions that is important in stochastic analysis; these are functions whose powers are Lebesgue integrable on some set in n-dimensional space (Adams, 1975). We motivate this class of functions by examining real-valued functions of a single variable.

Let $p \geq 1$ be an integer. The space of all functions for which

$$\int_a^b |f(x)|^p dx < \infty$$

is denoted by $L^p[a, b]$, or L^p for short. In words, these are functions whose powers are Lebesgue integrable on the interval $[a, b]$. A special case is when $p = 2$; we then speak of the class of *square-integrable* functions, thus

$$L^2[a, b] = \left\{ f : \int_a^b |f(x)|^2 dx < \infty \right\}$$

Another important case is when $p = \infty$. We shall discuss both of these cases in the context of convergence.

The p-integrable function class becomes a *metric space* (we discuss this in more detail in Chapter 2) and the corresponding *norm* is defined by

$$d(f, g) \equiv \|f - g\|_p = \left\{ \int_a^b |f(x) - g(x)|^p \right\}^{1/p}$$

For example, the *triangle inequality* holds for this space:

$$\|f - g\|_p \leq \|f - h\|_p + \|h - g\|_p \text{ where } f, g, h \in L^p[a, b]$$

We now state some useful inequalities (Rudin, 1970):

- Hölder's inequality:

$$\left| \int_a^b f(x)g(x)dx \right| \leq \|f\|_p \|g\|_q, \quad \frac{1}{p} + \frac{1}{q} = 1$$

- Schwarz's inequality (special case of Hölder's inequality with $p = q = 2$):

$$\left| \int_a^b f(x)g(x)dx \right| \leq \left\{ \int_a^b |f(x)|^2 dx \right\}^{1/2} \left\{ \int_a^b |g(x)|^2 \right\}^{1/2} = \|f\|_2 \|g\|_2$$

- Minkowski's inequality:

$$\|f + g\|_p \leq \|f\|_p + \|g\|_p, \quad 1 \leq p \leq \infty$$

These inequalities and the above theory generalise to general sets and measures. We take an example of proving that a function's power is integrable. We claim:

$$f \in L^1[0, 8] \text{ where } f(x) = \frac{1}{\sqrt[3]{x}}$$

To this end, define the function:

$$[f(x)]_p = \begin{cases} \frac{1}{\sqrt[3]{x}}, & \frac{1}{\sqrt[3]{x}} \leq p \text{ or equivalently } x \geq \frac{1}{p^3} \\ p, & \frac{1}{\sqrt[3]{x}} > p \text{ or equivalently } x < \frac{1}{p^3} \end{cases}$$

Then the following sequence of steps leads to the desired conclusion:

$$\int_0^8 \frac{dx}{\sqrt[3]{x}} = \lim_{p \to \infty} \int_0^8 [f(x)]_p dx$$

$$= \lim_{p \to \infty} \left[\int_0^{1/p^3} p\, dx + \int_{1/p^3}^8 \frac{dx}{\sqrt[3]{x}} \right]$$

$$= \lim_{p \to \infty} \left[[px]_0^{1/p^3} + \left[\frac{3}{2} x^{2/3} \right]_{1/p^3}^8 \right]$$

$$= \lim_{p \to \infty} \left[\frac{1}{p^2} + 6 - \frac{3}{2p^2} \right] = 6$$

We are finished. We note that this integral exists as an *improper Riemann integral*:

$$\lim_{\epsilon \to 0} \int_\epsilon^8 \frac{dx}{\sqrt[3]{x}} = \lim_{\epsilon \to 0} \left[\frac{3}{2} x^{2/3} \right]_\epsilon^8 = 6$$

In this case the Riemann and Lebesgue integrals have the same value.
We now discuss the relationship between L^p spaces and stochastic theory.

1.12   CONVERGENCE OF FUNCTION SEQUENCES

A sequence of functions $\{f_n(x)\}$ belonging to $L^p[a, b]$ is said to be a *Cauchy sequence* if

$$\lim_{\substack{m \to \infty \\ n \to \infty}} \int_a^b |f_m(x) - f_n(x)|^p dx = 0$$

or, if given $\epsilon > 0$, there exists a number $n_0 > 0$ such that

$$\|f_m - f_n\|_p \equiv \left(\int_a^b |f_m(x) - f_n(x)|^p dx \right)^{1/p} < \epsilon$$
$$\text{when } m > n_0, n > n_0$$

Furthermore, if there exists a function $f(x)$ in L^p such that

$$\lim_{n \to \infty} \int_a^b |f_n(x) - f(x)|^p dx = 0$$

we then say that $\{f_n(x)\}$ converges in the mean (or is mean convergent) to $f(x)$ in the space L^p. We write this property in the form:

$$\lim_{n \to \infty} f_n(x) = f(x)$$

We state that the space L^p is complete if every Cauchy sequence in the space converges in the mean to a function in the space.

Theorem 1.9 (Riesz-Fischer). Any L^p space is complete. Thus, if $\{f_n(x)\}$ is a sequence of functions in L^p and

$$\lim_{\substack{m \to \infty \\ n \to \infty}} \int_a^b |f_m(x) - f_n(x)|^p dx = 0$$

then there exists a function $f \in L^p$ such that f_n converges to f in the mean, that is $\lim_{n \to \infty} \int_a^b |f_n(x) - f(x)|^p dx < \infty$.

Now let $\{f_n(x)\}$ be a sequence of measurable functions defined almost everywhere. Then $\{f_n(x)\}$ converges in measure to $f(x)$ if $\lim_{n \to \infty} \mu\{x : |f_n(x) - f(x)| \geq \sigma\} = 0 \ \forall \ \sigma > 0$.

Theorem 1.10 (Convergence of a sequence of functions).

- If a sequence converges almost everywhere, then it converges in measure.
- If a sequence converges in the mean, then it converges in measure.
- If a sequence converges in measure, then there exists a subsequence that converges almost everywhere.

1.13   APPLICATIONS TO STOCHASTIC ANALYSIS

The above discussion leads naturally to the definition of some results in stochastic analysis. In this case we are interested in probability measures.

Let (Ω, A, P) be a probability measure space, that is

$\Omega =$ non-empty abstract set.
$\mathcal{F} = \sigma$-algebra of subsets of Ω.
$P =$ complete probability measure on A.

We denote the space $L^p(\Omega, \mathcal{F}, P)$, $1 \leq p < \infty$ as the set of measurable functions defined on $\mathbb{R}_+^1 = \{x \in \mathbb{R}^1; x > 0\}$ such that the inequality $\forall \ t \in \mathbb{R}_+^1$ is satisfied and we have $\int_\Omega |x(t; \omega)|^p dP(\omega) < +\infty$.

The norm in this space is

$$\|x(t; \omega)\|_p = \left\{ \int_\Omega |x(t; \omega)|^p dP(\omega) \right\}^{1/p} < \infty$$

If $x(t; \omega)$ is a vector-valued function with n components, then the norm becomes

$$\|x(t; \omega)\| = \left(\Sigma_{j=1}^n \|x_j(t; \omega)\|^2 \right)^{1/2}$$

Let X be a continuous random variable; then its *mean value* or *expected value* is given by:

$$E(X) = \int_\mathbb{R} x p(x) dx$$

where $p(x)$ is its probability density function.

We now define what we mean by convergence in this context; to this end, let X_1, $X_2, \ldots, X_n, \ldots$ be a sequence of random variables. We are interested in asymptotic behaviour of this sequence. In other words, does a random variable X that is the limit of X_n as $n \to \infty$ converge in some sense? The answer depends on the norm that we use (Kloeden, Platen and Schurz, 1997, page 27):

- *Mean-square convergence*:

$$E(X_n^2) < \infty, \quad n = 1, 2, \ldots, \quad E(X^2) < \infty$$

and

$$\lim_{n \to \infty} E(|X_n - X|^2) = 0$$

- *Strong convergence*:

$$E(|X_n|) < \infty, \quad n = 1, 2, \ldots \text{ with } E(|X|) < \infty$$

and

$$\lim_{n \to \infty} E(|X_n - X|) = 0$$

This is a generalisation of deterministic convergence; in particular, it is used when investigating convergence of numerical schemes.
- *Weak convergence*:

$$\lim_{n \to \infty} \int_{\mathbb{R}} f(x) dF_{X_n}(x) = \int_{\mathbb{R}} f(x) dF(x)$$

for all *test functions* $f(x)$ with compact support.
- *Convergence in distribution*:

$$\lim_{n \to \infty} F_{X_n}(x) = F_X(x) \text{ for all points of } F_X \text{ where it it continuous}$$

- *Convergence with probability one* (w.p.1):

$$P\left(\left\{\omega \in \Omega : \lim_{n \to \infty} |X_n(\omega) - X(\omega)|\right\} = 0\right) = 1$$

This is called *almost sure convergence*.

1.14   SUMMARY AND CONCLUSIONS

We have given an account of a number of important mathematical concepts that underpin the topics in succeeding chapters. We have attempted to be as complete as possible while at the same time avoiding those topics that are not absolutely essential to a full understanding of the material.

1.15   EXERCISES AND PROJECTS

1. (**) Find the sample spaces corresponding to the following random experiments:
   – Toss a die and observe the number that shows on top.
   – Toss a coin four times and observe the total number of heads obtained.
   – Toss a coin four times and observe the sequence of heads and tails observed.
   – A transistor is placed in an oven at high temperature and its operational lifetime is observed (this process is called *destructive testing*).
   – A launched missile's position is observed at n points in time. At each point the missile's height above the ground is recorded.
2. (**) Consider the experiment of tossing two dice. Answer the following questions:
   – What is the sample space?

- Find the event that the sum of dots on the two dice equals 7.
- Find the event that the sum of dots on the two dice is greater than 10.
- Find the event that the sum of dots on the two dice is greater than 12.

3. (***) Prove that the number of events in a sample space S with n elementary events is 2^n (this set is sometimes called the *power set* of S). Design an algorithm to compute the power set in C++.

4. (*) Based on the definition of the cumulative distribution function in equation (1.3) prove or deduce the following properties:

   (a) $0 \le F_X(x) \le 1$
   (b) $F_X(x_1) \le F_X(x_2), \quad x_1 \le x_2$
   (c) $\lim_{x \to \infty} F_X(x) = 1$
   (d) $\lim_{x \to -\infty} F_X(x) = 0$
   (e) $\lim_{x \to a^+} F_X(x) = F_X(a^+) = F_X(a)$ where $a^+ = \lim_{0 < \epsilon \to 0} a + \epsilon$

Remark: property (b) means that the cdf is a nondecreasing function while property (e) states that it is *continuous from the right*. Property (a) is obvious because the cdf is a probability function.

5. (**) A random variable X is called an *exponential r.v.* with parameter $\lambda > 0$ if its pdf is given by

$$f_X(x) = \begin{cases} \lambda e^{-\lambda x}, & x > 0 \\ 0, & x < 0 \end{cases}$$

Find the cdf as well as the mean and variance for this distribution.

6. (**) A random variable X is called a *Poisson r.v.* with parameter $\lambda > 0$ if its pmf is given by

$$p_X(k) = P(x = k) = e^{-\lambda} \frac{\lambda^k}{k!}, \quad k = 0, 1, 2, \ldots$$

Find the cdf as well as the mean and variance for this distribution. This distribution is important because it is a *building block* for stochastic processes with jumps. We shall discuss this topic in more detail in later chapters.

7. (***) The *covariance* of two random variables X and Y is defined as

$$Cov(X, Y) = \sigma_{XY} = E(XY) - E(X)E(Y)$$

The *correlation coefficient* is defined as

$$\rho(X, Y) = \rho_{XY} = \frac{Cov(X, Y)}{\sigma_X \sigma_Y} = \frac{\sigma_{XY}}{\sigma_X \sigma_Y}$$

where σ and σ are the standard deviations of X and Y, respectively. Prove that

$$|\rho_{XY}| \le 1 \text{ or } -1 \le \rho_{XY} \le 1$$

8. (**) Let X be a set. Prove that the following are σ-algebras over X:
   - The *trivial σ-algebra* consisting of X and the empty set.
   - The *power set* of X (this is the set of all subsets).
   - The collection of all subsets of X that are countable or whose complements are countable.

9. (***) Use *De Morgan's laws* to prove that a σ-algebra is closed under countable intersections. The laws are

$$(A \cup B)^c = A^c \cap B^c$$
$$(A \cap B)^c = A^c \cup B^c$$

where A^c is the complement of A.

10. (**) Define the function

$$g_n(x) \equiv ae^{-nax} - be^{-nbx} \quad (0 < a < b), \quad n = 0, 1, \ldots$$

Is the sum of the integral equal to the integral of the sum?

$$\sum_{n=0}^{\infty} \int_{\mathbb{R}} g_n(x)dx = \int_{\mathbb{R}} \sum_{n=0}^{\infty} g_n(x)dx$$

11. (**) Prove (by any means) that

$$\lim_{n \to \infty} \int_0^n \left(1 - \frac{x}{n}\right)^n x^{\alpha-1}dx = \int_0^{\infty} e^{-x}x^{\alpha-1}dx \ (\alpha > 1)$$

(We know that $\lim_{n \to \infty} (1 - \frac{x}{n})^n = e^{-x}$.)

12. (**) Prove that $f(x) = \frac{1}{\sqrt[3]{x}}$ does not belong to $L^3[0, 8]$.

13. (*) Prove that the functions $f(x) = x^2$ and $f(x) = |x|$ are convex.

14. (**) Let $f(x) = |x|^p$. For which value of p is this function convex? Prove that $f(x) = \sqrt{x}$ is not convex. Prove that the affine transformation $f(x) = ax + b$, where $a, b, x \in \mathbb{R}^2$ is convex.

15. (**) Compute $\lim_{n \to \infty} \int_0^n \left(1 \pm \frac{x}{n}\right)^n e^{-x/2}dx$ and $\lim_{n \to \infty} \int_0^n \left(1 \pm \frac{x}{n}\right)^n e^{-2x}dx$.

2

The Mathematics of Stochastic Differential Equations (SDE)

2.1 INTRODUCTION AND OBJECTIVES

The goal of this chapter is to create a mathematical framework for SDEs with particular emphasis on those SDEs that we use in later chapters of the current book. We discuss a number of methods that allow us to formulate an SDE in unambiguous terms. We provide necessary and sufficient conditions for an SDE to have a unique solution in a certain space of functions. We consider one-factor and n-factor models in Euclidean space as well as SDEs in more general Banach spaces. Knowing how to formulate the problem in this way improves our understanding of SDEs and we will be in position to create numerical algorithms that approximate their solution. We hope that this chapter will provide readers with a reference for the major categories of SDEs that they will encounter in finance. We also give a short summary of the major textbooks and literature on this subject.

The topics in this chapter can be classified into two major groups; first, an introduction to a number of mathematical concepts (notably, metric and Banach spaces and the *Contraction Mapping Theorem*), and second formulating SDEs and proving they have a unique solution.

Remark: *You should be familiar with the theory in Chapter 1 before embarking on the rest of the chapters in Part I of this book.*

2.2 A SURVEY OF THE LITERATURE

There are many textbooks on SDEs, ranging from introductory and intuitive treatments to more advanced mathematical and applied texts. However, in our opinion there is a dearth of textbooks that discuss the numerical solutions of SDEs, the notable exceptions being Kloeden and Platen (1995) and Kloeden, Platen and Schurz (1997).

In Chapter 0 we examined a special case of the one-factor SDE:

$$dX = \mu(t, X)dt + \sigma(t, X)dW \qquad (2.1)$$

where

$$X \equiv X_t \equiv X(t) \text{ (stochastic process)}$$

and

$$\mu(t, x) \in \mathbb{R} \text{ (drift)}$$
$$\sigma(t, x) \in \mathbb{R} \text{ (diffusion)}$$
$$W \equiv W_t \equiv W(t) \text{ (Wiener process)}$$

We need to interpret this equation in mathematical terms and this is done in Øksendal (1998) using measure theory. Other interpretations of this SDE can be found in Nefcti (1996) and Mikosch (1999). We can write the SDE in the equivalent *integral form* (it is then called a *stochastic* or *random integral equation* of Volterra type):

$$X(t) = X(0) + \int_0^t \mu(s, X(s))ds + \int_0^t \sigma(s, X(s))dW(s) \tag{2.2}$$

The first integral is a Lebesgue integral while the second integral is an Ito integral (see Øksendal, 1998, page 24). Special cases of this one-factor SDE are discussed in Shreve (2004), Karatsas and Shreve (1991) and Glasserman (2004).

We now discuss *n*-factor SDEs. A good source is Kloeden and Platen (1995), pages 148–154 where the term *vector SDE* is used. In this case we define the multi-dimensional equivalent of SDE (2.1); to this end, let n and m be positive integers; let $\mu : [0, T] \times \mathbb{R}^n \to \mathbb{R}^n$ be a *n*-dimensional vector function (the *drift vector*) and let $\sigma : [0, T] \times \mathbb{R}^n \to \mathbb{R}^{n \times m}$ be an $n \times m$ matrix function (the *diffusion matrix*). Finally, let $\underline{W} = \{\underline{W}(t), t \geq 0\}$ be an *m*-dimensional Wiener process whose components $W_1(t), \ldots, W_m(t)$ are independent scalar Wiener processes. Then the vector SDE is given by

$$d\underline{X} = \underline{\mu}(t, \underline{X})dt + \underline{\sigma}(t, \underline{X})d\underline{W} \tag{2.3}$$

where $\underline{X} = \underline{X}(t) = {}^t(X_1(t), \ldots, X_n(t))$ is an *n*-dimensional stochastic process. We can write equation (2.3) in the integral form for each component:

$$X_j(t) = X_j(0) + \int_0^t \mu_j(s, \underline{X}(s))ds + \sum_{k=1}^m \int_0^t \sigma_{jk}(s, \underline{X}(s))dW_j(s), \quad j = 1, \ldots, n \tag{2.4}$$

where

$$\underline{\mu} = {}^t(\mu_1, \ldots, \mu_n)$$
$$\underline{\sigma} = (\sigma_{jk})_{\substack{1 \leq j \leq n \\ 1 \leq k \leq m}}$$

Specific cases of equation (2.4) will be discussed in later chapters, for example spread options with stochastic volatility, the Heston model and others. An example in the case $n = 2, m = 1$ describes a random oscillator:

$$\begin{aligned} dX_1 &= -X_2 dt \\ dX_2 &= X_1 dt + \sigma dW \end{aligned} \tag{2.5}$$

Another two-factor SDE describes interest rates using the *Cheyette Model* (see Landgraf, 2007):

$$\begin{aligned} dX &= (Y - \kappa(t)X)dt + \eta(t)dW \\ dY &= (\eta^2(t) - 2\kappa(t)Y)dt \\ X(0) &= Y(0) = 0 \end{aligned} \tag{2.6}$$

where X and Y are state variables and represent Markovian processes.

We now describe SDEs in spaces that are generalizations of Euclidean space. We draw on the results in Tsokos and Padgett (1974) and Bharucha-Reid (1972). The form of the SDE in these cases is the same as before but we work in so-called *function spaces*. We shall discuss this topic in the coming sections.

The previous sections assumed that the random terms were based on *Geometric Brownian Motion (GBM)*. Researchers and practitioners know that GBM does not always model financial markets well and this awareness has led to the development of other, more appropriate models, for example (Cont and Tankov, 2004):

- Jump processes;
- Compound Poisson processes;
- Levy processes.

We shall discuss these processes and their applications in Part III of this book.

Finally, we mention the textbooks Skorokhod (1982) and Friedman (1976) (two combined volumes). These discuss SDEs from an advanced mathematical viewpoint. Existence and uniqueness theorems are proved.

2.3   MATHEMATICAL FOUNDATIONS FOR SDEs

We now introduce a number of mathematical concepts that we shall use when studying SDEs.

2.3.1   Metric spaces

We work with sets and other mathematical structures in which it is possible to assign a so-called *distance function* or *metric* between any two of their elements. Let us suppose that X is a set and let x, y and z be elements of X. Then a metric d on X is a non-negative real-valued function of two variables having the following properties:

$$D1 : d(x, y) \geq 0; \quad d(x, y) = 0 \text{ if and only if } x = y$$
$$D2 : d(x, y) = d(y, x)$$
$$D3 : d(x, y) \leq d(x, z) + d(z, y) \text{ where } x, y, z \in X$$

The concept of distance is a generalisation of the difference of two real numbers or the distance between two points in n-dimensional Euclidean space, for example.

Having defined a metric d on a set X we then say that the pair (X, d) is a *metric space*. We give some examples of metrics and metric spaces:

1. We define the set X of all continuous real-valued functions of one variable on the interval $[a, b]$ (we denote this space by $C[a, b]$) and we define the metric:

$$d(f, g) = \max \{|f(t) - g(t)|; \quad t \in [a, b]\}$$

   Then (X, d) is a metric space.
2. The n-dimensional Euclidean space, consisting of vectors of real or complex numbers of the form

$$x = (x_1, \ldots, x_n), \quad y = (y_1, \ldots, y_n)$$

   with metric

$$d(x, y) = \max \{|x_j - y_j|; j = 1, \ldots, n\} \text{ or using the notation for a norm}$$
$$d(x, y) = \|x - y\|_\infty$$

3. Let $L^2[a, b]$ be the space of all square-integrable functions on the interval $[a, b]$:

$$\int_a^b |f(x)|^2 dx < \infty$$

We can then define the distance between two functions f and g in this space by the metric:

$$d(f, g) = \|f - g\|_2 \equiv \left\{ \int_a^b |f(x) - g(x)|^2 \right\}^{1/2} \tag{2.7}$$

This metric space is important in many branches of mathematics, including probability theory and stochastic calculus.

4. Let X be a non-empty set and let the metric d be defined by

$$d(x, y) = \begin{cases} 0, & \text{if } x = y \\ 1, & \text{if } x \neq y \end{cases}$$

Then (X, d) is a metric space.

Many of the results and theorems in mathematics are valid for metric spaces and this fact means that the same results are valid for all specialisations of these spaces.

2.3.2   Cauchy sequences, complete metric spaces and convergence

In this book we are concerned with SDEs and their approximations using finite difference methods. Furthermore, we employ the Monte Carlo method in conjunction with these methods. To this end, we define the concept of convergence of a sequence of elements of a metric space X to some element that may or may not be in X. We introduce some definitions that we state for the set of real numbers but they are valid for any *ordered field*, which is basically a set of numbers for which every non-zero element has a multiplicative inverse and there is a certain ordering between the numbers in the field.

Definition 2.1   A sequence (a_n) of elements on the real line $\mathbb{R}$ is said to be *convergent* if there exists an element $a \in \mathbb{R}$ such that for each positive element ε in $\mathbb{R}$ there exists a positive integer n_0 such that

$$|a_n - a| < \varepsilon \text{ whenever } n \geq n_0$$

A simple example is to show that the sequence $\left\{ \frac{1}{n}, \geq 1 \right\}$ of rational numbers converges to 0. To this end, let ε be a positive real number. Then there exists a positive integer $n_0 > 1/\varepsilon$ such that $|\frac{1}{n} - 0| = \frac{1}{n} < \varepsilon$ whenever $n \geq n_0$.

We remark that Definition 2.1 also holds for any ordered field.

Definition 2.2   A sequence (a_n) of elements of an ordered field F is called a *Cauchy sequence* if for each $\varepsilon > 0$ in F there exists a positive integer n_0 such that

$$|a_n - a_m| < \varepsilon \text{ whenever } m, n \geq n_0$$

In other words, the terms in a Cauchy sequence get close to each other while the terms of a convergent sequence get close to some fixed element. A convergent sequence is always a Cauchy sequence but a Cauchy sequence whose elements belong to a field X does not necessarily converge to an element in X. To give an example, let us suppose that X is the set of rational numbers; consider the sequence of integers defined by the Fibonacci recurrence relation:

$$F_0 = 0$$
$$F_1 = 1$$
$$F_n = F_{n-1} + F_{n-2}, \quad n \geq 2$$

By solving this recurrence relationship (using the techniques in Chapter 4, or by using induction, for example) it can be shown that

$$F_n = \frac{1}{\sqrt{5}}[\alpha^n - \beta^n] \tag{2.8}$$

where

$$\alpha = \frac{1 + \sqrt{5}}{2}$$

$$\beta = \frac{1 - \sqrt{5}}{2}$$

Now define the sequence of rational numbers by

$$x_n = F_n/F_{n-1}, \quad n \geq 1$$

Then, by using equation (2.8) we can show that

$$\lim_{n \to \infty} x_n = \alpha = \frac{1 + \sqrt{5}}{2} \text{ (the } \textit{Golden} \text{ Ratio)} \tag{2.9}$$

and this limit is not a rational number. Incidentally, the Fibonacci numbers are useful in many kinds of applications such as optimisation (finding the minimum or maximum of a function) and random number generation.

We now define a *complete metric space* X as one in which every Cauchy sequence converges to an element in X. Examples of complete metric spaces are:

- Euclidean space $\mathbb{R}^n$.
- The metric space $C[a, b]$ of continuous functions on the interval $[a, b]$.
- By definition Banach spaces are complete normed linear spaces. A normed linear space has a norm based on a metric, as follows $d(x, y) = \|x - y\|$.
- $L^p(0, 1)$ is the Banach space of functions $f : [0, 1] \to \mathbb{R}$ defined by the norm $\|f\|_p = (\int_0^1 |f(x)|^p dx)^{1/p} < \infty$ for $1 \leq p < \infty$.

Definition 2.3 An *open cover* of a set E in a metric space X is a collection $\{G_j\}$ of open subsets of X such that $E \subset \cup_j G_j$.

Finally, we say that a subset K of a metric space X is *compact* if every open cover of K contains a *finite subcover*, that is $K \subset \cup_{j=1}^N G_j$ for some finite N.

2.3.3 Continuous and Lipschitz continuous functions

We now examine functions that map one metric space into another one. In particular, we discuss the *concepts of continuity* and *Lipschitz continuity* because they will be used when proving the existence and uniqueness of solutions of stochastic differential equations.

It is convenient to discuss these concepts in the context of metric spaces.

Definition 2.4 Let (X, d_1) and (Y, d_2) be two metric spaces. A function f from X into Y is said to be *continuous at the point* $a \in X$ if for each $\varepsilon > 0$ there exists a $\delta > 0$ such that

$$d_2(f(x), f(a)) < \varepsilon \text{ whenever } d_1(x, a) < \delta$$

We should note that this definition refers to the continuity of a function at a single point. Thus, a function can be continuous at some points and discontinuous at other points.

Definition 2.5 A function f from a metric space (X, d_1) into a metric space (Y, d_2) is said to be *uniformly continuous* on a set $E \subset X$ if for each $\varepsilon > 0$ there exists a $\delta > 0$ such that

$$d_2(f(x), f(y)) < \varepsilon \text{ whenever } x, y \in E \text{ and } d_1(x, y) < \delta$$

If the function f is uniformly continuous then it is continuous but the converse is not necessarily true. Uniform continuity holds for all points in the set E whereas 'normal' continuity is applicable at a single point.

Definition 2.6 Let $f : [a, b] \to \mathbb{R}$ be a real-valued function and suppose we can find two constants M and α such that $|f(x) - f(y)| \leq M|x - y|^\alpha, \forall x, y \in [a, b]$. Then we say that f satisfies a Lipschitz condition of order α and we write $f \in Lip(\alpha)$.

We take an example. Let $f(x) = x^2$ on the interval $[a, b]$.
Then:

$$\begin{aligned}
|f(x) - f(y)| &= |x^2 - y^2| = |(x + y)(x - y)| \\
&\leq (|x| + |y|)|x - y| \\
&\leq M|x - y|, \text{ where } M = 2\max(|a|, |b|)
\end{aligned}$$

Hence $f \in Lip(1)$. A concept related to Lipschitz continuity is *contraction*.

Definition 2.7 Let (X, d_1) and (Y, d_2) be metric spaces. A transformation T from X into Y is called a *contraction* if there exists a number $\lambda \in (0, 1)$ such that

$$d_2(T(x), T(y)) \leq \lambda d_1(x, y) \forall x, y \in X$$

In general, a contraction maps a pair of points into another pair of points that are closer together. A contraction is always continuous.

The ability to discover and apply contraction mappings has considerable theoretical and numerical value. For example, it is possible to prove that SDEs have unique solutions by the application of *fixed point theorems* (Bharucha-Reid, 1972; Tsokos and Padgett, 1974):

- Brouwer's fixed-point theorem.
- Kakutani's fixed-point theorem.
- Banach's fixed-point theorem.
- Schauder's fixed-point theorem.

Our interest here lies in the following fixed point theorem.

Theorem 2.1 (Banach Fixed-Point Theorem). Let T be a contraction of a complete metric space X into itself:

$$d(T(x), T(y)) \leq \lambda d(x, y), \quad \lambda \in (0, 1)$$

Then T has a unique fixed-point $\overline{x}$. Moreover, if x_0 is any point in X and the sequence (x_n) is defined recursively by the formula $x_n = T(x_{n-1}), n = 1, 2, \ldots$ then $\lim x_n = \overline{x}$ and

$$d(\overline{x}, x_n) \leq \frac{\lambda}{1 - \lambda} d(x_{n-1}, x_n) \leq \frac{\lambda^n}{1 - \lambda} d(x_0, x_1)$$

In general, we assume that X is a Banach space and that T is a linear or nonlinear mapping of X into itself. We then say that x is a fixed point of T if $Tx = x$.

We take some examples. Let X be the real line and define $Tx = x^2$. Then $x = 0$ and $x = 1$ are fixed points of T. Another example is the *deterministic integral equation*:

$$Tx = x(0) + \int_0^1 x(\xi)d\xi$$

where X is the set of continuous functions on the interval $[0, 1]$. The fixed points of this mapping are functions of the form $x(t) = ke^t, t \in [0, 1]$ *where k is a constant.*

It is important to distinguish between two classes of fixed-point theorems; first, *algebraic* (or *constructive*) *fixed-point theorems* give a method for finding the fixed point which can also be called the *iteration* or *successive approximation* procedure (see Bharucha-Reid, 1972). The second class is that of *topological fixed-point theorems* and they are strictly existence theorems, that is they establish conditions under which a fixed point exists but they do not provide an algorithm or a method for actually finding the fixed-point. We shall use fixed-point theorems in this chapter to prove the existence and uniqueness of the solution of stochastic differential equations (such as the Ito stochastic differential equation).

A generalisation of the above is due to Kolmogorov and it is used in proving a number of relevant theorems.

Theorem 2.2 If T is a mapping of a Banach space X into itself and if T^n is a contraction for some positive integer n, then T has a fixed point.

For a nice overview of fixed point theorems, see Smart (1974).

2.4   MOTIVATING RANDOM (STOCHASTIC) PROCESSES

A random process is a family of random variables defined on some probability space and indexed by the parameter t where t belongs to some *index set*. A random process is in fact a function of two variables:

$$\{\xi(t, x) : t \in T, x \in S\}$$

where T is the index set and S is the *sample space*. For a fixed value of t the random process becomes a random variable and for a fixed sample point x in S the random process is a real-valued function of t called a *sample function* or a *realisation* of the process. It is also sometimes called a *path*. The totality of all sample paths is called an *ensemble*.

The index set T is called the *parameter set* and the values assumed by $\xi(t, \omega)$ are called the *states*; finally, the set of all possible values is called the *state space* of the random process.

The index set T can be discrete or continuous; if T is discrete then the process is called a *discrete-parameter* or *discrete-time process* (also known as a *random sequence*). If T is continuous then we say that the random process is called *continuous-parameter* or *continuous-time*. We can also consider the situation where the state is discrete or continuous. We then say that the random process is called *discrete-state (chain) or continuous-state*, respectively.

2.5   AN INTRODUCTION TO ONE-DIMENSIONAL RANDOM PROCESSES

In this section we introduce random processes described by SDEs of the form:

$$d\xi(t) = \mu(t, \xi(t))\, dt + \sigma(t, \xi(t))\, dW(t) \tag{2.10}$$

where

$\xi(t) \equiv$ random process

$\mu(t, \xi(t)) \equiv$ transition (drift) coefficient

$\sigma(t, \xi(t)) \equiv$ diffusion coefficient

$W(t) \equiv$ Brownian process

$\xi(0) =$ given initial condition

defined in the interval $[0, T]$. We assume for the moment that the process takes values on the real line. We know that this SDE can be written in the equivalent integral form:

$$\xi(t) = \xi(0) + \int_0^t \mu(s, \xi(s))ds + \int_0^t \sigma(s, \xi(s))dW(s) \qquad (2.11)$$

This is a nonlinear equation because the unknown random process appears on both sides of the equation and it cannot be expressed in a closed form. We know that the second integral

$$\int_0^t \sigma(s, \xi(s))dW(s)$$

is a continuous process (with probability 1) provided $\sigma(s, \xi(s))$ is a bounded process. In particular, we restrict the scope to those functions for which

$$\sup_{|x| \leq C} (|\mu(s, x)| + |\sigma(s, x)|) < \infty, \ t \in (0, T] \text{ and for every } C > 0$$

Using this fact we shall see that the solution of equation (2.11) is bounded and continuous with probability 1.

We now discuss existence and uniqueness theorems. First, we define some conditions on the coefficients in equation (2.11):

- C1: $\exists \ K > 0$ such that $\mu(s, x)^2 + \sigma(s, x)^2 \leq K(1 + x^2)$
- C2: $\forall C > 0, \exists \ L$ such that $|\mu(s, x) - \mu(s, y)| + |\sigma(s, x) - \sigma(s, y)| \leq L|x - y|$ for $|x| \leq C, |y| \leq C$
- C3: $\mu(s, x)$ and $\sigma(s, x)$ are defined and measurable with respect to their variables where $s \in (0, T], x \in (-\infty, \infty)$
- C4: $\mu(s, x)$ and $\sigma(s, x)$ are continuous with respect to their variables for $t \in (0, T], x \in (-\infty, \infty)$

Condition C2 is called a *Lipschitz condition* in the second variable while condition C1 constrains the growth of the coefficients in the equation (2.11). We assume throughout that the random variable $\xi(0)$ is independent of $W(t)$.

Theorem 2.3 Assume conditions C1, C2 and C3 hold. Then equation (2.11) has a unique continuous solution with probability 1 for any initial condition $\xi(0)$.

Theorem 2.4 Assume that conditions C1 and C4 hold. Then the equation (2.11) has a continuous solution with probability 1 for any initial condition $\xi(0)$.

We note the difference between the two theorems: condition C2 is what makes the solution unique. Finally, both theorems assume that $\xi(0)$ is independent of the Brownian motion $W(t)$.

We now define another condition on the diffusion coefficient in equation (2.11):

- $C5$: $\sigma(t, x) > 0$ and for every $C > 0$ there exists an $L > 0$ and $\alpha > \dfrac{1}{2}$

such that

$$|\sigma(t, x) - \sigma(t, y)| \leq L|x - y|^{\alpha} \text{ for } |x| \leq C, |y| \leq C$$

Theorem 2.5 Assume that conditions C4, C1 and C5 hold. Then the equation (2.11) has a continuous solution with probability 1 for any initial condition $\xi(0)$.

For proofs of these theorems, see Skorokhod (1982), for example.

In some cases it is possible to find a closed-form solution of equation (2.10) (or equivalently, equation (2.11)). When the drift and diffusion coefficients are constant we see that the exact solution is given by the formula

$$\xi(t) = \xi(0) \exp\left(\left(\mu - \frac{1}{2}\sigma^2\right) t + \sigma W(t)\right) \tag{2.12}$$

Knowing the exact solution is useful because we can test the accuracy of finite difference schemes against it and this gives us some insights into how well these schemes work for a range of parameters. It is useful to know how the solution of (2.12) behaves for large values of time; the answer depends on a relationship between the drift and diffusion parameters:

(i) $\mu > \frac{1}{2}\sigma^2$, $\lim\limits_{t \to \infty} \xi(t) = \infty$ almost surely

(ii) $\mu < \frac{1}{2}\sigma^2$, $\lim\limits_{t \to \infty} \xi(t) = 0$ almost surely $\qquad$ (2.13)

(iii) $\mu = \frac{1}{2}\sigma^2$, $\xi(t)$ fluctuates between arbitrary large and arbitrary small values as $t \to \infty$ almost surely

In general it is not possible to find an exact solution and in these cases we must resort to numerical approximation techniques.

Equation (2.11) is a *one factor equation* because there is only one dependent variable (namely $\xi(t)$) to be modelled. It is possible to define equations with several dependent variables. The prototypical nonlinear stochastic differential equation is given by the system:

$$d\underline{X} = \underline{\mu}dt + \underline{\sigma}\,d\underline{W}(t) \tag{2.14}$$

where

$$\underline{\mu} : [0, T] \times \mathbb{R}^n \to \mathbb{R}^n \quad \text{(vector)}$$
$$\underline{\sigma} : [0, T] \times \mathbb{R}^n \to \mathbb{R}^{n \times m} \quad \text{(matrix)}$$
$$\underline{X} : [0, T] \to \mathbb{R}^n \quad \text{(vector)}$$
$$\underline{W} : [0, T] \to \mathbb{R}^m \quad \text{(vector)}$$

In general the drift and diffusion are nonlinear:

$$\underline{\mu} = \underline{\mu}(t, \underline{X})$$
$$\underline{\sigma} = \underline{\sigma}(t, \underline{X})$$

This is a generalisation of equation (2.11). Thus, instead of scalars this system employs vectors for the solution, drift and random number terms while the diffusion term is a rectangular matrix.

Existence and uniqueness theorems for the solution of the SDE system (2.14) are similar to those in the one-factor case. For example, theorem 5.2.1 in Øksendal (1998) addresses these issues. We shall also give a discussion of these topics when we introduce SDEs in Banach spaces.

2.6   STOCHASTIC DIFFERENTIAL EQUATIONS IN BANACH SPACES: PROLOGUE

In the rest of this chapter we generalise the results of section 2.5 (which had to do primarily with one-dimensional random equations). We define solutions of various types of *stochastic integral equations* (SIE) in Banach spaces and in particular we discuss SIEs of Ito type in detail. This approach offers a number of advantages; we can formulate SIEs in a general setting and prove existence and uniqueness results pertaining to them using a number of methods of applied functional analysis, in particular the *Banach fixed point theorem* and the *method of successive approximations*. We shall define SIEs in the combined space of time and the space of probability events as discussed in Chapter 1. Finally, we avoid the measure-theoretic approach in the discussion, an approach that we find is of little practical use when we wish to find numerical solutions to SIEs.

2.7   CLASSES OF SIEs AND PROPERTIES OF THEIR SOLUTIONS

We give a short overview of some SIEs and applications. We also introduce a number of Banach spaces because it is in these spaces that we seek a solution of the relevant SIE. As already stated, a random process is a function of two variables t (denoting time) and ω (denoting a point in probability space). We use the notation $f(t; \omega)$ to denote a stochastic process that depends on these two variables. Our first example is the *Volterra SIE*:

$$x(t; \omega) = h(t; \omega) + \int_0^t k(t, \tau; \omega) f(\tau, x(\tau; \omega)) d\tau \qquad (2.15)$$

This equation has applications in hereditary mechanics, population growth models and telephone traffic theory. A more general equation has the form

$$x(t; \omega) = h(t; \omega) + \int_0^t k(\tau, x(\tau; \omega); \omega) d\tau \qquad (2.16)$$

which has applications in turbulence theory and chemotherapy. In equations (2.15) and (2.16) we call $h(t; \omega)$ the *free random variable* while we call $k(t, \tau; \omega)$ and $k(\tau, x(\tau; \omega); \omega)$ the *stochastic kernel*. Another class of equations is called the *Fredholm SIE*:

$$x(t; \omega) = h(t; \omega) + \int_0^\infty k(t, \tau; \omega) f(\tau, x(\tau; \omega)) d\tau \qquad (2.17)$$

which has applications in stochastic control theory. Furthermore, it is possible to study *SIEs of mixed Volterra-Fredholm type*:

$$x(t; \omega) = h(t; \omega) + \int_0^t k(t, \tau; \omega) f(\tau, x(\tau; \omega)) d\tau + \int_0^\infty k_1(t, \tau; \omega) g(\tau, x(\tau; \omega)) d\tau$$
$$(2.18)$$

It is possible to define discrete analogues of the equations (2.15) to (2.18) by replacing the integrals (in the mean square sense) by discrete summations. For example, a *discrete Volterra system* is described as follows:

$$x_n(\omega) = h_n(\omega) + \sum_{j=1}^{n} c_{n,j}(\omega) f_j(x_j(\omega)), \quad j = 1, 2, \ldots \tag{2.19}$$

This system of equations is similar to the system of equations produced by approximating the SIE (2.15) or (2.16) by a numerical quadrature scheme. We can describe it as a semi-discretisation in t of an SIE. We shall discuss this topic in a later section. A *discrete Fredholm equation* (corresponding to equation (2.17)) is given by the equation

$$x_n(\omega) = h_n(\omega) + \sum_{j=1}^{\infty} c_{n,j}(\omega) f_j(x_j(\omega)), \quad j = 1, 2, \ldots \tag{2.20}$$

and this can be seen as the discrete equivalent of the SIE defined by equation (2.17). Our final example is a *stochastic integrodifferential equation* (SIDE) defined by

$$\dot{x}(t; \omega) = h(t, x(t; \omega)) + \int_0^t k(t, \tau; \omega) f(x(\tau; \omega)) d\tau, \quad t \geq 0 \tag{2.21}$$

where

$$\dot{x} \equiv \frac{dx}{dt}$$

Equation (2.21) arises in applications related to reactor dynamics, growth of biological populations, automatic systems and other applications in biology, physics and engineering.

2.8 EXISTENCE AND UNIQUENESS RESULTS

We now discuss the problem of proving that a given SIE or SIDE (for example, equations (2.15) to (2.21)) has a solution and that this solution is unique. We qualify this statement by saying that we seek a solution in a space of functions, typically continuous in time and square-integrable with respect to the probability measure in a probability measure space (we discussed this latter topic in Chapter 1).

Definition 2.8 Let I be a bounded or semi-infinite interval on the positive real axis. We define $C = C(I, L^2(\Omega, A, P))$ to denote the space of all continuous and bounded functions on I with values in $L^2(\Omega, A, P)$. We define C_c to be the set of all continuous functions on I with values in $L^2(\Omega, A, P)$ endowed with the topology of uniform convergence on intervals $[0, T]$ where $T > 0$.

Definition 2.9 We say that the Banach space B is *stronger* than the space C_c if every convergent sequence in B (with respect to its norm) will also converge in C_c.

We now describe SDEs in Banach spaces as *operator mappings*. For example, we can define the integral operator T as

$$(Tx)(t; \omega) = \int_0^t k(t, \tau; \omega) x(\tau; \omega) d\tau \tag{2.22}$$

where k is the stochastic kernel function. The operator T maps elements x of some Banach space B into another Banach space D.

Definition 2.10 The pair of spaces (B, D) is said to be *admissible* with respect to the operator $T : C_c(\mathbb{R}^+, L^2(\Omega, A, P)) \to C_c(\mathbb{R}^+, L^2(\Omega, A, P))$ where $\mathbb{R}^+ = \{x \in \mathbb{R}, x \geq 0\}$ if and only if $T(B) \subset D$.

Definition 2.11 The operator T is said to be *continuous* on $C_c(\mathbb{R}^+, L^2(\Omega, A, P))$ if and only if: $(Tx_n)(t; \omega) \to (Tx)(t; \omega)$ in $C_c(\mathbb{R}^+, L^2(\Omega, A, P))$ for every sequence $\{x_n(t; \omega)\}$ such that $x_n(t; \omega) \to x(t; \omega)$ in the same space.

Definition 2.12 The *norm* of a continuous and bounded operator $T : B \to D$ (where B and D are Banach spaces) is defined by the positive number

$$K = \sup_{x \in B} \frac{\|(Tx)(t; \omega)\|_D}{\|x(t; \omega)\|_B}$$

Theorem 2.6 Let us consider the SIE defined by equation (2.15). Assume that the following conditions are true:

- B and D are Banach spaces that are stronger than $C_c(\mathbb{R}^+, L^2(\Omega, A, P))$ and such that the pair (B, D) is admissible with respect to the operator T defined by (2.22).
- $x(t; \omega) \to f(t, x(t; \omega))$ is a continuous operator on the set $S = \{x(t; \omega) : x(t, \omega) \in D, \|x(t; \omega)\|_D \leq \rho\}$ with values in B and satisfying $\|f(t, x(t; \omega) - f(t, y(t; \omega))\|_B \leq \lambda \|x(t; \omega) - y(t; \omega)\|_D \; \forall \; x(t; \omega), y(t; \omega) \in S$ and λ is a positive constant.
- $h(t; \omega) \in D$.

Then there exists a *unique* solution of the SIE (2.15) provided that

$$\lambda < K^{-1}, \quad \|h(t; \omega)\|_D + K \|f(t, 0)\|_B \leq \rho(1 - \lambda K)$$

where K is the norm of the operator T as defined in equation (2.22).

The proof of this theorem uses the Banach fixed point theorem and is given in Tsokos and Padgett (1974). We have stated the theorem in order to prepare the way for the SIE of interest to us, namely the Ito equation.

2.9   A SPECIAL SDE: THE ITO EQUATION

We now discuss the SIE of Ito-Doobs type (Tsokos, 1974, page 214):

$$x(t; \omega) = \int_0^t f(\tau, x(\tau; \omega))d\tau + \int_0^t g(\tau, x(\tau; \omega))dW(\tau) \; t \in [0, T] \tag{2.23}$$

The first integral is of Lebesgue type while the second integral is of Ito type that is defined with respect to a scalar Brownian motion process $W(t)$. Our interest in this section is in proving that the SIE (2.23) has a unique solution in a given Banach space.

We need to introduce some more notation. First, we define $C^*([a, b], L^2(\Omega, A, P)$ to be the space of all continuous functions from $[a, b]$ to $L^2(\Omega, A, P)$ with corresponding norm $\|x\| \equiv \sup_{a \leq t \leq b} \left\{ \int_\Omega |x(t; \omega)|^2 dP(\omega) \right\}$.

Now we define the operators $W_1, W_2 \; : \; C^*([0, T], L^2(\Omega, A, P)) \; \to \; C^*([0, T], L^2(\Omega, A, P))$ by

$$(W_1 x)(t; \omega) \equiv \int_0^t x(\tau, \omega) d\tau$$

$$(W_2 x)(t; \omega) \equiv \int_0^t x(\tau; \omega) dW(\tau)$$

It can be shown (Tsokos, 1974) that there exist positive constants $K_1, K_2 (K_1 < 1, K_2 < 1)$ such that $\|(W_1 x)(t; \omega)\|_D \leq K_1 \|x(t; \omega)\|_B$ and $\|(W_2 x)(t; \omega)\|_D \leq K_2 \|x(t; \omega)\|_B$ where the Banach spaces B and D are stronger than C in Definition 2.8.

Theorem 2.7 Consider the stochastic integral equation (2.23) under the following conditions:

- B and D are Banach spaces in $C^*([0, 1], L_2(\Omega, A, P))$ which are stronger than $C^*([0, 1], L_2(\Omega, A, P))$ such that the pair (B, D) is admissible with respect to the operators W_1 and W_2.
- $x(t; \omega) \to f(t, x(t; \omega))$ is an operator on the space: $S = \{x(t; \omega) : x(t; \omega) \in D$ and $\|x(t; \omega)\|_D \leq \rho\}$ with values in B satisfying: $\|f(t, x(t; \omega)) - f(t, y(t; \omega))\|_B \leq \lambda_1 \|x(t; \omega) - y(t; \omega)\|_D$.
- $x(t; \omega) \to g(t, x(t; \omega))$ is an operator on S into B satisfying $\|g(t, x(t; \omega)) - g(t, y(t; \omega))\|_B \leq \lambda_2 \|x(t; \omega) - y(t; \omega)\|_D$, where λ_1 and λ_2 are constants.

Then there exists a unique random solution to equation (2.23) provided that

$$\lambda_1 K_1 + \lambda_2 K_2 < 1$$

and

$$\|f(t, 0)\|_B + \|g(t, 0)\|_B \leq \rho(1 - \lambda_1 K_1 - \lambda_2 K_2)$$

Proof:

Define the operator $U : S \to D$ by

$$(Ux)(t; \omega) - \int_0^t f(\tau, x(t; \omega)) d\tau + \int_0^t g(\tau, x(\tau; \omega)) dW(\tau) \tag{2.24}$$

What we need to prove now is that this operator is a contraction operator and hence that the equation $x(t; \omega) = (Ux)(t; \omega)$ has a unique solution. To this end, we shall use the Banach fixed-point theorem.

Let $x(t; \omega)$ and $y(t; \omega) \in S$. Since D is a Banach space we see that $(Ux)(t; \omega) - (Uy)(t; \omega) \in D$ and

$$\|(Ux)(t; \omega) - (Uy)(t; \omega)\|_D \leq \| \int_0^t [f(\tau, x(\tau; \omega)) - f(\tau, y(\tau; \omega))] d\tau \|_D$$

$$+ \| \int_0^t [g(\tau, x(\tau; \omega)) - g(\tau, y(\tau; \omega))] dW(\tau) \|_D$$

$$\leq K_1 \|f(t, x(t; \omega)) - f(t, y(t; \omega))\|_B + K_2 \|g(t, x(t; \omega)) - g(t, y(t; \omega))\|_B$$

$$\leq (\lambda_1 K_1 + \lambda_2 K_2) \|x(t; \omega) - y(t; \omega)\|_D$$

$$< \|x(t; \omega) - y(t; \omega)\|_D$$

Hence, the operator U is a contraction. We now must prove that the operator U maps elements of the set S into other elements of the set S, that is $US \subset S$. To this end, the following calculations prove this assertion.

Let $x(t; \omega) \in S$. Then using the assumptions of the theorem we get

$$\|(Ux)(t; \omega)\|_D$$

$$\leq \| \int_0^t f(\tau, x(\tau; \omega))d\tau \|_D + \| \int_0^t g(\tau, x(\tau; \omega))dW(\tau) \|_D$$

$$\leq K_1 \| f(t, x(t; \omega)) \|_B + K_2 \| g(t, x(t; \omega)) \|_B$$

$$\leq \lambda_1 K_1 \| x(t; \omega) \|_D + \lambda_2 K_2 \| x(t; \omega) \|_D$$

$$+ K_1 \| f(t, 0) \|_B + K_2 \| g(t, 0) \|_B$$

and since $x(t; \omega) \in S$ we finally get $\|(Ux)(t; \omega)\|_D \leq \rho(\lambda_1 K_1 + \lambda_2 K_2)$

$$+ \| f(t, 0) \|_B + \| g(t, 0) \|_B \leq \rho$$

We now conclude that the SIE (2.23) has a unique solution by appealing to the Banach fixed-point theorem.

2.10   NUMERICAL APPROXIMATION OF SIEs

In the previous section we gave sufficient conditions for an SIE to have a unique solution in a Banach space. We now ask the question: how do we numerically approximate the solution of an SIE? In order to reduce the scope, let us examine the SIE (2.15). There are a number of essential difficulties to be resolved:

1. The function f in equation (2.15) is usually nonlinear as a function of the unknown variable x and some kind of iterative scheme will be needed. Furthermore, we wish to determine the convergence rate of the resulting iterative scheme.
2. We approximate the integral in equation (2.15) by a numerical quadrature scheme, for example the extended trapezoidal method.

To address point (1) above we first of all apply the *method of successive approximations* to find a solution of equation (2.15): we define the sequence of successive approximations $\{x_n(t; \omega)\}$ by

$$\begin{cases} x_0(t; \omega) = h(t; \omega) \\ x_{n+1}(t; \omega) = (Ux_n)(t; \omega), \quad n \geq 0 \end{cases} \tag{2.25}$$

where the operator U has been defined by $(Ux)(t; \omega) = h(t; \omega) + \int_0^t k(t, \tau; \omega) f(\tau, x(\tau; \omega))d\tau$ (equation (2.24)).

It has been shown in Tsokos (1974), chapter III, that this sequence converges to the solution of (2.15) in the norm of the Banach space D already referred to. We also wish to determine the *rate of convergence* as a function of the iteration parameter n. The analysis in Tsokos and Padgett (1974) for the stochastic case is a generalisation of the analysis for the deterministic case as discussed in Rall (1969). The main convergence result is

$$\|x(t; \omega) - x_n(t; \omega)\|_{L^2(\Omega, A, P)} \leq \|x(t; \omega) - x_n(t; \omega)\|_D < (\lambda K)^n \rho \quad \forall \, t \in \mathbb{R}^+ \tag{2.26}$$

and hence (note $\lambda K < 1$)

$$
\begin{aligned}
E\left\{|x(t;\omega) - x_n(t;\omega)|^2\right\} &= \int_{\Omega} |x(t;\omega) - x_n(t;\omega)|^2 dP(\omega) \\
&= \|x(t;\omega) - x_n(t;\omega)\|^2_{L^2(\Omega,A,P)} < ((\lambda K)^n \rho)^2
\end{aligned}
\tag{2.27}
$$

This completes our attention to point (1) above.

We now discuss the combination of the method of successive approximations as just described when the integral in equation (2.15) is evaluated numerically. To this end, we partition the interval $[0, T]$ into N equal subintervals:

$$
0 = t_0 < t_1 < \ldots < t_N = T
\tag{2.28}
$$

with

$$
\Delta t = t_{n+1} - t_n, \quad n = 0, \ldots, N-1
$$

We now transform the SIE (2.15) into an *arithmetic fixed-point problem*; in this case the solution of the fixed-point problem $x = U(x)$, where U is an operator on the Banach space X if the function $U(x)$ can be calculated to any desired accuracy by a finite number of arithmetic operations. The main challenge is the estimation of the integral in equation (2.15) and we approximate it at time level n as follows:

$$
\int_0^{t_n} k(t_n, \tau; \omega) f(\tau, x(\tau; \omega)) d\tau = \sum_{j=0}^{n} W_{n,j} k_{n,j}(\omega) f_j(x_j(\omega)) - \delta^{(n)}(\omega)
$$

where

$x_j(\omega) \equiv x(t_j; \omega)$
$f_j(x_j(\omega)) \equiv f(t_j, x(t_j; \omega))$
$k_{n,j}(\omega) \equiv k(t_n, t_j; \omega)$
$W_{n,j} = $ weights of the numerical integration method
$\delta^{(n)}(\omega) = $ error of approximation

We now define the sequence $\left\{X_n^{(m)}\right\}$ of successive approximations to the solution of equation (2.15) at each time level n as

$$
\begin{aligned}
X_n^{(0)}(\omega) &= h_n(\omega) \\
X_n^{(m+1)}(\omega) &= h_n(\omega) + \sum_{j=0}^{n} W_{n,j} k_{n,j}(\omega) f_j(X_j^{(m)}(\omega)) \text{ for } m \geq 0
\end{aligned}
\tag{2.29}
$$

What can we say about the accuracy of scheme (2.29)? On the one hand we can choose Δt small enough in order to get a good approximation to the integral term and by taking enough iterations in equation (2.29), that is taking m large enough. In Tsokos and Padgett (1974) it is proved that

$$\|X_n^{(m+1)}(\omega) - x_n(\omega)\|_D$$

$$< \|\delta^{(n)}(\omega)\| \left\{ \frac{1 - (\lambda K)^{m+1}}{1 - \lambda K} \right\} + (\lambda K)^{m+1} \rho \qquad (2.30)$$

$$< \|\delta^{(n)}(\omega)\|/(1 - \lambda K) + (\lambda K)^{m+1} \rho$$

where K is defined in definition 2.12.

We now need to define some bounds on the right-hand terms in equation (2.30). First, we choose the mesh size Δt so that for every $\varepsilon_1 > 0$ $\|\delta^{(n)}(\omega)\| < \varepsilon_1(1 - \lambda K)$. Furthermore, for $\varepsilon_2 > 0$ we choose m so large to ensure that $(\lambda K)^{m+1} \rho < \varepsilon_2$. Having done that, we now have a final error estimate $\|X_n^{(m+1)}(\omega) - x_n(\omega)\|_D < \varepsilon_1 + \varepsilon_2 = \varepsilon$.

2.11   TRANSFORMING AN SDE: THE ITO FORMULA

In this section we introduce the Ito formula and it can be used for one-factor and multi-factor SDEs that are driven by a range of processes. We introduce it briefly and it has been discussed in many textbooks already (see Cont and Tankov, 2004).

Theorem 2.8 (One-dimensional Ito Formula). Let X be an Ito process defined by

$$dX = \mu(t, X)dt + \sigma(t, X)dW$$

Let $g(t, x) \in C^2([0, \infty] \times \mathbb{R})$, i.e. g is twice continuously differentiable in x and t. Then $y(t) \equiv g(t, x(t))$ is also an Ito process satisfying the SDE:

$$dY = \frac{\partial g}{\partial t}dt + \frac{\partial g}{\partial x}dX + \frac{1}{2}\frac{\partial^2 g}{\partial x^2}(dX)^2$$

where $(dX)^2 = dX.dX$ is computed using $dt.dt = dt.dW = dW.dt = 0$ and $dW.dW = dt$.

This formula is useful because we can transform an SDE into a simpler one that we can solve. To show how to use the formula, we examine the SDE that we introduced in Chapter 0:

$$dS = rSdt + \sigma SdW$$

Using the transformation $Y = f(t, S) = \log(S)$, checking that $\frac{\partial f}{\partial t} = 0$, $\frac{\partial f}{\partial S} = \frac{1}{S}$, $\frac{\partial^2 f}{\partial S^2} = -\frac{1}{S^2}$ we can deduce (by a bit of algebra) that

$$df = \left(r - \frac{1}{2}\sigma^2\right)dt + \sigma dW$$

We take another example. The SDE for an underlying commodity is defined by $dS = \mu Sdt + \sigma SdW$ and let the forward price F be defined by $F = Se^{r(T-t)}$. Then F satisfies the SDE:

$$dF = (\mu - r)F + \sigma FdW$$

(You should check this assertion.)

2.12 SUMMARY AND CONCLUSIONS

We have given a mathematical introduction to the theory of stochastic differential equations (SDEs). We proved existence and uniqueness results using a combination of probability theory and functional analysis. In particular, we used the Banach fixed-point theorem to prove the existence and uniqueness of the solution of SDEs. We discussed some types of SDE and paid particular attention to the Ito SDE because of its importance in financial engineering.

Having completed the mathematical formulation of SDEs, we need to show how to model them in C++ using a combination of object-oriented and generic programming techniques. We introduce these issues in Chapter 3.

2.13 APPENDIX: PROOF OF THE BANACH FIXED-POINT THEOREM AND SOME APPLICATIONS

We prove Theorem 2.1 that we introduced in section 2.3.3. We prove that the fixed-point is unique and that it exists. First, let us suppose that both x and y are solutions of the fixed-point problem $z = T(z)$, where T is a contraction operator. Then

$$d(x, y) = d(T(x), T(y)) \leq \lambda d(x, y) \text{ where } 0 < \lambda < 1$$

Hence $x = y$ and we conclude that the fixed point is unique. We now prove existence by creating a sequence of successive approximants of the operator equation and proving that this is a Cauchy sequence.

Take any point $x_0 \in X$ and let $x_n = T(x_{n-1}), n = 1, 2, \ldots$.

Then for $k > 0$, we have $d(x_k, x_{k+1}) = d(T(x_{k-1}), T(x_k)) < \lambda d(x_{k-1}, x_k)$.

Using this formula repeatedly we get $d(x_k, x_{k+1}) \leq \lambda^j d(x_{k-j}, x_{k-j+1})$, $j = 1, \ldots, k$.

Continuing, we use the triangle inequality repeatedly on $m > n \geq 1$ to get

$$d(x_n, x_m) \leq \sum_{j=0}^{m-n-1} d(x_{n+j}, x_{n+j+1}) \leq \sum_{j=0}^{m-n-1} \lambda^j d(x_{n-1}, x_n)$$
$$\leq \frac{\lambda}{1-\lambda} d(x_{n-1}, x_n) \leq \frac{\lambda^n}{1-\lambda} d(x_0, x_1)$$

Since $0 < \lambda < 1$, then for each $\varepsilon > 0$ we can choose a positive integer n_0 such that $\frac{\lambda^n}{1-\lambda} d(x_0, x_1) < \varepsilon$ where $n \geq n_0$.

We thus conclude that $\{x_n\}$ is a Cauchy sequence in the complete metric space X and thus converges to a point $\overline{x} \in X$. Since T is continuous we have $\overline{x} = \lim x_n = \lim T(x_{n-1}) = T(\overline{x})$. Hence $\overline{x}$ is a fixed point of T, and we are done.

We conclude this appendix with a short overview of applications in numerical analysis where fixed-point theorems are useful. Not only can we use them to prove existence and uniqueness results (as in this chapter) but it can be used as a *computational tool*. In general, the operator T can be linear or nonlinear and both cases occur in practice. One of the main challenges lies in transforming the original equation to be solved into one of the form $x = T(x)$ in such a way that T is a contraction. We gave a short overview of where fixed-point theorems are used as computational tools:

- Solution of matrix systems: In many applications we solve linear algebraic equations of the form

$$A\underline{x} = \underline{b} \tag{2.31}$$

where A is a given matrix, $\underline{b}$ is a given vector and $\underline{x}$ is the unknown vector. The objective is to develop an algorithm to compute the vector $\underline{x}$ in a finite number of steps. One class of algorithms for doing this is called *iterative methods*, which are based on a splitting of the matrix A as $A = M - N$. Then the problem (2.31) can be written in the equivalent form $(M - N)\underline{x} = \underline{b}$ or $M\underline{x} = N\underline{x} + \underline{b}$. Then this problem can be cast as a fixed-point problem in the form $\underline{x} = T(\underline{x})$, $T \equiv M^{-1}(N + \underline{b})$ leading to the iterative scheme:

$$\begin{cases} M\underline{x}^{(k+1)} = N\underline{x}^{(k)} + \underline{b}, & k \geq 0 \\ \underline{x}^{(0)} \text{ arbitrary} \end{cases} \tag{2.32}$$

Of course, we must be sure that the mapping is a contraction, in other words that $\|M^{-1}N\| < 1$ for some matrix norm $\|.\|$. In many cases it will be possible to find matrices M and N that do satisfy this inequality. Fortunately, in many cases (for example, when the matrix A is positive definite or diagonally dominant) we can find matrices M and N that lead to a contraction operator. For more information, see Varga (1962) and Golub and van Loan (1996).

- Solution of nonlinear equations: Let $f(x)$ be a real-valued function of the scalar variable x and let us suppose that we wish to solve the equation $f(x) = 0$ on the interval $[a, b]$. There are many methods for solving this problem, for example the Bisection method, Newton's method and the Secant method. But it is also possible to cast it as a fixed-point problem. To this end, let us suppose that $0 < m_1 \leq f'(x) \leq m_2, \forall x \in [a, b]$. We now convert the original problem to a fixed-point problem:

$$g(x) = x - \frac{1}{m} f(x)$$

By a suitable choice for m (see Haaser and Sullivan, 1991) we can ensure that g is a contraction of $[a, b]$ into itself. We have found this to be a useful technique for a number of finance problems, for example when calculating yield in fixed income applications.

- Integral equations: Fixed-point analysis can be used to prove the existence and uniqueness of solutions of the nonlinear Volterra equation of the second kind:

$$x(t) = \lambda \int_{t_0}^{t} f(t, s, x(s))ds + g(t) \tag{2.33}$$

and solutions of the nonlinear Fredholm equation of the second kind:

$$x(t) = \lambda \int_{a}^{b} f(t, s, x(s))ds + g(t) \tag{2.34}$$

In general, equation (2.33) will have a solution for all values of λ while for equation (2.34) this statement is not necessarily true; it does not have a solution for all values of λ.

- Ordinary differential equations: Consider the system of n first-order differential equations with initial condition:

$$\dot{x}(t) \equiv \frac{dx(t)}{dt} = f(t, x(t)), \quad x(t_0) = x_0 \tag{2.35}$$

We call problem (2.35) an *initial value problem* (IVP for short) and it can be transformed (by integration) to a nonlinear Volterra integral equation:

$$x(t) = \int_{t_0}^{t} f(s, x(s))ds + x_0 \qquad (2.36)$$

Theorem 2.9 Let the function $f : \mathbb{R}^{n+1} \to \mathbb{R}^n$ be continuous and satisfy the Lipschitz condition:

$$|f(t, x_1) - f(t, x_2)| \leq L|x_1 - x_2|, \quad L > 0$$

in some neighbourhood N of the point (t_0, x_0). Then, for each $a > 0$ such that

$$S = \{(t, x) : |t - t_0| \leq a, |x - x_0| < b\} \subset N \text{ for some } b > 0$$

there exists a unique solution of (2.36) on $I = [t_0 - a_1, t_0 + a_1]$ where $a_1 = min\{a, b/M\}$ and $M = \sup_{(t,x) \in S} |f(t, x)|$.

2.14   EXERCISES AND PROJECTS

1. (**) Let X be the set of all bounded real-valued functions defined on any set A. Show that

$$d(f, g) = \sup\{|f(t) - g(t)|; t \in A\}$$

   defines a metric on X (here 'sup $h(t)$' signifies the least upper bound function $h(t)$ on some interval).
2. (**) Prove that a convergent sequence in a metric space is a Cauchy sequence.
3. (*) Compute the first 15 Fibonacci numbers.
4. (***) Prove the following statements:

   if $f \in L_{ip}(\alpha)$ on $[a, b]$, then f is continuous

   if $f \in L_{ip}(\alpha)$ on $[a, b]$, with $\alpha > 1$ then f is constant

   if $f \subset L_{lp}(\alpha)$ on $[a, b]$, and if $|f'(x)| \leq M$ then $f \in L_{ip}(1)$

   Hint: use the *mean value theorem for derivatives*: if f is differentiable on $[a, b]$ and $|f'(t)| \leq m$ for all $t \in (a, b)$ then $|f(b) - f(a)| \leq m(b - a)$.
   Another form of the theorem states that there exists $x \in (a, b)$ such that $f(b) - f(a) = (b - a)f'(x)$.
5. (***) Fixed points and the solution of nonlinear equations
   We solve the equation $x = f(x)$ by the recursion $x_n = f(x_{n-1})$, $n \geq 0$, for a given x_0. The recursion converges to a root if $|f'(x)| \leq L < 1$ and the error e_n is given by $e_n \sim f'(r)e_{n-1}$.
   Apply this method to solving the equation

$$F(x) = x^3 + 2x^2 + 10x - 20 = 0$$

   by writing it in the form

$$x = 20/(x^2 + 2x + 10)$$

   (The approximate solution is $x = 1.368808107$ and it was originally calculated by Leonardo of Pisa in 1225.)

6. (**) Use the Banach fixed-point theorem to find the solutions of the following nonlinear equations:

   (a)

   $$x^2 = 2, \quad x_{n+1} = \frac{1}{2}\left(x_n + \frac{2}{x_n}\right), \quad n \geq 0 \quad x_0 = 1$$

   Can you motivate how we arrived at this iteration?

   (b)

   $$x = \sin(x + y)$$
   $$y = \cos(x - y)$$
   $$x_0 = y_0 = 0.5$$

7. (***) Consider the SDE $dX = \sigma dW$ and consider the general process $Y(t) = f(t, X(t))$. Prove the following by Ito's formula:

   $$dY = \frac{1}{2}\sigma^2 Y dt + \sigma Y dW \text{ when } f(t, x) = e^x$$

   and

   $$dY = \sigma Y dW \text{ when } f(t, x) = \exp\left(x - \frac{1}{2}\int_0^t \sigma^2(u)du\right)$$

3
Alternative SDEs and Toolkit
Functionality

3.1 INTRODUCTION AND OBJECTIVES

In this chapter we introduce a number of stochastic differential equations (SDEs) that are generalisations of the SDEs from previous chapters of this book. We use these in a Monte Carlo application to calculate option prices and we compare the solutions with an exact representation and with the finite difference method.

The second set of topics in the chapter is concerned with developing algorithms to compute random variates from a number of important distributions, for example gamma, beta and exponential distributions because of their relevance in Monte Carlo simulation. We also introduce a number of statistical distributions and other special functions from the Boost library and we recommend using them in applications rather than reinventing the wheel.

Finally, we introduce a number of topics related to the existence and uniqueness of the solutions of SDEs and PDEs (partial differential equations). In particular, we introduce the Feller condition and the Fichera function and we show how they are related.

A general goal in this chapter is to provide code that you can use in your applications.

3.2 BESSEL PROCESSES

Let $W = (W_1, \ldots, W_m)$ be a Brownian motion in $\mathbb{R}^m$, $m \geq 2$ and define the process:

$$R(t, \omega) = \|W(t, \omega)\| \equiv \left(\sum_{j=1}^m W_j^2(t, \omega) \right)^{1/2} \tag{3.1}$$

This process represents the distance to the origin of $W(t, \omega)$. It can be shown (Karatzas and Shreve, 1991) that this process satisfies the SDE:

$$dR = \frac{m-1}{2R} dt + \sum_{j=1}^m \frac{W_j dW_j}{R} \tag{3.2}$$

The process R is called the *m-dimensional Bessel process* and it can be shown that equation (3.2) is equivalent to

$$R(t) = R(0) + \int_0^t \frac{m-1}{2R(s)} ds + \tilde{W}(t) \tag{3.3}$$

where $\tilde{W}(t)$ is the standard one-dimensional Brownian motion or equivalently

$$dR = \frac{m-1}{2R} dt + d\tilde{W}, \quad 0 < t < \infty \tag{3.4}$$

where $d\tilde{W}$ is a one-dimensional Brownian process.

An interesting property of the Bessel process is that the origin is never attainable, that is:

$$P[R(t) > 0; \quad 0 < t < \infty] = 1 \tag{3.5}$$

We would also like to satisfy this property by finite difference schemes that approximate SDE (3.4).

We note (Jäckel, 2002) that the CEV process can be written as a Bessel process. We discuss the CEV process in detail in section 3.10.

3.3   RANDOM VARIATE GENERATION

In the following sections we discuss techniques to sample from a number of distributions. In particular, we discuss algorithms in C++ for the following distributions:

- exponential;
- beta;
- gamma;
- Poisson;
- geometric.

These distributions are used in financial models. In particular, they are used when modelling gamma and Lévy processes and processes based on *subordinated Brownian motion* (see Glasserman, 2004, page 143; Cont and Tankov, 2004, page 117). Other distributions are lognormal, Cauchy, chi-square and Student. We have provided C++ code on the CD to generate random variates from the above distributions. Please do not confuse this code with Boost library code.

3.4   THE EXPONENTIAL DISTRIBUTION

Definition 3.1 An *exponential variate* X with parameter $\beta > 0$ has the density (pdf):

$$f(x) = f_X(x) = \begin{cases} \frac{1}{\beta} e^{-x/\beta}, & 0 \le x < \infty, \quad \beta > 0 \\ \\ 0, \text{ otherwise} \end{cases} \tag{3.6}$$

and is denoted by exp (β).

The mean and variance are given by

$$E(X) = \beta$$
$$V(X) = \beta^2$$

respectively. We generate random exponential variates by the *inverse transform method*, as follows:

$$U = F_X(x) = \int_0^x \frac{1}{\beta} e^{-y/\beta} dy = 1 - e^{-x/\beta} \tag{3.7}$$

where U is a standard uniform variate. Then, since $1 - U$ and U are distributed in the same way, we have

$$X = -\beta \log(1 - U) \text{ or } X = -\beta \log U \tag{3.8}$$

and this is the basis for the C++ code on the CD for generating exponential variates. The function prototypes for generating exponential variates and arrays of these variates is

```
// Generate exp(1) (Standard distribution)
double exponential ();

// Using the inverse transform method, exp(beta)
double exponential (double UniformValue, double beta);
double exponential (double beta);

// Generate an array of exponential variates with the same
// factor, direct
vector<double> exponentialArrayDirect (long N, double beta);

// Generate array of exponential variates, using order
   statistics
vector<double> exponentialArrayOrderStasticsMethod
                   (long N, double beta);
```

Exponential random variables and their sums are used when defining Markov processes with jumps.

3.5   THE BETA AND GAMMA DISTRIBUTIONS

In order to define these distributions we first introduce the gamma function defined by

$$\Gamma(p) = \int_0^\infty x^{p-1} e^{-x} dx, \quad p > 0 \tag{3.9}$$

When $p > 0$ the above improper integral converges to a finite value. Using integration by parts we can show that

$$\Gamma(p) = (p-1)\Gamma(p-1)$$

In the special case when p is a positive integer, that is $p = n$, we obtain the representation:

$$\Gamma(n) = (n-1)! \quad \left(\text{use } \Gamma(1) = \int_0^\infty e^{-x} dx = 1\right)$$

We thus see that the gamma function is a generalisation of the factorial function. We note that the Boost library has an implementation of the gamma function.

Definition 3.2 A random variable X has a *beta distribution* on the interval $[0, 1]$ if its density (pdf) is defined by

$$f(x) = f_X(x) = \frac{\Gamma(\alpha + \beta)}{\Gamma(\alpha)\Gamma(\beta)} x^{\alpha-1}(1-x)^{\beta-1}, \quad \alpha, \beta > 0, \quad x \in [0, 1] \tag{3.10}$$

We denote this distribution by $B(\alpha, \beta)$.

This distribution has applications to the modelling of the random recovery rate (as a percentage) upon default of a bond subject to credit risk, for example. The algorithms for generating beta distribution variates are

1. Using the multivariate transform method.
2. Using order statistics.
3. Jöhnk's method (Jöhnk, 1964).
4. Acceptance-rejection methods.

We have created four methods for calculating beta variates using so-called *traits classes* (we discuss these in more detail in Chapter 11); these are template classes based on an integer parameter. Each specific value of the parameter corresponds to one of the above algorithms; for example the code for the class based on order statistics (option 2 above) is

```
template <int Type> class Beta {};
template <> class Beta<2>        // Be-2
{ // Using order statistics
private:
        long a;                    // Alpha
        long b;                    // Beta
public:
        explicit Beta(long delta, long beta);
        double generateVariate() const;

};
```

The body of this class is given by

```
Beta<2>::Beta(long delta, long beta)
{ // Be-2

    a = delta;
    b = beta;
}

double Beta<2>::generateVariate() const
{
    // From order statistics Be-2

    // Create the order statistics array
    long dim = a + b - 1;
    vector<double> UArr = generateUniformArray(dim);

    // Now have to sort this array (order statistics): ASCENDING
    sort(UArr.begin( ), UArr.end( ) );

    return UArr[a -1]; // +1 because null offset

}
```

An example of use is:

```
Beta<2> myBeta2(2, 1);
double var2 = myBeta2.generateVariate();
cout << var2 << endl;
```

Definition 3.3 The gamma distribution with *shape parameter* α and *scale parameter* β has the density function (pdf):

$$f(x) = f_X(x) = \begin{cases} \frac{1}{\Gamma(\alpha)\beta^\alpha} x^{\alpha-1} e^{-x/\beta}, & 0 \le x \le \infty, \quad \alpha > 0, \quad \beta > 0 \\ \\ 0, \text{ otherwise} \end{cases} \tag{3.11}$$

We denote this distribution by $G(\alpha, \beta)$. There is no explicit formula for the cdf of the gamma function and thus the inverse transform method cannot be used. Thus, we resort to other methods of generating gamma variates. We consider a number of algorithms (Rubinstein, 1981 and Glasserman, 2004). In some cases we can generate gamma variates from beta variates and in other cases we can generate beta variates from gamma variates. In section 3.13 we discuss how the Boost library implements statistical distributions.

The mean and variance of the gamma distribution are given by

$$E(X) = \alpha\beta$$
$$V(X) = \alpha\beta^2$$

We first consider algorithms for generating gamma variates:

1. Using the reproductive property: In this case we use the fact that if $X_j, j = 1, \ldots, n$ is a sequence of independent variables from

$$G(\alpha_j, \beta) \text{ then } X = \sum_{j=1}^{n} X_j \text{ is from } G(\alpha, \beta), \text{ where } \alpha = \sum_{j=1}^{n} \alpha_j$$

In the case when $\alpha = m$ is an integer we generate a random variate from $G(m, \beta)$ by summing m independent exponential random variates $\exp(\beta)$:

$$X = \beta \sum_{j=1}^{m} (-\log U_j) = -\beta \log \prod_{j=1}^{m} U_j$$

2. Jöhnk's method (Jöhnk, 1964): This is a technique for generating variates from $G(\delta, \beta)$ where $0 < \delta < 1$.

    Theorem 3.1 Let W and V be independent variates from the beta distribution $B(\delta, 1 - \delta)$ and the standard exponential distribution $\exp(1)$, respectively. Then $X = \beta V W$ is a variate from $G(\delta, \beta)$, where $0 < \delta < 1$.

3. Fishman's method (Fishman, 1976): This is a procedure for generating from $G(\alpha, 1)$ where $\alpha \ge 1$.
    The steps are
    1. Set $A = \alpha - 1$.
    2. Generate V_1 and V_2 from $\exp(1)$.
    3. If $V_2 < A(V_1 - \log V_1 - 1)$ goto step 2.
    4. Deliver V_1 as variate from $G(\alpha, 1)$.
4. Cheng's method (Cheng, 1977): This is a procedure for gamma variate generation from $G(\alpha, 1)$ where $\alpha > 1$ and whose execution time is independent of α.
    Define $\lambda = (2\alpha - 1)^{1/2}$, $b = \alpha - \log 4$, $d = \alpha + 1/\lambda$.

The steps are
1. Sample U_1 and U_2 from $U(0, 1)$.
2. Set $V = \lambda \log(U_1/(1 - U_2))$.
3. Set $X = \alpha e^V$.
4. If $b + d - X \geq \log(U_1^2 U_2)$, then deliver X.
5. Goto step 1.

We have created the various implementations of gamma variate generation using traits classes in the same way as we did for the beta distribution. Each specific algorithm has its own associated class, for example in the case of the Fishman's method this is

```
template <int Type> class Gamma {};
template <> class Gamma<3>              // Fishman
{ // G(alpha, 1), alpha >= 1
private:
      double a;          // Alpha
public:
      explicit Gamma(double alpha);
      double generateVariate() const;
};
```

The code for this class is given by

```
Gamma<3>::Gamma(double alpha)
{
      a = alpha;

}

double Gamma<3>::generateVariate() const
{
      double A = a - 1.0;
      double V1, V2;

L1:
      V1 = exponential();
      V2 = exponential();

      if ( V2 >= A * (V1 - log(V1) - 1.0))
      {
          return V1;          // This is a variate from G(alpha, 1)
      }

      goto L1;                // a 'do while' is also OK

}
```

An example of use is given by the following code:

```
Gamma<4> myGamma4(2.0);
double var4 = myGamma4.generateVariate();
cout << var4 << endl;
```

The results in this section can be used as *building-blocks* when simulating pure-jump and Lévy processes, for example (see Glasserman, 2004; see also the exercises in this chapter).

3.6 THE CHI-SQUARED, STUDENT AND OTHER DISTRIBUTIONS

A chi-squared distribution Y is described in terms of sums of squares of independent $N(0, 1)$ variables:

$$Y = \sum_{j=1}^{k} Z_j^2 \text{ where } Z_j \sim N(0, 1), \quad j = 1, \ldots, k \qquad (3.12)$$

where the parameter k is called the number of *degrees of freedom*. We have provided three functions on the CD to calculate these variates.

The variable X defined by

$$X = \frac{Z}{\sqrt{Y/k}} \qquad (3.13)$$

where

Z is a $N(0, 1)$ variable

Y is χ^2 variate

$k =$ number of degrees of freedom

has a *Student's t-distribution* with k degrees of freedom. Summarising, the function prototypes for some of the other continuous distributions are

```
double LogNormal(long mu, long sigma);
double Cauchy(long alpha, long beta);

template <int N> double ChiSquared(long k) {}
template <> double ChiSquared<1>(long k);
template <> double ChiSquared<2>(long k);
template <> double ChiSquared<3>(long k);     // For k > 30

double Student(long k);
```

3.7 DISCRETE VARIATE GENERATION

We discuss two distributions in this section. First, the Poisson distribution has the probability mass function (p.m.f.):

$$f(X) = \frac{\lambda^X e^{-\lambda}}{X!}, \quad X = 0, 1, 2, \ldots \qquad (3.14)$$

where $\lambda > 0$ is called the *arrival rate* while for the geometric distribution the p.m.f. is defined by

$$f(X) = p(1 - p)^X, \quad X = 0, 1, \ldots, \quad 0 < p < 1 \qquad (3.15)$$

We have provided the code for variates from the Poisson and geometric distributions. The function prototypes are

```
double Poisson(long lambda);
double Geometric(double p);
```

Please see the CD for the source code. Again, the Boost library also has an implementation for these distributions.

3.8   THE FOKKER-PLANCK EQUATION

In this section we give a short overview of a partial differential equation (PDE) that describes the evolution of state space density rather than that of a single trajectory (or path). This is called the *Fokker-Planck (FP) equation* (also known as the *Kolmogorov forward equation*) and in the one-dimensional case it is defined by

$$\frac{\partial f}{\partial t} = -\frac{\partial}{\partial x}(\mu f) + \frac{1}{2}\frac{\partial^2}{\partial x^2}(\sigma^2 f) \qquad (3.16)$$

where

$f = f(x, t)$ is the probability density function.

$\mu = \mu(x, t)$ is the drift function.

$\sigma = \sigma(x, t)$ is the diffusion function $x, t \in \mathbb{R}$

We have information about the state x of the system at time t, namely the probability density functions $f(x, t)$ at time $t = 0$, that is $f(x, 0)$. We integrate the equation *forward in time*.

One of the first applications of the FP equation was the statistical description of Brownian motion of a particle in a fluid. It is possible to describe the path of a single Brownian particle by the *Langevin SDE*:

$$dU(t) = -U(t)\frac{dt}{\tau} + \frac{2v^{1/2}}{\tau}dW(t) \qquad (3.17)$$

where

$U(t)$ is the velocity of the particle.

$dW(t)$ is a Wiener process.

v is a turbulence intensity.

τ is a Lagrangian time-scale

We can approximate the solution of equation (3.17) using the explicit Euler scheme:

$$U(t + \Delta t) = U(t) - U(t)\frac{\Delta t}{\tau} + \frac{2\sqrt{v\Delta t}}{\tau}N \qquad (3.18)$$

where N is a standard Gaussian random variable. The Kolmogorov backward equation is defined by the PDE:

$$-\frac{\partial f}{\partial t} = \mu \frac{\partial f}{\partial x} + \frac{1}{2}\sigma^2 \frac{\partial^2 f}{\partial x^2} \tag{3.19}$$

and subject to the *final condition*:

$$f(x, T) = \varphi(x) \tag{3.20}$$

In this case we are interested in answering the question: given time t, will the system be in a given subset of states at some future time $s(s > t)$? This is called the target set and is defined by the above final condition (3.20); in particular:

$$\varphi(x) = \begin{cases} 1, & \text{if state } x \text{ is in the target set} \\ 0, & \text{otherwise} \end{cases}$$

The FP equation is used for computing the probability densities of stochastic differential equations of the form:

$$dX = \mu(X, t)dt + \sigma(X, t)dW(t) \tag{3.21}$$

where $X = X(t)$. If the initial distribution $X_0 \sim f(x, 0)$ then the density $f(x, t)$ of the state $X(t)$ is given by the FP equation (3.16).

3.9   THE RELATIONSHIP WITH PDEs

We introduce a number of concepts and techniques that are related to stochastic processes and stochastic differential equations. These techniques are useful because they give us some insights into the solutions of SDEs and in particular the conditions that must hold in order for these equations to have a solution. To our knowledge, this discussion is new in the financial literature. To this end, we discuss the following topics.

- The Fichera function and the determination of boundary conditions.
- The Feller condition.

We bring together a number of results that relate the probabilistic and PDE approaches to option pricing. In particular, the Fichera function is a useful tool that determines where to define (or not to define) boundary conditions for a PDE that models the Black-Scholes equation in particular, and convection-diffusion equations in general. We see the Fichera function and the Feller conditions as two complementary views of the same problem.

3.9.1   The Fichera function

The Fichera function is applicable to a wide range of elliptic, parabolic and hyperbolic PDEs and it is particularly useful for PDEs whose coefficients are zero on certain boundaries of a bounded domain Ω in n-dimensional space (for more information, see Fichera, 1956, and

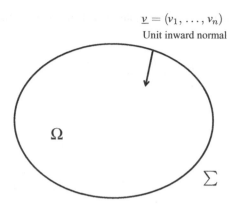

$$\underline{v} = (v_1, \ldots, v_n)$$
Unit inward normal

Ω

Σ

Figure 3.1 Region Ω and boundary Σ

Oleinik and Radkevič, 1973). We depict this domain, its boundary Σ and *inward* unit normal $\underline{v}$ in Figure 3.1. For the moment, let us examine the elliptic equation defined by

$$Lu \equiv \sum_{i,j=1}^{n} a_{ij} \frac{\partial^2 u}{\partial x_i \partial x_j} + \sum_{i=1}^{n} b_i \frac{\partial u}{\partial x_i} + cu = f \text{ in } \Omega \qquad (3.22)$$

$$\sum_{i,j=1}^{n} a_{ij} \, \xi_i \, \xi_j \geq 0 \text{ in } \Omega \cup \Sigma \text{ (characteristic form)}$$

$$\forall \, \xi = (\xi_1, \ldots, \xi_n) \in \mathbb{R}^n \qquad (3.23)$$

where

Σ is the boundary of Ω

Please note that the characteristic form is strictly positive in most cases but we are interested when it is identically zero, and in particular the subsets of the boundary Σ where it is identically zero. To this end, we partition Σ into two sub-boundaries:

$$\Sigma_3 = \left\{ x \in \Sigma : \sum_{i,j=1}^{n} a_{ij} \, v_i v_j > 0 \right\} \qquad (3.24)$$

$\Sigma - \Sigma_3$, where the characteristic form is zero

On the boundary where the characteristic form is zero (the *characteristic boundary*) we define the so-called *Fichera function*:

$$b \equiv \sum_{i=1}^{n} \left(b_i - \sum_{k=1}^{n} \frac{\partial a_{ik}}{\partial x_k} \right) v_i \qquad (3.25)$$

where v_i is the ith component of the inward normal $\underline{v}$ on Σ.

Having computed the Fichera function, we then determine its sign on all parts of the characteristic boundary; there are three mutually exclusive options:

$$\Sigma_0 : b = 0$$
$$\Sigma_1 : b > 0$$
$$\Sigma_2 : b < 0 \tag{3.26}$$

In other words, the boundary consists of the following sub-boundaries:

$$\Sigma \equiv \Sigma_0 \cup \Sigma_1 \cup \Sigma_2 \cup \Sigma_3$$

We demand that no boundary conditions are allowed when the Fichera function is zero or positive (in other words, Σ_0 and Σ_1) and the PDE (3.22) degenerates to a lower-order PDE. When $b < 0$ (that is, on Σ_2) we define a boundary condition. We pose parabolic PDEs in the form:

$$\frac{\partial u}{\partial t} = Lu + f \text{ or } -\frac{\partial u}{\partial t} + Lu = -f \tag{3.27}$$

where the elliptic operator L has already been defined in equation (3.22). Then the same conclusions hold concerning characteristic and non-characteristic boundaries as in the elliptic case. In other words, we focus on the elliptic part of the PDE to calculate the Fichera function.

Let us take an example. In this case we examine the PDE that prices a zero-coupon bond under a Cox-Ingersoll-Ross (CIR) interest-rate model:

$$\frac{\partial B}{\partial t} + \frac{1}{2}\sigma^2 r \frac{\partial^2 B}{\partial r^2} + (a - cr)\frac{\partial B}{\partial r} - rB = 0 \tag{3.28}$$

Please note that we are using backward time in this case, hence the sign difference when compared with equation (3.27). Using the definition in equation (3.25) we see that the Fichera function is given by

$$b = ((a - cr) - \sigma^2/2)\nu \text{ where } \nu \text{ is the inward unit normal} \tag{3.29}$$

We are particularly interested in the case $r = 0$ (because this is the only characteristic boundary) and we see that each choice in (3.26) can be valid depending on the relative sizes of the parameters a and σ:

$$\Sigma_2 : b < 0 \rightarrow \sigma > \sqrt{2a} \quad \text{(BC needed)}$$
$$\Sigma_0 : b = 0 \rightarrow \sigma = \sqrt{2a} \quad \text{(No BC needed)} \tag{3.30}$$
$$\Sigma_1 : b > 0 \rightarrow \sigma < \sqrt{2a} \quad \text{(No BC needed)}$$

In the last two cases we see that no boundary condition is allowed and then the PDE (3.28) evolves into the hyperbolic PDE:

$$\frac{\partial B}{\partial t} + a\frac{\partial B}{\partial r} = 0 \tag{3.31}$$

on $r = 0$. These results are consistent with the conclusions in Tavella and Randall (2000), pages 126–128. In general, we need to solve (3.31) either analytically or numerically. From a financial perspective, the third condition in (3.30) states that the interest rate cannot become negative. The inequality in this case is called the *Feller condition* for the CIR process. We have also investigated it for the process for the Heston square-root model and we have reproduced the well-known Feller condition:

$$\kappa\theta \geq \frac{1}{2}\sigma^2 \tag{3.32}$$

A full discussion of this topic is outside the scope of the current book. For a discussion on solutions of the Heston PDE using finite difference methods, see Sheppard (2007) (also available from the website www.datasimfinancial.com). See also exercise 3 (in section 3.14) for some examples from finance.

3.10   ALTERNATIVE STOCHASTIC PROCESSES

Some option pricing models assume that the underlying asset follows a geometric Brownian motion (GBM). This implies that the asset price is lognormally distributed and that returns are normally distributed. It is now clear that this model does not reflect real markets. For example, volatility is not constant but it can decrease or increase as a function of the asset price. In these cases we experience the heavy left and right tails and we speak of *volatility smile* and *volatility smirk*. A number of new models and modifications have been introduced in order to resolve the shortcomings:

- Modify the Black-Scholes equation to model skewness and kurtosis.
- Jump diffusions (Merton, 1976; Bates, 1991).
- Stochastic volatility models (Heston, 1993).
- Constant elasticity of variance (CEV) model (Cox, 1975).

We discuss the Heston and jump diffusion models in Part III of this book while a discussion of skewness-kurtosis models (with VBA code) can be found in Haug (2007). *Kurtosis* is a measure of the degree of peakedness of the probability distribution of a real-valued random variable. Higher kurtosis means more of the variance is due to infrequent extreme deviations, as opposed to frequent modestly-sized deviations. Some common formulae for kurtosis are

$$\frac{\sum_{j=1}^{N}(x_j - \bar{x})^4/N}{\sigma^4} \equiv \frac{\mu_4}{\sigma^4} \text{ (Pearson)} \tag{3.33}$$

$$\sum_{j=1}^{N}\frac{(x_j - \bar{x})/N}{\sigma^4} - 3 \equiv \frac{\mu_4}{\sigma^4} \text{ (Fisher, also known as \textit{excess kurtosis})}$$

where

N is the number of observations
$\{x_j\}_{j=1}^{N}$ is a set of observations
$\bar{x}$ is the mean of the observations
σ is the standard deviation
μ_4 is the fourth moment about the mean

These are called Pearson and Fisher kurtosis, respectively. In general, we define the nth moment about the mean as

$$\mu_n = \sum_{j=1}^{N} \frac{(x_j - \bar{x})^n}{N}, \quad N \geq 1 \tag{3.34}$$

We can categorise distributions based on this measure:

- *Mesokurtic*: These are distributions whose (Fisher) kurtosis is equal to zero, for example the normal distribution. Mesokurtic distributions are neither very peaked nor flat-topped.
- *Platykurtic*: These are distributions whose (Fisher) kurtosis is less than zero, for example the Bernoulli distribution. Platykurtic distributions have small means and thin tails.
- *Leptokurtic*: These are distributions whose (Fisher) kurtosis is greater than zero, for example the *logistic distribution* whose cumulative distribution is given by

$$F(x; \mu, s) = \frac{1}{1 + e^{-(x-\mu)s}} = \frac{1}{2} \left(1 + \tanh\left(\frac{x - \mu}{2s} \right) \right) \tag{3.35}$$

Leptokurtic distributions have high peaks and fat tails. Another example is the *Laplace distribution* (also known as the *double exponential distribution*) whose probability distribution function is given by

$$f(x; \mu, b) = \frac{1}{2b} \exp\left(-\frac{|x - \mu|}{b} \right)$$

$$= \frac{1}{2b} \begin{cases} \exp\left(-\frac{\mu - x}{b} \right), & x < \mu \\ \exp\left(-\frac{x - \mu}{b} \right), & x \geq \mu \end{cases} \tag{3.36}$$

The Laplace distribution is similar to the normal probability distribution. The Laplace distribution has fatter tails than the normal distribution. Its cumulative probability distribution is given by

$$F(x) = \begin{cases} \frac{1}{2} \exp\left(\frac{x - \mu}{b} \right), & x < \mu \\ 1 - \frac{1}{2} \exp\left(-\frac{x - \mu}{b} \right), & x \geq \mu \end{cases} \tag{3.37}$$

We now discuss a model that models pricing problems with heavy left and right tails.

3.10.1 The constant elasticity of variance (CEV) model

The CEV is a popular model because it is able to reproduce an implied volatility skew for plain options. It is used in a range of applications such as equity, commodity and interest rate modelling. In the case of equities, we define the SDE as

$$dS = (r - q)Sdt + \sigma S^\beta dW \tag{3.38}$$

where

r = risk-free rate

q = constant dividend

σ = volatility scale parameter

β = the volatility elasticity factor (a constant)

W = Wiener process

This model subsumes some well-known models as special cases; for $\beta = 1$ the process reduces to geometric Brownian motion and when $\beta = 0$ we get an *Ornstein-Uhlenbeck process*. For $\beta = 0.5$, we obtain the *square-root process*.

How do we interpret the CEV model? When $\beta < 1$ the local volatility increases as the stock price decreases. This implies a heavy left tail and a less heavy right tail, as witnessed with equity options. Empirical evidence suggests that a values $\beta = -3$ and $\beta = -4$ are appropriate for the S&P 500 index. When $\beta > 1$ local volatility increases as the stock price increases. This implies a heavy right tail and a less heavy left tail, as witnessed with options on futures. In general, the CEV parameters are estimated by a calibration process.

We now discuss how to price call and put options based on the process in equation (3.38). We write equation (3.38) in the form:

$$dS = (r - q)Sdt + (\sigma S^{\beta-1})SdW \tag{3.39}$$

The code on the CD is based on this form of the SDE.

3.10.2 Exact, quasi-exact and numerical solutions of CEV equation

In the case of European options it is possible to find exact solutions for puts and calls (Schroder, 1989). They are based on the *noncentral chi-squared distribution* that we now discuss. Let $X_j, j = 1, \ldots, k$ be k independent normally distributed random variables with means μ_j and variances σ_j^2; then the random variable defined by

$$\Sigma_{j=1}^{k} \left(\frac{X_j}{\sigma_j}\right)^2$$

is distributed according to the noncentral chi-square distribution having two parameters; the first parameter k is the *number of degrees of freedom* and the second parameter λ is the *noncentrality parameter* defined by

$$\lambda \equiv \sum_{j=1}^{k} \left(\frac{\mu_j}{\sigma_j}\right)^2 (\lambda > 0)$$

The probability density function (pdf) is given by

$$f_X(x; k, \lambda) = \frac{1}{2}e^{-(x+\lambda)/2} \left(\frac{x}{\lambda}\right)^{\frac{k}{4}-\frac{1}{2}} I_{\frac{k}{2}-1}\left(\sqrt{\lambda x}\right) \tag{3.40}$$

where $I_a(y)$ is a *modified Bessel function of the first kind*:

$$I_a(y) \equiv (y/2)^a \Sigma_{j=0}^{\infty} \frac{(y^2/4)^j}{j!\Gamma(a+j+1)} \tag{3.41}$$

The cumulative distribution function (cdf) is given by

$$\chi^2(x;k,\lambda) \equiv F_X(x;k,\lambda) \equiv \sum_{j=0}^{\infty} e^{-\lambda/2} \frac{(\lambda/2)^j}{j!} \frac{\gamma(j+\frac{k}{2},x/2)}{\Gamma(j+k/2)} \tag{3.42}$$

where

$$\Gamma(a) = \int_0^{\infty} t^{a-1} e^{-t} dt \text{ (gamma function)}$$

and

$$\gamma(a,x) = \int_0^x t^{a-1} e^{-t} dt \text{ (unnormalised incomplete gamma function)}$$

Notice that

$$\lim_{x \to \infty} \gamma(a,x) = \Gamma(a)$$

We are now in a position to price European options. We concentrate on put options:

for $\beta < 1$
$$P = K e^{-rT} \left[1 - \chi^2(d,c,b) \right] - S_0 e^{-qT} \chi^2(b,c+2,d)$$
for $\beta > 1$
$$P = K e^{-rT} \left[1 - \chi^2(b,2-c,d) \right] - S_0 e^{-qT} \chi^2(d,-c,b)$$
where
$$b = \frac{\left[K e^{-(r-q)T} \right]^{2(1-\beta)}}{(1-\beta)^2 w}, \quad c = \frac{1}{1-\beta}$$
$$d = \frac{S_0^{2(1-\beta)}}{(1-\beta)^2 w},$$
and
$$w = \frac{\sigma^2}{2(r-q)(\beta-1)} \left[e^{2(r-q)(\beta-1)T} - 1 \right]$$

and $\chi^2(x;k,\lambda)$ is the cumulative distribution function of the noncentral chi-squared random variable with noncentrality parameter λ and k degrees of freedom, in equation (3.42) above.

The computation of option prices using the above formulae can be done in languages such as Matlab, Mathematica or C++ (using the Boost library). The exact formula tends to become unstable near $\beta = 1$, for example, and the evaluation of the infinite series can be computationally expensive in some cases. However, we can use the formula to generate option prices and we compare them against those prices generated using the Monte Carlo method (and using partial differential equation methods).

3.10.3 Monte Carlo simulation of CEV models

We apply the finite difference methods from Chapter 0 to the CEV model in equation (3.38). We expect that the presence of the elasticity factor β will affect stability and convergence and to this end we have applied a number of finite difference schemes for various values of β (we take the same test cases as discussed in Wong and Jing, 2008). In general, the schemes give accurate results for most values of β; however, the schemes produce negative asset values for values of β smaller than -2 using the explicit Euler method.

Since we are interested in determining the usefulness of the Monte Carlo method when applied to the CEV model we focus on the essential algorithmic details; we have implemented the code using the following techniques:

- A1: Model option data as a struct.
- A2: Group option data, drift and diffusion into a namespace.
- A3: Implement the Monte Carlo algorithm.

For A1, we assemble all the data and payoff information in one place:

```cpp
struct OptionData
{ // Option data + behaviour

    double K;
    double T;
    double r;
    double sig;

    // Extra data
    double H;           // down and out barrier
    double D;           // dividend
    double betaCEV;     // elasticity factor (CEV model)
    double scale;       // scale factor in CEV model

    int type;           // 1 == call, -1 == put

    double myPayOffFunction(double S)
    { // Payoff function

        if (type == 1)
        { // Call

            return std::max(S - K, 0.0);
        }
        else
        { // Put

            return std::max(K - S, 0.0);
        }
    }
};
```

We now initialise this struct with test data:

```cpp
OptionData myOption;
myOption.K = 110.0;
myOption.T = 0.5;
myOption.r = 0.05;
```

```
myOption.D = 0.00;
myOption.H = 0.0;
myOption.betaCEV = -3.0;           // elasticity factor
myOption.scale = 0.20;
double S_0 = 100.0;                // where calculate option price
myOption.sig = myOption.scale *pow(S_0, 1.0 - myOption.betaCEV);
myOption.type = -1;
```

For activity A2, we define the related functionality in a *namespace* that models the SDE in equation (3.38):

```
namespace SDEDefinition
{ // Defines drift + diffusion + data

    OptionData* data;

    double drift(double t, double X)
    { // Drift term

        return (data->r - data->D)*X;     // r - D
    }

    double diffusion(double t, double X)
    { // Diffusion term

        return data->sig * pow(X, data->betaCEV);
    }

    double diffusionDerivative(double t, double X)
    { // Diffusion term, needed for the Milstein method

        return 0.5*(data->sig)*(data->betaCEV)*
                  pow(X, 2.0*data->betaCEV - 1.0);
    }

} // End of namespace
```

The algorithm that calculates the option price using the Euler method is given by (full code on CD):

```
for (long i = 1; i <= NSim; ++i)
{ // Calculate a path at each iteration

    VOld = initialCondition;

    for (long index = x.MinIndex()+1; index <= x.MaxIndex();++index)
    {
        dW = myNormal->getNormal();
        tmp = VOld   + (k * drift(x[index-1], VOld))
                     + (sqrk * diffusion(x[index-1], VOld) * dW);

        // Check for values crossing zero!!
        if (tmp > 0.0)
```

```
        {
                VNew = tmp;
                VOld = VNew;
        }
        else
        { // UGH, negative values, should not be
                break; // exits 'NT loop'
        }
    }

    if (VNew > 0.0)
    {
            tmp = myOption.myPayOffFunction(VNew);
            price += (tmp)/double(NSim);
    }

    // Finally, discounting the average price
    price *= exp(-myOption.r * myOption.T);
```

The code for other methods, for example the Milstein and derivative-free methods, can also be found on the CD.

The reader will have noticed that we test whether the generated path data becomes negative at time level $n + 1$. Can this situation occur? The answer is 'yes'! Let us take the Euler scheme:

$$S_{n+1} = S_n + (r - q)S_n \Delta t + \sigma S_n^\beta \Delta W_n$$

Then, we can see that the solution can become negative (that is, $S_{n+1} < 0$) if the Wiener increments satisfy the inequality:

$$\Delta W_n < -\left(\frac{S_n + (r - q)S_n \Delta t}{\sigma S_n^\beta} \right)$$

Even in the GBM case ($\beta = 1$), we can get negative values but the problem disappears after a log transformation:

$$d \log S = \left(r - q - \frac{1}{2}\sigma^2 \right) dt + \sigma dW$$

However, in the CEV case a transformation will not resolve the problem, as discussed in Jäckel (2002), pages 36–37. In general, we have seen that negative values are realised when β becomes less than –2. We have also seen these negative values with the Milstein and other methods that we introduced in Chapter 0.

There are a number of 'fixes' or 'fudges' to resolve the problem of producing negative values:

- *absorption fix*: set the value to zero when it becomes negative.
- *reflection fix*: reflect the value in the origin when it becomes negative.
- *'ignore' fix*: reject the path generation by breaking out of the loop, as can be seen in the above code.

None of these options is very elegant. We have seen that they give similar answers and that they are not accurate for extreme negative values of β.

3.10.4   American option pricing and hedging with the CEV model

We now discuss how to price options with early exercise features and how to calculate option sensitivities. The Monte Carlo is not the most suitable method in this case although a number of methods have been developed, as discussed in Glasserman (2004) and in Part III of the current book. In this section we give a short discussion of the application of the Finite Difference Method (FDM) to calculating option sensitivities. This is relatively easy because this method calculates the option price for all discrete asset prices and all time levels up to the expiry time T. We then approximate the sensitivities as divided differences. An alternative solution is to avoid negative values by developing an adaptive mesh strategy.

We formulate the problem as a partial differential equation (PDE):

$$-\frac{\partial V}{\partial t} + \frac{1}{2}\sigma^2 S^{2\beta}\frac{\partial^2 V}{\partial S^2} + (r-q)S\frac{\partial V}{\partial S} - rV = 0 \quad S \geq 0, \quad 0 < t \leq T \qquad (3.43)$$

This equation will have a unique, well-defined solution if we prescribe the payoff function (also known as the *initial condition*) where we assume that we price a *put* option:

$$V(S, 0) = V_0(S) = \max(K - S, 0), \quad S \geq 0 \qquad (3.44)$$

and the *boundary conditions*:

$$V(0, t) = Ke^{-(r-q)t}, \quad 0 < t \leq T \qquad (3.45)$$

$$V(S_{\max}, t) = 0 \qquad (3.46)$$

The value $S = 0$ and $S = S_{\max}$ are called the *near* and *far field boundaries*, respectively. In the latter case we can estimate the position of the far field (as discussed in Wong and Jing, 2008, for example).

We approximate the solution of system (3.43)–(3.46) using the finite difference method, as described in Duffy (2004a) and Duffy (2006b). We show the code for calculating sensitivities; we see that once we have calculated the option price vector it is easy to calculate the delta, gamma and theta sensitivities:

```
Vector<double, long> xArr = FDM.xarr();   // Mesh of Asset values
Vector<double, long> tArr = FDM.tarr();   // Mesh of Time values

double h = xArr[2] - xArr[1];
double k = tArr[2] - tArr[1];

Vector <double,long> Delta(xArr.Size(), xArr.MinIndex());
long min = Delta.MinIndex();
long max = Delta.MaxIndex();
for (long j = Delta.MinIndex() + 1; j < Delta.MaxIndex(); j++)
{ // Array 'result' contains asset price at expiry time t = T

     Delta[j] = (result[j+1] - result[j-1])/(2.0*h);
}
Delta[min] = (result[min+1] - result[min])/h;
Delta[max] = (result[max] - result[max-1])/h;

// Make and fill gamma vector
Vector <double,long> Gamma(xArr.Size(), xArr.MinIndex());
```

```
for (long j = Gamma.MinIndex() + 1; j<Gamma.MaxIndex(); j++)
{
      Gamma[j] = (Delta[j+1] - Delta[j-1])/(2.0*h);
}

Gamma[min] = (Delta[min+1] - Delta[min])/h;
Gamma[max] = (Delta[max] - Delta[max-1])/h;

long NP1 = result().MaxRowIndex();
long NP = result().MaxRowIndex() -1;

 Vector <double,long> Theta(xArr.Size(), xArr.MinIndex());
 for (long ii = Theta.MinIndex(); ii <= Theta.MaxIndex(); ii++)
{
      Theta[ii] = -(result()(NP1, ii) - result()(NP, ii) )/k;
}
```

We adapt system (3.43)–(3.46) to accommodate early exercise features. In this case, we model the *free boundary* $B(t)$ using the so-called *smooth pasting conditions*:

$$V(B(t), t) = K - B(t) \tag{3.47}$$

$$\frac{\partial V}{\partial S}(B(t), t) = -1 \tag{3.48}$$

In Duffy (2006b) we employ the *penalty method* to price options with early exercise feature. We report on the performance and accuracy of this method in the next section.

3.10.5   Test cases and numerical results

We now give a number of data sets and option values based on the Monte Carlo method. These sets are taken from Wong (2008); the test values are $r = 0.05, q = 0.0, \beta = 0.20, S_0 = 100.0$. The parameters K and β are variable and we concentrate on the put price (it is possible to run the code for a call option or by using put-call relationship). The exact values for European options are:

$$K = 90, \beta = 0, P = 1.4680$$
$$K = 110, \beta = 0, P = 9.9552$$

$$K = 90, \beta = 2/3, P = 1.3380$$
$$K = 110, \beta = 2/3, P = 10.1099$$

$$K = 90, \beta = -3, P = 2.2210$$
$$K = 110, \beta = -3, P = 9.3486$$

The Monte Carlo method gives good results in general, except in the case of $\beta = -3$, where the value is hovering around 8.83 irrespective of the number of time steps, number of simulations and the method used.

We have tested the CEV model using the FDM as described in Duffy (2004a) and Duffy (2006b); we produced the same option prices as in Wong (2008), although some of our values for the Greeks differed from theirs:

$$K = 90, \beta = -3, P = 2.2254$$
$$K = 100, \beta = -3, P = 4.6010$$
$$K = 110, \beta = -3, P = 10.227$$

You can experiment with the code on the CD and run your own examples.

3.11   USING ASSOCIATIVE ARRAYS AND MATRICES TO MODEL LOOKUP TABLES AND VOLATILITY SURFACES

In this section we introduce a number of generic classes that model one-dimensional and two-dimensional data structures whose elements we access using keys that have direct relevance to the problem domain in question. For example, in a portfolio sensitivity analysis we would create a matrix of profit and loss over time based on different values of some critical parameters. In this case we access the elements of the matrix by a given value of the parameter (row number) and a date that is the index of the column numbers. In this case we define an *associative matrix* because we access the elements – not by indices of integer type – but by another more generic index. This feature is very important and useful because it avoids us having to work with nonrealistic indices that are not directly related to the problem at hand. This behaviour can be seen in the Excel spreadsheet package in which we access cells in a worksheet as a combination of letters and integers. Some of the applications where associative data structures are needed are

- Volatility and correlation matrices and surfaces (Flavell, 2002).
- Profit/loss profiles for various kinds of option strategies (Fabozzi, 1993) and for sensitivity analyses.
- Cash flow matrices.
- Rates matrices.
- Creating associative matrices as *lookup tables*; for example, we could create a table of the cdf of the noncentral chi-squared distribution for various values of the degrees of freedom and noncentrality parameters.

We discuss how to *use* these associative data structures in applications and in order to reduce the scope we concentrate on matrices (the full C++ code is on the CD and we recommend that you compile and run the code to see how it works. Incidentally, you should be familiar with template programming in C++). An associative matrix is a wrapper for a numeric matrix and it contains two sets of indices, one for rows and the other one for columns. Let us take a simple example in which we try to give the look and feel of an Excel worksheet by defining an associative matrix; it has three template parameters for the types of the row indices, column indices and of the cell elements. We take an initial example in which the row indices are strings, the column indices are integers and the values are doubles. The main steps are

1. Create the row and column indices.
2. Create the matrix containing the numeric data.
3. Create the associative array.

First, step 1 is realised by

```
// Create the row indices using Datasim's set class
Set<string> names;
names.Insert("A");
names.Insert("B");
names.Insert("C");
names.Insert("D");

// Create the column indices
Set<long> columns;
long startRow = 3;
columns.Insert(startRow);
columns.Insert(startRow + 1);
columns.Insert(startRow + 2);
```

Second, we initialise the data matrix as follows:

```
// Create the embedded numeric matrix of appropriate dimensions
NumericMatrix<double, long> myMatrix(names.Size(), columns.Size());

// Fill in the values (this is just one way, there are others...)
for (long c = myMatrix.MinColumnIndex();
                    c <= myMatrix.MaxColumnIndex(); ++c)
{
    for (long r = myMatrix.MinRowIndex();
                    r <= myMatrix.MaxRowIndex(); ++r)
    {
        myMatrix(r,c) = double(c);

    }
}
```

Finally, we assemble the associative matrix by calling the appropriate constructor, as follows:

```
// Now create the associative matrix
AssocMatrix<string, long, double> myAssocMat(names, columns,
    myMatrix);
print(myAssocMat);

cout << "Single cell: " << myAssocMat(string("C"), 5) << endl;
```

Having taken a simple example, we now discuss how to create a lookup table for a representative example, namely the table of the noncentral chi-squared distribution for various degrees of freedom (rows) and noncentrality (columns) parameters. The code is more flexible than the first example because the row and column index sets are generated based on a starting value, an offset value and the number of elements in the index sets. To this end, we define a structure to hold this information:

```
template <typename Numeric, typename Type>
struct VectorCollectionGenerator // 1d array, heterogeneous
{
Numeric Start;    // The lowest or highest value
Type Increment; // Distance between values (+ or - possible)
long Size;        // Number of elements to be generated
};
```

We now create two instances of this structure that will represent the rows and columns of the table, respectively and we generate the sets by calling the function

```
// Now create the row and column indices; first, degrees
   of freedom
VectorCollectionGenerator<double, double> dofRows;
dofRows.Start = 2.0;
dofRows.Increment = 1.0;
dofRows.Size = 9;
Set<double> dofSet = createSet<double>(dofRows);

// Noncentral parameter
VectorCollectionGenerator<double, double>
   nonCentralParameterColumns;
nonCentralParameterColumns.Start = 2.0;
nonCentralParameterColumns.Increment = 2.0;
nonCentralParameterColumns.Size = 5;
Set<double> nonCentralParameterSet
              = createSet<double>(nonCentralParameterColumns);
```

The next step is to create the data matrix by using the functionality in the Boost library. First, we need to define some auxiliary variables:

```
// Start values for rows and columns
double r1 = dofRows.Start;
double c1 = nonCentralParameterColumns.Start;

// Lookup table dimensions
long NRows = dofRows.Size;
long NColumns = nonCentralParameterColumns.Size;
double incrementRow = dofRows.Increment;
double incrementColumn = nonCentralParameterColumns.Increment;
```

We are now ready to populate the data matrix; we use the template class for numeric matrices as introduced in Duffy (2004a) and (2006a):

```
NumericMatrix<double, long> mat(NRows, NColumns);
using namespace boost::math; // For convenience
// Basic case, no associativity
for (long r = mat.MinRowIndex(); r <= mat.MaxRowIndex();++r)
{
 c1 = nonCentralParameterColumns.Start;
 for (long c = mat.MinColumnIndex(); c<=mat.MaxColumnIndex();++c)
 {
  cs = quantile(complement(chi_squared(r1), 0.05));
  mat(r,c)=cdf(complement(non_central_chi_squared(r1,c1),cs));
       // Call the boost function
  c1 += incrementColumn;
 }

   r1 += incrementRow;
}
```

Finally, we create the associative matrix and then export its value to Excel:

```
// Now create the associative matrix
AssocMatrix<double, double, double>
    myAssocMat(dofSet, nonCentralParameterSet, mat);
print(myAssocMat);

printAssocMatrixInExcel(myAssocMat, string("NCCQT"));
```

The output matrix is:

	2	4	6	8	10
2	0.225545	0.415427	0.58404	0.717564	0.815421
3	0.192238	0.358534	0.518079	0.654111	0.761063
4	0.171467	0.320074	0.470102	0.604725	0.715986
5	0.156993	0.291756	0.432876	0.564449	0.677439
6	0.146212	0.269796	0.40283	0.530652	0.643848
7	0.137813	0.252152	0.377911	0.501722	0.614188
8	0.131052	0.237603	0.356823	0.476586	0.587734
9	0.125473	0.225361	0.338694	0.454489	0.563949
10	0.120777	0.214894	0.322908	0.434875	0.542418

It is possible to use the class for associative matrices in a range of applications, for example when the row and column index sets are *Date* and *Time*, *string* and other popular data types in finance. It is also possible to extend the structure and functionality by using design patterns (as discussed in GOF, 1995), for example *Composite* (recursive and nested matrices), *Decorator* (adding extra data members to matrices at run-time and *Visitor*. In the latter case we can define an associative matrix of volatilities for different strikes and maturities. We can define specific visitors (for example, for bilinear or bicubic interpolation) to compute new values at intermediate points in the matrix. This topic is outside the scope of this book. We discuss design patterns in detail in Part II of this book. Precomputing lookup tables in an application may result in performance improvements because there is no longer a need to call an expensive function.

3.12   SUMMARY AND CONCLUSION

In this chapter we introduced a number of topics that are directly and indirectly related to Monte Carlo simulation. First, we introduced several statistical distributions that are used in applications, in particular the exponential, chi-squared and gamma distributions. We shall need them in later chapters. We also stress that the Boost library supports these and other distributions and this implies that you do not have to write code in order to implement them but you can directly use the functionality that is provided by Boost. Second, we introduced the CEV (Constant Elasticity of Volatility) SDE and its numerical simulation using finite difference methods. We addressed some of the *essential difficulties* when using methods such as the explicit Euler scheme, especially for large negative values of the elasticity factor. Finally, we introduced a template class for *associative matrices* that allows us to precompute tables of data; the example taken was the table of the cumulative distribution function of the noncentral chi-squared distribution for a range of values of the number of degrees of freedom and the noncentrality parameter.

3.13   APPENDIX: STATISTICAL DISTRIBUTIONS AND SPECIAL FUNCTIONS IN THE BOOST LIBRARY

We give an overview of how the Boost library (www.boost.org) has implemented C++ modules and classes for special functions and statistical distributions. In particular, we show how to use these functions in C++ code. Much of the theory has been discussed in well-known textbooks such as Press *et al.* (2002), Glasserman (2004), Jäckel (2002) and Cont and Tankov (2004), for example. However, we use the C++ code from Boost because it offers many advantages. First, the library is well designed and is easy to use; second, the code is portable and has been standardised. Finally, in our opinion Boost is one of the best designed C++ libraries in the market place. We give an overview of Boost in Chapter 13; in this section we reduce the scope by concentrating on statistical distributions and other special functions.

We first discuss special functions in the Boost library. We introduce the main categories and give some code examples to show how to understand the intent of the library and how to use the code in applications. We give a synopsis of the functionality:

- gamma functions (gamma, log gamma, incomplete gamma);
- factorial and binomial coefficients (factorial, double factorial);
- beta functions (beta, incomplete beta and their derivatives);
- error functions (error function and its inverse);
- polynomials (Legendre, Laguerre, Hermite, spherical harmonics);
- Bessel functions (first and second order, modified functions, spherical);
- elliptic integrals (first, second and third kinds);
- logs, powers, roots and exponentials;
- sinus cardinal and hyperbolic sinus cardinal functions;
- inverse hyperbolic functions;
- polynomials and rational functions.

You may need to use these functions in your applications and it is advisable first to look in Boost to see if it has the functionality that you need instead of programming it yourself. We show how to use these functions by examining a number of representative examples (a discussion of all these special functions is outside the scope of this book).

3.13.1   The gamma functions

The *gamma function* is defined by

$$\Gamma(z) = \int_0^\infty t^{z-1} e^{-t} dt \quad (z \in \mathbb{R}) \tag{3.49}$$

When z is a positive integer (call it n) then we get the result: $\Gamma(n + 1) = n!$. We can show (use integration by parts) that the gamma function satisfies the recurrence relation: $\Gamma(z + 1) = z\Gamma(z)$.

The (normalised) incomplete gamma function is defined by

$$P(a, x) = \frac{1}{\Gamma(a)} \int_0^x t^{a-1} e^{-t} dt = \frac{\gamma(a, x)}{\Gamma(a)}, a > 0 \tag{3.50}$$

where $\gamma(a, x)$ is the unnormalised incomplete gamma function defined by

$$\gamma(a, x) = \int_0^x t^{a-1} e^{-t} dt, \quad a > 0$$

We note that

$$P(a, 0) = 0 \text{ and } \lim_{x \to \infty} P(a, x) = 1$$

We now present some code that computes these gamma functions. We note the presence of the include files and the appropriate namespace:

```
#include <boost/math/special_functions/gamma.hpp>
#include <boost/math/special_functions/erf.hpp>
#include <boost/math/special_functions/detail/erf_inv.hpp>


// Don't forget to tell compiler which namespace
using namespace boost::math;

// The famous gamma function gamma(n) = (n-1)! for n an integer
// Slow and accurate
double d = tgamma(5);
cout << "t gamma: " << d << endl;

double d2 = tgamma(5.01);
cout << "t gamma: " << d2 << endl;

// More accurate, due to Lanczos
// tgamma1pm1(z) = tgamma(z+1) - 1
double d3 = tgamma1pm1(4);
cout << "t gamma: " << d3 << endl;

// Normalised incomplete gamma function
double a1 = 3.0;
double a2 = 10.0;

double x = 2.0;
cout << "Normalised incomplete gamma function: " <<
                        gamma_p(a1, x) << endl;
cout << "Normalised incomplete gamma function: " <<
                        gamma_p(a2, x) << endl;
```

The gamma function is important in applications because it is needed by the gamma and beta distributions, for example.

3.13.2   The error function

The error function and the complementary error function are defined by

$$erf(z) = \frac{2}{\sqrt{\pi}} \int_0^z e^{-t^2} dt \tag{3.51}$$

and by

$$erfc(z) = 1 - erf(z) = \frac{2}{\sqrt{\pi}} \int_z^\infty e^{-t^2} dt, \qquad (3.52)$$

respectively. We now show the C++ code for the error function:

```
// Error function
// template <class T, class Policy, class Tag>
// T erf_imp(T z, bool invert, const Policy& pol, const Tag& t)
bool complement = false;
double dummy = 1.0;

double value = detail::erf_imp(1.0, complement,
                        policies::policy<>(), dummy);

cout << "Error function value: " << value << endl;

complement = true;

value = detail::erf_imp(2.0, complement,
                        policies::policy<>(), dummy);
```

Finally, we should use the exception handling mechanism to catch exceptions. For example, the error function expects its input arguments to be in the closed range $[-1,1]$, otherwise an error will occur:

```
double u = 1.3;

try
{ // The variable 'u' must be in the range [-1,1]

        cout << "erf inverse: " << erf_inv(u) << endl;
        cout << "erfc inverse: " << erfc_inv(u) << endl;
}
catch(const std::exception& e)
{
        cout << e.what() << endl;
}
```

3.13.3 An overview of statistical distributions in Boost

The Boost library has extensive support for univariate statistical distributions and functions that operate on them:

- beta distribution;
- chi-squared distribution;
- exponential distribution;
- gamma (and Erlang) distribution;
- F distribution;
- normal (Gaussian) distribution;
- Poisson distribution;

- Student's t-distribution;
- Weibull distribution;
- uniform distribution.

Each distribution has its defining parameters and it has been implemented in a template class structure. The underlying parameters are of numeric type but in many cases we work with double precision numbers. Finally, we can use so-called *policies* to customise how errors are handled or how quantiles of discrete distributions behave. We take a '101' example to show how to create instances of two distributions, namely uniform and gamma distributions:

```cpp
#include <boost/math/distributions/uniform.hpp>
#include <boost/math/distributions/gamma.hpp>
#include <iostream>
using namespace std;

int main()
{
    // Don't forget to tell compiler which namespace
    using namespace boost::math;

    uniform_distribution<> myUniform(0.0, 1.0); // Default 'double'
    cout << "Lower value: " << myUniform.lower()
            << ", upper value: " << myUniform.upper() << endl;

    // Choose another data type
    uniform_distribution<float> myUniform2(0.0, 1.0);
    cout << "Lower value: " << myUniform2.lower()
            << ", upper value: " << myUniform2.upper() << endl;

    // Distributional properties
    double x = 0.25;

    cout << "pdf: " << pdf(myUniform, x) << endl;
    cout << "cdf: " << cdf(myUniform, x) << endl;

    // Gamma distribution
    double alpha = 3.0; // Shape parameter, k
    double beta = 0.5; // Scale parameter, theta
    gamma_distribution<double> myGamma(alpha, beta);

    return 0;
}
```

The class' interfaces are small in the sense that they do not have functions for statistical functions, the latter being realised by overloaded generic nonmember functions. To this end, the main functions are

- probability distribution function;
- cumulative distribution function;
- quantile;
- hazard function;

- cumulative hazard function;
- mean, median, mode, variance, standard deviation;
- kurtosis, kurtosis_excess;
- range (the valid range of the random variable over a given distribution);
- support (smallest closed set outside of which the probability is zero).

We take an example to show how to use these functions. In this case we take a Student's
t-distribution with 30 degrees of freedom:

```
#include <boost/math/distributions/students_t.hpp>
students_t_distribution<float> myStudent(30);
```

Then the above list of functions translates into the following code for the current distribution
instance:

```
// Other properties
cout << "\n***Student's t distribution: \n";
cout << "mean: " << mean(myStudent) << endl;
cout << "variance: " << variance(myStudent) << endl;
cout << "median: " << median(myStudent) << endl;
cout << "mode: " << mode(myStudent) << endl;
cout << "kurtosis excess: "
              << kurtosis_excess(myStudent) << endl;
cout << "kurtosis: " << kurtosis(myStudent) << endl;
cout << "characteristic function: " << chf(myStudent, x) << endl;
cout << "hazard: " << hazard(myStudent, x) << endl;

// Range and support
pair<double, double> mySupport = support(myStudent);
cout << "Support: [" << mySupport.first << ","
              << mySupport.second << "]" << endl;
pair<double, double> myRange = range(myStudent);
cout << "Range: [" << myRange.first << ","
              << myRange.second << "]" << endl;
```

Finally, we show how to compute quantiles and the number of degrees of freedom needed in
the t-distribution for a given significance level:

```
// Quantiles and conversions between significance levels
// (fractions, 0.05)  and confidence levels (in percentages,
// e.g. 95%)
double Alpha = 0.25;
cout << "Confidence 1: "
        << quantile(myStudent, Alpha / 2) << endl;
cout << "Confidence, in %: "
        << quantile(complement(myStudent, Alpha / 2)) << endl;

// Required sample sizes for Students t-distribution
double M = 1.2;          // True mean
double Sm = 1.8;         // Sample mean
double Sd = 2.4;         // Sample standard deviation

try
```

```
{
        double df = students_t::find_degrees_of_freedom (
                            fabs(M-Sm), Alpha, Alpha, Sd);
        int dof = ceil(df) + 1;
        cout << "One-sided degrees of freedom: " << dof << endl;
}
catch(const std::exception& e)
{
        cout << e.what() << endl;
}
```

This completes our description of statistical distributions in Boost. The best way to learn how to use them is to examine, run and modify the code on the CD.

We consider our examples to be representative and you should be able to adopt them to your own needs.

3.14   EXERCISES AND PROJECTS

1. (**) Numerical Approximation of Bessel Process
   We approximate the solution of the SDE (3.4) by the family of finite difference schemes:

   $$R_{n+1} - R_n = \frac{m-1}{2R_{n,\theta}} dt + \Delta \tilde{W}_n$$

   where

   $$R_{n,\theta} \equiv \theta R_{n+1} + (1 - \theta) R_n$$
   $$\theta = 0 \Rightarrow \text{explicit Euler method}$$
   $$\theta = 1 \Rightarrow \text{implicit Euler method}$$

   In particular, test the explicit and implicit Euler methods (the latter method involves solving a quadratic equation at each time level). Investigate whether or not the approximate solutions hit the origin for a range of time steps. Now define the process $V = \frac{\sigma^2}{4} R^2$. Then prove by Ito's lemma that this process satisfies the SDE:

   $$dV + \frac{m\sigma^2}{4} dt + \sigma \sqrt{V} d\tilde{W}$$

   Approximate this SDE by the implicit and explicit Euler schemes. Do you get better results compared with those from the schemes for the original SDE? The above SDE is similar to the volatility process in the Heston model:

   $$dv = \kappa(\theta - v)dt + \sigma \sqrt{v} dW$$

   Prove that the origin is not attainable if $\kappa\theta \geq \frac{1}{2}\sigma^2$ (the Feller condition).
2. (**) Weibull Distribution
   This distribution has a p.d.f. defined by

   $$f_X(x) = \begin{cases} \dfrac{\alpha}{\beta} x^{\alpha-1} e^{-(x/\beta)^\alpha}, & 0 \leq x < \infty, \quad \alpha > 0, \quad \beta > 0 \\ 0, \text{ otherwise} \end{cases}$$

   To generate a random variate we use the inverse transformation method to get

   $$U = F_X(x) = 1 - e^{-(x/\beta)^\alpha} \text{ or } X = \beta(-\log(1 - U))^{1/\alpha}$$
   $$\text{or } X = \beta(-\log U)^{1/\alpha}$$

Create C++ code to implement this algorithm. Does the Boost library support this distribution?

3. (***) Fichera Functions
   Consider the three PDEs:

$$\alpha \frac{\partial u}{\partial x} + \beta \frac{\partial u}{\partial y} = f$$

$$\frac{1}{2} S^{2\beta} y^2 \frac{\partial^2 u}{\partial S^2} + \frac{1}{2} y^2 \frac{\partial^2 u}{\partial y^2} = 0$$

$$\frac{\partial V}{\partial t} + \frac{1}{2} \sigma^2 S^2 \frac{\partial^2 V}{\partial S^2} + \rho \sigma S w \frac{\partial^2 V}{\partial S \partial r} + \frac{1}{2} w^2 \frac{\partial^2 V}{\partial r^2}$$

$$+ (r - D_0) S \frac{\partial V}{\partial S} + (u - \lambda w) \frac{\partial V}{\partial r} - rV + kZ = 0$$

each of which is defined in a rectangle in (x, y) space. Answer the following questions:
 – Calculate the Fichera function in each case.
 – In the case of characteristic boundaries (find them) determine the form of the PDE on these boundaries.
 – Determine the Feller conditions in the third case (this is the PDE for a convertible bond).

4. (**) Error function
   Check – by using equations (3.51) and (3.52) – the following relationships:

$$erf(0) = 0, \quad erf(\infty) = 1, \quad erf(x) = -erf(-x)$$
$$erfc(0) = 1, \quad erfc(\infty) = 0, \quad erfc(x) = 2 - erfc(-x)$$

and

$$erf(x) = P\left(\frac{1}{2}, x^2\right) \text{ for } x \geq 0 \text{ where}$$

$$P(a, x) \text{ is defined in equation (3.50)}$$

5. (**) Cumulative Normal Function versus Error Function
   Investigate the problem of computing the cumulative normal function:

$$\Phi(x) = \frac{1}{\sqrt{2\pi}} \int_{-\infty}^{x} e^{-t^2/2} dt$$

and of its inverse

$$\Phi^{-1}(x)$$

by application of the error function. The transformations you need are (Glasserman, 2004)

$$erf(x) = 2\Phi(x\sqrt{2}) - 1$$
$$\Phi(x) = \frac{1}{2}[erf(x/\sqrt{2}) + 1]$$
$$erf^{-1}(u) = \frac{1}{\sqrt{2}}\Phi^{-1}\left(\frac{u+1}{2}\right)$$
$$\Phi^{-1}(u) = \sqrt{2} \, erf^{-1}(2u - 1)$$

Use the C++ code from the Boost library to compute these functions.

6. (***) Transform CEV Model to Bessel Process
   How would you transform the SDE (3.39) to the SDE (3.4)?

7. (***) The noncentral chi-squared distribution

We have discussed this distribution in section 3.10 and we used it to compute option prices under the CEV model. We note that the Boost library has support for this distribution. The following code is a sample to show how to use the distribution in C++:

```
#include <boost/math/distributions/non_central_chi_squared.hpp>
#include <boost/math/special_functions/cbrt.hpp>
#include <boost/math/distributions.hpp> // Non-member functions

#include <iostream>
using namespace std;

int main()
{

  boost::math::non_central_chi_squared_distribution<double>
  myNonCentralChiSquared(dof, lambda);


  // Distributional properties
  double x = 5.0;
  // Create a noncentral chi^2 distribution object, dd
  double dof = 3.0;
  double lambda = 1.5;

  cout << "pdf: " << pdf(myNonCentralChiSquared, x) << endl;
  cout << "cdf: " << cdf(myNonCentralChiSquared, x) << endl;

  // Other properties
  cout << "\n***Noncentral Chi^2 Distribution: \n";
  cout << "mean: " << mean(myNonCentralChiSquared) << endl;
  cout << "variance: " << variance(myNonCentralChiSquared) << endl;
  cout << "median: " << median(myNonCentralChiSquared) << endl;
  cout << "mode: " << mode(myNonCentralChiSquared) << endl;
  cout << "kurtosis excess: " <<
       kurtosis_excess(myNonCentralChiSquared) << endl;
  cout << "kurtosis: " << kurtosis(myNonCentralChiSquared) << endl;
  cout << "characteristic function: " <<
       chf(myNonCentralChiSquared, x) << endl;
  cout << "hazard: " << hazard(myNonCentralChiSquared, x) << endl;

  return 0;
}
```

Answer the following questions:
– Determine the member functions in `non_central_chi_squared_distribution`.
– Create the graphs of the p.d.f. and c.d.f. of this distribution on a given interval for a range of values of the number of degrees of freedom and the noncentrality parameter. You can use the *Excel Visualiser* to display the graphs.

– Calculate option prices based on the formulae in section 3.10.2 in conjunction with the
C++ Boost code. Check your answers.

8. (****) Applying the noncentral chi-squared distribution to SDE simulation
We discuss simulating discrete paths for the square-root diffusion process for the short rate
(see Glasserman, 2004, page 122):

$$\begin{cases} dr(t) = \alpha(b - r(t))dt + \sigma \sqrt{r(t)}dW(t) \\ \text{where} \\ 2\alpha b \geq \sigma^2 \text{ (Feller condition)} \end{cases}$$

Then, if $r(0) > 0$ we know that $r(t) > 0$ for all time t. The distribution of $r(t)$ in terms of
the value $r(u)$ where $u < t$ is a noncentral chi-squared distribution. In other words:

$$r(t) = c\chi_d^2(\lambda)$$

As usual, we employ one-step marching schemes for special values of u and t, namely:

$$t = t_{n+1}, \ u = t_n, \ n = 0, \ldots, N - 1$$

Answer the following questions:
– Calculate the path of the short rate based on the following algorithm:

```
for n = 0, N-1
{ // Assume d <= 1
    set t = meshPoint[n+1];
    set u = meshPoint[n];

  // generate a noncentral Chi^2 value X
    r[t[n+1]] = cX

}
```

– Compare the output from the above question with the solution delivered by the explicit
Euler method. Use the following values: $\sigma = 0.2, \alpha = 0.1, b = 5\%, r(0) = 4\%$.

An Introduction to the Finite Difference
Method for SDE

4.1 INTRODUCTION AND OBJECTIVES

In the previous chapters we developed the mathematical theory for SDEs and we discussed applications to computational finance. We examined some common examples of SDEs and we were able to give exact solutions in special cases. But in general it is not possible to find an exact solution, especially for multi-factor equations and equations whose diffusion and drift terms are nonlinear. For these cases we then resort to numerical methods that approximate the solution of the SDE; to this end, we use the finite difference method (FDM) to replace the SDE that is defined on a continuous interval by an equation that is defined on a discrete set of *mesh points*.

This chapter examines some theoretical foundations of finite difference schemes for SDEs; we continue this discussion in Chapter 5 by applying the schemes to a number of one-factor and multi-factor SDEs. Finally, in Chapter 6 we discuss a number of advanced theoretical and practical topics associated with these schemes.

4.2 AN INTRODUCTION TO DISCRETE TIME SIMULATION, MOTIVATION AND NOTATION

In this section we introduce the FDM and we apply it to finding approximate solutions of SDEs. We define the notation that we use in this and subsequent chapters.

The first step is to replace continuous time by discrete time. To this end, we divide the interval $[0, T]$ (where T is the expiry date) into a number of subintervals as shown in Figure 4.1. We define $N + 1$ *mesh points* as follows:

$$0 = t_0 < t_1 < \ldots < t_n < t_{n+1} < \ldots < t_N = T$$

In this case we define a set of *subintervals* (t_n, t_{n+1}) of size $\Delta t_n \equiv t_{n+1} - t_n, 0 \leq n \leq N - 1$. In general, we speak of a *non-uniform mesh* when the sizes of the subintervals are not necessarily the same. However, in this book we consider a large class of finite difference schemes where the N subintervals have the same size (we then speak of a *uniform mesh*), namely $\Delta t = T/N$.

Having defined how to subdivide $[0, T]$ into subintervals, we are now ready to motivate our finite difference schemes; for the moment we examine the scalar linear SDE with constant coefficients:

$$\begin{aligned} dX &= aX dt + bX dW, \quad a, b \text{ constant} \\ X(0) &= A \end{aligned} \tag{4.1}$$

Regarding notation, we do not show the dependence of variable X on t and when we wish to show this dependence we prefer to write $X = X(t)$ instead of the form X_t.

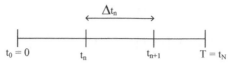

Figure 4.1 Mesh generation

We write equation (4.1) as a stochastic integral equation between the (arbitrary) times s and t as follows:

$$X(t) = X(s) + \int_s^t aX(y)dy + \int_s^t bX(y)dW(y), \quad s < t \tag{4.2}$$

We evaluate equation (4.2) at two consecutive mesh points and using the fact that the factors a and b in equation (4.1) are constant we get the exact identity:

$$\begin{aligned}
X(t_{n+1}) &= X(t_n) + \int_{t_n}^{t_{n+1}} aX(y)dy + \int_{t_n}^{t_{n+1}} bX(y)dW(y) \\
&= X(t_n) + a\int_{t_n}^{t_{n+1}} X(y)dy + b\int_{t_n}^{t_{n+1}} X(y)dW(y)
\end{aligned} \tag{4.3}$$

We now approximate equation (4.3) and in this case we replace the solution X of equation (4.3) by a new discrete function Y (that is, one that is defined at mesh points) by assuming that it is constant on each subinterval; we then arrive at the discrete equation:

$$\begin{aligned}
Y_{n+1} &= Y_n + aY_n \int_{t_n}^{t_{n+1}} dy + bY_n \int_{t_n}^{t_{n+1}} dW(y) \\
&= Y_n + aY_n \Delta t_n + bY_n \Delta W_n,
\end{aligned} \tag{4.4}$$

where

$$\Delta W_n = W(t_{n+1}) - W(t_n), \quad 0 \le n \le N - 1$$

This is called the (explicit) *Euler-Maruyama scheme* and it is a popular method when approximating the solution of SDEs. In some cases we write the solution in terms of a discrete function X_n if there is no confusion between it and the solution of equations (4.1) or (4.2). In other words, we can write the discrete equation (4.4) in the equivalent form:

$$\begin{cases} X_{n+1} = X_n + aX_n \Delta t_n + bX_n \Delta W_n \\ X_0 \quad = A \end{cases} \tag{4.5}$$

In many examples the mesh size is constant and furthermore the Wiener increments are well-known computable quantities:

$$\begin{cases} \Delta t_n \quad = \Delta t = T/N, \quad 0 \le n \le N - 1 \\ \Delta W_n = \sqrt{\Delta t}\, z_n, \text{ where } z_n \sim N(0, 1) \end{cases}$$

Incidentally, we generate increments of the Wiener process by a random number generator for independent Gaussian pseudo-random numbers, for example Box-Muller, Polar Marsaglia, Mersenne Twister or lagged Fibonacci generator methods. We discuss these methods in various chapters of the current book.

We generalise the approach taken in this section to multi-factor nonlinear SDEs. We deal almost exclusively with *one-step marching schemes*; in other words, the unknown solution at time level $n + 1$ is calculated in terms of known values at time level n.

4.3   FOUNDATIONS OF DISCRETE TIME APPROXIMATION: ORDINARY DIFFERENTIAL EQUATIONS

We introduced the Euler-Maruyama scheme in section 4.2. But we now must determine whether the accuracy of the scheme is 'good' in some sense and if we can give an estimate of the difference between the exact solution of the SDE (4.1) and the solution of the finite difference scheme (4.5).

There arc two special cases to investigate when we approximate SDEs. The first is called *pathwise approximation* and in this case we are interested in computing the difference between the approximate and exact solutions at specific mesh points. The second approach focuses on *approximating the expectations* of the Ito process, for example its probability distribution and moments. In this book we are interested in calculating the values of the underlying variables at the expiry time $t = T$ (and possibly at other mesh points in the interval $[0, T]$) and for this reason we focus on pathwise approximation.

A stochastic differential equation (SDE) can be viewed as an ordinary differential equation (ODE) with an additional random term. There are many books on the numerical solution of ODEs (see, for example, Henrici (1962) and Lambert (1991)) but there are few books that deal with the numerical solution of SDEs (notable exceptions being Kloeden and Platen (1995) and Kloeden, Platen and Schurz (1997). Some of the numerical schemes for SDEs are extensions of schemes that have been used for the solution of ODEs. This is not a book on the numerical solution of ODEs but we think it is useful to give a short introduction to the underlying principles. To this end, we discuss the following properties of a finite difference approximation to an ODE:

- consistency;
- stability;
- convergence.

In order to reduce the scope of the problem (for the moment), we examine the simple scalar *initial value problem* (IVP) defined by

$$
\begin{cases}
\dfrac{dX}{dt} = \mu(t, X), \quad 0 < t \leq T \\[2mm]
X(0) = X_0 \quad \text{given}
\end{cases}
\tag{4.6}
$$

We assume that this system has a unique solution in the interval $[0, T]$. In general it is impossible to find an exact solution of (4.6) and we resort to some kind of numerical scheme. To this end, we can write a generic *k-step method* in the form (Henrici, 1962; Lambert, 1991):

$$
\sum_{j=0}^{k} (\alpha_j X_{n-j} - \Delta t \beta_j \mu(t_{n-j}, X_{n-j})) = 0, \quad k \leq n \leq N
\tag{4.7}
$$

where α_j and β_j are constants, $j = 0, \ldots, k$ and Δt is the constant step-size.

Since this is a k-step method we need to give k *initial conditions*:

$$X_0; X_1, \ldots, X_{k-1} \tag{4.8}$$

We note that the first initial condition is known from the continuous problem (4.6) while the determination of the other $k - 1$ numerical initial conditions is a part of the numerical problem. These $k - 1$ numerical initial conditions must be chosen with care if we wish to avoid producing unstable schemes. In general, we compute these values by using Taylor's series expansions or by one-step methods.

We now discuss the *consistency* of scheme (4.7). This is a measure of how well the exact solution of (4.6) satisfies (4.7). Consistency states that the difference equation (4.7) formally converges to the differential equation in (4.6) when Δt tends to zero. In order to determine whether a finite difference scheme is consistent, we define the *generating polynomials*:

$$\rho(\zeta) = \sum_{j=0}^{k} \alpha_j \zeta^{k-j}$$

$$\sigma(\zeta) = \sum_{j=0}^{k} \beta_j \zeta^{k-j} \tag{4.9}$$

It can be shown that consistency (see Henrici, 1962; Dahlquist, 1974) is equivalent to the following conditions:

$$\rho(1) = 0, \quad \frac{d\rho}{dx}(1) = \sigma(1) \tag{4.10}$$

Let us take the explicit Euler method applied to system (4.6):

$$X_n - X_{n-1} = \Delta t \mu(t_n, X_{n-1}), \quad n = 1, \ldots, N$$

The reader can check the following:

$$\rho(\zeta) = \alpha_0 \zeta + \alpha_1 = \zeta - 1$$
$$\sigma(\zeta) = 1 \tag{4.11}$$

from which we deduce that the explicit Euler scheme is consistent with the IVP (4.6) by checking with equation (4.10)

The class of difference schemes (4.7) subsumes well-known specific schemes, for example:

- The one-step ($k = 1$) explicit and implicit Euler schemes.
- The two-step ($k = 2$) leapfrog scheme.
- The three-step ($k = 3$) Adams-Bashforth scheme.
- The one-step trapezoidal ($k = 1$) scheme.

Each of these schemes is consistent with the IVP (4.6) as can be checked by calculating their generating polynomials (see exercise 2 at the end of this chapter).

We now discuss what is meant by the *stability* of a finite difference scheme. To take a simple counterexample, a scheme whose solution is exponentially increasing in time while the exact solution is decreasing in time cannot be stable. In order to define stability, it is common practice to examine *model problems* (whose solutions are known) and apply various finite difference schemes to them. We then examine the stability properties of the schemes. The model problem in this case is the constant-coefficient scalar IVP in which the coefficient μ is a complex number:

$$\begin{cases} \frac{dX}{dt} = \mu X, & 0 < t \leq T \\ X(0) = 1 \end{cases} \tag{4.12}$$

and whose solution is given by

$$X(t) = e^{\mu t} \tag{4.13}$$

Thus, the solution is increasing when μ is positive and real and decreasing when μ is negative and real. The corresponding finite difference schemes should have similar properties. We take an example of the one-step trapezoidal method:

$$\begin{cases} X_{n+1} - X_n = \frac{\mu \Delta t}{2}(X_{n+1} + X_n), & 0 \leq n \leq N - 1 \\ X_0 = 1 \end{cases} \tag{4.14}$$

The solution of (4.14) is computable and is given by

$$X_n = \left[\frac{1+\alpha}{1-\alpha} \right]^n, \quad \alpha \equiv \frac{\mu \Delta t}{2} \tag{4.15}$$

We see that X_n is bounded if and only if $|1 + \alpha| \leq |1 - \alpha|$ and this implies $\Re\left(\frac{\mu \Delta t}{2}\right) < 0$ (recall that μ is a complex number).

This example leads us to our first encounter with the concept of stability of finite difference schemes. In particular, we define the *region of absolute stability* of a numerical method for an IVP as the set of complex values of $\mu \Delta t$ for which all discrete approximations to the test problem (4.12) remain bounded when n tends to infinity. For example, for the trapezoidal method (4.14) the left-half plane is the stability region.

Theorem 4.1 (The Root Condition). A necessary and sufficient condition for the stability of a linear multistep method (4.7) is that all the roots of the polynomial ρ defined in equation (4.9) are located inside or on the unit circle and that the roots of modulus 1 are simple.

We now discuss convergence issues. We say that a difference scheme has *order of accuracy* p if:

$$\max |X_n - X(t_n)| \leq M \Delta t^p, \quad \text{for } 0 \leq n \leq N$$

where X_n = approximate solution, $X(t_n)$ = exact solution and M is independent of Δt.

We conclude this section by stating a convergence result that allows us to estimate the error between the exact solution of an initial value problem and the solution of a multistep scheme that approximates it. To this end, we consider the n-dimensional *autonomous* initial value problem:

$$(IVPI) \begin{cases} \underline{y}' = \dfrac{d\underline{y}}{dt} = \underline{f}(\underline{y}), \text{ in the interval } [a, b], \quad \underline{y}(a) = \underline{c} \\[2mm] \text{where} \\[2mm] \underline{y} = {}^t(y_1, \ldots, y_n) \\[2mm] \underline{f}(\underline{y}) = {}^t(f_1(\underline{y}), \ldots, f_n(\underline{y})), \quad \underline{c} = {}^t(c_1, \ldots, c_n) \end{cases}$$

By 'autonomous' we mean that $f(\underline{y})$ is a function of the dependent variable $\underline{y}$ only and is thus not in the form $f(\underline{y}, t)$.

We approximate this IVP using the multistep method:

$$\sum_{j=0}^{k}(\alpha_j \underline{X}_{n-j} - \Delta t \beta_j \underline{f}(\underline{X}_{n-j})) = 0$$

Theorem 4.2 Assume that the solution $\underline{y}$ of the IVPI is $p + 1$ times differentiable with $\|\underline{y}^{(p+1)}(x)\| \le K_0$, $p \ge 1$ and assume that $\underline{f}$ is differentiable for all $\underline{y}$.

Suppose now that the sequence $\{\underline{X}_n\}$ is defined by the equations:

$$\underline{X}_n = \underline{y}(t_n) + \underline{\epsilon}_n, \quad n = 0, \ldots, k - 1$$

$$\sum_{j=0}^{k}(\alpha_j \underline{X}_{n-j} - \Delta_t \beta_j \underline{f}(\underline{X}_{n-j})) = \underline{\epsilon}_n, \quad k \le n \le \frac{b - a}{\Delta t}$$

If the multistep method is stable and satisfies

$$\sum_{j=1}^{k}(\alpha_j \underline{y}(t - j\Delta t) - \Delta t \beta_j \underline{y}'(t - jh) \sim C \Delta^{p+1} \underline{y}^{p+1}(t)$$

where C is a positive constant independent of Δt, then there exist constants K_1, K_2 and Δt_0 such that for all $t_n \in [a, b]$, $\Delta t \le \Delta t_0$

$$\|\underline{X}_n - \underline{y}(t_n)\| \le (C \Delta t^p (t_n - a) K_0 + \sum_{j=0}^{n} \|\underline{\epsilon}_j\|) K_1 e^{K_2(t_n - a)}$$

In all cases we define the norm $\|.\|$ for a vector $\underline{z} \in \mathbb{R}^n$ as

$$\|\underline{z}\| = \left(\sum_{j=1}^{n} |z_j|^2\right)^{1/2} \quad \text{or} \quad \|z\| = \max_{j=1,\ldots,n} |z_j|$$

We state this theorem in more general terms: consistency and stability of a multistep scheme are sufficient for convergence.

Finally, the discussion in this section is also applicable to systems of ODEs. For more discussions, we recommend Henrici (1962) and Lambert (1991).

4.4 FOUNDATIONS OF DISCRETE TIME APPROXIMATION: STOCHASTIC DIFFERENTIAL EQUATIONS

We extend the results of the previous section to SDEs. The construction and analysis of finite difference schemes for SDEs is more complicated than for ODEs because of the presence of random terms. We introduce a number of topics that allow us to determine the quality of difference schemes for SDEs. *This area of research is relatively new*. We determine how 'good' a finite difference scheme is. To this end, we discuss and elaborate some of the techniques in Kloeden, Platen and Schurz (1997)

- *Absolute error criterion*: In this case we define a statistic that represents the error between the exact solution of the SDE and the approximate solution of the finite difference scheme at the expiry time $t = T$. We need to have a closed form representation for the exact solution. This technique is useful when we wish to test the accuracy of finite difference schemes for SDEs whose solutions we can compute exactly (see Kloeden, Platen and Schurz (1997) pages 115–125).
- *Confidence intervals for absolute error*: If we take a large number of simulations we know from the *Central Limit Theorem* that the absolute error behaves asymptotically like a Gaussian random variable. We partition the experiment into M batches of NSIM simulations (where NSIM is usually a large positive integer) and we estimate the variance of the error by constructing a confidence interval using Student's t-distribution.
- *Dependence of the absolute error on the step size*: In this case we create M batches in which each batch has NSIM simulations. We repeat the experiment for a range of monotonically decreasing step sizes.
- *Strong and weak convergence*: There are several norms that measure the error between the exact and approximate solutions. We investigate the weak and strong convergence properties of a number of well-known finite difference schemes. In particular, we discuss the *order of convergence* of these schemes.

We now discuss each of these topics in more detail.

4.4.1 Absolute error criterion

This is the expectation of the absolute value of the difference between the approximate and exact solutions:

$$\epsilon = E(|X_T - Y_T|) \tag{4.16}$$

where

$Y_T =$ Euler solution at time T

$X_T =$ Exact solution at time T (Ito process)

The main use is to give a measure of the pathwise error at $t = T$. In Kloeden, Platen and Schurz (1997) the authors estimate this error using a statistical approach in combination with computer experiments. In this regard they compute a trajectory NSIM times for the exact and approximate solutions (using the same set of Wiener increments for both solutions!) and they compute the average error as follows:

$$\hat{\epsilon} = \tfrac{1}{NSIM} \sum_{k=1}^{NSIM} |X_{T,k} - Y_{T,k}| \qquad (4.17)$$

where $Y_{T,k}$ = value at time T of the kth simulated trajectory (Euler scheme) and $X_{T,k}$ = value at time T of the kth simulated trajectory (exact Ito solution).

We note that the exact solution is known at $t = T$. In general, we calculate the expression in (4.17) with a given value of NSIM and a given value of the step size Δt. We then carry out the same operation with smaller step sizes.

In Chapter 6 we shall discuss a number of techniques that allow us to determine the order of convergence when the exact solution of the SDE is not known. To this end, we compare the approximate solutions on meshes of size Δt and $\Delta t/2$.

4.4.2 Confidence intervals for the absolute error

We now examine the error between the exact and approximate solutions in more detail. In particular, we estimate the average error as defined in equation (4.17). When the number of simulations NSIM is large we know from the *Central Limit Theorem* that the error becomes a Gaussian random variable in the asymptotic sense and it then converges to the nonrandom expectation of the absolute value of the error as NSIM approaches infinity.

In this section we simulate M batches with each batch consisting of NSIM draws. We assume that M is small (around 20 or 30) so that we can apply some techniques from *small sampling theory*. For large samples ($M \geq 30$) the sampling distributions of many statistics is approximately normal while for $M \leq 30$ this is not a good approximation and we resort to Student's t-distribution in these cases. To this end, we introduce and use the *Student t-distribution* to create a *confidence interval* that will contain the error that is the mean of the batch averages. We examine a set of independent, approximate Gaussian variables $X_1, \ldots, X_n$ with unknown variance. We define the *sample mean* and unbiased estimate of the variance (the *sample variance*) by

$$\overline{X} = \sum_{j=1}^{n} \frac{X_j}{n}$$

$$\hat{\sigma}_n^2 = \tfrac{1}{n-1} \sum_{j=1}^{n} \left(X_j - \overline{X} \right)^2$$

respectively. We give a short overview of the Student's t-distribution and to this end we now define the random variable:

$$t_n = \frac{(\overline{X} - \mu)}{\sqrt{\hat{\sigma}_n^2/n}}$$

where μ is the expected value. Then this variable satisfies the Student t-distribution with $n - 1$ degrees of freedom having mean zero and variance $(n - 1)/(n - 3)$ for $n > 3$. A standard result allows us to obtain the following confidence interval for μ:

$$\left(\overline{X} - \frac{\hat{\sigma}_n}{\sqrt{n}} t_{1-\alpha,n-1}, \quad \overline{X} + \frac{\hat{\sigma}_n}{\sqrt{n}} t_{1-\alpha,n-1} \right)$$

We find the numbers $t_{1-\alpha/2,n-1}$ from tables and hence we can produce a confidence interval for the unknown mean. We note that the C++ Boost library supports this distribution.

We now apply the above statistical technique to finding confidence intervals for the error between the solutions of the Ito process and the Euler approximation at $t = T$. In this case we compute the error quantity in equation (4.17) a number of times; we create a simulation of M *batches* of NSIM simulations. As before, we calculate the absolute error of each simulation in the batch as

$$\hat{\epsilon}_j = \frac{1}{NSIM} \sum_{k=1}^{NSIM} |X_{T,k,j} - Y_{T,k,j}| \quad j = 1, \ldots, M \tag{4.18}$$

and these are independent and approximately Gaussian for large NSIM. We now apply the Student t-distribution to construct confidence intervals for the sum of these random Gaussian variables having unknown variance. The batch averages are

$$\hat{\epsilon} = \frac{1}{M} \sum_{j=1}^{M} \hat{\epsilon}_j \tag{4.19}$$

and we take the quantity

$$\hat{\sigma}_\epsilon^2 = \frac{1}{M-1} \sum_{j=1}^{M} (\hat{\epsilon}_j - \hat{\epsilon})^2 \tag{4.20}$$

as an approximation of the variance of the batch averages. Then the confidence interval is given by

$$(\hat{\epsilon} - \Delta\hat{\epsilon}, \hat{\epsilon} + \Delta\hat{\epsilon}) \tag{4.21}$$

where

$$\Delta\hat{\epsilon} = t_{1\ \alpha,M-1} \sqrt{\frac{\hat{\sigma}_\epsilon^2}{M}} = \frac{\hat{\sigma}_\epsilon}{\sqrt{M}} t_{1-\alpha,M-1} \tag{4.22}$$

Summarising, the unknown mean lies in an interval whose length is halved by increasing the number of batches four-fold (you can see this by examining equation (4.22)); the number M is under the square root sign:

$$M = \hat{\sigma}_\epsilon^2 \left(\frac{t_{1-\alpha,M-1}}{\Delta\hat{\epsilon}}\right)^2$$

Of course, the greater the accuracy desired, the larger the value of M that we need.

4.4.3   Dependence of the absolute error on the step size

We now determine how the error behaves as a function of the step-size Δt. In general, the smaller the value of Δt the better the accuracy, but there are exceptions to this rule, for example when *round-off errors* occur, thus destroying the accuracy of the scheme.

In order to determine the relationship between the absolute error and the step size we carry out the experiment of section 4.4.2 with a sequence of step sizes:

$$\begin{cases} \Delta t_0 = T/16 \text{ (for example)} \\ \Delta t_n = \frac{\Delta t_{n-1}}{2}, \quad n = 1, \ldots, K \\ \text{where } K \text{ is the number of time intervals} \\ \text{to use in the experiment} \end{cases}$$

We then plot the size of the confidence interval as a function of the step size on a graph, for example. We can use logarithmic coordinates to give us some intuition concerning the *order of convergence* of the scheme; if we assume that the order is

$$\Delta \hat{\epsilon} = C \Delta t^{\beta}, \quad C \text{ is a constant}, \beta > 0$$
$$\text{then } \log_2 \Delta \hat{\epsilon} = \log_2(C \Delta t^{\beta}) = \log_2 C + \beta \log_2 \Delta t$$

When plotted using log coordinates we see that the value of the parameter β can be computed. For the Euler scheme, for example, we can determine experimentally that $\beta = 0.5$. We now discuss the two major kinds of convergence, namely strong and weak convergence.

4.4.4   Strong and weak convergence

We say that a discrete time approximation Y *converges strongly* to the exact solution X at time T if

$$\lim_{\Delta t \to 0} E(|X_T - Y_T|) = 0 \tag{4.23}$$

Continuing, we say that Y_T converges strongly with order $\gamma \geq 0$ at time T if

$$\epsilon(\Delta t) = E(|X_T - Y_T|) \leq C \Delta t^{\gamma}, \quad \Delta t \in (0, \Delta t_0), \text{ where } \Delta t_0 > 0 \text{ is given} \tag{4.24}$$

Some applications do not require a good pathwise approximation and in this case we introduce the concept of *weak convergence*. Using the same notation as above, we say that the discrete approximant Y_T is *weakly convergent* if: $\lim_{\Delta t \to 0} |E(g(X_T)) - E(g(Y_T))| = 0$ where g is a continuous function, for example a polynomial.

The approximation is of weak order $\beta \geq 0$ if

$$|E(g(X_T)) - E(g(Y_T))| \leq C \Delta t^{\beta} \text{ for } \Delta t \in (0, \Delta t_0)$$

We can set up an environment to test the weak convergence of a finite difference scheme. To this end, we define the quantity called the *mean error*:

$$\mu = E(X_T) - E(Y_T) \tag{4.25}$$

where X_T is the solution of the SDE (4.1) at $t = T$. Its mean is given by

$$E(X_T) = E(X_0) \exp(\mu T) \tag{4.26}$$

As before, we create M batches with each batch having NSIM paths

$$\hat{\mu}_j = \frac{1}{NSIM} \sum_{k=1}^{NSIM} Y_{T,k,j} - E(X_T), \quad j = 1, \ldots, M \tag{4.27}$$

Then we take the average

$$\hat{\mu} = \frac{1}{M} \sum_{j=1}^{M} \hat{\mu}_j \tag{4.28}$$

The estimated variance of the batch is

$$\hat{\sigma}_\mu^2 = \frac{1}{M-1} \sum_{j=1}^{M} (\hat{\mu}_j - \hat{\mu})^2 \tag{4.29}$$

Finally, the confidence interval is

$$(\hat{\mu} - \Delta\hat{\mu}, \ \hat{\mu} + \Delta\hat{\mu}) \tag{4.30}$$

where

$$\Delta\hat{\mu} = t_{1-\alpha, M-1} \sqrt{\frac{\hat{\sigma}_\mu^2}{M}} \tag{4.31}$$

We conclude this section with the remark that the analysis in this section rests on the fact that the exact solution of the SDE (4.1) is known. This is a restriction because in general we model systems of SDEs as well as SDEs with non-constant and nonlinear coefficients and then the above techniques break down because an exact solution is almost impossible to find. In Chapter 6 we adapt the analysis to accommodate cases in which the exact solution is not known.

4.5   SOME COMMON SCHEMES FOR ONE-FACTOR SDEs

In this book we concentrate on *one-step marching schemes*; in other words, given the solution at time level n we calculate the solution at time level $n + 1$. Some important schemes are

- Implicit and explicit Euler schemes.
- Implicit and explicit Milstein schemes.
- Predictor-Corrector method.
- Schemes that use Richardson extrapolation techniques.

We mention that there are many schemes for approximating the solution of nonlinear SDE systems. In Part III of the book we shall introduce a number of special schemes (for example, Andersen's QE method) for the Heston model.

We now discuss some popular one-step schemes.

4.6   THE MILSTEIN SCHEMES

This scheme is a variation of the Euler-Maruyama scheme. In this case we add an extra term that depends on the derivative of the diffusion term with respect to the (unknown) dependent variable. Let us consider the general one-factor nonlinear SDE:

$$dX = \mu(t, X)dt + \sigma(t, X)dW$$

In order to use the Milstein scheme we define the term

$$\frac{1}{2}\sigma\sigma' \left\{(\Delta W_n)^2 - \Delta t\right\} \text{ where } \sigma' = \frac{\partial\sigma}{\partial X} \tag{4.32}$$

In general, a derivative needs to be calculated. In the special case of equation (4.1) this quantity is just the constant volatility term. There are two forms of the Milstein scheme; first, the Ito Milstein scheme is

$$X_{n+1} = X_n + \mu X_n \Delta t + \sigma X_n \Delta W_n + \frac{1}{2}\sigma^2 \left\{(\Delta W_n)^2 - \Delta t\right\} \tag{4.33}$$

whereas the *Stratonovich Milstein* scheme is

$$X_{n+1} = X_n + \tilde{\mu} X_n \Delta t + \sigma X_n \Delta W_n + \frac{1}{2}\sigma^2 (\Delta W_n)^2 \tag{4.34}$$

where

$$\tilde{\mu} = \mu - \frac{1}{2}\sigma^2$$

It can be shown that the Milstein method is strongly consistent of strong order 1.0.

It is possible to define a generalised Milstein method by approximating the drift term by a combination of explicit and implicit terms. This is called the *implicit Milstein scheme*:

$$X_{n+1} = X_n + \mu \left\{\alpha X_n + (1-\alpha)X_{n+1}\right\} \Delta t + \sigma X_n \Delta W_n + \frac{1}{2}\sigma^2 \left\{(\Delta W_n)^2 - \Delta t\right\} \tag{4.35}$$

where $0 \le \alpha \le 1$.

4.7 PREDICTOR-CORRECTOR METHODS

Predictor-corrector schemes are suitable for nonlinear equations because they allow us to linearise them. This means that we can solve the problem without having to use nonlinear solvers such as the Newton-Raphson method, for example. We consider system (4.1) again. The idea is simple; first, we define a so-called *predictor* value that is the solution of an explicit scheme at level n, for example explicit Euler:

$$\tilde{X}_{n+1} = X_n + \mu X_n \Delta t + \sigma X_n \Delta \hat{W}_n \tag{4.36}$$

where $\Delta \hat{W}_n$ is a two point distributed random variable with $P(\Delta \hat{W} = \sqrt{\Delta t}) = 1/2, n = 0, \ldots, N-1$.

We then use the predictor to calculate the solution (called the *corrector*) at time level $n+1$, for example using the modified trapezoidal method:

$$X_{n+1} = X_n + \mu \left\{\alpha X_n + (1-\alpha)\tilde{X}_{n+1}\right\} \Delta t + \sigma X_n \Delta W_n \tag{4.37}$$

where $0 \le \alpha \le 1$.

It is possible to define other kinds of predictor-corrector schemes for nonlinear SDEs; see Kloeden, Platen and Schurz (1997) for more details. Finally, we introduce a number of finite difference schemes for SDEs in Chapters 5, 6 and 16.

4.8   STIFF ORDINARY AND STOCHASTIC DIFFERENTIAL EQUATIONS

We now discuss special classes of ODEs and SDEs that arise in practice and whose numerical solution demands special attention. These are called *stiff systems* whose solutions consist of two components; first, the *transient solution* that decays quickly in time and the *steady-state solution* that decays slowly. We speak of *fast transient* and *slow transient*, respectively. As a first example, let us examine the scalar linear initial value problem:

$$\begin{cases} \frac{dy}{dt} + ay = 1, & t \in (0, T], \quad a > 0 \text{ is a constant} \\ y(0) = A \end{cases} \tag{4.38}$$

whose solution is given by

$$y(t) = Ae^{-at} + \frac{1}{a}[1 - e^{-at}]$$

In this case the transient solution is the exponential term and this decays very fast (especially when the constant a is large) for increasing t. The steady-state solution is a constant and this is the value of the solution when t is infinity. The transient solution is called the *complementary function* and the steady-state solution is called the *particular integral*, the latter including no arbitrary constant (Ince, 1967). The stiffness in the above example is caused when the value a is large; in this case traditional finite difference schemes can produce unstable and highly oscillating solutions. One remedy is to define very small time steps. Special finite difference techniques have been developed that remain stable even when the parameter a is large. These are the *exponentially fitted* schemes and they have a number of variants (Duffy, 1980; Liniger and Willoughby 1970, Duffy, 2004a). The variant described in Liniger and Willoughby (1970) is motivated by finding a fitting factor for a general initial value problem and is chosen in such a way that it produces an exact solution for a certain model problem. To this end, let us examine the scalar ODE:

$$\frac{dy}{dt} = f(t, y(t)), \quad t \in (0, T] \tag{4.39}$$

and let us approximate it using the *Theta method*:

$$y_{n+1} - y_n = \Delta t[(1 - \theta)f_{n+1} + \theta f_n], \quad f_n = f(t_n, y_n) \tag{4.40}$$

where the parameter θ has not yet been specified. We determine it using the heuristic that the Theta method should be exact for the linear constant-coefficient *model problem*:

$$\frac{dy}{dt} = \lambda y \text{ (exact solution } y(t) = e^{\lambda t}) \tag{4.41}$$

Based on this heuristic and by using the exact solution in scheme (4.40) we get the value (you should check that this formula is correct):

$$\theta = -\frac{1}{\Delta t \lambda} - \frac{\exp(\Delta t \lambda)}{1 - \exp(\Delta t \lambda)} \tag{4.42}$$

We need to determine whether this scheme is stable (in some sense). To answer this question, we introduce some concepts.

Definition 4.1 The *region of (absolute) stability* of a numerical method for an initial value problem is the set of complex values $\Delta t \lambda$ for which all discrete solutions of the model problem (4.41) remain bounded when n approaches infinity.

Definition 4.2 A numerical method is said to be *A-stable* if its region of stability is the left-half plane, that is:

$$R = \{\Delta t \lambda \in \mathbb{C}; \mathbb{R}_e h\lambda < 0\}$$

Returning to the exponentially fitted method we can check that it is A-stable because for all $\Delta t \lambda < 0$ we have $\theta \leq \frac{1}{2}$ and this condition can be checked using the scheme (4.40) for the model problem (4.41).

We can generalise the exponential fitting technique to linear and nonlinear systems of equations. In the case of a linear system stiffness is caused by an isolated real negative eigenvalue of the matrix $\mathbf{A}$ in the equation:

$$\frac{d\underline{y}}{dt} = \mathbf{A}\underline{y} + \underline{f}(t) \tag{4.43}$$

where $\underline{y}, \underline{f} \in \mathbb{R}^n$, $\mathbf{A}$ is a constant $n \times n$ matrix with eigenvalues

$$\lambda_j \in \mathbb{C}, \quad j = 1, \ldots, n \text{ and eigenvectors } \underline{x}_j \in \mathbb{C}^n, \quad j = 1, \ldots, n.$$

The solution of this equation is given by

$$\underline{y}(t) = \sum_{j=1}^{n} c_j \exp(\lambda_j t)\underline{x}_j + \underline{g}(t) \tag{4.44}$$

where $c_j, j = 1, \ldots, n$ are arbitrary constants and $\underline{g}(t)$ is a particular integral.

If we assume that the real parts of the eigenvalues are less than zero we can conclude that the solution tends to the steady state. Even though this solution is well behaved the cause of numerical instabilities is the presence of quickly decaying transient components of the solution.

Let us take an example whose matrix has already been given in diagonal form:

$$\frac{d}{dt}\begin{pmatrix} y_1 \\ y_2 \end{pmatrix} = \begin{pmatrix} -\alpha_1 & 0 \\ 0 & -\alpha_2 \end{pmatrix}\begin{pmatrix} y_1 \\ y_2 \end{pmatrix}$$

$$y_1(0) = y_2(0) = 1, \quad 0 \leq \alpha_2 \ll \alpha_1 \tag{4.45}$$

The solution of this system is given by

$$\begin{aligned} y_1(t) &= e^{-\alpha_1 t} \\ y_2(t) &= e^{-\alpha_2 t} \end{aligned} \tag{4.46}$$

The solutions decay at different rates and in the case of the explicit Euler method the inequality:

$$\Delta t \leq \frac{2}{\alpha_1}$$

must be satisfied if the first component of the solution is to remain within the region of absolute stability. Unfortunately, choosing a time step of these proportions will be too small to allow for control over the round-off error in the second component.

In this case we fit the dominant eigenvalue. For variable coefficient systems and nonlinear systems we periodically compute the *Jacobian matrix* and carry out fitting on it.

4.8.1 Robust schemes for stiff systems

The presence of different time scales in ODEs leads to a number of challenges when approximating them using the standard finite difference schemes. In particular, schemes such as explicit and implicit Euler, Crank Nicolson and Predictor-Corrector do not approximate these systems well, unless a prohibitively small time step is used. Let us take the example (Dahlquist and Björck, 1974)

$$\frac{dy}{dt} = 100(\sin t - y), \quad y(0) = 0$$

with exact solution

$$y(t) = \frac{\sin t - 0.01 \cos t + 0.01 e^{-100t}}{1.0001}$$

This is a stiff problem because of the different time scales in the solution. We carried out an experiment using the explicit Euler method and we had to divide the interval $[0, 3]$ into 1.2 million sub-intervals in order to achieve accuracy to three decimal places. The implicit Euler and Crank Nicolson methods are not much better. The code used is

```
int main()
{
    // Input
    double a = 0.0;    // Initial value of independent variable (IV)
    double b = 3.0;    // The value of IV where we calculate solution

    double exact = sin(b) - 0.01*cos(b) + 0.01*exp(-100.0*b);
    exact = exact/1.0001;

    cout << "Exact solution is: " << exact << endl;

    // Euler method
    cout << "Give num steps: ";
    int M; cin >> M;

    double k = (b - a)/double(M);

    double VOld = 0.0;
    double VNew;
    double t = k;

    // EE
    for (int n = 0; n <= M; n++)
    {
        VNew = VOld + k * alpha * (sin(t) - VOld);
```

```
        VOld = VNew;
        t += k;
}

cout << "Explicit Euler solution: " << VNew << endl;

// IE
t = k;
for (int n = 0; n <= M; n++)
{
    VNew = VOld + k * alpha * sin(t);
    VNew = VNew / (1.0 + k*100.0);

    VOld = VNew;
    t += k;
}

cout << "Implicit Euler solution: " << VNew << endl;

// CN
t = k/2.0;
for (int n = 0; n <= M; n++)
{
    VNew = VOld*(1.0 - (k * alpha)/2.0) + k * 100.0 * sin(t);
    VNew = VNew / (1.0 + (k*alpha)/2.0);

    VOld = VNew;
    t += k;
}

cout << "Crank Nicolson: " << VNew << endl;

    return 0;
}
```

The schemes are not suitable for this stiff problem. For this reason, we need schemes that converge without having to use very small time steps. In this section, we discuss the Bulirsch-Stoer method (Stoer and Bulirsch, 1980) that performs well for stiff systems. This is an extrapolation method and it uses function values on meshes of varying sizes. It depends on the fact that the asymptotic expansion for the difference between the exact and approximate solutions can be expressed in even powers of the step-length Δt:

$$\underline{y}(t_n) - Y^n = \sum_{j=1}^{\infty} \Delta t^{2j} e_{2j}(t_n) \tag{4.47}$$

where

$\underline{y}()$ is the exact solution of the IVP

Y is the approximate solution of the IVP

$e_{2j}(t)$ is independent of Δt

This is called *Gragg's formula* and it allows us to remove oscillating terms. We then approximate the solution of the IVP using rational functions (a rational function is the quotient of two polynomials):

$$R(t) = \frac{P_\mu(t)}{Q_\nu(t)} = \frac{\sum\limits_{j=0}^{\mu} p_j t^j}{\sum\limits_{j=0}^{\nu} q_j t^j} \tag{4.48}$$

Finally, the method builds a tableaux of numbers that we calculate by means of an interpolation formula. The details can be found in Stoer and Bulirsch (1980).

We have used some open source software to test stiff ODE systems. It is easy to find on the Internet. The accuracy and performance of the Bulirsch-Stoer method are very good.

4.8.2 Stiff stochastic differential equations

We generalise the discussion on stiff ODEs and to this end we introduce the concept of *Lyapunov exponents*. These measure the asymptotic rates of expansion or contraction of the solutions of dynamical linear systems, a generalisation of the real parts of the eigenvalues of autonomous deterministic linear systems such as equation (4.43). In particular, we can use Lyapunov exponents to study the properties of solutions of SDEs.

Let us consider a continuous time dynamical system whose solution is denoted by $f(t)$ for any non-negative value of t. We are interested in the rate of separation of two trajectories given that they differ by a certain amount at $t = 0$. If the following relationship holds:

$$|\delta f(t)| \equiv e^{\lambda t} |\delta f(t_0)|, \quad t \geq t_0 \tag{4.49}$$

then the constant λ is called the *Lyapunov exponent*. In this case $f(t)$ is some trajectory in space. In general, the number of Lyapunov exponents in a system is equal to the number of state variables in the system. Thus, a one-dimensional system has one exponent. The signs of the exponents provide qualitative information about the dynamics of the system; if they are negative then there is convergence between close trajectories whereas if they are positive the system is chaotic. When $\lambda = 0$ the initial perturbations neither diverge nor converge, in other words their initial distance remains constant. We say that a system is *conservative* if all its Lyapunov exponents are zero while the system is said to be *dissipative* if the sum of the Lyapunov exponents is negative. The predictability of a dynamical system is determined by the *maximal (top) Lyapunov exponent* that we define as

$$\lambda = \lim_{t \to \infty} \frac{1}{t} ln \frac{|\delta f(t)|}{|\delta f(t_0)|} \tag{4.50}$$

where $ln(x)$ is the natural logarithm (base e) of the variable x. You can check that equation (4.50) follows from equation (4.49). For discrete systems of the form

$$x_n = f(x_{n-1}), \quad n \geq 1, \quad x_0 = u_0 \tag{4.51}$$

where f is a real-value function of a real variable, we can define the Lyapunov exponent as follows:

$$\lambda = \lim_{n \to \infty} \frac{1}{n} ln |f^n(u) - f^n(u_0)|$$

where

$$f^n(u) = f(f^{n-1}(u)), \quad n \geq 1$$

and

$$f^0(u) \equiv f(u)$$

(4.52)

Having introduced this concept we now describe how Lyapunov exponents relate to stochastic differential equations. First, we write the SDEs in Stratonovich form. For convenience, we take a one-factor Ito SDE:

$$dX = a(t, X)dt + b(t, X)dW \tag{4.53}$$

The Stratonovich SDE is written in the form:

$$dX = \underline{a}(t, X) + b(t, X)dW \tag{4.54}$$

where the original drift and modified drift functions are related by

$$a(t, x) = \underline{a}(t, x) + \frac{1}{2} b(t, x) \frac{\partial b}{\partial x}(t, x)$$

Let us now consider the n-dimensional Stratonovich SDE having an m-dimensional standard Wiener process:

$$d\underline{X} = \underline{a}(t, \underline{X})dt + \sum_{k=1}^{m} \underline{b_k}(t, \underline{X})dW_k \tag{4.55}$$

$$\underline{W} = {}^t(W_1, \ldots, W_m), \quad \underline{X} = {}^t(X_1, \ldots, X_n)$$

where

$$\underline{a} = {}^t(a_1, \ldots, a_n), \quad b = (b_{ij})_{\substack{1 \leq i \leq n \\ 1 \leq j \leq k}}$$

We linearise this equation around a given vector

$$\underline{Z}(t) = \underline{X}(t) - \tilde{\underline{X}}(t), \text{ where}$$

$$\tilde{\underline{X}}(t) \text{ is a stochastically stationary solution}$$

to give the linearised SDE:

$$d\underline{Z} = A(t, \omega)\underline{Z}dt + \sum_{k=1}^{m} B^k(t, \omega)\underline{Z} \circ dW_k$$

where the $n \times n$ matrices $A, B^1, B^2, \ldots, B^m$ are defined by:

$$\left. \begin{array}{l} A_{ij}(t, \omega) = \dfrac{\partial \underline{a_i}(t, \tilde{X}(t, \omega))}{\partial x_j} \\[4mm] B_{ij}^k(t, \omega) = \dfrac{\partial b_{k,i}(t, \tilde{X}(t, \omega))}{\partial x_j} \end{array} \right\} i, j = 1, \ldots, n, \quad k = 1, \ldots, M \tag{4.56}$$

In the one-dimensional case ($n = 1$) we can solve (4.56) explicitly (see Kloeden and Platen, 1995) and we define the Lyapunov exponent as

$$\lambda = \lim_{t \to \infty} \frac{1}{t} |Z(t)|$$

And since we get the following expression for the exponent:

$$ln|Z| = ln|Z_0| + \int_0^t A(s, \omega)ds + \int_0^t B(t, \omega)dW(s)$$

since

$$\lim_{t \to \infty} \frac{1}{t} \int_0^t B(s, \omega)dW(S) = 0 \text{ with probability } 1$$

we then get

$$\lambda = \lim_{t \to \infty} \frac{1}{t} \int_0^t A(s, \omega)ds \text{ with probability } 1$$

In the n-dimensional case we use *Oseledets' Multiplicative Ergodic Theorem* (Oseledets, 1968) to assert the existence (with probability 1) of n non-random Lyapunov exponents:

$$\lambda_n \geq \lambda_{n-1} \geq \ldots \gg \lambda_1$$

In general, it is difficult to find the Lyapunov exponents for an SDE exactly and we then need to resort to numerical methods.

Definition 4.3 The linearised SDE (4.56) is called *stochastically stiff* if its largest and smallest exponents satisfy:

$$\lambda_n \gg \lambda_1$$

This definition is consistent with the theory for ODEs because the real parts of the eigenvalues of the coefficient matrix in that case are its Lyapunov exponents. Thus, stochastic stiffness refers to the presence of two or more wide time scales in the solutions. Finally, a stiff linear ODE is also stochastically stiff. Explicit finite difference schemes will suffer severe difficulties when applied to stiff SDEs due to the fact that we must choose very small time steps in order to get any sort of decent accuracy.

We have provided some examples on the CD of the computation of Lyapunov exponents, for example SDEs and chaotic fractal systems.

4.9   SOFTWARE DESIGN AND C++ IMPLEMENTATION ISSUES

When writing code that implements numerical schemes for SDEs we need to satisfy a number of requirements:

- *Accuracy*: How well should the discrete solution approximate the exact solution? Are we interested in strong or weak convergence?
- *Efficiency and performance*: Numerical schemes should be fast because we use them many times in a simulation; the response time of the program will be dependent on how much effort is needed to achieve a given level of accuracy.
- *Maintainability*: Once we have found the most appropriate scheme for the problem at hand, we need to integrate the corresponding code in the software framework.

As developer, it is important to determine what your goals are. Then you can then decide which *software process* to use to achieve them. One process that we use is to develop the software systems as a sequence of prototypes; each prototype delivers a tangible software product that we use in the next iteration. Typical scenarios are

1. Select a scheme and develop code to test it; focus on the accuracy of the results and whether the scheme is suitable for the problem at hand. Do not worry about the object-oriented niceties for the moment. One useful ploy is to define C++ namespaces to group related functions and data. For this step, we recommend taking a *model problem* that contains most of the essential difficulties.
2. Re-engineer the code from step 1. This could entail creating C++ classes that implement the functions and data in step 1.
3. Scale the model problem to the full problem. The model problem could be a one-factor linear SDE while the full problem could be a two-factor nonlinear SDE (for example, the SDE that describes the Heston stochastic volatility model). Go to step 1 and repeat steps 1 and 2. When you are satisfied with the performance and accuracy, proceed to step 4.
4. This is an optional step (in some cases, you may not have time to execute it). In this case we integrate the classes and code from step 3 into the software framework. In many cases, we use the GOF (see GOF, 1995) design patterns to drive the software process. We build on proven software design techniques.

We discuss these software-related issues in more detail in Part II of the book. In particular, we use the Unified Modeling Language (UML) to document software designs.

4.10   COMPUTATIONAL RESULTS

A requirement when approximating SDEs using finite differences is that the error between the exact and approximate solutions at the expiry date $t = T$ (and possibly at other points in $[0, T]$, for example when modelling path-dependent Asian and barrier options) is within a certain predefined tolerance. We also need to determine whether we are interested in strong or weak convergence (see Kloeden, Platen and Schurz (1997) for a discussion on which option is more appropriate in a given context).

We also mention the effects of round-off error when computing numerical quantities. A *round-off error* occurs in computers with a finite precision. For example, we can get round-off errors when a computer cannot handle numbers with more than s digits. Then the exact product of two numbers cannot be used in subsequent calculations because the product has $2s$ digits; it must be rounded. The same problem occurs when we approximate irrational numbers by numbers with finite precision.

Thus, increasing the number of simulations NSIM in a Monte Carlo application or increasing the number of mesh points NT may result in more inaccurate results than with smaller values of these parameters. We have experienced this disconcerting phenomenon when performing numerical experiments on a range of SDEs and finite difference schemes. In general, we achieve better accuracy when pricing put options (because the payoff is bounded) whereas for call options the payoff is unbounded. We recommend pricing the put option and then using *call-put parity relationships* to find the call price if these relationships are applicable.

4.11   ASIDE: THE CHARACTERISTIC EQUATION OF A DIFFERENCE SCHEME

When developing homogeneous finite difference schemes (no right-hand side term) for ODEs it is useful to examine constant-coefficient model problems. In these cases we find an exact solution to a scheme by constructing its *auxiliary* or *characteristic equation* (see Goldberg, 1986). To this end, let us consider the *homogeneous linear difference equation of kth order with constant coefficients*:

$$y_{n+k} + a_1 y_{n+k-1} + \cdots + a_k y_n = 0 \tag{4.57}$$

We wish to find a solution to this equation; it is satisfied by a sequence

$$\{y_j\} \text{ where } y_j = cm^j \ (m \neq 0, \quad c \neq 0)$$

if and only if

$$cm^{n+k} + a_1 cm^{n+k-1} + \cdots + a_k cm^n = 0$$

that is, when (divide by c and the common powers of m):

$$\varphi(m) \equiv m^k + a_1 m^{k-1} + \cdots + a_k = 0$$

This is called the *characteristic equation* and $\varphi(m)$ is called the *characteristic polynomial*.

Theorem 4.3 If the characteristic equation has k different roots $m_1, m_2, \ldots, m_k$ then the general solution of this equation (4.57) is given by

$$y_n = \sum_{j=1}^{k} c_j m_j^n \text{ where } c_1, \ldots, c_k \text{ are arbitrary constants}$$

We conclude that we can produce a unique solution of the difference scheme if we can compute the above k constants. There are several ways of doing this. Let us take some examples. The first example is

$$y_{n+2} - 5y_{n+1} + 6y_n = 0$$
$$y_0 = 0, \quad y_1 = 1$$

The characteristic equation is $m^2 - 5m + 6 = 0$ and the roots are $m_1 = 3$ and $m_2 = 2$. Hence a general solution is given by $m_n = c_1 3^n + c_2 2^n$ and we can find the constants as follows:

$$n = 0 \Rightarrow c_1 + c_2 = 0$$
$$n = 1 \Rightarrow 3c_1 + 2c_2 = 1$$
$$(c_1 = 1, \quad c_2 = -1)$$

Hence $y_n = 3^n - 2^n$.

Another example is to find an explicit formula for *Tchebycheff polynomials* of the first kind defined by the following recurrence relation:

$$T_{n+1}(x) - 2xT_n(x) + T_{n-1}(x) = 0, \quad n \geq 1, \quad -1 < x < 1$$
$$T_0(x) = 1, \quad T_1(x) = x$$

Characteristic equation
$$m^2 - 2xm + 1 = 0, \quad m_\pm = x \pm i\sqrt{1 - x^2}, \quad i = \sqrt{-1}$$
Set $x = \cos\varphi$, then $m_\pm = \cos\varphi \pm i\sin\varphi$
Hence $m_1 = \exp(i\varphi), \quad m_2 = \exp(-i\varphi), \quad m_1 \neq m_2$

Initial condition
$$n = 0 \Rightarrow c_1 + c_2 = 1$$
$$n = 1 \Rightarrow c_1 \exp(i\varphi) + c_2 \exp(-i\varphi) = \cos\varphi$$
Hence $c_1 = c_2 = \frac{1}{2}$, and thus
$$T_n(x) = \cos(n\varphi), \quad x = \cos\varphi$$

We note that the Boost C++ library has extensive support for orthogonal polynomials, such as Bessel and Hermite, Tchebycheff, Legendre, Laguerre and Jacobi. You do not need to write the code yourself.

4.12   SUMMARY AND CONCLUSIONS

In this chapter we have given an introduction to some issues related to the approximation of one-factor SDEs using finite difference schemes. We have concentrated on examining the theoretical properties of these schemes and we discussed a number of popular one-step schemes. We shall extend, apply and generalise the methods that we introduced here in Chapters 5 and 6.

We conclude this chapter with the remark that there are many ways to approximate the solutions of SDEs that are needed in financial applications. We have discussed a subset of these techniques.

4.13   EXERCISES AND PROJECTS

1. (*) Solution of Difference Equations
   The *Fibonacci numbers* are defined by the recurrence relation:

   $$\begin{cases} y_n = y_{n-1} + y_{n-2}, & n \geq 2 \\ y_0 = 0, & y_1 = 1 \end{cases}$$

   Use the techniques of section 4.11 to find an explicit representation for the nth Fibonacci number.

2. (**) Consistency, Stability and Convergence for Initial Value Problems
   We present four consistent schemes for the initial value problem (IVP) defined by equation (4.6) and their corresponding generating polynomials. It is useful to write these polynomials

in their most general form for one-step and two-step schemes, respectively:

$$\rho(\zeta) = \alpha_0 \zeta + \alpha_1$$
$$\sigma(\zeta) = \beta_0 \zeta + \beta_1$$

$$\rho(\zeta) = \alpha_0 \zeta^2 + \alpha_1 \zeta + \alpha_2$$
$$\sigma(\zeta) = \beta_0 \zeta^2 + \beta_1 \zeta + \beta_2$$

Verify the formula using equation (4.9) and convince yourself that the consistency relations (4.10) hold for the following schemes:

Leap frog scheme:

$$\frac{X_{n+1} - X_{n-1}}{2\Delta t} = \mu(t_n, X_n), \quad 1 \le n \le N - 1$$

$$\rho(\zeta) = \zeta^2 - 1, \quad o(\zeta) = 2\zeta$$

Trapezoidal scheme:

$$\frac{X_{n+1} - X_n}{\Delta t} = \frac{1}{2}[\mu(t_n, X_n) + \mu(t_{n+1}, X_{n+1})], \quad 0 \le n \le N - 1$$

$$\rho(\zeta) = \zeta - 1, \quad \sigma(\zeta) = \tfrac{1}{2}(\zeta + 1)$$

Implicit Euler scheme:

$$\frac{X_{n+1} - X_n}{\Delta t} = \mu(t_{n+1}, X_{n+1}), \quad 0 \le n \le N - 1$$

$$\rho(\zeta) = \zeta - 1, \quad \sigma(\zeta) = \zeta$$

Adams-Bashforth scheme:

$$\frac{X_{n+1} - X_n}{\Delta t} = \frac{1}{12}[23\mu(t_n, X_n) - 16\mu(t_{n-1}, X_{n-1}) + 5\mu(t_{n-2}, X_{n-2})], \quad 2 \le n \le N$$

$$\rho(\zeta) = \zeta - 1$$

$$\sigma(\zeta) = \tfrac{23}{12}\zeta^2 - \tfrac{16}{12}\zeta + \tfrac{5}{12}$$

Verify that these schemes satisfy the root condition of Theorem 4.1.

3. (***) Exact Solutions of SDEs

Set up an environment to test the accuracy of finite difference schemes for one-factor SDEs. In particular, examine several SDEs for which we have an analytic solution; and to this end take some of the problems from Kloeden and Platen (1995), pages 120–124. The cases of interest are

$$dX = \tfrac{1}{2}a^2 X dt + a\sqrt{X^2 + 1}\, dW$$
$$X(t) = \sinh(aW(t) + \operatorname{arcsinh} X_0)$$

$$dX = 1 dt + 2\sqrt{X}\, dW$$
$$X(t) = (W(t) + \sqrt{X_0})^2$$

$$dX = \tfrac{1}{2}a^2 X dt + aX dW$$
$$X(t) = X_0 \exp(aW(t))$$

Ito exponential SDE (multiplicative noise)
$$dX = \tfrac{1}{2}X dt + X dW$$
$$X(t) = X_0 \exp(W(t))$$

Drift-free SDE (multiplicative noise)
$$dX = X dW$$
$$X(t) = X_0 \exp(W(t) - t/2)$$

Homogeneous (multiplicative noise)
$$dX = aX dt + bX dW$$
$$X(t) = X_0 \exp\left\{(a - \tfrac{1}{2}b^2)t + bW(t)\right\}$$

Homogeneous (additive noise)
$$dX = -\alpha X dt + \sigma dW$$
$$X(t) = e^{-\alpha t}(X_0 + \int_0^t e^{\alpha s} dW(s))$$

In all cases, X_0 is the value of the stochastic process at $t = 0$. You may need to use the mathematical functions that are defined in the standard C++ math library <cmath >. We summarise these functions for completeness and you can find out more about them by using the online help facility in your C++ IDE (*Integrated Development Environment*):

```
acosf, asinf, atanf, atan2f, ceilf, cosf, coshf, expf, fabsf,
floorf, fmodf, frexpf, ldexpf, logf, log10f, modff, powf, sinf,
sinhf, sqrtf,tanf, tanhf, acosl, asinl, atanl, atan2l, ceill,
cosl, coshl, expl, fabsl, floorl, fmodl, frexpl, ldexpl, logl,
log10l, modfl, powl, sinl, sinhl, sqrtl, tanl, tanhl, abs, acos,
asin, atan, atan2, ceil, cos, cosh, exp, fabs, floor, fmod, frexp,
ldexp, log, log10, modf, pow, sin, sinh, sqrt, tan, tanh
```

For example, we show how to use the hyperbolic tangent function for various data types:

```
int main()
{

    double xd = 1.0;
    float xf = 1.0;
    long double ld = 1.0;
```

```
      double d = tanh(xd);
      float f = tanh(xf);
      float f2 = tanhf(xf);
      long double l = tanh(ld);

      cout << "double: " << d << endl;
      cout << "float: " << f << endl;
      cout << "float, tanhf function: " << f << endl;
      cout << "long double " << l << endl;

      return 0;
}
```

Answer the following questions:
- Use the classes for SDEs that we introduced in Chapter 0 to model the above SDEs at any point t in the interval $(0, T]$ where $T > 0$.
- Compute an approximate solution to these SDEs using (1) Milstein's method (see section 4.6) and (2) predictor-corrector method (section 4.7).
- Apply the techniques of section 4.4.3 to compute (by halving the step size successively) the order of convergence of these two schemes. Use logarithms of the data and plot on log paper.

4. (****) Richardson-Romberg Extrapolation and Higher-Order Accuracy
A well-known technique in numerical analysis is called the *Richardson Extrapolation technique*, which allows us to improve the accuracy of finite difference schemes by calculating the approximate solution on two consecutive meshes. The numerical cost of the Richardson procedure is much smaller than the cost corresponding to some other schemes to produce the same order of accuracy. Furthermore, the code can be parallelised.

Let us take the example of the explicit Euler method. We know that it is first-order weakly convergent and we thus write the error as an asymptotic expansion as follows:

$$E(g(X_T)) - E(g(Y_T^{\Delta t})) = m_1 \Delta t + O(\Delta t^2)$$

where

$$X_T = \text{exact solution at } t = T$$
$$Y_T^{\Delta t} = \text{approximate solution at } t = T$$
$$g = \text{is a test function}$$
$$m_1 \text{ is a constant independent of } \Delta t$$

We now examine the solutions on two consecutive meshes and using some basic algebra we see that

$$V_T^{\Delta t/2} \equiv 2Y_T^{\Delta t/2} - Y_T^{\Delta t}$$

has second-order accuracy (in the weak sense).

The objective of this exercise is to create C++ code that implements this extrapolation method. You should integrate the code into the *Visitor* hierarchy that we introduced in

Chapter 0. Test your results; do you indeed get second-order accuracy? How did you model the random numbers?

A number of authors have applied this extrapolation technique using the implicit Euler method to achieve second-order and oscillation-free finite difference schemes for the partial differential equations for Heston and SABR stochastic models (see, for example, Sheppard, 2007).

5. (*****) Testing the Accuracy of Finite Difference Schemes, Project
In this exercise we apply Student's t-distribution and the results in section 4.4 to find a confidence interval for the error in equation (4.16). The objective is to design and implement a C++ module whose responsibility is to compute the confidence interval that contains the error between the Ito process (this solution must be known) and its numerical approximation. The code is an implementation of the formulae (4.21) and (4.22). The output will be a Range<T> instance representing the confidence interval.

The input to the module is:
– A function pointer (or function object as discussed in Chapter 21) and initial condition that together represent the exact solution of the stochastic differential equation. Alternatively, we could provide the module with an SDE<double, 1> instance.
– The type of FDM scheme to be used. You could use the *Visitor* pattern for FDM classes that we introduced in Chapter 0.
– The number of batches M.
– A vector of discrete values as in equation (4.18) representing the vector of the variance of the simulation.
– The desired confidence interval value α (you will need to have access to a table of values for the t-distribution).
The steps that harmonise input and output are:
– Compute the average error (4.18) (note that you have to calculate the exact and approximate solutions NSIM times up to $t = T$).
– Calculate the batch average in equation (4.19).
– Calculate the variance (4.20).
– Read the values for the t-distribution from the table of values.
Having carried out these steps we are then able to compute the desired quantity (4.21).

6. (****) Experimental Determination of the Order of Convergence
Write C++ code to determine the order of convergence of a finite difference scheme that approximates the solution of an SDE whose exact solution is known. You should use the software modules from exercise 5. The code must support the sequence of step sizes:

$$\begin{cases} \Delta t_0 = T/16 \text{ (for example)} \\ \Delta t_n = \frac{\Delta t_{n-1}}{2}, \quad n = 1, \ldots, K \\ \text{where } K \text{ is the number of time intervals to use in the experiment} \end{cases}$$

Use the *Excel Visualiser* to present your results. The code should test common schemes such as explicit Euler, Milstein and Predictor-Corrector. Base your analysis on section 4.4.3.

7. (*****) Interpolation of Discrete Time Approximations
The finite difference schemes in this book calculate the values of the dependent variable at (discrete) mesh points. The values are not defined at intermediate points. So, what can we do if we wish to approximate the solutions at these points? The answer is to deploy an *interpolation scheme*, for example linear, cubic spline or exponential interpolation. In

this exercise we discuss the application of linear interpolation. The problem is to find the approximate solution at *any* point t in the interval $[0, T]$. In order to produce code for this problem, we need to execute two steps:

– Find the subinterval that contains the value t.

– Interpolate between the end points of this subinterval to find the approximate value at the intermediate value t. Then we are done.

For the first step, we need to find the index number of the subinterval that contains the value t. We use the following algorithm:

$$n_t = \max \{n : 0 \le n \le N; t_n \le t\} \text{ where } \{t_n\}_{n=0}^{N-1}$$

are the mesh points as discussed in section 4.2

Having found this index we know the endpoints of the corresponding interval and then we can apply the interpolation scheme:

$$X(t) = X_{n_t} + \frac{t - t_{n_t}}{t_{n_t+1} - t_{n_t}}(X_{n_t+1} - X_{n_t})$$

The objective of this exercise is to implement this scheme as part of your C++ software framework. For example, you could add it to the class `Mesher` that is responsible for the creation and management of mesh points. Of course, you can first implement the code as a global C function, test the code and then afterwards integrate it into `Mesher`. One special attention area is to develop the code that computes the index of the subinterval containing the value t; in a first version of the software you could iterate sequentially from $t = 0$ to $t = T$ until you find the subinterval that contains t. This approach is acceptable for prototyping but it will become progressively slower when we use large values of N (the number of subdivisions of the interval $[0, T]$). In this latter case the performance of the program will degrade and we need to use a different algorithm, for example the *Bisection method* (the code for this is in Duffy, 2006a).

It is important to note that linear interpolation incurs an error that is bounded by the second derivative of the function being approximated. We compute this error. Let us define the function $f(x)$ to be interpolated and let the linear polynomial $p(x)$ approximate it at the points $x = a$ and $x = b$. Define the error term

$$R_T = f(x) - p(x), \quad a \le x \le b$$

Then by an application of *Rolle's theorem* (see Spiegel, 1969; Widder, 1989) we can show that

$$p(x) = f(a) + \frac{f(b) - f(a)}{b - a}(x - a)$$

with the error term bounded by

$$|R_T| \le \frac{(b - a)^2}{8} \sup_{a \le x \le b} |f''(x)|$$

We must be careful in the current case because the Wiener process is almost surely non-differentiable everywhere!

(**Rolle's theorem** is: Let $f(x)$ be continuous in $[a, b]$ and suppose $f(a) = f(b) = 0$. Then if the derivative $f'(x)$ exists in $[a, b]$, there is a point c in (a, b) such that $f'(c) = 0$.)

8. (**) Computation of Orthogonal Polynomials

In section 4.11 we used a technique to find the solution of homogeneous finite difference schemes with constant coefficients. As an example, we showed how to give a representation for Tchebycheff polynomials that belong to the wider class of orthogonal polynomials. Orthogonal polynomials have numerous applications in finance, including:

– Numerical integration, in particular Gauss quadature (Davis, 1975).
– Spectral analysis of partial differential equations (Voigt, 1984).
– Fitting of data (Rivlin, 1969).
– Solving SDEs with Stochastic FEM and Polynomial Chaos (Ghanem and Spanos, 1991; Xiu and Karniadakis, 2002).

A discussion of these topics is outside the scope of this book, but in this exercise we discuss how to define and compute two special kinds, namely Hermite and Legendre polynomials. Some others are called Laguerre, Tchebycheff, ultraspherical and Jacobi orthogonal polynomials. These polynomials can also be generalised to n dimensions. All orthogonal polynomials have a number of defining features:

– They satisfy a three-term recurrence relationship:

$$Q_{n+1}(x) = \alpha_n(x - \beta_n)Q_n(x) - \delta_n Q_{n-1}(x), n \geq 1$$
$$Q_0(x) = a(x), Q_1(x) = b(x)$$

– They satisfy the generalised Rodrigues formula:

$$Q_n(x) = \frac{1}{w(x)} \frac{d^n}{dx^n}[w(x)s^n(x)]$$

We use the values of the polynomial when $n = 0$ and $n = 1$ as the initial values for the above recurrence relationship.

– They satisfy a differential equation:

$$a(x)\frac{d^2Q}{dx^2} + b(x)\frac{dQ}{dx} + \lambda Q = 0$$

where

$a(x) =$ quadratic polynomial (at most) in x
$b(x) =$ linear polynomial
$\lambda =$ constant, the eigenvalue of the differential equation

– They satisfy an integral orthogonality principle on some interval S:

$$\int_S Q_n(x)Q_m(x)w(x)dx = h_n^2\delta_{nm}, \quad \text{with } n, m \in N$$

where $\delta_{n,m}$ is the Kronecker delta defined by

$$\delta_{nm} = \begin{cases} 1, \text{ if } n = m \\ 0, \text{ if } n \neq m \end{cases} \text{ and } h_n^2 > 0$$

We examine Hermite polynomials as a representative case. In this case:

$$w(x) = e^{-x^2}, -\infty < x < \infty$$
$$\alpha_n = 2, \beta_n = 0, \delta_n = 2n$$
$$H_n(x) = (-1)^n e^{x^2} \frac{d^n}{dx^n}[e^{-x^2}]$$

Answer the following questions:
– Find the values of the Hermite polynomials in the case $n = 0$ and $n = 1$.

- Use the values found above to compute the value of the polynomial for arbitrary values of n.
- Create C++ code to test your algorithm. Plot a graph (using the Excel *Visualiser*, for example) for various values of n.
- Now adapt and test your code for Legendre polynomials:

$$w(x) = 1, \quad -1 < x < 1$$
$$(n+1)P_{n+1}(x) = (2n+1)x\,P_n(x) - n\,P_{n-1}(x), \quad n \geq 1$$
$$P_n(x) = \frac{1}{2^n n!}\frac{d^n}{dx^n}(x^2 - 1)^n, \quad n \geq 0$$

Apply what you have learned for Hermite polynomials to the current situation.

9. (**) Stability of Difference Scheme

For which values of the constant a does the following difference scheme produce an oscillating solution?

$$y_{n+1} - 2y_n + (1-a)y_{n-1} = 0, \quad n \geq 1$$
$$y_0 = A, \; y_1 = B$$

(Hint: use results from section 4.11.)

5

Design and Implementation of Finite Difference Schemes in Computational Finance

5.1 INTRODUCTION AND OBJECTIVES

In this chapter we apply the results from the first four chapters of this book to a number of examples in computational finance. In particular, we model the following types of derivatives using the Monte Carlo method:

- A two-factor spread option with stochastic volatility.
- Barrier options.
- The Heston stochastic volatility model.
- Asian options.

We analyse these models by first defining the corresponding SDEs, then we approximate the solutions of these SDEs using finite differences. Finally, we calculate the option price by the Monte Carlo method.

The main goals of this chapter are

- To show the applicability of the mathematical and numerical methods that we discussed in the first four chapters of this book to solving option pricing problems.
- To design the C++ code that solves these problems in such a way that it can be extended and generalised to a wider range of problems in later chapters.
- To prepare the reader for more advanced issues that we introduce in Parts II and III of the book, in particular system and design patterns and complex option pricing applications.
- To show the relationships between our approach and other textbooks in this area. In particular, we model two well-known models (namely, stochastic spread and Heston models). We formulate them as systems of SDEs, approximate them using finite differences and finally implement the schemes using C++. In other words, we delineate the full process from theory to code and in this way we hope that the reader will get some insights into the software.

This is a key chapter because it maps some examples to C++. Furthermore, the patterns and examples will reappear in later chapters. In this chapter we concentrate on the essential details so that the reader can get a good overview of what is taking place. We recommend that you experiment with the code on the CD.

5.2 MODELLING SDEs AND FDM IN C++

We have learned from experience with software projects that it is almost impossible to develop flexible, robust and accurate software for applications without going through a number of phases. First, we write a prototype software system (where the software metaphor may be *modular*) in order to ensure that the crucial algorithms produce accurate output. Second, having tested and reviewed the prototype solution we then embark on upgrading it in order to make it more adaptable to new requirements. We can achieve these ends by introducing object-oriented classes, design patterns and standard data structures (see, for example, GOF (1995), Josuttis (1999)). Finally – once we understand the problem – we then apply system-level patterns and other architectural models in conjunction with standardised inter-component interfaces to help us create a framework that can be customised and extended by the developer. In this chapter we concentrate on discussing the first software phase. We stress that all three phases implement the same kind of systems; in general, the software architectures that we deploy have three major components:

- S1: The components that model the underlying assets, market data and other related information. In this book we use stochastic differential equations (SDEs) to model the behaviour of the underlying assets. We note that this component uses other components for random number generation, correlation analysis and calibration data.
- S2: The components that model the derivatives products associated with the assets in component S1. For example, in this component we define C++ classes that model the properties of options and other derivatives products. Furthermore, we define numerical methods that are responsible for the path evolution of the SDEs in component S1, for example the Finite Difference Method (FDM) and other numerical methods.
- S3: The components that calculate the price (and possibly the sensitivities) of derivatives products using the Monte Carlo method. Included in the functionality is the calculation of the standard error and standard deviation and other relevant information.

Each example in this chapter will implement these components. Attention points are

1. Structuring the components S1, S2 and S3.
2. Defining the software interfaces.
3. Structuring a working program that the reader can use and extend.

After having read this chapter and run the code on the CD, you will be able to appreciate which major components are needed, and how to effect the following modifications:

- How to add a scheme to the framework.
- How to add a payoff (Barrier, Asian, etc.).
- How to add a new finite difference scheme.
- How to add a random number generator.

The chapters in Part III deal with these issues in more detail.

5.3   MATHEMATICAL AND NUMERICAL TOOLS

In this section we give a short introduction to a number of supporting techniques that we use in our C++ codes.

5.3.1 Analytical solution and numerical solution of SDEs

In general, it is not possible to find a closed-form solution of an SDE but in some cases it is possible by an application of Ito's lemma. For example, the constant-coefficient scalar SDE

$$\begin{cases} dX = aXdt + bXdW, & 0 < t \leq T \\ X(0) = X_0 \end{cases} \tag{5.1}$$

has solution:

$$X(t) = X_0 \exp((a - b^2/2)t + bW(t)), \quad 0 \leq t \leq T \tag{5.2}$$

Having a solution that we can compute is useful because we can compare numerical solutions against it. For completeness, we give the 'didactic' C++ code that computes the solution of equation (5.2) on N equal subintervals on the interval $[0, T]$:

```cpp
// Exact solution of linear SDE dX = aXdt + bXdw (a, b are constant)
Vector<double, long> GBMRandomWalk(double X0, double a, double b,
                                   double T, int N,
                                   const RNG<double, 1>& myRandom)

{ // Kloeden (1997) et al page 112, a == drift, b == diffusion

    // Define a mesh
    Mesher mesh(0.0, T);
    Vector<double, long> x = mesh.xarr(N);
    double k = (T - 0.0)/double(N);        // Assume interval is [0,T]
    double sk = sqrt(k);

    const int dim = 1;

    VectorSpace<double, dim> dW;           // 1d Array of random
                                           values, (compile-time!)

    double c = a - (0.5 * b * b);

    Vector<double, long> result(N+1, 1); // the path of the
                                         process in (5.1)

    result[result.MinIndex()] = X0;

    double wT = 0.0;

    // create the path

    for (int n = result.MinIndex()+1; n <= result.MaxIndex(); ++n)
    {
        dW = myRandom.getRandomArray();    // Array of length 1
        wT += dW[1] * sk;
        result[n] = X0 * ::exp(c*x[n] + b*wT);
    }
    return result;
}
```

We now turn our attention to the n-factor case and we examine the system of equations representing a multidimensional geometric Brownian motion:

$$dS_j(t) = \mu_j S_j(t)dt + \sigma_j S_j(t)dW_j(t), \quad j = 1, \ldots, M \tag{5.3}$$

where W_j is a standard one-dimensional Brownian motion; furthermore, W_i and W_j have correlation ρ_{ij}.

The individual solutions have the representation

$$S_j(t) = S_j(0)\exp\left(\left(\mu_j - \frac{\sigma_j^2}{2}\right)t + \sigma_j W_j(t)\right), \quad j = 1, \ldots, M \tag{5.4}$$

Now, define the $M \times M$ *covariance matrix* $\Sigma = (\Sigma_{ij})$ as follows (Glasserman, 2004, page 104):

$$\sum_{ij} = \sigma_i \sigma_j \rho_{ij} \text{ for } i \neq j, \quad i, j = 1, \ldots, M$$

$$\sum_{ii} = \sigma_i^2, \quad i = 1, \ldots, M$$

where ρ_{ij} is the correlation between assets i and j.

We know that this matrix can be written in the form $\sum = \mathbf{A}^t \mathbf{A}$, where $\mathbf{A}$ is a matrix and $^t\mathbf{A}$ is the transpose of $\mathbf{A}$. From this, we can compute the values at given mesh points as follows:

$$S_j(t_{n+1}) = S_j(t_n)\exp\left(\left(\mu_j - \frac{\sigma_j^2}{2}\right)\Delta t_n + \sqrt{\Delta t_n}\sum_{i=1}^{M} A_{ji}Z_{n+1,i}\right) \tag{5.5}$$

$$j = 1, \ldots, M, \quad n = 0, \ldots, N - 1$$

where

$$\Delta t_n = t_{n+1} - t_n$$

and

$Z_n = (Z_{n,1}, \ldots, Z_{n,M}) \sim N(0, I)$ where $Z_{n,1}, \ldots, Z_{n,M}$

independent and I is the $M \times M$ identity matrix

We shall see in section 5.5 how to compute the matrix $\mathbf{A}$ in equation (5.5) using Cholesky decomposition. Spectral decomposition (see Jäckel, 2002) is superior to Cholesky since it also works for non-positive definite matrices. We discuss the spectral decomposition method in Part II of the current book.

5.3.2 Brownian Bridge

When approximating the solutions of SDEs using finite difference methods (for example) it is necessary to simulate Brownian motion as defined by

$$dW = Z\sqrt{dt}, \text{ where } Z \sim N(0, I) \tag{5.6}$$

and by its discrete version:

$$W(t_{n+1}) = W(t_n) + \sqrt{\Delta t_n}Z_{n+1}, \quad n = 0, \ldots, N - 1 \tag{5.7}$$

where

$$t_0 = 0, \; W(0) = 0 \text{ and } \Delta t_n = t_{n+1} - t_n$$

The C++ code for this scheme is given by

```
Vector<double, long> RandomWalk(const Vector<double, long>& mesh,
                                const RNG<double, 1>& myRandom)
{ // Create a 1d random walk (Glasserman page 81)

    Vector<double, long> result(mesh.Size(), 1);

    const int dim = 1;
    VectorSpace<double, dim> Z;            // 1d array of random values

    result[result.MinIndex()] = 0.0;       // Wiener initial value

    double wT;                             // Brownian term
    double tn;                             // Redundant value for mesh
                                               points

    for (int n = result.MinIndex()+1; n <= result.MaxIndex(); ++n)
    {
        Z = myRandom.getRandomArray();   // Array of length 1

        result[n] = result[n-1] + (sqrt(mesh[n]-mesh[n-1]) * Z[1]);
    }

    return result;
}
```

We now continue with an introduction to the Brownian Bridge construction that gives better results in some cases than the random walk construction as described by equation (5.7). There are two ways to construct a Brownian Bridge:

• Using an analytic formula (Kloeden, Platen and Schurz, 1997).
• Using a discrete recursive scheme (Morokoff, 1998; Sobol, 1994).

We concentrate on the former method in this section. The idea underlying the Brownian Bridge construction is that we can generate values of the Wiener process in any order, and not only by starting at $t = 0$ as in equation (5.7). In fact (Kloeden, Platen and Schurz, 1997, page 59):

$$Y(t, \omega) = a + W(t, \omega) - \tfrac{t}{T}\{W(T, \omega) - b + a\} \qquad (5.8)$$

where

$$Y(0, \omega) = a, \quad Y(T, \omega) = b$$

In this case the paths of the Brownian Bridge process Y all pass through the initial point a (not necessarily 0) as well as the given point b at $t = T$. We now discuss the code that implements equation (5.8). The input parameters are

• The expiry time T.
• The mesh-point vector.

- The vector of Brownian motion values at these mesh points.
- The boundary values a and b.

The output is a vector of values based on the Brownian Bridge construction. The code is given by

```
Vector<double, long> BrownianBridgeExact(double T,
                        const Vector<double, long>& t,
                        const Vector<double, long>& dW,
                        double a, double b)
{ // Exact Solution BB, Kloeden page 59

    long N = t.Size() - 1;
    double k = (T - 0.0)/double(N);        // Assume interval is [0,T]
    double sk = sqrt(k);

    Vector<double, long> result(N+1, 1);

    result[result.MinIndex()] = a;

    double finalValue = dW[dW.MaxIndex()];

    for (int n = result.MinIndex()+1; n <= result.MaxIndex(); ++n)
    {
        result[n] = a + dW[n] - (t[n] * (finalValue - b + a))/T;
    }

    return result;
}
```

Another way to examine a Brownian Bridge is to examine its defining SDE (Øksendal, 1998, page 75):

$$dY = \frac{b - Y}{1 - t}dt + dW, \quad 0 \le t < 1, \quad Y_0 = a \tag{5.9}$$

where $\lim_{t \to 1} Y(t) = b$ almost surely.

The solution of (5.9) is given by

$$Y(t) = a(1 - t) + bt + (1 - t)\int_0^t \frac{dW(s)}{1 - s}, \quad 0 \le t \le 1$$

5.3.3   Finite difference methods for Brownian Bridges

We can approximate SDE (5.9) by a finite difference method, for example implicit Euler:

$$Y_{n+1} - Y_n = \left(\frac{b - Y_{n+1}}{1 - t_{n+1}}\right)\Delta t + \Delta W_n, \quad n = 0, \ldots, N - 1 \tag{5.10}$$

The code for scheme (5.10) is given by

```
Vector<double, long> BrownianBridge(double T,
        const Vector<double, long>& t, const Vector<double, long>& dW,
        double a, double b)
```

```
{ // Approximate the Brownian Bridge using Implicit Euler,
  // Oksendal 1998, page 75

     long N = t.Size() - 1 T = 1.0;
     double k = (T - 0.0)/double(N);      // Assume interval is [0,T]
     double sk = sqrt(k);

     Vector<double, long> result(N+1, 1);

     result[result.MinIndex()] = a;

     double wT;           // Brownian term
     double temp;         // Redundant value for mesh points

     for (int n = result.MinIndex()+1; n <= result.MaxIndex(); ++n)
     {
          wT = dW[n] * sk;
          temp = 1.0 - t[n];

          result[n]=((temp * result[n-1]) + (b * k) + (temp * wT))
                     / (temp + k);
     }

     return result;
}
```

5.4 THE KARHUNEN-LOEVE EXPANSION

One problem – from a numerical viewpoint – is that a Wiener process consists of an *uncountable number* of random variables. This number is one representation of infinity. We say that a set is uncountable if its cardinal number (size) is larger than that of the natural numbers. An example of an uncountable set is the set of real numbers.

When we approximate SDEs we deal with abstract measure spaces that have limited physical intuitive appeal. One approach is to compute paths using finite difference methods, as we have already seen in this book. We solve problems on the abstract spaces that are represented on the σ-field of random events. When using Monte Carlo methods in this context, we must sample a large number of points if we wish to achieve good results. In this section we expand a general random process as a Fourier expansion:

$$f(\underline{x}, \omega) = \sum_{n=0}^{\infty} \sqrt{\lambda_n} \xi_n(\omega) f_n(\underline{x})$$

where

- $\omega \in \Omega$ = sample space.
- $\{\xi_n(\omega)\}$ is a set of random processes to be determined.
- λ_n = constant.
- $\underline{x}$ is an element of some domain (for example, the real line).
- $\{f_n(\underline{x})\}$ = an orthonormal set of deterministic functions.

This is the so-called Karhunen-Loeve expansion (see Karhunen, 1947; Ghanem and Spanos, 1991, for an overview and applications). In the current context – Wiener processes – we have an expansion of the form (Kloeden, Platen and Schurz, 1997):

$$W(t, \omega) = \sum_{n=0}^{\infty} Z_n(\omega)\varphi_n(t), \quad 0 \le t \le T \tag{5.11}$$

where

$Z_0, Z_1, \ldots$ are independent standard normal random variables

The orthogonal functions in this case are

$$\varphi_n(t) = \frac{2\sqrt{2T}}{(2n+1)\pi} \sin\left(\frac{(2n+1)\pi t}{2T}\right) \tag{5.12}$$

We define these functions with respect to the inner product:

$$(\varphi_i, \varphi_j) \equiv \int_0^T \varphi_i(t)\varphi_j(t)dt$$

In general, we determine the independent random variables in equation (5.11) in much the same way as we do it with classical Fourier series (see Tolstov, 1962):

$$Z_n(\omega) = \frac{2}{T} \left(\frac{(2n+1)\pi}{2\sqrt{2T}}\right)^2 \int_0^T W(t, \omega)\varphi_n(t)dt, \quad n = 0, 1, 2, \ldots \tag{5.13}$$

From a computational viewpoint, we evaluate the series in equation (5.11) by series truncation to a finite number of terms and we also calculate a set of independent standard Gaussian random variates. We give an example in C++ on the CD to show how to implement the algorithm for the truncated series.

5.5   CHOLESKY DECOMPOSITION

This decomposition allows us to express the covariance matrix Σ in the form:

$$\Sigma = C\,{}^tC, \text{ where } {}^tC \text{ is the transpose of the matrix } C$$

Then it is possible to generate a correlated random vector X with mean m from an uncorrelated vector Z by application of the formula:

$$X = CZ + m$$

The C++ code for this process is given by

```
template <int N>
    VectorSpace<double, N> generateMultiNormalVariates(
            const VectorSpace<double, N>& mean,
            const MatrixVectorSpace<double, N, N>& covMatrix)
{

        // 1. Generate N(0,1) vector
        VectorSpace<double, N> Z = generateUniform2<N>();
```

```
// 2. Calculate the Cholesky matrix
MatrixVectorSpace<double, N, N>
                        C = Cholesky<N>(covMatrix);

// 3. New vector
VectorSpace<double, N> X = C*Z + mean;

// 4. Deliver it
return X;
}
```

In this case we are using compile-time matrices and vectors (*tiny matrices*) because we are assuming that the number of rows and columns is relatively small. In the current book we work with examples where $N = 4$ (for example, spread options with stochastic volatility), $N = 2$ (Heston model) and $N = 40$ (for basket options) and for this reason we see that compile-time structures – whose data is situated on the stack – is more efficient than data structures whose data is defined on the heap. The actual function that performs the Cholesky decomposition in the above process has the signature (input is a covariance matrix and output is the matrix C that we need)

```
template <int N>  MatrixVectorSpace<double, N, N>
            Cholesky(const MatrixVectorSpace<double, N, N>& covMat)
{ // Cholesky decomposition covMat = C * transpose (C)


    // code on CD

    // Notice that the size N is a template parameter
}
```

We take an example of use when $N = 4$. First, we need to define a covariance matrix (note the use of operator overloading to define the values of elements in the matrix):

```
// Set up the covariance matrix
MatrixVectorSpace<double, N, N> CovarianceMatrix;
CovarianceMatrix(1,1) = 1.0; CovarianceMatrix(2,2) = 1.0;
CovarianceMatrix(3,3) = 1.0; CovarianceMatrix(4,4) = 1.0;

CovarianceMatrix(1,2) = CovarianceMatrix(2,1) = 0.50;
CovarianceMatrix(1,3) = CovarianceMatrix(3,1) = 0.20;
CovarianceMatrix(1,4) = CovarianceMatrix(4,1) = 0.01;

CovarianceMatrix(2,3) = CovarianceMatrix(3,2) = 0.01;
CovarianceMatrix(2,4) = CovarianceMatrix(4,2) = 0.30;

CovarianceMatrix(3,4) = CovarianceMatrix(4,3) = 0.30;


// Calculate the Cholesky matrix
MatrixVectorSpace<double, N, N>
        C = Cholesky<N>(CovarianceMatrix);
```

We now define the two vectors that we need, one is correlated, the other one is not. In this case the mean is zero:

```
VectorSpace<double, N> Z, X;
X = NormalVector<N>(); // Generate N(0,1) vector, uncorrelated
Z = C * X;
```

In this case we have used a simple algorithm to generate random numbers:

```
template <int N> VectorSpace<double, N> NormalVector()
{ // Create an array of uncorrelated Normal numbers

        double N1;
        double N2;

        VectorSpace<double, N> vec;

        for(long i=vec.MinIndex(); i<=vec.MaxIndex()-1; i += 2 )
        {

                //BoxMuller(N1, N2);      // Beware: Neave effect
                PolarMarsaglia(N1, N2);

                vec[i] = N1;
                vec[i+1] = N2;
        }

        vec[vec.MaxIndex()] = N2;

        return vec;
}
```

In later chapters we use more advanced and flexible algorithms for calculating random numbers.

5.6   SPREAD OPTIONS WITH STOCHASTIC VOLATILITY

In this section we examine a two-factor model. The two underlying assets have stochastic volatility and in these cases we shall have four loosely-coupled SDEs. Thus, we model both the assets and their volatilities and we shall do this using an Euler scheme; first, we simulate the variances and then we use their updated values in the numerical scheme that calculates asset prices at each time level. In order to scope the problem, we model a two-factor spread option. By definition, a *spread call option* between two assets is one whose payoff at expiry T is given by

$$\max(0, [S_1(T) - S_2(T)] - K)$$

where

$$S_1 = \text{first asset value}$$
$$S_2 = \text{second asset value}$$
$$K = \text{strike price}$$

Similarly, a put option is defined as follows:

$$\max(0, K - [S_1(T) - S_2(T)])$$

The most general case is when we have a quantity α of asset 1 and a quantity β of asset 2. In this case, the payoff function for a call option is given by

$$\max(0, [\alpha S_1(T) - \beta S_2(T)] - K)$$

where $\alpha, \beta > 0$ are constants.

There are many examples of such options (see Geman, 2005), for example:

- *Crack spread option*: An option on the spread between heating oil and crude oil futures.
- *Spark spread*: The difference between the price of electricity and the price of the corresponding quantity of primary fuel. For example, we could have a spread between electricity and natural gas.

The volatilities may be modelled as deterministic functions of the underlying assets. We discuss the case where the volatilities are stochastic and in particular we examine a European spread option when the underlying prices follow Geometric Browian Motion (GBM) and the variance of returns follow mean-reverting square-root processes (Clewlow and Strickland, 1998). In this case we have a system of SDEs defined by

$$dS_1 = rS_1 dt + \sigma_1 S_1 dW_1$$
$$dS_2 = rS_2 dt + \sigma_2 S_2 dW_2$$
$$dV_1 = \alpha_1(\mu_1 - V_1)dt + \xi_1\sqrt{V_1}dW_3$$
$$dV_2 = \alpha_2(\mu_2 - V_2)dt + \xi_2\sqrt{V_2}dW_4$$

where

$$S_1 = \text{first underlying asset}$$
$$S_2 = \text{second underlying asset}$$
$$V_1 = \sigma_1^2, \quad \sigma_1 \text{ is volatility of } S_1$$
$$V_2 = \sigma_2^2, \quad \sigma_2 \text{ is volatility of } S_2$$

and

$$\alpha_j = \text{rate of mean reversion of variance } V_j, \quad j = 1, 2$$
$$\xi_j = \text{volatility of variance } V_j, \quad j = 1, 2$$
$$W_j = \text{Wiener process}, \quad j = 1, \ldots, 4$$
$$\mu_j = \text{mean reversion factor}, \quad j = 1, 2$$

We now discuss the C++ code for this model. We have two versions. The first C++ version is based on the pseudocode in Clewlow and Strickland (1998) and the second solution uses a more object-oriented approach. The full source code for both solutions can be found on the CD. Please note that we checked both solutions with the answers given in Clewlow and Strickland (1998).

We discuss the first solution that is based on a modular strategy. We note this solution is procedural and not much use has been made of objects or design patterns (this choice was deliberate because we wish to program the major steps without getting bogged down in design details). First, the defining variables and their initialised values are

```
// 1. Underlyings
double r;               // Interest rate
double div1, div2;      // Dividends
double sig1, sig2;      // Volatilities of underlyings S1 and S2
                        // Calculated from V1 and V2, V = sig^2
// 2. Variances
double alpha1, alpha2;  // alpha * (mu - V) drift term
double mu1, mu2;
double eta1, eta2;      // eta * sqrt(V) * dZ diffusion term

// 3. Initial conditions
double S1_0, S2_0;
//double V1_0, V2_0;

// 4. Other vital input
double T; // Expiry
double K; // Strike
// Initialise the data, N.B. covariance matrix already done
r = 0.06;
div1 = 0.03; div2 = 0.04;
alpha1 = 1.0; alpha2 = 2.0;
mu1 = 0.04; mu2 = 0.09;
eta1 = 0.05; eta2 = 0.06;
S1_0 = 100.0; S2_0 = 110.0;
sig1 = 0.20; sig2 = 0.30;    // Initial volatilities
T = 1.0; K = 1.0;
```

Having defined the input variables we need to create two loops; the (inner)-loop creates a path from $t = 0$ to $t = T$ while the (outer)-loop executes the inner loop based on the number of simulations or draws:

```
double CallValue;
double SumCallValue = 0.0;
double SumCallValueSquared = 0.0;

for (int i = 1; i <= NSIM; ++i)
{

    logSt1 = log(S1_0); logSt2 = log(S2_0);
    //St1 = S1_0; St2 = S2_0;
    Vt1 = sig1*sig1; Vt2 = sig2*sig2;

    for (int n = 1; n <= NT; ++n)
    {

        X = NormalVector<N>();     // Generate N(0,1) vector
        Z = C * X;

        // Simulate Variances
```

```
Vt1 = Vt1 + (alpha1 * k * (mu1 - Vt1)) +
                      (eta1 * sqrk * sqrt(Vt1) * Z[3]);
Vt2 = Vt2 + (alpha2 * k * (mu2 - Vt2)) +
                      (eta2 * sqrk * sqrt(Vt2) * Z[4]);

// Simulate the underlying asset prices
logSt1 = logSt1 + (r - div1 - 0.5 * Vt1)*k +
                      (sqrt(Vt1) * sqrk * Z[1]);
logSt2 = logSt2 + (r - div2 - 0.5 * Vt2)*k +
                      (sqrt(Vt2) * sqrk * Z[2]);

} // Next time level

St1 = exp(logSt1);
St2 = exp(logSt2);

CallValue = SpreadPayoffFunction(St1, St2, K);

SumCallValue += CallValue;
SumCallValueSquared += CallValue * CallValue;


} // Next simulation
```

Finally, the postprocessing phase delivers the option price and other relevant statistics:

```
CallValue = exp(-r * T) * SumCallValue / NSIM;
double SD = sqrt( (SumCallValueSquared -
        SumCallValue*SumCallValue/NSIM)*exp(-2.0*r*T)/(NSIM -1));
double SE = SD/sqrt(double(NSIM));
cout << "Standard Deviation, Error: " << SD << "," << SE << endl;
cout << "Call value: " << CallValue << endl;
```

We now turn our attention to the second solution and we use the generic class for n-factor SDE (we discuss this class in more detail in later chapters). In the current case we use the system form of the SDE and we then initialise the drift vector and diffusion matrix with appropriate functions. We write the system of equations as

$$dX = \mu(t, X)dt + \sigma(t, X)dW$$

where

$$X = {}^t(S_1, S_2, V_1, V_2)$$

$$dW = {}^t(dW_1, dW_2, dW_3, dW_4) \quad \text{and 't' denotes transpose}$$

We use the notation

$$X(0) = X_0$$
$$X \equiv (S_1, S_2, V_1, V_2)$$

We do not show *all* the functions due to reasons of space; the reader can find them on the CD. We do discuss the most important ones:

```
    // Drift terms
    double drift1(double x, const VectorSpace<double,dim>& input)
    { // S1 drift

            return (r - div1) * input[1];

    }

        // S2, V1 drift

    }

    double drift4(double x, const VectorSpace<double,dim>& input)
    { // V2 drift

            return alpha2 * (mu2 - input[4]);

    }

    // Diffusion terms
    double diffusion1(double x, const VectorSpace<double,dim>& input)
    { // S1 diffusion

            return input[1] * sqrt(input[3]);

    }

    // ã S2, V1 diffusion

    double diffusion4(double x, const VectorSpace<double,dim>& input)
    { // V2 diffusion

            return eta2 * sqrt(input[4]);

    }
```

Having defined the SDE's functions we are now in a position to create an instance of the SDE class:

```
SDE<double, dim, dim> SpreadOptionSDE(const Range<double>& range,
                            const VectorSpace<double, dim>& VOld)
{

    SDE<double, dim, dim> result(range, VOld);


    // Define the drift vector and diffusion matrix;
    // Later INCORPORATE THIS INTO THE sde CONSTRUCTOR
    for (int i = 1; i <= dim; ++i)
    {
        result.setDriftComponent(ZeroFunction, i);
        for (int j = 1; j <= dim; ++j)
```

```
      {
            result.setDiffusionComponent(ZeroFunction,i, j);
      }
}

// Override the non-zero functions
result.setDriftComponent(drift1, 1);
result.setDriftComponent(drift2, 2);
result.setDriftComponent(drift3, 3);
result.setDriftComponent(drift4, 4);

result.setDiffusionComponent(diffusion1, 1, 1);
result.setDiffusionComponent(diffusion2, 2, 2);
result.setDiffusionComponent(diffusion3, 3, 3);
result.setDiffusionComponent(diffusion4, 4, 4);

return result;

}
```

We mention that all the data, functions and other code pertaining to this spread option have been grouped into a convenient namespace:

```
namespace SpreadOptionDataEnvironment
{ // Construct the SDE that models a European spread option
  // where the variance of returns follow a mean-reverting square
  // root process.
  // This is a 4-vector (S1,S2, V1, V2)

    //
}
```

The next stage in this solution is to model the SDE using finite differences. We use Euler and predictor-corrector methods. We first define the initial condition for the SDE:

```
VectorSpace<double, N> VOld;
VOld[1] = S1_0;
VOld[2] = S2_0;
VOld[3] = sig1 * sig1;
VOld[4] = sig2 * sig2;
```

We then define an instance of the SDE class that we wish to model:

```
Range<double> range(0.0, T);
SDE<double, N, N> mySDE = SpreadOptionSDE(range, VOld);
```

We now discuss the finite difference schemes to approximate the SDE for the spread option. The simplest scheme is explicit Euler:

$$\underline{X}_{n+1} = \underline{X}_n + \mu(t_n, \underline{X}_n)\Delta t + \sigma(t_n, \underline{X}_n)\Delta W_n, \quad n \geq 0$$

In this section we discuss the application of the predictor-corrector method:

$$\tilde{\underline{X}}_{n+1} = \underline{X}_n + \mu(t_n, \underline{X}_n)\Delta t + \sigma(t_n, \underline{X}_n)\Delta W_n, \quad n \geq 0 \text{ (predictor)}$$

$$\underline{X}_{n+1} = \underline{X}_n + \frac{\Delta t}{2}\left\{\mu(t_n, \underline{X}_n) + \mu(t_{n+1}, \tilde{\underline{X}}_{n+1})\right\}$$

$$+ \frac{1}{2}\left\{\sigma(t_n, \underline{X}_n) + \sigma(t_{n+1}, \tilde{\underline{X}}_{n+1})\right\}\Delta W_n, \quad n \geq 0 \text{ (corrector)}$$

The code is

```
for (int i = 1; i <= NSIM; ++i)
{
     VOld[1] = S1_0;
     VOld[2] = S2_0;
     VOld[3] = sig1 * sig1;
     VOld[4] = sig2 * sig2;

     // 1 step == 1 simulation of a MC method
     int index = 2;
     double t = 0.0;

L1:  // excuses for not using a do-while loop
     X = NormalVector<N>(); // Generate N(0,1) vector
     Z = C * X;

     // Explicit Euler
     if (choice == 1)
     {

     // OPTIMISED CODE
     //tmp1 = mySDE.calculateDrift(t, VOld);
     //tmp2 = mySDE.calculateDiffusion(t, VOld, Z);

     //VNew = VOld + (k * tmp1)+ (sqrk * tmp2);
     TripleSum(VNew, VOld, mySDE.calculateDrift(t, VOld),
          mySDE.calculateDiffusion(t, VOld, Z), k, sqrk);
     }
     else
     {
          // UNOPTIMISED CODE
          // Predictor-Corrector
          VMid = VOld +
               (k * mySDE.calculateDrift(t, VOld)) +
               (sqrk * mySDE.calculateDiffusion(t, VOld, Z));

          VNew = VOld + 0.5 *
               k * (mySDE.calculateDrift(t, VOld) + mySDE.
               calculateDrift(t + k, VMid))+
               0.5*sqrk*(mySDE.calculateDiffusion(t,VOld,Z) +
               mySDE.calculateDiffusion(t+k,VMid,Z));
     }

     if (index <= NT + 1)
     {
```

```
        t += k;
        VOld = VNew;
        index++;
        goto L1; // Student exercise: do-while loop
    }

    CallValue = SpreadPayoffFunction(VNew[1], VNew[2], K);

    SumCallValue += CallValue;

    } // Simulations
```

Finally, we use discounting to compute the call price:

```
    CallValue = exp(-r * T) * SumCallValue / NSIM;

    cout << "\nCall value, FDM style: " << CallValue << endl;
```

Incidentally, the payoff function in this case is defined in the namespace `Spread` `OptionDataEnvironment` and is given by:

```
double SpreadPayoffFunction(double S1, double S2, double K)
{ // Spread option

    return max (0.0, S1 - S2 - K);
}
```

We have now finished the discussion of the second solution to the European spread option problem.

5.7 THE HESTON STOCHASTIC VOLATILITY MODEL

In Part III we discuss the Heston stochastic volatility model in detail. In this section, however, we are mainly interested in applying a number of finite difference schemes to the model. It is an interesting problem to study for a number of reasons:

- It is popular in finance because of its ability to model option pricing problems with stochastic volatility. It allows correlation between volatility and spot-asset returns which explains the skewness and strike-price biases in the Black-Scholes model (Heston, 1993).
- It is an example of a two-factor model with a square root nonlinearity in the SDE component for the variance. It is thus a good benchmark example to test a range of finite difference schemes on. We can then apply the same schemes to other kinds of problems.
- We code the model in C++ and it is relatively easy to adapt the code to other kinds of SDEs. In our opinion, coding algorithms for finite difference schemes is a good way to gain hands-on experience with C++.

    The SDE for the Heston model is given by

$$dS = (r - d)Sdt + \sqrt{v}\, SdW_1$$
$$dv = \kappa(\theta - v)dt + \xi\sqrt{v}\, dW_2$$

(5.14)

where

$$S = \text{asset price}$$
$$v = \text{variance}$$
$$r = \text{interest rate (domestic rate, usually)}$$
$$d = \text{dividend (or foreign interest rate)}$$
$$\kappa = \text{strength of mean reversion}$$
$$\theta = \text{long-term average}$$
$$\xi = \text{volatility of variance}$$
$$\rho = \text{correlation}$$
$$S(0) = \text{initial asset price}$$
$$v(0) = \text{initial variance price and } dW_1 dW_2 = \rho dt$$

This system is mean-reverting in the variance while there is a nonlinear term in both diffusion terms. Furthermore, the Wiener process increments are correlated and we need to take this fact into account when generating the corresponding random numbers for the finite difference schemes.

From a numerical viewpoint, we see that the drift term is linear in the asset price and in the variance whereas the diffusion terms are nonlinear. This means that some methods cannot be used (for example, the implicit Euler method) precisely because of this nonlinearity but on the other hand we can use implicit methods for the drift terms and explicit methods for the diffusion terms. This realisation leads us to a number of schemes that we use and we introduce the following finite difference schemes to approximate the solution of the system (5.14):

- The explicit Euler scheme.
- The Milstein scheme.
- The semi-implicit Euler scheme.
- The implicit Milstein scheme.
- The weak predictor-corrector scheme.
- The transformed semi-implicit Euler scheme.
- The transformed explicit Euler scheme.

These one-step schemes advance the solution (a two-dimensional vector) from time-level n to time-level $n + 1$ by first calculating the variance (it does not depend on the asset) and then using this value in the finite difference scheme for the asset. Furthermore, we can write the Heston SDE in three equivalent forms, namely:

- The original form (5.14) as already been discussed.
- By defining untransformed, correlated Wiener increments and incorporating the correlation as an explicit parameter in the new SDE:

$$dS = (r - d)Sdt + \sqrt{v}S \, dW_1$$
$$dv = \kappa(\theta - v)dt + \xi\sqrt{v}(\rho dW_1 + \sqrt{1 - \rho^2} \, dW_2) \tag{5.15}$$
$$dW_1 dW_2 = 0$$

- By using a logarithmic transformation:

$$dX = (r - d - \tfrac{1}{2}v)dt + \sqrt{v}dW_1$$
$$dv = \kappa(\theta - v)dt + \xi\sqrt{v}dW_2 \tag{5.16}$$

where

$$X = \log(S), \quad S = e^X$$

We now have three equivalent formulations for the Heston model and we propose several finite difference schemes to solve them. It is obvious that we wish to produce accurate and stable algorithms. At this stage, we assume that the parameters in equation (5.14) are known. We now enumerate the schemes for the current problem based on equation (5.14).

Explicit Euler scheme

$$S_{n+1} = S_n + (r - d)S_n \Delta t + \sqrt{V_n} S_n \Delta W_{1,n}$$
$$V_{n+1} = V_n + \kappa(\theta - V_n)\Delta t + \xi \sqrt{V_n} \Delta W_{2,n} \quad n = 0, \dots, N - 1 \qquad (5.17)$$
$$S_0 = S(0), \quad V_0 = v(0)$$

where

$$\Delta W_{j,n} = \sqrt{\Delta t} N_j, \quad N_j \sim N(0, 1) \quad j = 1, 2, \quad n = 0, \dots, N - 1$$
and N_1, N_2 have correlation ρ

Rearranging, we can write this scheme in the computational form:

$$S_{n+1} = S_n(1 + (r - d)\Delta t + \sqrt{V_n}\Delta W_{1,n})$$
$$V_{n+1} = V_n(1 - \kappa \Delta t) + \kappa\theta \Delta t + \xi \sqrt{V_n}\Delta W_{2,n} \qquad (5.18)$$
$$n = 0, \dots, N - 1$$

Milstein scheme

We now introduce the Milstein scheme. In the interest of readability we define some notation for operators that act on the mesh functions:

$$L_1^{\Delta t}(S_n, V_n) \equiv S_n(1 + (r - d)\Delta t + \sqrt{V_n}\Delta W_{1,n})$$
$$L_2^{\Delta t}(S_n, V_n) \equiv V_n(1 - \kappa \Delta t) + \kappa\theta \Delta t + \xi \sqrt{V_n}\Delta W_{2,n} \qquad (5.19)$$

Then the Milstein scheme is defined by

$$S_{n+1} = L_1^{\Delta t}(S_n, V_n) + \tfrac{1}{2}S_n V_n(\Delta W_{1,n} * \Delta W_{1,n} - \Delta t)$$
$$V_{n+1} = L_2^{\Delta t}(S_n, V_n) + \tfrac{\xi^2}{4}(\Delta W_{2,n} * \Delta W_{2,n} - \Delta t), \quad n = 0, \dots, N - 1 \qquad (5.20)$$

with

$$S_0 = S(0), \quad V_0 = v(0)$$

Semi-implicit Euler scheme

$$S_{n+1} = S_n + (r - d)S_{n+1}\Delta t + \sqrt{V_n} S_n \Delta W_{1,n}$$
$$V_{n+1} = V_n + \kappa(\theta - V_{n+1})\Delta t + \xi \sqrt{V_n}\Delta W_{2,n}, \quad n = 0, \dots, N - 1 \qquad (5.21)$$

with

$$S_0 = S(0), \quad V_0 = v(0)$$

In this case we evaluate the drift terms at time level $n+1$ while we evaluate the diffusion terms at time level n. We rewrite equation (5.21) in the computational form:

$$
\begin{aligned}
&S_{n+1}(1 - (r-d)\Delta t) = S_n + \sqrt{V_n}S_n\Delta W_{1,n} = S_n(1 + \sqrt{V_n}\Delta W_{1,n})\\
&V_{n+1}(1 + \kappa\Delta t) = V_n + \kappa\theta\Delta t + \xi\sqrt{V_n}\Delta W_{2,n}, \quad n = 0,\ldots,N-1
\end{aligned}
\tag{5.22}
$$

Implicit Milstein scheme

$$
\begin{aligned}
&S_{n+1} = S_n + (r-d)S_{n+1}\Delta t + \sqrt{V_n}S_n\Delta W_{1,n} + \tfrac{1}{2}S_nV_n(\Delta W_{1,n}*\Delta W_{1,n} - \Delta t)\\
&V_{n+1} = V_n + \kappa(\theta - V_{n+1})\Delta t + \xi\sqrt{V_n}\Delta W_{2,n}\\
&\quad + \tfrac{\xi^2}{4}(\Delta W_{2,n}*\Delta W_{2,n} - \Delta t), \quad n = 0,\ldots,N-1
\end{aligned}
\tag{5.23}
$$

with

$$S_0 = S(0), \quad V_0 = v(0)$$

Weak predictor-corrector scheme

Predictor:

$$
\begin{aligned}
&\overline{S}_{n+1} = S_n + (r-d)S_n\Delta t + \sqrt{V_n}S_n\Delta W_{1,n}\\
&\overline{V}_{n+1} = \kappa(\theta - V_n)\Delta t + \xi\sqrt{V_n}\Delta W_{2,n}, \quad n = 0,\ldots,N-1
\end{aligned}
\tag{5.24}
$$

Corrector:

$$
\begin{aligned}
&S_{n+1} = S_n + (r-d)\overline{S}_{n+1}\Delta t + \sqrt{V_n}S_n\Delta W_{1,n}\\
&V_{n+1} = V_n + \kappa(\theta - \overline{V}_{n+1})\Delta t + \xi\sqrt{V_n}\Delta W_{2,n}, \quad n = 0,\ldots,N-1
\end{aligned}
\tag{5.25}
$$

with

$$S_0 = S(0), \quad V_0 = v(0)$$

Transformed semi-implicit Euler method (using equation (5.16))

$$
\begin{aligned}
&X_{n+1} = X_n + (r - d - \tfrac{1}{2}V_{n+1})\Delta t + \sqrt{V_n}\Delta W_{1,n}\\
&V_{n+1} = V_n + \kappa(\theta - V_{n+1})\Delta t + \xi\sqrt{V_n}\Delta W_{2,n}\\
&X_n \equiv log(S_n), \quad n = 0,\ldots,N-1
\end{aligned}
\tag{5.26}
$$

with

$$S_0 = S(0), \quad V_0 = v(0)$$

Transformed explicit Euler scheme (using equation (5.16))

$$
\begin{aligned}
&X_{n+1} = X_n + (r - d - \tfrac{1}{2}V_n)\Delta t + \sqrt{V_n}\Delta W_{1,n}\\
&V_{n+1} = V_n + \kappa(\theta - V_n)\Delta t + \xi\sqrt{V_n}\Delta W_{2,n} \quad n = 0,\ldots,N-1
\end{aligned}
\tag{5.27}
$$

with

$$S_0 = S(0), \quad V_0 = v(0)$$

In this case we define a namespace that logically relates all information pertaining to the Heston model including procedures in the C language that implement the algorithms in equations (5.17) to (5.27). This is an effective strategy because it is easy to add your own procedures to the namespace. We say that 'the code is not beautiful but it works'. Ensuring that the algorithms were properly implemented has the highest priority in this case. The namespace (subset of functionality, see CD for code) is

```
namespace HestonNamespace
{

    const int dim = 2;

    double r, q;
    double kappa, theta, epsilon;
    double rho;                    // Correlation

    // Initial conditions
    double IC_S;
    double IC_V;

    // Other redundant variables
    // ...

    // Explicit Euler method
    VectorSpace<double, 2> EE(const VectorSpace<double, 2>& VOld,
                             double WI1, double WI2)
    { // Solution at n+1 in terms of solution at time level n
        result[2] = VOld[2] * (1 - kappa * deltaT)
                            + kappa * theta * deltaT
                            + (epsilon * sqrt(VOld[2]) * sqrk * WI2);
        result[1] = VOld[1]*(1.0 ⌐ (r - q) * deltaT
                            + sqrt(VOld[2]) * sqrk * WI1);

        return result;
    }



    // Implicit Milstein method
    VectorSpace<double, 2> ImplicitMilstein(
        const VectorSpace<double, 2>& VOld, double WI1, double WI2)
    {
        // Milstein corrections
        double corr1 = 0.5 * VOld[1] * VOld[2]* ( deltaT * WI1 *
                        WI1 - deltaT);
        double corr2 = 0.25 * epsilon * epsilon * ( deltaT * WI2 *
                        WI2 - deltaT);
```

```
        double denom1 = 1.0 - ((r - q) * deltaT);
        double denom2 = 1.0 + (kappa * deltaT);

        result[2] = (corr2 + VOld[2] + (kappa * theta * deltaT)
                 + (epsilon * sqrt(VOld[2]) * sqrk * WI2) )/ denom2;

        result[1] = (corr1 + VOld[1]*(1.0
                 + sqrt(VOld[2]) * sqrk * WI1) )/ denom1;

        return result;

    }


    // Other schemes here



}
```

You can experiment with the schemes using your own data. Here is a test program that you can use as a skeleton for your examples:

```
int main()
{

    using namespace HestonNamespace;

    double T = 1.0;

    // Set 2 parameters K = 123.4!! C = 13.85!

    r = 0.1; q = 0.0; kappa = 1.98937; theta = 0.011876;
    epsilon = 0.15; rho =  -0.9; IC_S = 123.4; IC_V = 0.1414*.1414;

    const int dim = 2;
    VectorSpace<double, dim> VOld;
    VOld[1] = IC_S;
    VOld[2] = IC_V;

    // Now the numerical work
    // Get input steps and simulations
    long NSIM = 10000;
    int NT = 100;
    cout << "Number of time steps: "; cin >> NT;
    cout << "Number of MC simulations: "; cin >> NSIM;
    deltaT = (T - 0.0) / double(NT);
    sqrk = sqrt(deltaT);

    // Generate the random numbers' seed, ONCE
    setSeed();
```

```
VectorSpace<double, dim> VNew;

// Work space variables
double CallValue;
double SumCallValue = 0.0;
double SumCallValueSquared = 0.0;
double WI1; double WI2;

// Monte Carlo loop
for (long i = 1; i <= NSIM; ++i)
{
      VOld[1] = IC_S;
      VOld[2] = IC_V;

      for (long index = 1; index <= NT; ++index)
      { // Generate two correlation RNs with correlation rho

            CorrelatedNumbers(WI1, WI2, rho);

            // !! Fill in YOUR SCHEME HERE
            //VNew = SIETransform(VOld, WI1, WI2);
            //VNew = SIE(VOld, WI1, WI2);
            // etc. See CD

            VNew = PredictorCorrector(VOld, WI1, WI2);

            VOld = VNew;

            CallValue = PayoffFunction(VNew[1]);

      }

      SumCallValue += CallValue;
      SumCallValueSquared += CallValue * CallValue;

} // Simulations

CallValue = exp(-r * T) * SumCallValue / NSIM;
double SD = sqrt( (SumCallValueSquared
      -SumCallValue*SumCallValue/NSIM)*exp(-2.0*r*T)/(NSIM -1));
double SE = SD/sqrt(double(NSIM));

return 0;
}
```

Once we have tested the schemes using this approach we do a redesign to create an object-oriented solution. We address these issues in Part II of the book when we discuss design patterns.

Finally, we note that there are several approaches in the literature for defining the parameters in the Heston model. You must realise this when comparing your results with those of others' work! It can be confusing.

5.8   PATH-DEPENDENT OPTIONS AND THE MONTE CARLO METHOD

We have discussed the pricing of options whose payoff was calculated at the expiry date $t = T$ only. In this section we discuss the pricing of so-called *exotic* or complex options whose payoffs depend on the path taken by the underlying asset in the interval $[0, T]$. There are two main forms of path dependence; first, *strong path dependence* refers to problems in which the payoff depends on some extra property in addition to the asset value. In particular, it is often necessary to sample the asset prices *discretely* or *continuously*. In the latter case the asset value is continuously monitored whereas in the former case we sample the asset value at predefined discrete times. In general, we need to introduce one or more new independent variables in addition to the variable that models the underlying asset. In other words, we need to model in a higher dimension. The second form of path dependence is called *weak path dependence*; the payoff is determined by the values of the underlying asset at certain points but the introduction of new variables is not necessary.

We discuss three major kinds of path-dependent options:

- Barrier options.
- Asian options.
- Lookback options.

A barrier option has a payoff that depends on the underlying asset reaching a given value (the barrier) before expiry. There may be several barrier levels and barrier options are weakly path dependent because no new independent variable is needed in order to model them. We do not need other information about the path. There are two main kinds of barrier options; a *knockin* barrier option is one that has a payoff only if the barrier is reached before expiry, otherwise it is zero. A *knockout* barrier is one that has a payoff only if the barrier is not reached before expiry. Thus, for barrier options the price is determined by the current level of the asset and the expiry time. A *down-and-out* barrier option is a knockout option that has no payoff if the asset price reaches a given barrier level H. In this case the barrier level is below the initial asset price. A *down-and-in* barrier option is one that comes into existence only if the asset price reaches the barrier level before expiry. The payoff for barrier options has the following form:

$$
\begin{aligned}
\max(0, S_T - K)\theta \quad \text{(call)} \\
\max(0, K - S_T)\theta \quad \text{(put)}
\end{aligned}
\tag{5.28}
$$

where the factor θ is a shorthand notation and is an indicator that is either 1 or zero. It is needed because a barrier option can either become worthless or get some worth if a barrier level is reached. For example, a down-and-out call option has the following payoff:

$$
\max(0, S_T - K)\,\mathbf{1}_{\{\min\{(S(t); t \,\in (0,T))\} > H\}}
\tag{5.29}
$$

when $\mathbf{1}$ is the indicator function.

An *Asian option* has a payoff that depends on the average value of the underlying asset in the interval $[0, T]$. To this end, we need to calculate a running average of the asset value. There are two kinds of averaging, namely *arithmetic* and *geometric* and the averaging process can be *continuous* or *discrete*:

$$A = \frac{1}{t} \int_0^t S(y)dy \text{ (continuous arithmetic)}$$

$$A = \exp\left(\frac{1}{t} \int_0^t S(y)dy\right) \text{ (continuous geometric)}$$

(5.30)

for continuous averaging and

$$A = \frac{1}{N} \sum_{n-1}^{N} S(t_n) \text{ (discrete arithmetic)}$$

$$A = \left(\prod_{n=1}^{N} S(t_n)\right)^{1/N} \text{ (discrete geometric)}$$

(5.31)

for discrete averaging. For payoffs, there are various forms (in these formulae the average A may be any of the forms (5.30) and (5.31)):

$$\begin{aligned}
&\text{Average strike call: } \max(0, S - A) \\
&\text{Average strike put: } \max(0, A - S) \\
&\text{Average rate call: } \max(0, A - K) \\
&\text{Average rate put: } \max(0, K - A)
\end{aligned}$$

(5.32)

It is possible to find the exact solution of certain kinds of Asian options (see Haug, 2007) but in general we must resort to numerical methods in order to price them. Finally, a *lookback option* has a payoff that is determined by the difference between the maximum and minimum values of the underlying asset over the life of the option. There are two basic kinds of lookback options, namely *fixed strike* and *floating strike*. For example, the payoff for a fixed strike option is given by

$$\max(0, M(T) - K)$$

(5.33)

where

$$M(t) = \max_{0 \le y \le t} S(y) \text{ for } t \in (0, T] \text{ in the continuous case and}$$

$$M(t) = \max_{1 \le n \le N} S(t_n), \quad t \in \{t_m : m = 0, \ldots, N\} \text{ in the discrete case}$$

Thus, the payoffs are similar to those for vanilla options except that we replace $S(T)$ by the maximum $M(T)$ of the underlying asset up to the expiry date. We discuss the modelling of Asian, barrier and lookback options in Part III of the book.

5.9   A SMALL SOFTWARE FRAMEWORK FOR PRICING OPTIONS

We give a short preview of C++ code for pricing options and we build the software in stages. Our eventual objective is to develop a flexible software architecture that can model a range of path-dependent options using the Monte Carlo. The advantages of this approach are:

- Incremental development: We develop the code in a step-by-step fashion, thus adding to its robustness and reliability.
- Insight is gained into how path-dependent options are modelled.

- This architecture can be generalised, extended and used as a building block in a larger software framework.

These points will be elaborated in Parts II and III of this book. We give an example of this proccess on the CD where we price barrier options.

5.10   SUMMARY AND CONCLUSIONS

We introduced a number of finite difference schemes and applied them to several popular option models. We focused on two-factor SDEs with a square root nonlinearity in the diffusion terms.

Having described the SDEs and the finite difference schemes for these problems the objective is that you should be able to apply the same process – namely from SDE to FDM to C++ – to your own applications. We hope that the examples in this chapter will provide a basis for further experimentation.

5.11   EXERCISES AND PROJECTS

1. (*) Brownian Bridge
   Create paths based on the Brownian Bridge construction. In particular, calculate the paths using the exact and approximate solutions in equations (5.8) and (5.9), respectively. Compare these solutions with the scheme devised in Morokoff (1998).
2. (***) Two-factor Model with and without Correlation
   We consider a generic SDE (call it model A) for random processes X and Y:

$$dX = a\,dt + b\,dW$$
$$dY = c\,dt + f\,dZ$$

In this case the variables a, b, c and f are nonlinear functions of t, X and Y. The random processes X and Z are correlated as follows:

$$dW\,dZ = \rho\,dt, \text{ where } \rho \text{ is the correlation coefficient}$$

It is known that we can define an equivalent SDE by using a change of variables (call it model B) in which the correlation between the random processes is zero:

$$dX = a\,dt + b\,dW$$
$$dY = c\,dt + f(\rho\,dW + \sqrt{1 - \rho^2}\,d\tilde{Z})$$

and

$$dW\,d\tilde{Z} = 0$$

In general, we convert correlated to non-correlated variables and vice versa using the following formula:

$$z_1 = \epsilon_1$$
$$z_2 = \rho\epsilon_1 + \sqrt{1 - \rho^2}\,\epsilon_2$$

when z_1 and z_2 are drawn from a standard bivariate normal distribution with correlation ρ; ϵ_1 and ϵ_2 are independent normal variables.

The objective of this exercise is to compare the efficiency and accuracy of finite difference schemes that approximate the solutions of models A and B. In particular, answer the following questions:
- Choose a number of problems for which you know the analytical solution for models A and B. Then compare these solutions with those produced by finite difference schemes.
- Experiment with the explicit Euler scheme for various values of the mesh size. Use extreme values of the drift and diffusion terms as well as extreme values of the correlation coefficient (this coefficient has values in the interval $[-1, 1]$).

3. (**) Performance Improvement of Predictor-Corrector Code for Spread Option

The objective of this exercise is to improve the performance of the code in section 5.6, especially the code for the predictor-corrector method. We optimised the code for the Euler method by eliminating the need for temporary variables and assigning them to other ones. We have noticeable improvements of 20–30% when compared with the original non-optimised code:

```
// Explicit Euler
if (choice == 1)
{
     //tmp1 = mySDE.calculateDrift(t, VOld);
     //tmp2 = mySDE.calculateDiffusion(t, VOld, Z);

     //VNew = VOld + (k * tmp1)+ (sqrk * tmp2);
     TripleSum(VNew, VOld, mySDE.calculateDrift(t, VOld),
               mySDE.calculateDiffusion(t, VOld, Z), k, sqrk);
}
```

The new function ensures that no temporary objects are created and it is hoped that this improves the performance. The basic assignment operation is given by

$$D = A + bB + cC$$

where A, B and C are vectors; a and b are scalars. The optimised code becomes:

```
template <typename V, int N>
    void TripleSum(VectorSpace<V,N>& D,
              const VectorSpace<V,N>& A,
              const VectorSpace<V,N>& B,
              const VectorSpace<V,N>& C,
              V b, V c)
{

     // Precondition: all vectors have same size

     for (int j = D.MinIndex(); j <= D.MaxIndex(); ++j)
     {
          D[j] = A[j] + (b*B[j]) + (c*C[j]);
     }

}
```

Thus, we ask you to optimise this code (which is about three times slower than the optimised Euler code at the moment) by employing tactics similar to those used for Euler:

```
// Predictor-Corrector
VMid = VOld + (k * mySDE.calculateDrift(t, VOld)) +
              (sqrk * mySDE.calculateDiffusion(t, VOld, Z));

VNew = VOld + 0.5 * k * (mySDE.calculateDrift(t, VOld) +
            mySDE.calculateDrift(t + k, VMid)) +
            0.5 * sqrk * (mySDE.calculateDiffusion(t, VOld, Z) +
            mySDE.calculateDiffusion(t + k, VMid, Z));
```

(In Chapter 21 we shall discuss performance issues in more detail; one particular solution is to use *function objects* (which can be inlined) instead of function pointers which we have used here.)

4. (***) Barrier Options

In this exercise we develop the code for the exact solution of a barrier option and we use it to compare it with the Monte Carlo simulations. The formula for the exact solution is given by:

$$C(S, t) = C_v(S, t) - C_v(H^2/S, t) \left(\frac{S}{H}\right)^{1-2r/\sigma^2}$$

where C_v is the Black-Scholes value of a call option with the same expiry and payoff as the barrier option and H is the barrier level.

The code for this formula is on the CD:

```
// Price D&O barrier option with barrier H
double CalculateDownAndOut(const OptionData& optData,
                           double H, double S)
{
    // Steps
    // 1. Calculate vanilla C(S, t)
    // 2. Calculate C(H^2/S, t)
    // 3. Apply the well-known formula

    double factor1 = PlainCallOption(optData, S);

    double U = (H*H)/S;
    double factor2 = PlainCallOption(optData, U);

    double tmp1 = 1.0 - (2.0 * optData.r /
                            (optData.sig * optData.sig));
    double tmp2 = pow(S/H, tmp1);

    return factor1 - (tmp2 * factor2);

}
```

The objective of this exercise is to use this code (on the CD), test it and debug it.

5. (***) Asian Options
The price of a geometric continuous average-rate call option due to Kemma and Vorst (1990) is given by:

$$C = Se^{(q_A - r)T} N(d_1) - Ke^{-rT} N(d_2)$$

where

$$d_1 = \frac{log(S/K) + (q_A + \sigma_A^2/2)T}{\sigma_A \sqrt{T}}$$

$$d_2 = d_1 - \sigma_A \sqrt{T}, \quad \sigma_A = \sigma/\sqrt{3} \text{ (adjusted volatility)}$$

$$q_A = \frac{1}{2}\left(q - \frac{\sigma^2}{6}\right) \text{ (adjusted cost of carry)}$$

and $N(x)$ is the cumulative normal distribution function:

$$N(x) = \frac{1}{\sqrt{2\pi}} \int_{-\infty}^{x} e^{-z^2/2} dz$$

We now give the approximation for an arithmetic average-rate option due to Turnbull and Wakeman (1991). The form of the solution is the same as that for the above continuous average-rate call option. We use different values for the volatility and the cost of carry (Haug, 2007, page 186):

$$\sigma_A = \sqrt{\frac{log(M_2)}{T} - 2q_A}$$

$$q_A = log(M_1)/T$$

The first and second moments of the arithmetic average are

$$M_1 = \frac{e^{qT} - e^{qt_1}}{q(T - t_1)}, q \neq 0$$

$$M_2 = \frac{2e^{(2q+\sigma^2)T}}{(q + \sigma^2)(2q + \sigma^2)(T - t_1)^2} + \frac{2e^{(2q+\sigma^2)t_1}}{q(T - t_1)^2}\left[\frac{1}{2q + \sigma^2} - \frac{e^{q(T-t_1)}}{q + \sigma^2}\right], \text{ respectively}$$

q = cost of carry (not equal to zero)
t_1 = time to the beginning of the average period

Code these formulae in C++ and compare the solutions with those from the Monte Carlo method.

6. (**) Asian Options with Stochastic Volatility
We wish to price an arithmetic strike call option where the underlying asset is simulated using the Heston model (5.14). The payoff in the current case is defined as

$$V(S(T)) = \max(0, S(T) - \frac{1}{T}\int_0^T S(t)dt)$$

and we calculate the option price using the approximate formula:

$$V = \max(0, \alpha)$$

where

$$\alpha \equiv e^{-rT} \frac{1}{NSIM} \sum_{k=1}^{NSIM} \left(S(t)^{(k)} - \frac{1}{NT} \sum_{n=1}^{NT} S_{t_n}^{(k)} \right)$$

where

$NSIM$ = number of simulations
NT = number of time steps
$S(t)^{(k)}$ = stock price at time t for the kth iteration of the MC simulation

Answer the following questions:
- Adapt the C++ code for the Heston model in this chapter to implement the algorithm for this Asian option problem. Choose the appropriate parameters and calculate the call price.
- Now price a put payoff for this problem and calculate the put option price. Regarding the simulation parameters, take a range of values for the number of draws $NSIM$ and the number of subdivisions NT of the interval $[0, T]$.

7. (***) 'To Err is Human'
Examine the code on the CD for schemes (5.17) to (5.27). Do a code review to convince yourself that it is a consistent implementation.

The forum for discussions is **www.datasimfinancial.com**.

6

Advanced Finance Models
and Numerical Methods

6.1 INTRODUCTION AND OBJECTIVES

In this chapter we discuss a number of topics related to pricing options using the Monte Carlo method:

- Jump processes.
- Estimating the accuracy of a finite difference (FD) scheme without having to know the exact solution of the corresponding SDE.
- Smoothing payoff functions using *mollifiers* and *bump functions*.
- Using the C ANSI function `rand()`: the dangers and pitfalls.
- Numerical methods that fail when applied to SDEs.
- Approximating SDEs using strong Taylor (explicit and implicit) schemes.

The section on jump-diffusion processes describes formulae and methods as discussed in Glasserman (2004) and Cont and Tankov (2004). We also provide exercises to help the reader produce C++ code for these problems. An application involving jumps will be presented in Part III of this book.

Some of the literature on the numerical solution of SDEs using finite difference methods assumes that exact solutions are known and from there it is possible to find estimates for the error between exact and approximate solutions, as discussed in Kloeden, Platen and Schurz (1997) and Chapter 4 of the current book. Of course, this is an ideal situation because we can find exact solutions only in rare cases. So, how do we find *computable error estimates* when no exact solution is known? One approach is to estimate the error between two discrete solutions on meshes of size Δt and $\Delta t/2$. It is possible to compute this error as a function of the step size Δt. Knowing this, we can then compute the error between the exact and discrete solutions using numerical experiments as discussed in Schmitz and Shaw (2005). We obtain similar results by mathematical analysis based on previous work of one of the authors (see Duffy, 1980). The analysis uses general convergence principles using Cauchy sequences and the theory of Banach spaces.

Finally, we discuss a well-known (and potentially dangerous) pseudo-random number generator (called `rand()`) that is used in Monte Carlo simulation. We describe its shortcomings and we recommend other more robust methods. We also give an example of a Monte Carlo simulation that does not converge (or converges very slowly) when applied to a call option but which converges very quickly when we use it for a put payoff. Having found the put price we can then use put-call parity relationships to find the call price.

6.2 PROCESSES WITH JUMPS

It is now accepted that asset price movements do not have continuous sample paths (Cont and Tankov, 2004; Glasserman, 2004). Instead, prices have jumps and for this reason we wish to create SDEs that are able to model these jumps. Real markets exhibit a number of deviations from the ideal Black-Scholes model. In energy markets, for example, we see unanticipated large changes in energy and electricity prices called 'jumps' or 'spikes'. If we examine the logarithms of prices we see *leptokurtotic* behaviour which means that the distribution has a relatively high peak, in contrast to *platykurtotic* behaviour in which the distribution is flat-topped. The normal distribution is neither flat-topped nor peaked and for this reason we say that it is *mesokurtic*. A popular assumption is to allow prices to have discrete jumps in time. One of the first models for jumps was due to Merton (1976):

$$\frac{dS(t)}{S(t_-)} = \mu dt + \sigma dW(t) + dJ(t) \tag{6.1}$$

where μ and σ are constants, W is standard one-dimensional Wiener process and J is a process that is independent of W having piecewise constant sample paths.

Since the values of the underlying quantity S are discontinuous we define the notation for the value of the underlying to the left of a potential jump as

$$S(t_-) \equiv \lim_{y \uparrow t} S(y)$$

In other words, we approach the value at t *from below*. In equation (6.1) the process J is defined as

$$J(t) = \sum_{j=1}^{N(t)} (Y_j - 1) \tag{6.2}$$

where

$Y_1, Y_2, \ldots$ are random variables

$N(t)$ = counting process

We need to say some more about the processes J and $N(t)$. First, we assume a set of arrival times:

$$0 < t_1 < t_2 < \ldots \text{ and } N(t) = \sup\{n : t_n \le t\}$$

is the number of arrivals in the interval $[0, t]$. Furthermore, $dJ(t)$ signifies the jump in the process J at time t. The size of the jump is $Y_j - 1$ if $t = t_j$, and zero otherwise.

The solution of (6.1) is given by (Glasserman, 2004, page 136)

$$S(t) = \left(S(0)e^{((\mu - \frac{1}{2}\sigma^2)t + \sigma W(t))} \right) \prod_{j=1}^{N(t)} Y_j \tag{6.3}$$

and this is a generalisation of the solution to the SDE with geometric Brownian motion as already discussed in previous chapters.

We now discuss a number of issues concerning jump processes:

- Modelling the process $N(t)$, and specific choices for the process $J(t)$.
- Simulating equation (6.1) at fixed dates.

- Simulating equation (6.1) and simulating jump times explicitly.
- Approximating equation (6.1) using the finite difference method.

We devote a sub-section to each of these topics.

6.2.1   Specific choices for jump processes

We now constrain the form of the process J. In many cases we take $N(t)$ to be a Poisson process having a rate parameter, or intensity λ. Then the inter-arrival times $t_{n+1} - t_n$ are independent and are described by an exponential distribution:

$$P\,(t_{n+1} - t_n \leq t) = 1 - e^{-\lambda t}, \quad t \geq 0 \tag{6.4}$$

We can interpret λ as the expected frequency of events per unit interval of time. Furthermore, if $Y_j, j = 1, \ldots, N(t)$ are independent and identically distributed (i.i.d.), independent of N and independent of J, then we say that J is a *compound Poisson process*.

6.2.2   Simulating jumps, fixed dates

In this case we define a fixed set of dates:

$$0 < t_0 < t_1 < \cdots < t_N = T$$

and we make no distinction between jump and diffusion terms. We now consider applying the formula (6.3) between time levels n and $n + 1$; the reader can check that the solution is given by

$$S(t_{n+1}) = S(t_n)\exp((\mu - \tfrac{1}{2}\sigma^2)\Delta t_n + \sigma\,\Delta W_n)\prod_{j=N(t_n)+1}^{N(t_{n+1})} Y_j \tag{6.5}$$

where

$$\Delta t_n \equiv t_{n+1} - t_n$$
$$\Delta W_n \equiv W(t_{n+1}) - W(t_n)$$

Using a log transformation $X(t) = \log S(t)$, we see that equation (6.5) is equivalent to

$$X(t_{n+1}) = X(t_n) + (\mu - \tfrac{1}{2}\sigma^2)\Delta t_n + \sigma\,\Delta W_n + \sum_{j=N(t_n)+1}^{N(t_{n+1})} \log Y_j \tag{6.6}$$

Once we have calculated the Xs we can then revert to the S values since $S = \exp(X)$. In exercise 1 at the end of this chapter, we describe the algorithm for simulating equation (6.6) from time level n to time level $n + 1$.

6.2.3   Simulating jump times

We now discuss the problem where the jump times are explicitly modelled. Between jump times, the price $S(t)$ behaves like a geometric Brownian motion because we have assumed that the Wiener process W and the compound Poisson process J are independent of each other.

This means that the value just before time level $n + 1$ is defined in terms of the solution at time level n as being

$$S(t_{n+1}-) = S(t_n)\exp\left(\left(\mu - \frac{1}{2}\sigma^2\right)\Delta t_n + \sigma \Delta W_n\right) \tag{6.7}$$

The equation from just before the time level $n + 1$ to time level $n + 1$ is given by

$$S(t_{n+1}) = S(t_{n+1}-)Y_{n+1} \tag{6.8}$$

If we now take logarithms on both sides of equations (6.7) and (6.8) and eliminate the term $X(t_{n+1}-)$ we then get the formula:

$$X(t_{n+1}) = X(t_n) + (\mu - \frac{1}{2}\sigma^2)\Delta t_n + \sigma \Delta W_n + \log Y_{n+1} \tag{6.9}$$

where

$$\Delta t_n = t_{n+1} - t_n \quad \text{and} \quad X = \log(S)$$

See exercise 2 at the end of this chapter for a discussion of the algorithm for simulating equation (6.9).

6.2.4   Finite difference approximations

In general, it is difficult to find exact solutions of jump-diffusion differential equations such as equation (6.1). A more general form of the jump-diffusion SDE is given by (we drop the dependence of the process X on t for convenience):

$$dX = \mu(t, X)dt + \sigma(t, X)dW + c(t, X_-)dJ \tag{6.10}$$

where

$$X_-(t) \equiv \lim_{u\uparrow t} X(u)$$

This equation can be written in integral form:

$$X(t) = X(t_0) + \int_{t_0}^{t} \mu(s, X(s))ds + \int_{t_0}^{t} \sigma(s, X(s))dW(s) + \int_{t_0}^{t} c(s, X(s_-))dJ(s) \tag{6.11}$$

The first integral is a Riemann integral, the second integral is an Ito integral while the third integral is a stochastic integral with respect to a Poisson random measure. It can be shown that the solution of equation (6.11) exists and is pathwise unique under the assumptions of growth restriction, uniform Lipschitz continuity and smoothness of the coefficients of this equation (see Gikhmann and Skorokhod, 1972). The simplest scheme for equations (6.10) and (6.11) is called the *Cauchy-Euler scheme*:

$$Y_{n+1} = Y_n + \mu_n \Delta t + \sigma_n \Delta W_n + c_n \Delta J_n \tag{6.12}$$

where

$$\mu_n = \mu(t_n, Y_n), \quad \sigma_n = \sigma(t_n, Y_n), \quad c_n = c(t_n, Y_n)$$
$$\Delta W_n = \text{increment of Wiener process in } (t_n, t_{n+1})$$
$$\Delta J_n = \text{increment of Poisson process in } (t_n, t_{n+1})$$
$$\Delta t = \text{(constant) mesh size}$$

This scheme is first-order accurate in the mean-square sense (see Maghsoodi, 1998, where the Cauchy-Euler scheme and higher-order accurate schemes are proposed). The Cauchy-Euler scheme can be generalised to n-factor problems.

6.3   LÉVY PROCESSES

In this section we give a short introduction to a general class of processes that subsumes the Wiener and Poisson processes as special cases (Cont and Tankov, 2004).

Definition 6.1 A function $f : [0, T] \to \mathbb{R}^d$ is said to be *cadlag* if it is right-continuous with left limits:

$$\forall\, t \in [0, T], \text{ the limits}$$
$$f(t-) \equiv \lim_{s \uparrow t} f(s) \text{ and } f(t+) \equiv \lim_{s \downarrow t} f(s) \text{ exist and } f(t) = f(t_+)$$

A continuous function is a cadlag function but a cadlag function is not necessarily continuous because it can have discontinuities. To this end, we can define the *jump* of a function f at a point of discontinuity t (Cont and Tankov, 2004):

$$\Delta f(t) \equiv f(t) - f(t_-) \tag{6.13}$$

In general, a cadlag function has a finite number of large jumps and at most a countable number of small jumps (a *countable set* is one that is either finite or is an infinite set that is equivalent to the set of natural numbers (in this case we call it *denumerable*). A set that is not countable is called *non-countable*; an example is the set of real numbers in the interval [0, 1]). An example of a cadlag function is the step-function:

$$f(t) = \begin{cases} 0, & t < t_0 \\ 1, & t_0 \le t \le T \end{cases}$$

Alternatively, we write this function as

$$f(t) = \mathbf{1}_{[t_0, T]}(t)$$

Then:

$$f(t_{0-}) = 0$$
$$f(t_{0+}) = f(t_0) = 1$$

Cadlag functions are useful when modelling the trajectories of paths with jumps. In general terms, a *Lévy process* is a stochastic process that allows cadlag modifications and that possesses the following properties:

- independent increments;
- stationary increments;
- stochastic continuity.

The last condition has to do with the fact that discontinuities occur at random times. Mathematically, it is defined as follows:

$$\forall\, \epsilon > 0, \quad \lim_{h \to 0} \mathbb{P}(|X(t+h) - X(t)| \geq \epsilon) = 0 \tag{6.14}$$

where $\mathbb{P}$ is a probability measure.

We finish with a short introduction to the solution of SDEs that are driven by Lévy processes. In this case we apply finite difference methods, in particular the explicit Euler method. We write the SDE in integral form:

$$X(t) = X(0) + \int_0^t f(X(s_-))dZ(s) \tag{6.15}$$

where

$X(0)$ is an $\mathbb{R}^n$ valued random variable

$f(\cdot)$ is an $n \times d$ matrix valued function of $\mathbb{R}^n$

$Z(t)$ is a d-dimensional Lévy process

Then the explicit Euler method is defined by

$$Y_{n+1} = Y_n + f(Y_n)(Z_{n+1} - Z_n), \quad n = 0, \ldots, N-1$$
$$Y_0 = X_0 \tag{6.16}$$

This scheme is similar to the Euler scheme that used the Wiener process in previous chapters. Instead of generating Wiener increments, we now generate Lévy increments in the interval between the time levels n and $n+1$.

In Chapter 20 we shall introduce a class of Lévy models whose increments have a *normal inverse Gaussian* distribution when we introduce NIG processes and their implementation in C++.

6.4 MEASURING THE ORDER OF CONVERGENCE

In previous chapters we estimated the error between discrete and exact solutions of SDEs based on the assumption that an exact solution was known. But what do we do if an exact solution in not known? In this case we use a number of results and theorems that allow us to calculate the order of convergence by examining the discrete solution on two meshes and then comparing the error between these two solutions. One of the authors (Duffy, 1980) used such techniques for proving the convergence of the solutions of finite difference schemes for partial differential equations. We give a summary of these techniques here. Furthermore, we report on some recent work that uses similar techniques and that is applied to SDEs (Schmitz and Shaw, 2005).

The topics in this section can be found in much of the numerical analysis literature, such as extrapolation methods, multigrid methods (see Brandt, 1977) and general convergence results in Banach spaces.

6.4.1 A general convergence principle

We reduce the scope by examining a real-valued function F of one variable. This function is otherwise unspecified but in our example it could be the solution of a differential equation or the integral of a function, for example.

Theorem 6.1 (*General Convergence Principle*). Let F be a real-valued function of one variable and let $G(h)$ be some finite-dimensional approximation to F, depending on the positive parameter h. We assume the following *consistency condition*:

$$\lim_{h \to 0} \| F - G(h) \| = 0 \text{ where } \| \cdot \| \text{ is some appropriate norm} \qquad (6.17)$$

Suppose:

$$\| G(h) - G(h/2) \| \leq \varphi(h) \qquad (6.18)$$

where φ is a *strictly increasing function* of h such that $\varphi(0) = 0$. Then we get the following error estimate between exact and discrete solutions:

$$\| F - G(h) \| \leq \sum_{j=0}^{\infty} \varphi(2^{-j}h) \qquad (6.19)$$

Proof: First, we observe that the sum on the right-hand side of inequality (6.19) is a bounded quantity. To prove this, we use the *ratio test* (Rudin, 1964, page 57) to prove the convergence of this series; in general, the statement of the ratio test is

Let $\sum a_n$ be a series and define the quantities $\rho = \lim_{n \to \infty} \left| \dfrac{a_{n+1}}{a_n} \right|$

Then, if:
$\rho < 1$, the series converges
$\rho > 1$, the series diverges
$\rho = 1$, the series may diverge or converge

In the current case, we have the inequality

$$\frac{a_{n+1}}{a_n} = \frac{\varphi(2^{-(n+1)}h)}{\varphi(2^{-n}h)} < 1$$

because the function $\varphi(h)$ is strictly monotonically increasing. By repeated application of inequality (6.18) on a sequence of decreasing mesh sizes we can see that

$$\left\| G(h) - G\left(\frac{h}{2^m}\right) \right\| \leq \sum_{n=0}^{m-1} \left\| G\left(\frac{h}{2^n}\right) - G\left(\frac{h}{2^{(n+1)}}\right) \right\|$$
$$\leq \sum_{n=0}^{m-1} \varphi\left(\frac{h}{2^n}\right) \text{ for } m \geq 1 \qquad (6.20)$$

Now, using the triangle inequality we get

$$\| F - G(h) \| \leq \| F - G(2^{-m}h) \| + \| G(2^{-m}h) - G(h) \| \qquad (6.21)$$

Taking the limits as m goes to infinity and using the assumption (6.17) we finally get the desired result, namely the inequality (6.19).

We take a specific example; this is the case where the function φ in inequality (6.18) is some power of h (a polynomial) and this corresponds to applications in numerical analysis such as numerical integration and finite difference approximations to differential equations, for example. Then we can compute the term

$$\| G(h) - G(h/2) \| \leq \varphi(h) = Mh^2 \qquad (6.22)$$

where M is a positive constant that is independent of h. Then, the error in inequality (6.19) takes the form

$$\|F - G(h)\| \leq \sum_{n=0}^{\infty} \varphi(2^{-n}h) \leq$$

$$M \sum_{n=0}^{\infty} (2^{-n}h)^2 = Mh^2 \sum_{n=0}^{\infty} 2^{-2^n} = \frac{4Mh^2}{3} \tag{6.23}$$

6.4.2 Applications to ordinary differential equations

We give a simple example of the application of the general convergence principle to the solution of the scalar, linear initial value problem (IVP):

$$\begin{cases} \dfrac{du}{dt} + au = f(t), & 0 < t < 1, \quad a > 0 \text{ constant} \\[2mm] u(0) = A \end{cases} \tag{6.24}$$

We approximate this problem using the implicit Euler method:

$$\begin{cases} L^{\Delta t} u_n^{\Delta t} \equiv \dfrac{u_{n+1}^{\Delta t} - u_n^{\Delta t}}{\Delta t} + a u_{n+1}^{\Delta t} = f_{n+1}^{\Delta t}, & n \geq 0 \\[2mm] u_0^{\Delta t} = A \end{cases} \tag{6.25}$$

We use a modified notation here to denote the dependence of the approximate solution on the time step and the mesh point.

Lemma 6.1 (*Maximum Principle* for scheme (6.25)). Let the mesh function $w_n^{\Delta t}$ satisfy $L^{\Delta t} w_n^{\Delta t} \geq 0$ for $n \geq 0$ and assume $w_0^{\Delta t} \geq 0$. Then $w_n^{\Delta t} \geq 0 \, \forall \, n \geq 0$.

Lemma 6.2 (Stability of scheme (6.25)). Let $u_n^{\Delta t}$ be the solution of (6.25). Then $|u_n^{\Delta t}| \leq \frac{N}{a} + |A|$, where $N = \sup_{x \geq 0} |f(x)|$.

From Lemma 6.2 and the fact that scheme (6.25) is consistent with (6.24) we can deduce from the *Lax Equivalence Theorem* (see Duffy, 2006a) that inequality (6.17) is true in the current context, in other words:

$$\lim_{\Delta t \to 0} \|u(t_n) - u_n^{\Delta t}\| = 0$$

where

$u(t)$ is the solution of (6.24)

$u_n^{\Delta t}$ is the solution of (6.25)

and where we use the notation

$\|g_n\| = \max_{0 \leq n \leq N} |g_n|$ for a mesh function

It now remains to estimate the quantity that represents the difference of solutions of (6.25) on two consecutive meshes. In particular, we wish to estimate the quantity

$$\|u^{\Delta t} - u^{\Delta t/2}\| = \max_{0 \leq n \leq N} |u_n^{\Delta t} - u_{2n}^{\Delta t/2}| \tag{6.26}$$

This process involves some algebraic manipulation. To this end, we apply Lemma 6.2, and some algebra shows that

$$L^{\Delta t}(u_{2n}^{\Delta t/2} - u_n^{\Delta t}) = L^{\Delta t}u_{2n}^{\Delta t/2} - f_{n+1}^{\Delta t} = A_{2n}^{\Delta t/2}u_{2n}^{\Delta t/2} + B_{2n}^{\Delta t/2} \tag{6.27}$$

where

$$A_{2n}^{\Delta t/2} \equiv \frac{\delta^{\Delta t/2} - 1}{\Delta t} + a^{\Delta t/2}$$

$$\alpha^{\Delta t/2} = \left(1 + a\frac{\Delta t}{2}\right)^{-1}$$

$$\delta^{\Delta t/2} = \alpha^{\Delta t/2} * \alpha^{\Delta t/2}$$

$$A_{2n}^{\Delta t/2} = \frac{\delta^{\Delta t/2} - 1}{\Delta t} + u\delta^{\Delta t/2}$$

$$B^{\Delta t/2} \equiv (a + \Delta t)^{-1}\left[\delta^{\Delta t/2} f_{2n}^{\Delta t/2} + \alpha^{\Delta t/2} f_{2n+1}^{\Delta t/2}\right]\Delta t - f_n^{\Delta t}$$

Using the inequalities

$$|A_{2n}^{\Delta t/2}|, \quad |B_{2n}^{\Delta t/2}| \leq M\Delta t$$

and the fact that the solution at time level $2n$ is bounded, we can recreate it as if it were the already well-known convergence result:

$$\max_{0 \leq n \leq N} |u(t_n) - u_n^{\Delta t}| \leq M\Delta t, \text{ where } M \text{ is independent of } \Delta t \tag{6.28}$$

6.4.3 Applications to stochastic differential equations

We give an introduction to a method for measuring the order of convergence of finite difference schemes for SDEs in the case where the exact solution is not known; in order to measure the convergence we introduce a technique from Schmitz and Shaw (2005). The authors discuss strong and weak convergence schemes for both the Euler and Milstein schemes for SDEs, including the Heston stochastic volatility model. We concentrate on the weakly convergent schemes only.

Theorem 6.2 If a time discrete approximation has the following *weak convergence* between the exact and discrete solutions $(S(T)$ and $\tilde{S}(T))$:

$$|E[g(S(T)] - E[g(\tilde{S}(T), \Delta t)]| \leq M_1 \Delta t^{\beta} \tag{6.29}$$

for all $\Delta t < \infty$, using the same Wiener process then there exists a positive constant M_2, independent of Δt and β such that

$$\left|E[g(\tilde{S}(T), \Delta t)] - E\left[g\left(\tilde{S}\left(T, \frac{\Delta t}{2}\right)\right)\right]\right| \leq M_2 \Delta t^{\beta} \tag{6.30}$$

The advantage of this approach is that we can compute the order of convergence of the weak scheme. In fact, running a number of experiments allowed the authors to deduce that

$$M_2 \approx \frac{2M_1}{3}$$

This relationship is similar to that seen in inequality (6.23). It is an open problem in our opinion on applying the general convergence principle to SDEs.

6.5   MOLLIFIERS, BUMP FUNCTIONS AND FUNCTION REGULARISATION

We introduce a useful technique to smooth functions with discontinuities. This is important in derivatives pricing problems because many payoff functions and/or their mathematical derivatives can be discontinuous at certain points, for example at one or more strike prices in the one-factor case. There are various ways to smooth these kinds of functions:

- Projecting the payoff function onto a set of basis functions (Rannacher, 1984).
- Averaging the payoff function (Kreiss, 1970; Thomée and Wahlbin, 1974); for example, in the one-factor case for the underlying variable S this technique is

$$f_j = \frac{1}{S_{j+1/2} - S_{j-1/2}} \int_{S_{j-1/2}}^{S_{j+1/2}} f(S_j - y)dy \tag{6.31}$$

where

$$S_{j\pm1/2} = \frac{1}{2}(S_{j+1} \pm S_j), \quad j = 1, \ldots, J - 1$$

and

$f = f(S)$ is the payoff function

J = number of subdivisions of the interval of integration

- Mollifiers (Adams, 1975), the topic we discuss in this section.

In order to describe what a mollifier is we introduce some notation concerning functions and their continuity. In general, we consider real-valued functions in n-dimensional Euclidean space; we define a number of spaces:

- $\Omega \subset \mathbb{R}^n$ is a domain.
- $C^\infty(\Omega)$ = vector space of functions φ all of whose derivatives are continuous in Ω.
- $C_0^\infty(\Omega)$ = functions in $C^\infty(\Omega)$ that have compact support in Ω, that is the closure of the set where the function is not zero, namely $supp(\varphi) = \{x \in \Omega : \varphi(x) \neq 0\}$.
- $L^p(\Omega) = \left\{ f : \Omega \to \mathbb{R}, \int_\Omega |f(x)|^p dx < \infty \right\}$.
- $C^0(\Omega)$ = space of real-valued continuous function on Ω.

Let J be a non-negative, real-valued function belonging to $C_0^\infty(\mathbb{R}^n)$ such that

(a) $J(x) = 0$, if $|x| \geq 1$

(b) $\int_{\mathbb{R}^n} J(x)dx = 1$

Here $x = (x_1, \ldots, x_n)$ and $|x| = \left(\sum_{j=1}^n x_j^2 \right)^{1/2}$

We now define the function $J_\varepsilon(x) = \varepsilon^{-n} J(x/\varepsilon)$ for $\varepsilon > 0$. This function has the following properties:

(a) J_ε is non-negative and $J_\varepsilon \in C_0^\infty(\mathbb{R}^n)$

(b) $J_\varepsilon(x) = 0$ if $|x| \geq \varepsilon$

(c) $\int_{\mathbb{R}^n} J_\varepsilon(x) = 1$

An example of a mollifier is the function

$$J(x) = \begin{cases} k \exp[-1/(1 - |x|^2)], & |x| < 1 \\ 0, & |x| \geq 1 \end{cases} \tag{6.32}$$

where the constant k is chosen to ensure that condition (c) above is satisfied.

We now come to the main topic. The function J_ϵ is called a *mollifier* and its use is to create sequences of smooth functions that approximate non-smooth and generalised functions using *convolution*.

This new function is called a *mollification* or *regularisation* of the function u.

Theorem 6.3 Let

$$f \in C^0(\Omega), \text{ then } J_\varepsilon * f \to f \text{ uniformly on } \Omega,$$

where $J_\varepsilon * f(x) = \int_{\mathbb{R}^n} J_\varepsilon(x - y) f(y) dy$

If $f \in L^p(\Omega), 1 \leq p < \infty$ then $\|J_\varepsilon * f\|_{L^p(\Omega)} \leq \|f\|_{L^p(\Omega)}$ and

$J_\varepsilon * f \to f$ in $L^p(\Omega)$ as $\varepsilon \to 0$

Here, $\| \cdot \|_{L^p(\Omega)}$ is the norm defined by $\|f\|_{L^p(\Omega)} = \left(\int_\Omega |f(x)|^p dx \right)^{1/p}$.

We shall see some examples of mollifiers in Part III where we discuss the smoothing of payoff functions.

6.6   WHEN MONTE CARLO DOES NOT WORK: COUNTEREXAMPLES

In this section we give a short overview of some of the unexpected events that can occur when we model SDEs using their exact representations and by application of the finite difference method. Furthermore, we say a few words on random number generators.

6.6.1   How good is the random number generator rand()?

An important issue to address when using the Monte Carlo method is how to choose a good pseudo random number generator. We discuss random number generators in more detail in Chapter 22. In this section we discuss the use of the standard C library function rand(). This function generates a pseudorandom number between 0 and RAND_MAX = 32767. It is based on a linear congruential generator of the form

$$X_{n+1} = a X_n + b \ (mod \ c) \tag{6.33}$$

This is a difference scheme and the generated values will lie in the interval $[0, c - 1]$. A simple example of use is

```cpp
#include <time.h>
#include <iostream>
using namespace std;
void RandDemo( int n )
{
    // Print n random numbers.
    for(int i = 0; i < n; ++i)
        cout << rand() << endl;
}
```

In this case we call the random number generator a number of times and we print the value on the console. The value will be somewhere between 0 and RAND_MAX . We now show how to generate random numbers in a given interval $[A, B]$:

```cpp
void RangedRandDemo( int A, int B, int n )
{
    // Generate random numbers in the half-closed interval
    // [A, B).
    for (int i = 0; i < n; ++i)
    {
    int u = (double)rand() / (RAND_MAX + 1) * (B - A)
                                            + A;
    cout << u << endl;
    }
}
```

Finally, we need to define a value for the *seed* (start value) in the iteratve process in equation (6.33) and we can see how this is achieved in the followng test program:

```cpp
int main()
{
    // Create the seed for the random-number generator with the
        current
    // time so that the numbers will be different for each run.
    srand((unsigned)time( NULL));

    cout << "Demo 1\n";
    RandDemo( 10 );
    cout << "\nDemo 2\n";
    RangedRandDemo( -4, 4, 10);

    return 0;
}
```

The current random number generator is not good because the value 32767 is not a very big number. The generated numbers contain more duplicates in the data than the corresponding Random class function in Visual Basic produces, for example. This latter class generates 32-bit integer values instead of 16-bit integer values as with the C function rand(). As already mentioned, we shall propose a number of more reliable pseudo-random number generators in later chapters. Furthermore, we introduce a Microsoft-specific extension to rand() in exercise 10 at the end of this chapter.

6.6.2 Special stochastic differential equations

In the previous chapters we concentrated on solving SDEs in which drift and diffusion terms are present. We now take an example of an SDE in which the drift term is absent and we call it a *pure-diffusion SDE*:

$$dX = \sigma X dW \tag{6.34}$$

Instead of using an FD scheme to approximate the solution of (6.34) we calculate the path using the exact representation

$$X(t) = X_0 \exp\left(-\frac{\sigma^2}{2}t + \sigma W(t)\right), \quad 0 < t \le T \tag{6.35}$$

We now calculate the value at $t = T$ and we use this in the payoff function for a plain call option. We take $NT = 1$ so we do not have to partition the interval $[0, T]$ in order to achieve a good approximation. Taking $NSIM = 10\,000\,000$ (ten million) draws, calculating the discounted average price using the Monte Carlo method as discussed in Chapter 0 and comparing with the exact Black-Scholes price we find for prices a range of values for σ as follows:

σ	Exact	Simulated
0.3	58.8687	58.8462
0.5	82.9111	81.9162
0.7	94.4751	93.8009
0.9	98.6268	126.62
1	99.3815	48.2532

We see that the accuracy becomes progressively worse as σ approaches one. On the other hand, if we use the payoff function for a put option, the results are very good indeed! Why should this be so? For large T, the probability is concentrated near $S = 0$. This contributes to good put statistics, because almost every trial counts towards the value. Furthermore, since the put payoff is bounded, it has good errors. On the other hand, the call value has to rely on rare events, and, being unbounded, has big errors. Now, in order to recover the call price we used the call-put parity relationship

$$C = P + S - Ke^{-rT}$$
$$C = \text{call price}, \; P = \text{put price} \tag{6.36}$$

6.7 APPROXIMATING SDEs USING STRONG TAYLOR, EXPLICIT AND IMPLICIT SCHEMES

We extend the discussion in Chapter 4 by introducing a number of advanced finite difference equations for stochastic differential equations. We focus on strong schemes and we reduce the scope to one-factor models but many of the schemes are applicable in the n-factor case as well.

6.7.1   Stability analysis of SDEs with multiplicative and additive noise

This topic has received relatively little attention when compared with the number of publications for ordinary differential equations. In this section we discuss the stability of finite difference schemes for two model SDEs based on multiplicative noise. We define different kinds of stability; in general, we wish to determine whether the solution of a finite difference scheme tends to zero at infinity when the solution of the SDE that it approximates also tends to zero for large time. To this end, we first examine the scalar SDE with constant coefficients and multiplicative noise:

$$
\begin{cases} dX = \mu X dt + \sigma X dW \\ X(0) = 1 \end{cases}
\tag{6.37}
$$

The solution of this SDE is given by

$$
X(t) = \exp\left\{ \left(\mu - \frac{1}{2}\sigma^2 \right) t + \sigma W(t) \right\}
\tag{6.38}
$$

In general this type of SDE has complex coefficients. Based on the qualitative theory of SDEs, the trivial solution $X(t) \equiv 0$ is asymptotically stable if $\Re(\mu - \frac{1}{2}\sigma^2) < 0$ and is unstable if $\Re(\mu - \frac{1}{2}\sigma^2) \geq 0$. In particular, we examine the condition

$$
\lim_{t \to \infty} \|X(t)\|, \text{ where } \|X(t)\| = \left\{ \mathbf{E}|X|^2 \right\}^{1/2}
\tag{6.39}
$$

Necessary and sufficient conditions for (6.39) to hold are given in Saito (1996) and are described by the inequality

$$
2\Re\mu + |\sigma|^2 < 0
\tag{6.40}
$$

We now determine the conditions that should be imposed on a numerical approximation of equation (6.37) that leads to the following discrete asymptotic behaviour:

$$
\lim_{n \to \infty} \|X_n\| = 0
\tag{6.41}
$$

To this end, we define $Y_n = \mathbf{E}|X_n|^2$. Let us suppose that $\{X_n\}$ is an approximation to equation (6.37) at discrete mesh points. Then taking the mean-square norm, we get a finite difference scheme of the form

$$
Y_{n+1} = R(\overline{\Delta t}, \beta) Y_n
\tag{6.42}
$$

where

$$
\overline{\Delta t} = \mu \Delta t
$$

$$
\beta = -\frac{\sigma^2}{\mu}
$$

Definition 6.2 The scheme (6.42) is said to be MS (mean-square) stable for those values of $\overline{\Delta t}$ and β for which the inequality

$$
|\Re(\overline{\Delta t}, \beta)| < 1 \text{ holds}
\tag{6.43}
$$

When $\overline{\Delta t}$ and β are real numbers we call the domain of stability the region of MS-stability. A number of finite difference schemes are discussed in Saito and Mitsui (1996) and the authors calculate the stability function R as defined in equation (6.42). In fact, they discuss the schemes (0.28) to (0.33) that we introduced in Chapter 0.

The way to calculate this function is as follows: compute the discrete solution to equation (6.37), square it and use known expected values of Wiener increments, namely:

$$\left.\begin{array}{l} \mathbf{E}(\Delta W_n) = 0 \\ \mathbf{E}(\Delta W_n^2) = \Delta t \end{array}\right\} n = 0, \ldots, N$$

See exercise 4 for some more details and examples. We now discuss the stability of finite difference schemes for the model SDE with additive noise (Kloeden and Platen, 1995, pages 334–337).

We introduce the concept of A-stability by examining one-step finite difference schemes with constant mesh size applied to the model SDE (6.37):

We call the set of complex numbers μ with

$$\Re(\mu) < 0 \text{ and } |\Re(\mu \Delta t)| < 1 \tag{6.44}$$

the region of absolute stability of the given scheme. We then say that a scheme is A-stable if its region of absolute stability is the whole of the left half of the complex plane. Let us take an example, namely the explicit Euler method:

$$X_{n+1} = X_n + \mu X_n \Delta t + \Delta W_n = (1 + \mu \Delta t)X_n + \Delta W_n \tag{6.45}$$

Some analysis with complex numbers shows that the region of absolute stability of this method is the unit disk with centre $(-1, 0)$. The reader can check that the implicit Euler scheme is A-stable. The concept of A-stability is a generalisation of similar concepts from ODE theory.

The following three sections are based on discussions in Kloeden and Platen (1995).

6.7.2 Strong Taylor approximants

These schemes are based on truncated Taylor expansions. The simplest strong Taylor scheme is the Euler method and its strong order of convergence is 0.5. It is useful when the drift and diffusion terms are nearly constant but the method is unsuitable in more complex cases and when we wish to achieve higher accuracy. The Milstein scheme has strong order of convergence equal to 1.0. It is essentially the Euler scheme with an extra added term. To this end, consider the SDE:

$$dX = \mu(t, X)dt + \sigma(t, X)dW \tag{6.46}$$

Then the Milstein scheme is

$$X_{n+1} = X_n + \mu_n \Delta t + \sigma_n \Delta W_n + \tfrac{1}{2}\sigma_n \sigma_n' \left\{ (\Delta W_n)^2 - \Delta t \right\} \tag{6.47}$$

where

$$\mu = \mu(t_n, X_n)$$
$$\sigma_n = \sigma(t_n, X_n)$$
$$\sigma' = \frac{\partial \sigma}{\partial X}$$

Finally, the following Ito-Taylor scheme (due to Platen and Wagner) has strong convergence order equal to 1.5 (Kloeden and Platen, 1995, page 351):

$$
\begin{aligned}
X_{n+1} = {} & X_n + \mu \Delta t + \sigma \Delta W_n + \tfrac{1}{2}\sigma\sigma' \left\{(\Delta W_n)^2 - \Delta t\right\} \\
& + \mu'\sigma \Delta Z_n + \tfrac{1}{2}(\mu\mu' + \tfrac{1}{2}\sigma^2\mu'')\Delta t^2 \\
& + (\mu\sigma' + \tfrac{1}{2}\sigma^2\sigma'')\left\{\Delta W_n \Delta t - \Delta Z_n\right\} \\
& + \tfrac{1}{2}\sigma(\sigma\sigma'' + (\sigma')^2)\left\{\tfrac{1}{3}(\Delta W_n)^2 - \Delta t\right\}\Delta W_n
\end{aligned}
\tag{6.48}
$$

where we use the notation:

$$\mu = \mu(t_n, X_n)$$
$$\sigma = \sigma(t_n, X_n)$$
$$\sigma'' = \frac{\partial^2 \sigma}{\partial x^2}, \; \mu' = \frac{\partial \mu}{\partial x}, \; \mu'' = \frac{\partial^2 \mu}{\partial x^2}$$

and ΔZ_n is normally distributed.

Finally,

$$\mathbf{E}(\Delta Z_n) = 0$$

Variance $\mathbf{E}((\Delta Z_n)^2) = \tfrac{1}{3}\Delta t^3$

Covariance $\mathbf{E}(\Delta Z_n, \Delta W_N) = \tfrac{1}{2}\Delta t^2$

We calculate the pair $(\Delta W, \Delta Z)$ as follows:

$$
\begin{aligned}
\Delta W &= U_1 \sqrt{\Delta t} \\
\Delta Z &= \tfrac{1}{2}\Delta t^{3/2}(U_1 + \tfrac{1}{\sqrt{3}}U_2)
\end{aligned}
\tag{6.49}
$$

where U_1 and U_2 are two independent $N(0, 1)$ distributed random variables.

6.7.3 Explicit strong schemes

The strong Taylor approximations that we discussed in the previous section have a number of disadvantages, such as the necessity of calculating derivatives of the drift and diffusion functions (which may not be continuous); the performance may not be optimal due to many function evaluations and the generation of pairs of standard normal random variates. Some of these drawbacks can be mitigated by employing schemes that avoid the use of derivatives. To motivate this class of schemes, we examine equation (6.46) again. We consider the following derivative-free method (a variation of Milstein scheme (6.48)):

$$
\begin{aligned}
X_{n+1} &= X_n + \mu \Delta t + \sigma \Delta W_n + \frac{1}{2\sqrt{\Delta t}}\left\{\sigma(t_n, \overline{X}_n) - \sigma\right\}\left\{(\Delta W_n)^2 - \Delta t\right\} \\
\overline{X}_n &= X_n + \mu \Delta t + \sigma \sqrt{\Delta t}
\end{aligned}
\tag{6.50}
$$

where we use the same notation as in equation (6.48). We see that this scheme is similar to scheme (6.47) when we realise that the term

$$
\frac{1}{\sqrt{\Delta t}}\left\{\sigma(t_n, X_n + \mu\Delta t + \sigma\sqrt{\Delta t}) - \sigma(t_n, X_n)\right\}
\tag{6.51}
$$

is a difference approximation to $\sigma\sigma'$ at (t_n, X_n).

This is an explicit order 1.0 strong scheme.

6.7.4 Implicit strong schemes

We now discuss a number of schemes that are used for stiff SDEs (we introduced the concept of stiffness in Chapter 4). A feature of implicit methods – in contrast to explicit methods – is that they support a wide range of step sizes and are able to handle problems with different time scales. But the fact that the schemes are now implicit necessitates our solving a nonlinear system at each time level, for example using the Newton-Raphson method. Let us look at equation (6.46) and approximate it using the implicit Euler method of order 0.5:

$$X_{n+1} = X_n + \mu(t_{n+1}, X_{n+1})\Delta t + \sigma(t_n, X_n)\Delta W_n, \quad n = 0, \ldots, N - 1 \qquad (6.52)$$

In the multi-dimensional case with N underlyings and m random terms we have the generalisation of equation (6.52):

$$X_{n+1}^k = X_n^k + \mu^k(t_{n+1}, X_{n+1})\Delta t + \Sigma_{j=1}^m \sigma^{k,j}\Delta W_n^j, \quad n = 0, \ldots, N - 1 \qquad (6.53)$$

We can then solve this system at each time level using the Newton-Raphson method.

The second example is the implicit Milstein scheme:

$$X_{n+1} = X_n + \mu(t_{n+1}, X_{n+1})\Delta t + \sigma\Delta W_n + \tfrac{1}{2}\sigma\sigma'\left\{(\Delta W_n)^2 - \Delta t\right\} \qquad (6.54)$$

where

$$\sigma = \sigma(t_n, X_n)$$
$$\sigma' \equiv \frac{\partial\sigma}{\partial x}(t_n, X_n)$$

We give an example of an implicit order 1.0 Runge-Kutta method that avoids the use of derivatives:

$$X_{n+1} = X_n + \mu(t_{n+1}, X_{n+1})\Delta t + \sigma\Delta W_n + \frac{1}{2\sqrt{\Delta t}}(\sigma(t_n, \overline{X}_n) - \sigma)\left\{(\Delta W_n)^2 - \Delta t\right\} \qquad (6.55)$$

where

$$\overline{X}_n = X_n + \mu\Delta t + \sigma\sqrt{\Delta t}$$

Summarising: we have introduced a number of finite difference schemes that extend the simpler methods that we have discussed in the first five chapters of this book. Our recommendation would be to experiment with them on a range of problems in order to build your intuitive feeling for the different schemes. Numerical analysis is as much an art as a science, especially when modelling nonlinear problems that do not have closed solutions.

6.8 SUMMARY AND CONCLUSIONS

In this chapter we introduced a number of special SDEs. We also examined numerical approximations of SDEs from a new perspective when compared with previous chapters of this book.

We have provided a set of exercises below. Designing and programming them in C++ will improve your understanding of the algorithmic and computational aspects of the Monte Carlo method.

6.9   EXERCISES AND PROJECTS

1. (****) Simulating Jump Processes, Fixed Dates

   We wish to set up the algorithm for solving equation (6.6) and then we implement it in C++. In particular, we find the solution at time level $n + 1$ in terms of the solution at time level n (Glasserman, 2004, page 138). We use the fact that the increment $N(t_{n+1}) - N(t_n)$ has a Poisson distribution with mean $\lambda(t_{n+1}) - \lambda(t_n)$ and that this increment is independent of process N in the interval $[0, t_n]$.

   The steps are

   (a) Generate a standard normal random number $Z \sim N(0, 1)$.

   (b) Generate $N \sim$ Poisson $(\lambda(t_{n+1} - t_n))$.

   (c) If $N = 0$ then $M = 0$.

   else

   $$M = \sum_{j=1}^{N} \log Y_j$$

   where

   $$Y_j \sim \log(a, b^2) \Leftrightarrow \log Y_j \sim N(a, b^2)$$

   (d) Apply equation (6.6) (all input is known):

   $$X(t_{n+1}) = X(t_n) + \left(\mu - \frac{1}{2}\sigma^2 \right) \Delta t_n + \sigma \sqrt{\Delta t_n} Z + M$$

   In the special case where we use the lognormal distribution we see that the sum of terms can be written as

   $$\sum_{j=1}^{N} \log Y_j \sim N(aN, b^2 N) = aN + b\sqrt{N} Z$$

   Generate a standard normal random number $Z \sim N(0, 1)$. Then $M = aN + b\sqrt{N} Z$. Write C++ code to implement this algorithm.

2. (***) Simulating Jump Processes, and Jump Times

   We set up the C++ code that implements equation (6.9) to simulate a path where the jump times are simulated as part of the process. The steps in the algorithm to calculate a solution at time level $n + 1$ based on a solution at time level n are

   (a) Generate R_{n+1} from the exponential distribution with mean $1/\lambda$.

   (b) Generate $Z_{n+1} \sim N(0, 1)$.

   (c) Generate $\log Y_{n+1}$.

   (d) Apply the formula using a modified equation (6.9):

   $$X(t_{n+1}) = X(t_n) + (\mu - \tfrac{1}{2}\sigma^2)R_{n+1} + \sigma \sqrt{R_{n+1}} Z_{n+1} + \log Y_{n+1}$$
   $$\text{where } R_{n+1} = t_{n+1} - t_n$$

   Write C++ code to implement this algorithm. The CD contains code for generating the appropriate exponential and uniform variates. In particular, we generate an exponential variate by

   $$R_{n+1} = -\log(u)/\lambda \text{ where } u \sim U(0, 1)$$

3. (**) Simulating Jump Processes, Finite Difference Method

For most problems it is not always possible to find exact solutions to SDEs with jumps and we then resort to solving them using finite difference methods.

The objective of this exercise is to approximate equation (6.10) (or its integral form (6.11)) using the finite difference method defined by equation (6.12). You can use modular programming techniques. In a later version you can *reverse engineer* the code and integrate it into the Monte Carlo framework.

4. (****) Mean-Square Stability

Apply the stability analysis in section 6.7.1 to find the region of absolute stability of the schemes that we discussed in Chapter 0, namely (0.29) to (0.33).

5. (***) Smoothing of Payoff Functions

We implement the algorithm in equation (6.31) using C++. Define input using (1) a function and (2) an array of mesh points and output as a discrete array of function values. Test your code using the payoff function for a *supershare binary call option*:

$$V(t = T) = \begin{cases} 0, & S < K \\ 1/d, & K \leq S \leq K + d \\ 0, & S > K + d \end{cases}$$

It may be possible to calculate the integral exactly depending on the complexity of the integrand; otherwise, we need to resort to numerical integration techniques such as the midpoint rule or Simpson's rule, for example.

6. (**) n-Dimensional Mollifiers

Consider the function defined in equation (6.32). We now wish to construct the mollifier in n variables by taking the product of n copies of this function:

$$\Phi(x_1, x_2, \ldots, x_n) = J(x_1) \ldots J(x_n) = \prod_{j=1}^{n} J(x_j)$$

Write C++ code to implement this functionality.

7. (***) SDEs with Complex Coefficients

It is possible to define SDEs whose coefficients are complex numbers. To this end, let $W(t)$ be a real-valued Wiener process and let $Z(t)$ be a complex-valued Ito process. Consider the three complex-valued SDEs with exact solutions (Kloeden and Platen, 1995, page 125):

$$dZ = -\tfrac{1}{2} Z dt + i Z dW$$
$$Z(t) = Z_0 \exp(i W(t)), \quad i = \sqrt{-1}$$

$$dZ = i Z dW$$
$$Z(t) = Z_0 \exp(i W(t) + \tfrac{1}{2} t)$$

$$dZ = \lambda Z dt + \gamma Z dW$$
$$Z(t) = Z_0 \exp((\lambda - \tfrac{1}{2} \gamma^2) t + \gamma W(t))$$

The objective of this exercise is to approximate the solutions of these equations using the finite difference method and in order to reduce the scope we apply the Euler method using two different approaches: (1) by writing the SDE as two uncoupled real-valued SDEs for the real and imaginary parts of the complex-valued process; and (2) directly solving the complex-valued SDE; this is possible because we have created template SDE classes and we can use the class `Complex` (which is provided on the CD or alternatively you can use STL). Then this class has all the numeric operators defined that we need. You will use a class such as `SDE<Complex, N>`. We also mention that STL has a class for complex numbers.

8. (*) Linear SDEs with Two-dimensional Noise
   Consider the SDE (Kloeden and Platen, 1995)

   $$dX = \mu X dt + \sigma_1 X dW_1 + \sigma_2 X dW_2$$

   having the solution

   $$X(t) = X_0 \exp((\mu - \frac{1}{2}(\sigma_1^2 + \sigma_2^2))t + \sigma_1 W_1(t) + \sigma_2 W_2(t))$$

   How would you design numerical schemes for this kind of problem? How will you model these problems as C++ classes?

9. (*) Using the `rand()` Function
   We wish to determine the applicability (or otherwise) of the random number generator `rand()` and to this end we create arrays of varying sizes and we then check for duplicates:

   ```
   const int N = 10000000; // 10^7

   int* x; // A pointer type on stack
   x = new int[N]; // All values == 0 on the heap

   for(int i=0; i < N; ++i)
   {
       x[i] = rand(); // new values on heap

   }

   delete [] x;
   ```

   The objective of this exercise is to extend the above code so that we can count the number of occurrences of each generated value. Run the program with values of $N = 1000, 10000, 100000, 1000000$ and 10000000.

10. (*) 32-bit Random Number Generators, `rand_s()`
    In this exercise we test the Microsoft random number generator `rand_s()` that is meant to be a more secure version of `rand()`. It generates a random number in the interval `[0, UINT_MAX]` (UINT_MAX is maximum unsigned `int` value). Our interest is in generating arrays of such random numbers. First, the appropriate functions are defined in the library:

    ```
    #include <stdlib.h>
    ```

    Second, we must define the following constant prior to calling the random number generator:

    ```
    #define _CRT_RAND_S
    ```

    Finally, here is the code that generates the random array:

```
// Variables for rand_s()
errno_t           err;
unsigned int      number;

int* x;
x = new int[N];

for(int i=0; i < N; ++i)
{
    err = rand_s( &number );
    x[i] = number;
}
delete [] x;
```

The objective of this exercise is to extend the above code so that we can count the number of occurrences of each generated value. Run the program with values of $N = 1000, 10000, 100000, 1000000$ and 10000000. Do the results give an improvement when compared with rand()?

11. (*) Difficult SDEs
   Calculate the call price of a plain option with initial stock price $= 100$, strike $= 100, r = 0$, sig $= 1$, and $T = 30$ (the exact price is C = 99.383). Simulate the process, first using the call payoff function, then using the put payoff function in conjunction with the put-call parity relationship (6.36). Compare the results based on *accuracy* and *performance* of the two simulation methods. Try a simulation with $T = 100$. What do you notice?

12. (*****) Advanced Schemes for SDEs (Could be a student project)
   This exercise is based on section 6.7. We wish to investigate the robustness and accuracy of the schemes that we introduced in that section and whether they represent an improvement on well-known schemes such as the Euler method. We focus on the schemes we discussed in section 6.7:
   – Ito-Taylor.
   – Derivative-free.
   – Implicit Milstein.
   – Runge-Kutta.
   Answer the following questions:
   (a) Create code to implement these schemes. It is not necessary to integrate the code into an object-oriented framework just yet. To this end, create a namespace (as we did in Chapter 5, for example) that encapsulates the data and functions that model the SDE; for example, for scheme (6.48) we need representations for the derivatives of the drift and diffusion functions up to order two. You may prefer to model this information as a struct or as a class (for example, you could use the *Decorator* design pattern in conjunction with the SDE class hierarchy in Chapter 0).
   Create a separate function for each scheme; the function uses the information in the namespace and should create one path (the output is a vector).
   (b) Test the code by comparing the solutions produced with the exact solution (0.11) of the constant-coefficient case of the SDE (0.9), Chapter 0. Choose the coefficients of drift and diffusion to be in a range [a, b], where a is 'small' and b is 'large'. In this way we wish to model stiff problems.

(c) Test the accuracy of the schemes when applied to the CEV model in section 3.10. Use various values of the elasticity factor (use the input values in section 3.10.5).
(d) Integrate the schemes into the object-oriented framework in Chapter 0 by creating a new class for each scheme (see section 0.8).
(e) Test the framework by running the examples in part (b) again.

Foundations of the Monte Carlo Method

If you have to simulate, simulate often, but not too often

7.1 INTRODUCTION AND OBJECTIVES

The No-Arbitrage theory gives us the opportunity to derive option prices by computing the expectation of their payoffs with respect to the risk-neutral measure, see for example Boyle, Broadie and Glasserman (1997) or Musiela and Rutkowski (2004). If we denote this expectation by $\mathbb{E}$ and the asset price dynamics by the stochastic process defined on a given probability space $(\Omega, \mathcal{F}, \mathbb{P})$:

$$S : [0, T] \times \Omega \to \mathbb{R} \, (t, \omega) \mapsto S(t, \omega)$$

We write $(S(t))_{t \in [0,T]}$ as shorthand for this stochastic process because this is the standard notation in probability theory. The value of the option with payoff function h, possibly depending on the spot price of the asset at several time points in the interval $[0, T]$, is

$$\mathbb{E}[h(S(t_1), \ldots, S(t_N))], \quad t_1, \ldots, t_n \in [0, T] \tag{7.1}$$

Computing the expectation is equivalent to the evaluation of an integral with respect to a given probability measure. To this end, we can apply *Monte Carlo simulation*. The Monte Carlo method uses probabilistic, geometric and analytic methods to compute an approximation for the integral expression (7.1). The approximation is known as the *Monte Carlo Estimator*.

We give a brief introduction to the mathematics of Monte Carlo simulation and the concepts behind it. Here we discuss the probabilistic theory in a financial setting.

In section 7.2 we introduce the mathematical concepts and we discuss the *Laws of Large Numbers* in section 7.3. Section 7.4 introduces the *Central Limit Theorem* and gives its application to problems from quantitative finance, especially error estimates for the Monte Carlo estimator. In financial applications there is yet another version of the Monte Carlo method called *Quasi Monte Carlo simulation*. We also discuss this method and describe the theory behind it.

7.2 BASIC PROBABILITY

We recall some definitions from Chapter 1 and add useful definitions. First, we consider a family $(X_t)_{t \in \mathbb{R}^+}$ of random variables on a probability space $(\Omega, \mathcal{P}, \mathcal{F})$. A stochastic process can either be seen as a collection of distributions $(F_{X_t})_t$ of the random variables $(X_t)_t$ or as a mapping $t \mapsto X_t(\omega)$ for fixed $\omega \in \Omega$. In the latter case we call $X_.(\omega)$ a path.

To further explore stochastic processes, especially regarding the index set as time, we have to take care of the information content available in the market and its evolution. Describing the revelation of information with mathematical rigour we need the notion of a *filtration*. A filtration $(\mathcal{F}_t)_t$ is a collection of σ-algebras such that $\mathcal{F}_s \subset \mathcal{F}_t \subset \mathcal{F}, s \leq t$.

The σ-algebra $\mathcal{F}_t$ can be seen as the information available up to time t.

A probability space together with a filtration is called *filtered probability space*. We can then distinguish information currently available in the market from that which is still a possible scenario and therefore random. All this leads to studying *non-anticipating* processes. For a given filtration $(\mathcal{F}_t)_t$, that is an information structure, such a process is called *adapted* to the filtration if X_t is $\mathcal{F}_t$-measurable.

An important property of a stochastic process is the *martingale property*. If the process $(X_t)_t$ possesses this property the best prediction of the future value of X_t at time $s < t$, denoted by $\mathbb{E}[X_t|X_s]$, is the present value X_s. In finance this property plays an important rôle since the *No-Arbitrage Theory* is based on this concept and allows prices of derivative products to be computed as expectations and therefore we can use methods such as Monte Carlo simulation to compute it.

In the following we give two examples for stochastic processes. The examples serve as prototypes of different stochastic movement.

7.3   THE LAW OF LARGE NUMBERS

How can we apply probabilistic concepts to compute the value of integrals? To illustrate the link between these concepts we consider a simple integral given by

$$\int_0^1 f(x)dx \tag{7.2}$$

We consider a sequence of random variables U_i that are identically distributed with $U_i \sim \mathcal{U}(0, 1)$. Then, we hope that the estimator given by

$$\hat{I}_n(f) := \frac{1}{n}\sum_{i=1}^n f(U_i) \tag{7.3}$$

approximates the integral (7.2) in some sense.

That this is really the case is a result from probability theory known as the *Law of Large Numbers*. It states that the sum (7.3) converges to the expression (7.2) with probability one. For example, we can evaluate the integral $\int_0^1 \cos(x)dx$. Figure 7.1 shows the convergence of the approximation using Monte Carlo simulation in this case.

In the financial setting we use another formulation. We take $N \in \mathbb{N}$ simulated trajectories denoted by $S_i, i = 1, \ldots, N$. We evaluate the payoff function V on each of the trajectories and obtain a sequence of payoffs $V_i := (V(S_i))$. The random variables $(V_i)_{i=1,\ldots,N}$ are independent and identically distributed with expectation $\mathbb{E}[V(S_i)] = V_0$ for all $i = 1, 2, \ldots, N$. We then have

$$\mathbb{P}\left[\lim_{N \to \infty} \frac{1}{N}\sum_{i=1}^N V_i\right] = 1 \tag{7.4}$$

This implies that with probability 1 the value of the estimator

$$\hat{V}_N := \frac{1}{N}\sum_{i=1}^N V_i \tag{7.5}$$

converges to the current value of the option, which is V_0.

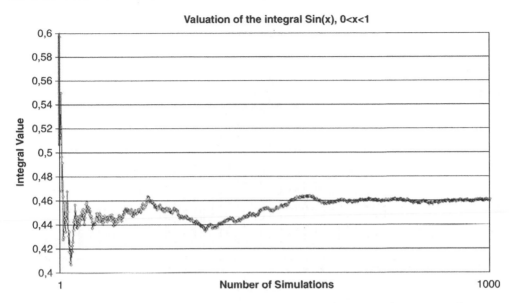

Figure 7.1 The figure shows the convergence to the true value which is $\text{Cos}(0) - \text{Cos}(1) = 0.45969769413186$ using equation (7.3)

We can numerically test the result for functions such as *sin*, *cos*, *sqrt* or *exp* by using the following piece of C++ code:

```
//Init a random generator
PseudoRandGen<MersenneTwister> rangenerator_Func(234567);
//Generate a vector of uniforms
rangenerator_Func.GenerateUniformsVector(Func_Samples);
//Use them to evaluate the integral
for(long i = Func_Samples.MinIndex(); i <= Func_Samples.MaxIndex();
    i++)
    MC_Estimator += exp(Func_Samples[i]);
    MC_Estimator /= number_of_samples;
```

The reader can change the functions to test the Monte Carlo integration method.

7.4   THE CENTRAL LIMIT THEOREM

If we wish to apply the Monte Carlo method we need some kind of criteria for when to abort the simulation. The law of large numbers does not yield any information on when to stop it.

To see this we take the sequence $(V_i)_{i=1,\ldots,N}$ of independent, identically distributed random variables with $\mathbb{E}[V_i^2] = \sigma^2 < \infty, i = 1, \ldots$. For example, each of the random variables can be a payoff function h applied to a sample X. As above, we denote by $\hat{S}_n$ the estimator of the arithmetic average of the first n outcomes. We denote by V_0 the expectation $\mathbb{E}[V_i]$ which is the same for all V_i as well as the variance denoted by $\sigma^2 = \mathbb{V}[V_1]$. The convergence speed of

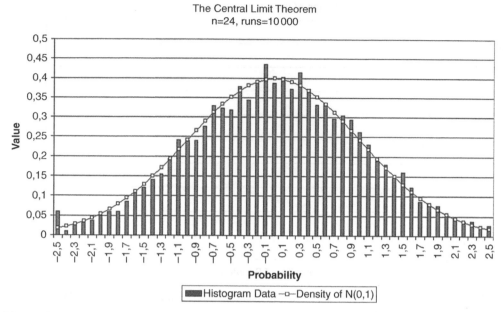

Figure 7.2 Equation (7.6) for $n = 24$ and $10\,000$ runs to create a histogram

the estimator $\hat{V}_n$ is determined by its variance $\sigma_{\hat{V}_n}$. We have

$$\hat{V}_n := \frac{\hat{S}_n - V_0}{\sigma/\sqrt{n}} \rightarrow \mathcal{N}(0, 1) \text{ as } n \rightarrow \infty \tag{7.6}$$

This result is known as the *Central Limit Theorem* in the Feller-Lévy version and it states that for rescaled independent identically distributed random variables the limiting distribution is the standard normal.

To come back to our example (7.2) we could use

$$\hat{\sigma}_n := \sqrt{\left(\frac{1}{n-1} \sum_{i=1}^{n} (V_i - \hat{V}_n) \right)^2} \tag{7.7}$$

as the sample standard deviation and the discussion below to derive a criterion for the quality of our estimate.

Figure 7.2 shows the convergence of the estimator to that of a normal variable.

7.4.1 Lindeberg-Feller Central Limit Theorem

The Feller-Lévy version of the Central Limit Theorem is the basic form of the Central Limit Theorem. This version has been extended in several ways. One result, the Lindeberg-Feller version of the Central Limit Theorem, is widely applied in financial mathematics. Therefore, we give this result here.

Let $(V_i)_i$ be independent random variables with $\mu_i := \mathbb{E}[V_i]$ and $\sigma_i^2 := \mathbb{V}[V_i] \leq +\infty$. If we denote $s_N^2 = \sigma_1^2 + \ldots + \sigma_N^2$ and for $\epsilon > 0$ the following relation holds:

$$\lim_{N \to \infty} \frac{1}{s_N^2} \sum_{n=1}^{N} \int_{\{|X_n - \mu_n| \in s_N\}} (X_n - \mu_n)^2 \, d\mathbb{P} = 0 \tag{7.8}$$

Then, we have

$$\frac{1}{s_N} \sum_{n=1}^{N} (V_n - \mu_n) \longrightarrow \mathcal{N}(0, 1) \tag{7.9}$$

Equation (7.8) is known as the Lindeberg criterium.

7.4.2   Explicit calculations of the confidence intervals

We choose a confidence level α, $\alpha \in (0, 1)$ such that the true value of V_0 lies within the interval $[L(\alpha, S), R(\alpha, S)]$ with probability $1 - \alpha$. The latter notation indicates that the left and the right boundary depend on the chosen α and on the random variable S. This interval is called the *confidence interval* and we denote it by I_α. It is a random interval characterised by

$$\mathbb{P}[I_\alpha] = 1 - \alpha$$

But if $h(X)$ is replaced by a realisation x of X the interval $[L(h(x)), U(h(x))]$ is a real interval. From the Tschebyshev inequality, which relates the probability to the variance, we guess that smaller values for the variance $\mathbb{V}[\cdot]$ improve the estimate of V_0. In our setting this inequality is

$$\mathbb{P}\left[\left|\hat{V}_n - V_0\right| \geq k\right] \leq \frac{\mathbb{V}\left[\hat{V}_n - V_0\right]}{k^2}$$

and therefore assures that the width of the confidence interval is reduced as a function of the number of simulations. This inequality cannot be used in practice to construct confidence intervals and is of theoretical interest only. To construct confidence intervals we use the central limit theorem.

To state this theorem let $z_{1-\alpha/2}$ denote the α-quantile of the $\mathcal{N}(0, 1)$-distribution:

$$P_{\mathcal{N}}(-z_{1-\alpha/2} \leq Z \leq z_{1-\alpha/2}) = 1 - \alpha$$

We now compute the quantiles for the normal distribution in C++. To this end we define two doubles `quantile = 0.9` and `quantile_step = 0.01`. The value 0.9 indicates that we start the calculation for the 90%-quantile and step 1% forward. The code for computing is

```
double quantile = 0.9; //specify the quantile
double quantile_step = 0.01; //the stepping in quantile
for(long i = 1; i $<=$ 10; ++i)
{
    result = InverseCumulativeNormal(quantile);
    cout << quantile * 100 << "\%-quantile= " << result << endl;
    quantile += quantile_step;
}
```

The confidence interval is now determined as follows:

$$\mathbb{P}_{\mathcal{N}}\left[-z_{1-\alpha/2} \le \frac{\sqrt{n}\left(\hat{V}_n - V_0\right)}{\sigma} \le z_{1-\alpha/2}\right] \approx 1 - \alpha$$

$$\mathbb{P}_{\mathcal{N}}\left[-z_{1-\alpha/2}\frac{\sigma}{\sqrt{n}} \le \hat{V}_n - V_0 \le z_{1-\alpha/2}\frac{\sigma}{\sqrt{n}}\right] \approx 1 - \alpha$$

$$\mathbb{P}_{\mathcal{N}}\left[\hat{V}_n - z_{1-\alpha/2}\frac{\sigma}{\sqrt{n}} \le V_0 \le \hat{V}_n + z_{1-\alpha/2}\frac{\sigma}{\sqrt{n}}\right] \approx 1 - \alpha$$

Thus, the confidence interval I_α is given by

$$I_\alpha = \left[\hat{V}_n - z_{1-\alpha/2}\frac{\sigma}{\sqrt{n}}, \hat{V}_n + z_{1-\alpha/2}\frac{\sigma}{\sqrt{n}}\right]$$

In general we do not know the standard deviation σ used to construct I_α. To overcome this difficulty we use the sampled standard deviation given by equation (7.7). Then, the confidence interval becomes

$$I_\alpha = \left[\hat{V}_n - z_{1-\alpha/2}\frac{\hat{\sigma}_n}{\sqrt{n}}, \hat{V}_n + z_{1-\alpha/2}\frac{\hat{\sigma}_n}{\sqrt{n}}\right]$$

In fact, when using the estimated standard deviation, we find that

$$\frac{\hat{V}_n - \mu}{\hat{\sigma}_n/\sqrt{n}} \sim t_{n-1}$$

has t-distribution with $n - 1$ degrees of freedom. According to this fact we have to replace the quantile $z_{1-\alpha/2}$ by the quantile of the t-distribution; that is

$$I_\alpha = \left[\hat{V}_n - t_{n-1,\alpha/2}\frac{\hat{\sigma}_n}{\sqrt{n}}, \hat{V}_n + t_{n-1,\alpha/2}\frac{\hat{\sigma}_n}{\sqrt{n}}\right]$$

In the sequel we use the normal quantile as a good approximation. The real value V_0 lies within I_α with probability $1 - \frac{\alpha}{2}$.

Let us briefly discuss some properties of I_α. The total width of the interval is given by

$$\frac{2z_{1-\alpha/2}\hat{\sigma}_n}{\sqrt{n}}$$

Therefore, the width does depend on α, n and $\hat{\sigma}_n$. For a fixed α by increasing the number of simulations we get smaller intervals and therefore more accurate estimates of V_0. Since length $(I_\alpha) \propto \frac{1}{\sqrt{n}}$ it follows that decreasing the length of I_α by $1/2$ the number of simulations has to be increased by a factor 4. It can be shown that it is the symmetric interval which has the smallest width.

We remark that there is a possibility to reduce the error for our simulation by reducing the variance of the problem. Such methods are called *Variance Reduction Methods*. We come back to such methods when discussing option pricing problems.

7.5   QUASI MONTE CARLO METHODS

The discussion up to now has shown how we can use probabilistic concepts to compute integrals. Using the central limit theorem it is possible to determine the convergence behaviour of the estimator. A closer look at the result shows that we derive an averaged error using probabilistic methods. There is another approach to this topic that leads to higher order convergence. This is known as *Quasi Monte Carlo simulation*. The aim of Quasi Monte Carlo methods is to use number sequences called *Low discrepancy numbers* together with a numerical procedure to evaluate integrals. Mimicking randomness is not desired here, but rather using auto-correlation among the numbers to achieve tighter estimates in the sense of low variance. There are numerous algorithms for generating low discrepancy sequences. For quantitative finance the most relevant method is called the *Sobol* sequence. We give a short introduction to the construction in Chapter 22. The C++ code to generate Sobol numbers is provided on the CD.

In Quasi Monte Carlo simulation the averaged probabilistic error bound coming from the Central Limit Theorem is replaced by a deterministic bound based on the *Koksma-Hwlaka inequality*.

The Koksma-Hwlaka inequality is the theoretical underpinning of the method. Let d denote the dimension. For a continuous function f, $f : [0, 1]^d \to \mathbb{R}$ with finite variation on $[0, 1]^d$ and a sequence $\xi = (\xi_n)_{n \in \mathbb{N}}$ in $[0, 1]^d$ we have for any $n > 0$

$$\left| \int_{[0,1]^d} f(x)dx - \frac{1}{n} \sum_{j=1}^{n} f(\xi_n) \right| \leq V(f)D_{\infty}^*(\xi, n) \tag{7.10}$$

$V(f)$ denotes the variation of f in the sense of Hardy and Krause. Since we do not need this concept we do not give the definition here. $D_{\infty}^*(\xi, n)$ is known as the $*$-discrepancy. Formally, $*$-discrepancy is defined for a sequence ξ_i, $i = 1, \ldots, N$ taking values in the d-dimensional set $[0, 1]^d$. For a given number $p = 1, 2, \ldots, \infty$ and a vector $\underline{x} \in [0, 1]^d$ we define the $*$-discrepancy by

$$D_p(\xi, N) = \left\| \frac{1}{N} \sum_{k=1}^{N} \prod_{1}^{d} 1_{\{\xi_{k,i} \leq \underline{x}_i\}} - \prod_{i=1}^{d} \underline{x}_i \right\|_p$$

Let us comment on this result:

- The bound given by equation (7.10) is a deterministic bound. It is strict.
- The $*$-discrepancy as well as the Hardy-Krause variation are hard to compute in general. Therefore, the bound is not easy to obtain.
- In cases where the variation and the $*$-discrepancy are known, the bound grossly overestimates the true error.
- The condition of the variation that must be bounded is very restrictive.

This method has been successfully applied to financial engineering applications as the examples in Acworth, Broadie and Glasserman (1998), Berman (1997), Paskov (1997) or Boyle, Broadie and Glasserman (1997) show. These authors found that Quasi Monte Carlo methods outperform simple Monte Carlo methods even for a small number of simulations.

We now discuss the upper bound of equation (7.10) and the notions of variation and $*$-discrepancy. Under certain smoothness conditions on the integrand f it can be shown that certain number sequences taken as an input to our Monte Carlo procedure lead to convergence estimates to be bounded by

$$c(d)\frac{\ln(N)^d}{N} = O\left(\frac{\ln(N)^d}{N}\right) \tag{7.11}$$

The constant $c(d)$ depends on the dimension and therefore we use the notion 'O()' to indicate that the bound is controlled by the notion in brackets. A function $f(x)$ is $O(g(x))$ with respect to another function $g(x)$ if there exist positive numbers c and d such that

$$f(x) \leq cg(x) \text{ for all } x \geq d$$

The error bound mainly depends on the discrepancy and therefore on the used number sequence and it is a theoretical worst case bound. Deriving error bounds in practice is useless, for example, because taking $d = 50$ and $N = 10000$ we find $\ln(N)^d/N = 6.6279$. For many financial problems it has been shown empirically that the error bound is of order $1/N$, see Paskov and Traub (1995), Paskov (1997) or Radovic, Sobol and Tichy (1996). This depends on a mathematical concept called *effective dimension*. Problems where the effective dimension is low can be approximated using Quasi Monte Carlo simulation with an error of order close to $1/N$. We refer to Wang and Fang (2003) for a discussion of effective dimension and the references therein.

Low discrepancy sequences are constructed such that the integral estimator is close to the integral to be approximated. Let $d \geq 2$ and $\xi = (\xi_n)_{n\in\mathbb{N}}$ be a sequence in $[0, 1]^d$. One can show that for every $n \geq 1$

$$D_\infty^*(\xi, n) \geq D_2^*(\xi, n) \geq c(d)\frac{\ln(n)^{\frac{d-1}{2}}}{n} \tag{7.12}$$

where $c(d)$ is a constant depending only on d. By taking the logarithm to base 2 we get $c(d) = \frac{1}{4^{d+2}(d-1)^{(d-1)/2}}$.

This implies that for infinitely many n

$$D_\infty^*(\xi, n) \geq c'(d)\frac{\ln(n)^{d/2}}{n} \tag{7.13}$$

where $c'(d)$ is a constant depending only on d. This is the worst case bound from the Koksma-Hwlaka inequality and shows that the bound is indeed determined by the $*$-discrepancy and therefore by the number sequence.

We now study how the concept of discrepancy is related to geometry and probability theory.

7.5.1 Uniform distribution and its geometric interpretation

To understand the Quasi Monte Carlo method let us first give a geometrical interpretation in the case of the uniform distribution.

A sequence $\xi = (\xi_n)_{n\in\mathbb{N}}$ in $[0, 1]^d$ is called uniformly distributed in $[0, 1]^d$ if for every $x = (x_1, \ldots, x_d) \in [0, 1]^d$

$$\lim_{n\to\infty} \frac{1}{n} \sum_{k=1}^{n} \prod_{i=1}^{d} 1_{\{\xi_{k,i} \leq x_i\}} = \text{Volume}\left(\prod_{i=1}^{d}[0, x_i]\right) = \prod_{i=1}^{d} x_i \tag{7.14}$$

This equation suggests that the number of points of the sequence ξ lying in the box with upper right endpoint x converges to the volume of the corresponding box.

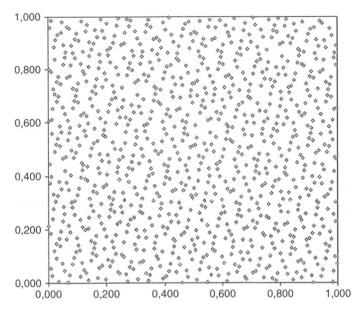

Figure 7.3 The figure shows a slice for the Halton sequence using base 2 and 7

For illustration purposes we give an example (Figure 7.3) by computing $n = 100, 500$ and 1000 points from a two-dimensional Halton sequence and compare the area of a rectangle, right-hand side of (7.14), and the counted Halton numbers lying within the rectangle, left-hand side of (7.14), see Chapter 22 for details.

Discrepancy

Discrepancy can be seen as a measure of how inhomogeneously a sequence of d-dimensional vectors ξ_n is distributed in the unit hypercube.

Discrepancies are used as measures of distance of number sequences to uniformly distributed numbers.

We use the $*$-discrepancy. Let $1 \le p \le \infty$ and define

$$D_p^*(\xi, n) = \left\| \frac{1}{n} \sum_{k=1}^n \prod_{i=1}^d 1_{\{\xi_n^i \le x^i\}} - \left(\prod_{i=1}^d x^i \right) \right\|_{L^p(dx)} \tag{7.15}$$

$$= \int \ldots \int \left(\frac{1}{n} \sum_{k=1}^n \prod_{i=1}^d 1_{\{\xi_n^i \le x^i\}} - \left(\prod_{i=1}^d x^i \right) \right)^p dx_1 \ldots dx_d \tag{7.16}$$

Therefore, $*$-discrepancy penalises the distance for the empirical discrepancy to the volume. To demystify the above definition we interpret the discrepancy in terms of a uniform distribution. The following statements are equivalent:

- The sequence ξ is uniformly distributed in $[0, 1]^d$.
- For every $p \in [1, \infty]$, $D_p^*(\xi, n) \to 0$ as $n \to \infty$.

- There exists $p \in [1, \infty]$ such that $D_p^*(\xi, n) \to 0$ as $n \to \infty$.
- Let δ_{ξ_j} denote the Dirac measure in ξ_j. Then, $\frac{1}{n} \sum_{j=1}^{n} \delta_{\xi_j}$ converges weakly to the volume element dx.

The evaluation procedure stays the same but there might be interaction between low discrepancy numbers and methods for computing variates due to given distributions. See for example the *Neave effect* explained in Jäckel (2005).

7.6 SUMMARY AND CONCLUSIONS

We have reviewed probabilistic concepts to motivate the main theory behind Monte Carlo simulation. The Laws of Large Numbers and the Central Limit Theorem give the underpinning of the practical application. We have shown how to use the theoretical results to obtain useful error bounds for the Monte Carlo estimator. This theory is applied by using the implementation of the C++ classes on the CD. Finally, we gave a short introduction to low discrepancy numbers and their properties as well as the relationship to simulation. Quasi Monte Carlo is a version of Monte Carlo simulation based on the concept of low discrepancy numbers. We give a detailed discussion and show how to implement Sobol numbers in Chapter 22. Now, we are prepared to study real life quantitative finance problems with the help of Monte Carlo methods.

   We have not touched on other relevant theory such as the theory of *Large Deviations* and *rare event simulation* which might lead to more sophisticated error bounds. This is beyond the scope of this book because our goal is to map the Monte Carlo method to C++ classes.

7.7 EXERCISES AND PROJECTS

1. (**) Bounds
   Let S be the number of ups in $1\,000\,000$ oberservations of daily stock prices. Use (a) Tchebycheff's inequatility and (b) the central limit theorem to estimate the probability that S lies between $490\,250$ and $500\,550$.
2. (**) Independence
   Suppose we choose 30 numbers independently from the interval [0, 1], using for example a random number generator. These variates are converted into variates with respect to a distribution having the densities given below. If we repeat this experiment 1500 times and plot the graph of the densities and a bar graph for the outcome of the experiment, how well does the normal fit?
   - $f(x) = 1$
   - $f(x) = 2x$
   - $f(x) = \exp(-x)$
   - $f(x) = 2 - 4|x - 0.5|$
3. (**) The Central Limit Theorem
   Examine why there is in fact a Student distribution for estimating the quantile and not a normal one.
4. (**) Discrepancy
   We want to explore discrepancy. To this end we can write C++ code to determine the discrepancy of the sequences determined by our random number generators given on the CD.

5. (**) Halton Sequences

We consider a d-dimensional setting. For dimension n choose the nth prime and denote it by p_n. Now, we proceed as follows for each draw i:
– Choose some integer $\gamma(i)$, for example we may choose $\gamma(i) = i$ for simplicity.
– Write $\gamma(i)$ in the base given by the prime p_n, $n = 1, \ldots, d$. This leads to coefficients a_k of

$$\gamma(i)_{\text{base } 10} = \gamma(i)_{\text{base } p_n} = \sum_{k=1}^{m_{i,n}} a_{k,n} p_n^{k-1}$$

Here, $m_{i,n}$ has to be chosen large enough to assure that all non-zero digits in the base p_n are accounted for and $a_{k,n} < p_n$.
– Construct the mth uniform u_{mn} for dimension n by transforming the sequence of coefficients using

$$u_{i,n} = \sum_{k=1}^{m_{i,n}} a_{k,n} p_n^{-k}$$

For example, we take $\gamma(i) := 15_{10}$ and the primes 2, 3 and 5:

15_p	Transform	Transform	$u_{n,i}$
1111_2	0.1111	$1 \cdot 2^{-1} + 1 \cdot 2^{-2} + 1 \cdot 2^{-3} + 1 \cdot 2^{-4}$	0.9375
120_3	0.021	$2 \cdot 3^{-1} + 1 \cdot 3^{-1}$	0.777778
30_5	0.03	$2 \cdot 5^{-2}$	0.08

Refer to the implementation on the CD and reproduce the example. Then, compute the Halton sequence for some big numbers of d. For example, choose $d = 100$. Randomly pick dimensions $d_1 \neq d_2 < d$. Plot the Halton sequences corresponding to dimension d_1 against those of d_2. What do you observe? Are Halton sequences likely to be used for Quasi Monte Carlo methods in high dimensions?

Part II
Design Patterns

8

Architectures and Frameworks for Monte Carlo Methods: Overview

8.1 GOALS OF PART II OF THIS BOOK

In this part of the book we discuss the design and implementation of the numerical methods that we introduced in Part I. In particular, we map numerical algorithms to code and each major mathematical concept will be realised by a C++ class. Furthermore, we introduce software modelling and design techniques that allow us to create flexible and maintainable Monte Carlo frameworks. To this end, we employ a number of techniques to analyse, design and implement complex software systems.

There are six chapters in this part of the book; each chapter deals with one aspect of the problem of translating higher-level *design blueprints* to more detailed ones. In general, our starting point is a description of a system that we wish to implement while the end result is a set of C++ classes that realise the requirements that the system should satisfy. The main steps are

1. Create the highest-level software architecture for the system (using *domain architectures* (Duffy, 2004b)): this chapter.
2. Detailed component design using system patterns (POSA, 1996): Chapter 9.
3. Detailed object design blueprints using design patterns (GOF, 1995): Chapter 10.
4. Translate the design blueprints to C++ code: Chapters 11 to 13.

In this way we show how we arrived at the running program based on a defined process. The reader can follow the steps in the process and we have provided hints, guidelines and exercises so that he or she can understand the design intent of the current framework. We create code at various levels of generality:

- '*get it working*' (here we focus on accuracy).
- '*get it right*' (here we focus on the problem at hand but we do pay some attention to maintainability and functionality issues).
- '*get it optimised*' (here we focus on creating a framework that can be used by clients without having to know all the internal details).

8.2 INTRODUCTION AND OBJECTIVES OF THIS CHAPTER

The main goals of this first chapter in Part II are to introduce techniques to help us decompose problems into simpler ones and having done that to create UML (Unified Modeling Language) diagrams to document what we have created. In particular, we approach the software development process as a series of activities.

One of the authors (see Duffy, 2004b) has discovered and documented a number of *domain architectures* that describe the structure and functionality of a range of applications. In fact, these are *metamodels* that function as 'cookie cutters' for specific applications:

- *Manufacturing Systems* (code MAN): These are systems that create finished products based on some 'raw' input data. Instance systems in the MAN category are compilers and computer aided design (CAD) applications. Another example is a system to create SDEs.
- *Resource Allocation and Tracking Systems* (code RAT): These systems process information, entities and objects by assigning them to resources. In fact, we schedule these entities by executing algorithms and informing client systems of the status of the success (or otherwise) of the execution of these algorithms. Instance systems in the RAT category track objects from entry point to exit point; between these two points the objects are modified in some way. Examples of RAT systems are helpdesk systems and real-time tracking systems. Another example is a system to compute numerical solutions of SDEs using the finite difference method.
- *Management Information Systems* (code MIS): These systems accept entities, data and objects from other server systems (usually of the RAT type). We aggregate these by applying *consolidation algorithms* to produce decision-support information. Instance systems in the MIS category include all kinds of reporting and decision-support systems in which we merge historical and operational data. An example is a portfolio risk management system. Another example is a Monte Carlo pricing and hedging engine.

We discuss these three categories and we use them to create a Monte Carlo framework. Finally, we mention that there are three other domain architecture types:

- *Process Control Systems* (code PCS): These systems monitor and control the values of certain critical parameters in a system. When a value crosses one or more thresholds action is taken to bring the system back to an acceptable state. Systems in this category include environment controllers (for example, home heating systems), exceptional reporting systems and systems for pricing and hedging barrier options, for example.
- *Access Control Systems* (code ACS): These are systems that allow clients to access resources and objects based on authentication and authorisation mechanisms. These systems are usually proxies to other systems.

(A discussion of these two categories is outside the scope of this book.)

- *Lifecycle Systems and Models* (code LCM): These *aggregate or composite* systems model the life of entities and objects from the time they are created to when they are no longer needed in the system. Thus, each LCM system has a MAN, RAT and MIS component. These components have well-defined responsibilities (we can view them as *black boxes*) and they (ideally) communicate with other systems using standardised interfaces.

8.3   THE ADVANTAGES OF DOMAIN ARCHITECTURES

We discovered and subsequently documented domain architectures after having worked on small, medium and large software systems. We classify systems based on a dominant core process, which by definition produces the main products, services and output that the system delivers to potential client systems. We now describe the products from MAN, RAT and MIS basic types that we introduced in section 8.2 (the other categories are described in Duffy, 2004b):

- *MAN*: Creates finished products and objects that potential client systems can use. The core process is one of *conversion* of raw data to usable data.
- *RAT*: These systems process objects (typically from MAN systems) and assign resources to them. These assigned objects are then planned, scheduled or executed in some way. The core process is one of knowing what the *status* of the assigned object is in time and space, or more generally in some multi-dimensional datastructure.
- *MIS*: We aggregate and merge many objects (typically from RAT systems) and we store these objects in *multi-dimensional data structures*. The product from MIS systems is typically a high-level data structure representing a *report* for use in decision-support systems.

We note that domain architectures give us guidelines on *what* a system should do. We do not become embroiled with low-level implementation details in the early stages of the software development process. This is in contrast to traditional object-oriented technology where the development process tends to begin with the discovery of classes and objects, the relationships between these entities (using inheritance, aggregation and association relationships, for example) as well as the discovery of member functions and interfaces. This approach can lead to networks of tightly-coupled classes that are difficult to maintain. In this chapter we are concerned with the *decomposition* of a given system into subsystems. In Chapters 9 and 10 we shall see how to *design* the subsystem using POSA system patterns (see POSA, 1996) and GOF class-level design patterns (see GOF, 1995), respectively. Having discovered which patterns to use we are then in a position to implement them using C++ classes and modules. The advantages of a software development process using system decomposition techniques are

- They allow us to *scope* the problem by forcing us to think about what the system should deliver. Furthermore, we are able to determine the *system context*; this describes the external systems that interact with the current *system under discussion* (the so-called SUD). Finally, we strive to pin down the interfaces between the SUD and the external systems as soon as possible.
- Having defined the boundaries of the SUD we decompose it using a number of architectural and design techniques, such as the *Whole-Part* and *Presentation-Abstraction-Control* (PAC) models that we shall introduce in Chapter 9.
- Identifying the SUD as an instance of a domain category or as an aggregate of a number of domain categories reduces the time it takes to decide what kind of system we are really trying to design.
- Developers can implement the models in an incremental fashion. There are different possible strategies but an important requirement is that the development team should be able to produce a working system (albeit a simple prototype) in the early phases of the software lifecycle.
- Domain architectures are a valuable cognitive tool for project managers and software architects. In general, we decompose a system into subsubsystems and an initial high-level analysis allows these stakeholders to determine how much effort is needed to implement each subsystem. Let us take an example, in this case a system S having subsystems S1, S2

and S3. We design four systems namely S, S1, S2 and S3 with each one having its own sets of responsibilities and interfaces. We give more specific examples of these systems in later chapters.

Based on a number of factors such as time-to-market, system risk and desired functionality, the project team can choose from a number of scenarios:

- *Scenario A*: Create a *scale model* in which we design a smaller system instead of the full system. We have seen an example of this in Chapter 0 where the system and subsystems were defined as follows:
  - S1: models a one-factor SDE.
  - S2: models the finite difference schemes using a *Visitor* pattern in combination with the *Template Method* pattern.
  - S3: the code that implements the Monte Carlo method. This code needs modules for random number generation, for example Box Muller, Mersenne Twister or lagged Fibonacci.
  - S: this is the system that integrates the subsystems S1, S2 and S3 and is an instance of the *Mediator* and *Whole-Part* patterns.

  The main requirements in this scenario are that the algorithms should be accurate and efficient. Finally, we adopt this incremental approach when developing new software; it is a low-risk process because we either get results in a week or the project runs into difficulties. Unforeseen problems will surface sooner rather than later.
- *Scenario B*: Having determined the inter-system interfaces (which we discover from Scenario A, for example) we then decompose S1, S2, S3 and possibly S into sub-components using the system patterns described in POSA (1996). The decision to use these patterns is determined by a number of requirements, such as:
  - R1: Suitability of the software for a range of products.
  - R2: Accuracy of the software algorithms.
  - R3: Interoperability with other systems.
  - R4: Security issues.
  - R5: Conformance and compliance with standards.
  - R6: Time and resource efficiency (performance).
  - R7: Different kinds of user interfaces supported.
  - R8: Separation of core application code from volatile user interface and driver code.
  - R9: Should our code be portable between different operating systems?
  - R10: Should the software system be maintainable?

  These are the main requirements that most software systems must satisfy. They tend to be major implicit assumptions held by the project stakeholders. Unfortunately, many of these requirements are resolved during the later implementation phase. Instead, we determine what the requirements are during the early stages of the software lifecycle and we then decide which patterns will realise these requirements. We discuss these requirements in more detail in Chapters 9 and 10 where we show how to implement them in software. Requirements R2 and R6 must be satisfied by many systems in computational finance.
- *Scenario C*: This is an (optional) optimisation step. In this case we develop extendible systems using system patterns such as the *Broker* and the *Blackboard* (see POSA, 1996) because we can add new systems (for example, a calibration engine) to them without destroying the stability of the SUD while at the same time we can model them as distributed or shared memory systems, thus allowing us to take advantage of hardware that supports

multi-threading and parallel programming models. For an introduction to the design of parallel programs using parallel design methods, see Mattson, Sanders and Massingill (2005). We introduce multi-threaded and parallel processing models in Chapters 24 and 25 of the current book.

8.4 SOFTWARE ARCHITECTURES FOR THE MONTE CARLO METHOD

In this section we describe the rationale for a proposed software architecture that can be customised to suit Monte Carlo applications. The main goal of this project is to produce a generic framework that allows us to price and hedge a range of equity derivatives. In the future we would expect the framework to be adapted to other financial applications such as interest rate and risk management products.

We design the system and we identify three major systems with each system having one major *responsibility*. The systems correspond to the most important activities in the framework. We call them

• Market Model Systems.
• Numerical Simulator Systems.
• Pricing, Hedge and Risk Systems.

We now describe each of these systems in more detail.

8.4.1 Market model systems

These systems are primarily of the *manufacturing* type and their responsibility is to create the equations and algorithms that model the underlying assets. In this book we use SDEs to model these assets and in particular we focus on SDEs driven by Geometric Brownian Motion (GBM). In Part III we extend the set of SDEs to those that model Poisson and Lévy processes.

When creating an SDE we need to address a number of issues:

• How to choose the most appropriate SDE model for the problem at hand.
• Having chosen an SDE model, determine how to initialise the data and functions that define the SDE.
• Determining how to present the SDE as a service (using programmatic interfaces) to potential clients, for example C++ classes that model the finite difference method.

We model and design this system in a number of ways. How we design the system is secondary to the services it delivers to clients; in this case, we have created a template class that is able to model a range of linear and nonlinear SDEs; the current version of the software in this book is

```
template <typename V, int N, int D> class SDE : public SdeThing
{ // Non-linear SDE; N is the number of independent variables and
  // D is the number of Brownian motions

private:
    //
```

```
public:
    SDE();
    SDE(const Range<V> range,
            const VectorSpace<V,N>& initial_condition);
    SDE(const SDE<V, N, D>& source);


    // Define components of the drift and diffusion functions
    void setDriftComponent (V (*fun) (V value,
            const VectorSpace<V,N>& arguments), int row);
    void setDiffusionComponent (V (*fun) (V value,
            const VectorSpace<V,N>& arguments),int row,
            int column);

    // Calculate drift and diffusion functions at a given time value
    const VectorSpace<V,N>& calculateDrift (V value,
            const VectorSpace<V,N>& arguments);
    const VectorSpace<V,N>& calculateDiffusion (V value,
            const VectorSpace<V,N>& arguments,
            const VectorSpace<V,D>& dW);

    // Calculate diffusion using Dynamic Vector<double, long>
    const VectorSpace<V,N>& calculateDiffusion (V value,
            const VectorSpace<V,N>& arguments,
            const Vector<V,long>& dW);

    const MatrixVectorSpace<V, N, D>&  calculateDiffusionMatrix(
        V value, const VectorSpace<V,N>& arguments);

    //

    // Selector functions
    const Range<V>& range() const;
    const VectorSpace<V,N>& startValue() const;

    // Extend functionality with Visitor pattern
    void Accept(SdeVisitor<V,N,D>& sv);


};
```

We may need to extend and adapt this class as new requirements emerge, for example when supporting jump processes. We can add new functionality with (we hope) minimal impact on the stability of the code by using object-oriented and generic programming techniques in combination with the appropriate software patterns. In this system the *Builder, Prototype, Whole-Part* and *Decorator* patterns play an important role. Please note that the functionality of the class SDE `<V,N,D>` can be extended by means of the *Visitor* pattern, as already discussed in Chapter 0.

8.4.2   Numerical simulator systems

These systems *associate* the SDEs with finite difference schemes. In particular, we calculate one or more *paths* of an SDE. A path contains information about the underlying asset in the interval $[0, T]$, where T is the expiry date. Depending on the kind of derivative being priced we may need information at certain discrete points in $[0, T]$, for example:

- For plain options we only need the value of the underlying at $t = T$.
- For path-dependent options we need the values over the life of the asset (for example, its average value or its maximum and minimum values in $[0, T]$).

We also must decide how to approximate the SDE. Some options are:

- By finding the exact solution (if possible).
- By finite difference schemes (weak and strong schemes).
- By other methods, for example Stochastic FEM (SFEM), Karhunen-Loeve methods.

In Chapter 0 we used a hierarchy of C++ classes that implements various finite difference methods. We used the *Visitor* pattern and we can easily extend it to support code for the computation of the exact solutions and for SFEM (Stochastic Finite Element Method); in these cases we implement each numerical scheme as a separate visitor class. The base class interface is

```
class OneFactorSDEVisitor
{
private:

public:
    // Constructors and Destructor
    OneFactorSDEVisitor() {}                    // Default constructor
    OneFactorSDEVisitor(const OneFactorSDEVisitor& source) {}
    virtual  OneFactorSDEVisitor() {}

    // The visit functions
    virtual void Visit(SDETypeA& sde)=0;    // Linear/linear

    // Type B and C are student exercises!

    //virtual void Visit(SDETypeB& sde)=0; // Linear/Nonlinear
    //virtual void Visit(SDETypeC& sde)=0; // Visit Nonlinear/linear
    virtual void Visit(SDETypeD& sde)=0;    // Nonlinear/Nonlinear


    // Operators
    OneFactorSDEVisitor& operator =
            (const OneFactorSDEVisitor& source) {}
};
```

The class of finite difference schemes is defined as follows (there are quite a few, the others can be found on the CD):

```
class FDMVisitor : public OneFactorSDEVisitor
{ // Base class for all schemes
```

```
private:

    // ...
public:
    FDMVisitor(long NSteps, const Range<double>& interval,
               double initialValue);
    FDMVisitor(long NSteps, const OneFactorSDE& sde);

    void SetRandomArray(const Vector<double,long>& randomArrray);

    virtual Vector<double, long> path() const;

    long getNumberOfSteps() const;
};

class ExplicitEuler : public FDMVisitor
{
public:
    ExplicitEuler(long NSteps, const Range<double>& interval,
                  double initialValue);
    ExplicitEuler(long NSteps, const OneFactorSDE& sde);

    void Visit(SDETypeA& sde);
    void Visit(SDETypeD& sde);
};

class SemiImplicitEuler : public FDMVisitor
{
public:
    SemiImplicitEuler(long NSteps, const Range<double>& interval,
                      double initialValue);
    SemiImplicitEuler(long NSteps, const OneFactorSDE& sde);

    void Visit(SDETypeA& sde);
    void Visit(SDETypeD& sde);

};
```

This code is the implementation of a *Visitor* pattern. In Monte Carlo systems we need several supporting software modules and classes for

- Mesh generation.
- Classes for dates, calendars, day count conventions.
- Random number generation.
- Compile-time and run-time vectors and matrices.

We implement each of these chunks of functionality as a dedicated C++ class or class hierarchy. Furthermore, each class has one major responsibility.

The main goal of the current system is to approximate the solution of SDEs by numerical schemes. The product (output) is typically a vector, matrix or some other data structure. The steps in the core process are

1. Register the SDE object for further processing; it may be necessary to transform it into some internal format.
2. Choose a finite difference scheme to approximate the SDE.
3. Determine the kind of desired path and then calculate this path.
4. Postprocess and present the path for use by client systems.

Client systems will need many paths and the current system should be designed for performance and accuracy.

8.4.3   Pricing, hedge and risk systems

These are the highest-level *management systems* and these are clients of the systems for path calculation. We have seen a simple example of these MIS systems in Part I; in these cases we created a large number of paths, calculated the payoff for each corresponding path, then we discounted the averaged value. The main goal of the current system is to aggregate and to consolidate the numeric data from the *Numerical Simulator Systems* to produce high-level decision-support and reporting data. We summarise some of the features that we implement in this book:

• Pricing one-factor and *n*-factor vanilla options.
• Pricing options with early exercise features.
• Calculating option sensitivities (delta, gamma and theta, for example).

The main activities in the core process for this system are

1. Register all necessary path information; filter the relevant information for your application.
2. Determine which *merging* and *consolidation* algorithms to use, then execute them and store the results in the *permanent/historical database*.
3. Provide interfaces so that clients can access the decision-support data that they need.

At this level we would expect the software to be integrated with Excel, for example. We discuss C++ and Excel integration in Chapter 27.

As already stated, we have given a special case of the above framework in Chapter 0. In that case we created a class hierarchy representing various finite difference schemes using the *Visitor* pattern. Finally, we aggregated the classes for SDEs, FD schemes and random number generators using a *Whole-Part* structural pattern that subsequently played the role of *Mediator* between the subsystems.

What are the most important requirements for this software system? To answer this question, we need to know who the system stakeholders are. First, we have the group of quant analysts and developers who create, design and implement new models. The algorithms and the related data must be *accurate*. Second, the software system should be *suitable* for a wide spectrum of users and hence it must offer them sufficient *functionality*. The code should also be *maintainable* and *understandable* for the benefit of model validators and those quants who extend and support the software system. And the resulting code should be efficient.

We summarise the relationships between the three systems as an UML component diagram (Figure 8.1).

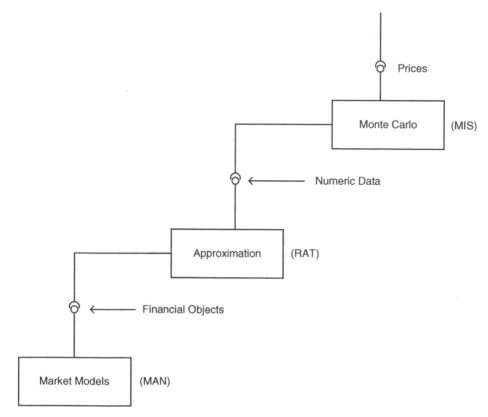

Figure 8.1   Generic model for the Monte Carlo method

8.5   SUMMARY AND CONCLUSIONS

In this chapter we discussed the major architectural issues that we address when developing systems for the Monte Carlo method. We identified three subsystems called the *Market Data Model* (the SDEs in question), the *Numerical Simulator Systems* (in the main, the finite difference schemes that approximate the solutions of the SDEs) and the *Monte Carlo* (the management system that calculates the option price). We examined the responsibilities of each of these systems and the core process in each one.

In the following chapters we shall discuss how to design these systems at ever-increasing levels of detail. In particular, we model the system depicted in Figure 8.1 using the Unified Modeling Language (UML) in combination with POSA and GOF patterns. In Chapter 24 we examine this figure in more detail.

Figure 8.2 is a concept map for the methods and techniques that we describe in the later chapters. We identify three major stages in the development process; first, we determine which domain architecture or category a given system is an instance of; second, we decompose the system into smaller subsystems using POSA patterns, and finally we design and implement the subsystems using the GOF patterns that we introduce in Chapters 10–13. These are proven technologies and we shall see that using them leads to flexible and maintainable software

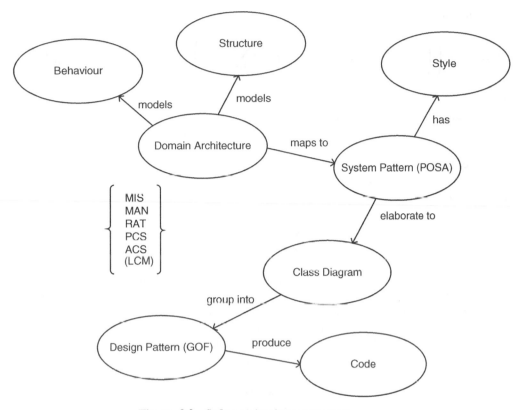

Figure 8.2 Software development process

systems. We shall see that system decomposition is not a luxury but essential when we write multi-threaded applications. We discuss this topic in Chapters 24 and 25.

8.6   EXERCISES AND PROJECTS

1. (****) Monte Carlo Method for Claims on Many Underlying Stocks

   We consider the problem of pricing a derivative that is contingent on a number of underlying assets. In general we will be given a payoff function and we use Monte Carlo simulation techniques to calculate asset prices and discount the averaged payoff function (Glasserman, 2004, page 104; Benth, 2004, page 106). We describe the sequence of steps to calculate the price of the derivative:

   – We calculate a matrix of standard normal numbers; it has $n \times N$ elements where n is the number of underlying assets and N is the number of simulations (or draws):

$$(y_1^1, y_2^1, \ldots, y_n^1), \ldots, (y_1^N, y_2^N, \ldots, y_n^N)$$

   where

$$y_j^k \sim N(0, 1), \quad j = 1, \ldots, n, \quad k = 1, \ldots, N$$

– We define the paths:

$$s_i^k = x_i \exp\left(\left(r - \frac{1}{2}\sum_{j=1}^{n}\sigma_{ij}^2\right)(T-t) + \sqrt{T-t}\sum_{j=1}^{n}\sigma_{ij}y_j^k\right), i = 1,\ldots,n, k = 1,\ldots,N$$

where

x_i = value of underlyings at time $t, i = 1,\ldots,n$
s_i^k = value of underlying at time $T, i = 1,\ldots,n, k = 1,\ldots,N$
T = expiry
r = interest rate
$\Sigma = (\sigma_{ij})_{\substack{1 \le i \le n \\ 1 \le j \le n}}$ is the volatility matrix
– Calculate the price given by

$$e^{-r(T-t)}\frac{1}{N}\sum_{k=1}^{N}h(s_1^k, s_2^k, \ldots, s_n^k)$$

where h is a real-valued function of n variables that represents the payoff function. Answer the following questions:

(a) Describe this problem in terms of the architectures as described in section 8.4 and summarised in Figure 8.1. Pay particular attention to the identification of the instances of MAN, RAT and MIS categories and the specification of the interfaces between the systems. In particular, determine the data that is produced and used by the various subsystems in the current application.

(b) Which of the requirements R1 to R10 in section 8.3 would you realise first if you were to create a software prototype in C++ for this problem?

(c) Which design patterns, libraries and classes would you need for (i) random number generation, (ii) Cholesky decomposition, (iii) payoff class hierarchy and (iv) data structures (for example, matrices and vectors)? How long would it take to develop them?

2. (****) Domain Architectures and some Common Finance Applications
In this exercise we wish to categorise a specific application. At this stage we concentrate on the *core process* that is defined by the following characteristics: (i) the products, data or services that the application delivers to potential client systems, (ii) the input data that is needed by the application and (iii) the sequence of steps or activities that we need to execute in order to produce output from input.

The problem is to apply a random walk in a partial differential equation (PDE) setting. We scope the problem by examining the time-independent *convection-diffusion equation*:

$$\frac{\partial^2 u}{\partial x^2} + \frac{\partial^2 u}{\partial y^2} + \alpha_1 \frac{\partial u}{\partial x} + \alpha_2 \frac{\partial u}{\partial y} = 0 \tag{8.1}$$

defined in the unit rectangle $R = (0, 1) \times (0, 1)$ and *Dirichlet* boundary conditions given on the boundary of R, that is the solution of equation (8.1) is a known function on the boundary. We find the solution of the boundary value problem for equation (8.1) at special *hot spots*; this is in contrast to finite difference schemes where an approximate solution is found at many points in the rectangle R. The steps are
1. Create a mesh of discrete points in the rectangle.
2. Approximate the derivatives in equation (8.1) by divided differences.

3. Choose the point P where we wish to approximate the solution of the boundary value problem.

4. Construct a random walk procedure starting at P to calculate the solution (Klahr, 1960).

Answer the following questions:

(a) What is the core process for this application?

(b) Determine the subsystems in the current problem, their responsibilities and the data that they exchange with each other.

(c) Create a simple prototype in C++.

9

System Decomposition and
System Patterns

9.1 INTRODUCTION AND OBJECTIVES

In this chapter we refine the high-level components that we discovered from the architectural models in Chapter 8. We elaborate these components before we commence with a detailed design and implementation of the system under consideration. The process in this chapter is one of *recursive decomposition*. This term refers to the fact that we partition a component into smaller, more dedicated components. We are also interested in the interaction *between* components at this stage and we are not yet interested in the design of their internals (this latter topic will be dealt with in Chapters 10–12).

When do we stop with the decomposition process? There are several possible answers to this question. One answer is that we stop when it becomes *obvious* (in some sense) on how to proceed to detailed design and implementation. In many cases we will be able to use system and design patterns (see POSA, 1996; GOF, 1995).

9.2 SOFTWARE DEVELOPMENT PROCESS; A CRITIQUE

Before we discuss software design methods and patterns, we look at some work practices that we have used and that we have replaced with more robust ones. We focus on the influence that the object-oriented programming (OOP) model has had on how developers think about software and the creation of software products.

The main problem is that the object-oriented paradigm is not a suitable cognitive technique for analysing and partitioning complex systems in the early stages of the software development process. Instead, we need to disassociate ourselves from the member data/member function mindset in these stages of software development. However, during detailed design and implementation, the application of the object-oriented paradigm *will* be useful. Detailed design is the subject of the following chapters in Part II.

9.3 SYSTEM DECOMPOSITION, FROM CONCEPT TO CODE

We give an overview of the process of developing software systems and frameworks for the Monte Carlo method. We restrict the scope to problems that involve the pricing of derivatives using the finite difference method, random number generators, stochastic differential equations and Monte Carlo simulators. The software techniques are applicable to large, medium and small systems. The sources for the current chapter are POSA (1996), GOF (1995) and Duffy (2004b).

9.3.1 Phases

We identify several phases when developing software systems. Each phase consists of a number of activities to help the developer discover, model and document software products. We start with general and high-level requirements and we progressively map these to more detailed design blueprints and then to C++ classes. In general we are assuming that a software system – which we call the *System Under Discussion* (SUD) – is to be designed and implemented. The phases are:

- *System Decomposition*: We partition the SUD into loosely-coupled subsystems as shown in Figure 9.1(a). Each subsystem has one major responsibility and it cooperates with the SUD and with the other subsystems to satisfy system requirements. This phase is also known as *Architectural Design* and we use a number of the partitioning techniques as described in Duffy (2004b).
- *Component Discovery and Component Diagrams*: We map subsystems to more concrete entities called *components*. A component is an entity that realises the behaviour of a system by *providing services* to other components while at the same time *requiring services* from other components. These relationships are described by the de-facto standard UML *ball-and-socket* notation as shown in Figure 9.1(b); the ball represents service provision while the socket corresponds to the service requirement aspect. A component can be partitioned into lower-level components, each one having its own interfaces. This phase is also known as *Logical Design*.

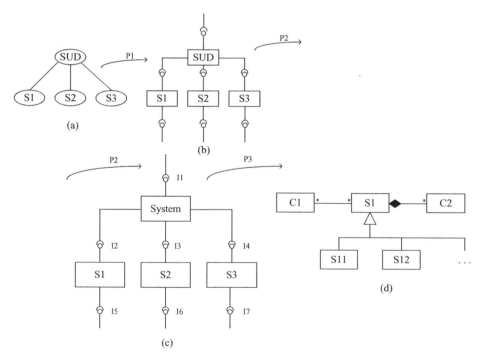

Figure 9.1 Phases in system decomposition from concept map to class diagram: (a) initial system decomposition as a concept map; (b) systems and responsibilities; (c) component diagram with detailed interfaces; (d) class diagrams and detailed design

- *Class and Interface Discovery*: In this phase we discover and document the *interfaces* between the components from Figure 9.1(b) and we decide how to implement these interfaces using classes and the associated modelling techniques such as *aggregation* and *inheritance*. An interface is similar to an abstract class; it consists solely of abstract methods. It is a pure specification.

An example of an interface in C++ that models essential one-factor derivative functionality is

```
class IDerivative
{
public:
        virtual double price(double S) const = 0;
        virtual double delta(double S) const = 0;
};
```

In applications, we implement these functions using a combination of inheritance (*provides* interface) and composition (*requires* interface), for example:

```
class OneFactorOption : public IDerivative
{ // Implementing an interface
public:
        double price(double S) const  { // code }
        double delta(double S) const  { // code }
};
```

The following code is an example of the *requires* interface, in this case a given class has a pointer to the interface IDerivative:

```
class Client
{ // Client requires services
private:
        IDerivative* impl;
public:
        double calculate (double S)
        {
                //
                return impl -> price(S);
        }
};
```

Thus, the above code is one way of implementing the *ball-and-socket notation* from Figure 9.1(b) and in Figure 9.1(c) where the discovered interfaces are shown as annotation near the appropriate ball-and-socket symbol. In Chapter 11 we shall see how to implement this functionality using templates (the so-called *policy-based design*) (Alexandrescu, 2001). It is in this phase that we discover and apply the GOF design patterns. They allow us to satisfy certain requirements in the software framework. For example, the following requirements must be satisfied in Monte Carlo software programs:

- *Accuracy*: The program should give correct and expected results. In this case computed option prices must be accurate, for example.

- *Suitability*: It must be possible to customise the framework to suit a wide range of products. For example, even though the framework focuses on equities it can be adapted to other models such as the Libor Market Model (LMM), for example.
- *Efficiency*: This refers to time efficiency (response time of a program) and resource efficiency (the amount of memory needed).
- *Maintainability*: This means that the software framework remains stable and testable under modifications to the code and that the code is easy to test after modifications have been introduced into the framework.

We realise these four requirements by the application of the appropriate GOF patterns. For example, in Figure 9.1(d) we show how the component S1 from Figure 9.1(c) has been elaborated based on certain requirements and subsequently documented using UML. This phase is also known as *Detailed Design* and it is the phase in which we use the design patterns from GOF (1995) when they are applicable. The focus is on producing accurate and efficient data structures and algorithms.

- *Implementing the Products from Detailed Design*: In this phase we implement the UML class diagrams in C++. We use a combination of object-oriented, generic and modular (procedural) programming techniques in order to arrive at a solution. The focus is on producing efficient algorithms to solve a given problem. Once the algorithms are working properly we can then incorporate them into an object-oriented framework. To this end, the GOF patterns (which we discuss in Chapter 10) are useful because they allow us to encapsulate volatile behaviour. For example, we create finite difference schemes by encapsulating the functionality of each scheme in a separate class. This class is derived from a base class and client code can use the classes by employing a reference or pointer to this base class.

9.4   DECOMPOSITION TECHNIQUES, THE PROCESS

We solve problems by breaking them down into smaller sub-problems. This *divide-and-conquer* technique is well accepted in many disciplines. We note that the technique can be applied in all phases of the software lifecycle.

In this section we are assuming that we need to design some software system. In other words, the *core process* of the system is to create output (products) based on certain kinds of input. The core process consists of a number of steps or *activities* that together realise system output. For example, going back to the Monte Carlo problem in Chapter 8 we see that the core process produces a value which is the price of an option. There are three activities, namely the SDE model, the FDM model and the MC model. Each activity produces its own output and has its own input. More generally, all programs process and produce data. We need to model this data and determine the tasks that manipulate it. To this end, there are two main decomposition techniques:

- Task (or process) decomposition.
- Data decomposition.

In the first case the core process is partitioned into a network of *tasks* that may execute in parallel. We need to know what the computationally intensive tasks and key data structures are. In many cases we see that a task is implemented by a subsystem. *Data decomposition* is appropriate when an application needs to manipulate and organise a large data structure. The data structure is partitioned into independent subparts. These parts can in principle be operated upon independently of each other. Some common examples of data structures in computational finance applications are

- *Arrays and matrices*: These structures can be partitioned into segments. For example, we decompose a matrix into rows or columns; a one-dimensional array can be decomposed into contiguous chunks based on a start index and an end index.
- *Recursive data structures*: These are structures that contain substructures of the same type. These are typically tree structures and we update each subtree concurrently. A special case of a recursive data structure is the *Composite* design pattern. We discuss this structural pattern in Chapters 11 and 12.

9.4.1 A special case: geometric decomposition

In many cases the data in an application can be visualised in some way. The corresponding problem space is decomposed into discrete subspaces and the core process is realised by a number of tasks with each task operating on its own subspace. In general, the subspaces are not completely independent but ideally a given subspace should require data from a small number of other subspaces.

The *Geometric Decomposition* pattern is found in many scientific applications. In general, we model a region in n-dimensional Euclidean space and we break up this region into smaller n-dimensional regions. Suitable application areas are

- Numerical solution of partial differential equations (PDE).
- Numerical integration in n-dimensional space.
- Random number and quasi-random number generation in n-dimensional space.

We take an example. Consider calculating the integral of a real-valued function in some bounded n-dimensional region D using the *stratified sampling* method (see, for example, Rubinstein, 1981). To this end, we examine the problem of calculating the integral:

$$I = \int_D g(x)f(x)dx \tag{9.1}$$

where $f(x)$ is a given probability density function. Let

$$D = \bigcup_{j=1}^{m} D_j \text{ and } D_i \bigcap D_j = \emptyset \text{ for } i \neq j$$

be a partition of D into m disjoint subregions. Then we can write the integral in equation (9.1) in the equivalent form:

$$I = \sum_{j=1}^{m} I_j \tag{9.2}$$

where

$$I_j = \int_{D_j} g(x)f(x)dx, \quad j = 1, \ldots, m$$

Each integral can now be evaluated using any suitable numerical integrator, for example the *sample-mean Monte Carlo* (which is similar to the midpoint rule) or using the *hit-or-miss* Monte Carlo method (these integrators will be introduced in Chapter 10). One of the advantages of this approach is that we can take more observations in the parts of region D that are more *important* in some sense, by using variance reduction techniques, for example.

9.4.2   Examples of task and data decomposition

We now give an example of decomposition techniques in applications that use Monte Carlo simulation. We concentrate on the neutron transport problem because many of the conclusions concerning this problem are transferrable to the current Monte Carlo framework. To this end, we examine the problem of computing neutron transmission through a plate (Sobol, 1994, page 47). We track the path of an elementary particle through a two-dimensional slab. The slab is of finite thickness in the x-direction and has infinite extent in the y-direction. Neutrons are bombarded at the plate; the angle of incidence is 90 degrees and we assume that the slab is defined as an interval $[A, B]$ in the x-direction. The possible fate of these neutrons is one of the following:

- It is transmitted through the slab and makes its exit at $x = B$.
- It is absorbed in (A,B) and it does not make an exit at $x = B$.
- It is reflected by the plate; at some point in (A,B) the path changes direction and eventually it makes an exit at $x = A$.

Each of these events has a probability of occurrence. The Monte Carlo method is one way to calculate this probability and we can choose between a task decomposition and a data decomposition of this problem. For convenience, we truncate the slab in the y-direction; we assume the slab's y coordinate is in the bounded interval (C,D). In the first case we associate each path with a task. Another approach is to partition the slab into sections and then we assign each section to a separate task.

We now give an introduction to two system decomposition techniques. We discuss this topic in Chapter 24:

- Whole-Part.
- Presentation-Abstraction-Control.

These patterns lay the basis for the Gamma (GOF) patterns and their C++ implementations in later chapters.

9.5   WHOLE-PART

This important pattern is documented in POSA (1996) and it is used to aggregate components and classes to form a semantic unit. In this case we speak of a *whole* object that encapsulates and contains its constituent *parts*. Some essential aspects of this pattern are

- The whole is a component in its own right, has member data and organises the collaboration between its parts. In the latter case we say that it plays the role of a *mediator*.
- The whole offers a common interface to its clients without their knowing – or their having to know – what its parts are or how they are organised. Thus, it becomes a black box and it adheres to the principle of *Information Hiding*. This means that clients can only use the whole's public interface.

- The parts in a whole can themselves be wholes. In this way, we can carry out the hierarchical decomposition to any level of detail.

Whole-Part structures abound in nature, engineering, science and everyday life. We also model software objects and components using this pattern. There are three main categories:

- *Assembly-Parts*: In this case we differentiate between the whole (the *assembly*) and its parts (the *subassemblies*). The number of distinct parts and their multiplicity is fixed at configuration time. The parts are tightly integrated and they communicate with the whole. An example of an assembly-parts pattern from everyday life is an automobile. Another example is an object that consists of an SDE, finite difference scheme and a random number generator.
- *Collection Members*: In this case we aggregate similar objects into one whole; we speak of an *organisation* and its members. We make no distinction between the members of the collection. The whole provides functionality to clients for iterating over the members and performing operations on them. An example of a collection-members object from everyday life is when we model a house that consists of a number of rooms. Each room has the same interface. Another example is a portfolio of assets.
- *Container-Contents*: This relationship models independent sets of objects that are contained in a bag-like structure. The contents or parts are loosely coupled with the whole. In this sense the container does not have member data in general.

In general, we apply the *Assembly-Parts* pattern at system and subsystem level (based on data or task decomposition methods, for example) whereas the collection-members and container-contents objects are found during detailed design and when we apply the GOF patterns.

9.6 WHOLE-PART DECOMPOSITION; THE PROCESS

We have described what Whole-Part structures are. We now prescribe *how* to discover, create and integrate these structures.

9.6.1 Task-based decomposition

The first technique corresponds to task decomposition and it allows us to find the functional subsystems of an application; the application itself plays the role of the whole. We first focus on the categories of applications (the so-called *Domain Architectures*) that we introduced in Chapter 8. A domain architecture is a meta-model because it describes families of applications having common structure and behaviour. What is of interest in the current situation is that such applications can be modelled as a whole-part structure and in particular we can attribute meaningful names to each part. In general, we partition an instance system of any domain category as an assembly-parts as shown in Figure 9.2(a). We provide some standard names that help us when determining the responsibilities of each subsystem. We present these names in Figure 9.2(b). You can use them to help you with the decomposition process. For example, the MAN category has the following subsystems:

- *Preprocessing*: Map external raw data to internal (working) data.
- *Conversion*: Map internal data to *half-products*.
- *Postprocessing*: Transform and display half-products on output media.

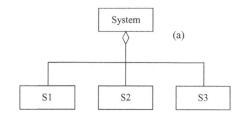

MAN	Preprocessing	Conversion	Postprocessing
PCS	Delivery	Regulator	Panel UI
MIS	Registration	Merging	Reporting
RAT	Registration	Assignment	Dispatching
ACS	Registration	Authentication	Status

Figure 9.2 Whole-Part Pattern and Domain Architecture

These names are guidelines only and you can choose your own names if it is more appropriate to do so.

Let us take the example from Chapter 8 again. We present this application as an instance of the MAN category and we present it as an assembly-parts structure in Figure 9.3. The specific names for the parts now become

- SDE (Preprocessing): Creates an SDE object based on the type of underlying model and market data.
- FDM (Conversion): Creates paths (arrays and matrices) for a given SDE object.
- MC (Postprocessing): Extracts relevant information from FDM in order to create the payoff function and the price of the derivative product.

We have given the code and detailed UML diagrams for this problem in Chapter 0.

9.6.2 Data decomposition

Many objects can be modelled as tangible entities that consist of other entities. In this case we model them as Whole-Part structures. These kinds of objects are found in Computer Aided Design (CAD) applications in which complex objects are *decomposed* into smaller objects (this is a recursive process in general) or in which complex objects are *composed* of simpler

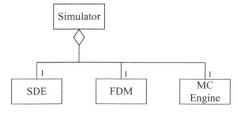

Figure 9.3 Assembly-parts relationship

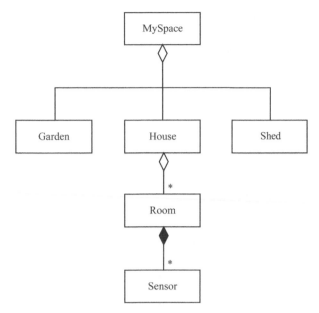

Figure 9.4   Whole parts in CAD

objects. These features support parts changeability and the ability to combine constituent parts
to form other aggregates. The term used in CAD is *parts explosion or bill-of-materials*.

We give some examples. The first example is a model for a homestead as shown in Figure 9.4.
At the highest level it is an assembly-parts structure while the house and room are collection-
members structures. In the latter case the room has sensors for measuring the temperature,
humidity and other physical properties. Intuitively, we start thinking about the data in each
of the classes in Figure 9.4; for example, each class has a name, area and other physical
properties. What we do not see in Figure 9.4 is the set of services that the classes provide
and require. This step is discussed in Chapter 10. In particular, we can imagine that different
stakeholders may wish to define *views* such as

- Calculate the total area of the homestead.
- Save data to a database.
- Maintenance issues and service-level agreements.

Another example is a model of a portfolio object as a collection-members structure as shown
in Figure 9.5. In fact, this is data decomposition; we define the attributes of bonds, options and
other instruments.

Summarising: when decomposing a system we apply task-decomposition (using the domain
architecture approach, for example) at a high level and data decomposition at the lower, class
level.

The steps to execute the *Whole-Part* pattern are

1. Design the public interface of the Whole.
2. Separate the Whole into Parts.
3. Bottom-up approach: use existing parts to create a whole object.
4. Partition the Whole's services into smaller collaborating services.

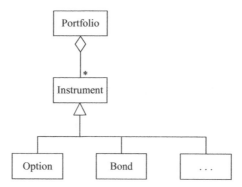

Figure 9.5   Collection members relationship

5. Specify the Whole's services in terms of the Part's services.
6. Implement the parts.
7. Implement the Whole; the Whole delegates to its parts.

   This is an iterative process and the structure will eventually converge to one that satisfies our requirements.

9.7   PRESENTATION-ABSTRACTION CONTROL (PAC)

In the previous section we showed how to decompose a problem into smaller subproblems. In order to promote cohesiveness (that is, spending too much time working solely on analysis models) we address the following issues:

- A1: The (domain) classes that we model in the application.
- A2: The algorithms and functionality in the application.
- A3: The system's user-interface and external device drivers.
- A4: The synchronisation of the user-interface with the data in the domain objects.

   These are the issues that concern us in daily development work; creating classes and defining algorithms for them. A useful pattern that allows us to design the activities A1 to A4 is the *Presentation-Abstraction-Control (PAC)* pattern. This pattern defines a structure for software systems in the form of a hierarchy of cooperating *agents*. Each agent consists of three components (which we call P, A and C):

- *Presentation*: The visible behaviour of the agent. This component contains the user-interface elements, external device drivers and real-time data feeds, for example. Please note that this component contains both input and output components.
- *Abstraction*: Contains the data model, including the business (entity) objects and the associated functionality, algorithms and synchronisation mechanisms.
- *Control*: The component that connects the presentation and abstraction components. It plays the role of a mediator. Furthermore, it also provides functionality to allow the agent to communicate with other agents (by means of their control components).

There are four main agent types:

- *Top-level agent*: This provides the core functionality of the system. In our case it corresponds to the system to be developed.
- *Bottom-level agents, I*: These are self-contained, cohesive units that implement semantic concepts on which users act. Examples are charts and spreadsheets.
- *Bottom-level agents, II*: These are bottom-level agents that implement system services, for example error handling functionality and configuration routines (in particular, creational patterns).
- *Intermediate-level agents*: These are combinations or aggregations of lower-level agents. An agent can also represent relationships between lower-level agents.

The steps needed in order to execute the *PAC* pattern are described in POSA (1996) in the general case. In this chapter we apply the *Whole-Part* pattern before embarking on PAC, which simplifies the design process somewhat. The steps are

1. Define a model of the application. We realise this phase by the *Whole-Part* pattern.
2. Define a general strategy for organising the PAC hierarchy. This phase could be realised using concept mapping techniques (Duffy, 1995). Each concept is a potential PAC agent.
3. Specify the top-level PAC agent. This agent implements the functional core of the system.
4. Specify the bottom-level (type I) PAC agents.
5. Specify the bottom-level (type II) PAC agents.
6. Specify intermediate-level agents. These are composed of other low-level agents and those that coordinate communication between low-level agents.
7. Separate core functionality from human-computer and external driver interaction.
8. Provide the external interface. In this case we determine the interfaces between the control components of related agents.

For example, taking the classes in Figure 9.3 and applying the eight steps in this process allows us to construct the more detailed class diagram in Figure 9.6. Finally, it is possible to design a PAC agent using an alternative layers model as shown in Figure 9.7. During the execution of these steps we apply GOF patterns because they fall naturally into place as it were. These patterns will be discussed in Chapter 10 where we produce running C++ code that implements the classes in the PAC model.

Closely related to *PAC* pattern is the *Model-View-Control (MVC)* pattern. Like PAC, it separates the functional code (corresponding to PAC's A component) from information display (the View) and user-input (the Control). We do not discuss MVC in this book because of its inherent shortcomings, one of which is the difficulty of using it with modern user-interface tools.

Finally, the advantages of the *PAC* pattern are

- *Separation of concerns*: Each *PAC* agent encapsulates tightly-coupled concepts in an application. This is beneficial because it promotes the cohesiveness in the application. Each agent has its own state, user-interface and it communicates with other agents from its control component.
- *Support for change and extension*: This pattern promotes maintainability because changes in the Presentation and Abstraction components do not affect other agents. All agents should communicate with each other through predefined and standardised interfaces.

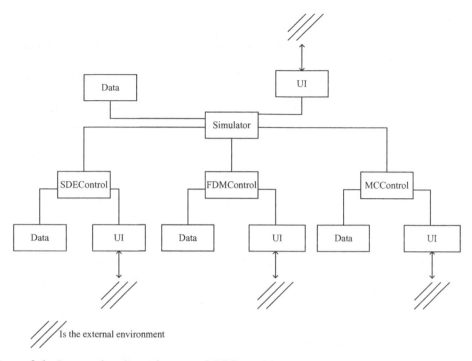

Figure 9.6   Presentation abstraction control (PAC) model

- *Support for multi-tasking*: We can implement *PAC* agents as independent processes and threads and we can distribute them to processors in shared memory and distributed memory environments. All that is needed is to introduce *IPC* (InterProcess Communication) code into the control component.

  Some possible disadvantages of the *PAC* pattern are

- *Efficiency*: There is some overhead between *PAC* agents. This may reduce system performance.
- *Increased system complexity*: Designing a hierarchical system consisting of agents is a nontrivial task. In general, each agent should have one major responsibility.

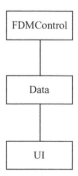

Figure 9.7   Layered agent

- *Complex control component*: This is the mediator between the presentation and abstraction components and it is also responsible for sending data to, and receiving data from, other agents.
- *Applicability*: The PAC pattern is not suitable for all applications. The semantic concepts and components need to be medium-grained or even large-grained in order to be useful. Otherwise, we end up with a bunch of small-grained interfaces that are difficult to integrate.

9.8 BUILDING COMPLEX OBJECTS AND CONFIGURING APPLICATIONS

In this and the previous chapter we introduced a number of patterns that describe the structure of objects of varying complexity. For example, we have seen that an object can be decomposed into orthogonal parts using the *Whole-Part* pattern and that each part can be modelled as a *PAC* agent containing a control, abstraction and presentation component.

Furthermore, each component in its turn may contain *composite objects*. Having determined the structure of an object or of an object network we then determine how to create it. In other words, we devise a *plan* to create and initialise the objects in the network by using more detailed patterns. To this end, we propose a number of *creational patterns* (see GOF, 1995). These patterns are classes whose instances are responsible for the creation of objects in an application. In this section we discuss three major creational patterns:

- The *Builder* pattern: This pattern is suitable for the creation of Whole-Part configurations, PAC agents, composites and recursive aggregates. There is a clear separation between the construction of a complex object and its representation. In other words, we describe *what* objects need to be created on the one hand and we also describe *how* they should be created on the other hand. This pattern is also suitable as a configuration tool for a complete application.
- The *Abstract Factory* pattern: This pattern defines an *interface* (that is, a collection of pure virtual functions defined in an abstract class) for creating families of related or dependent objects (usually in a class hierarchy) without specifying the specific derived classes that actually create these objects. This pattern is suitable when configuring systems that need *families of products*.
- The *Factory Method* pattern: This is the lowest-level pattern and it provides an interface for creating instances of a single class. Derived classes decide how to create these instances.

We now discuss each of these patterns and we focus on specific examples.

9.8.1   The Factory Method pattern

We take an example to show how this pattern works. To this end, we model some well-known one-factor interest rate models as SDEs. These equations describe the short rate:

$$
\begin{aligned}
dr &= \mu dt + \sigma dW \text{ (Merton)} \\
dr &= \kappa(\theta - r)dt + \sigma dW \text{ (Vasicek)} \\
dr &= \kappa(\theta - r)dt + \sigma\sqrt{r}dW \text{ (CIR)} \\
dr &= \kappa(t)(\theta(t) - r)dt + \sigma(t)r^\beta dW \text{ (Hull-White)}
\end{aligned}
\tag{9.3}
$$

We model these SDEs as a C++ class hierarchy as shown in Figure 9.8. This consists of a hierarchy of C++ classes that implement the SDEs in equation (9.3) and a hierarchy of

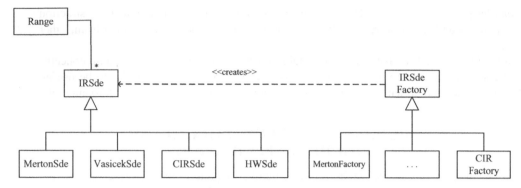

Figure 9.8   Structure for Factory Method pattern

factory classes. Furthermore, we create instances of these classes using the *Factory Method* pattern; in this case we create a class for each type as can be seen in Figure 9.8.

The classes in question are derived from a base class IrSde that implements the structure of an SDE and that has abstract member functions to calculate the drift and diffusion terms. For convenience, we define all functions to be *default inline*. The interface is

```
class IrSde
{
private:
     double ic;                // Initial condition
     Range<double> ran;        // Time Interval where SDE 'lives'

public:
     IrSde()
     {
         ic = 0.0;
         ran = Range<double> (0.0, 1.0);
     }

     IrSde(double initialCondition, double Expiry)
     {
         ic = initialCondition;
         ran = Range<double> (0.0, Expiry);
     }

     IrSde(double initialCondition, const Range<double>& interval)
     {
         ic = initialCondition;
         ran = interval;
     }

     const double& InitialCondition() const
     {
         return ic;
     }
```

```
      const Range<double>& Interval() const
      {
            return ran;
      }

      double getExpiry() const
      {
            return ran.high();
      }

      // Selector functions
      virtual double calculateDrift (double t, double r) const = 0
      virtual double calculateDiffusion (double t, double r)
      const = 0;

};
```

We have created C++ classes for the CIR and Merton models (the construction of the other models is left as a student exercise). The CIR class is defined as

```
class CIRSde : public IrSde
{ // Cox, Ingersoll, Ross

private:
      double m_kappa, m_theta, m_sigma; // Use MS notation
public:
      CIRSde() : IrSde()
      {
            m_kappa = m_theta = m_sigma = 0.0;
      }

      CIRSde(double initialCondition, double Expiry,
            double kappa, double theta, double sigma)
                              : IrSde(initialCondition, Expiry)
      {
            m_kappa = kappa;
            m_theta = theta;
            m_sigma = sigma;
      }

      CIRSde(double initialCondition, const Range<double>& interval,
            double kappa, double theta, double sigma)
                              : IrSde(initialCondition, interval)
      {
            m_kappa = kappa;
            m_theta = theta;
            m_sigma = sigma;
      }

      // Selector functions
      double calculateDrift (double t, double r) const
```

```
    {
        return m_kappa * (m_theta - r);
    }

    double calculateDiffusion (double t, double r) const
    {
        return m_sigma * sqrt(r);
    }
};
```

The class for the Merton model is similar to the above description and the code can be found on the CD. We now turn our attention to the factory classes. The base class (an interface) is

```
class IrSdeFactory
{
public:
    virtual IrSde* CreateIrSde() const = 0;
};
```

Derived classes must implement the function `CreateIrSde()`; for example, here is the code for the class that creates instances of the CIR class (the parameter values of the SDE are initialised from the system console):

```
class CIRSdeFactory : public IrSdeFactory
{
public:
    virtual IrSde* CreateIrSde() const
    {
        double T, kappa, theta, sigma, IC;
        cout << "Factory for CIR\n";
        cout << "Kappa: "; cin >> kappa;
        cout << "Theta: "; cin >> theta;
        cout << "Sigma: "; cin >> sigma;
        cout << "Expiry T: "; cin >> T;
        cout << "Initial condition: "; cin >> IC;

        return new CIRSde(IC, T, kappa, theta, sigma);
    }
};
```

An advantage of using this pattern is that client code does not need to know which specific C++ class is being used nor does it need to know which specific factory is being used. In other words, client code receives a pointer to the base class for all SDEs and a pointer to the base class for all SDE factories. This is an extremely useful feature when developing extendible software frameworks because we eliminate the need to bind application-specific classes into code. In other words, we move the knowledge on how to create objects out of the framework, thus making it applicable to a wide range of applications. To take an example, we first note that all the SDEs in equation (9.3) can be written in the generalised form:

$$dr = A(t, r)dt + B(t, r)dW$$

Let us now simulate the short rate based on this general form using the explicit Euler method:

$$r_{n+1} = r_n + A(t_n, r_n)\Delta t + B(t_n, r_n)\Delta W_n, \quad 0 \le n \le N - 1$$

where

$$\Delta t = t_{n+1} - t_n \text{ and } r_n \equiv r(t_n)$$

where we use the notation from Part I of this book. This scheme can be used with any SDE and we would like to write C++ code with a similar level of generality. This is possible because of subtype polymorphism that we realise using the functions

```
virtual double calculateDrift (double t, double r) const = 0;
virtual double calculateDiffusion (double t, double r)
const = 0;
```

All derived classes implement these functions. Finally, the code that implements the Euler scheme for an arbitrary SDE is

```
Vector<double, long> Simulation(const IrSde& irsde,
                                Vector<double, long> mesh)
{ // Simulate a short-rate using explicit Euler method

    long N = mesh.Size();

    Vector<double, long> result(N, mesh.MinIndex());

    // Step size
    double k = irsde.Interval().spread()/double(N - 1);
    double sk = sqrt(k);

    double rOld;

    // Generate array of normal random numbers
    TerribleRandGenerator myTerrible; // rand()
    NormalGenerator* myNormal = new BoxMuller(myTerrible);
    Vector<double, long> arr2 = myNormal->getNormalVector(N);

    // Initial condition
    result[result.MinIndex()] = irsde.InitialCondition();

    for (long n = result.MinIndex()+1; n <= result.MaxIndex(); ++n)
    {
        rOld = result[n-1];
        result[n] = rOld
                + (irsde.calculateDrift(mesh[n], rOld) * k)
        + (irsde.calculateDiffusion(mesh[n], rOld) * sk * arr2[n]);
    }
    delete myNormal;
    return result;
}
```

In this case we use functions to generate standard normal random numbers. The code is very generic. Here is some code to show how to use the *Factory Method* pattern. Please note that we use a handy function that returns a pointer to a factory base class:

```
// Function to allow you to choose a specific factory
IrSdeFactory* ChooseFactory(int j)
{
    if (j == 1)
    {
        return new CIRSdeFactory;
    }

    if (j != 1)
    {
        return new MertonSdeFactory;
    }
}
```

The actual test program is

```
int main()
{
    // Choose your factory
    cout << "1. CIR, 2. Merton: "; int choice; cin >> choice;
    IrSdeFactory* myFactory = ChooseFactory(choice);

    IrSde* mySde = myFactory->CreateIrSde();

    // Now simulate a path using Euler method
    cout << "Number of sub-intervals: "; long N; cin >> N;
    Vector<double, long> myMesh = mySde->Interval().mesh(N);
    // Do an Euler simulation with the current SDE
    Vector<double, long> result = Simulation(*mySde, myMesh);
    print(result);

    // Clean up
    delete mySde;
    delete myFactory;
    return 0;
}
```

Finally, it is possible to avoid having to create new derived classes for each kind of factory by using C++ templates. We discuss this topic in Chapter 11.

9.8.2 Abstract Factory pattern

This pattern can be seen as an extended *Factory Method* pattern. In the latter case we create an instance of a single class but in the current case we are interested in creating so-called *product families*, that is related groups of objects. It is possible to replace these objects by objects from another product family. It is relatively easy to discover and model product families as C++ class hierarchies:

Figure 9.9   Structure for Abstract Factory pattern

- Creating hierarchies of GUI controls, such as buttons, text boxes and dialog boxes.
- Vendor-specific classes for sensors and actuators.
- Applications that need and use interchangeable parts, for example structured products in fixed income.

We give an example in this section of how to apply the pattern. We extend the functionality of the code in section 9.8.1 by defining product families that allow us to create SDE instances based on console input, as copies of other objects (called prototypes) or by calibration, for example. The UML class diagram is shown in Figure 9.9. In this case, the factory classes have member functions for each SDE class. As always, these are abstract:

```
class IrSdeAbstractFactory
{
public:
      virtual IrSde* CreateMertonSde() const = 0;
      virtual IrSde* CreateCIRSde() const = 0;

      // Student exercise, other models . . .
      // virtual IrSde* CreateMertonSde() const = 0;
      // virtual IrSde* CreateMertonSde() const = 0;
};
```

Each derived class implements these member functions, for example the class `ConsoleFactory` that creates instances of the classes corresponding to the SDEs in equation (9.3) using the system console:

```
class ConsoleFactory : public IrSdeAbstractFactory
{
public:
        virtual IrSde* CreateCIRSde() const
        {
            double T, kappa, theta, sigma, IC;

            cout << "Factory for CIR n";
            cout << "Kappa: "; cin >> kappa;
            cout << "Theta: "; cin >> theta;
            cout << "Sigma: "; cin >> sigma;
            cout << "Expiry T: "; cin >> T;
            cout << "Initial condition: "; cin >> IC;
            return new CIRSde(IC, T, kappa, theta, sigma);
        }
```

```
        virtual IrSde* CreateMertonSde() const
        {
              double T, drift, sigma, IC;

              cout << "Factory for Merton\n";
              cout << "Drift: "; cin >> drift;
              cout << "Sigma: "; cin >> sigma;
              cout << "Expiry T: "; cin >> T;
              cout << "Initial condition: "; cin >> IC;

              return new MertonSde(IC, T, drift, sigma);
        }
};
```

Finally, in an application the client code can choose both a factory object and an SDE object at run-time, for example:

```
IrSdeAbstractFactory* ChooseAbstractFactory(int j)
{
      if (j == 1)
      {
            return new ConsoleFactory;
      }

      if (j != 1)
      {
            // Student: return new PrototypeFactory;
      }
}

int main()
{
      // Choose your factory
      cout << "1. Console, 2. Prototype: "; int choice; cin >> choice;
      IrSdeAbstractFactory* myFactory = ChooseAbstractFactory(choice);

      cout << "1. CIR, 2. Merton: "; cin >> choice;
      IrSde* mySde;
      if (choice == 1)
      {
            mySde = myFactory->CreateCIRSde();
      }
      else
      {
            mySde = myFactory->CreateMertonSde();
      }

      // Now simulate a path using Euler method
      cout << "Number of sub-intervals: "; long N; cin >> N;
      Vector<double, long> myMesh = mySde->Interval().mesh(N);
```

```
    // Do an Euler simulation with the current SDE
    Vector<double, long> result = Simulation(*mySde, myMesh);
    print(result);

    // Clean up
    delete mySde;
    delete myFactory;

    return 0;
}
```

Summarising, the Factory Method and Abstract Factory patterns are useful when we con-figure an application. They uncouple code for object creation from algorithmic code.

9.8.3   Builder pattern

This strategic pattern is useful for configuring arbitrary object networks, Whole-Part assemblies and composites. It is documented in GOF (1995) and we see it as a special case (or instance system) of the manufacturing domain architecture (code name MAN) that we introduced in Chapter 8. In all cases we are interested in creating a product based on some given input data. We sometimes speak of *raw materials* when referrring to the input data. The best way to understand the Builder pattern is to consider it to be the implementation of a process that creates products from raw materials. It is important to focus on the *data flow* aspects of the process. To this end, the process is broken down into three major activities:

- *Processing*: Parses raw materials and creates the building blocks that will form the final product. This phase is implemented by a *Director* object.
- *Conversion*: Creates the final products by assembling its parts. This phase is implemented by a *Builder* object. This is a step-by-step process.
- *Postprocessing*: Optimises the product and formats it so that it can be used by client systems. This system produces the final *Product*.

The class diagram is shown in Figure 9.10. The *Director* class parses the input data. The parsed data is sent to the *Builder* which then creates the product in a step-by-step fashion. This class has member functions for building the parts and for returning the finished product to client systems. An example of a sequence diagram showing the steps is given in Figure 9.11.

Focusing on the data flow issues instead of the more static class diagrams (as is done in GOF, 1995) makes it easier to understand and apply this patten in software projects.

We have already given an example of the *Builder* pattern in Chapter 0. A typical candidate for this pattern is the complex object network as shown in Figure 9.12 and this is the basis for a Monte Carlo software engine. The top-level object MCEngine is a Whole-Part object and its parts correspond to stochastic differential equations, finite difference methods and random number generators. In future versions the class network will need to be extended to support more requirements (for example, the requirements R1 to R10 as we discussed in Chapter 8). The implementation of a given requirement implies the design of new C++ classes that are then integrated in the class diagram in Figure 9.12.

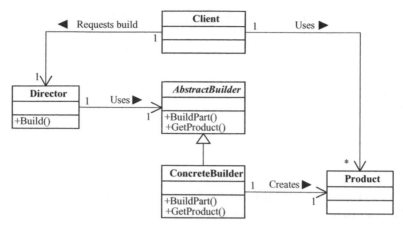

Figure 9.10   Class diagram for Builder

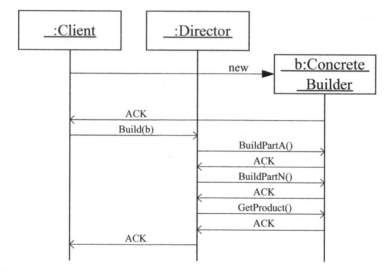

Figure 9.11   Sequence diagram for Builder

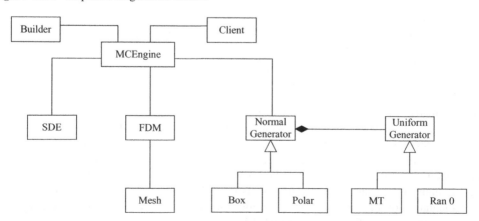

Figure 9.12   Class diagram for Monte Carlo framework

Some final remarks on the design and implementation of the classes in Figure 9.12:

- We could design the builder object in such a way that it delegates parts of its creational activities to factory objects. In this case we use so-called subcontractors to create the parts of the MCEngine object. For example, we could use *subcontractor* factories to create SDE, FDM and random number generator objects.
- An important issue is to determine the structure and format of the input data that the *Director* needs to process. In Chapter 0 we used enumerated types to distinguish between the different kinds of derived classes. In more complex applications we need to define a language to describe the input data and a parser to extract the tokens and building blocks that eventually form the parts of the finished product. To this end, the *Interpreter* pattern (GOF, 1995) allows us to
  - define a representation for the grammar of the language that we have chosen; and
  - use the representation to interpret sentences in the language. Fortunately, the boost library provides us with much of the functionality we need, for example Boost.Regex (pattern matching), Boost.Spirit (parser generator framework) and other libraries. Alternatively, we can use XML and its associated parsers to achieve the same ends.

In section 13.10 of Chapter 13 we describe the class diagram in Figure 9.12 in more detail. It is an end-of-term project as it were, because it will be designed and implemented using all the techniques to date.

9.9   SUMMARY AND CONCLUSIONS

In this chapter we have introduced a number of key decomposition methods and patterns to reduce cognitive overload during the development process and to give the developer a chance to create stable and flexible software systems. This *separation of concerns* approach ensures that we can concentrate on one particular aspect of the problem at one time. Finally, the *design blueprints* in this chapter are the input for the later chapters in Part II of the book. In general, we execute the steps in the *Whole-Part* pattern before applying the *PAC* pattern. In particular, we first discover an agent, after which time we partition it into its P, A and C components. We determine how to design and implement these components and in general they will be populated by classes and GOF patterns.

9.10   EXERCISES AND PROJECTS

1. (****) How Flexible should Software Be?
   The objective of this exercise is to determine how the *Whole-Part* and *PAC* patterns add to the overall *quality* of a software product. We use to the same quality criteria as introduced in Chapter 8:
   - R1: Suitability of the software for a range of products.
   - R2: Accuracy of the software's algorithms.
   - R3: Interoperability with other systems.
   - R4: Security.
   - R5: Conformance and compliance with standards.
   - R6: Time and resource efficiency (performance).
   - R7: Different kinds of user interface for different purposes.
   - R8: Separation of core application code from volatile user interface and driver code.

– R9: Should our code be portable between different operating systems?
– R10: Should the software system be maintainable?
Answer the following questions:
(a) Discuss in general terms how the use of *Whole-Part* and *PAC* patterns helps in realising the features R1 to R10. Then, for each feature determine in more detail how you would realise it. For example, examining feature R6 (Efficiency), we could realise it using the following techniques:
   – Creating efficient algorithms (for example, various FDM schemes).
   – Avoiding the creation of temporary objects; using redundant data.
   – Using efficient data structures; *Complexity Analysis* estimates (*O(nlogn)*).
   – Using call-by-reference and avoiding *volatile* variables.
   – Using the *Proxy* pattern to cache objects in memory that are expensive to create.
(b) In section 8.4 we discussed some features that need to be supported in a Monte Carlo framework. In which subsystems in Figure 9.12 should these features be implemented? Do the subsystems satisfy the *Single Responsibility Principle* (SRP)? If not, you should partition them into lower-level parts, thus avoiding components with more than one major responsibility.
(c) In which parts of the component network in Figure 9.12 is the following functionality needed?
   – Mesh generation algorithms.
   – Classes for dates, calendars, day conventions.
   – Random number generators.
   – Compile-time and run-time vectors and matrices.
   – SDE class hierarchy.
   – Calculating option sensitivities.
   – Quasi-random number generation.
   – Calibration algorithms.
   – Statistical distributions (Normal, exponential, gamma, for example).

2. (***) Factory Method Pattern
   This exercise is concerned with the topics in section 9.8.1. We have created the classes for the CIR and Merton models as well as a test program and a function to simulate the short rate path using the explicit Euler method. Answer the following questions:
   – Create the C++ classes (for the SDEs as defined in equation (9.3) and the corresponding factories) for the Vasicek and Hull-White models.
   – Test these classes using the explicit Euler method.
   – Implement the Milstein method and apply it to the classes that you have created.
   – Display the results in Excel (using the software on the CD, for example).

3. (**) Prototype Pattern
   Extend and test the class hierarchy in Figure 9.8 to support the construction of objects as copies of other (prototypical) objects. This option is useful in applications where the user can clone objects from other objects that are selected from a *palette* or *toolbox*. This concept underlies the *Prototype* pattern (GOF, 1995).

4. (****) Creating Software Models for Interest Rate Applications
   In this exercise we discuss how to design a simple interest rate application. We assume that the reader has some knowledge of this area (for an introduction, see Hull (2006) and Flavell (2002)). A short summary of the application is:

The goal of the system is to price simple interest rate derivatives such as interest rate futures, various kinds of swaps and interest rate options. In particular, we must be able to value future cash flows. The system should be flexible and the design should facilitate the maintainability of the software that implements this system. Furthermore, it must be possible to manage historical data as well as data corresponding to different currencies.

- Day count: a convention for quoting interest rates. Examples are actual/actual, 30/360, actual/360 and other possibilities.
- Ability to model bonds, interest rate caps and floors, currency and equity swaps.
- Simulation and sensitivity analyses (for example, 'bumping' a portfolio).
- Flexible curve construction, including support for a range of interpolation schemes (for example, linear, loglinear and cubic).
- Historical data to be stored in a range of formats, for example XML, relational databases and CSV files.
- Generation of cash flow dates and values; calculation of discounting factors.
- Pricing formulae based on Flavell (2002) and commercial standards, for example Reuters Powerplus.
- Excel support; we use this spreadsheet for both input and output. We also need to support Automation COM Addins to support worksheet functions and computationally-intensive algorithms.
- In a later version, we will need to produce a multi-threaded version of the system using OpenMP, C# threads or Boost threads, for example.

The objective of this exercise is to scope this problem by determining what goes into the system, what the external systems are and the discovery of the main subsystems. The background reading is based on Chapters 8 and 9. We are not (yet) concerned with low-level design using the GOF patterns.

Answer the following questions:

(a) Describe in your own words what the core process is, that is the primary output from the system, the different inputs to the system and the steps (activities) that map input to outputs. In other words, what is the workflow in the system?

(b) In which domain category (or combination of categories) does this system belong (see section 8.3)? Based on your answer decompose the system based on the guidelines in Figure 9.2. Alternatively, you can propose your own system decomposition.

(c) Based on the above nine requirements listed above, find the main components in the system. Does each one have one major responsibility, in other words each component must satisfy SRP (Single Responsibility Principle)?

(d) Create an initial PAC model (as in Figure 9.6, for example) using the components from part (c) of this exercise. These components are candidates for PAC agents (see section 9.7 for a description). In particular, find those Presentation components that communicate with Excel, disk files, databases, user dialog boxes as well as the Abstraction components that model algorithms and business logic.

(e) Create class hierarchies of Abstraction objects using the *Whole-Part* pattern (section 9.6). It is not necessary to start worrying about class hierarchies yet as this aspect is part of detailed design. The desired answer from this exercise is a UML diagram in the spirit of Figure 9.6 (or Figure 10.1).

10
Detailed Design using the GOF Patterns

Thus, it is often appropriate to start the work with the question: Do we know a related problem?
Look at the unknown! and try to think of a familiar problem having the same or similar unknown.

Georg Pólya

10.1 INTRODUCTION AND OBJECTIVES

In this chapter we continue our discussion of the design process that we introduced in Chapters 8 and 9. The components in those chapters are large-grained and are not yet amenable to a direct implementation in C++. We now discover the classes and objects that *realise* or implement the functionality of these components. Furthermore, we model the static relationships between classes. This step involves possible optimisation of the class design by creating *inheritance hierarchies* as well as the application of the *delegation* mechanism. The resulting product will be a network of classes that we can subsequently implement in C++. There is just one proviso when developing real applications: the software requirements tend to change after a product has been created. For example, here are some of the modifications that might need to be made:

- Replace the current user-interface by another one.
- Ensure the ability to model new kinds of derivatives or other domain classes.
- Replace an algorithm for calculating the option sensitivities by a more accurate or more efficient one.
- Portability: ensure that our core application code is independent of the driver software, for example raw data feeds.
- A general requirement that it takes a week instead of a month to effect a software change request.

There are examples of *software volatility* and we develop a number of techniques in this chapter that help us pinpoint these potential sources of change. Having done that we shall be able to determine which gamma patterns (also known as the *Gang Of Four* or *GOF* patterns, for short) to use.

There are 23 GOF patterns and we have seen that a relatively small percentage of them – when used in combination with each other – realise the highest productivity gains for the developer.

In the current book that deals with Monte Carlo applications we have seen that the following patterns are crucial:

- *Builder* (creating complex objects and configuring a system).
- *Bridge* (providing multiple implementations of some *domain classes*).
- *Facade* (creating a simpler, unified interface to a subsystem).
- *Composite* (creating nested objects and tree-like object structures).
- *Visitor* (adding extra functionality to a class hierarchy in a non-intrusive manner).
- *Template Method* (the *refactoring* pattern).
- *Strategy* (implementing algorithms as classes).

We discuss these patterns in this and the following chapters. We also include simple and not-so-simple exercises and projects based on these patterns and we advise the reader to study and implement them.

10.2   DISCOVERING WHICH PATTERNS TO USE

In Chapter 9 we discussed the *Whole-Parts* and *PAC* patterns. We can apply these to many kinds of applications in computational finance and at various levels of system complexity. The *Whole-Part* pattern is more critical to a successful design than PAC because of its universal applicability whereas PAC focuses on lower-level issues such as user-interfaces, data and algorithms.

In this chapter we elaborate the designs from Chapter 9 by concentrating on the PAC *agents* that we have discovered. In particular, these agents are elaborated to support the needed functionality and requirements. What normally happens is that we add new C++ classes to the design. Once we arrive at this stage we are in *programming mode* and most of the developer resources will now be spent on developing and testing new functionality for the framework.

This section functions as a bridge between the high-level decomposition techniques and patterns from Chapters 8 and 9 and the more detailed GOF patterns and their implementation in C++. In particular, we design a simple C++ model to solve the one-factor Black-Scholes partial differential equation (PDE) using finite-difference methods (see Duffy, 2004a; Duffy, 2006a). The decomposition in this case is based on the *Whole-Part* pattern in which each part is a PAC agent. We show the resulting UML diagram in Figure 10.1. Our strategy is as follows: we implement the classes in C++ and we carry out a *code inspection* in combination with defining a list of *features* or *requirements* that new versions of the software product should support.

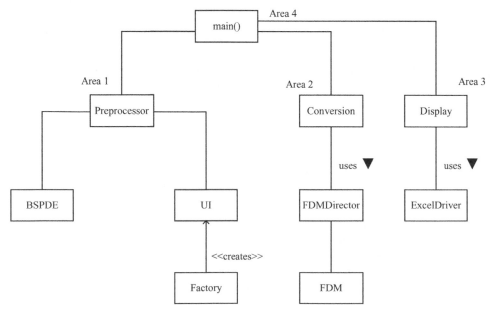

Figure 10.1   UML class diagram for model problem

For convenience, we have numbered the classes in Figure 10.1. For example, Area 1 is the *Preprocessor* agent that is responsible for the definition of the Black-Scholes PDE. The techniques can also be applied to Monte Carlo applications.

10.2.1 *Whole-Part* structure for a finite difference scheme

The *core process* in this case is to price a one-factor plain put (or call) option using the explicit Euler finite difference method. We have chosen this method because it is easy to explain and to program and it allows us to focus on the essential design issues related to the implementation of the classes in Figure 10.1. In most applications we would use other, more robust and accurate numerical methods (see Duffy, 2006a). The core process has the following steps:

1. Define the Black-Scholes PDE (Area 1).
2. Approximate the PDE using finite difference methods (Area 2).
3. Display the result in Excel using the Excel driver (Area 3).

Each of these areas is a *PAC* agent containing user-interface, data and control components. The Area 4 (which is just a `main()` function in this case) plays the role of the component that coordinates all data traffic between the individual parts (incidentally, Figure 10.1 is an example of *Assembly-Parts* structure as already discussed in Chapter 9).

The Black-Scholes PDE (written in a generic form!) is given by

$$\frac{\partial u}{\partial t} = \sigma \frac{\partial^2 u}{\partial x^2} + \mu \frac{\partial u}{\partial x} + bu + f \tag{10.1}$$

This is a convection-diffusion equation and it is augmented by *Dirichlet boundary conditions* and an *initial condition* in order to produce a unique solution (in a Black-Scholes environment the initial condition corresponds to the payoff function at the expiry date). We discretise the PDE (10.1) using centred differencing in space and forward differencing in time (this is known as an FTCS scheme or explicit Euler scheme; the acronym 'FTCS' means *forward in time, centred in space*) and in this case the scheme is

$$\frac{u_j^{n+1}}{\Delta t} - \frac{u_j^n}{\Delta t} = \frac{\sigma_j^n}{h^2} \left(u_{j+1}^n - 2u_j^n + u_{j-1}^n \right) + \frac{\mu_j^n}{2h} \left(u_{j+1}^n - u_{j-1}^n \right) + b_j^n u_j^n + f_j^n \tag{10.2}$$

We thus replace a PDE in a continuous (x, t) space by a finite difference scheme defined in a discrete space. We rewrite the scheme (10.2) in a useful computational form:

$$u_j^{n+1} = A_j^n u_{j-1}^n + B_j^n u_j^n + C_j^n u_{j+1}^n + \Delta t f_j^n \quad 1 \le j \le J - 1$$

$$\left. \begin{aligned} A_j^n &\equiv \Delta t \left(\frac{\sigma_j^n}{h^2} - \frac{\mu_j^n}{2h} \right) \\ B_j^n &\equiv 1 - 2\Delta t \frac{\sigma_j^n}{h^2} + \Delta t b_j^n \\ C_j^n &\equiv \Delta t \left(\frac{\sigma_j^n}{h^2} + \frac{\mu_j^n}{2h} \right) \end{aligned} \right\} \quad 1 \le j \le J - 1 \tag{10.3}$$

We take a different approximation to the free term in order to improve the stability of the FTCS scheme:

$$b_j^n u_j^n \to b_j^n u_j^{n+1} \tag{10.4}$$

This is the technique that is used in Hull (2006), which has a short section on implicit and explicit finite difference methods for the one-factor Black-Scholes equation. More robust schemes are discussed in Duffy (2004a).

10.2.2 The Preprocessor agent

This is the Area 1 agent (see Figure 10.1) and its main responsibility is to define the Black-Scholes PDE as well as its boundary conditions and initial condition. Since we wish to support a wide range of PDEs (and not just the Black-Scholes PDE) we design Area 1 in such a way that its client systems access a more generic PDE class; in this version we implement it as a namespace and this namespace models all features that unambiguously define the PDE:

```
namespace ParabolicPde
{
    // Abstract PDE description
    // The ranges in which the PDE is defined
    Range<double> XInterval;
    Range<double> TInterval;

    // Coefficients of PDE equation
    double (*sigma)(double x, double t); // Diffusion term
    double (*mu)(double x, double t);   // Convection term
    double (*b)(double x, double t);    // Free term
    double (*f)(double x, double t);    // The forcing term


    // (Dirichlet) boundary conditions
    double (*BCL)(double t); // The left-hand boundary condition
    double (*BCR)(double t); // The right-hand boundary condition

    // Initial condition
    double (*IC)(double x); // The condition at time t = 0


}
```

This namespace is defined in terms of seven function pointers and two ranges that represent the intervals in the x and t directions. We implement the above PDE by instantiating the function pointers and ranges. In this case we define a namespace that defines the essential features of the Black-Scholes PDE as follows:

```
namespace BSPde
{
    // Implementing a PDE
    // All option data contained in a struct
    OptionData data;

    // The ranges in which the PDE is defined
    Range<double> XInterval;
    Range<double> TInterval;
```

```
double BlackSholesSigma (double x, double t)
{ // x is stock, not necessarily log(S)

    return 0.5 * data.sig * data.sig * x * x;

}

double BlackScholesMu (double x, double t)
{
    return (data.r) * x;
}

double BlackScholesB (double x, double t)
{

    return  -data.r;

}

double BlackScholesF (double x, double t)
{
    return 0.0;
}

double BlackScholesBCL (double t)
{
    return data.K*exp(-data.r * (data.T - t));
}

double BlackScholesBCR (double t)
{
    return 0.0; // P
}

double BlackScholesIC (double x)
{
    // Put option
    if (data.K > x)
        return data.K - x;
    return 0.0;

    // Call option
    /* if (x >= data.K)
        return x - data.K;
    return 0.0;*/
}

} // end of namespace
```

We see that the Black-Scholes PDE needs data; to this end, we model all relevant option data in a *struct*:

```
struct InstrumentData ;

struct OptionData : public InstrumentData
{
    double r;        // Interest rate
    double sig;      // Volatility
    double K;        // Strike price
    double T;        // Expiry date
    double SMax;     // Far field condition

    OptionData()
    {
        r = 0.05;
        sig = 0.02;
        K = 100.0;
        T = 1.0;
        SMax = 4.0 * K;      // Magic number, make more general
    }

    void print()
    {

        cout << "Interest: " << r << endl;
        cout << "Vol: " << sig << endl;
        cout << "Strike: " << K << endl;
        cout << "Expiry: " << T << endl;
        cout << "Far field: " << SMax << endl;
    }

};
```

We need to create option data and in this case we employ a *Factory Method* pattern because we do not wish to have hard-coded values (so-called *magic numbers*) in the application. Instead, we define dedicated classes whose instances create the data in an `OptionData` instance. We define an abstract base class containing the virtual function to create the desired data:

```
class InstrumentFactory
{
public:

    virtual OptionData* CreateOptionData() const = 0;
};
```

We have created two specialisations of this class; the first derived class is an interactive console appliction that prompts the user to give the values of the option data, as follows:

```
class ConsoleInstrumentFactory : public InstrumentFactory
{
public:

    OptionData* CreateOptionData() const
```

```
    {

        double dr;       // Interest rate
        double dsig;     // Volatility
        double dK;       // Strike price
        double dT;       // Expiry date
        double dSMax;    // Far field boundary

        cout << "Interest rate: ";
        cin >> dr;

        cout << "Volatility: ";
        cin >> dsig;

        cout << "Strike Price: ";
        cin >> dK;
        dSMax = 6.0 * dK; // Magix Number !!!!

        cout << "Expiry: ";
        cin >> dT;

        OptionData* result = new OptionData;

        result->r = dr;
        result->sig = dsig;
        result->K = dK;
        result->T = dT;
        result->SMax = dSMax;

        return result;

    }

};
```

The second factory class creates a default data object; in other words, it creates a *prototype object* that the user can use in the application:

```
class PrototypeInstrumentFactory : public InstrumentFactory
{
public:

    OptionData* CreateOptionData() const
    {

        OptionData* result = new OptionData;

        result->r = 0.08;       // call price == 2.1334
        result->sig = 0.30;
        result->K = 65.0;
        result->T = 0.25;
```

```
        result->SMax = 4.0 * result->K;

        return result;
    }
};
```

In client code we work with pointers to the base factory class. This is useful because we create a function to allow the user to choose the desired factory; a pointer to the base class is returned:

```
InstrumentFactory* GetInstrumentFactory()
{ // A kind of Yellow Pages, i.e. choose your factory

    cout << "1. Console Factory, 2. Prototype Factory: ";
    int c; cin >> c;

    if (c == 1)
    {
        return new ConsoleInstrumentFactory;
    }
    else
    {
        return new PrototypeInstrumentFactory;
    }
    // etc.
}
```

We now complete the discussion of the *Preprocessor* agent (Area 1 and its components). The main steps are (1) choose an option factory, (2) initialise the current PDE object (in our case it corresponds to the Black-Scholes PDE, and (3) clean up pointer memory. The code is given by

```
void init()
{

            // UI part of the preprocessor (P layer)
            InstrumentFactory* myFactory = GetInstrumentFactory();
            OptionData* myOption = myFactory ->CreateOptionData();
            myOption->print();


            // Now build up the object
            using namespace ParabolicPde;


            // Data
            BSPde::data = *myOption;

            BSPde::XInterval = Range<double>(0.0, BSPde::data.SMax);
            BSPde::TInterval = Range<double>(0.0, BSPde::data.T);
```

```
        // Assignment of functions; use explicit namespace scoping
        // for Black Scholes PDE (Bridge implementation)
        sigma = BSPde::BlackSholesSigma;
        mu = BSPde::BlackSholesMu;
        b = BSPde::BlackSholesB;
        f = BSPde::BlackSholesF;
        BCL = BSPde::BlackSholesBCL;
        BCR = BSPde::BlackSholesBCR;
        IC = BSPde::BlackSholesIC;

        // Clean up pointers
        delete myFactory;
        delete myOption;
}
```

We are now ready to approximate the PDE using finite differences.

10.2.3   The Conversion agent

This is Area 2 and its responsibility is to calculate option prices using the FTCS difference scheme, as already discussed in section 10.2.1. We partition the problem into two main classes because we do not want to mix control flow and time marching with the actual process of calculating new values of the option price:

- FDM: This class contains the code that implements the scheme in equation (10.2) (or equivalently equation (10.3)).
- FDMDirector: This class is responsible for driving the solution at all time levels up to the expiry date. It is a client of FDM and it delegates to the latter object.

The C++ (inline) code for the class FDM has a constructor and a member function called solve() to calculate the solution at time level $n + 1$ in terms of the solution at time level n:

```
using namespace ParabolicPde;

class FDM
{
private:

        // Coefficients of system at each time level
        double A, B, C, RHS;

        // Solutions at time levels n and n+1, respectively
        Vector<double, long> vecOld;
        Vector<double, long> vecNew;

        Vector<double, long> mesh;

        // Other redundant variables
        double tmp1, tmp2, k, h;
```

```
public:
    FDM() {}
    FDM(const Vector<double, long>& meshArray)
    {

    // Initialise the solution at time zero. This occurs only
    // at the interior mesh points of mesh (and there are J-1
    // of them).


    mesh = meshArray;
    h = mesh[mesh.MinIndex()+1] - mesh[mesh.MinIndex()];

    vecOld = Vector<double, long> (mesh.Size(), mesh.MinIndex());
    vecNew = Vector<double, long> (mesh.Size(), mesh.MinIndex());

    // Initialise at the boundaries
    vecOld[vecOld.MinIndex()] = BCL(0.0);
    vecOld[vecOld.MaxIndex()] = BCR(0.0);

    // Now initialise values in interior of interval using
    // the initial function 'IC' from the PDE
    for (long j = mesh.MinIndex()+1; j <= mesh.MaxIndex()-1; ++j)
    {
        vecOld[j] = IC(mesh[j]);
    }

    }

    const Vector<double, long>& current()
    {
        return vecNew;
    }

    void solve (double tprev, double tnow)
    { // Calculate the solution at n+1 in terms of that at level n

        k = tnow - tprev;

        // Explicit method

        vecNew[vecNew.MinIndex()] = BCL(tprev);
        vecNew[vecNew.MaxIndex()] = BCR(tprev);

        for (long i = vecNew.MinIndex()+1;
                        i <= vecNew.MaxIndex()-1; ++i)
        {

            tmp1 = (k * sigma(mesh[i], tprev))/(h*h);
            tmp2 = (k * 0.5 * mu(mesh[i], tprev))/h;
```

```
                A = tmp1 - tmp2;
                //B = 1.0 - (2.0 * tmp1) + (k * b(mesh[i], tprev));
                B = 1.0 - (2.0 * tmp1);
                C = tmp1 + tmp2;
                RHS = k * f(mesh[i], tprev);
                vecNew[i] = (A * vecOld[i-1])
                                + (B * vecOld[i])+(C * vecOld[i+1])+ RHS;

                vecNew[i] /= (1.0 - (k * b(mesh[i], tprev)));

            }
            vecOld = vecNew;
        }
};
```

Finally, we show the code that calculates the solution at all time levels:

```
class FDMDirector
{

private:

        double T;
        double Xmax;

        double k;
        long J, N;
        double tprev, tnow;
        Vector<double, long> xarr; // Useful work array
        FDM fdm;


public:

        FDMDirector (double XM, double TM, long JSteps, long NSteps,
                    const Vector<double, long>& mesh)
        {

            T = TM;
            J = JSteps;
            N = NSteps;
            Xmax = XM;
            tprev = tnow = 0.0;
            fdm = FDM(mesh);

            xarr = mesh;
            k = T / double (N);

        }

        const Vector<double, long>& current()
```

```
{
     return fdm.current();
}

void doit()
{
     // Step 4, 5: Get new coefficient arrays + solve

     tnow = tprev + k;
     fdm.solve(tprev, tnow);
     tprev += k;
}


bool isDone()
{
     if (tnow < T)
     {
           return false;
     }

     cout << "done";
     return true;
}
};
```

10.2.4   The Display agent and Top-level agent

We now discuss Areas 3 and 4. Area 4 is implemented as a main() function in the current version while we use a print function from the Excel Visualisation library to implement Area 3. The code is given by

```
int main()
{ // The main program plays the of the Whole object

     // Preprocessor
     init();

     // Conversion
     int J= 200; int N = 4000-1;
     cout << "Number of space steps: ";
     cin >> J;
     cout << "Number of time steps: ";
     cin >> N;

     // Create the mesh
     double T = BSPde::data.T;
     Mesher mesh(BSPde::XInterval,T);
```

```
Vector<double, long> xresult = mesh.xarr(J);

double Smax = BSPde::TInterval.high();
FDMDirector fdir(Smax, T, J, N, xresult);

do
{ // No goto's used anymore!

    fdir.doit();

} while(fdir.isDone() == false);

// Output, area 3
try
{
    printOneExcel(xresult, fdir.current(), string("Value"));
}
catch (DatasimException& e)
{
    e.print();
    return 0;
}

return 0;
}
```

You can run this program and test it using different parameter values. We shall also use this small application to motivate the need for design patterns.

10.3   AN OVERVIEW OF THE GOF PATTERNS

The origins of design patterns for software systems date back to the 1980s and 1970s. It was not until 1995 that they were published by Eric Gamma and co-authors (GOF, 1995). This influential book spurred interest in the application of design patterns to software development projects in C++ and Smalltalk.

The motivation for using design patterns originated from the work of architect Christopher Alexander who used the following description:

Each pattern describes a problem which occurs over and over again in our environment, and then describes the core of the solution to that problem, in such a way that you can use this solution a millions times over, without ever doing it the same way twice.

The current authors have been working with design patterns since 1993 and they have applied them in different kinds of applications such as Computer Aided Design (CAD) and computer graphics, process control, real time and finance applications. Once you learn how a pattern works in a certain context, you will find that it is easy to apply in new situations. The GOF patterns are applicable to objects and to this end they model *object lifecycle*, namely object creation, the structuring of objects into larger configurations and finally modelling how objects communicate with each other using a form of *message passing*. The main categories are

- *Creational*: These patterns abstract the instantiation (object creation) process. The added-value of these patterns is that they ensure that an application can use objects without having to be concerned with how these objects are created, composed or internally represented. To this end, we create dedicated classes whose instances (objects) have the sole responsibility of creating other objects. In other words, instead of creating all our objects in `main()`, for example, we can delegate the object creation process to dedicated *factory objects*. This approach promotes the single responsibility principle.
     The specific creational patterns are
  - *Builder* (for complex objects).
  - *Factory Method* (define an interface for creating an object).
  - *Abstract Factory* (define an interface for creating hierarchies of objects or families of related objects).
  - *Prototype* (create an object as a copy of some other object).
  - *Singleton* (create a class that has only one instance).
  For more details on these and other patterns, we refer the reader to GOF (1995).
- *Structural*: These patterns compose classes and objects to form larger structures. We realise these new relationships by the appropriate application of structural modelling techniques such as *inheritance*, *association*, *aggregation* and *composition*.
     The specific structural patterns are
  - *Composite* (recursive aggregates and tree structures).
  - *Adapter* (convert the interface of a class into another interface that clients expect).
  - *Facade* (define a unified interface to a system instead of having to access the objects in the system directly).
  - *Bridge* (a class that has multiple implementations).
  - *Decorator* (add additional responsibilities to an object at run-time).
  - *Flyweight* (an object that is shared among other objects).
  - *Proxy* (an object that is a surrogate/placeholder for another object to control access to it).
- *Behavioural*: These are patterns that are concerned with inter-object communication, in particular the implementation of algorithms and sharing of responsibilities between objects. These patterns describe run-time control and data flow in an application. We can further partition these patterns as follows:
  - *Variations*: Patterns that customise the member functions of a class in some way. In general, these patterns externalise the code that implements member functions. The main patterns are
    * *Strategy* (families of interchangeable algorithms).
    * *Template Method* (define the skeleton of an algorithm in a base class; some variant steps are delegated to derived classes; common functionality is defined in the base class).
    * *Command* (encapsulate a request as an object; execute the command).
    * *State* (allows an object to change behaviour when its internal state changes).
    * *Iterator* (provide a means to access the elements of an aggregate object in a sequential way, without exposing its internal representation).

- *Notifications*: These patterns define and maintain dependencies between objects:
  * *Observer* (define one-to-many dependency between a *publisher* object and its dependent *subscribers*).
  * *Mediator* (define an object that allows objects to communicate without being aware of each other; this pattern promotes *loose coupling*).
  * *Chain of Responsibility* (avoid coupling between *sender* and *receiver* objects when sending requests; give more than one object a chance to handle the request).
- *Extensions*: Patterns that allow us to add new functionality (in the form of member functions) to classes and to classes in a class hierarchy. There is only one such pattern:
  * *Visitor* (define an operation on the classes in a class hierarchy in a non-intrusive way).
  There are some other, somewhat less important behavioural patterns in GOF (1995):
- *Memento* (capture and externalise an object's internal state so that it can be restored later).
- *Interpreter* (given a language, define a representation for its grammar and define an interpreter to interpret sentences in the language).

Which GOF patterns are useful when developing applications? An initial answer is that 20% of the patterns are responsible for 80% of developer productivity in our experience.

10.3.1   Strengths and limitations of GOF patterns

Design patterns are an essential technique in the software developer's toolbox. They are based on the object-oriented paradigm that became popular in the 1990s. The GOF book uses inheritance, composition and subtype polymorphism that languages such as C++ support. However, GOF patterns are not a panacea for all problems and it is important to know in which situations their use is suboptimal and in which situations they do not function properly. We give a list of these limitations and we propose how to resolve them:

- GOF patterns are *micro-patterns*; they are not suitable as a tool for high-level architectural or logical design. We resolve this shortcoming by first applying appropriate POSA patterns (for example, *Whole-Part* and *PAC*). The POSA patterns evolve naturally into GOF patterns. This is a process of elaboration.
- Support for other software paradigms: Most textbooks describe and apply GOF patterns from a pure object-oriented perspective. But it is also possible to describe design patterns by posing them as *generic design patterns*. For example, we have created the following patterns as C++ template classes:
  - *Singleton< T >*
  - *Composite< T >*
  - *Command< Receiver, Action >*

We introduce these templated patterns in Chapters 11 and 12 and we discuss their advantages when compared with the classic GOF patterns.

10.4   THE ESSENTIAL STRUCTURAL PATTERNS

We have already discussed a strategic structural pattern in Chapter 9, namely the *Whole-Part* pattern. This pattern partitions an object (or system) into smaller objects where each object has a well-defined responsibility at its level of abstraction. The GOF structural patterns are subsumed by the higher-level POSA patterns such as *PAC, Layers* and *Whole-Part* patterns. GOF structural patterns should partition objects into networks of dedicated objects in such a way as to satisfy the *Single Responsibility Principle (SRP)*. What kinds of object decomposition problems lead to the discovery of GOF structural patterns? Some scenarios are

- Allow an object to have several implementations or realisations.
- Create a unified interface to a collection of objects.
- Place a surrogate/proxy object between two objects.
- Create trees of objects and recursive aggregates.
- Convert the interface of a class into another interface that clients expect.

The discovery and implementation of structural patterns is crucial to the quality of software applications and it is for this reason that we introduce structural patterns followed by a discussion of creational and behavioural patterns. In more general terms, we worry first about the structure and then about the decorating, as it were.

10.4.1   Facade pattern

This pattern is used to make a subsystem (consisting of a network of classes) easier to use. In general, the facade object provides a simple and unified interface to a collection of objects. The client communicates with the facade which in its turn delegates to the objects in the subsystem. There are two main scenarios when looking for facades:

- We discover them in the early stages of the software development process when we use the *Whole-Part* pattern, for example. Many GOF patterns are facades.
- We discover the need for them when client code interfaces with too many objects, resulting in code that becomes difficult to maintain. We then need to reduce the degree of coupling between objects.

In the second scenario we group objects in some way and we consider this to be a reengineering or *refactoring* process. This is an option when you start realising that your object network is becoming too complex and when corrective action needs to take place, sooner rather than later.

An example of a facade in the current book is the application we took in Chapter 0; the client communicates with an object that delegates to dedicated objects for SDEs, calculations using FDM and Monte Carlo simulation. The unified interface in this case consists of a number of functions to price options.

The facade pattern is a general concept and many of the specific GOF patterns are instances of it.

10.4.2   Bridge pattern, template version

This is an exceedingly important pattern in computational finance because domain classes can have several implementations. Again, we separate concerns by defining an *abstraction* (the domain class) and its implementations as classes. We take an example (discussed in Chapter 5) in which we model the Heston SDE. The abstraction in this case is a class containing the essential parameters of the Heston model; the implementation classes correspond to the different ways of implementing the Heston SDE, for example in the original form (Heston, 1993) or using a logarithmic transformation. The UML structural diagram is given in

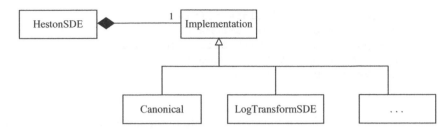

Figure 10.2 Bridge pattern

Figure 10.2. First, we discuss the implementation-independent class and this consists of the parameters in the Heston model in combination with functions that delegate to an implementation. In this case we implement the *Bridge* pattern using C++ generic code, in particular *template template parameters* in the definition of the class (we discuss template template parameters in more detail in Chapter 11). The code for the Heston parameters is defined as a struct:

```
template <typename V> struct HestonStruct
{ // Defining properties of class, already discussed in chapter 5

    V T;
    V r, q;
    V kappa, theta, epsilon;
    V rho;          // Correlation

    V IC_S;         // initial conditions S, V
    V IC_V;
};
```

The class corresponding to the abstraction role in the *Bridge* pattern is given by

```
template <typename V, template <typename S> class HestonImpl>
class HestonClass
{
private:

    HestonImpl<V> imp; // Which implementation to use
    Range<V> ran;
    VectorSpace<V, N> ic;
    HestonStruct<V> data;

    // Other private data and functions..

public:
    HestonClass(const Range<V> range,
            const VectorSpace<V,N>& initial_condition,
            const HestonStruct<V>& myData);

    // Calculate the drift and diffusion functions
```

```
        const VectorSpace<V,N>& calculateDrift(V value,
              const VectorSpace<V,N>& arguments);
        const VectorSpace<V,N>& calculateDiffusion(V value,
              const VectorSpace<V,N>& arguments,
              const VectorSpace<V,D>& dW);
};
```

The bodies of the drift and diffusion functions delegate to the implementation class and hence we see that the abstraction is independent of the implementation. We concentrate on the drift function to show how this process works:

```
// Calculate the drift and diffusion functions at a given time value
template <typename V, template <typename S> class HestonImpl>
const VectorSpace<V,N>& HestonClass<V, HestonImpl>::calculateDrift
 (V value, const VectorSpace<V,N>& arguments)
{

    V tmp1 = driftS(value, arguments);
    V tmp2 = driftV(value, arguments);

    result[1] = tmp1;
    result[2] = tmp2;

    return result;

}
```

where we have used the 'internal' drift functions:

```
template <typename V, template <typename S> class HestonImpl>
    V HestonClass<V, HestonImpl>::driftS(V t, const VectorSpace
        <V,N>& input)
{
    return imp.driftS(t, input, (*this).data);
}

template <typename V, template <typename S> class HestonImpl>
    V HestonClass<V, HestonImpl>::driftV(V t, const VectorSpace
     <V,N>& input)
{
    return imp.driftV(t, input, (*this).data);
}
```

We define the standard implementation of the Heston SDE as introduced in Chapter 5:

```
template <typename V>
    class HestonImplCanonical    // Canonical class
{
public:
```

```
V driftS(V t, const VectorSpace<V,N>& input, const HestonStruct
   <V>&  sdeData)
{ // S component drift term

     return (sdeData.r - sdeData.q) * input[1];
}


V driftV(V t, const VectorSpace<V,N>& input, const HestonStruct
   <V>&  sdeData)
{ // V component is drift

      return sdeData.kappa * (sdeData.theta - input[2]);

}

V diffusionSS(V t, const VectorSpace<V,N>& input, const
   HestonStruct<V>& sdeData)
{ // Main square root term

      return input[1] * sqrt(input[2]);

}

V diffusionVV(V t, const VectorSpace<V,N>& input, const
   HestonStruct<V>& sdeData)
{ // V component drift

     return sdeData.epsilon * sqrt(input[2]);
}

 V diffusionSV(V t, const VectorSpace<V,N>& input, const
    HestonStruct<V>&  sdeData)
{ // Mixed term (1,N) == (S,V)


     return 0.0;
}

V diffusionVS(V t, const VectorSpace<V,N>& input, const
   HestonStruct<V>&  sdeData)
{ // Mixed term (2,1) == (V,S)


      return 0.0;
}


};
```

An example shows how to use this particular implementation and how to define the corresponding Heston parameters:

```
/////////////////// Data Area ////////////////////////////////
    HestonStruct<double> data;

    data.T = 1.0;

    data.r = 0.1;
    data.q = 0.0;

    data.kappa = 1.98837;
    data.theta = 0.1089;
    data.epsilon = 0.15;

    data.rho =  -0.9;

    data.IC_S = 123.4; // ATM
    data.IC_V = 0.37603 * 0.37603;// Not sqrt(V), but V
```

We define the implementation as follows:

```
    Range<double> range(0.0, data.T);
    VectorSpace<double, N> VOld;
    VOld[1] = data.IC_S;
    VOld[2] = data.IC_V;

    HestonClass<double, HestonImplCanonical>
                myHeston(range, VOld, data);
```

Please see the source code on the CD for a full discussion of this code, including how to apply the Monte Carlo in this context. We recommend that you run the code and experiment with the parameters. This makes it easier to understand how this pattern works.

10.4.3   Bridge pattern, run-time version

The implementation of the *Bridge* pattern in the previous section uses the template mechanism. The original *Bridge* pattern is based on the object-oriented paradigm (GOF, 1995) and in this section we give an example based on the test case in Duffy (2004a), pages 290–294 where the abstraction is a class that models scalar-valued functions defined in an interval and the implementations are classes for numeric quadrature schemes based on the midpoint rule and a rule based on the tanh (hyperbolic tangent) function. In this section we extend the implementation hierarchy by adding a number of quadrature schemes based on the Monte Carlo method (Rubinstein, 1981, pages 114–121).

The *Bridge* pattern identifies two main classes; first, the *abstraction class* that encapsulates the application knowledge and second the *implemenation classes* (and there are usually several of them), each one of which implements specific algorithms. In the current case the abstraction is a wrapper for a function defined in a bounded interval and it has a pointer to a base class implementation. We note that the abstraction class has no knowledge of the derived classes of the base implementaion class and this adds to the maintainability of the software. The interface for the abstraction is

```
class NumIntegrator
{
private:
      int nSteps;                    // Number of subdivisions of interval
      Range<double> interval;   // Interval of interest

      double (*f)(double x);    // C style function

      IntegratorImp* imp;       // The 'real' integrator

public:
      NumIntegrator(double (*fp)(double x),
                    const Range<double>& myRange,
                    IntegratorImp& implementor, int numSteps = 30);


      // Modifiers
      void function(double (*fp)(double x));
      void range (const Range<double>& myRange);

      // Selectors
      int numberSteps() const;
      Range<double> getInterval() const;
      double calculate(double x) const;      // Calculate value at x

      // Calculating the integral of the function. Functions that are
      // delegated to the Bridge implementation.
      double value() const;

};
```

Each derived class corresponds to a deterministic or Monte Carlo-based integration method, the latter group being

- Hit or Miss Monte Carlo method.
- Sample-Mean Monte Carlo method.
- Weighted Monte Carlo method.
- Antithetic Variate method.

We mention that we have implemented the code for these four methods on the CD.

A mathematical discussion of these methods is outside the scope of this book (for more information see Rubinstein, 1981, for example) and we give a short discussion of the first method in order to make the transition to C++ code as easy as possible. Let us assume that we wish to integrate a non-negative bounded function $f = f(x)$ in the bounded interval (a, b):

$$I \equiv \int_a^b f(x)dx, \text{ assume } 0 \leq f(x) \leq c, \ x \in [a, b]$$

Define the rectangle:

$$\Omega = \{(x, y) : a \le x \le b, \quad 0 \le y \le c\}$$

The idea behind the *Hit or Miss* method is based on a geometric interpretation; we generate N random points in Ω and we count the number of times M that the points fall under the curve $y = f(x)$, that is, the number of hits. Then the integral is estimated by the quantity:

$$I \approx \theta_1 = c(b - a)\frac{M}{N} \tag{10.5}$$

The steps of the algorithm are:

1. Create a sequence of $2N$ random numbers $U(1), \ldots, U(2N)$.
2. Arrange these numbers into N pairs $(U(1), V(1)), \ldots, (U(N), V(N))$ where each random number $U(j)$, $j = 1, \ldots, N$ is used exactly once.
3. Compute $X(j) = a + U(j)(b - a)$ and $f(X(j))$ for $j = 1, \ldots, N$.
4. Count the number of cases M for which $f(X(j)) > cV(j)$.
5. Estimate the integral I by the formula in equation (10.5).

The code that implements this algorithm is given by:

```
class HitorMissMonteCarlo: public IntegratorImp
{ // The Hit or Miss method ('throwing darts at a board')
  // Assume in this version that 0 <= f(x) <= C

private:

    double C; // Maximum value of function in interval [a,b]

public:
    HitorMissMonteCarlo(double YMax);
    virtual double value(const NumIntegrator& f) const;
};
HitorMissMonteCarlo::HitorMissMonteCarlo(double YMax)
{

    C = YMax;
}


double HitorMissMonteCarlo::value(const NumIntegrator& f) const
{

    Range<double> range = f.getInterval();
    int N = f.numberSteps();
    double A = range.low();
    double B = range.high();
    double d = B - A;

    // 1. Generate 2N U(0,1) numbers
    // 2. And arrange them in N pairs
    vector<pair <double, double> > pairs = generateUniformPairs(N);
```

```
// 3. Translate U(0,1) to U(a, b) and test where the dart falls

long NH = 0;       // Number of hits
double tmp;

for (long j = 0; j < pairs.size(); ++j)
{

        tmp = A + (pairs[j].first * d);
        if (f.calculate(tmp) > C * pairs[j].second)
        {
                NH++;
        }
}

return C * d * double (NH) / double (N);

}
```

An example of use is

```
double myfuncx3 (double x)
{
// Function to be integrated
        return x * x;
}

double FMax = 10.0;
IntegratorImp* imp4 = new HitorMissMonteCarlo(FMax);
context = NumIntegrator(myfuncx3, r, (*imp4), N);

result = context.value();
cout << "Hit or Miss Monte Carlo value is: " << result << endl;
```

Some final remarks concerning the *Bridge* pattern are

• It is one of the most useful patterns in the authors' opinion when you need to define domain classes whose implementations or realisations can change.
• You can choose between compile-time (using templates) and run-time (using inheritance and base class pointers) variants of the *Bridge* pattern; the choice depends on whether you are interested in efficiency or flexibility.
• The alternative to using this pattern is to employ inheritance; in the case of numerical quadrature we would have a single class-based inheritance hierarchy. This approach results in inflexible code because we cannot change implementations at run-time whereas *Bridge* avoids these so-called *permanent bindings*. For a more detailed discussion of this topic, we refer the reader to GOF (1995).

We have seen a very simple implementation of the *Bridge* pattern in section 10.2.2; in this case namespace ParabolicPde is the abstraction and namespace BSPde is its implementation. An object-oriented design and implementation of these classes can be found in Duffy (2006a).

10.4.4 Adapter pattern

This pattern can be used to created a *wrapper object*. We use this pattern in combination with the Standard Template Library (STL) (in general we like to wrap STL containers in user-defined containers). We give some examples in the following chapters and we provide numerous examples on the CD.

A good example of an adapter is a class for a stack (these are *Last In First Out* (LIFO)) data structures. This class is part of the STL but we have created our own stack class that is composed of (or implemented by) a list and which delegates to that latter class. The header file is given by

```
#include <list>
using namespace std;

class Stack
{
private:
     list<double> elements;
public:

     // Default constructor, initialise parts
     Stack();

     // Manipulating elements
     double pop();
     void push(double value);
};
```

You can apply the same principles to the classes that you create for Monte Carlo applications. For example, you can adapt the SDE class to model stochastic equations with jumps.

10.4.5 Layers pattern

This pattern is discussed in detail in POSA (1996). We use it in a particular context in this book, as shown in Figure 10.3 where we use it in a three-layer (case (a)) and a two-layer (case (b)) context. The most common use for us is when we model a *PAC* agent, a simple example of which we have seen in section 10.2.2 (the *Preprocessor*, see Figure 10.1). In all cases, we have decomposed an agent into three independent components corresponding to the data, the user interface and the control aspect. This initial separation of concerns will help us when we elaborate the design of these components using the GOF patterns.

10.5 THE ESSENTIAL CREATIONAL PATTERNS

A creational pattern is realised by a class (or a hierarchy of classes) whose instances are responsible for the creation of other objects. The former objects are specialised *factories* whose main responsibility is to create objects that will subsequently be used by client code.

There are a number of concerns when discovering the most appropriate patterns to use in an application, assuming of course that the context warrants it:

• Separating the object construction process from the clients that use newly-created objects.
• The object lifecycle policy.

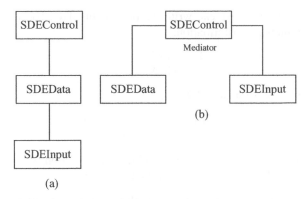

Figure 10.3 *Layers* pattern: (a) three-layer case; (b) two-layer case

The first concern is related to the structural patterns that we discussed in section 10.4. We need to identify the reasons why we wish to use a given creational pattern. In this book we use the *Builder* pattern that creates complex aggregate objects and object networks and the *Factory Method* pattern that offers an interface to create instances of specific classes. We have already discussed creational patterns in Chapter 9. We now discuss some of their uses in the context of this book.

10.5.1 Factory Method pattern

This is a useful pattern for the applications in this book because it provides an interface for creating an object while derived classes decide which class to instantiate. The most important application of the pattern in this book is when we create instances of C++ classes that model SDEs. We give some examples and we show the use of SDEs in a range of application areas:

- *Heston* (equities): The SDE in this case has already been discussed in Chapter 5.
- *CIR* (interest rate model): This is an equilibrium model containing a square-root process:

$$dr(t) = \alpha(b - r(t))dt + \sigma\sqrt{r(t)}dW(t) \quad (\text{where } 2\alpha b \geq \sigma^2) \tag{10.6}$$

- *Swing option SDE* (energy markets): The two-factor connects the spot price S and the equilibrium price L (Pilopović, 1997; Geman, 2005):

$$\begin{aligned} dS &= \alpha(L - S)dt + \sigma S^\gamma dW_1 \\ dL &= \mu L dt + \xi L^\delta dW_2 \end{aligned} \tag{10.7}$$

- *Haken* (experimental psychology and neuronal activity): This is a model for the coordination of human movement. The one-factor SDE is given by

$$dX = -(a \sin X + 2b \sin 2X)dt + \sigma dW \tag{10.8}$$

where a and b are positive parameters that must be determined from external data; the variable X represents the phase difference between two fingers, for example, and it is interpreted modulo 360 degrees. We can write the one-factor SDE (10.8) as a two-factor SDE by using a trigonometric transformation:

$$Y = \cos X$$
$$Z = \sin X$$

to give the following SDE in Stratonovich form:

$$dY = (a + 4bY)(Z)^2 dt - \sigma Z \circ dW$$
$$dZ = -(a + 4bY)YZ dt + \sigma Y \circ dW \qquad (10.9)$$

(note that we need to take a modified drift term and then the solution of (10.9) will be the same as the solution of the Ito SDE with the modified drift term).

We have chosen these examples to show the applicability of design patterns to a range of SDEs and to test these patterns.

We show how we have developed the SDE in equation (10.7) in C++. In this case we have used a namespace for convenience. The code is given by

```
namespace Swing2DFactories
{ // SDE for swing options S = spot price , L = equilibrium price

    double alpha, mu, eta, sigma; // parameters of SDE
    double gamma, delta;

    double driftS(double x, const VectorSpace<double,2>& input)
    { // S component is pure diffusion


        return alpha * (input[2] - input[1]);
    }

    double driftL(double x, const VectorSpace<double,2>& input)
    { // L component

        return mu * input[2];
    }

    double diffusionS(double x, const VectorSpace<double,2>& input)
    {


        return sigma * ::pow(input[1], gamma);

    }

    double diffusionL(double x, const VectorSpace<double,2>& input)
    {


        return eta * ::pow(input[2], delta);
    }
```

```
double zeroFunc(double x, const VectorSpace<double,2>& input)
{
        // No mixed terms
        return 0.0;
}


SDE<double, 2, 2> SwingSDE(const Range<double>& range,
                          const VectorSpace<double, 2>& VOld)
{
// Function that actually creates the SDE instance

     cout << "In Swing\n";
     SDE<double, 2, 2> result(range, VOld);

    // Define the drift terms
    result.setDriftComponent(driftS, 1);
    result.setDriftComponent(driftL, 2);
    // Define the diffusion matrix
    result.setDiffusionComponent(diffusionS, 1, 1);
    result.setDiffusionComponent(diffusionL, 2, 2);
    result.setDiffusionComponent(zeroFunc, 2, 1);
    result.setDiffusionComponent(zeroFunc, 1, 2);

    return result;

}
}
```

We have tried to make the cognitive distance between the symbols in equation (10.7) and their realisation in C++ as small as possible by choosing good variable names. A test program to show how to use the factory is

```
using namespace SDEFactories::Swing2DFactories;

// Initialise its parameters
alpha = 0.2;
mu = 0.4;
eta = 0.1;
sigma = 0.20;
gamma = 1.0;
delta = 1.0;

// Initial conditions
VectorSpace<double, dim> VOld;
VOld[1] = 0.10;
VOld[2] = 1.0;

SDE<double, dim, dim2> result = SwingSDE(myRange, VOld);
```

We note that you need to include the *namespace* directive when using this particular factory and it needs to be done at compile time. In other cases we may need to choose a factory at run-time, in which case a different variant of the pattern will be needed. We have seen a simple example of a *Factory Method* pattern in section 10.2.2. In this case we used namespaces when creating a PDE that models the Black-Scholes equation. But using namespaces is just one particular solution.

10.5.2 Builder pattern

The Builder pattern is in a league of its own as it were because – in contrast to other creational patterns – it is used for the creation of complex objects and for the configuration of objects in a complete application. By 'complex' we mean any of the following:

- Whole-Part hierarchies.
- The agent in a *PAC* pattern.
- The components of a *PAC* agent.
- Composites and recursive aggregates.
- The complete application (a network of objects).

The last example pertains to creating and initialising the objects corresponding to the application. The Builder pattern offers many advantages:

- It takes care of the tedious and potentially unsafe work of creating data, objects and links between objects. Clients do not have to know how the objects are created and how the links are realised. In GOF terminology, it is stated as:

   Builder separates the construction of a complex object from its representation so that the same construction process can create different representations.

- The Builder pattern is particularly useful when we create an application to test a Monte Carlo application. The main() function will delegate to a builder object, thus making the code easier to maintain and to understand.
- Since the builder is responsible for the creation of heap-based objects, among other things, we can also agree that the same builder should be responsible for the destruction of these objects. This can take place in the builder's destructor. In this way we avoid infamous memory leaks when using 'raw' C++ pointers. In Chapter 13 we introduce smart pointers and in this case the developer does not need to worry about memory deallocation; it is taken care of by the compiler.

10.6 THE ESSENTIAL BEHAVIOURAL PATTERNS

Once we have discovered the classes, class hierarchies and class relationships in the application we need to design their member functions. In particular, requirements evolve and code may need to be changed. Some scenarios are

- S1: The body of a member function is replaced by new code.
- S2: Define a family of interchangeable algorithms that clients can use.
- S3: Extend the functionality of all classes in a class hierarchy in a non-intrusive way.
- S4: Promote common data and functionality (so-called *commonality*) from derived classes to a common base class.

Scenarios S1 and S2 are realised by the *Strategy* pattern (and sometimes by the *State* pattern); the *Visitor* pattern realises scenario S3 while the *Template Method* pattern is used to realise scenario S4. These patterns compete in certain contexts but they can also collaborate to form so-called small *pattern languages*. A pattern language is a structured method of describing good design practices within a field of expertise. It is characterised by

- Noticing and naming the common problems in a field of interest.
- Describing key characteristics of effective solutions that meet some stated goal.
- Helping the designer move from problem to problem in a logical way.
- Allowing for many different paths through the design process.

We shall see some examples of these patterns in the following sections.

10.6.1   *Visitor* **pattern**

We have given some examples of the application of *Visitor* to computational finance in Duffy (2004a) and Duffy (2006a). The focus was on partial differential equations and finite difference methods. We have already shown its applicability to the Monte Carlo applications in Chapter 0. In general, we use this pattern when we extend the essential functionality of classes in a class (context) hierarchy or when we wish to write input and output functionality for these classes. This pattern addresses a fundamental design problem in software development, namely defining classes in a class hierarchy with each class having its own data structure and subsequently defining new operations for these classes. However, we do not wish to implement these operations as member functions of the classes themselves because this increases code bloat and makes the classes more difficult to maintain. Instead, we create another class hierarchy and the classes in this hierarchy contain functions that implement the new functionality associated with the context classes. This is the intent of the *Visitor* pattern.

We have provided several examples of this pattern on the CD and have used it to model finite difference schemes. One particularly useful application of the *Visitor* pattern is when we write object data to disk or when we re-create an object by reading in its data from disk. We gave an example in the context of XML interoperability in Duffy (2004a).

10.6.2   *Strategy* **and** *Template* **Method patterns**

These are two related behavioural patterns and they are used when we are working with *algorithms* (a common activity in computational finance). In particular, these patterns allow the developer to design and implement algorithms as classes (usually they are part of a class hierarchy having standard interfaces). The actual body of the code that implements an algorithm is hidden in member functions. Furthermore, it is desirable to standardise the types of the input and output parameters of the algorithm. This leads to maintainable code because format changes tend to be hidden from sight.

We first discuss *Strategy*. This pattern allows us to define a family of algorithms by encapsulating each one in a class. We make the algorithms interchangeable by deriving the corresponding classes from a general abstract base class. The added value is that the algorithms and clients can vary independently, thus allowing the algorithms to become more reusable.

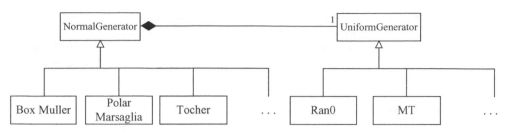

Figure 10.4 Normal and uniform variate generators

When designing strategy classes we can choose between an object-oriented approach (base and derived classes, as discussed in GOF, 1995) or we can use *policy classes* and templated strategies. We discuss the latter topic in Chapter 11.

We now discuss the *Template Method Pattern*. It is similar to the *Strategy* pattern in that it models algorithms, but in contrast to Strategy – where the complete code body of an algorithm is replaced by other code – this pattern describes an algorithm as a series of steps, some of which are *invariant* (which means that the corresponding code does not need to be replaced by other code) and some of which are *variant* (may need to be replaced by other code). In short, the algorithm has customisable (variant) and non-customisable (invariant) parts. The advantage is that we can replace variant code by other variant code while retaining the structure and the semantics of the original or 'main' algorithm.

So, how do we implement the *Template Method* pattern in C++? The general idea is to define a base class B and one or more derived classes (let's call them D1, D2, . . .). The tactic is as follows:

1. Define the member function for the main algorithm in B.
2. Define 'hook' (variant) functions as pure virtual functions in B.
3. Implement these hook functions in D1 and D2.

Thus, this solution employs a combination of inheritance and polymorphism to implement the pattern.

Let us take an example. In this case we create a small object-oriented framework that calculates normal variates, arrays of normal variates and matrices of normal variates. In order to compute normal variates we first produce uniform random variates and we then use them in an algorithm to compute the normal variates. The requirements are that it should be easy to extend the framework and that all common code should be situated in the base class (this process is called *refactoring*). To this end, we now discuss the classes that are documented in Figure 10.4 and we first concentrate on the class hierarchy for uniform variate generation. The interface for the base class is

```
class UniformGenerator
{
private:

public:
    UniformGenerator();

    // Initialisation and setting the seed
```

```
    virtual void init(long Seed_) = 0;

    // Getting random structures (Template Method pattern)
    virtual double getUniform() = 0;// Number in range (0,1),
      variant part
    Vector<double, long> getUniformVector(long N); //
      Invariant part

};
```

We have *hook functions* for initialising the seed and for calculating a uniform random number in the range (0, 1). The template method calculates an array of uniform variates and it is inherited by all derived classes. The code for this function is given by

```
// Getting random structures (Template Method itself)
Vector<double, long> UniformGenerator::getUniformVector(long N)
{ // Invariant part

    Vector<double, long> vec(N);

    for(long i=vec.MinIndex(); i<=vec.MaxIndex();  ++i)
    {
        vec[i] = getUniform(); // Variant part
    }

    return vec;
}
```

Derived classes must implement the pure virtual member function getUniform() but this is not so much work and you get the functionality from the base class for free! We have created derived classes for a number of uniform generators; we show the code for the well-known and shaky generator based on the C function rand(). The interface is

```
class TerribleRandGenerator : public UniformGenerator
{ // Based on the infamous rand()

private:
    double factor;

public:
    TerribleRandGenerator();

    // Initialise the seed, among others
    void init(long Seed_);

    // Implement (variant) hook function
    double getUniform();

};
```

The code for this class is given as

```
TerribleRandGenerator::TerribleRandGenerator()
{
        factor = 1.0 + double(RAND_MAX);
}


void TerribleRandGenerator::init(long Seed_)
{
    // Call this function ONCE ONCE ONCE before calling
    // the other 'generator' functions

    srand((unsigned) time (0));

}



// Implement (variant) hook function
double TerribleRandGenerator::getUniform()
{

    return  double(rand())/factor;
}
```

We now discuss the other class hierarchy in Figure 10.4. The base class interface is given by

```
class NormalGenerator
{
protected:

    UniformGenerator* ug;      // This is a strategy object

public:
    NormalGenerator(UniformGenerator& uniformGen);

    // Getting random structures (Template Method pattern)
    virtual double getNormal() = 0;      // Number in (0,1)

    // Two template methods
    Vector<double, long> getNormalVector(long N);
    NumericMatrix<double, long> getNormalMatrix(long N, long M)

};
```

In this case we have one hook function and two template methods that produce arrays and matrices of normal variates, respectively. The code in the latter case is given by

```
NumericMatrix<double, long>
                    NormalGenerator::getNormalMatrix(long N, long M)
{ // Invariant part
```

```
NumericMatrix<double, long> result(N, M);

for(long i=result.MinRowIndex(); i<= result.MaxRowIndex(); ++i)
{
     for(long j=result.MinColumnIndex();
              j<= result.MaxColumnIndex(); ++j)
     {
        result(i,j) = getNormal();
     }
}
return result;
}
```

We have created a number of classes for popular methods such as the *Box-Muller* scheme:

```
class BoxMuller : public NormalGenerator
{
private:
     double U1, U2;      // Uniform numbers
     double N1, N2;      // 2 Normal numbers as product of BM

     double W;
     const double tpi;
public:
     BoxMuller(UniformGenerator& uniformGen);

     // Implement (variant) hook function
     double getNormal();
};
```

The code for this class is

```
BoxMuller::BoxMuller(UniformGenerator& uniformGen) :
 NormalGenerator(uniformGen), tpi(2.0 * 3.1415)
{
}


// Implement (variant) hook function
double BoxMuller::getNormal()
{

          U1 = ug->getUniform();
          U2 = ug->getUniform();
          W = sqrt( -2.0 * log(U1));

          N1 = W * cos(tpi * U2);
          N2 = W * sin(tpi * U2);

          return N1;
}
```

Finally, we show how to use this code in an application; in this case we generate (1) an array of uniform variates and (2) an array and a matrix of normal numbers using the `rand()` function and the *Box-Muller* method:

```
TerribleRandGenerator myTerrible;
myTerrible.init(0);

Vector<double, long> arr = myTerrible.getUniformVector(20);
print(arr);

NormalGenerator* myNormal = new BoxMuller(myTerrible);
Vector<double, long> arr2 = myNormal->getNormalVector(100);

print(arr2);

cout << "Random matrix\n";
NumericMatrix<double, long> mat
    = myNormal -> getNormalMatrix(5, 6);
print(mat);

delete myNormal;
```

We have now completed our discussion of patterns for implementing algorithms. The test case is interesting in itself and the experience can be applied to other problems in computational finance. The Template Method pattern can be used to build small frameworks.

10.7   SUMMARY AND CONCLUSIONS

In this chapter we have given a detailed description of the most important GOF design patterns. By the use of appropriate and relevant examples we showed how to implement them using C++. We recommend that you experiment with the code on the CD. Finally, we strongly recommend your doing the exercises in this chapter.

Another way to learn the 'mechanics' of design patterns in C++ is to examine the appropriate code on the CD and adapt it to suit your own needs. The implementation of a given design pattern is always the same; it is just the class name and the code in the corresponding member functions that differ.

10.8   EXERCISES AND PROJECTS

1. (**) General Questions on Patterns
   The following questions are aimed at identifying the most appropriate design patterns in a given context. The questions are structured in such a way that each question should lead to an answer that involves one major design pattern. Which pattern realises the following requirements?
   - Configuring the data and parameters for a stochastic differential equation, for example using GUI, XML or from a calibration engine.
   - Configuring objects and global data in an application prior to start-up.
   - Defining prototypical objects in some kind of toolbox; the user can select a copy of an object from the toolbox, modify it (if necessary) and use it in the application.

- Creating a C++ class for an SDE that includes jumps. This class is based on a class that already models Brownian motion (as in the chapters in Part I of the book).
- Creating run-time compile-time implementations for uniform and normal variate generators.
- Creating a hierarchy of C++ classes that model finite difference schemes for a range of one-factor and n-factor SDEs.
- The ability to save critical data to disk, as well as restoring that data for use in objects.
- Comparing the advantages and disadvantages of using the *Strategy* and *Visitor* patterns to approximate the solution of SDEs using the finite difference method. Base your answers on Efficiency, Maintainability and Functionality requirements.

2. (****) Creating C++ Classes for Polynomials

In this exercise we model a class of functions that can be written in the form

$$p_n(z) = \sum_{j=0}^{n} a_j z^{n-j}$$

These are called polynomials of degree n in the variable z (which can be of any type but in many applications it will be a real or complex number). The coefficients in the polynomial expansion have the same data type as that of z. We model these functions using C++ and we apply the design patterns in this chapter to help us write an extensible class that can be used in a variety of applications, ranging from numerical integration and interpolation, Padé approximants to the exponential function and finite element analysis, to name just a few. Another application (when the coefficients are of Boolean type, that is they have the value 0 or 1) is when we construct *Sobol numbers* using *primitive polynomials* (see Press *et al.*, 2002; Jäckel, 2002).

For the current exercise we would like to add, subtract and multiply two polynomials:

$$p_n(z) \pm q_m(z) = \sum_{j=0}^{n} (a_j \pm b_j) z^{n-j}$$

where

$$q_m(z) = \sum_{j=0}^{m} b_j z^{m-j}, \quad n \geq m \text{ and } b_j = 0, \quad j > m$$

We assume that addition and subtraction of polynomials of different degrees is possible; in that case you need to 'pad' the lower-degree polynomial with zero-valued coefficients.

Multiplication of polynomials is defined by

$$p_n(z) * q_m(z) = \sum_{j=0}^{N} c_j z^{N-j}$$

where

$$N = n + m$$

and

$$c_j = \sum_{i=0}^{j} a_i b_{j-i}$$

Answer the following questions:
- Create a C++ template class called `Polynomial<typename T, int N>` where T is the data type and N is the degree of the polynomial. In this case we would like you to use the *Adapter* pattern by coding the polynomial class using the class `VectorSpace<T, N>` as embedded implementation. Define and implement constructors and the operators corresponding to the above mathematical operations.
- Implement *Horner's method* that evaluates a polynomial for a given value of z:

$$p_n(z) = a_n + z(a_{n-1} + \ldots + z(a_3 + z(a_2 + z(a_1 + za_0))))$$

This is more efficient than building the powers of z one by one and then evaluating by the standard polynomial form. Use a member function to realise Horner's method.
- We wish to make the coefficients of a polynomial *persistent*. In other words, we wish to create an instance of `Polynomial<typename T, int N>` by reading its coefficient data from disk and we save the data to disk after it has been changed. Which patterns would you employ in order to realise this requirement? We note that the Boost library has support for polynomials.

3. (**) Single Reponsibility Principle (SRP) and Cohesion
   We define *cohesion* as a measure of how well the lines of source code within a module work together to provide a specific piece of functionality. In object-oriented programming this is the degree to which a method implements a single function. Methods that implement a single function are described as having high cohesion. SRP states that every object should have a single responsibility, and that all its services should be narrowly aligned with that responsibility.

   We examine Figure 10.1 again and the C++ code that implements the classes in that diagram. Answer the following questions:
   - Do the classes satisfy SRP and are they highly cohesive?
   - We shall upgrade the code in this problem and we wish to know what the consequences are. To this end, we must address the following aspect:

     The essence of this interpretation is that a responsibility is a reason to change, and that a class or module should have one, and only one, reason to change.

   Using this example as a model guideline you should make an inventory of the reasons why the code for this problem would change. Relate your answer to the areas in Figure 10.1.

4. (****) Payoff Functions in a Finite Difference Scheme
   In section 10.2 we restricted our attention to call and put payoff functions. We now wish to price options with payoffs such as *binary (digital), super-share, asset-or-nothing* and *shout*, for example (see Haug, 2007 and Duffy, 2004a, page 189 for the formulae). Answer the following questions that have to do with the C++ code corresponding to Figure 10.1:
   - Which parts of the code need to be changed in order to support these new payoffs?
   - Which combination of creational, structural and behavioural patterns do you need to use in order to configure the application in section 10.2?
   - Modify the UML diagram in Figure 10.1 to reflect these new features.

5. (***) PAC Model for Monte Carlo Simulator
   The objective of this exercise is to create a software design for the simple Monte Carlo simulator from Chapter 0 by using the PAC model for the explicit Euler finite difference scheme for a one-factor PDE as an analogy. The underlying assumption is that the solution in section 10.2 can be used as a template as it were for the current problem in the sense

that each problem is concerned with option pricing using PDE and stochastic methods, respectively.

Summarising, the input to this exercise is discussed in sections 0.8 (initial MC framework in C++) and 10.2 (PAC model that implements the explicit Euler finite difference scheme for a one-factor PDE). We will attempt to 'morph' Figure 0.1 into Figure 10.1 in the sense that we wish to produce a diagram similar to Figure 10.1 but using classes from Figure 0.1. We call the solutions A and B, for convenience.

Answer the following questions:
- Identify the input and output for solutions A and B. What are the similarities?
- Identify the activities in linking the input to output in solution A. Find the relationships between these activities and the areas in Figure 10.1 (ideally, there should be a one-to-one mapping between them).
- Design each new area for solution A based on the analogous classes in Figure 10.1. The product of this part is a new UML diagram. Having done that, we now wish to use the *Builder* and *Mediator* patterns in the new solution. Where will you place them in the UML diagram?
- Implement the new solution in C++. Can you reuse code from solution A (for example, classes for random number generation)?

6. (****) Version 2 of PAC Model Figure 10.1

In this exercise we wish to generalise the design in section 10.2 to accommodate a wider range of one-factor derivative products and numerical schemes. We focus on the PDE solution but the conclusions can also be applied to the new Monte Carlo solution from exercise 4 (above).

Answer the following questions:
- Instead of using namespaces, create a hierarchy of classes that model a range of one-factor option types (for example, CEV, barriers, Asian, plain). Consider using the *Bridge* pattern in order to improve portability.
- Support for implicit Euler and Crank Nicolson schemes; create a hierarchy of classes to model finite difference schemes. The classes have common functionality and this should be promoted to base class level (refactoring). Use a class to create mesh points in the underlying and time variables. The Template Method pattern will be useful.
- Use the *Singleton* pattern to store default settings such as mesh sizes, choice of scheme, for example. Finally, apply the *Builder* pattern to construct the objects in the application. We have already produced a solution to this problem in Duffy (2004a) (see Figure 16.1 in that book). The difference in this case is that we show how to arrive at a fully-fledged object-oriented solution in an incremental fashion. In short, we advocate the following tactic: get it working, then get it right, then get it optimised.

Combining Object-Oriented and Generic Programming Models

We can solve any problem by introducing an extra level of indirection.

Butler Lampson

11.1 INTRODUCTION AND OBJECTIVES

In this chapter we implement patterns and design blueprints using a combination of object-oriented and generic programming models. The process of mapping patterns to code is well documented (see GOF, 1995; for examples in computational finance, see also Duffy, 2004a and Duffy, 2006a). However, the literature tends to focus on the object-oriented approach with its emphasis on inheritance and *subtype polymorphism* while many of the Gamma patterns can be implemented as C++ template classes using *parametric polymorphism*. We define these two kinds of polymorphism in this chapter. We review the possibilities, choices and the consequences of their use in applications.

We use template classes and function templates extensively in this book to help us create reusable code and frameworks. It is for this reason that we devote a chapter to generic programming and its integration with the object-oriented model. This chapter also extends a number of object-oriented and generic patterns from Alexandrescu (2001) and GOF (1995).

We discuss the following topics in this chapter:

- Choosing between compile-time and run-time data structures.
- Using template classes to write reusable components.
- Template member functions; template template parameters.
- Traits classes.
- Policy-based design using templates.
- Combining object-oriented programming (OOP) and generic programming (GP) models.
- Template-based design patterns.

This list of techniques forms the building blocks when we design and implement C++ applications. Many of the source files on the CD use the above techniques.

11.2 USING TEMPLATES TO IMPLEMENT COMPONENTS: OVERVIEW

This section discusses the various ways of implementing template classes. It can be seen as a summary of some useful features from the C++ language.

The fundamental questions and action points that we resolve when developing a software module or component are

- A1: What are its (potential) client components?
- A2: What are its (potential) server components?
- A3: Do we define clients and servers at run-time or at compile time?
- A4: How do clients and servers communicate?

In general, these are issues that all developers have in their daily work. The advantage of addressing these issues and choosing the appropriate C++ code to realise them is that it will help us create flexible software that satisfies current (and future) requirements. This will become even more evident when we discover that an arbitrary software application is a network of communicating components and that the communication mechanism is built on a *provides-requires* metaphor; in other words, for each software module we determine the services it provides to (potential) clients and the services it needs or requires from servers.

Let us consider the case where we create a component that provides functionality in the form of member functions and that requires functionality from other components. We call these the *client* and *server* components, respectively. We address the fundamental design issues:

- A5: What kinds of interfaces does the server component offer to potential clients?
- A6: Does the client component have explicit knowledge of its server components?
- A7: Do we wish to have run-time or compile-time behaviour?

We first examine the structural relationships between client and server components. The main relationships are inheritance and composition, and it is also possible to use a server object as a parameter in a client member function. The next step is to decide if the client has explicit knowledge of the names of its servers (as in the OOP approach) or whether it interfaces with a generic data type. The specific server type needs to be instantiated at some stage and in the case of template classes this takes place using template instantiation. It is possible to combine OOP and GP to create inheritance and composition structures.

Having defined client-server relationships between components we now determine how they interact. In practical terms, a client component calls a member function in a server component and to this end, we address the following issues:

- A8: The name of the function.
- A9: The input parameters of the function.
- A10: The return type of the function.

The major challenge is to determine if we need generic, extendible and flexible parameters and return types or whether hard-coded parameters and return types are sufficient. Finally, we need some way of grouping collections of functions to form interfaces:

- A11: Gather functions into logically related interfaces.

We address the action points A1 to A11 in this chapter and we show how to realise them using a combination of generic and object-oriented programming techniques. We give a number of examples to show how to apply design techniques when building software frameworks for the Monte Carlo method.

11.3   TEMPLATES VERSUS INHERITANCE, RUN-TIME VERSUS COMPILE-TIME

A fundamental issue when developing object-oriented and generic software systems lies in determining how a given class (which we call the *client*) delegates to another class (which we call the *server*). The client may need to know about the existence of the server at run-time or at compile-time. There are four main scenarios:

- Client has a server base class pointer as (private) member data (stateful, non-templated).
- Client is a template class using template template parameters (stateful, templated). We discuss this mechanism in section 11.4.5.
- Client has a non-template base class reference as input argument in its member function (stateless, non-templated).
- Client has a template object as input argument in one of its member functions (stateless, templated). This is called a *template member function* which we shall discuss in section 11.4.3.

Let us take a very simple but illustrative example to show how to create client and server classes using object-oriented and generic programming techniques. The relevant diagram is in Figure 11.1 and we first discuss part (a) of that diagram. An instance of the class C is composed of an S1 instance and it has a dependency on an instance of class S2. These two latter classes have polymorphic functions to which C delegates. This is a common configuration in many

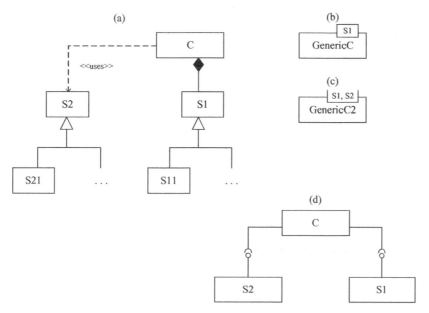

Figure 11.1   Clients and servers: (a) OOP solution using inheritance and composition; (b) and (c) generic classes; (d) component diagrams

applications and it is in fact the way in which many design patterns are implemented. The source code for the server classes in Figure 11.1(a) is

```
struct S1
{
    S1() {}
    virtual int func1() const = 0;
};

struct S11 : public S1
{
    int func1() const
    {
        return +99;
    }
};
struct S2
{
    S2() {}
    virtual int func1() const = 0;
};

struct S21 : public S2
{
    int func1() const
    {
        return -99;
    }
};
```

The code for the client class C is given by:

```
class C
{ // Client class
private:
    S1* m_srv;
    C() { m_srv = 0;}
public:
    C(S1& s1) { m_srv = &s1;}

    // Functions that use delegation
    int func1() { return  m_srv->func1();} // Stateful variant
    int func2(S2& s2) { return s2.func1();} // Stateless variant
};
```

We can then use these classes as follows:

```
    S1* s1 = new S11;
    S2* s2 = new S21;

    // OOP variant
    C myC(*s1);
```

```
cout << myC.func1() << endl;
cout << myC.func2(*s2) << endl;
delete s1; delete s2;
```

It is possible to extend the functionality of this configuration by creating derived classes of S1 and S2 as well as implementing their pure functions. This is a well-known approach. However, it is possible to achieve the same effects by using templates, as shown in Figure 11.1(b). In this case the client class has a template parameter S1 (note S1 is not a 'real' class now) whose policy is to implement a function that the client expects. Furthermore, we use a *template member function* to implement the desired functionality of S2:

```
template <typename S1>
        class GenericC
{ // Generic version
private:
    S1* m_srv;
    GenericC() { m_srv = S1();}

public:
    GenericC(S1& server) { m_srv = &server;}

    // Functions that use delegation
    int func1() { return m_srv->func1();}      // Stateful variant

    template <typename S2>                     // Template member
                                               // function
    int func2(S2& s2) { return s2.func1();}    // Stateless variant

};
```

In this case the client has no knowledge of its specific server classes; instead it will work with *any* class that implements the functions func1() and func2().

```
struct AnotherClass
{
    int func1() const
    {
        return +77;
    }
};
```

An example of use shows that we can achieve the same functionality as with the OOP approach:

```
    // GP variant
    GenericC<S1> myGC(*s1);
    cout << myGC.func1() << endl;
    cout << myGC.func2<S2>(*s2) << endl;

    // Choose implementation using template member function
    AnotherClass other;
    cout << myGC.func2<AnotherClass>(other) << endl;
```

Finally, we can create a second template class by promoting the status of the template parameter
S2 to that of a class template parameter as shown in Figure 11.1(c):

```
template <typename S1, typename S2>
        class GenericC2
{ // Generic version 2
private:
    S1* m_srv;
    GenericC2() { m_srv = S1();}

public:
    GenericC2(S1& server) { m_srv = &server;}

    // Functions that use delegation
    int func1() { return m_srv->func1();}    // Stateful variant

    // NON-template member function
    int func2(S2& s2) { return s2.func1();}  // Stateless variant
};
```

We now give an example of how to use this class:

```
GenericC2<S1, AnotherClass> myGC2(*s1);
cout << myGC2.func1() << endl;
cout << myGC2.func2(other) << endl;
```

Finally, we note that all solutions use the *provide-require* metaphor; in this case the client C
uses the functions in the classes S1 and S2. We show this behavioural relationship using a
UML *component diagram* in 11.1(d).

On a related issue, the experience gained when migrating an object-oriented solution (as
depicted in Figure 11.1(a)) to a templated one (as depicted in 11.1(b) or Figure 11.1(c)) can
be applied in more general cases. This could be a useful way to upgrade your non-templated
code to support a wider range of data types.

11.4   ADVANCED C++ TEMPLATES

In this section we give an overview of a number of useful techniques that C++ supports and
that we use to promote the reusability and robustness of template classes and functions.

11.4.1   Default values for template parameters

When creating template classes with several template parameters it is possible to define default
policy. In other words, template parameters are used to express *policies* and *traits* (we shall
discuss traits in detail in section 11.5). The default argument provides the most common or
default policy. To give an example, we examine a class for one-dimensional vectors:

```
template <typename Value = double, int N = 10>
        class SimpleVector
{ // Simple vector class
```

```
private:
     Value arr[N];
public:
     // member functions
};
```

In this case there are two default parameters. Thus, it is possible to create vectors with two, one or zero parameters, for example:

```
SimpleVector<double, 20> vec1;
SimpleVector<string> vec2;
SimpleVector<> vec3;
```

In this case the first vector contains 20 doubles; the second vector contains 10 strings while the third vector contains 10 doubles.

We note that default template arguments can be user-defined types. For example, the following declaration defines a matrix class in which the default structure is a full matrix (see Duffy, 2004a where we introduced this class):

```
template <class V, class I=int, class S=FullMatrix<V> >
class Matrix
{// Default structure is FullMatrix. Default integral type is int.

private:
     S m_structure;            // The array structure
     I m_rowstart;             // The row start index
     I m_columnstart;          // The column start index

     // Redundant data
     I nr, nc;

public:
     //
};
```

The main advantage of using default template parameters in code is that it reduces cognitive overload by allowing the developer to use the most common policy in a transparent way. Both the STL and Boost libraries use this feature. It is pervasive.

11.4.2 Template nesting

An effective way to create new generic data structures is to use template classes as parameters for other template classes. We say that one class is *nested* in another one. We speak of an *inner class* and an *outer class*, respectively.

This tactic promotes reusability because the new nested classes can be used in a variety of situations. Furthermore, the amount of testing and debugging is reduced because we are creating a class from existing classes. The only thing to watch out for is that the template parameters must be compatible, in particular that the interface of the inner class conforms to the type that the outer class expects. For example, a templated vector class that expects a numeric underlying type cannot be specialised using strings because the vector class would expect the string class to have mathematical operators for addition, subtraction and multiplication, which it obviously does not have.

We take an example to show the power of nesting. Let us consider creating a square sparse matrix class. In the past, this would have been a non-trivial task in the C language but thanks to templates and STL we can create such a data structure in a few lines of code. To this end, we view a dynamic sparse matrix as a map of maps. We specialise the underlying parameter types for convenience and we define a synonym for readability purposes:

```
// Specific data types, can be generalised
typedef map<int, double> SparseRow;
```

Now we define a sparse matrix structure as follows:

```
template <int N> struct SparseMatrix
{ // Compile-time matrix (stack-based)
    map<int, SparseRow> data;
};
```

The complete code can be found on the CD. We now take an example of using this class. In this case we create a sparse matrix by populating its rows. We also print the sparse matrix using the following function:

```
template <int N> void print(const SparseMatrix<N>& sm)
{
    SparseRow sr;
    SparseRow::const_iterator it;

    for (int row = 0; row < N; ++row)
    {
        SparseRow sr = sm.data[row];
        // Now iterate over row
        for (it=sm.data[row].begin();it!=sm.data[row].end(); ++it)
        {
            cout << (*it).second << ", ";
        }
        cout << endl;
    }
}
```

The code for initialisation is

```
int main()
{
    const N = 500000;
    // Create some rows
    SparseRow current;
    current.insert(pair<int, double> (0, -2.0));
    current.insert(pair<int, double> (1, 1.0));

    // Create a sparse matrix and populate its first row
    SparseMatrix<N> sparseMat;
    sparseMat.data[0] = current;
```

```
int currentIndex = 0;

// Populate the matrix with multiple rows
for (int row = 1; row < N-1; row++)
{
    current.clear();
    current.insert(pair<int, double> (currentIndex, 1.0));
    current.insert(pair<int, double> (currentIndex+1, -2.0));
    current.insert(pair<int, double> (currentIndex+2, 1.0));
    sparseMat.data[row] = current;
    currentIndex++;
}

print(sparseMat);

return 0;
}
```

This sample shows how it is possible to write reliable and flexible code using C++ templates. There are a number of applications where nested classes could be used to good effect:

- Modelling complex volatility surfaces, for example two-dimensional data structures where the first dimension represents the expiry date and the second dimension represents strike price. We have discussed an example in Chapter 3 (section 3.13).
- Modelling a variety of matrix structures and pattern types (as discussed in Duffy, 2004a).
- Statistical information pertaining to Monte Carlo simulations, for example matrices containing path information and data structures to hold information such as standard deviation and standard error.
- Modelling data pertaining to discrete monitoring dates and the modelling of payoff functions. For example, when modelling options we could choose a data structure such as `map<DatasimDate, vector<T> >`.

11.4.3   Template member functions

A *template member* function can be defined in any class to add an extra template parameter to one of the class member functions. In other words, we define a member function that uses one or more additional template parameters in addition to those defined in the class containing that member function. For example, returning to the example in section 11.4.1 (the *Simple Vector* class), let us suppose that we wish to multiply the elements of a vector by a scalar; this scalar belongs to a so-called field type and the corresponding template member function is defined as follows:

```
// Member function version of the scaling function
template <typename F> void scale(const F& scalar)
{
    for (int i= 0; i < N; ++i)
    {
        arr[i]  = scalar * arr[i];
    }
}
```

An example of use is

```
// Multiplication by a scalar
double value = 10.0;
SimpleVector<double, 6> vec4(value);
// Now scale using a member function; notice the use of
      data type
vec4.scale<double>(factor);
vec4.print();
```

Please note that in the call to the scaling function we have inserted the type of the scaling factor. This makes calls unambiguous and ensures we do not get cryptic compiler error messages. Finally, another example is to define a scaling function (non-member) using operator overloading:

```
// Premultiplication by a field value
template <typename F> SimpleVector<Value, N>
      friend operator * (const F& scalar,
                          const SimpleVector<Value, N>& myArray)
{
      SimpleVector<Value, N> result;
      for (int i= 0; i < N; ++i)
      {
            result.arr[i]  = scalar * myArray.arr[i];
      }
      return result;
}
```

An example of use is

```
// Scale using a templated friend function
double factor = 0.5;
SimpleVector<double, 6> scaledVector = factor * vec4;
scaledVector.print();
```

Another important application of template member functions is when the associated generic data type is a *function object*. In that case we can implement a compile-time version of the *Strategy* pattern. We discuss this topic in Chapter 21.

11.4.4 Partial template specialisation

Partial template specialisation is a particular form of class template specialisation. It allows the programmer to specialise only some arguments of a class template, as opposed to explicit specialisation where all the template arguments are specialised. We take an example of a class that calculates Fibonacci numbers (in real life we would not program them in this way). We define a template class as follows:

```
template <unsigned N>
        struct Fibonacci
{
      enum { value = Fibonacci<N-1>::value + Fibonacci<N-2>::value};
};
```

This is an implementation of the well-known recursive scheme for calculating Fibonaccci numbers. We need two initial values and we calculate them using specialisations of the above template class:

```
template <> struct Fibonacci<0>
{
    enum { value = 0 };
};
```

and

```
template <> struct Fibonacci<1>
{
    enum { value = 1 };
};
```

What is going on here? By default, a template gives a single definition to be used for every template argument. We wish to customise this default behaviour by using an implementation that overrules a default implementation by a specific one. This is what we have done when implementing the Fibonacci classes in the cases $n = 0$ and $n = 1$.

An example of use is

```
int main()
{
    cout << Fibonacci<21>::value << endl;
    return 0;
}
```

In general, it is possible to specialise one or more parameters in template classes by using specific parameter types.

11.4.5   Template template parameters

This is a relatively new feature in C++ and at first sight it may not be obvious why we would need it. Let us take the example of a generic collection class to show how this technique works. The code for the class is on the CD and for now the relevant information is given by

```
template<typename T, typename Container = vector<T> >
                class MyCollection2
{ // Generic class without using 'template template' parameters

private:
    // This is the implementation class of the Collection
    Container items;
public:
    MyCollection2()
    {
        items = Container();
    }
    void add(T const& t)
    {
        items.push_back(t);
```

```
    }
    T operator [](int index) const
    {

        typedef typename Container::const_iterator Iter;
        for(Iter i = items.begin(); i != items.end(); ++i,
            --index)
        {
            if(index == 0)
                return *i;
        }

        throw runtime_error("Index out of bounds");
    }
    void clear()
    {
        items.clear();
    }
    int size() const
    {
        return items.size();
    }
};
```

We can now instantiate this class in the usual way. For example, the following code creates a collection of strings using a list:

```
    // Second alternative
    MyCollection2 <string, list<string> > coll3;
    coll3.add("D");
    coll3.add("E");
    coll3.add("F"); cout << endl;

    for (int j = 0; j < coll3.size(); ++j)
    {
        cout << coll3[j] << ", ";
    }
```

So far, so good, but now comes the nasty part; what happens if the first underlying type is different from the underlying type associated with the container? At best we will get a compiler error and at worst we run the real risk of loss of precision (*silent corruption of data*) by copying a double to an int, as in the example:

```
    MyCollection2 <double, list<int> > coll4;
    coll4.add(2.0);
    coll4.add(3.0);
    coll4.add(4.888); cout << endl;

    for (int j = 0; j < coll4.size(); ++j)
    {
        cout << coll4[j] << ", ";
    }
```

What we would really like to write is the following: `MyCollection2 <double, list> coll4;`. However, this syntax leads to a compiler error and one solution to the problem is to use the so-called *template template parameter* feature. In this case we define a new collection class as follows:

```
template<typename T,
     template <typename S, typename Alloc> class Collection,
     typename TAlloc = allocator<T> >

class MyCollection
{
private:
     Collection<T, TAlloc> items;
public:
     MyCollection()
     {
     items = Collection<T, TAlloc>();
     }
     void add(T const& t)
     {
     items.push_back(t);
     }
     T operator [](int index) const
     {
     typedef typename Collection<T>::const_iterator Iter;
     for(Iter i = items.begin(); i != items.end(); ++i, --index)
     {
          if(index == 0)
          return *i;
     }

      throw runtime_error("Index out of bounds");
     }
     void clear()
     {
          items.clear();
     }
     int size() const
     {
          return items.size();
     }
};
```

In this case we define a template that accepts a parameter that is itself the name of a template, thus:

```
template<typename T,
    template <typename S, typename Alloc> class Collection, typename
      TAlloc = allocator<T> >
```

where the first parameter `T` is the underlying type, the second parameter `Collection` is the collection that will hold data and the last parameter `TAlloc` is the allocator that is a memory model; this parameter is used as an abstraction to translate the *need* to use memory into a raw *call* for memory (see Josuttis, 1999). Now, we can create specific collections without getting compiler errors or suffering a loss in precision:

```
// Produce a list of strings
MyCollection<string, list> coll2;
coll2.add("A");
coll2.add("B");
coll2.add("C"); cout << endl;

for (int j = 0; j < coll2.size(); ++j)
{
      cout << coll2[j] << ", ";
}
```

Template template parameters represent a way to implement policies. A *policy* is a description of what a class expects or requires from its server classes. Future releases of C++ will use C++ concepts (Dos Reis, 2006)

11.5   TRAITS AND POLICY-BASED DESIGN

We introduce two design techniques that are used in many C++ libraries and applications. In particular, we can implement components with their associated provided and required interfaces using so-called *policies*, while *traits* are small objects whose main purpose is to encapsulate specific structure.

11.5.1   Traits

In general, a trait is a small object whose main purpose is to carry information that is used by another object or algorithm, thus allowing us to determine 'policy' or 'implementation details'. The main reason for using a trait is to provide a consistent interface to clients and to avoid embedding *magic numbers* in code. Let us take an example and suppose that we wish to create a portable *linear congruential pseudo-random number generator* (LCG) defined by a recursion (Kloeden, Platen and Schurz, 1997: in practice, we would not implement our own LCGs but instead use the Boost Random Number Library, for example):

$$X_{n+1} = aX_n + b \quad (\text{mod } c) \text{ with } X_0 \text{ given (the seed)} \tag{11.1}$$

This formula generates a sequence of integer values in the range $(0, c - 1)$ and these are the remainders when the term $aX_n + b$ is divided by c. Different values of a, b, c and X_0 will lead to different sequences. In practice, the choice depends on a number of factors such as the hardware being used, for example. When developing code that uses LCGs we would like it to be independent of any specific values of the above parameters and to this end we create traits or *template baggage classes* that encapsulate specific and consistent combinations of these parameters. The traits class will be generic because it depends on one or more generic parameters which, when instantiated, will deliver the specific values for a, b, c and X_0. We must be careful because certain values lead to sequences with negative values and hence will not produce uniform numbers. The constraints on these numbers are

$$0 < c \text{ (modulus)}$$
$$0 \leq a < c \text{ (multiplier)}$$
$$0 \leq b < c \text{ (increment)} \tag{11.2}$$
$$0 \leq X_0 < c \text{ (the seed)}$$

LCGs produce reasonable pseudo-random numbers but the quality is highly dependent on the choices of a, b and c. Having produced the sequence in equation (11.1) we can now produce a sequence of numbers that seem to be uniformly distributed on the unit interval [0, 1] by defining the numbers:

$$U_n = X_n/c$$

We now discuss how to model LCGs using C++. In particular, we localise the different sets of parameters in structures, thus avoiding magic numbers, switch statements and the use of default values in constructors and member functions. To this end, we create traits types and classes. In this particular case we have created an empty template class:

```
template <int ParameterType> struct LCG_traits {};
```

We have created some specific classes by instantiating this template class. The values of the parameters correspond to some well-known models from the literature:

```
template <> struct LCG_traits<1>
{ // Kloeden page 9, example

    long a; long b; long c;
    LCG_traits<1>()
    {
        a = 1229; b = 1; c = 2048;
    }
};
template <> struct LCG_traits<2>
{ // IBM 360 parameters (Park and Miller), not perfect

    long a; long b; long c;

    LCG_traits<2>()
    {
        a = 16807;          // 7^5
        b = 0;
        c = 2147483647;   // long(pow(2.0, 31)) - 1;is
                                    a prime number
    }
};

template <> struct LCG_traits<3>
{ // Numerical Recipes recommendation

    long a; long b; long c;
    LCG_traits<3>()
```

```
    {
         a = 16807;
         b = 1;
         c = 2048;
    }
};
```

Having created the traits classes we must determine how to use them in client code. To this end, we create a class that models LCGs as defined in equation (11.1) while taking the constraints in (11.2) into consideration. The complete interface is given by

```
template <int Type> struct LCGClient
{ // A simple class to show to generate a sequence of numbers
          that seem
  // to be uniformly disributed on [0,1]
private:
    LCG_traits<Type> traits;
    long X0;
public:
    LCGClient()
    {
         // Define the specific parameters
         traits = LCG_traits<Type>();
         X0 = 0;
    }
    void InitSeed()
    {   // Initialise seed

         // Call ONCE ONCE ONCE before other 'generator' functions
         srand((unsigned) time (0));
         // Get the seed
         X0 = rand();
    }

    void print() const
    {
         cout << "\na, b, c: (" << traits.a << "," << traits.b
                              << "," << traits.c << ")" << endl;
         cout << "Seed value: " << X0 << endl;
    }

    Vector<double, long> RandomSequence(long N)
    {   // Generate N U(0,1) random numbers
         // In practice use ran0, ran1 or other generator
         long si = 0; // Start index
         Vector<double, long> result (N, si);

         // Recursion
         long Xn, Xnm1;
         Xnm1 = X0;
```

```
        for (long n = result.MinIndex();n <= result.MaxIndex();++n)
        {  // In practice use ran0, ran1 or Mersenne Twister code
            Xn = (traits.a * Xnm1 + traits.b) % traits.c;
            result[n] = Xn / double (traits.c);
            Xnm1 = Xn;
        }

        return result;
    }
};
```

We now have a class that can use different sets of parameters in a *non-intrusive* way; there is no *if-else-then* code that needs to be modified when we wish to define or use a new set of parameters. Instead, we use a new instantiated traits class. An example of use shows what we mean; in this case we create vectors of uniform numbers based on the different parameter sets:

```
long N = 20;
Vector<double, long> randomVector(N);

LCGClient<1> c1; c1.InitSeed();
randomVector = c1.RandomSequence(N);
print(randomVector);
c1.print();

LCGClient<2> c2; c2.InitSeed();
randomVector = c2.RandomSequence(N);
print(randomVector);
c2.print();

LCGClient<3> c3; c3.InitSeed();
randomVector = c3.RandomSequence(N);
print(randomVector);
c3.print();
```

You can use this code in order to experiment with the random number generation process. It was written for pedagogical reasons only. In practice, the function rand() produces terrible results.

We are now finished with the first example of using traits in the context of Monte Carlo applications and frameworks. In order to find traits for your code we suggest the following tips:

- Traits deal with structural issues such as member data, default values in functions and similar characteristics where the structure is the same but the specific values are different.
- Traits are small and are used by client code to determine 'policy' or to enforce a consistent interface.
- Traits are compile-time mechanisms and they eliminate the need for run-time binding. They help improve the efficiency of code that uses data structures.
- Traits help improve the portability of applications by removing hardware and software-specific code from clients.

Our first example of a traits class was user-defined. We note that the STL and Boost libraries contain built-in traits classes that you can use in your applications. An important trait is `numeric_limits<T>`; this class contains a wealth of information on numeric data types, for example:

- Minimum and maximum values.
- Binary and decimal accuracy estimates.
- Whether a numeric type is signed.
- Whether a numeric type is integer.
- Machine precision information.
- Details about rounding behaviour.

This class should be used when creating scientific and numeric applications that use a range of numeric data types such as `float` and `double`, for example. By instantiating the traits class you will be given the appropriate set of parameters and values. A simple template function to print some of these numerical properties is

```
template <typename Numeric>
    void print(string& s)
{ // Numeric properties

    Numeric largest = numeric_limits<Numeric>::max();
    Numeric smallest = numeric_limits<Numeric>::min();

    //calculations done on a type are free of rounding errors.
    bool exactYN = numeric_limits<Numeric>::is_exact;

    // has integer representation
    bool integerRepYN = numeric_limits<Numeric>::is_integer;

    // etc. for the interested developer, see online documentation

    cout << endl << "Numeric type is: " << s << endl;

    cout << "Max, min: " << largest << ", " << smallest << endl;

    // This function ensures values are printed as text, not 0 or 1
    boolalpha(cout);
    cout << "Free of rounding errors: " << exactYN << endl;
    cout << "Integer representation: " << integerRepYN  << endl;
}
```

We can then instantiate this template function by replacing the generic data type by built-in types:

```
print<double> (string("double"));
print<int> (string("int"));
print<long> (string("long"));
print<unsigned int> (string("unsigned int"));
print<unsigned long> (string("unsigned long"));
```

The output from this program is:

```
Numeric type is: double
Max, min: 1.79769e+308, 2.22507e-308
Free of rounding errors: false
Integer representation: false

Numeric type is: int
Max, min: 2147483647, -2147483648
Free of rounding errors: true
Integer representation: true

Numeric type is: long
Max, min: 2147483647, -2147483648
Free of rounding errors: true
Integer representation: true

Numeric type is: unsigned int
Max, min: 4294967295, 0
Free of rounding errors: true
Integer representation: true

Numeric type is: unsigned long
Max, min: 4294967295, 0
Free of rounding errors: true
Integer representation: true
```

Concluding, the use of traits in this case promotes portability and reusability of code because it operates on a wide range of numeric data types.

We conclude this section with an example from matrix algebra. We note that numerical analysis applications need matrices having various structures, for example (Bronson, 1989):

- Dense (full) matrix.
- Band matrices (for example, tridiagonal and pentagonal matrices).
- Sparse matrices.
- Block-banded matrices.
- Lower-diagonal and upper-diagonal matrices.
- Symmetric matrices.
- Diagonal matrices.

Each kind of matrix needs its own storage scheme and to this end we model these structural aspects using traits. We use template parameters as the following pseudo-code shows:

```
Matrix<typename DataType, typename Structure>
```

We have two template parameters, the first parameter for the underlying data type and the second parameter that tells us which storage scheme is being used. Some instantiations are:

```
Matrix<double, Full>
Matrix<double, Tridiagonal>
Matrix<string, Sparse>
Matrix<Complex, Tridiagonal>
```

We used traits classes in Duffy (2004a) and Duffy (2006a) to model some of the above storage schemes for one-dimensional and two-dimensional data structures. For example, we define a class for matrices having an embedded traits class for its storage scheme. The interface is

```
// Default structure is FullMatrix with default allocator.
template <class V, class I=int, class S=FullMatrix<V> >
class Matrix
{
private:
    S m_structure;          // The array structure
    I m_rowstart;           // The row start index
    I m_columnstart;        // The column start index

    // Redundant data
    size_t nr, nc;
public:
    // public functions here
};
```

We see that the default trait is a full matrix of data called `FullMatrix<V>` whose interface is defined in terms of a nested data structure:

```
template <class TValue, class TA=std::allocator<TValue> >
class FullMatrix: public MatrixStructure<TValue>
{
    FullArray<FullArray<TValue, TA>,
          std::allocator<FullArray<TValue, TA> > > m_structure;

    // Redundant data
    size_t nr, nc;

public:
    //

};
```

Thus, a two-dimensional storage scheme is constructed by nesting two one-dimensional storage schemes. The one-dimensional structure `FullArray<TValue, TA>` is defined as follows:

```
template <class V, class TA=std::allocator<V> >
                class FullArray: public ArrayStructure<V>
{
private:
    std::vector<V, TA> m_vector;    // Use STL vector class
                                          for storage
public:
    //
};
```

We can create other similar data structures as discussed in Duffy (2004). Summarising, a traits class is a template class that is used instead of template parameters or default parameters. As a class, it aggregates useful types and constants and as a template it provides a way to achieve an 'extra level of indirection' to solve a number of software problems.

11.5.2   Policy-based design (PBD)

The authors saw this term in Alexandrescu (2001) where it is used in the context of C++ template programming. We generalise it here to make it applicable to a wider range of software techniques including component-based design, UML modelling and template programming.

The need for, and power of, the PBD approach is that we can think about design of any system by decomposing it into loosely coupled components. A component is a piece of software that offers services in the form of groups of functions (called *interfaces*) to other potential client components. In order to design a component we need to address the following activities:

- The products, services and data that the component provides.
- The input data that the component requires from other components.
- The steps that map the input data to output data.

Carrying out these activities is part of the software design process and the end result is a network of components, each one having well-defined responsibilities. This software design process is outside the scope of the current book. We model these responsibilities by interfaces. The resulting UML component diagram is shown in Figure 11.2 for the case of a component called C1 that provides an interface I3 to potential clients and that requires interfaces I1 and I2. In other words, C1 offers services but it also needs services from other server components. These components C2 and C3 typically have responsibilities for services such as

- S1: Object creation and initialisation of simple and complex objects.
- S2: Authentication and authorisation (allowing access to C1).
- S3: Execution of commands on behalf of component C1.
- S4: Execution of algorithms and extended functions of C1 (for example, *Strategy* and *Visitor* patterns).

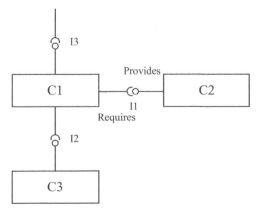

Figure 11.2   Dimensions of policy-based design

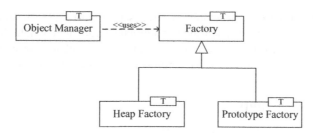

Figure 11.3   Creational policies

In particular, we should strive to create the components in Figure 11.2 so that they have little overlapping functionality and each one should have one major responsibility. Let us take an example in which we model scenario S1 above. In this case we wish to model template components that create objects (this example is based on Alexandrescu, 2001, page 8). Clients then delegate to these factory components when they need an object to be created. We depict the situation in Figure 11.3. A client object delegates to factory objects. The base factory describes an interface:

```
template <class T> class Factory
{ // Base class for all factories
public:
    virtual T* Create() = 0;
};
```

Derived classes must implement this interface:

```
template <class T> class HeapFactory : public Factory<T>
{
public:
    virtual T* Create()
    {
        cout << "Creating heap object\n";
        return new T();
    }
};

template <class T> class PrototypeFactory : public Factory<T>
{
private:
    T* proto;
public:
    PrototypeFactory () {T t; proto = &t;}
    PrototypeFactory (T* prototype) { proto = prototype; }

    virtual T* Create()
    {
        cout << "Creating prototype object\n";
        return new T(*proto);
    }
};
```

We now define the client classes that use these generic factory classes:

```
template <class CreationPolicy>
class ObjectManager : public CreationPolicy
{
public:
    ObjectManager() {}
};
```

We can also define some synonyms to make our code more readable:

```
// Define host classes; app code
typedef ObjectManager<HeapFactory <Point> > MyHeapPointMgr;
```

Now we can use these classes in applications; in this case we manage two-dimensional points. First, we create a useful template function that prompts the user to choose which specific factory to use in subsequent code:

```
template <class T> Factory<T>* GetFactory()
{
    int choice = 1;
    cout << "Factories: 1) Heap 2) Prototype ";
    cin >> choice;

    if (choice == 1)
    {
        return new HeapFactory<T>();
    }
    else
    {
        return new PrototypeFactory<T>();
    }
}
```

Finally, we can write code that is independent of the way memory is allocated; we call a factory to create memory:

```
int main()
{
    // Create a double
    Factory<double>* fac = GetFactory<double>();

    double* myval = fac->Create();
    *myval = 0.001;
    cout << "double is: " << *myval << endl;

    // Create a point by choosing a factory
    Factory<Point>* fac2 = GetFactory<Point>();
    Point* pt2 = fac2->Create();
    (*pt2).print();
```

```
// Create a point using heap allocation
MyHeapPointMgr myPoint;
Point* pt = myPoint.Create();
pt->x = 1.0;
pt->y = 2.0;
(*pt).print();

delete pt;
delete pt2;
delete myval;
delete fac;
delete fac2;

return 0;
}
```

11.5.3   When to use inheritance and when to use generics

We have employed two software programming models in this book, namely the object-oriented and generic programming paradigms. A problem that we need to resolve when developing software systems is to determine which paradigm to choose in a given context and how to combine the two paradigms to produce flexible and extendible software. But what do we mean by these terms? Generic programming implements the concept of an *Abstract Data Type* (ADT) that models data together with operations or functions operating on the data. In order to use the ADT we need to replace the abstract type by a specific type. Having done this we can then use all of the functions 'as is' without any modifications whatsoever. This is called *parametric polymorphism*. Object-oriented programming uses *subtype polymorphism* to define a set of abstract or pure virtual functions in an abstract base class. The developer overrides these functions in derived classes. Thus, in this case the emphasis is on defining various implementations of a common interface with less emphasis on the data types. Based on these observations, these paradigms may or may not satisfy the software requirements in a given context. In an ideal world, we would like to use the features from both paradigms but again it depends on our requirements:

1. Flexible data types necessarily imply generic data structures.
2. Applying the *Principle of Substitutability*: We write a function using a reference to a base class as input parameter. We can then call this code with an instance of any derived class. This principle allows us to define any number of derived classes and use them in applications but they must implement the pure virtual functions that are defined in their base classes. We assume that the reader is familiar with this statement.
3. We would like to combine features 1 and 2 in applications.

We take an example to show how to combine these two programming paradigms. This is the template class that models an n-factor stochastic differential equation based on geometric Brownian motion. It does not model other kinds of random processes such as compound Poisson processes, variance gamma processes or Lévy processes (Cont and Tankov, 2004). To this end, we define a base class that models stochastic differential equations and that subsumes all current and future specialisations. At the moment this non-templated base class has minimal functionality. However, it does define a function that allows us to extend functionality using the *Visitor* pattern (this is needed when we develop various kinds of finite difference schemes for SDEs, for example):

```
class SdeThing
{
public:

        // No virtual functions, yet
        // Extend functionality with Visitor pattern
        template <typename V, int N, int D>
                void Accept(SdeVisitor<V,N,D>& sv) = 0;
};
```

The most important class for SDEs in this book is

```
template <typename V, int N, int D> class SDE : public SdeThing
{ // Non-linear SDE; N is the number of independent variables and
  // D is the number of Brownian motions

private:
    FunctionWrapper<V, N> drift[N];
    FunctionWrapper<V,N> diffusion[N][D];

    Range<V> ran;           // Interval in which SDE is defined
    VectorSpace<V,N> ic;    // Initial condition
                            //
public:
    // see CD for full interface
};
```

We model an SDE's drift vector and diffusion matrix using compile-arrays of function pointers. What are the consequences of taking this approach? First of all, the major advantages are

- A single template class can model any number of specific SDEs; this means that we do not need to create a separate class for each kind of SDE (Heston, Asian, Spread) but we instantiate the template class by giving the number of factors, underlying data type and specific drift and diffusion functions. This feature also promotes code maintainability.
- New kinds of stochastic differential equations can be created and incorporated into the class hierarchy by using the GOF patterns, in particular, *Decorator, Bridge* and *Composite*. Furthermore, we use factory patterns to instantiate the data and functions that we need in order to create a specific SDE instance. Finally, the class hierarchy is structured in such a way that makes it possible to extend the functionality of the classes in the hierarchy using the *Visitor* pattern.
- There is a focus on compile-time structures and stack-based data; we can also create redundant data structures in the SDE class so that they are initialised only once instead of having to create and delete them (as volatile variables) each time they are called in a function body.
- We hide low-level details concerning the construction of the SDE; we only need to know about calculating the drift and diffusion functions.
- We can extend the SDE class if the need arises by deriving new classes from it and by letting the new class delegate to one of its Bridge implementations

Some of the possible disadvantages of this design are

- Possible performances degradation; we use function pointers to implement the drift and diffusion functions and these are slower than function objects. Furthermore, function objects may have state (member data) and this is not possible with function pointers. We discuss function objects in Chapter 21.
- Extendibility problems; it is difficult to add extra structure to the SDE class in order to accommodate new requirements. In particular, we may need to calibrate the data that the SDE needs or we may need to interface to external files and databases. Furthermore, it is also possible that an SDE can have a number of implementations for its drift and diffusion functions (a good example of this last requirement is the case of the Heston 2-factor model that has three representations, which we discussed in Chapter 5).

We are not saying that the above design is the one that should be taken in all situations. There are other, equally valid approaches to the design of the current problem. If the design satisfies the stipulated requirements (whatever they might be) then you are finished.

In general, we are modelling data and operations on that data and we can think of many ways of implementing these features in C++:

- Create a struct to define the data and use function pointers to access the data in the struct. This would be the approach in classic C.
- Define the data and functions in a namespace and use this namespace in applications. This approach is useful when we wish to develop a prototype solution. The advantage is also that we can migrate the code to an object-oriented model in later versions of the software.
- Create an empty base class for all stochastic differential equations and derive your specialised classes from this base class.
- Using the *Bridge* pattern in combination with class hierarchies to separate application-specific behaviour from implementation details.

11.6   CREATING TEMPLATED DESIGN PATTERNS

The GOF patterns are based on a small number of fundamental assumptions, namely:

- They are implemented by defining a class hierarchy in which the base class is abstract and its derived classes – which represent specialisations in general – implement the pure virtual member functions from the base class.
- Client code accesses the classes in the hierarchy by defining a pointer to the base class or by using a reference to it in a function. In this way we achieve high levels of maintainability in the code because of support for the Principle of Substitutability and subtype polymorphism.

There are many examples in this and other books (Duffy, 2004a, GOF, 1995) and the technique should be familiar to the reader at this stage.

Notwithstanding the advantages of the object-oriented realisation of the GOF patterns, there are some shortcomings that severely reduce their applicability. In general, these inherent limitations are caused by the use of (class-based) inheritance and the lack of support for generic data types:

- Using class hierarchies implies that clients must derive their classes from the base class if they wish to avail of the features in the patterns. This action is not always desirable because it introduces more coupling into the application code; furthermore, it could impact performance because calling a virtual function is more expensive than calling a non-virtual function (in general, we have seen that calling a virtual function is between two and ten times as costly as calling the equivalent non-virtual function; we discuss performance issues in Chapter 21).

- Inheritance is the C++ way of realising the ISA or *Generalisation/Specialisation* relationship between classes. This is a semantic relationship and there is a possibility that the developer has modelled the wrong relationship. The consequences are that the corresponding code is hard to maintain at best, or semantically incorrect at worst.
- The data types used in the GOF patterns are hard-coded; they do not discuss how the patterns could be adapted to support generic data types; in all fairness, the original patterns book was written when C++ did not (fully) support the template mechanism. Furthermore, the only way to support different data structures when implementing a Whole Part or object composite structure is to create a separate derived class for each specific implementation (for example, one class that uses a list, another that uses a vector and so on).

We discuss these problems in the following sections and we resolve them using templates. In general, genericity is achieved by defining template classes having one or more template parameters; each parameter corresponds to a specific design dimension.

11.7   A GENERIC *SINGLETON* PATTERN

The intent of this pattern is to create a class that has one instance and one instance only. It is not possible – by accident or deliberately – to create a second instance of the class because of the way the pattern is implemented. The pattern provides a global access point to the Singleton object. The GOF implementation of this pattern uses inheritance to create specialised Singleton classes. There are memory problems associated with this GOF pattern but a discussion of this well-documented problem is outside the scope of this book (see Alexandrescu, 2001, for example). In our opinion, it is better not to fret about the *Singleton* pattern at all because the added value in applications is not commensurate with the effort needed to implement and maintain it.

We discuss our implementation of the generic Singleton pattern. First, it is a template class and second, it contains an embedded object (a destroyer) whose role is to delete the Singleton when the destroyer goes out of scope. The interface is similar to that of the *GOF Singleton* but instead of defining a class whose member data is a static pointer to itself we define a template class as follows:

```
template<class Type>
     class Singleton
{ // Templated Singleton class, full code on CD

private:
     static Type* ins;

     // This class deletes singleton at destruction time
     static Destroyer<Type> des;

protected:
     Singleton();
     Singleton(const Singleton<Type>& source);
```

```
    virtual ~Singleton();
    Singleton<Type>& operator = (const Singleton<Type>& source);

public:
    static Type* instance();
};
```

The *Singleton* pattern is used when we need to be sure that we are working with a unique, globally accessible object. For Monte Carlo applications, we see some examples of where the pattern can be used:

- Global data and settings (for example, a calendar).
- A global algorithm to be applied on multiple data sets.
- User settings and preferences.
- Many of the GOF patterns are best modelled as Singletons (for example, a builder).

We take three examples. The first example shows how to create a Singleton object class and it is for pedagogical reasons. First, the embedded class is defined as:

```
class AnyOldThing
{ // Hello world, 101 example

private:
    int j;
public:
    AnyOldThing() { j = 0;}

    int& coeff(){ return j;}

};
```

We show how to use the *Singleton* pattern in combination with this class; we note that although the embedded object is unique it is not read-only and hence can be modified:

```
    // 101 example, get it working
    AnyOldThing* pp = Singleton<AnyOldThing>::instance();
    cout << "Old value: " << pp -> coeff() << endl;

    Singleton<AnyOldThing>::instance()->coeff() = 3.0;
    cout << "New value: " << pp -> coeff() << endl;
```

The second example creates a Singleton object representing a set of dates. This could be useful when creating calendars, sets of special business days and other temporal types in fixed-income applications, for example:

```
    // Unique set of dates
    DatasimDate today;
    DatasimDate tomorrow = today + 1;
    DatasimDate theDayAfterTomorrow = tomorrow + 1;

    // Create the singleton set of dates
    Set<DatasimDate>* birthdays =
                    Singleton<Set<DatasimDate> >::instance();
```

```
// Add some birthdays
birthdays->Insert(today);
birthdays->Insert(tomorrow);
birthdays->Insert(theDayAfterTomorrow);

// Now print the singleton
Set<DatasimDate>::const_iterator iter;
for (iter = birthdays->begin(); iter != birthdays->end();
    ++iter)
{
     cout << *iter << endl;
}
```

The third example is interesting for data-driven applications (for example, for the Monte Carlo method). In particular, many applications are based on a *Blackboard* or *Data Repository* (POSA, 1996) pattern in which a global data structure can be accessed and modified by multiple threads. For example, let us take the data in the Heston model. The structure is

```
template <typename V> struct HestonStruct
{ // Defining properties of class, already discussed in chapter 5

    V T;
    V r, q;
    V kappa, theta, epsilon;
    V rho;          // Correlation

    V IC_S;         // initial conditions S, V
    V IC_V;
};
```

We initialise the data in this structure as follows:

```
// Defining a global data structure
HestonStruct<double> data;

data.T = 1.0; data.r = 0.1; data.q = 0.0;

data.kappa = 1.98837; data.theta = 0.1089;
data.epsilon = 0.15;   data.rho =  -0.9;

data.IC_S = 123.4; // ATM
data.IC_V = 0.37603 * 0.37603;
```

Next, we create a Singleton object that contains the data:

```
HestonStruct<double>* SharedDataArea =
            Singleton<HestonStruct<double> >::instance();

// Modify the shared data structure
SharedDataArea->r = 0.1;
cout << "Interest rate: " <<
        (*Singleton<HestonStruct<double> >::instance()).r
            << endl;
```

We have now completed the examples to show how the *Singleton* pattern is used. Finally, we note that the *Singleton* pattern is not *thread-safe*. We discuss multi-threading in Chapters 24 and 25.

11.8   GENERIC COMPOSITE STRUCTURES

The composite pattern models nested objects and tree structures that represent Whole-Part hierarchies. The pattern allows clients to treat individual objects and compositions of objects in a uniform way. Some examples of composites are:

- Directories (may contain files, symbolic links and other directories).
- GUI dialog boxes can contain controls (such as buttons and text boxes) and other dialog boxes.
- Hardware systems can be decomposed into logical areas; each area can contain other areas.
- A region in *n*-dimensional Euclidean space consists of subregions (recursive data pattern).
- Objects in CAD applications are typically composites.
- An algorithm consists of other algorithms.
- A portfolio consists of sub-portfolios.

In general, a composite object is a *recursive aggregate*, which is an object that may contain *simple* (or *atomic*) objects as well as other composite objects. For example, in the graphical user interface (GUI) example above the simple objects correspond to GUI controls such as text boxes, buttons and other simple 'toolbox' controls, while the composite objects correspond to list boxes, group boxes, panel and split containers.

The authors have developed applications that use the above composite objects by implementing the steps that are advocated in GOF (1995). We adopted the object-oriented approach and this entails code duplication because the code is always the same except that the base class name is different in each case. In particular, the first composite that we ever developed was for geometric objects in CAD. The structure is defined as

```
class ShapeComposite: public Shape // Shape is abstract base class
{
private:
     // The shapelist using the STL list
     std::list<Shape*> sl;

public:

     // Member functions here
};
```

Developing composite classes for other hierarchies – for example, dialog boxes – involved copying the code and replacing the word Shape by Control:

```
class ControlComposite: public Control
{ // Control = abstract base class

private:
```

```
     // The Controllist using the STL list
     std::list<Control*> sl;

public:

     // Member functions here
};
```

Eventually, we came to the realisation that a template-based approach was the correct way to implement a composite class; this tactic saves unnecessary code duplication:

```
template <typename T>
                    class GenericComposite: public T
{
private:
     // The element list using the STL list
     std::list<T*> sl;
     void Copy(const GenericComposite<T>& source);

public:
     // member functions

};
```

The code for the public member functions is written once because all specific composites will now be created using template specialisation, for example:

```
GenericComposite<Shape> nestedShape;
GenericComposite<Control> dialogBox;
```

The advantage is that the developer only has to write the code for the templated composite class once. The current implementation uses an STL list to hold the data while all memory allocation and deallocation issues are taken care of in the composite class, in particular, the composite's destructor deletes all the pointers in the embedded list.

We now describe the public member functions in this class:

• Constructors and destructor:

```
     GenericComposite();                    // Default constructor
     GenericComposite(const GenericComposite& source);
     virtual  GenericComposite();       // Destructor
```

• Adding an element to the composite:

```
     void push_front(T* s);             // Add element at the
                                            beginning
     void push_back(T* s);              // Add element at the end
```

• Other removal operations:

```
     void RemoveFirst();                    // Remove first element
     void RemoveLast();                     // Remove last element
     void RemoveAll();                      // Remove all elements
     void Remove(T* t);                     // Delete ptr+remove from list
```

- Defining iterators in order to navigate in the composite:

```
iterator begin();                     // Return iterator at begin
const_iterator begin() const;         // Return const iterator
                                      //    at begin
iterator end();                       // Return iterator after end
const_iterator end() const;           // Return const iterator
                                      //    after end
```

We take a simple example to show how to use the new templated composite class. The current example shows the essential syntax. To this end, we define a base class and two derived classes:

```
class Base
{ // Class with non-virtual destructor
private:

public:
    Base() { }
    virtual  Base() { cout << "Base destructor\n\n"; }
    virtual void Print() const {cout << "base class print\n ";};
    virtual Base* Copy() const { return new Base(*this); }
};

class Derived : public Base
{ // Derived class
private:

public:
    Derived() : Base() { }
    virtual  Derived() { cout << "Derived destructor\n"; }
    virtual void Print() const { cout << "\tDerived object\n";}
    virtual Base* Copy() const { return new Derived(*this); }
};

class Derived2 : public Base
{ // Derived class
private:

public:
    Derived2() : Base() { }
    virtual  Derived2() { cout << "Derived2 destructor\n"; }
    virtual void Print() const { cout << "\tDerived2 object\n";}
    virtual Base* Copy() const { return new Derived2(*this); }
};
```

When using the generic composite class we have the option of instantiating the class or creating a derived class of the instantiated composite class as follows:

```
class CompositeClass: public GenericComposite<Base>
{ // Define a nested class, note we must implement *print()*!
public:
```

```
     // Other functions here

     void Print() const
     {
          cout << "\n*** Big GC\n";

          GenericComposite<Base>::const_iterator it;

          for (it= this->begin(); it!=this->end(); it++)
          {
               (*it)->Print();
          }
     }

     // Don't forget the deep copy
     Base* Copy() const { return new CompositeClass(*this); }
};
```

We are now ready to use the composite:

```
     // Create a composite with two leaves
     CompositeClass* myComp1  = new CompositeClass;

     myComp1->push_front(new Derived);
     myComp1->push_back(new Derived2);


     // Create a composite containing a leaf and another composite
     CompositeClass* myComp2  = new CompositeClass;

     Base* d11 = new Derived;

     myComp2->push_front(d11);
     myComp2->push_front(new Derived);
     myComp2->push_back(myComp1);
     myComp2->Print();

     // Delete 'root' composite
     delete myComp2;

     // The next line will give a run-time error because
     // myComp1 has been deleted from within myComp2
     // !!!!! delete myComp1;
```

Please note the memory deallocation regime; we need only to delete the *root* composite object;
its destructor recursively deletes its parts. Ideally, if we use the Boost library's *shared pointers*
then no explicit delete is needed at all. We discuss this topic in Chapter 13.

11.8.1   Applications of generic composites

Composite structures are found in many applications:

- Composite data structures (for example, portfolios/structured products).
- In applications (for example, composite algorithms acting on a data structure).
- Creating new classes from composites using inheritance, composition and other semantic modelling techniques.
- Composite GOF patterns.

Regarding this last category we can think about composite creational, structural and behavioural patterns. This is not to say that all combinations are of practical applicability but some are important:

- *Builder* (contractors and subcontractors).
- *Proxy* (combining different kinds of proxy).
- *Command* (composite commands are macros and we use them for scripting purposes).
- *Strategy* (an algorithm may consist of other algorithms).
- *Visitor* (similar to how a composite *Strategy* works).

In exercise 4 of this chapter (below) we give an exercise concerning nested intervals in one dimension. We can then use them when developing adaptive mesh strategies, for example.

11.9   SUMMARY AND CONCLUSIONS

This chapter discussed a number of modern design techniques and C++ syntax that we use as building blocks in complex applications. We introduced traits, template template parameters and policy-based design. We ported a number of the GOF patterns to their generic equivalents. Finally, the synergy between the object-oriented and generic programming models leads to code that helps in the construction of C++ software frameworks.

C++ is evolving and it has the most extensive support for the generic programming models of all the object-oriented programming languages at the time of writing. We only need to witness how the Boost library is evolving to convince ourselves of this fact. Finally, software developers are becoming acquainted with C++ template programming.

11.10   EXERCISES AND PROJECTS

1. (***) Traits and Pseudo-Random Number Generators
   We discuss the implementation of Schrage's method (Schrage, 1979) using traits. This is an algorithm for multiplying two 32-bit integers modulo a 32-bit constant without having any intermediate value larger than 32 bits. It is implemented in Press *et al.* (2002). The objective in this exercise is to re-engineer the algorithm using traits. We first describe the method and we show the C++ code that needs to be re-engineered.

   Again, we start with equation (11.1) but now we wish to factorise the modulus c in the approximate form:

   $$c = aq + r, \text{ or } q = [c/a] \text{ where } [c/a]$$

   denotes the integer part of c/a, and $r = c \bmod a$

   if r is small $(r < q)$ and $0 < z < c - 1$ we have

$$az \bmod c = \begin{cases} a(z \bmod q) - r[z/a] \\ \text{when this expression} \geq 0 \\ a(z \bmod q) - r[z/q] + c \\ \text{when this expression} < 0 \end{cases}$$

We now come to coding issues and we give the header and code files for the original implementation based on Press *et al.* (2002). First, the header file:

```
class Ran0
{
public:

    Ran0(long Seed = 1, long Dim = 1, long a = 16807,
            long c = 2147483647, long q = 127773, long r = 2836);

    double GetRandomNumber(unsigned long NthElement);
    void SetSeed(long Seed);

private:

    long Seed;
    long Dim;
    long a;
    long c;
    long q;
    long r;

};
```

Please note that we use default values in the constructor and these will be replaced by trait values in the new version. The source file is

```
Ran0::Ran0(long Seed_, long Dim_, long a_, long c_, long q_, long r_)
: Seed(Seed_), a(a_), c(c_), q(q ), r(r_)
{
  if (Seed ==0)
        Seed=1;
if (a == 0)
        a = 16807;
if (c == 0)
        c = 2147483647;
if(q==0)
        q = 127773;
if(r==0)
        r = 2836;
if (Dim ==0)
        Dim = 1;
}

void Ran0::SetSeed(long Seed_)
{
    Seed=Seed_;
```

```
            if (Seed ==0) // To ensure RNG does not only return
                zeroes
            Seed=1;
}

double Ran0::GetRandomNumber(unsigned long NthElement)
{
    long k;
    k=Seed/q;
    Seed=a*(Seed-k*q)-r*k;
    if (Seed < 0)
        Seed += c;
    return Seed * 1.0/(1.0+c);
}
```

Create a new traits class by re-engineering this code. Test the code using the LCG class as discussed in section 11.5.1.

2. (**) Improving Portability and Maintainability of LCG class
The LCG class uses the well-known and unreliable ANSI C function `rand()` to generate seeds and random numbers, as seen in the code:

```
void InitSeed()
{// Initialise seed

    // Call ONCE ONCE ONCE before other 'generator' functions
    srand((unsigned) time (0));

    // Get the seed
    X0 = rand();
}
```

In order to make the code more portable we would like to use different and more robust functions. One example is to be found in Windows XP. It is called `rand_s()`. It offers a number of advantages; it is *re-entrant* (this means that it can be safely executed concurrently; that is, this function can be re-entered while it is already running), it is secure and no seed value is needed. An example of use is

```
// Define _CRT_RAND_S prior to inclusion statement.
#define _CRT_RAND_S

#include <stdlib.h>
#include <stdio.h>
#include <limits.h>
#include <iostream>
using namespace std;

int main()
{
    unsigned int    number;
    errno_t         err;
```

```
      // Display 10 random integers in the range [ 1,10 ].
      for(int i = 0; i < 10; ++i)
      {
            err = rand_s( &number );
            if (err != 0)
            {
                  cout << "The rand_s function failed!\n";
            }
            cout <<  (unsigned int)
                  ((double)number /(double) UINT_MAX * 10.0) + 1 <<
                      endl;
      }
      cout << endl;
      // Display 10 random doubles between 0 and max.
      for (int i = 0; i < 10; ++i)
      {
            err = rand_s( &number );
            if (err != 0)
            {
              cout << "The rand_s function failed!\n";
            }
              cout << endl << (double)number / (double)UINT_MAX
                  * max;
      }
      return 0;
}
```

The objective of this exercise is to apply a design pattern or some other design technique that allows clients to choose the appropriate random number generator at compile-time. No hard-wired if-else or switch statements are allowed.

3. (***) Implementing C++ Traits for Matrix Storage Schemes
   In section 11.5.1 we discussed how to create matrix classes having a variety of data structures; in this case we used nested STL vectors. The question now is to determine how to implement the other matrix structures using a combination of vectors and maps, for example bounded and unbounded triangular and sparse matrices.

4. (***) Composite Range
   We use a class called Range<T> that models one-dimensional intervals. The interface is (code on CD)

```
template <class Type> class Range
{

private:

      Type lo;
      Type hi;

public:
      // Constructors
      Range();                                      // Default
                                                    constructor
```

```
Range(const Type& low, const Type& high); // Low and high value
Range(const Range<Type>& ran2);           // Copy constructor
// Destructor
virtual ~Range();

// Modifier functions
void low(const Type& t1);      // Sets the low value of
                                  range
void high(const Type& t1);     // Sets the high value of range

//Accessing functions
Type low() const;              // Lowest value in range
Type high() const;             // Highest value in the range

Type spread() const;           // High - Low value

// Boolean functions
bool left(const Type& value) const;      // Is the value to
                                            left
bool right(const Type& value) const;     // Is the value to
                                            right
bool contains(const Type& value) const;  // Range contain
                                            value?

// Utility functions
Vector<Type, long> mesh(long nSteps) const;// Mesh

// Operator overloading
Range<Type>& operator = (const Range<Type>& ran2);

};
```

Create a class that models nested ranges (use the generic composite class), as in:

```
typedef GenericComposite<Range> AdaptiveRange;
```

This class can then be used to model adaptive meshes for the finite difference method, for example.

Data Structures and their Application to the Monte Carlo Method

12.1 INTRODUCTION AND OBJECTIVES

In this chapter we introduce a number of classes and structures that model data. We categorise the structures as follows:

- Memory issues (run-time structures versus compile-time structures).
- Linear structures (for example, vectors) or nonlinear structures (for example, graphs and trees).
- Modelling generic and associative structures (for example, the STL map).
- 'Polymorphic data types'; containers for generic data types.
- Specific structures for dates and calendars.
- Modelling discrete data structures from mathematics (for cxample, vector-valued functions).

We motivate why we need these structures and give some examples of where they are used. We summarise where we will need them below:

- Modelling member data of various kinds of derivatives products.
- Compile-time and run-time classes for vectors and matrices.
- Transferring data from C++ to other systems, for example Excel.
- Modelling multi-dimensional arrays in the Boost library.
- Modelling a function's input and output parameters.

The code in this chapter is generic in order to be able to support a range of application requirements. It is for this reason that we use the template mechanism and STL. We discuss other relevant data structures in Chapter 13 when we introduce the Boost library.

12.2 ARRAYS, VECTORS AND MATRICES

In technical applications we model various kinds of data structures, for example:

- One-dimensional arrays and vectors.
- Two-dimensional matrices.
- Three-dimensional tensors.
- n-dimensional structures.

In this book we are concerned with the first two categories and we can choose from the following possible implementations:

- Using the STL vector<T>.
- Using the STL valarray<T>.

- Associative arrays and the STL map<K,V>.
- The Boost multi-dimensional array library.
- Creating your own specific array types.
- Using some open-source library (for example, GSL).

In this chapter, we choose for the data containers in STL in combination with the classes that the authors have created.

We have already discussed a number of template classes to model data structures in Duffy (2004a) and Duffy (2006a). The two most important classes are Vector (for one-dimensional arrays) and NumericMatrix (for two-dimensional arrays). These are *adapter classes* because they wrap STL containers. Thus, the functions in these two classes delegate to the functions in the STL classes of which they are composed. This approach promotes code reusability and reliability.

Where do we need these classes in the current book? In general, we use them when we define array structures whose size is determined at run-time, for example:

- Arrays and matrices of random numbers.
- Arrays and matrices of paths when simulating SDEs using the finite difference method.
- Aggregated and merged data in a Monte Carlo simulation.
- Slices and cross-sections in *n*-dimensional data structures.

We now give some illustrative examples to show how to use these classes. First, we create a function that returns an array of pseudo-random numbers using the (in)famous rand() function:

```
Vector<double, long> generateUniform(long N)
{ // Generate N U(0,1) numbers

    long startIndex = 1;
    Vector<double, long> result(N, startIndex);

    double factor = 1.0 + double(RAND_MAX);

    for (long j = result.MinIndex(); j <= result.MaxIndex(); ++j)
    {

        result[j] = double(rand())/factor;
    }

    return result;
}
```

Please note the use of array indexing; in contrast to C-style arrays and STL vector – where indexing begins at 0 – we iterate between well-defined index boundaries and this reduces the chances of getting *array bounds exceptions* in the code. It also makes the code much more readable.

We now examine some code that uses matrices; in this case we create a matrix of random numbers. We do this by first calling a function to initialise each row of the computed matrix by returning a vector of random numbers:

```
void Normal(Vector<double, long>& vec)
{ // Create an array of uncorrelated Normal numbers

        double N1;
        double N2;

        for(long i=vec.MinIndex(); i<=vec.MaxIndex()-1; i += 2 )
        {

                //BoxMuller(N1, N2);
                PolarMarsaglia(N1, N2);

                vec[i] = N1;
                vec[i+1] = N2;
        }

        vec[vec.MaxIndex()] = N2;
}
```

The code for generating the matrix of random data is then

```
template <class V>
    NumericMatrix<V, long> createRandomNumbersMatrix(
                    long NSIM, long N)
{

    NumericMatrix<V, long> result(NSIM, N+1, 1, 1);


    Vector<V, long> temp(result.Columns(),
                            result.MinColumnIndex(), 0.0);

    for (long i = result.MinRowIndex();i<=result.MaxRowIndex(); ++i)
    {

        Normal(temp);

        for (long j = temp.MinIndex(); j <= temp.MaxIndex(); ++j)
        {
                result(i, j) = temp[j];
        }


    }

    return result;
}
```

This code shows how to use vectors and matrices in applications; we can optimise the code in order to improve performance, especially avoiding the creation of temporary objects. We discuss this issue in Chapter 21.

Our final example shows how to create pairs of correlated random numbers; in this case the number of columns in the matrix is 2:

```
NumericMatrix<double, long> CorrelatedNormalMatrix(
                        long Size,double rho)
{ // Create an array of correlated Normal numbers;
  // these are pairwise correlated.

        // Create an correlated matrix
        long Col = 2;
        NumericMatrix<double, long> UCM =
                    createRandomNumbersMatrix<double>
                    (Size, Col);

        // Matrix has the same number of rows as size of input
        // array, and two columns
        long startIndex = 1;
        NumericMatrix<double, long> result(
                        UCM.Rows(), UCM.Columns(),
                        UCM.MinRowIndex(),
                        UCM.MinColumnIndex());

        double SqrtRho = sqrt(1.0 - rho*rho);
        double tmp;

        for(long i=result.MinRowIndex();
                        i<=result.MaxRowIndex(); ++i)
        {

            tmp = result(i, 1) = UCM(i,1);

            result(i, 2) = (rho * tmp) + (SqrtRho *  UCM(i, 2));
        }

        return result;
}
```

The next examples show how vectors are used when creating finite difference schemes for SDEs. In general, the trajectories or paths of an SDE are stored in a vector. Here is an example of use. First, we define the data containers (vectors) to store mesh data, the solution and random numbers:

```
// Initial conditions
double initVal, VOld;
// Solution at time level n+1
double VNew;

// Mesh data
```

```
Vector<double, long> x;
double k;          // Time step
double sqrk;       // Square root of k (for dW stuff)

// Result path
Vector<double, long> res;

// Random numbers
Vector<double, long> dW;

// Number of steps
long N;
```

We now take the explicit Euler method for a one-factor SDE as discussed in Chapter 0:

```
FDMVisitor::FDMVisitor(long NSteps, const OneFactorSDE& sde)
{
    k = sde.Interval().spread()/ double (NSteps);
    sqrk = sqrt(k);
    x = sde.Interval().mesh(NSteps);

    res = Vector<double, long>(x.Size(), x.MinIndex());

    dW = Vector<double, long>(x.Size(), x.MinIndex());

    initVal = VOld = VNew = sde.InitialCondition();
    N = NSteps;

}
```

Finally, the code for the algorithm is

```
void ExplicitEuler::Visit(SDETypeD& sde)
{
    VOld = initVal;
    res[x.MinIndex()] = VOld;
    for (long index = x.MinIndex()+1; index <= x.MaxIndex(); ++index)
    {
        VNew = VOld  + k * sde.calculateDrift(x[index-1], VOld)
        + sqrk * sde.calculateDiffusion(x[index-1], VOld)
                                                    * dW[index-1];

        res[index] = VNew;
        VOld = VNew;
    }
}
```

These examples show that it is easy to use vectors and matrices in your code. More examples are to be found on the CD. Finally, we give an introduction to the Boost matrix library in Chapter 13.

12.3   COMPILE-TIME VECTORS AND MATRICES

In this section we create compile-time data structures. Why do we need such structures? Some reasons are

- *Efficiency*: Pushing data onto the stack is faster than creating data on the heap.
- *Reliability*: We model the size(s) of a compile-time structure as a template parameter and this forces adherence to proper dimensionality. For example, assigning a compile-time vector of length 10 to a vector of length 20 will result in a compiler error. A follow-on remark is that it is not necessary to include code that executes array bounds checking at run-time (in combination with the exception handling mechanism). Again, this improves performance and reliability.
- *Functionality*: In many applications we model objects in n-dimensional Euclidean space. The parameter n is a fixed number so that it will never be necessary to change it. Furthermore, we wish to model the parameter n directly.

12.3.1   One-dimensional data structures: vectors

In order to motivate compile-time data structures we first discuss one-dimensional vectors. These are implementations of finite-dimensional vector spaces. A vector space over a field F has three defining parameters:

- Its size or dimension.
- The data type of its elements.
- The data type of the field F.

We have reduced the scope by assuming that the element data type and the data type of F are the same. The specification of the new vector class (developed by the current authors) is then given by

```
template<typename Type, int N> class VectorSpace
{
private:

    Type arr[N];

public:

    // All public service functions

};
```

The size of the array is parametrised by a template parameter N. The constructors for this class are defined as follows:

```
// Constructors
VectorSpace();
VectorSpace(const Type& value);// All elements get this value
VectorSpace(const VectorSpace<Type, N>& source);
```

We need functions to return the size and index bounds of a vector:

```
// Selectors
int Size() const;
int MinIndex() const;
int MaxIndex() const;
```

Having defined a vector we can access its elements using the operator []:

```
// Operators
Type& operator[](int index);                    // Non const
const Type& operator[](int index) const;    // Const
```

We can create instances of the class by giving the size of the vector as a template parameter. Here are examples to show how the above member functions are used:

```
const int N = 3;
VectorSpace<double, N> myArray;

// All elements in vector have the same value, 2.2
double value = 2.2;
VectorSpace<double, N> myArrayB(2.2);

for (int j = myArray.MinIndex(); j <= myArray.MaxIndex(); j++)
{

     myArray[j] =  double (j); // Indexing begins at 1!

}
```

We now discuss operator overloading in this class. We have defined a number of operators:

```
VectorSpace<Type, N> operator - () const;    // The negative
VectorSpace<Type, N> operator + (const VectorSpace<Type,
                                 N>& v2) const;
VectorSpace<Type, N> operator - (const VectorSpace<Type,
                                 N>& v2) const;
VectorSpace<Type, N> operator + (const Type& offset) const;
// Add offset to each coord
VectorSpace<Type, N> operator - (const Type& offset) const;
// Subtract offset
```

Some examples of use are:

```
VectorSpace<double, N> myArray1 = - myArray;
VectorSpace<double, N> myArray2 = myArray;   // No other works!!
VectorSpace<double, N> myArray3 = myArray2 - myArray;
myArray5 = myArray - offset;
myArray5 = myArray - myArray;
```

We see that we can assign vectors that have the same dimensions; if you assign vectors of different dimensions you will get a compiler error, as in the following code:

```
/* This code will not compile, no conversions between
the two different classes
const int N1 = 3;
const int N2 = 4;
VectorSpace<double, N1> ArrOne;
VectorSpace<double, N2> ArrTwo;
ArrOne = ArrTwo; */
```

A defining feature of a vector space is that it can be premultiplied by a scalar value. To effect this, we use operator overloading (notice that we use a *template member function* as discussed in Chapter 11):

```
// ** Template member functions ** Premult by a field value
template <typename F> VectorSpace<Type, N> friend operator *
        (const F& scalar, const VectorSpace<Type, N>& pt);
```

An example of how to use this functionality is

```
// Calling a template member function (operator)
double factor = 0.5;
VectorSpace<double, N> myArray4 = factor * myArray;
```

We use `VectorSpace<double, N>` in a number of examples and applications in the book:

- As input parameters to, or as return types of, functions.
- As *building blocks* for higher-dimensional data structures (for example, matrices and tensors).
- Implementing classes for differential equations (ODE, SDE, PDE and others).

We finish this section with some initial examples of using vectors as input arguments in functions; we take a two-dimensional example:

```
double func1(const VectorSpace<double,2>& input)
{

    return -(input[1] + input[2]);
}

double func2(const VectorSpace<double,2>& input)
{

    return -(input[2] - input[1]);
}
```

We use this style when defining drift and diffusion functions for SDEs. Mathematically speaking, this vector class models n-dimensional Euclidean space.

12.3.2   Two-dimensional data structures: matrices

We now define a template class to model matrices. The class declaration has three template parameters that represent the underlying data type, the number of rows and the number of columns of the structure:

```
template <typename V, int NR, int NC> class MatrixVectorSpace
{// Numeric Matrix class. This is a COMPILE-TIME Matrix
 // class for numeric data.

    private:

        V mat[NR][NC];
public:

    // Public interface functions

};
```

This class has constructors, functions to access the elements of the matrix and operators for matrix multiplication. For example, here is *inline* code that realises the multiplication of two matrices:

```
template <int NC2>
    MatrixVectorSpace<V, NR, NC2> operator *
            (const MatrixVectorSpace<V, NC, NC2>& source)
{
    MatrixVectorSpace<V, NR, NC2> result;

    for (int i = 0; i < NR; ++i)
    {
        for (int j = 0; j < NC2; ++j)
        {
            result.mat[i][j] = V(0.0);
            for (int k = 0; k < NC; ++k)
            {
                result.mat[i][j] +=
                (*this).mat[i][k] * source.mat[k][j];
            }
        }
    }

    return result;
}
```

A nice feature in this case is that you can never multiply two matrices that have *incompatible* bounds. Some examples of operator overloading for this matrix class are

```
const int NR = 4;
const int NC = 4;
const int dim = 2;
```

```
MatrixVectorSpace<double, dim, dim> myMat0(2.0);
MatrixVectorSpace<double, dim, dim> myMat2(1.0);

MatrixVectorSpace<double, dim, dim> myMat3 = myMat0 + myMat2;
MatrixVectorSpace<double, dim, dim> myMat4 = myMat0 - myMat2;
MatrixVectorSpace<double, dim, dim> myMat4A = myMat0 * myMat2;
```

12.3.3 Application: modelling N-factor SDEs

We have already discussed what an SDE is. We have given a number of examples to show how to map an SDE to C++. In this section we create a single template class (it has no derived classes at the moment) that models SDEs having the following properties:

- It uses generic underlying data types.
- It models N-factor equations.
- It models an arbitrary number of Brownian motions.
- All vectors and data are defined at compile-time (on the stack).
- It uses the template classes `VectorSpace` and `MatrixVectorSpace`.

First, we create a base class for all kinds of SDEs; it also supports *Visitor* functionality that we can use to extend its functionality:

```
template <typename V, int N, int D> class SdeVisitor;
  // forward declaration

class SdeThing
{
public:

    // No virtual functions, yet

    // Extend functionality with Visitor pattern
    template <typename V, int N, int D>
                    void Accept(SdeVisitor<V,N,D>& sv) = 0;

};
```

The class that we work with in most cases is modelled by a vector of functions for drift terms and a matrix of functions for the diffusion terms. We use function pointers in this case and we need to create a wrapper for them:

```
template <typename V, int N> struct FunctionWrapper
{ // Models a scalar-valued function

// Call by value first argument
    V (*f) (V value, const VectorSpace<V,N>& arguments);
};
```

Now, the SDE class of interest has the following structure:

```
template <typename V, int N, int D> class SDE : public SdeThing
{ // Non-linear SDE; N is the number of independent variables and
  // D is the number of Brownian motions
```

```
private:

    // INDEXING STARTS AT 0 IN THESE ARRAYS
    FunctionWrapper<V, N> drift[N];           // Drift
    FunctionWrapper<V,N> diffusion[N][D];   // Diffusion

    Range<V> ran;                       // Interval in which
                                        // SDE is defined
    VectorSpace<V,N> ic;                // Initial condition


    // Generated, redundant arrays (performance)
    //


    // Private functions
    //


public:
    // Public interface

};
```

Thus, we model the SDE class by defining its drift and diffusion terms. We also define the interval in which the SDE is defined as well as giving its initial condition. The main member functions in the class SDE<V, N, D> are

- Constructors (input: an interval and an initial condition).
- Functions to set the drift and diffusion terms.
- Calculating the drift and diffusion terms at a given time value and for a given value of the underlying variable.

Please note that this class does not model the Wiener process directly but clients will need to define vectors of Wiener increments when working in discrete time space. For this reason we provide two functions to calculate the diffusion term, as we shall presently see. The constructors are

```
SDE();
SDE(const Range<V> range,
            const VectorSpace<V,N>& initial_condition);
SDE(const SDE<V, N, D>& source);
```

Having defined the interval in which the SDE is defined and its corresponding initial condition we then define the components of its drift and diffusion terms:

```
// Define individual components of drift and diffusion
   functions
void setDriftComponent (V (*fun) (V value, const VectorSpace
   <V,N>& arguments), int row);
void setDiffusionComponent (V (*fun) (V value, const VectorSpace
   <V,N>& arguments),
int row, int column);
```

Function pointers are null pointers by default, so you must define all components of these vector-valued and matrix-valued functions if you wish to avoid a run-time error. Client code (for example, FDM classes) will need to calculate drift and diffusion values at discrete points in (S, t) space and this is achieved using the following functions:

```
// Calculate drift and diffusion functions at given time value
const VectorSpace<V,N>& calculateDrift (V value, const
    VectorSpace<V,N>& arguments);
const VectorSpace<V,N>& calculateDiffusion (V value, const
    VectorSpace<V,N>& arguments, const VectorSpace<V,D>& dW);
```

In some cases we calculate the Wiener increments using dynamic vectors and we have included an extra function for compatibility reasons:

```
// Calculate diffusion using Dynamic Vector<double, long>
const VectorSpace<V,N>& calculateDiffusion (V value, const
VectorSpace<V,N>& arguments,
const Vector<V,long>& dW);
```

Finally, it is useful to calculate the diffusion as a matrix independently of the Wiener increment vector:

```
// Calculate the diffusion matrix (coefficient of dW)
const MatrixVectorSpace<V, N, D>& calculateDiffusionMatrix
                (V value, const VectorSpace<V,N>& arguments);
```

We have optimised the code here because these functions return a reference to an object that has been initialised in the constructor.

Finally, we define selector functions for the SDE's interval and initial condition, respectively:

```
// Selector functions
const Range<V>& range() const;
const VectorSpace<V,N>& startValue() const;
```

Let us take an example; we create an instance of class SDE<double, 2, 2>. We first define two functions that will be used as components of the drift and diffusion terms:

```
double func1(double t, const VectorSpace<double,2>& input)
{

    return -input[2];

}

double func2(double t, const VectorSpace<double,2>& input)
{

    return input[1];

}
```

Next, we create the initial condition and interval in which the SDE is defined:

```
// Number of equations
const int dim = 2;              // Dimension of deterministic part
const int dim2 = 2;             // Dimension of array of Brownians

// Initial conditions
VectorSpace<double, dim> VOld;
VOld[1] = 1.0;
VOld[2] = 0.0;
double T = 1.0;
Range<double> myRange(0.0, T);
```

Next, we define the SDE and set its drift and diffusion terms:

```
// Now the new SDE problem
SDE<double, dim, dim2> mySDE(myRange, VOld);
mySDE.setDriftComponent(func1, 1);
mySDE.setDriftComponent(func2, 2);

// Define the diffusion matrix
mySDE.setDiffusionComponent(func1, 1, 1);
mySDE.setDiffusionComponent(func2, 2, 2);
mySDE.setDiffusionComponent(func1, 1, 2);
mySDE.setDiffusionComponent(func2, 2, 1);
```

We are now finished. We can now use the class as input to a finite difference scheme, for example.

12.4 CREATING ADAPTERS FOR STL CONTAINERS

STL is a framework and we can extend it to suit our needs. In this case we use inheritance, composition and aggregation to create new containers, iterators and algorithms. The three main techniques are (Josuttis, 1999):

- *Invasive approach*: In this case we provide interfaces that STL requires, for example begin() and end(). It is invasive because the developer must write the container in a certain way. The advantage is that many STL algorithms can be used directly with the new container.
- *Noninvasive approach*: In this case the developer writes special iterators that act as mediators between the STL algorithms and the new containers. The main challenge is to ensure that we can navigate in the container.
- *Wrapper approach*: This combines the first two approaches. In this case we use aggregation or composition techniques by creating a new wrapper or adapter class and offering STL container-like interfaces.

We have used the last approach in practice and it is in fact an application of the *Adapter* pattern as discussed in GOF (1995). Some of the examples in this book are

- *Property Sets* (wrappers for STL map<K,V>).
- *Set* (a wrapper for STL set<K>).
- *Relation* (this models many-to-many relationships and we use two multimap<K1, K2> instances to implement it).

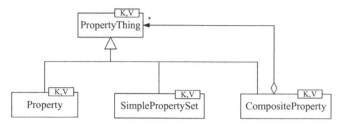

Figure 12.1   Class hierarchy for property pattern

The UML diagram for properties is shown in Figure 12.1. Let us take an example.

In order to implement a wrapper container we create a C++ class that represents mathematical sets. It hides much of the complicated function calls to the STL set<T> container and it also extends its functionality (for example, we have the ability to create the Cartesian product of two sets with different underlying types).

The C++ wrapper class for sets has the following functionality:

- Constructors.
- Set operations (union, intersection, ...).
- Inserting elements into, and removing elements from, a set.
- Boolean relationships between sets (subset of, superset of).
- Implementing STL iterator functionality.

The structure of the class, including iterators and related functions, is

```
template <class V> class SetThing {};

template <class V> class Set : public SetThing<V>
{
private:
    set<V> s;

public:
    // Iterator functions; Navigating in a set
    typedef typename set<V>::iterator iterator;
    typedef typename set<V>::const_iterator const_iterator;

public:
    //

    iterator begin();              // Return iterator at
                                   // begin of set
    const_iterator begin() const;  // Return const iterator

    iterator end();                // Return iterator after
                                   // end of set
    const_iterator end() const;    // Return const iterator

};
```

We embed an STL `set<T>` in the current C++ class. We create the same kinds of iterators as in STL. The constructors are defined as follows:

```
// Constructors
Set();                          // Empty set
Set(const set<V>& stlSet);      // Create a Set from STL set
Set(const Set<V>& s2);          // Copy constructor
Set(const list<V>& con);        // From an STL list
```

Set operations are very easy to understand and to use. We have two options for each operation: the first option uses a non-member function while the second option uses operator overloading:

```
// Standard set operations from High School
template <class V>
    friend Set<V> Intersection(const Set<V>& s1,
                                    const Set<V>& s2);
Set<V> operator ^ (const Set<V>& s2);       // Intersection

template <class V>
    friend Set<V> Union(const Set<V>& s1,
                            const Set<V>& s2);
Set<V> operator + (const Set<V>& s2);       // Union

template <class V>
    friend Set<V> Difference(const Set<V>& s1,
                                const Set<V>& s2);
Set<V> operator - (const Set<V>& s2);       // Difference

template <class V>
    friend Set<V> SymmetricDifference(const Set<V>& s1,
                                        const Set<V>& s2);
Set<V> operator % (const Set<V>& s2);       // Symmetric
                                            // Difference
```

Finally, the other member functions are

```
// Operations on a single set
long Size() const;                          // Number of elements
void Insert(const V& v);                    // Insert an element
void Insert(const Set<V>& v);               // Insert another set
void Remove(const V& v);                    // Remove an element
void Replace(const V& Old, const V& New);   // Replace old by new
void Clear();                               // Remove all
                                            // elements
bool Contains(const V& v) const;            // Is v in set?
bool Empty() const;                         // Contains no
                                            // elements

// Relations between sets (s1 == *this)
bool Subset(const Set<V>& s2) const;        // s1 a subset
                                            // of s2?
```

```
bool Superset(const Set<V>& s2) const;      // s1 a superset
                                            of s2?
bool Intersects(const Set<V>& s2) const;    // common elements?
```

These functions are easy to use because they have relatively few input parameters when compared to what is needed if we use the equivalent STL functions. For example, here is the body of the function that computes the union of two sets:

```
template <class V>
    Set<V> Union(const Set<V>& s1, const Set<V>& s2)
{
    set<V> myunion;
    set<V>::iterator i = myunion.begin();
    insert_iterator<set<V> > insertiter(myunion, i);
    set_union(s1.s.begin(), s1.s.end(), s2.s.begin(),
                s2.s.end(), insertiter);

    return Set<V>(myunion);
}
```

We shall give some applications of the Set<T> class in section 12.5.
    The advantages of using wrapper classes are

- *Functionality*: The developer can build new classes using patterns and design techniques such as *Whole-Part, Composition, Aggregation* and *Inheritance*.
- *Efficiency*: STL containers and algorithms have been optimised for speed.
- *Reliability*: It is easy to test and debug wrapper classes because they delegate to STL components that have already been tested. It remains to test the code that uses the STL functionality. For example, the authors' set class has a member function to replace an element by another element and this uses two functions from the STL set container:

```
template <class V>
      void Set<V>::Replace(const V& Old, const V& New)
{ // Replace old by new

    s.erase(Old);
    s.insert(New);
}
```

- *Code inspection*: One can see at a glance that the code is correct.
- *Maintainability*: Software that is built in an incremental fashion is relatively easy to modify and to extend. In the current case clients of the wrapper class have no direct interaction with the wrapped class. This principle is called *Information Hiding* and we say that the wrapper object is a *black box* because it hides irrelevant details from the client.

12.5   DATE AND TIME CLASSES

In some applications we need to model dates and time as C++ classes. We now discuss some ways of using them.

12.5.1 Basic functionality in date class

We have created a C++ class that models dates (as discussed in Duffy, 2004a). The class is called `DatasimDate` and it has the following categories of member functions:

- Constructors: default constructor, copy constructor and constructor with day, month and year as input.
- Comparing two dates using operators $<$, $>$, $==$ and $!=$, for example.
- Offsetting a date by one day, a number of days, of months, of quarters and years.
- Calculating the number of days between two dates.

We take an example. We create two dates, one of which is today's date and the other date is one year from now. Then we print the dates and find the number of days between them; furthermore, we compute the date that is seven days away from today:

```cpp
#include "DatasimDate.hpp"
#include <iostream>
using namespace std;


int main()
{

    DatasimDate now;
    cout << "First Date: " << now << endl;

    int year_offset  = 2;
    DatasimDate d2 = now.add_years(year_offset);
    cout << "Second Date: " << d2 << endl;

    // Two ways to find number of days between 2 dates
    int diff = d2.difference(now);
    cout << "Difference in days is: " << diff << endl;
    diff = d2 - now;
    cout << "Difference in days is: " << diff << endl;

    // Add number of days offset to a date
    DatasimDate nextWeek = now + 7;
    cout << "Next week: " << nextWeek << endl;

    return 0;
}
```

12.5.2 Creating sets of dates and using set operations

We now turn our attention to creating collections of dates. In this case we create sets of dates using the authors' `Set` class. This adaptor class for the STL `set` container has functions for set operations such as union, intersection and so on as already discussed in section 12.4. First, we define the kinds of offset we wish to use by defining an enumeration (you can extend it to suit your own needs):

```
enum DateOffsetUnit
{

    DAYS,
    MONTHS,
    QUARTERS,
    HALFYEARS,
    YEARS
};
```

Second, we define a function that creates a date at a certain offset from another date:

```
DatasimDate nextDate(const DatasimDate& now, DateOffsetUnit
    type)
{ // Calculate date as offset(of certain unit) from a given date


    DatasimDate result;

    if (type == DAYS)
            result = now + 1;
    if (type == MONTHS)
            result = now.add_months(1);
    if (type == QUARTERS)
            result = now.add_quarter();
    if (type == HALFYEARS)
            result = now.add_halfyear();
    if (type == HALFYEARS)
            result = now.add_years(1);

    return result;
}
```

Finally, we define a function that creates a set of dates whose input is

- a start date;
- the number of dates in the set;
- the offset between consecutive dates in the set.

The code is given by:

```
Set<DatasimDate> DateCollection(const DatasimDate& start,
    DateOffsetUnit offset, int NumberOfDates)
{ // Creat a set of dates based on an equal offset

    // Initialise the array
    Set<DatasimDate> result;

    DatasimDate tmp = start;
```

```
    for (int i = 1; i <= NumberOfDates; ++i)
    {

        result.Insert(tmp);
        tmp = nextDate(tmp, offset);

    }

    return result;
}
```

We also define a function to print a set of dates:

```
template <class T> void print(const Set<T>& l, const string& name)
{   // Print the contents of a Set.

    cout << endl << name << ",size of set is " << l.Size() << "\n[ ";

    Set<T>::const_iterator i;

    for (i = l.begin(); i != l.end(); ++i)
    {
                cout << *i << ", ";

    }

    cout << "]\n";
}
```

The test program is

```
int main()
{

    // Input dates
    DatasimDate start;
    DateOffsetUnit offset = MONTHS;
    int N = 9;

    Set<DatasimDate> result = DateCollection(start, offset, N);
    print(result, string ("set of offsetted dates, 1:"));

    DatasimDate start2 = start.add_halfyear(); // 6 months on
    Set<DatasimDate> result2 = DateCollection(start2, offset, N);
    print(result2, string ("set of offsetted dates, 2: "));

    // Set operations
    Set<DatasimDate> currSet;

    currSet = Union(result, result2);
    print(currSet, string ("Union: "));
```

```
    currSet = Intersection(result, result2);
    print(currSet, string ("Intersection: "));

    currSet = Difference(result, result2);
    print(currSet, string ("Difference: "));

    currSet = SymmetricDifference(result, result2);
    print(currSet, string ("Symmetric Difference: "));

    return 0;
}
```

The output from this program is

```
set of offsetted dates, 1:, size of set is 9
[ 10/1/2008, 10/2/2008, 10/3/2008, 10/4/2008, 10/5/2008, 10/6/2008,
  10/7/2008, 10/8/2008, 10/9/2008, ]

set of offsetted dates, 2: , size of set is 9
[ 10/7/2008, 10/8/2008, 10/9/2008, 10/10/2008, 10/11/2008,
  10/12/2008, 10/1/2009, 10/2/2009, 10/3/2009, ]

Union: , size of set is 15
[ 10/1/2008, 10/2/2008, 10/3/2008, 10/4/2008, 10/5/2008, 10/6/2008,
  10/7/2008, 10/8/2008, 10/9/2008, 10/10/2008, 10/11/2008,
  10/12/2008, 10/1/2009, 10/2/2009, 10/3/2009, ]

Intersection: , size of set is 3
[ 10/7/2008, 10/8/2008, 10/9/2008, ]

Difference: , size of set is 6
[ 10/1/2008, 10/2/2008, 10/3/2008, 10/4/2008, 10/5/2008,
  10/6/2008, ]

Symmetric Difference: , size of set is 12
[ 10/1/2008, 10/2/2008, 10/3/2008, 10/4/2008, 10/5/2008, 10/6/2008,
  10/10/2008, 10/11/2008, 10/12/2008, 10/1/2009, 10/2/2009,
  10/3/2009, ]
```

12.5.3 Mapping dates to mesh points

In finite difference applications we use non-dimensional numbers to represent mesh points but in some cases these numbers are generated from dates. Two scenarios are:

• Convert a set of dates to a vector of numbers.
• Associate dates with numbers.

For example, we can create an array of mesh points between two given dates as follows:

```
Vector<double, int> convertDateArray(
                     const DatasimDate& start,
                     const DatasimDate& end,
                     int nSteps, double initialValue)
```

```
{

        // Initialise the array
        Vector<double, int> result (nSteps + 1, 1);

        double delta = double(end - start) / double(nSteps);


        result[result.MinIndex()] = initialValue;

        for (int i = result.MinIndex()+1;i<=result.MaxIndex(); ++i)
        {

                        result[i] = result[i-1] + delta;

        }

        return result;

}
```

There are other functions on the CD that are of relevance in applications. The above code will hopefully provide you with some guidelines.

12.5.4   Calendars, business days and business conventions

Many finance applications define and use calendars. They may need to know a myriad of details concerning dates and the relationships between them:

• Defining a calendar of dates.
• Defining business days and non-business days in a calendar.
• Finding the first business day after a holiday.

Some of the features that we would like to see in a C++ class that implements calendars are:

• Add a holiday.
• Remove a holiday.
• Find all business days between two dates in the calendar.
• Make provision for weekend dates.
• Give all holidays in the calendar.

It is possible to create code for a calendar class because we already have a C++ class for dates and the Set<T> template class is also very useful when we wish to store dates and execute set-like operations. The Boost library has extensive support for date and time types, which are an alternative to our own implementations.

12.6   THE CLASS STRING

Strings and string manipulation functions are important in many kinds of applications. In the past, programmers used the C-style character pointer types (char*) to represent arrays of characters. Programmers were responsible for allocating and deallocating memory for these types. Now C++ has a standard class to represent strings and it can be used as a built-in type. The programmer does not have to worry about memory allocation and deallocation issues.

It may be necessary in some applications to create and manipulate strings, for example when interfacing to external systems, files and database systems. We may also need to convert strings to numeric types and vice versa. The base class `basic_string` for all strings is a container that enables the use of strings as normal types, such as using comparison and concatenation operations, iterators and STL algorithms. It has two specialisations, namely `string` (that we discuss here) and `wstring` that contains the wide character type `wchar_t`. This class can model the *Unicode* character set.

In this section we learn about strings by choosing a number of examples. The main challenge is learning the syntax; the full source code is on the CD.

12.6.1   String constructors and string properties

It is possible to create strings by using constructors and the assignment operator:

- Create an empty string.
- Create a string from a C-style, null-terminated string.
- Create a string as an extraction of another string.
- Create a string as N duplications of a single character.

Sample code for using these members is

```
// Empty string
string s1;
if (s1.empty() == true)
{
    cout << "An empty string, indeed\n";
}

// Copy constructor
string s2(s1);

// String from a C-string
string s3("ABCDE");

// From another string starting at a given index (starts at 0)
string s4(s3, 1);

// From another string starting at given index (starts at 0)
// But at most _strlen_ chars
int strlen = 2;
string s4A(s3, 1, strlen);
cout << "s4A " << s4A << endl;

// N occurrences of a character
int N = 5;
char c = 's';
string s5(N, c);
```

```
cout << "s5 " << s5 << endl;

// Using iterators
char carr[] = '1', '2', '3';
int end = 3;              // Just beyond the last character
string s6(carr, carr + end);
cout << "s6 " << s6 << endl;
```

In some cases a string will need to contain a certain number of characters and in these cases we reserve some memory to hold them. For example, we create an empty string and we then reserve 100 characters for it (the size (the length) of the string is still zero but its capacity is now 100):

```
// Create a string and reserve memory
string S1;
S1.reserve(100); // Reserve memory for 100 characters

cout << "size, length, max_size, capacity: "
        << S1.size() << ", " << S1.length() << ", "
        << S1.max_size() << ", " << S1.capacity() << endl;
```

We can now add 10 characters to the string; the size is now 10 but the capacity is as it was before:

```
// Now fill in some values
for (int i = 0; i < 10; ++i)
{
      S1.push_back('z');
}
```

It is now possible to print the string using an iterator:

```
// Print S1
string::iterator it;
cout << endl;
for (it = S1.begin(); it != S1.end(); ++it)
{
     cout << *it << "-";
}
     cout << endl;
```

We have noticed that one compiler reserves more memory than what is given by the programmer; in the above case we reserved memory for 100 characters but the compiler in use reserved memory for 111 characters.

Finally, it is possible to create strings by a combination of the assignment and concatenation operators:

```
// Concatenation of strings and characters
string S2("987654321");
string S6 = "ABCD";
string S7 = S2 + '-' + S6 +  '-' + S2;
```

Please note that temporary objects may be created in this case; this may affect performance in some applications.

12.6.2 Extracting characters and substrings

Having created a string, we may then wish to access its elements, for example its characters or substrings. In the first case we use operator overloading:

```
// Indexing operator
string S2("987654321");
cout << endl;
for (int i = 0; i < S2.size(); ++i)
{
        cout << S2[i] << ",";
}
cout << endl;
```

In the second case we can extract contiguous arrays of characters from strings, as the following examples show:

```
// Substrings, index starts at 0
string S3 = S2.substr();            // Return a copy of S2
cout << "S3 " << S3 << endl;

int startPos = 3;
string S4 = S2.substr(startPos);
cout << "S4 " << S4 << endl;

int len = 4;
string S5 = S2.substr(startPos, len);
cout << "S5 " << S5 << endl;
```

We can compare strings in a straightforward way by using the `compare()` member function; the return type is an `int` and it performs a case-sensitive comparison with a specified string to determine if the two strings are equal or whether one is lexicographically less than the other:

```
// Comparisons
string S10("ABCD987");
string S11("ABCD987");
string S12("ABCD987123");
if (S10.compare(S11) == 0)
{
     cout << "Strings are equal, OK \n";
}


string A("A");
string B ("B");
if (A.compare(B)< 0)
{
     cout << "A before B, OK \n";
}
if (B.compare(A)< 0)
```

```
{
    cout << "B before A, not OK \n";
}
```

12.7   MODIFYING STRINGS

We can modify the contents of a string in a number of ways:

- Clear its contents (erase all its characters).
- Add and remove strings and characters.
- Place insertions into the string at given positions.
- Replace a range of characters by a string.

The code for these features is easy to follow and is given by

```
string S6 = "ABCD";
string S7 = S2 + '-' + S6 +  '-' + S2;
// Erase all characters
S7.erase();

// Add and remove strings
S7 = S2 + '-' + S6 +  '-' + S2;
S7.append(string("*Boris"));
cout << S7 << endl;
S7 += string("Appendage");
cout << S7 << endl;

// Insert at a specific position
string S8("ABCDE");
int atPos = 2;
string aString("-123-");
S8.insert(atPos, aString);
cout << S8 << endl;

S7.push_back('Z'); cout << S7 << endl;

// Replacing characters
string S9("AB987");
int startIndex = 2; int size = 1;
S9.replace(startIndex, size, string("-XY-123"));
 cout << S9 << endl;
```

12.7.1   Searching and finding in strings

An important feature is the ability to search a string for occurrences of characters or strings.
C++ allows us to search in a string in both the forward and reverse directions:

```
// Searching and Finding
string S13("ABCD1234");

// Forward find
string::size_type index; // This is a typedef for size_t
```

```
index = S13.find(string("12"));
if (index != string::npos)
{
        cout << index << "\n in range " << endl;
}
else
{
        cout << index << "\n out of range\n";
}
```

In this example the functionality tells us whether the search has been successful, namely checking that the index is (or is not) equal to string::npos (an unsigned integral value initialized to −1 that indicates either 'not found' or 'all remaining characters' when a search function fails). Finally, we can search a string by navigating in a backward direction. In this code we search for the first occurrence of a substring that matches a specified sequence of characters:

```
// Reverse find
index = S13.rfind(string("D1"));
cout << index << endl;
```

For more advanced string manipulation applications and regular expression handling, we recommend the use of the *Regex* library in Boost.

12.7.2   Conversions between strings and other data types

Working with strings is very convenient when developing applications because they can be used as wrappers for different data types such as double, int and even user-defined types. We thus need to have conversion functions. We concentrate on converting data types to strings and to this end we use *stringstreams* (see Stroustrup, 1997, page 640). We can avail of the formatting facilities in the streams library. First, we have created a template function to convert an arbitrary type to a string:

```
#include <sstream>
#include <string>
#include <iostream>
using namespace std;

template <typename T>
        string getString(const T& value)
{
    stringstream s;
    s << value;

    return s.str();
}
```

We now show how to use this function for built-in data types:

```
int main()
{

    // Hard-coded example for starters
```

```
double myDouble = 1.0;
stringstream s;
s << myDouble;
string result = s.str();
cout << "String value is: " << result << endl;

long j = 1234567890;
float f = 3.14f;

myString = getString<long>(j);
cout << myString << endl;

myString = getString<float>(f);
cout << myString << endl;

return 0;
}
```

Finally, in some cases we may wish to convert a string's characters to upper or lower case. This feature is needed in interactive applications, for example when we write *case-insensitive comparisons*.

The following example shows how this is done by converting lower-case characters to upper-case characters in a string:

```
// Conversions
string Alphabet("abcdefgh");
cout << Alphabet << endl;

for (int i = 0; i < Alphabet.size(); ++i)
{
    Alphabet[i] = toupper(Alphabet[i]);
}
cout << Alphabet << endl;
```

The new value of the string will be 'ABCDEFGH'.

12.8   A FINAL LOOK AT THE GENERIC COMPOSITE

In Chapter 11 we introduced the generic composite; this is a template class representing recursive structures. In this section we discuss how to create *hierarchical data structures* using this pattern. In other words, we structure data in a certain way. We reduce the scope here by taking an example and you can generalise it to other applications. The example creates a tree structure where each node has a name (identified as a string) as well as a reference to some data or other node. To this end, we encapsulate this data in properties. We have already discussed the Property Pattern in Duffy (2004a) and Duffy (2006a). This pattern models key-value pairs and it is a wrapper class for the STL map<K,V> container. We give a short review of this pattern. The class hierarchy has already been shown in Figure 12.1. In particular, we have developed the code for the classes Property<K,V> and SimplePropertySet<K,V> while all we need to do is to instantiate the generic composite class in order to generate the code for composite properties. In other words, no extra coding is needed.

We now examine the essential C++ structure. The base class has the following interface:

```
template <class Name, class Value> class PropertyThing
{
public:
    PropertyThing() {}
    virtual  PropertyThing() {}
    virtual PropertyThing<Name, Value>* Copy() const {return 0;}
    virtual void print() const {}; // FOR CONVENIENCE
    PropertyThing<Name, Value>& operator = (const PropertyThing
                                   <Name, Value>& source) {}

};
```

The basic property class (name-value pair) has the interface:

```
template <class Name = string, class Value = double>
            class Property : public PropertyThing<Name, Value>
{
private:
    Name nam;
    Value con;
public:

    // See CD for full set of functions
    void print() const;
};
```

The property set class has the interface:

```
template <class N = string, class V = double> class SimplePropertySet
          : public PropertyThing<N, V>
{
private:
    N nam;            // The name of the set
    // The SimplePropertySet list using the STL map
    map<N, V> sl;
    Set<N> keys;
public:
    // Full interface on CD
};
```

Please consult the CD for the full source code.

We now come to the issue at hand. In this case we create composite property sets and we reduce the scope by using strings for the key type and double precision numbers for the value type. First, a common tactic when using templates is to use shorthand notation to make the resulting code more readable:

```
typedef GenericComposite<PropertyThing<string, double> >
   CompositeProperty;
```

What we now propose is to create a data structure that models the data in a bull spread option strategy. This is a long position in a call option with a given strike price K1 combined

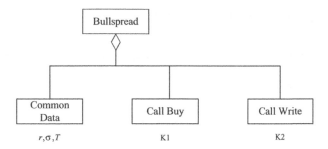

Figure 12.2 Bullspread as a Whole-Part object

with a short position in a call with strike price K2 where K2 > K1. A simple model is shown
in Figure 12.2. In this case the top-level object models a bull spread and it is a composite
containing the common option data and two properties representing the strikes, respectively.
The following code creates the parts of the bull spread composite in Figure 12.2:

```
Property<string, double>
    r = Property<string, double> ("Interest rate", 0.08);
Property<string, double>
    sig= Property<string, double> ("Volatility",0.30);
Property<string, double>
    T = Property<string, double>("Expiry date", 0.25);

SimplePropertySet<string, double>*
CommonProps = new SimplePropertySet<string,double>("CommonProps");
    CommonProps->add(r);
    CommonProps->add(sig);
    CommonProps->add(T);
Property<string, double>*
        CallBuy = new Property<string, double>("CallBuy", 100.0);
Property<string, double>*
        CallWrite= new Property<string, double>
        ("CallWrite", 120.0);
```

Finally, we create the top-level composite as follows:

```
    CompositeProperty BullSpread;
    BullSpread.push_back(CommonProps);
    BullSpread.push_back(CallBuy);
    BullSpread.push_back(CallWrite);
    print(BullSpread);
```

The output from this program is

```
* Name of Pset: CommonProps
    Expiry date, 0.25
    Interest rate, 0.08
    Volatility, 0.3

* Property name: CallBuy, value: 100
* Property name: CallWrite, value: 120
```

where the code for the `print()` function is given by

```
template <class K, class V>
    void print(const GenericComposite<PropertyThing<K,V> >& pset)
{
    GenericComposite<PropertyThing<K,V> >::const_iterator it;

    for (it= pset.begin(); it!=pset.end(); it++)
    {
        (*it)->print();
    }
}
```

We can apply the same approach to tree structures containing arbitrary data types. We apply the *Property* pattern in Part III of this book.

12.9 SUMMARY AND CONCLUSIONS

This chapter discussed a number of data structures and classes that we use in a variety of applications. The focus is on organising data so that it can be used by other parts of a program. In particular, we have discussed the following data structures:

- Dynamic (run-time) vectors and matrices.
- Compile-time vectors and matrices.
- Modelling SDEs using compile-time data structures.
- STL wrapper and adapter classes.
- C++ classes for date and time.
- Strings in C++.
- Sorting algorithms.

We recommend the use of these and similar data structures in applications. You can use them without modification and you can extend them using well-documented design patterns in combination with object-oriented and generic programming principles. We discuss more data structures in Chapter 13.

12.10 EXERCISES AND PROJECTS

1. (**) Manipulations with Dates
   Given a date and an offset generate a set of dates between them. The set contains both end points. The function prototype is

   ```
   Set<DatasimDate> DateCollection(const DatasimDate& start,
       DateOffsetUnit offset, int NumberOfDates)
   ```

   Write the code for this function and test it as we did in section 12.5.2. Write a function to generate all dates between two given dates.
2. (*) Stringstreams and Output Precision
   Explain what is happening in this code:

   ```
   template <typename T>
       string getString(const T& value, int prec = 4)
   ```

```
    {

        stringstream s;
        s.precision(prec);

        s << value;

        return s.str();
    }
```

Write a program to test this function. Furthermore, investigate what the following functions do (notice we have discussed toupper()):

```
namespace std {
        using ::isalnum;
        using ::isalpha;
        using ::iscntrl;
        using ::isdigit;
        using ::isgraph;
        using ::islower;
        using ::isprint;
        using ::ispunct;
        using ::isspace;
        using ::isupper;
        using ::isxdigit;
        using ::tolower;
        using ::toupper;}
```

3. (***) Project: Using Lookup Tables of Strings

In this exercise we create a front-end to the *Command* design pattern. We recall that this pattern encapsulates user commands as *functors* or *function objects*. In the current case we associate a string with code that executes on a supplier object. For example, the string 'price' could correspond to an action to calculate the price of an option. But in interactive applications the user might type the string incorrectly and for this reason we would like to associate a set of synonyms or aliases with the unique string name. We thus have a many-to-one relationship between synonyms and original names and for this reason we model the relationship as an STL *multimap<string, string >* in which the keys correspond to the synonyms and the values correspond to the original string.

The class that you create should be able to support the following functionality:
- Defining a set of original value type (of string type).
- Defining any number of synonyms for a given original value.
- Removing synonyms and/or values from the relationship.
- Dealing with exceptions (no synonym found, no value found).

You can decide to write the C++ class using the STL *multimap* as the embedded data structure; alternatively, you can use the adapter template class *Relation<D, R>* from the accompanying CD and this option will save you having to reinvent the wheel.

4. (***) Sorting Algorithms

It is sometimes necessary to sort arrays and vectors of numbers, for example when we create arrays of uniformly distributed random variates as we have seen in Part I. It is possible to create your own sorting algorithms but this approach is not optimal in general because STL has implemented these algorithms and in our opinion it would be difficult to improve on them.

STL has four main algorithms for sorting data:

- `sort()`: This is based on the *quicksort* algorithm developed by Sid Hoare in 1960. It guarantees run-time $O(n * log(n))$ complexity in general but in the worst case it has quadratic complexity. It is a comparison-based sort by which we mean that it reads the list elements through a single abstract comparison operation (often a 'less than or equal to' operator) that determines which of two elements should occur first in the final sorted list.

- `stable_sort()`: This is based on the *mergesort* algorithm invented by John von Neumann in 1945. It is a comparison-based sort and it guarantees run-time $O(n * log(n))$ complexity in general but at the expense of additional memory. Stable sorting algorithms maintain the relative order of records with equal keys (sort key values). That is, a sorting algorithm is stable if whenever there are two records R and S with the same key and with R appearing before S in the original list, R will appear before S in the sorted list. Some features of this algorithm are

  – It parallelises well.

  – It is a stable sort.

  – It is one of the best methods for sorting linked lists.

  – It is suitable for slow-to-access sequential media (for example, tape drives).

  A variation on the two above algorithms is the *introsort()* developed by David Musser in 1997; by default, it is a *quicksort* but it switches to *heapsort* when recursion depth exceeds a predefined value. We must be careful about portability issues between compilers.

- `partial_sort()`: This algorithm is based on *heapsort*, originally invented by Robert W. Floyd and J.W.J. Williams in 1964. It guarantees run-time $O(n * log(n))$ complexity *in all cases* but is a factor of two to five times as slow as quicksort. It never achieves quadratic complexity.

- `heap_sort()`: A *heap* can be viewed as a binary tree that is implemented by a sequential collection. Some properties of a heap are that the first element is always the largest element and we can add or remove elements in logarithmic time. Heaps are useful as implementations of *priority queues*. STL has four algorithms for heaps:

  – *make_heap()*: convert a range of elements to a heap.

  – *push_heap()*: add an element to the heap.

  – *pop_heap()*: remove an element from the heap.

  – *sort_heap()*: convert the heap into a sorted collection using a binary predicate as sorting criterion, after which time it is no longer a sorted collection.

In general, *quicksort* is considered to be the fastest of these four algorithms, followed by *mergesort*, *partial sort* and then *heapsort*. An example of using these sort algorithms is:

```
#include <iostream>
#include "clock.hpp"
#include <vector>
#include <list>
#include <algorithm>
#include <functional>      // For greater<int>( )
using namespace std;
size_t Size = 10000000;    // 10^7
vector<int> vec(Size);
```

```
list<int> myList;
for(size_t ii=0; ii < Size; ++ii)
{
    vec[ii] = rand();
}

cout << "Start sorting\n";
myClock.start();
sort(vec.begin(), vec.end());
myClock.stop();
cout << myClock.duration() << endl;
```

We are now ready to formulate the exercise. We are interested in coding the following algorithm: we wish to construct a collection of standard exponential variates (that is, with rate = 1) from a collection of independent uniformly distributed random variates. The algorithm is as follows (Rubinstein, 1981):

- Generate $2n - 1$ uniformly distributed random variates $U_1, \ldots, U_n, U_{n+1}, \ldots, U_{2n-1}$.
- Arrange the collection $U_{n+1}, \ldots, U_{2n-1}$ consisting of $n - 1$ elements from above in increasing magnitude, that is the *order statistics* $U_{(1)}, \ldots, U_{(n-1)}$ corresponding to the random sample in the above step (assume $U_{(0)} = 0$ and $U_{(n)} = 1$).
- Calculate the collection

$$Y_j = (U_{(j-1)} - U_{(j)}) \log \left(\prod_{k=1}^{n} U_k \right) \text{ for } j = 1, \ldots, n$$

This is the desired collection each of whose elements is in exp(1).

Write C++ code to implement this algorithm. You need to decide on (i) the most appropriate containers to hold input and output data (for example, lists, vectors) and (ii) which of the above sorting algorithms is the most appropriate? One last question: what are the consequences if you sort an already-sorted container?

5. (***) Print Functions in Property Sets using *Visitor* pattern

In section 12.8 we created a tree of properties and property sets. We also created a function `print()` in each class for pedagogical reasons but we do not recommend this in general. The objective of this exercise is to redesign the code in such a way that the code in section 12.8 works as before but all console printing takes place using the *Visitor* pattern.

13

The Boost Library: An Introduction

13.1 INTRODUCTION AND OBJECTIVES

In the previous chapters of Part II we introduced system decomposition techniques to partition a system into more manageable subsystems (POSA, 1996), namely in Chapters 8 and 9. We then designed each subsystem using design patterns (GOF, 1995), namely Chapter 10. Eventually, the design is detailed enough to allow it to be implemented in C++ as discussed in Chapters 11 and 12.

In this chapter we give an introduction to the Boost library. The library will become part of the official C++ standard in due course and the authors of this book plan to migrate their code to support these libraries in the future. This chapter is an overview of what the Boost library offers. We provide exercises on how to use it. Due to scoping problems we are only able to discuss a small subset of the functionality in the library.

13.2 A TAXONOMY OF C++ POINTER TYPES

One of the most difficult topics to master in C++ is heap memory management. In C++ we use pointers in conjunction with the *new* and *delete* operators to realise object lifecycle. The developer is responsible for cleaning up heap memory when it is no longer needed. The main action points that we address are

- A1: Who (which object) creates the memory?
- A2: Who deletes the memory?
- A3: Who is the owner of the memory?
- A4: Can memory ownership be transferred to another object?
- A5: When is memory allocated/deallocated?
- A6: Can memory become corrupted?

It is a major challenge to resolve these problems using raw C++ pointers (as has been experienced in many applications) and for this reason we decide to use the so-called *smart pointers* from the Boost library (see www.boost.org and Karlsson, 2006). As developer, you need to decide which specific smart pointer type to use in a particular context:

- Avoiding *dangling pointers* (pointers that do not point to a valid object).
- Making shared ownership of resources effective and safe.
- Automatically deleting pointers when they go out of scope (or at the right time).

We now discuss memory allocation in the following subsections.

13.2.1 The smart pointer types

Smart pointers solve the problem of managing the lifecycle of resources, and in particular dynamically allocated objects. There are five smart pointer types in the library `Boost.Smart_ptr`.

We discuss scoped and shared pointers only in this book. In general, we use smart pointers for the following scenarios (Karlson, 2006):

- *Shared ownership*: In this case two or more objects use a third, shared object. They may be able to modify the third object and the vital issue is to decide when to delete this object. To this end, we use a smart pointer whose sole responsibility is to decide when and where a shared object may be deleted.
- *Exception safety*: In general, dynamically allocated objects using 'raw' C++ pointers are not deleted when an exception is thrown. What happens is that the stack is unwound, thus deleting the pointer but not the associated resources which remain inaccessible until the program terminates. Smart pointers resolve these problems, even when exceptions occur.
- *Avoiding common errors*: Programmers are human and they can forget to clean up memory after they have created it and when that memory is no longer needed. Smart pointers hide deallocation details, thus removing the burden from the developer's shoulders.

We advise the use of smart pointers in projects, especially in large-scale applications. They are more robust and safer than using 'raw' C++ pointers or the STL `auto_ptr`.

13.2.2 Scoped pointers

We use `scoped_ptr` to ensure that a dynamically allocated object is deleted when it goes out of scope; in other words, we create an object in a function body and it is then automatically deleted when it is popped from the stack. Here is an example:

```
#include "boost/scoped_ptr.hpp"
#include "Point.hpp"


int main()
{

    // Create dynamic memory
    boost::scoped_ptr <Point> myPoint (new Point(1.0, 23.3));

    // The memory is cleaned up automatically
    // NO delete needed

    // Check by placing print statement in the destructor
    // of the Point class

    return 0;
}
```

Next, having defined a scoped pointer, what can we do with it? First, a scoped pointer assumes ownership of the resource to which it points and this ownership will never be surrendered. In particular, you will get a compiler error if you try to assign one scoped pointer to another one. The use of scoped pointers does not affect performance and it improves the robustness of code. It overloads the major operators that raw pointers use and this makes it easy to understand, as the following documented code shows:

```
#include "boost/scoped_ptr.hpp"
#include "Point.hpp"


int main()
{
        // Create dynamic memory
        boost::scoped_ptr <Point> myPoint (new Point(1.0, 23.3));

        // Scoped pointer has same syntax as a raw pointer
        if (myPoint != 0)
        {
            cout << *myPoint;
        }

        // Assign to another point
        Point yourPoint (7.3, -9.9);

        *myPoint = yourPoint;
        cout << *myPoint;

        // Use operator '->'
        myPoint -> X(8.8);
        cout << *myPoint;

        // Cannot assign scoped pointers, operator '=' is private
        boost::scoped_ptr <Point> myPoint2 (new Point(1.0, 23.3));
        // THIS CODE DOES NOT COMPILE ' myPoint = myPoint2;

        // Illegal, cannot convert
        // boost::scoped_ptr <Point> illegalVar (new double);

        return 0;
}
```

Finally, we discuss the *pimpl* idiom and its relationship with scoped pointers. This idiom was used in early C++ applications and it can still be found in some legacy systems. Its main advantage is that it insulates clients from having to know about the private parts of a class. In particular, the constructor of the class allocates the pimpl type while the destructor deletes it, hence removing implementation dependencies from the header file. Here is an example in which we create a simple class that uses a struct. We forward declare the struct in the header file of the pimpl class:

```
#ifndef PIMPL_HPP
#define PIMPL_HPP
```

```
template <typename V>
    struct HestonStruct; // Forward reference


template <typename V>
    class Pimpl
{
private:
    HestonStruct<V>* data;
public:
    Pimpl();
    ~Pimpl();

    void initialiseData();
    void print() const;

};

#endif
```

The declaration of the struct containing the Heston data is

```
#ifndef HestonStructure_HPP
#define HestonStructure_HPP

template <typename V> struct HestonStruct
{ // Defining properties of class, already discussed in chapter 5

    V T;
    V r, q;
    V kappa, theta, epsilon;
    V rho;                      // Correlation

    V IC_S;                     // Initial conditions S, V
    V IC_V;

    void initialiseData();   // Default data
    void print() const;
};
```

The code for the pimpl class is given by

```
template <typename V>
    Pimpl<V>::Pimpl() : data(new HestonStruct<V>)
{

}

template <typename V>
    Pimpl<V>::~Pimpl()
{
```

```
        delete data;
}

template <typename V>
    void Pimpl<V>::initialiseData()
{

    data -> initialiseData();
}

template <typename V>
    void Pimpl<V>::print() const
{
    data->print();
}
```

The code looks robust enough. Unfortunately, it is not *exception safe*, which means in this case that if the constructor in the pimpl class throws an exception after the embedded pointer has been created then the latter's destructor will not be called when the stack is unwound. In other words, we get a *memory leak* and for this reason we advise against the use of the idiom. Instead, we use scoped pointers.

Scoped pointers should be used in the following situations:

- The lifetime of a dynamically allocated object is limited to a specific scope.
- A pointer is used in a scope where exceptions may be thrown.
- There are several control paths in a function.
- Exception safety is important (for example, when an exception occurs in a constructor of a class having pointer member data, then this pointer should be cleaned up).

13.2.3   Shared pointers

In this case we are interested in the dynamic creation of objects that are subsequently shared by two or more other objects (this is an implementation of the GOF *Flyweight* pattern). The major problem is to know when to delete the dynamically allocated object. If we delete it when another object needs it we will probably get a run-time error at some stage, whereas if it is no longer needed we would like to remove it from memory. The solution is to use the *reference counting* principle; we define an integral reference count that is incremented (by one) when an object creates or accesses the shared object and it is decremented (by one) when the shared object is no longer needed. Only when the reference count is zero are we allowed to delete the shared object; this is done automatically.

We discuss the shared pointer class in the Boost library: it allows us to *non-intrusively* manage the lifecycle of a shared object. To this end, we have programmed some representative scenarios:

- Two classes that share common member data (built-in types or user-defined types).
- Determining the reference count of an object.
- Using shared pointers with STL containers.

In the first example we create two disjoint classes (that is, they have no common base class) C1 and C2 but they have shared member data:

```
#include "boost/shared_ptr.hpp"
class C1
{
private:
     //double* d; OLD WAY
     boost::shared_ptr<double> d;
public:
     C1(boost::shared_ptr<double> value) : d(value) {}
     virtual ~C1() { cout << "\nC1 destructor\n";}
     void print() const { cout << "Value " << *d; }
};

class C2
{
private:
     //double* d; // OLD WAY
     boost::shared_ptr<double> d;
public:
     C2(boost::shared_ptr<double> value) : d(value) {}
     virtual ~C2() { cout << "\nC2 destructor\n"; }
     void print() const { cout << "Value " << *d; }
};
```

We now create instances of these classes; even when the first instance `object1` goes out of scope we see that the shared memory `commonValue` is still accessible to the instance `object2` of C2:

```
     boost::shared_ptr<double> commonValue(new double (3.1415));
     {
          C1 object1(commonValue);

     }

     C2 object2(commonValue);
```

In the second example, we use the `shared_ptr` member function `use_count()` that tells us how many objects are accessing a shared object at any given time. To this end, we create two classes D1 and D2 that share a common instance of class `Point`:

```
class D1
{
private:

     boost::shared_ptr<Point> p;
public:
     D1(boost::shared_ptr<Point> value) : p(value) {}
     virtual ~D1() { cout << "\nD1 destructor\n";}
     void print() const { cout << "\nValue " << *p; }
};
```

```
class D2
{
private:

    boost::shared_ptr<Point> p;
public:
    D2(boost::shared_ptr<Point> value) : p(value) {}
    virtual ~D2() { cout << "\nD2 destructor\n";}
    void print() const { cout << "\nValue " << *p; }
};
```

The test code is:

```
boost::shared_ptr <Point> myPoint (new Point(1.0, 23.3));
cout << "Reference count: " << myPoint.use_count() << endl;
{
        D1 point1(myPoint);
        cout << "Reference count: " << myPoint.use_count()
         << endl;
        D1 point2(myPoint);
        cout << "Reference count: " << myPoint.use_count()
         << endl;

}
cout << "Reference count: " << myPoint.use_count() << endl;
{
        D2 object3(myPoint);
        cout << "Reference count: " << myPoint.use_count()
         << endl;
}
cout << "Reference count: " << myPoint.use_count() << endl;
```

When we run this code, the following values for the reference count will be printed: 1, 2, 3, 1, 2, 1.

Finally, in the third case we show how to use shared pointers in STL containers. In this case we create vectors whose elements are shared pointers. The base and derived class interfaces are defined as

```
class Base
{ // Class with non-virtual destructor
private:

public:
    Base() { }
    virtual ~Base() { cout << "Base destructor\n\n"; }
    virtual void print() const = 0;
};

class Derived : public Base
{ // Derived class
private:
```

```
public:
    Derived() : Base() { }
    ~Derived() { cout << "Derived destructor\n"; }
    void print() const { cout << "derived object\n";}
};
```

We define a useful function that gives us a pointer to the base class (in real applications it would return the address of one of a number of derived classes):

```
// Simple creator function
boost::shared_ptr<Base> createBase()
{
    boost::shared_ptr<Base> result(new Derived());
    return result;
}
```

The data container is defined as

```
    // Use in STL containers
    typedef std::vector<boost::shared_ptr<Base> > ContainerType;
    typedef ContainerType::iterator iterator;
```

We add elements to the container as follows:

```
    // Create a vector of objects
    ContainerType con;
    for (int j = 0; j < 10; ++j)
    {
        con.push_back(createBase());      // Add pointers to vector
    }
```

Finally, we print the elements of the container using an iterator:

```
    // Now iterate and print
    iterator myIter;
    for (myIter = con.begin(); myIter != con.end(); ++myIter)
    {
        (*myIter) -> print();
    }
```

All memory management is taken care of. This example gave the essentials of using shared pointers with STL containers. Shared pointers are useful in the following situations:

- When we implement the *Flyweight* design pattern (GOF, 1995); we create objects on the heap and they can be shared by other objects.
- Storing pointers in STL containers.
- When there are multiple clients of an object, but no explicit owner.
- When passing objects to and from libraries without any clear ownership regime.
- When managing resources that need special cleanup procedures, for example using *custom deleters*. A customer deleter is one that augments the simple C++ delete keyword. For example, resource handles are good candidates for customer deleters. This feature could be implemented in conjunction with the *Builder* pattern.
- As a replacement for the *pimpl* idiom.

13.2.4   Using smart pointers in Monte Carlo applications

We now step back from the details of smart pointers and think about where they can be used in Monte Carlo applications. In this book we used raw pointers for readability and understandability reasons and also because smart pointers are – strictly speaking – not (yet) part of the C++ standard. In future applications we shall use smart pointers and our advice to readers is to apply them whenever possible because they improve the reliability of the code.

Since we use a number of high-level structural patterns (such as *Whole-Part* and *PAC*) to model the classes and objects in Monte Carlo applications it is relatively easy to define object creational policies and object lifecycles. In general, scoped and shared pointers are to be recommended when

- We need to create an object whose lifetime is limited (for example, a factory object), then we can use scoped pointers. Factories are typically objects whose scope is a single subsystem and do not have to be known outside that subsystem.
- We need to create an object that will be shared among several parts and subsystems, then we used shared pointers.
- We could consider the use of the *Builder* pattern that creates objects in the *Whole-Part* pattern. The builder then creates the parts. The advantage of this approach is that all object creation and destruction is localised in one place, namely the builder object itself.
- Shared objects are not needed in an application, then the use of shared pointers is probably superfluous. In that case, the use of raw C++ pointers (don't forget `delete`) is recommended.

13.3   MODELLING HOMOGENEOUS AND HETEROGENEOUS DATA IN BOOST

In Chapter 12 we discussed some ways of modelling data in C++. But Boost has some of the same capabilities. As already mentioned, these libraries will become part of the standard C++ language in due time.

When determining which library to use when modelling data we need to ask some questions:

- Is data homogeneous or heterogeneous?
- Are data collections of fixed size or of variable size?
- Is the data defined at compile-time or can be it changed at run-time?

13.3.1   Tuples

The *Boost Tuple* library can be seen as a generalisation of `std::pair` (this is a struct that groups pairs of objects). It is now possible to define so-called *n-tuples*; these structures model fixed-sized collections of values of specified types (for example, STL pairs are considered to be 2-tuples). Tuples correspond to *record structures* in languages such as Cobol and we need them in many kinds of applications and in C++ code, for example:

- When we wish to have multiple return types from functions.
- When we need tuples input arguments to functions.
- When we group logically related types (for example, defining records and tables).

Some languages have built-in support for n-tuples, but not C++. In order to fill the gap, the Boost library developers created the *Tuple* library.

We now take some examples to show how to create and use tuples. The first example creates 2-tuples and populates them using a constructor and the *convenience function* make_tuple():

```
#include "boost/tuple/tuple.hpp"
#include <string>
#include <iostream>
using namespace std;

int main()
{
    // Using declaration, for readability purposes
    using boost::tuple;

    // Creating tuples
    tuple<string, double> myTuple(string("Hello"), 3.1415);
    tuple<string, int>
    myTuple2 = boost::make_tuple(string("position x"), 0);

    return 0;
}
```

We now show how to retrieve the elements of a 3-tuple using the template member functions get<>() which accepts an index value that must be less than the number of elements in the tuple:

```
    // Retrieving values from a tuple
    tuple<long, double, string>
            newTuple(100, 2.17, string("a new tuple"));

    long first = newTuple.get<0>();
    double second = newTuple.get<1>();
    string third = newTuple.get<2>();

    cout << "Elements of tuple: " << first << ", " << second
            << ", " << third << endl;
```

Summarising, we use tuples when modelling fixed sized collections whose elements can be of heterogeneous data type; the data types can be built-in or user-defined types.

13.3.2   Variants and discriminated unions

The *Variant* library is used for typesafe storage and retrieval of a bounded set of types, that is *discriminated unions*. The main uses are

- Typesafe storage and retrieval of user-specified sets of types.
- Storing heterogeneous types in STL containers.
- Compile-time checked visitation of variants (using *Visitor* pattern).
- Efficient, stack-based storage for variants.

We describe the functionality in this library and we refer the reader to Karlsson (2006) for a more detailed description, in particular the application of the *Visitor* pattern. We take an example of a variant with three different types in the discriminated union:

```
#include "boost/variant.hpp"
int main()
{
    // Using declaration, for readability purposes
    using boost::variant;

    variant<long, string, Point> myVariant;

    myVariant = 24;
    print(myVariant);

    myVariant = string("It's amazing");
    print(myVariant);
    myVariant = Point();
    print(myVariant);
    return 0;
}
```

The function for printing the current value in the variant is given by

```
template <typename V> void print(V& v)
{
    if (long* pi = boost::get<long> (&v))
    {
        cout << "It's a long value" << *pi;
    }
    else
    if (string* st = boost::get<string> (&v))
    {
        cout << "It's a long " << *st;
    }
    else
    if (Point* pt = boost::get<Point> (&v))
    {
        cout << "It's a point " << *pt;
    }

    cout << endl;
}
```

The *Variant* library complements the *any* library, which we now describe.

13.3.3 Any and undiscriminated types

The *any* library resolves a number of the shortcomings of C++, in particular when we create collections whose elements can be of any type. In the past, some developers modelled these collections with void* but this lacks type safety. The *any* library resolves this problem by ensuring that there is no way to get a value without knowing its type; in this way we preserve type safety. Some of the advantages and uses of this library are:

- Storing heterogeneous types in STL containers.
- Typesafe storage and safe retrieval of arbitrary types.
- In layered applications, objects send and receive data without having to know anything about the precise types of the data that they send or receive.
- We can use the any class as a kind of variant data type.

The any class preserves the type of the data that it stores and you cannot get at the stored value unless you know the correct type. It is possible to query for the type using run-time type information (RTTI) and casting functions in C++. We use the any class in cases when we do not wish to know about the type. At some stage we determine what the actual type is, but this can be done in a specialised function.

We take an example of a list of any types:

```
#include "boost/any.hpp"
#include <string>
#include <list>
#include <iostream>
using namespace std;

int main()
{
    // Using declaration, for readability purposes
    using boost::any;
    list<any> myList;

    long v = 123;
    double d = 3.14;
    string s = string("D");
    Point p;

    // Populate the list with all kinds of types
    myList.push_back(v);
    myList.push_back(d);
    myList.push_back(s);
    myList.push_back(p);
    myList.push_back(make_pair<bool, double>(true, 3.14));

    return 0;
}
```

The list also contained a variable *p* that is an instance of class Point:

```
struct Point
{
    double x, y;

    Point() { x = y = 0.0;}

    friend ostream& operator << (ostream& os, const Point& pt)
```

```
    {
        os << "(" << pt.x << "," << pt.y << ")" << endl;
        return os;
    }
};
```

Summarising, we see that this is very generic and flexible!

13.3.4   A Property class

A useful application of the *any* library is to define a class that represents *name-value pairs*. We call this the *Property class* and we have used it in the past as well as in the current book to model class attributes (see Duffy, 2004a and Duffy, 2006a). To this end, we define a simple property class as follows:

```
using boost::any;
template <typename Key>
        class Property
{
private:
        Key nam;
        any val;
public:
    Property(const Key& key, const any& value)
        : nam(key), val(value)
    {
    }

    string Name() const { return nam;}
    any& Value() { return val; }

    // Allows storage in STL containers
    friend bool operator < (const Property<Key>&lhs,
                            const Property<Key>&rhs)
    {
        return lhs.nam < rhs.nam;
    }
};
```

We now create a number of instances of this class and we add them to a vector. In this way we can create simple *property maps* (which we call *property sets* in Duffy, 2004a):

```
int main()
{
    // Using declaration, for readability purposes
    using boost::any;

    long v = 123;
    double d = 3.14;
    string s = string("D");
```

```
Property<string> myProp(string("1"),v);
Property<string> myProp2(string("2"),d);
Property<string> myProp3(string("3"),s);

vector<Property<string> > properties;
properties.push_back(myProp);
properties.push_back(myProp2);
properties.push_back(myProp3);

return 0;
}
```

13.3.5 Boost arrays

The array class in the *Array* library is close in spirit to the authors' VectorSpace<V, N> class that we have already discussed in Part II. Instead of providing the semantics of dynamic arrays, we note in this case that the size of a Boost array is fixed at initialisation time and it is a template parameter. The interface of this class has most of the member functions that you would expect:

- No constructors, only the assignment statement.
- Indexing operator [].
- Iterators.
- Functions to retrieve the first and last elements of the array.
- It is possible to compare arrays (lexicographical compare).

We take an example to show how to use the class:

```
#include "boost/array.hpp"
#include "Point.hpp"


int main()
{

    boost::array<long, 4> myArr = { 1, 2, 3, 4};


    // Using iterators
    boost::array<long, 4>::const_iterator it;

    for (it = myArr.begin(); it != myArr.end(); ++it)
    {
        cout << *it << endl;
    }

    // Indexing operator
    for (long i = 0; i < myArr.size(); ++i)
    {
        cout << myArr[i] << endl;
```

```
}

boost::array<Point, 4> myPointArr;
myPointArr[0] = Point();
myPointArr[1] = Point();
myPointArr[2] = Point();
myPointArr[3] = Point();

return 0;
}
```

We now review some other libraries in Boost. The objective is to help the reader become aware of the many useful resources that Boost has to offer.

13.4   BOOST SIGNALS: NOTIFICATION AND DATA SYNCHRONISATION

The *Signals* library is the boost implementation of the *Observer* or *Publisher-Subscriber* pattern (GOF, 1995, POSA, 1996). It allows developers to manage events while ensuring that inter-object dependencies are kept to a minimum, a problem that plagues the more traditional object-oriented approach taken in the *Observer* pattern. Using the *Signals* library ensures that the emissions of signals or events (by *subjects*) are decoupled from the slots (also known as *observers* or *subscribers*). The *Signals* library is similar to the *Delegates mechanism* in the .NET framework.

Some of the features of *Signals* are

- Flexible multicast callbacks for functions and function objects.
- A robust method for triggering and handling events.
- Compatible with function object factories (for example, *Boost.Bind* and *Boost.Lambda*).
- In general, implementing *callbacks*.

We take a simple example to show how the *Signals* library works. The main steps are

1. Create a signal.
2. Define functions or function objects (these are slots).
3. Connect the slot to the signal.
4. Emit the signal (and the slots are called immediately).
5. Optionally, disconnect a slot.
6. Emit the signal, again.

The corresponding C++ code is given by

```
#include "boost/signals.hpp"
#include <iostream>
using namespace std;

// Define a normal function (a Slot)
void mySlot()
{
    cout << "a slot \n";
}
```

```
// 2. Define a function object (a Slot)
struct SecondSlot
{
    void operator () () { cout << "a second slot \n";}
};

int main()
{

    // 1. Create signal
    boost::signal<void ()> signal;

    // 3. Connect slots
    signal.connect(&mySlot);
    signal.connect(SecondSlot());

    // 4. Emit the signal
    signal();

    // 5. Disconnect first slot
    signal.disconnect(&mySlot);

    // 6. Emit signal (one slot less)
    signal();


    return 0;
}
```

A good example of where the *Signals* library can be used is when we separate GUI code from business logic code. In general, it supersedes old-style callbacks. Finally, it is possible to define so-called *Combiners* that allow developers to write event mechanisms that are tailor-made for a given domain. For more on this, see Karlsson (2006).

13.5   INPUT AND OUTPUT

We discuss two libraries in this section. The first one allows the developer to write data to, and retrieve data from, a disk while the second library supports portable file systems.

13.5.1   Boost.Serialisation

This portable library allows us to save C++ data structures to archives and to restore these structures from archives. In this case we are referring to *persistent data*, that is objects whose lifetime survives the scope in which they are defined. An archive can be a text file or an XML file, for example. The library offers support for class versioning, for STL classes and shared data, for example. Another way to define serialisation is to say that it is the reversible deconstruction of an arbitrary set of C++ data structures to a sequence of bytes. We can then reconstitute an equivalent structure in another program context.

We take an example. In this case we model the parameters of the Heston model that are defined in a struct and we apply the archiving functionality to save the data to disk and then we restore the data from disk:

```
#include <fstream>
#include <iostream>

// Include headers that implement a archive in simple text format
#include "boost/archive/text_oarchive.hpp"
#include "boost/archive/text_iarchive.hpp"
```

We define the persistent data structure that we introduced in Chapter 5:

```
template <typename V> struct HestonStruct
{ // Defining properties of class, already discussed in chapter 5

        V T;
        V r, q;
        V kappa, theta, epsilon;
        V rho;                // Correlation

        V IC_S;               // Initial conditions S, V
        V IC_V;

        // Template member function
        template <typename Archive>
            void serialize(Archive& arc, unsigned int version)
            { // Classes must implement this function

                    arc & T; arc & r; arc & q;
                    arc & kappa; arc & theta; arc & epsilon;
                    arc & rho; arc & IC_S; arc & IC_V;

            }

};
```

We note that each persistent class must implement the serialize() function, as above. Finally, the code for two-way input-output is given by

```
int main()
{
        /////////////////// Data Area ///////////////////////////////////
        HestonStruct<double> data;

        data.T = 1.0; data.r = 0.1; data.q = 0.0;

        data.kappa = 1.98837; data.theta = 0.1089; data.epsilon = 0.15;

        data.rho =   -0.9;

        data.IC_S = 123.4; // ATM
        data.IC_V = 0.37603 * 0.37603;
```

```
// Create and open a character archive for output
std::ofstream ofs("Heston.dat");

// Save data to archive
{
      boost::archive::text_oarchive oa(ofs);

    // Change some data
    data.r = 0.08;

    // Write class instance to archive
    oa << data;

}


// ... Some time later, restore the class
HestonStruct<double> newData;
{
    // Create and open an archive for input
    std::ifstream ifs("Heston.dat", std::ios::binary);
    boost::archive::text_iarchive ia(ifs);

    // Read class state from archive
    ia >> newData;

// Just checking
std::cout << "Interest rate is: "
                << newData.r << std::endl;

}

    return 0;
}
```

For completeness, we show the contents of the archived file:

```
22 serialization::archive 4 0 0 1 0.080000000000000002 0 1.98837
   0.1089
0.14999999999999999 -0.90000000000000002 123.40000000000001
   0.14139856089999997
```

The *Serialisation* library allows us to build a simple and effective data storage system.

13.5.2   Boost.Filesystem

This is a portable library for the manipulation of paths, directories and files. The developer can write code using script-like operations. For example, algorithms are provided for iterating in directories and files. Here is an example of use (more information on www.boost.org):

```
#include "boost/filesystem.hpp"
#include <iostream>
```

```
int main()
{

    boost::filesystem::path my_path( "Heston.dat" );

    return 0;
}
```

13.6   LINEAR ALGEBRA AND uBLAS

The uBLAS library consists of a number of linear algebra operations for vectors and matrices based on operator overloading. It has facilities for efficient code generation using so-called *expression templates* (see Abrahams and Gurtovoy (2005) for a discussion of this topic in particular and C++ *template metaprogramming* in general).

The library contains much of the functionality that has already been created by one of the current authors (see Duffy, 2004a), in particular basic vector and matrix operations. Furthermore, the uBLAS library supports different kinds of *banded matrices*, for example:

- Dense matrices.
- Triangular matrices.
- Symmetric matrices.
- Hermitian matrices.
- Banded matrices.
- Sparse matrices.

It is also possible to define how the data is stored in memory, for example *row-major order* or *column-major order*. The choice has an impact on performance.

Here is an example to show how to use the library by creating a dense matrix:

```
#include <boost/numeric/ublas/matrix.hpp>
#include <boost/numeric/ublas/io.hpp>

int main()
{
    using namespace boost::numeric::ublas;
    matrix<double> m (3, 3);
    for (unsigned i = 0; i < m.size1(); ++i)
    {
        for (unsigned j = 0; j < m.size2(); ++j)
        {
            m(i,j) = 3 * i + j;
        }
    }
    std::cout << m << std::endl;
    return 0;
}
```

In future applications we will use these patterned matrices as a basis for advanced numerical applications.

13.7   DATE AND TIME

The *Date_time* library supports date and time types and the corresponding operations on them. Programming with dates and times becomes almost as simple as programming with strings and integers. The following classes are supported:

- *Date*: The primary interface for date programming.
- *Date Duration*: Simple day count used for arithmetic with *Date*.
- *Date Period*: Direct representation for ranges between two dates.
- *Date Iterators*: A standard mechanism for iterating through dates.

Furthermore, the library has algorithms for generating dates and schedules of dates. For example, we can represent concepts such as 'the first Sunday in February', 'the first Sunday after Jan 1, 2009' and so on.

The following simple example shows how to use the functionality. In this case we create a date based on a string:

```cpp
// TestDate.cpp
//
// Testing boost Date_time (large!) library
//
// (C)Datasim Education BV 2008
//

#include "boost/date_time/gregorian/gregorian.hpp"
#include <string>
using namespace std;

int main()
{

    using namespace boost::gregorian;

    // ISO 8601 extended format CCYY-MM-DD
    string s("2009-10-9"); // 10 October 2009
    date myDate(from_simple_string(s));

    // Now convert to a string
    string converted = to_simple_string(myDate);
    cout << "String: " << converted << endl; // OUTPUT is
                                                2009-Oct-09

    return 0;
}
```

13.8   OTHER LIBRARIES

We conclude this chapter with a short description of some other libraries in Boost. For more information, please consult **www.boost.org** and the CD accompanying this book where we have provided numerous C++ code examples to help the reader understand the essentials of these libraries.

13.8.1   String and text processing

There are three major libraries in Boost for analysing and parsing text and strings:

- *Regex*: A library for pattern-matching applications, in particular support for regular expressions in C++ and improving the robustness of input validation.
- *Spirit*: A recursive-descent parser generator framework. It makes use of meta-programming techniques and expression templates that approximate the syntax of Extended Backus Naur Form (EBNF). It is possible to create grammar rules in C++ and the library can be used to define command-line parsers, for example.
- *Tokenizer*: This library offers functionality for separating character sequences into tokens, for example finding data in delimited text streams. The user determines how the character sequence is delimited and the library finds the tokens as the user requests new elements.

An example of use is

```cpp
#include<iostream>
#include<boost/tokenizer.hpp>
#include<string>

int main()
{
    using namespace std;
    using namespace boost;


    // Default delimiter, white space
    string s = "This is,  a test";
    tokenizer<> tok(s);
    for(tokenizer<>::iterator beg=tok.begin(); beg!=tok.end();++beg)
    {
        cout << *beg << "\n";
    }

    // Delimiter is '\'
    string s2 =
    "Fld 1,\"putting quotes around fields, allows commas\",Fld 3";

    tokenizer<escaped_list_separator<char> > tok2(s2);

    for(tokenizer<escaped_list_separator<char> >::iterator
                beg=tok2.begin(); beg!=tok2.end();++beg)
    {
        cout << *beg << "\n";
    }
}
```

This is a useful library when you wish to define delimited ASCII files, for example.

13.8.2 Function objects and higher-order programming

We describe three libraries that allow developers to bind functions to function pointers and function objects, implement callback functions and provide support for *lambda expressions* (unnamed functions).

- *Bind*: This library binds arguments to anything that behaves like a function (for example, a function pointer, function object or a member function pointer) and it is an improvement on the STL binders `bind1st` and `bind2nd`. The advantage is that syntax is now uniform. This library is useful for *functional composition*. This is a mechanism to combine simple functions to build more complicated ones. Like the composition of functions in mathematics, the result of the composed function is passed to the composing one via a parameter. Because of this similarity, the syntax in program code tends to closely follow that in mathematics.
- *Function*: This is a library that implements generalised callback mechanisms. It allows us to store and invoke function objects, function pointers and member function pointers. This library works with *Boost.Bind* and *Boost.Lambda*.
- *Lambda*: This is a library that supports unnamed functions, especially in combination with STL algorithms. The term originates from *functional programming* and *lambda calculus*, where a lambda abstraction defines an unnamed function. The primary motivation is to provide a flexible and convenient way to define unnamed function objects for STL algorithms.

13.8.3 Concurrent and multi-threading programming

The *Thread* library allows us to write programs as multiple, asynchronous, independent threads-of-execution. Each thread has its own machine state including program instruction counter and registers.

13.8.4 Interval arithmetic

This library implements mathematical intervals that are used in numerical analysis applications. This is especially important when computations produce inexact results. Furthermore, intervals allow us to quantify the propagation of rounding errors.

13.9 SUMMARY AND CONCLUSIONS

We have given an overview of the Boost library that extends and improves STL and brings C++ to a higher level. In particular, we gave a short overview of some of its libraries and some examples to show how to use them. The libraries are very well written and if you know C++ templates and STL syntax you will not have much difficulty understanding and applying them.

We recommend that you look in Boost first to see whether it has functionality that you used for your applications.

This chapter is meant as a short introduction to the Boost library and we give an overview of some of its major functionality and some generic examples and some examples that are relevant to the Monte-Carlo method.

13.10 EXERCISES AND PROJECTS

1. (**) Using Arrays of Tuples
   We create an array structure whose elements represent average promised yields on corporate bonds based on quality rating; in particular, for each year (which we model by a

`DatasimDate` class) we give the ratings such as Aaa, Aa, A and Baa. A typical record (row) is given as:

Year Aaa Aa A Baa 1976-1-1 8.43 8.75 9.09 9.75

Answer the following questions:

– Design the data structure for this problem using Boost tuples and STL vectors.
– Populate the data structure using a combination of tuple constructors, the convenience function `make_tuple()` and the vector indexing operator [].
– Create a function to print each record in the data structure.

2. (**) Using the *any* Library
Complete the code in section 13.3.3 by printing all the values of the types in the list of any types (use casting and exception handling).

3. (**) Which Data Structure to Use
In section 13.3 we discussed a number of attention points when choosing a suitable data structure in applications:
– A1: Is data homogeneous (all of the same type) or heterogeneous?
– A2: Are data collections of fixed or of variable size?
– A3: Is the data defined at compile-time or can be it changed at run-time?
Determine how far the following libraries satisfy the above three attention points: `tuple`, `any`, `variant`, `array`.

4. (****) Re-engineering Finite Difference Engine of Chapter 10
The objective of this exercise is to upgrade the code and design that we introduced in section 10.2. In this case we apply a more flexible design than the basic one we used in section 10.2 and we use a number of the specific Boost libraries to improve the maintainability, performance and functionality of the resulting software system.

5. (****) End-Of-Part II Project
This exercise represents a medium-sized project to test your knowledge of the first 13 chapters of this book. We base the exercise on the *initial* UML diagram in Figure 13.1 and we extend it based on the requirements and desired features that we presently describe:
– `MCEngine`: The class that offers pricing services to clients.
– `SDE`: C++ class hierarchy that models stochastic differential equations.
– `FDM`: C++ class hierarchy for finite difference schemes.
– `NormalGenerator`: Classes for generating normal random variates.
– `UniformGenerator`: Classes for generating uniform random variates.
– `Builder`: Creates the objects in Figure 13.1.
– `Client`: This is your main program.
We examine this problem from four perspectives in the software lifecycle, namely (1) defining the scope of the problem, (2) object-oriented design of the problem, (3) C++ implementation and (4) evolution of the software product.

Problem Scope: We describe the kinds of derivatives products that we support:
– R1: 1, 2 and *n*-factor models.
– R2: Path-dependency (for example, Asian options).
– R3: Calculating Greeks using finite differences.
– R4: Various random number generators.
– R5: Different kinds of payoff functions.

Design: We discover and document the classes that realise requirements R1 to R5:
– R6: System configuration using the *Builder* and other *factory* patterns.

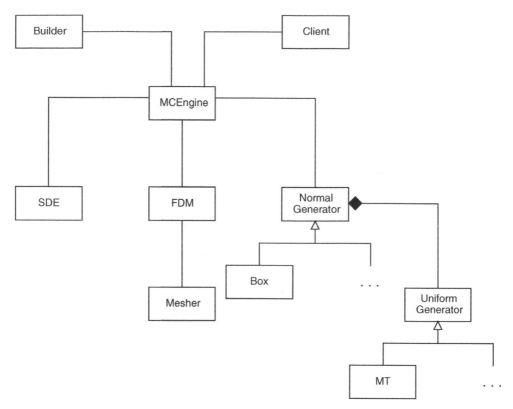

Figure 13.1   End-of-term project

- R7: Modelling SDEs as a template SDE<V, N, D> class.
- R8: Using the *Visitor, Strategy* and *Template Method* pattern to implement FDM.
- R9: Choosing between OO and policy-based design approaches.
- R10: Displaying results in Excel.
   C++ Implementation: We decide which particular software tools to use:
- R11: boost shared (and scoped) pointers.
- R12: vector<T>, Vector<V, I> and VectorSpace<V,N> classes.
- R13: Using the *Property* pattern to model payoff parameters.
- R14: Multi-threading (for example, OpenMP).
   Software Evolution: We deliver a running system as a series of prototypes:
- R15: One-factor plain vanilla option.
- R16: Asian option.
- R17: Two-factor spread option with stochastic volatility.
- R18: Heston model.
6. (**) Cholesky Decomposition
   Use the classes in the uBlas library to create Cholesky decomposition code. This entails
   some research into the Boost uBlas library.

Part III
Advanced Applications

Instruments and Payoffs

What kind of result is that? Siobhan asked, not for the first time
Ian Rankin, *The Naming of the Dead*

14.1 INTRODUCTION AND OBJECTIVES

In this part of the book we apply the Monte Carlo method to a number of financial problems. In particular, we cover instrument hierarchies, path-dependent derivatives and multi-asset problems. We consider stochastic volatility models as well as models where the underlying stochastic movement is a pure jump process, for example in the case of a *Normal Inverse Gaussian* dynamic. We focus our attention on the calculation of hedge sensitivities and the pricing of early exercise features.

Monte Carlo simulation can be applied to a wide range of problems in a variety of scientific disciplines. In this book we focus on using the method to model financial problems. We discuss the building blocks for financial instruments. To this end, we create a hierarchy of instruments to model financial contracts such as bonds, rates and equities.

The structure can be extended by readers to suit their own needs. We give the main ideas and suggest mechanisms for software development. Our focus lies in modelling options and payoffs because we wish to apply the Monte Carlo method to derive prices of such instruments.

This chapter is meant to familiarise the reader with the structure and the C++ involved to model derivative structures.

This chapter is organised as follows. We describe the hierarchy for instruments in section 14.2 and create the base class from which all other instruments inherit. The focus is on the relation between option and its underlying. The following section, 14.3, discusses payoffs in detail because these are the main building blocks of an option and are used by the Monte Carlo solver to compute prices and sensitivities. A key building block is a *Property Set*. This container stores the necessary information to describe the characteristics of an option as well as its payoff. It has to be very flexible because it is used in both simple and complex multi-asset path-dependent applications. In section 14.3 we show how we can handle heterogeneous data. We finally give hints on how to implement exception handling within our framework.

14.2 CREATING A C++ INSTRUMENT HIERARCHY

To model financial markets we first need to deal with the entities to be modelled. The instruments are securities such as bonds or shares. Another category is derived from the basic securities. These products are known as derivatives. For example, options are financial instruments that are also derivatives.

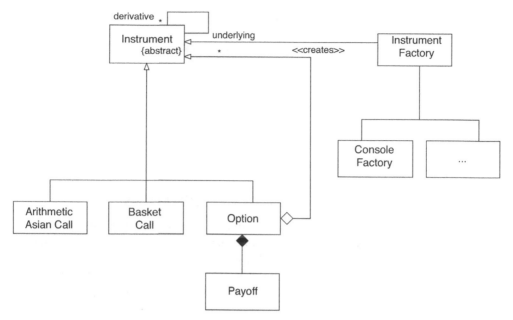

Figure 14.1 UML diagram for the class hierarchy

14.2.1 Instrument hierarchy

For our purposes we model the financial market as a class hierarchy. The basic building block is an instrument. In an application an instrument can be an equity, a bond or an option. All implementations may need different member data as well as different member functions. For example, an equity does not have a payoff whereas this is essential for an option. This consideration leads us to the following setting described by the UML diagram shown in Figure 14.1. The base class is

```
class Instrument
{
public:
    Instrument(){};
    virtual void print() const=0; \\ For illustration purposes only!
    virtual ~Instrument(){ };
};
```

In the following section we discuss two implementations of financial objects within the instrument hierarchy as well as the Design Patterns used to create instruments at run-time. This method is called a *Factory Method*.

14.2.2 Underlyings and derivatives

Having created the base class we apply the inheritance mechanism of C++ to derive financial instruments in the Monte Carlo application. In general a class representing a financial instrument has private and public member data and functions. In our setting the class from which all specific instruments inherit is the base class Instrument. An important point here is that new functionality can be added. Details on the inheritance mechanism can be found in Duffy (2006a), chapter 7. For illustration in the Monte Carlo setting we supply the code for an equity as well as an option. Both classes are template classes. For modelling an equity we specify the template arguments to be `Dates` and `Spot` representing the data types used to model dates, for example, `double` or `date` and spot values.

```
template<class Dates, class Spot>
    class Equity : public Instrument
{
private:
    Spot spotvalues;       // Stores the spot values
    Dates dates;           // Stores the dates for the spot values
public:
    string Company;           // Companies name
    string instrument_type;   // Underlying or derivative
    Equity();                 // Default Constructor
    Spot GetSpotValues();     // Get Spot Values;

    Dates GetDates();                            // Get Dates
    void SetSpotValues(const Spot& spots);       // Set spot values
    void SetDates(const Dates& dates2);          // Set Dates
    virtual void print() const;                  // for illustration
                                                 // only!

}
```

An example for using the class `Equity` is

```
int main()
{
    Equity<double, double> pb;      // Define an equity
    pb.SetSpotValues(65.35);        // Set the current spot value
    pb.SetDates(1.0);               // Number of Spot dates
    pb.print();
}
```

Our next example shows how an option can be mapped into the instrument hierarchy in Figure 14.1. To this end, we give the definition of the class `Option` derived from the base class `Instrument`. The class `Option` has different private member data than the previously discussed class `Equity`. It has a `vector` of pointers to `Instruments` which serve as underlyings.

```
class Option : public Instrument
{
private:
    vector<Instrument*> underlying; // Stores the underlying(s)
public:
    double T;                     // Maturity
    string OptionType;            // Call or Put
    string EvaluationType;        // Path-dependent or non
                                  //   path-dependent
    string ExerciseType;          // European or American
    string instrument_type;       // Underlying or derivative
```

```
    SimplePropertySet<string, AnyType*>        // Property Set
     optionsprops;
    Option();                                  // Default Constructor
    Option(const SimplePropertySet$<$string,   // Constructor
     AnyType*>& pset);
    virtual void print() const;      // For illustration only!
}
```

We have used a pointer to the class `AnyType`. This acts as a wrapper class if we want to consider heterogeneous data. We will discuss this class later. Notice the usage of `SimplePropertySet` in the above code. This container stores the information necessary to evaluate options and register payoffs. To create instruments we use a mechanism called the *Factory Method* pattern. We discuss this concept in detail below and show how to implement it in C++.

Before we describe the *Factory Method* pattern, we discuss a program to test the class `Option`:

```
int main()
{
    SimplePropertySet<string, AnyType*> bset;

    // Add values to the bset
    // ... code to add values to the Property Set bset should be
    // placed here

    // Init BarrierOption using bset
    BarrierOption opt(bset);
    opt.print();
    cout <<"\nTheoretical Price is: " << opt.TheoreticalPrice()
     << "\n";
}
```

The implementation of a factory in C++ is

```
class InstrumentFactory
{
public:
    virtual Instrument*
        CreateOption(const SimplePropertySet<string, AnyType*>&
        pset) const = 0;
}
```

and the factory that implements the console application is

```
class ConsoleInstrumentFactory : public InstrumentFactory
{
public:
   Instrument* CreateOption(const SimplePropertySet<string,
   AnyType*>& pset)
const
   {
       Instrument* result = new Option(pset);
```

```
        (*result).print();// For illustration only!
        return result;
    }
}
```

Since we have a base class with a pure virtual member function the actual implementation must implement the member function `CreateOption`. In this case it accepts an instance of a `SimplePropertySet` and returns a pointer to an `Instrument`. It is an `Option`. The following program illustrates its use:

```
int main
{
    // Using the Instrument Factory
    ConsoleInstrumentFactory mycif;
    Instrument* barrieroption;
    barrieroption = mycif.CreateOption(bset);
    (*barrieroption).print();
}
```

14.3   MODELLING PAYOFFS IN C++

An option payoff is a function to be evaluated given the spot prices of the underlying(s) to compute the value of the option. For example, a European call option on a single asset S with maturity T and strike price K has the payoff:

$$\mathrm{Max}\,(S(T) - K, 0) \tag{14.1}$$

An example of a trade with more complex payoffs is locally floored at y, globally capped at x Min/Max Cliquet option on several assets. If we denote by t_j, $j = 0, \ldots, t_n$ time points and consider m assets, S_i, $i = 1, 2, \ldots, m$, the payoff is:

$$\frac{1}{n} \sum_{j=1,\ldots,n} \mathrm{Min}\left(\mathrm{Max}\left(\mathrm{Max}_{i=1,2,3,\ldots,m}\left(\frac{S_i(t_j)}{S_i(t_{j-1})} - 1 \right), x \right), y \right) \tag{14.2}$$

We give examples for different kinds of payoffs when we discuss path-dependent options in Chapter 15, stochastic volatility models in Chapter 16 and multi-asset options in Chapter 17. We focus on the implementation that should be flexible enough to allow any kind of payoff and choose it at run-time using a *Factory Method* pattern.

14.3.1   Simple property sets

Our discussion is based on Duffy (2006a). We use the STL container map to store the data and in this case the `SimplePropertySet` class is a wrapper (or adapter) object that hides much of the low-level functionality of map from clients (see Figure 14.2).

Basic functionality

We discuss the functionality of a `SimplePropertySet`. This gives us deeper understanding and helps us in later sections. The implementation in C++ is

```
template <class N = string, class V = double>
  class SimplePropertySet : public PropertyThing<N, V>
```

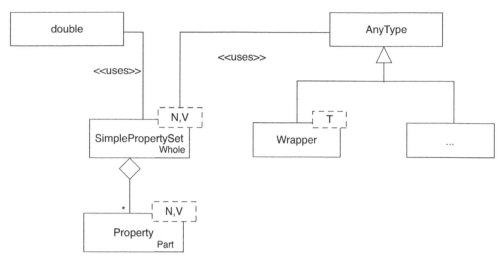

Figure 14.2   UML diagram for simple property sets

```
{
   private:
    N nam;   // The name of the set
    // The SimplePropertySet list using the STL map
    map<N, V> sl;
    Set<N> keys;
   Public:
    Public members
}
```

The construction of Property Set instances can be realised by default, giving an existing property set to initialise the private data, from another simple property set and via a given set of data. Use the following constructors:

```
SimplePropertySet();
SimplePropertySet(const N& name);
SimplePropertySet(const SimplePropertySet<N,V>&source);
SimplePropertySet(const N& name, const Set<N>&keySet);
```

Addition of properties is achieved via the member functions:

```
void add(const Property<N,V>& p);
void add(const N& key, const V& value);
```

Thus, it is possible to add a single property to the set as well as a pair consisting of a key and its value. For removal we use two functions:

```
void remove(const N& key);
void remove(const Property<N, V>& prop);
```

Please keep in mind that these lines are based on the assumption that the second data type is known explicitly, for example a `double`. If we have to handle heterogeneous data the coding is not that straightforward. C++ supports heterogeneous sets but we have to use *run-time type information*. Such data types are also supported by the Boost library, which we have already discussed in Chapter 13.

Setting up the instrument hierarchy and putting all the data into property sets is error prone. To keep track of the implementation is not easy. A method to catch occurring errors is known as *exception handling*. This is discussed in detail in Duffy (2006a). For example, for implementing an option we get the strike price from the property set. However, we may have made a mistake and the key "strike" gives us not data of type double but of type string. If we execute a program it will crash and throw an exception. We can try to catch the exception using a class for error handling. In the exercises at the end of this chapter we suggest what can be done using the exception classes supplied on the CD. For a short introduction see section 14.3.6.

Accessing data of a property set

We give an example to show how to set and access data in a property set.

First, we define an object for storing properties by

```
SimplePropertySet<string, double> myset;
```

We declare double Strike = 98.0; and a property consisting of an identifier represented by a string and the data represented by a double by

```
Property<string, double> Prop_Strike;
```

We name the identifier "Strike" and assign the value of the previously declared variable Strike by

```
Prop_Strike = Property<string, double> ("Strike",Strike);
```

Finally, we add this property to myset using the member function add():

```
myset.add(Prop_Strike);
```

We can use the object myset. For example, we can pass it to a constructor of an Option or PayOff. In these classes the data can be accessed by calling the member function value with the identifier as follows:

```
double Option_Strike = PayOffOption_Properties.value("Strike");
```

The variable Option_Strike is initialised with the value corresponding to the identifier Strike. This is very useful because if you use self-explaining names as identifiers you may not get into trouble with variables.

We can print a list of all the stored data of the set myset using the following code:

```
SimplePropertySet<string, double>::const_iterator it;
for(it = myset.Begin(); it!=myset.End(); it++)
{
   cout << endl << (*it).first << "    " << (*it).second << endl;
}
```

14.3.2   Extending the payoff class

The payoff classes discussed in the previous section allow us to model a wide range of options such as path-dependent options and simple European options with complex payoffs and instantiate them at run-time. Let us suppose we wish to use the current classes to implement a basket option. For simplicity we take a European basket call option on N assets with maturity T and strike price K has payoff

$$B(T, K) := \text{Max} \left(\sum_{i=1}^{N} \omega_i S_i(T) - K, 0 \right) \tag{14.3}$$

Here, ω_i denotes the weight of the ith asset S_i in the basket $B = \sum_i \omega_i S_i$. What is worth mentioning here is that in general we would like to consider baskets chosen at run-time and not at compile-time. The basket is a sum of weighted assets. This information is supplied at run-time. Thus, we have to provide and store the necessary data to evaluate the payoff.

Our classes currently allow for multiple underlyings because the payoff class is a template allowing matrices as input, for example. We can model any number of assets at run-time. Clearly, we do not want to implement a separate payoff class for baskets with two or more assets. This would demand a flexible implementation of basket option payoffs.

We examine what we can do to extend the payoff class to some problem. One solution would be to further extend the template class such that another class may be supplied as a vector for the weights. But such a class would be useless for single factor options and does not make sense in our setting. Therefore, we have chosen to extend the property set such that it can handle different data structures. What we want to achieve is to create sets of heterogeneous data.

14.3.3   Heterogeneous property sets

What happens if we wish to create property sets where elements are arbitrary data types? We might want to have a set gathering together objects like `double`, `Vector`, `string` or user-defined (template) classes. The solution is to define a new data hierarchy and bring any data type into the hierarchy by building a wrapper. Using `Wrapper<T>` we can support any object or data type in the hierarchy by just wrapping it into this class. The code for the classes is given below. We start with a base class for all wrapped types:

```
class AnyType
{
    AnyType() {};
    virtual ~AnyType(){};
};
```

As the name may suggest `AnyType` can be any data type such as `double` or `Vector<>` but also any other class. The inline code for the wrapper class used to set up heterogeneous property sets is given by

```
template<class T>
    class Wrapper : public AnyType
{// Generic wrapper for any data type
public:
    T obj;
```

```
Wrapper(){ obj = T();}
virtual  Wrapper(){};
T GetObj(){return T(obj);};
Wrapper(T wrappedObject) {obj = wrappedObject;}
template <class T2> bool sameType (const T2& t2)
{
    if (typeid(Wrapper<T>) == typeid(t2))
    {
        return true;
    }
    return false;
}
}
```

We use this code for wrapping and accessing the wrapped data. In the following section we give an example by discussing the same option we used for illustrating the case for non-heterogeneous property sets.

A more efficient and standard way to solve this problem is to apply the data structures of the Boost library. As discussed in Chapter 13 there is a library called *Any* to handle heterogeneous data, tuples and variant types. In a future version of the software we will use this Boost implementation.

Accessing data of a heterogeneous property set

First, we define a set for storing properties:

```
SimplePropertySet<string, AnyType*> myset;
```

The type is not explicitly given since we want to use all kinds of objects. We declare `double Strike = 98.0`, a property consisting of an identifier represented by a `string` and the data represented by a `double` object by

```
Property<string, Wrapper<double> > Prop_Strike;
```

We name the identifier `"Strike"` and give it the value of the previously declared variable `Strike` by

```
Prop_Strike = Property<string, double> ("Strike",Strike);
```

Finally, we add this property to `myset` using the member function `add()`. This can be done as in the simple case:

```
myset.add(Prop_Strike);
```

We can use `myset`. For example, we can pass it to a constructor of an `Option` or `PayOff`. The data in these classes is accessed by retrieving it by calling the member function `value()` with the identifier, as in the following example:

```
AnyType* type_double = PayOff_Option_Properties.value("Strike");
Wrapper<double>* Wrapped_Strike =
    dynamic_cast<Wrapper<double>*> (type_double);
double Option_Strike =(*Wrapped_Strike).GetObj();
```

The variable Option_Strike is initialised with the value corresponding to the identifier Strike. At first sight this might look complex. But this is the way we have to do it to allow heterogeneous data. For example, for basket options we supply the weights which are of type vector<double> as well as the strike price which is of type double. But we will discuss this in later chapters when we are going to model complex payoffs for exotic options.

Simply printing all the stored data is not possible anymore. Executing the statement

```
SimplePropertySet<string, double>::const_iterator it;
for(it = myset.Begin(); it!=myset.End(); it++)
{
    cout << endl << (*it).first << "   " << (*it).second << endl;
}
```

does not lead to the result as in the simple example. See also the exercises at the end of this chapter.

The heterogeneous property set offers a fundamental tool for financial engineering applications. As a user one should carefully decide if it is meaningful to use heterogeneous sets at all. Often a more hard-coded approach might be preferable for performance issues and to avoid problems using advanced techniques such as RTTI, run-time type information, and dynamic casting. Let us briefly discuss how Property Sets are used. For illustrative examples we refer to Chapters 15 to 20 of this book where we discuss several types of options with increasing complexity.

14.3.4   The payoff base class

We consider the payoff base class:

```
template<class D, class T>
    class PayOff
{
public:
    PayOff(){};
    virtual double operator()(D& Discount, T& Spot) const=0;
    virtual PayOff<D, T>* clone() const=0;
    virtual ~PayOff(){};
private:
}
```

The data types D and T are the data types for the discount and the spot prices, respectively. In the simplest setting the discount factor is of type double but can also be a discount curve implemented by some class to model curves. For the spot prices we may wish to use a double to model one single price but we may also wish to use a vector or matrix class. The latter is useful for implementing payoffs for path-dependent or multi-asset options. To implement payoffs in the following chapters we use the inheritance mechanism in C++.

Let us consider the following cases:

* one-factor non-path-dependent options;
* one-factor path-dependent options;
* multi-factor non-path-dependent options;
* multi-factor path-dependent options.

This is necessary because the data structure for passing the spot prices to evaluate the payoff function differs in each case. It is a `double`, a `Vector` or a `NumericMatrix` type object. For example, if we consider one factor path-dependent options we need spot prices at given discrete points in time up to the lifetime of the option. Therefore, we would like to model a whole path as a vector in C++. For example, an implementation of a one-factor path-dependent payoff would be, for example, as follows:

```
class PayPathDependent : public PayOff<double,Vector<double> >
```

Thus, the payoff of an arithmetic Asian call option, for instance, inherits from the base class PayOff initialised with `double` and `Vector<double>`. For all the other cases and many different payoffs we refer the reader to Chapter 15. The final class hierarchy is given in Figure 14.3.

14.3.5   Abstract factories for payoff classes

We now discuss a specific problem, namely creating instances of the class `PayOff` to be used in our Monte Carlo simulation application. This concept is known as an *Abstract Factory* pattern. It is further discussed in Part II of this book. We summarise what we have achieved so far and how the abstract factory is put to work by the UML diagram, shown in Figure 14.4.

In short, for each implemented payoff object one has to tell the abstract factory that it exists and therefore can be instantiated. The first idea that comes to our mind is to use global variables. But with global variables one does not have any influence on when they are created. Everything is done by the compiler. But C++ offers the user a way to control the process. We have made the factory into a static variable at registration. If the registration routine is called it

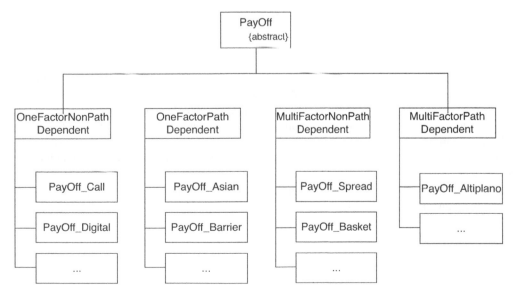

Figure 14.3   UML diagram for the `PayOff` class hierarchy

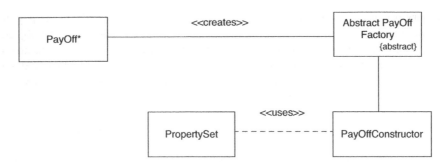

Figure 14.4 UML diagram for payoff abstract factory

comes into existence and behaves like a global variable. We shall now describe how we create the code. The implementation in C++ has the following structure:

```
template<class D, class T> class PayOffFactory
{
public:
    typedef PayOff<D, T>* (*CreatePayOffFunction)
                (SimplePropertySet<string,AnyType*>);
    static PayOffFactory<D, T>& Instance();
    void RegisterPayOff(string, CreatePayOffFunction);
    PayOff<D, T>* CreatePayOff(string PayOffId,
    SimplePropertySet<string, AnyType*> pset);
    virtual ~PayOffFactory(){};

private:
    std::map<string, CreatePayOffFunction> TheCreatorFunctions;
    PayOffFactory(){}
    PayOffFactory(const PayOffFactory<D, T>&){}
    PayOffFactory& operator=(const PayOffFactory<D,T>&)
    {return *this;}
}
```

The above code implements the general form using heterogeneous property sets. The data types D and T have the same meaning as in the class PayOff. To use it in the simple setting when we only consider double data types, just change the lines containing AnyType* to double. The same procedure has to be applied to the other parts of the code. The code for the implementations can be found on the CD. Please note that we have used a typedef to add a new name to an existing type PayOff<D,T>*. This is extremely useful for coding the actual factory.

The *Abstract Factory* pattern is discussed in detail in Chapter 9. Therefore, we only describe the main mechanism and the usage:

```
template <class D, class T, class P>
  class PayOffConstructor
{
public:
  PayOffConstructor(string);
  static PayOff<D, T>* Create(SimplePropertySet<string, AnyType*>);
};
```

This class consists of a constructor and one member function. The constructor takes in a `string` which is the name of the payoff and uses the member function to return a pointer to a new `PayOff` object.

The functionality to return the `PayOff` object is given by

```
template <class D, class T, class P> PayOff<D, T>*
PayOffConstructor<D, T, P>
    ::Create(SimplePropertySet<string, AnyType*> pset)
        {return new P(pset);}

template <class D, class T, class P>PayOffConstructor<D,T,P>
    ::PayOffConstructor(string id)
    {
    PayOffFactory<D, T>& thePayOffFactory =
                    PayOffFactory<D,T>::Instance();
    thePayOffFactory.RegisterPayOff(id,PayOffConstructor
                                <D,T,P>::Create);
    }
```

The last step is to register a class `PayOff`. To this end, we have to specify the template arguments and the actual payoff class:

```
namespace
{
    PayOffConstructor<double, double, PayOff_XY>
    RegisterCall("call");
}
```

The file can be extended with other payoffs. For example, to add a payoff for a path-dependent option where the spots are given as a `Vector<double>` type, the corresponding entry would be

```
namespace
{
    PayOffConstructor<double, Vector<double>, PayOff_XY>
    RegisterCall("path-dependent");
}
```

We have used an unnamed namespace to implement *Information Hiding*. No other part of the application should be aware of the implementation of the registration. Therefore, it should not be seen from any other part of the project.

Let us further stress one point. We have to invoke all created payoffs by the same factory. To this end we have chosen the *Singleton* design pattern which fulfils all our needs for this case. See Part II of the book for further information on the *Singleton* design pattern.

14.3.6   Exception handling

For applications, the above setup can be used but errors can occur due to missing data. For example, we might forget to add data necessary for evaluation purposes to a `SimpleProp-ertySet`. This is where exception handling should be applied.

We describe a first adjustment to the function:

```
V SimplePropertySet<N,V>::value(const N& name).
```

The modified function is now

```
template <class N, class V>
V SimplePropertySet<N,V>::value(const N& name) const
{
    // ;( Sledgehammer, use find!!
    // We iterate over the list until we find the value
    map<N,V>::const_iterator it;

    // Here we have to include exception handling!
    for (it=sl.begin(); it!=sl.end(); it++)
    {
        if ((*it).first == name)
        {
            return (*it).second;
        }
    }

    // If we have not found anything return exception

    throw DatasimException(string(name),
            string("does not exist to evaluate function: value()"),
            string("Check the definition of your property set!"));
}
```

In the exercises we suggest a more efficient way to get a value from the property set. This modified version throws an exception if for a supplied key no corresponding value can be found. How can we use this modified version of the `value()` function? If we wish to retrieve data from a `SimplePropertySet` we put a `try{} ... catch{}` statement around the assignment of the value to the variable of type `anytype` as follows:

```
try
{
    anytype = PayOff_Spread_Properties.value("Strike");
}
catch(DatasimException& e)
{
    e.print();
    return 0;
}
```

In the `catch` statement, an error message gets printed to the console.

14.4   SUMMARY AND CONCLUSIONS

We discussed how to model an instrument hierarchy in C++ using object-oriented methods. We have distinguished between building blocks called underlyings and derived classes, for example options. Underlyings are bonds, equities and rates whereas options refer to an underlying. An option class has to store all the necessary data for evaluation purposes such as maturity, volatility and the payoff. We elaborated on the implementation of the payoff class because it is the function we have to evaluate after generating sample paths. We gave a detailed introduction to the factory mechanism and showed how to apply it to mapping `PayOff` functions in our framework. We apply this framework in later chapters.

Hint: You may consider storing your information needed to evaluate payoffs in private data of the corresponding payoff class. The use of large (heterogeneous) property sets is time consuming because at any call we have to extract the data from the set and assign the corresponding variables. However, setting it up this way is very instructive because you can use the names for the model parameters, for example 'mean' or 'drift'.

14.5   EXERCISES AND PROJECTS

1. (**) Compound Options
   Define an option with another option as the underlying instrument. Use the underlyings function `TheoreticalPrice` to compute the theoretical price of the option. This type of option is known as a *Compound Option*.
2. (*) Heterogeneous Property Sets
   Use the iterator for heterogeneous property sets. What is going wrong?
   Create a heterogeneous property set of different types of objects, for example `string`, `double`, `Vector<double>`. Display the values and print them to the console using `dynamic_cast()`.
3. (***) Exception Handling
   We have given an illustrative example of an error which might occur and how to handle this error. The classes needed are supplied on the CD.
   Find the main errors that may occur when applying the framework discussed in this chapter and think about how to identify them using C++. Finally, try to implement the corresponding routines for exception handling.
4. (**) Referenced Versions
   We have used a template class `PayOff` given by

```
template<class D, class T> class PayOff
{
public:
    PayOff(){};
    virtual double operator()(D Discount, T& Spot) const=0;
    virtual double PayOff_Value(D Discount,
                                T& Spot,
                                D Strike) const=0;
    virtual PayOff<D, T>* clone() const=0;
    virtual ~PayOff(){};
private:
};
```

Note: Our objects for payoffs must implement the functions `operator()` and `Pay-Off_Value()`. Since the object `T` might be a complex type such as a `Vector` or a `NumericMatrix` it might be better to implement the functions as:

```
virtual double operator()(D Discount, const T& Spot) const=0;
```

and

```
virtual double PayOff_Value(D Discount, const T& Spot, D Strike)
const=0;
```

to achieve a better performance. See also Chapter 21, where we cover performance issues. Change the current implementation in this way.

5. (***) Boost Version

   The Boost library offers many data types such as Any. Use the Boost library to base the implementation of the template class PropertySet on this data type. To this end consider the class AnyType together with the class Wrapper and modify the code such that AnyType is replaced by boost::any.

6. (**) Exception Handling

   We have shown how to retrieve data from a property set consisting of heterogeneous data in section 14.3.6. We iterate until we find the key and return the result:

```
for (it=sl.begin(); it!=sl.end(); it++)
{
    if ((*it).first == name)
    {
        return (*it).second;
    }
}
```

Use the map.find() to replace this part of the code. Do you notice any performance improvements?

15

Path-Dependent Options

15.1 INTRODUCTION AND OBJECTIVES

In the previous chapters we studied the Monte Carlo method in an object-oriented flexible framework in C++. We also wish the method to be accessible to people working in the financial industry. To this end, we give another implementation that we think is very easy to use since it avoids heavy use of design patterns.

Since the Monte Carlo method is always the method of choice for pricing path-dependent derivatives we apply it in this chapter to price *Asian, barrier, lookback* and *cliquet options*. These options are well known and accurate approximation formulae for pricing them exist. We use these formulae to compare our results obtained via Monte Carlo simulation.

By considering these options we introduce methods for improving the accuracy of the approximation. We study well-known variance reduction methods such as *control variates, antithetic sampling* and *importance sampling*. We show the implementation in C++ for the options mentioned above and we illustrate the variance reduction method for the Asian option and barrier option cases.

For each option we give a short introduction to its structure and we supply the code for the corresponding approximation formula. Finally, we map the contract into our framework. To this end, we set up payoff classes for path-dependent options by extending the framework introduced in Chapter 14. Having this implementation at hand means that we are able to use the main framework to perform the simulation.

The second part of this chapter is devoted to a family of path-dependent derivatives called *cliquet options*.

The cliquet option in its simplest form is a sum of simple *forward start options*. Some special cliquet option structures are *reverse cliquet* or *swing cliquet options*. Furthermore, cliquet options will be considered again in Chapter 16 when we consider (*stochastic volatility models*) since such options are very sensitive to the volatility and its (forward) skew.

In this chapter we focus on the Black-Scholes model. We assume an asset dynamic governed by the stochastic differential equation:

$$\begin{cases} dS(t) = (r - d)S(t)dt + \sigma S(t)dW(t) \\ S(0) = S_0 \end{cases} \tag{15.1}$$

The values S_0, r, d and σ denote the spot value, the risk-less rate, the dividend yield and the volatility. This assumption is that we compare the results obtained by simulation with the results computed using analytical approximation formulae. Using the Monte Carlo implementation we only need a path of underlying spot prices in order to price the contract. Therefore, any model for the asset dynamic can be applied. The theory corresponding to the models and the options can be found in Glasserman (2004).

15.2   MONTE CARLO – A SIMPLE GENERAL-PURPOSE VERSION

We structure this section into three parts, namely the model, the scheme and the evaluation of the payoff.

A model is a collection of parameters. It represents all of the underlying needed to discretise the SDE which governs the time evolution. For example, in the Black-Scholes model we need the volatility σ, the risk-less rate r, the dividend yield d and the initial spot price S_0. The scheme uses this information and implements the algorithm for discretisation of the model using the finite difference method. Finally, the evaluation takes place after all the spot prices have been calculated. The generated path is evaluated on a given payoff function. For example, if we value a call option with strike K, the payoff class needs this strike price and an implementation of the function $\max(x - K, 0)$.

15.2.1   The structure

We give an overview of the C++ classes and how they are combined. Figure 15.1 shows the UML class diagram for the interaction of the classes representing the model, the scheme and the Monte Carlo engine. The model is used to store the data. This can be seen as an analogue to the SDE class of the general framework. Together with the RandomNumberTemplate, designed in Chapter 22 and the class MCModel, the class MCSampleScheme that we discuss in the next section uses the random numbers and the information on the model to generate a path due to a given finite difference scheme or using the exact solution if it is available. Finally, the class MCMonteCarlo takes the generated paths as an input to compute the value

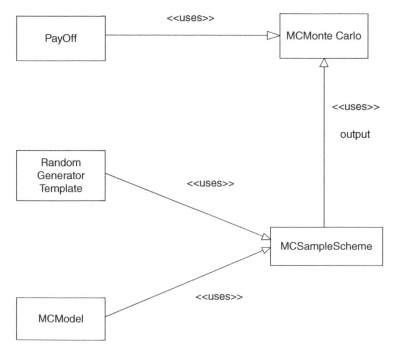

Figure 15.1   The UML diagram for the current MC framework

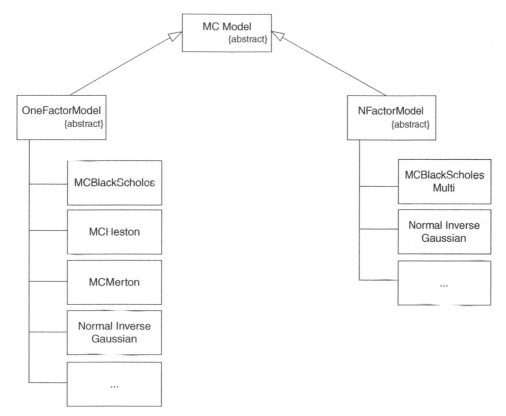

Figure 15.2 The UML class diagram for `MCModel`

of a derivative. The derivative is represented as a `PayOff` object. We discuss the Monte Carlo engine in the next section.

15.2.2 Adding models

To explain the functionality we begin with the class `MCModel`. The UML representation is given in Figure 15.2. It models one factor and multi-factor problems represented by the classes `OneFactorModel` and `NFactorModel`, respectively.

As described in the previous section a model is a class storing all the necessary data to cope numerically with the model. For illustration purposes we give the class `MCBlackScholes`:

```
class MCBlackScholes : public OneFactorModel
{
public:
    MCBlackScholes();
    MCBlackScholes(double r, double d, double sigma, double Maturity,
       double Spot);
    virtual ~MCBlackScholes();
```

```
    // Get functionality
    double getdrift() const;
    double getvol() const;
    double getdividend() const;
    double getmartcorrection() const;
    double getmaturity() const;
    double getspot() const;

private:
    double drift;              // drift r
    double vol;                // volatility
    double martcorrection;     // (r-d-0.5 * vol * vol) for exponential
                                  spots
    double dividend;           // dividend
    double maturity;           // T
    double spot;               // Spot
};
```

Adding models is straightforward by adding the data as illustrated above for the Black-Scholes model.

As usual we put the main definition into some .hpp file and the implementation in the corresponding .cpp file. To use the class we have to include the preprocessor directive which includes the .hpp file.

To implement the model we call the constructor with the necessary data S_0, r, d and σ:

```
    MCBlackScholes MCBS(r, d, sigma, Maturity, Spot);
```

We give a full example on the usage when we discuss Asian options in section 15.3.

15.2.3 Adding schemes

The next ingredient we discuss is the class MCSampleScheme. This class uses the class MCModel and a random number generator described to calculate the spot price path with respect to the model data and a certain numerical scheme as shown in Figure 15.3. We discuss several schemes in the following sections and chapters.

For a sample scheme we use the simplest base class given by

```
class MCSampleScheme
{
public:
    MCSampleScheme(){};
    virtual ~MCSampleScheme(){};

private:
    // No private data nor member functions
};
```

from which all other classes inherit. Furthermore, we define two abstract classes called One-FactorScheme and NFactorScheme. These classes inherit from the base class MCSampleScheme. For example, the OneFactorScheme:

```
template<class RanGen, class Model, class V = Vector<double> >
    class OneFactorScheme : public MCSampleScheme
```

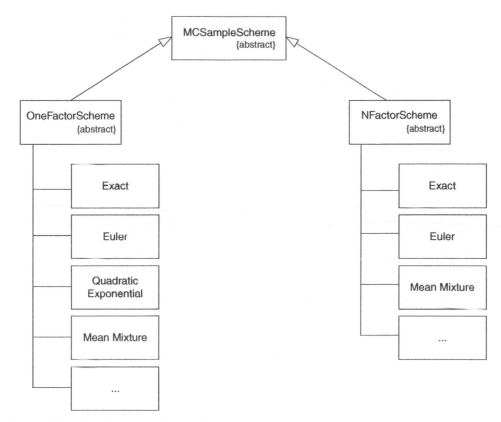

Figure 15.3 The UML class diagram for `MCSampleScheme`

```
{
    public:
        OneFactorScheme(){};
        virtual ~OneFactorScheme(){};

        virtual Vector<V> calcST(RanGen& rg, Model& model, long Paths,
                            int Factors, long Steps) const = 0;

    private:
        // No private data nor member functions
};
```

We use inheritance to implement a new sample scheme. As an example we give the design of the exact solution for geometric Brownian motion used in the Black-Scholes model:

```
template<class RanGen,class Model>
    class MCExactGeoBrownian : publicOneFactorScheme<RanGen,Model>
{
    public:
        MCExactGeoBrownian();
        virtual ~MCExactGeoBrownian();
```

```
            // Implements the usual incremental discretisation scheme
            Vector<Vector<double>> calcST(RanGen& rg, Model& model,
                                    long Paths,
                                    int Factors, long Steps) const;
            // Implements Antithetic Variance Reduction
            Vector<Vector<double>> calcST_anti(RanGen& rg, Model& model,
                                    long Paths,
                                    int Factors, long Steps) const;

    private:
            // No private member data nor functions
};
```

The functions `calcST()` and `calcST_anti()` give the spot prices and the spot prices obtained using antithetic sampling, respectively. Since we use a template class we have to use the directive:

```
#include "mcexactgeometricbrownian.cpp"
```

Adding schemes is easy too. The following code snippet illustrates how to set up a scheme in the case of the exact solution to the Black-Scholes model, equation (15.1). We define the scheme by

```
MCExactGeoBrownian<RandGen<MersenneTwister>, MCBlackScholes> MCE;
```

We provide a mechanism to generate random numbers and a model. Again, a full example will be given when we discuss Asian options.

15.2.4   The Monte Carlo evaluation

The Monte Carlo engine takes in a vector of sample paths and evaluates a payoff along all the paths stored in this vector. A single path can either be a vector or a matrix if several underlyings are considered. Therefore we have set up the class as a compile-time *Strategy*; see the description of design patterns in Part II for details on the *Strategy* pattern.

```
template<class Path>
    class MCMonteCarlo
{
public:
    MCMonteCarlo();                 // Default Constructor
    virtual ~MCMonteCarlo();        // Destructor
    MCMonteCarlo(Path& mcpath);     // User defined Constructor

    // Sets the private member data
    void setpath(Path& MCPath);

    // Simple Monte Carlo pricer
    template<typename Pay>
    Vector<double> mcprice(const double discount const Pay*
                        PayOffPtr);

    // Antithetic variables Monte Carlo pricer
    template<typename Pay>
    Vector<double> mcprice_anti(const double discount const Pay*
                        PayOffPtr);
```

```
// This version of Simple Pricer allows for several
// batches updating mcresults
template<typename Pay>
void mcprice2(const double discount const Pay* PayOffPtr,
              Vector<double>& mcresult);

// This version is the same as mcprice for use with antithetics
template<typename Pay>
void mcprice2_anti(const double discount const Pay* PayOffPtr,
                   Vector<double>& mcresult);

// Control Variate Monte Carlo pricer
template<typename Pay>
Vector<double> mcprice_cv(const double discount const Pay*
                          PayOffPtr,
                          const Pay* PayOffPtr_CV,
                          double KnownExpectation);

// As above for mcprice2 for using with Control Variates
template<typename Pay>
void mcprice2_cv(const double discount const Pay* PayOffPtr,
                 const Pay* PayOffPtr_CV, double KnownExpectation,
                 Vector<double>& mcresult);

private:
    Path mcpath;
};
```

The class implements several necessary features for applying the Monte Carlo method, including basic variance reduction methods and batch-based sampling. The member function mcprice returns the price as well as the standard error given a pointer to a payoff, whereas the function mcprice2 operates on a Vector<double> and stores the price as well as the standard error into the given vector. The two functions can be used to calculate the Monte Carlo price by one simulation as well as for a set of batches of Monte Carlo simulations, for example running n batches of m simulations.

In the latter we wish to use the object mcresult to accumulate the results into one object and evaluate it after all the batches are executed. The same functionality is implemented to be used for variance reduction methods. We have the functions mcprice_anti and mcprice2_anti to be used with antithetic variables. The latter is a technique used to reduce the variance of the sample. The usage and the application are discussed later in this chapter.

We have not commented on the function mcprice_cv and mcprice2_cv. These implement a method for reducing the variance by adding a *Control Variate*.

15.3   ASIAN OPTIONS

The payoff for an *Asian option* depends on the average price of the underlying asset up to maturity. We consider a financial contract with maturity T and a discrete set of time points $\mathcal{T} :=$ $\{t_0, t_1, \ldots, t_N\}$, $N \in \mathbb{N}$. We assume that $t_0 < t_1 < \ldots < t_N$, with $t_i < t_{i+1}, i = 1, \ldots, N$ and $t_N = T$. The *arithmetic average*, denoted by S_{AA}, and the *geometric average*, denoted by S_{GA}, are respectively given by:

$$S_{AA} := \frac{1}{N} \sum_{n=1}^{N} S(t_n) \tag{15.2}$$

$$S_{GA} := \sqrt[N]{\prod_{n=1}^{N} S(t_n)} \tag{15.3}$$

The payoff for Asian options is given by:

$$h(S_{Av}) = \text{Max}\left(\pm(S_{Av} - K), 0\right), \quad S_{Av} = S_{AA} \text{ or } S_{GA} \tag{15.4}$$

Average price options are not as expensive as standard call or put options and hence they are useful for hedging parts of the risk of a transaction over a given time period.

The period on which the average is calculated might be a subset of the time interval $[0, T]$, for example. The averaging period could start, for example, at a future time T_1 and the discrete time points $\mathcal{T} \subset [T_1, T]$.

Another type of Asian option is known as an *Average Strike Asian option*. For such an option the strike price is given by either the arithmetic or the geometric average and we compare it to the value of the underlying asset at its maturity. The payoff for such options is given by:

$$h(S, S_{\text{Average}}) = \text{Max}\left(\pm(S(T) - S_{\text{Average}}), 0\right), \quad S_{\text{Average}} = S_{AA} \text{ or } S_{GA} \tag{15.5}$$

For this option another variant to compute the average exists. The average strike could be calculated using a set of time points $\mathcal{T}$ lying in an interval $[T_1, T_2] \subset [0, T]$.

Since the sum of logarithmic normal distributed random variables does not obey a logarithmic normal distribution there are no closed form solutions for the option price of an arithmetic Asian option. Monte Carlo simulation, finite difference methods or analytical approximations must be used. In the following we describe the implementation of Asian options in our framework.

15.3.1 Mapping Asian options into our framework

Since in the Black-Scholes model analytical approximation or exact formulae are available for Asian options they serve as a test case of our implementation. We integrate Asian options into our framework by defining another payoff class. To this end we consider the instrument hierarchy from Chapter 14. By using inheritance we can implement the Asian option as follows:

```
class AsianOption : public Option
{
private:
    vector<Instrument*> underlying;         // Stores the underlying(s)
public:
    AsianOption();
    AsianOption(const SimplePropertySet<string, AnyType*>& pset);

    // Pointer to a payoff created by payoff factory
    const PayOff<double, vector<double> >* PayOffPtr;
```

```
    // Property set stores all the stuff needed to define option
    SimplePropertySet<string, AnyType*> asianoptionsprops;

    double TheoreticalPrice();

    double T;                 // Maturity
    string OptionType;        // Call or put
    string EvaluationType;    // Path dependent / Non Path dependent
    string ExerciseType;      // European / American
    string instrument_type;   // underlying or derivative

    virtual void print() const; // For illustration only
};
```

The class `AsianOption` inherits all member functions from the class `Option`. In our example we add the function `TheoreticalPrice()` and member data such as `Pay-Off<double, vector<double> >` reflecting the fact that an approximation is available to the real price and that it is a path-dependent option.

If we wish to use other data types and other container classes, for instance we may wish to replace the STL `vector<T>` by a proprietary template class (Datasim `Vector<T>`), we can customise the given class as follows:

```
class AsianOption : public Option
{
...
    vector<Instrument*> underlying; //Stores the underlying(s)
...
    // Pointer to a payoff
    const PayOff<double, vector<double> >* PayOffPtr;
...
}
```

We use the other data and container types. We have included an example on the CD where we use the STL `vector` as well as the `Vector`. The following code snippet is a test program to price an arithmetic Asian call option:

```
int main()
{
    // Define the Property Set to use
    SimplePropertySet<string, AnyType*> mc_myset_asian;

    double Spot = 100.0;     // current spot price
    double Maturity = 3.0;   // option maturity
    double r = 0.03;         // riskless rate
    double d = 0.0;          // dividend yield
    double sigma = 0.20;     // volatility


    // values for usage with the property set
    static Wrapper<double> Strike = 100;
    static Wrapper<std::string> PayOffType = "call";
    static Wrapper<std::string> AverageType = "arithmetic";
```

```
// Add properties to the set
mc_myset_asian.add("Strike", &Strike);          // add properties
mc_myset_asian.add("PayOffType", &PayOffType);   // add properties
mc_myset_asian.add("AverageType", &AverageType); // add properties


// Specify the name of your payoff used for registration
// with the factory
string mc_name = "asian_v";

// Create a pointer to the payoff for Multi Factor
PayOff<double, Vector<double> >* asianptr =
    PayOffFactory<double, Vector<double> >::Instance().
        CreatePayOff(mc_name, mc_myset_asian);

// Define the path
Vector<Vector<double>> mc_path_asian;

// Define the model
MCBlackScholes MCBS(r, d, sigma, Maturity, Spot);

// Define the scheme
MCExactGeoBrownian<RandGen<MersenneTwister>, MCBlackScholes> MCE;

// Define the Monte Carlo object
MCMonteCarlo<Vector<Vector<double>>> mc;

// The variable for outputting mean and standard deviation
Vector<double> mcvalue(2);
mcvalue[1] = 0.0; mcvalue[2] = 0.0;

int NoOfBatches = 10;    // Number of Monte Carlo batches
long NoOfPaths = 1000;   // Number of paths for each batch
long Timesteps=12;   // Timesteps

unsigned long Seed = 123456; // The seed we use to generate
//   uniforms
RandGen<MersenneTwister> rangen(Seed);   // The generator we use

// This is the Monte Carlo simulation
resetmc(mcvalue);          // Init the simulation

for(int i = 1; i <= NoOfBatches; i++)
{
   mc_path_asian = MCE.calcST(rangen, MCBS,NoOfPaths,1,Timesteps);
   mc.setpath(mc_path_asian);
   mc.mcprice2(1.0,asianptr,mcvalue);
}
// Output
cout << "PV:" << exp(-r * Maturity)*mcvalue[1] / NoOfBatches;
cout << " SE:" << mcvalue[2] / NoOfBatches << ")" << " ";
```

```
    delete asianptr;

    return 0;
}
```

The above program calls the function `resetmc`. This function sets the components of the result vector to 0:

```
void resetmc(Vector<double>& mc)
{// simple function to reset a path
    for(long i = mc.MinIndex(); i<= mc.MaxIndex(); i++)
        mc[i] = 0.0;
}
```

15.3.2   Approximation formulae for Asian options

To backtest our prices obtained via Monte Carlo simulation within a Black-Scholes framework we give some approximation formulae for arithmetic Asian options. All pricing formulae used are given on the accompanying CD.

The Turnball-Wakeman approximation

To price an arithmetic Asian call option, Turnball and Wakeman (1991) use the approximation:

$$Se^{(d-r)(T-t)}\mathcal{N}(d_1) - Ke^{-r(T-t)}\mathcal{N}(d_2) \tag{15.6}$$

with d_1 and d_2 denoting the quantiles used in the Black-Scholes formula; see equation (15.1), but with

$$\sigma_{Av} = \sqrt{\ln(M_2 e^{-T}) - 2\ln(M_1 e^{-T})}$$

to derive an approximate solution within the model given by (15.1). This method is based on moment matching for a comparable log normal dynamic with the first two moments given by

$$M_1 = \frac{e^{(r-d)(T-t)} - e^{(r-d)\hat{T}}}{(r-d)(T-\hat{T})} \tag{15.7}$$

$$M_2 = \frac{2e^{2(r-d)+\sigma_{Av}^2}S^2}{m(2r-2d+\sigma_{Av}^2)T^2} + \frac{2S^2}{(r-d)T}\left(\frac{1}{2(r-d)+\sigma_{Av}^2} - \frac{e^{(r-d)T}}{m}\right), \tag{15.8}$$

where we used $m = (r - d + \sigma_{Av}^2)$.

If the averaging begins before T then the strike price needs to be adjusted by the amount $K = \frac{T}{\hat{T}}K - \frac{T-\hat{T}}{\hat{T}}S$. The C++ implementation is based on the representation of the underlying data as a property set in combination with the Black-Scholes option pricing formula. Approximate solutions to the pricing problems for continuous and for discrete arithmetic and geometric Asian options can be found on the CD.

15.3.3   Control variates

Asian options serve as the standard examples to illustrate the mechanism of applying *control variates*. Let us discuss the corresponding theory of applying control variates in detail.

Suppose that Z is a random variable with known expectation, $\mathbb{E}[Z]$, or at least an expected value that can easily be calculated.

Let $\hat{V}$ be an estimator of the expected value of the option with payoff h, $\mathbb{E}[h(X)]$. For $c \in \mathbb{R}$ we consider the estimator $\hat{V}_c$ for $h(X) - c(Z - \mathbb{E}[Z])$. By taking the expected value we have

$$\mathbb{E}[\hat{V}_c] = \mathbb{E}[h(X)] - c\,(\mathbb{E}[Z] - \mathbb{E}[Z]) \tag{15.9}$$
$$= \mathbb{E}[h(X)] \tag{15.10}$$

Thus, $\hat{V}_c$ is an unbiased estimator for the option price.

To reduce the variance and to sharpen the confidence interval for the estimator we attempt to find a parameter $c_{\min}$ such that $\hat{V}_c$ has lower variance than that of $\hat{V}$. The variance of $\hat{V}_c$ is

$$\mathbb{V}[\hat{V}_c] = \mathbb{V}[Y] + c^2\mathbb{V}[Z] - 2c\mathrm{Cov}[Y, Z] \tag{15.11}$$

The maximum variance reduction is achieved if

$$c_{\min} = \frac{\mathrm{Cov}[Y, Z]}{\mathbb{V}[Z]} \tag{15.12}$$

This can be seen from the following calculations:

$$
\begin{aligned}
\mathbb{V}(\hat{V}_c) &= \mathbb{E}[(\hat{V}_c - \mathbb{E}[\hat{V}_c])^2] = \mathbb{E}[\hat{V}_c^2] - \mathbb{E}[\hat{V}_c]^2 \\
&= \mathbb{E}[(Y - c(Z - \mathbb{E}[Z])^2] - V^2 \\
&= \mathbb{E}[Y^2] - V^2 + c^2\mathbb{E}[(Z - \mathbb{E}[Z])^2] - 2c\mathbb{E}[Y(Z - \mathbb{E}[Z])] \\
&= \mathbb{V}[Y] + c^2\mathbb{V}[Z] - 2c\mathrm{Cov}[Y, Z] \\
&= \mathbb{V}[Y] + c\mathbb{V}[Z]\left[c - 2 \cdot \frac{\mathrm{Cov}[Y, Z]}{\mathbb{V}[Z]}\right]
\end{aligned}
$$

Substituting this result into equation (15.11) and dividing by the variance of $\hat{V}_c$, $\mathbb{V}[\hat{V}_c]$ gives:

$$\frac{\mathbb{V}[\hat{V}_{c_{\min}}]}{\mathbb{V}[\hat{V}_c]} = 1 - \frac{\mathrm{Cov}[Y, Z]^2}{\mathbb{V}[\hat{V}]\mathbb{V}[Z]} = 1 - \rho_{Y,Z}^2 \tag{15.13}$$

We have reduced the variance if for the random variables Y and Z the covariance is negative, that is $\mathrm{Cov}[Y, Z] \neq 0$.

The random variable Z is called a *control variate*. For sampling purposes we modify our algorithm to take advantage of the reduced variance estimator. For example, we can use the estimator:

$$\hat{V}_{c_{\min}} = \frac{\sum_{i=1}^{n}(Y_i + c_{\min}(Z_i - \mathbb{E}[Z]))}{n} \tag{15.14}$$

In practice we cannot use the estimator, equation (15.14), because we do not know $\mathrm{Cov}(Y, Z)$.

To overcome this problem we do p pilot-simulations first to estimate the covariance. This leads to an estimator $\widehat{\text{Cov}}(Y, Z)$ of the covariance given by

$$\widehat{\text{Cov}}[Y, Z] = \frac{\sum_{j=1}^{p}(Y_j - \bar{Y}_p)(Z_j - \mathbb{E}[Z])}{p - 1}$$

where $\bar{Y}_p$ denotes the expectation after p simulations.

Furthermore, it might also be necessary to simulate the variance $\mathbb{V}[Z]$ of the control variate Z. The corresponding estimator is $\hat{\mathbb{V}}[Z]$. To compute the estimator further simulations are necessary. We use $\hat{\mathbb{V}}[Z]$ to estimate

$$\hat{c}_{\min} = \frac{\widehat{\text{Cov}}[Y, Z]}{\hat{\mathbb{V}}[Z]}$$

for the optimal value $c_{\min}$ in equation (15.14).

The following algorithm implements the mechanism of using a control variate. We add an element function to our Monte Carlo class by

```
template<class Path>
template<typename Pay> Vector<double>
MCMonteCarlo<Path>::mcprice_cv(const Pay* PayOffPtr,
                               const Pay* PayOffPtr_CV,
                               double KnownExpectation)
{
    double sum = 0.0;
    double sum_cv = 0.0;
    double sumsum = 0.0;
    double sumsum_cv = 0.0;
    double mixedsum = 0.0;
    double payoff = 0.0;
    double payoff_cv = 0.0;

    double cv = 0.0;

    long N = mcpath.MaxIndex() - mcpath.MinIndex() +1;

    long minindex_Sims = mcpath.MinIndex();
    long maxindex_Sims = mcpath.MaxIndex();

    Vector<double> result(2);    // returns the price and the standard
       error

    // Estimate the parameter c
    for(long i = minindex_Sims; i <= maxindex_Sims; i++)
    {
        // compute PayOff
        payoff = (*PayOffPtr)(1.0, mcpath[i]);
        // compute PayOff for ControlVariate
        payoff_cv = (*PayOffPtr_CV)(1.0, mcpath[i]);

        sum += payoff;                      // Standard Estimator
        sum_cv += payoff_cv;                // CV Estimator
```

```
          sumsum += payoff * payoff;          // Standard to compute
                                                  Variance
          sumsum_cv += payoff_cv * payoff_cv; // CV to compute Variance
          mixedsum += payoff * payoff_cv;      // Mixed to compute
                                                  Covariance
   }

double cov = mixedsum
        - sum * (sum_cv / N + (1.0 - 1.0 / N) * KnownExpectation);
double c = cov / (sumsum_cv - KnownExpectation * KnownExpectation);

result[1] = sum / N - c / N * sum_cv + c * KnownExpectation;
result[2] = (sumsum / N - sum * sum / N / N) - 2.0 * c * cov / N
            + c * c * (sumsum_cv / N
            - KnownExpectation * KnownExpectation);

result[2] >= 0.0 ? result[2] = sqrt(result[2] / N) : 0.0;

return result;
}
```

Table 15.1 and Figure 15.4 show the variance reduction using a control variate estimator in contrast to the simple estimator for an arithmetic Asian option. Finding good candidates acting as a control variate can be achieved by analysing the dependence of the option payoff and the possible control variate. For the arithmetic Asian option we consider three possible options. Figure 15.5 shows the dependence for a geometric Asian option, a call option and the asset itself. As the figures indicate, the geometric Asian option is perfectly correlated to the arithmetic Asian option and hence the ideal choice for a control variate.

Finally, we compare the results obtained by applying Monte Carlo simulation with the approximate results in the Black-Scholes model. We summarise the results in Table 15.1.

The following test program computes the price of an arithmetic Asian call option using a geometric Asian call option as a control variate:

Table 15.1 Numerical results for arithmetic and geometric Asian call options with and without control variates

Steps	MC Price	SE	MC Price CV	SE	Approx Price
Type:	arithmetic				
12	1.93457	(0.0513482)	1.93775	(0.0281949)	1.9919
52	1.82024	(0.0495297)	1.79058	(0.0264867)	1.7852
365	1.78388	(0.0470935)	1.75843	(0.0259633)	1.7329
Type:	geometric				
12	1.90451	(0.0495511)	1.93785	(0.0277948)	1.99676
52	1.70041	(0.0461792)	1.79132	(0.0248705)	1.845032
365	1.63944	(0.0442717)	1.75982	(0.0240016)	1.81189

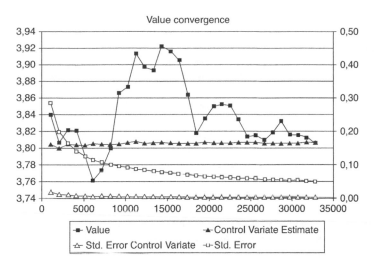

Figure 15.4 Convergence estimate of an arithmetic Asian option with a geometric Asian option as control variate

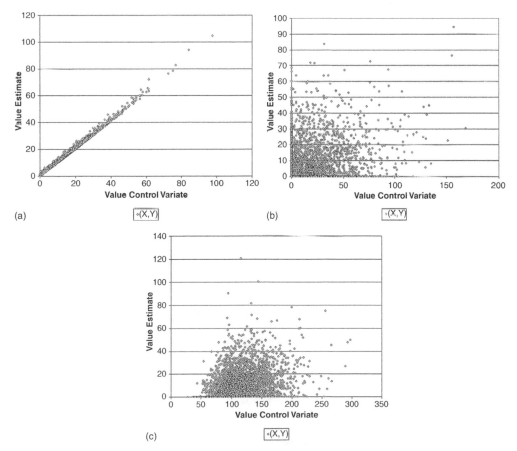

Figure 15.5 Correlation estimate of an arithmetic Asian option with (a) a geometric Asian option, (b) call option and (c) underlying as control variate

```
int main()
{
    // Define the Property Set to use
    SimplePropertySet<string, AnyType*> mc_myset_asian;
    SimplePropertySet<string, AnyType*> mc_myset_asian_cv;

    double Spot = 100.0;      // current spot price
    double Maturity = 3.0;    // option maturity
    double r = 0.03;          // riskless rate
    double d = 0.0;           // dividend yield
    double sigma = 0.20;      // volatility

    // values for usage with the property set
    static Wrapper<double> Strike = 100;
    static Wrapper<std::string> PayOffType = "call";
    static Wrapper<std::string> AverageType = "arithmetic";
    static Wrapper<std::string> AverageType_CV = "geometric";

    // Add properties to the set
    mc_myset_asian.add("Strike",
        &Strike);                                 // add properties
    mc_myset_asian_cv.add("Strike",
        &Strike);                                 // add properties
    mc_myset_asian.add("PayOffType",
        &PayOffType);                             // add properties
    mc_myset_asian_cv.add("PayOffType",
        &PayOffType);                             // add properties
    mc_myset_asian.add("AverageType",
        &AverageType);                            // add properties
    mc_myset_asian_cv.add("AverageType",
        &AverageType_CV);                         // add properties

    // Specify the name of your payoff used for registration with the
    // factory
    string mc_name = "asian_v";

    // Create a pointer to the payoff for Multi Factor
    PayOff<double, Vector<double> >* asianptr =
        PayOffFactory<double, Vector<double> >::Instance().
         CreatePayOff(mc_name, mc_myset_asian);
    PayOff<double, Vector<double> >* asianptr_cv =
        PayOffFactory<double, Vector<double> >::Instance().
         CreatePayOff(mc_name, mc_myset_asian_cv);


    // Define the path
    Vector<Vector<double>> mc_path_asian;

    // Define the model
    MCBlackScholes MCBS(r, d, sigma, Maturity, Spot);
```

```
// Define the scheme
MCExactGeoBrownian<RandGen<MersenneTwister>, MCBlackScholes> MCE;

// Define the Monte Carlo object
MCMonteCarlo<Vector<Vector<double>>> mc;

// The variable for outputting mean and standard deviation
Vector<double> mcvalue(2);
mcvalue[1] = 0.0; mcvalue[2] = 0.0;

int NoOfBatches = 10;    // Number of Monte Carlo batches
long NoOfPaths = 1000;   // Number of paths for each batch
long Timesteps=12;   // Timesteps

unsigned long Seed = 123456; // The seed we use to generate
                             uniforms
RandGen<MersenneTwister> rangen(Seed);   // The generator we use

// This is the Monte Carlo simulation
resetmc(mcvalue_cv);            // Init the simulation
for(int i = 1; i <= NoOfBatches; i++)
{
  mc_path_asian = MCE.calcST(rangen, MCBS,NoOfPaths,1,Timesteps);
  mc.setpath(mc_path_asian);
  mc.mcprice2_cv(1.0 asianptr, asianptr_cv, Timesteps,
  mcvalue_cv););
}

// Output
cout << "PV:" << exp(-r * Maturity)*mcvalue_cv[1] / NoOfBatches;
cout << " SE:" << mcvalue_cv[2] / NoOfBatches << ")" << " ";

return 0;
}
```

15.4   OPTIONS ON THE RUNNING MAX/MIN

We study two classes of exotic path-dependent options. The first class we have to check if trigger events up to maturity have occurred. *Barrier options* belong to this class of options. The second class is based on the maximum or the minimum value of the asset during the lifetime of the option. *Lookback options* belong to this class. *Lookback barrier options* combine both features in arbitrary combinations.

We further subdivide both classes. The trigger event, respectively the minimum or maximum, can occur at any time point and is thus continuously monitored. If we prescribe a discrete set of time points up to the maturity of the option we consider discretely monitored options. We simulate a trajectory of the spot price process and consider:

$$S_{Max} := \text{Max}_{t \in \mathcal{T}} (S(t)) \qquad (15.15)$$

$$S_{Min} := \text{Min}_{t \in \mathcal{T}} (S(t)) \qquad (15.16)$$

By evaluating the payoff operator we can check if S_{Max} or S_{Min} has or has not triggered the option.

In the continuous case, however, there is a possibility that the trigger event occurs between two consecutive time points of our discretisation. This makes it necessary to adjust the payoff adequately and account for that probability.

Corresponding formulae and theorems do exist not only for the case of the Black-Scholes model but also for more general stochastic processes. Often, the adjustment can be integrated into the corresponding payoff function as discussed in section 15.9. To this end the payoff object needs additional data, for instance the discretisation or the volatility.

Another possibility to overcome this difficulty of storing the data is to simulate additional path variables such as the running maximum or minimum. For processes following simple dynamics this is manageable because the distribution of the maximum and minimum may be explicitly known. Based on Asmusson, Glynn and Pitman (1995), section 6.4, we describe a general way to simulate the running maximum. Since we simulate another asset the method is computationally burdensome.

15.5   BARRIER OPTIONS

Barrier options are options where the payoff depends on whether the underlying asset has reached a certain level during the lifetime of the option.

We consider an *up-and-in call option*. The current spot price, $S(0)$, is assumed to be 0.97, its strike, K, is set to 1.0 and the barrier it should breach is 1.2. If the path breaches the barrier during the lifetime of the option we compare the spot price and the strike price at maturity. Figure 15.6 shows two paths. One path does not contribute to the price estimator since the payoff is zero. For the other path the payoff is nonzero and therefore it contributes to the price.

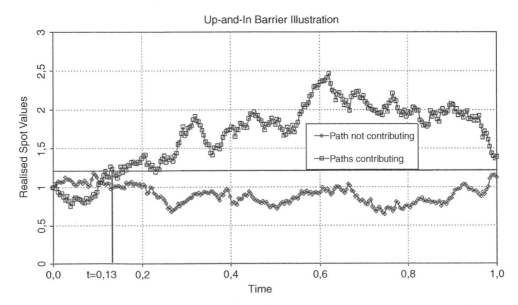

Figure 15.6 Two simulated paths. One path contributes to the price because it breaches the barrier at $t = 0.13$. The other path does not contribute.

Correspondingly, if the option is triggered or knocked out we consider two categories of barrier options, namely:

- knock-out options;
- knock-in options.

For a knock-out option the payoff is evaluated if the asset price never reaches the barrier level and it is *knocked out* if the asset reaches or crosses the level. For knock-in options the payoff function is computed if the asset reaches or crosses the barrier level. If an option has a trigger event that is higher than the current spot price we name it up-and-in or up-and-out respectively if it is a knock-out or knock-in option. The situation is reversed if the trigger event refers to a barrier currently lying below the spot value. We refer to this option as a down-and-in or down-and-out option.

Take, for example, the payoff of a European call option with payoff $\max(S(T) - K, 0)$ and extend the payoff function by adding a trigger event. The option pays the premium of a European call if the price of the underlying asset remains above a barrier level b. In this example the payoff is given by

$$h(S(t_1), \ldots, S(t_N)) = 1_{\{\inf_{t_n}\{S(t_n) < b\} > T\}} \text{Max}(S(T) - K, 0) \tag{15.17}$$

The indicator function $1_{\{\inf_{t_n}\{S(t_n) < b\} > T\}}$ is 1 if the asset price at the points t_n is above the b, but it is 0 if the asset price drops below b.

The complexity of barrier options can be increased by allowing *moving barriers*. Such barrier options involve time-dependent barrier levels. The barrier levels may depend also on the level of interest rates, the current level of the asset or on an exchange rate.

Barrier options are widespread. They are used to hedge *auto-callable* products often involved in structured equity certificates. Auto-callables are options that are automatically triggered if a certain event has happened. This event is modelled as a barrier.

15.5.1 Mapping barrier options into our framework

We use the general class hierarchy for mapping barrier options into our framework. The class `BarrierOption` has a pointer to a payoff object which has to implement a function that evaluates the payoff function for a given path. The implementation is given by

```
class PayOff_Barrier : public PayOff<double,Vector<double> >
{
public:
    PayOff_Barrier();
    PayOff_Barrier(const SimplePropertySet<string,AnyType*>& pset);

    virtual double operator()(double Discount,
                              Vector<double>& Spot) const;
    virtual double PayOff_Value(double Discount,
                                Vector<double>& Spot,
                                double Strike) const;

    virtual PayOff<double, Vector<double> >* clone() const;
```

```
    virtual ~PayOff_Barrier(){}

    SimplePropertySet<string,AnyType*> PayOff_Barrier_Properties;

private:
};
```

We have already mentioned that adjustments are necessary to compute prices for continuously monitored barrier options. See the exercises at the end of this chapter.

15.5.2   Approximation formulae for barrier options

Approximate formulae have been found in Merton (1976) and Reiner and Rubinstein (1992). We use the formulae presented by Haug (2007).

To price a barrier option we have to account for the possible `barriertype`. The option can be of knock-in or knock-out type. We implement this choice using a `switch` statement:

```
    char c;
if(barriertype == "di")
    c = 'a';
if(barriertype == "ui")
    c = 'b';
if(barriertype == "do")
    c = 'c';
if(barriertype == "uo")
    c = 'd';
if(Spot > Barrier){
if(payofftype == "call"){
    switch(c){
    case 'a' : result = C + E; break;
    case 'b' : result = A + E; break;
    case 'c' : result = A - C + F; break;
    case 'd' : result = F; break;}}
...
```

The result is computed by using the variables

```
mu = ((r-d) - sigma*sigma / 2.0) / (sigma * sigma);
lambda = sqrt(mu*mu + 2 * r /(sigma*sigma));
x1 = log(Spot / Strike) / (sigma * sqrt(Mat)) + (1+mu) *
    sigma * sqrt(Mat);
x2 = log(Spot / Barrier) / (sigma * sqrt(Mat)) + (1+mu) * sigma *
    sqrt(Mat);
y1 = log(Barrier * Barrier / (Spot * Strike)) / (sigma * sqrt(Mat))
        + (1 + mu) * sigma * sqrt(Mat);
y2 = log(Barrier / Spot) / (sigma * sqrt(Mat)) + (1 + mu) * sigm
    a * sqrt(Mat);
z = log(Barrier / Spot) / (sigma * sqrt(Mat)) + lambda * sigma *
    sqrt(Mat);
```

by a Black-Scholes type formula. For example, let us take the variable A to compute the price in cases b and c:

```
A = phi * Spot * exp(-d*Mat) * CumulativeNormal(phi * x1)
    - phi * Strike * exp(-r*Mat)
    * CumulativeNormal(phi * x1 - phi * sigma * sqrt(Mat));
```

The full source code, including all the other cases, is on the CD and can be studied in detail by the reader.

15.5.3 Importance sampling

Barrier options serve as the standard example to illustrate another very useful method to reduce the variance of a Monte Carlo estimator. It is called *importance sampling*. We give a short introduction and an example for computing the price of an *up-and-out* call option.

For all variance reduction techniques we apply our knowledge of the pricing problem and observe that discretisation of the asset price path and the evaluation of the payoff are not necessarily distinct parts of the simulation. We can use information on the payoff and incorporate it into the construction of the paths. This is essentially the case by applying importance sampling. For example, we incorporate a mechanism that transforms the generated paths to paths which end up in the money and therefore contribute to the calculation of the price. The importance sampling estimator does exactly that transformation and keeps track of how we have changed the problem under consideration by applying the transformation. Finally, we have to remove the artefacts from applying the transformation.

Our aim is to estimate the price $V := \mathbb{E}[h(S)]$ of an option with payoff function h. If the distribution of the asset S has a (multivariate) distribution with density f and there exists a density function g such that

$$f(x) \neq 0 \text{ whenever } g(x) \neq 0, \text{ that is } g \text{ has the same support as } f$$

we have

$$V = \mathbb{E}[h(S)] = \int h(x)f(x)dx$$

$$= \int h(x)\frac{f(x)}{g(x)}g(x)dx$$

$$= \mathbb{E}_g\left[\frac{h(S)f(S)}{g(S)}\right]$$

How can we apply this result to improve the variance of the sample? For example, we can use

$$\hat{V}_n^{IS} := \frac{1}{n}\sum_{j=1}^{n}\frac{h(X_j)f(X_j)}{g(X_j)}$$

as an alternative for the simple estimator.

$\hat{V}_n^{IS}$ is called the *importance sampling estimator*. We fix a barrier level H and time points $t_1, \ldots, t_N = T$ as well as a strike K. The payoff of this option is

$$(S_T - K)^+ \prod_{n=1}^{N} 1_{\{S(t_n)<H\}} \tag{15.18}$$

By importance sampling we restrict the scope to the case where the asset at all time points is lower than the barrier level and ends up in the money at maturity. Instead of using standard Gaussian random numbers $Z_n, n = 1, 2, \ldots, N$ computed by transforming uniform variates u_n

$$z_n = \mathcal{N}^{-1}(u_n) \tag{15.19}$$

we compute the probability that the asset at time point t_n is lower than the barrier value H. This probability is

$$h_i := \mathcal{N}\left(\frac{\ln(H/S(t_i)) + 1/2\sigma^2 \Delta t}{\sigma\sqrt{\Delta t}}\right) \tag{15.20}$$

Now, construct a normal variate z_i from the conditional distribution by

$$z_n = \mathcal{N}^{-1}(u_n h_n) \tag{15.21}$$

For the last step, both the barrier and the strike level have to be taken into account. We sample from the conditional distribution that the asset price $S(T)$ is lower than the barrier level H and larger than the strike level K. This leads us to consider

$$z_N = \mathcal{N}^{-1}(u_N(h_N - k) + k) \tag{15.22}$$

and

$$\mathcal{N}\left(\frac{\ln(K/S(T)) + \sigma^2/2\Delta T}{\sigma\sqrt{\Delta T}}\right) \tag{15.23}$$

The implementation of the importance sampling estimation for such options is given as an exercise in section 15.9.

15.5.4 Antithetic variables

We present a general variance reduction method called *antithetic variables*. To illustrate the functionality of this method suppose we generate two series of samples Y_1 and Y_2 representing the payoff function applied to an underlying asset to compute the value of an option. We consider the unbiased estimator of the option value $\hat{V}$ given by

$$\hat{V} = \frac{Y_1 + Y_2}{2} = \frac{1}{2N}\sum_{n=1}^{N}(Y_{1,n} + Y_{2,n}) \tag{15.24}$$

and the corresponding variance

$$\mathbb{V}[\hat{V}] = \frac{\mathbb{V}[Y_1] + \mathbb{V}[Y_2] + 2\text{Cov}(Y_1, Y_2)}{4}$$

The guiding idea is to reduce variance by the introduction of negative dependence.

We apply this method to normal variates and a given discretisation scheme that computes the drift as $\mu_n(S_n)$ and the diffusion term as $\sigma_n(S_n)$.

Instead of using only S_n to construct the asset's path in the usual way:

$$S_{n+1} = S_n + \mu_n(S_n)\Delta_n + \sigma_n(S_n)\sqrt{\Delta_n}Z_n, \quad Z_n \sim \mathcal{N}(0, 1)$$

we also take the variates $-S_n$ as follows:

$$S_{n+1} = S_n + \mu_n(S_n)\Delta_n - \sigma_n(S_n)\sqrt{\Delta_n}Z_n$$

Here we use the same random numbers Z_n but we change the sign. The path is called the *shadow path* and it is used to compute another price for the option under consideration. The main loop of the corresponding schemes needs to be modified:

```
template<class Path> template<typename Pay>
Vector<double> MCMonteCarlo<Path>::mcprice_anti(const Pay* PayOffPtr)
{
    double sum = 0.0;
    double sumsum = 0.0;
    double payoff = 0.0;

    long N = mcpath.MaxIndex() - mcpath.MinIndex() + 1;
    N /= 2;

    long minindex_Sims = mcpath.MinIndex();
    long maxindex_Sims = mcpath.MaxIndex() - N;

    Vector<double> result(2);    // returns the price and the standard
                                 // error

    for(int i = minindex_Sims; i<=maxindex_Sims;i++)
    {
        payoff = 0.5 * ((*PayOffPtr)(1.0, mcpath[i])
                        +(*PayOffPtr)(1.0, mcpath[i+N]));
        sum += payoff;
        sumsum += payoff * payoff;
    }

    result[1] = sum / N;
    double sesquare = (sumsum / N - sum * sum / N / N)/N;
    result[2] =  sesquare >= 0 ? sqrt(sesquare) : -999.0;

    return result;
}
```

After constructing the paths `result` and `result_anti` we store both values in the array `ST[]`. Since we have to evaluate the payoff for both paths and take the average the Monte Carlo class has also to be adjusted to be usable with antithetics.

Antithetic sampling is an easy-to-use method and often leads to a reduction in variance.

15.5.5 Numerical results

We test our framework by giving some numerical results (see Tables 15.2 and 15.3). We have simulated option prices using 20 000 paths. The spot price and the strike are set to 100. The rebate is set to 0 whereas the barrier is equal to 105 for a maturity of one year. Thus, we start below the barrier level and the option pays nothing if the barrier is breached.

Table 15.2 Numerical results for barrier options. The spot price dynamics assumes a geometric Brownian motion with $S(0) = 100$, $r = 3\%$, $\sigma = 20\%$ in the case of a call option. The down-and-out version is obviously 0.0 and therefore not included

Steps	PV (SE)	sec.	PVAnti (SE)	sec.	PV (BS)
down-and-in					
12	7.63607 (0.0913414)	0.672	7.52469 (0.0642582)	0.969	9.4134
52	9.3378 (0.102833)	2.172	9.2582 (0.0723942)	2.484	9.4134
365	9.48636 (0.103755)	13.781	9.26278 (0.0717847)	15	9.4134
up-and-in					
12	9.30489 (0.103668)	0.656	9.37783 (0.0731398)	0.844	9.3446
52	9.41367 (0.103891)	2.156	9.41477 (0.0731698)	2.438	9.3860
365	9.57216 (0.104207)	13.719	9.37032 (0.0726379)	14.89	9.3992
up-and-out					
12	0.0510099 (0.00281176)	0.656	0.0474204 (0.00193993)	0.844	0.0688
52	0.0206635 (0.00177713)	2.157	0.023089 (0.00129945)	2.453	0.0275
365	0.013789 (0.0013742)	13.734	0.0131654 (0.000933029)	14.797	0.0142

For the case of a down-and-in option the Black-Scholes prices remain the same for all discretisation levels. The reason is that we deal with the continuous case here. Therefore, the Monte Carlo price gets closer to the approximative price if we refine the level of discretisation. In all cases we observe that the use of antithetics not only leads to better prices but also the variance becomes smaller. For the considered test cases the prices computed by analytical approximation compare well to the results obtained by Monte Carlo simulation. We can improve the simulation results by considering further adjustment techniques when dealing with minima or maxima for continuous paths. This is further discussed in the exercises in section 15.9.

15.6   LOOKBACK OPTIONS

We review *lookback options* as the last application of path-dependent options. The payoff for a lookback option depends on the maximum or the minimum of the underlying asset over a certain time interval. Using the notation of section 15.1 we examine the closing prices at the time points of the discrete set $\mathcal{T}$. We consider the following types of options:

- $\text{Call}_{\text{fixed}} = \max(0, S_{\text{Max}} - K)$
- $\text{Put}_{\text{fixed}} = \max(0, K - S_{\text{Min}})$
- $\text{Call}_{\text{float}} = \max(0, S(T) - S_{\text{Min}})$
- $\text{Put}_{\text{float}} = \max(0, S_{\text{Max}} - S(T))$

Table 15.3 Numerical results for barrier options. The spot price dynamics assumes a geometric Brownian motion with $S(0) = 100$, $r = 3\%$, $\sigma = 20\%$ in the case of a put option. The down-and-out version is obviously 0.0 and therefore not included

Steps	PV (SE)	sec.	PVAnti (SE)	sec.	PV (BS)
down-and-in					
12	6.32457 (0.0675705)	0.656	6.48347 (0.0485253)	0.844	6.4580
52	6.50056 (0.0682784)	2.141	6.45884 (0.0481508)	2.437	6.4580
365	6.37209 (0.0679446)	13.687	6.44643 (0.0480667)	14.766	6.4580
up and-in					
12	1.87602 (0.0370372)	0.657	1.91036 (0.026377)	0.844	1.9442
52	2.60393 (0.0441855)	2.14	2.60969 (0.0310822)	2.437	2.6054
365	3.14613 (0.0487903)	13.75	3.01606 (0.0335294)	14.828	3.0537
up-and-out					
12	4.53314 (0.0644645)	0.656	4.52442 (0.0455395)	0.843	3.4042
52	3.85068 (0.061786)	2.141	3.79131 (0.0430937)	2.438	3.8526
365	3.39821 (0.058747)	13.734	3.4327 (0.0419185)	14.812	3.4042

The first two cases belong to the class of fixed strike options whereas the latter two cases belong to the floating strike class. Given a path Spot we evaluate the payoff for the case of a fixed and floating type as follows:

```
if(paytype == "call")
        if(type == "fixed")
        {
            Extreme = Spot[minindex_spot];
            for(int i=minindex_spot + 1; i <= maxindex_spot; ++i)
                Extreme = max(Extreme, Spot[i]);
            return max(0.0, Extreme - strike);
        }
        else
        {
            Extreme= Spot[minindex_spot];
            for(int i=minindex_spot +1; i <= maxindex_spot; ++i)
                Extreme = min(Extreme, Spot[i]);
            return max(0.0, Spot[maxindex_spot]-Extreme);
        }
```

The evaluation for the corresponding put option is omitted as it can be found on the CD.

15.6.1   Approximation formulae for lookback options

Approximation formulae for lookback options were first proposed in Goldman, Sosin and Gatto (1979). For the approximation of a European lookback put we refer also to Haug (2007). Our implementation of the approximation formula is based on the function

```
double LookbackOption::TheoreticalPrice()
```

We retrieve the necessary data from the property set:

```
type_double = dynamic_cast<Wrapper<double>*>
    (lookbackoptionsprops.value("Strike"));
Strike = (*type_double).GetObj();
```

We distinguish between fixed and floating strike options. The mathematical formulae for the approximation in the floating strike case are (see Haug, 2007):

$$Call_{float} = S(T)e^{-dT}N(a_1) - e^{-rT}S_{Min}N(a_2)$$

$$+ S(T)e^{-rT}\frac{\sigma^2}{2(r-d)}\left[\left(\frac{S(T)}{S_{Min}}\right)^{-\frac{2(r-d)}{\sigma^2}}N\left(-a_1 + \frac{2(r-d)}{\sigma}\sqrt{T}\right)e^{-dT}N(-a_1)\right]$$

$$Put_{float} = S_{Max}e^{-rT}N(b_2) - S(T)e^{-rT}N(-b_1)$$

$$+ S(T)e^{-rT}\frac{\sigma^2}{2(r-d)}\left[-\left(\frac{S_{Max}}{S(T)}\right)^{-\frac{2(r-d)}{\sigma^2}}N\left(b_1 + \frac{2(r-d)}{\sigma}\sqrt{T}\right)e^{-dT}N(b_1)\right]$$

with $a_1 = \frac{\ln(S(T)/S_{Min})+(r-d+0.5\sigma^2)T}{\sigma\sqrt{T}}$, $a_2 = a_1 - \sigma\sqrt{T}$, $b_1 = \frac{\ln(S_{Max}/S(T))+(r-d+0.5\sigma^2)T}{\sigma\sqrt{T}}$ and $b_2 = b_1 - \sigma\sqrt{T}$.

For the fixed strike versions of the options we use the following approximation formulae:

$$Call_{fixed} = S(T)e^{-dT}N(a_1) - e^{-rT}KN(a_2)$$

$$+ S(T)e^{-rT}\frac{\sigma^2}{2(r-d)}\left[e^{(r-d)T}N(a_1) - \left(\frac{S(T)}{K}\right)^{-\frac{2(r-d)}{\sigma^2}}N\left(a_1 - \frac{2(r-d)}{\sigma}\sqrt{T}\right)\right]$$

$$Put_{fixed} = Ke^{-rT}N(-a_2) - e^{-dT}S(T)N(-a_1)$$

$$+ S(T)e^{-rT}\frac{\sigma^2}{2(r-d)}\left[e^{(r-d)T}N(-a_1) - \left(\frac{S(T)}{K}\right)^{-\frac{2(r-d)}{\sigma^2}}N\left(-a_1 - \frac{2(r-d)}{\sigma}\sqrt{T}\right)\right]$$

If the strike price is greater than the maximum for the call option or the minimum in the case of a put option, then

$$Call_{fixed} = e^{-rT}\left[(S_{Max} - K) - S_{Max}N(b_2)\right] + S(T)e^{-dT}N(b_1)$$

$$+ S(T)e^{-rT}\frac{\sigma^2}{2(r-d)}\left[e^{(r-d)T}N(b_1) - \left(\frac{S(T)}{S_{Max}}\right)^{-\frac{2(r-d)}{\sigma^2}}N\left(b_1 - \frac{2(r-d)}{\sigma}\sqrt{T}\right)\right]$$

$$Put_{fixed} = e^{-rT}\left[(K - S_{Min}) - S_{Min}N(-c_2)\right] - S(T)e^{-dT}N(-c_1)$$

$$+ S(T)e^{-rT}\frac{\sigma^2}{2(r-d)}\left[e^{(r-d)T}N(-c_1) - \left(\frac{S(T)}{S_{Min}}\right)^{-\frac{2(r-d)}{\sigma^2}}N\left(-c_1 - \frac{2(r-d)}{\sigma}\sqrt{T}\right)\right]$$

where we use the abbreviations

$$a_1 = \frac{\log(S(T)/K) + (r - d + \sigma^2/2)T}{\sigma\sqrt{T}}$$

$$a_2 = a_1 - \sigma\sqrt{T}$$

$$b_1 = \frac{\log(S(T)/S_{\mathrm{Max}}) + (r - d + \sigma^2/2)T}{\sigma\sqrt{T}}$$

$$b_2 = b_1 - \sigma\sqrt{T}$$

$$c_1 = \frac{\log(S(T)/S_{\mathrm{Min}}) + (r - d + \sigma^2/2)T}{\sigma\sqrt{T}}$$

$$c_2 = c_1 - \sigma\sqrt{T}$$

15.6.2   Results

Table 15.4 summarises the results obtained by Monte Carlo simulation for a geometric Brownian motion running 10 000 paths starting at a spot value of 100. The risk-free rate is set to 3% and the volatility is 20%. We assume no dividends and an option strike of 100. Since lookback options involve the minimum or the maximum of the simulated spot price up to maturity

Table 15.4   Numerical results for lookback options

Steps	MC Price	SE		
PayOffType:	Call			
	fixed	Black-Scholes price:	26.995	
12	22.0052	(0.236424)		
52	24.9144	(0.245352)		
365	25.6685	(0.24416)		
730	26.4082	(0.246693)		
1460	26.8432	(0.247672)		
Type:	Float	Black-Scholes price:	23.113	
12	18.6694	(0.213046)		
52	21.3196	(0.228263)		
365	22.2266	(0.225452)		
730	22.5219	(0.223511)		
1460	22.7955	(0.225658)		
PayOffType:	Put			
	fixed	Black-Scholes result:	17.289	
12	13.9278	(0.129885)		
52	15.7828	(0.127045)		
365	16.7904	(0.126106)		
730	16.7871	(0.126193)		
1460	17.0719	(0.125958)		
Type:	Float	Black-Scholes result:	21.172	
12	15.377	(0.139729)		
52	18.5498	(0.145766)		
365	20.1222	(0.146632)		
730	20.4094	(0.147064)		
1460	20.7455	(0.147178)		

the price depends on the refinement of the discretisation. As the Black-Scholes formula is an approximation to the continuous case we expect that the results obtained by Monte Carlo simulation should better fit those values if we use a very fine discretisation. The results using daily data are therefore the best approximation. Again we can refine our Monte Carlo scheme using variance reduction methods or adjustment techniques.

Many problems in finance are discrete problems and therefore the approximated Black-Scholes price does not fit the traded prices. In this case we can directly use the results from Monte Carlo simulation. Another reason why a discrete view is very useful stems from the fact that hedges can only be done at discrete times and not continuously during the life of the option.

15.7   CLIQUET OPTIONS

One well-known product that is challenging to price is a *cliquet option*. There are many variants of such options, for example the *reverse cliquet* or the *swing cliquet*. Furthermore, each single transaction may depend on multiple assets.

To fix ideas and to define the general cliquet option on one underlying we introduce the return R_n, which is also known as the performance of an asset S over the time interval $[t_{n-1}, t_n]$, by

$$R_n := \frac{S(t_n)}{S(t_{n-1})} - 1 \tag{15.25}$$

The value $S(t_n)$ represents the closing price at time t_n. Typically, the time period differs from values of one month to one year. Thus, typical values for $t_n - t_{n-1}$ are $1/12, 0.25, 0.5$ or 1.

The maximum loss to be taken is reflected by a local floor LF. The maximum gain is reflected by a local cap LC:

$$U_n := \text{Min} \left(\text{Max} \left(LF, R_n \right), LC \right) \tag{15.26}$$

Now, we have the valuation rule for each period. Since the cliquet is an average over such periods we have to glue all components together by the overall rule to compute the price. We consider the arithmetic or the geometric cliquet, depending on the average technique we apply.

We can further control the overall payment by introducing a maximum loss level, the global floor denoted by GF, and a maximal upside level, the global cap denoted by GC. The arithmetic cliquet option pays

$$\text{Min} \left(\text{Max} \left(GF, \sum_{n=1}^{N} U_n \right), GC \right) \tag{15.27}$$

The geometrically averaged cliquet option is represented by the payoff

$$\text{Min} \left(\text{Max} \left(GF, \prod_{n=1}^{N} U_n \right), GC \right) \tag{15.28}$$

15.7.1   Remarks on cliquet options

The basic product implements an option strategy that consists of going periodically long a bull spread which is floored and capped.

Since a sufficiently large number of negative returns above the local floor destroy earnings over the long run, a protection, called the global floor, is added. In contrast, a large number of positive returns below the local cap amount lead to a large payout. This is the rationale for adding a global cap.

The product is designed for periods in which the performance is bound between local floor and local cap, that is there are no positive trends expected to break the global floor or cap.

The protection levels, namely the strikes of the floors and caps involved, may be tuned leading to costs or further earnings.

In mathematical terms the global floor and cap introduce an additional level of convexity and concavity respectively.

In financial markets the variant locally floored and globally capped and locally capped and globally floored are traded instruments.

15.7.2   C++ implementation

To implement the function

```
double PayOffCliquet::operator () (double Discount,
                                   Vector<double>& Spot) const
```

we extract all the necessary data from the underlying Property Set Pay-Off_Cliquet_Properties as we have shown in section 15.6.1. The payoff is then given by:

```
double result = 0.0;
for(size_t i = 0; i < NrOfCliqs; i++)
   result += min(max<double>(Spot[i+1]/Spot[i] - 1.0,
           LocalFloor), LocalCap);
result = min(max<double>(result,GlobalFloor),GlobalCap);
return result;
```

This means that we have implemented formulae (15.25) and (15.26).

15.7.3   Version of the basic cliquet option

Reverse cliquet

The are many variants of the basic cliquet option. First, we consider the reverse cliquet option. Here we consider

$$RC_n := \text{Min} \left(\text{Max} \left(LF, -R_n \right), LC \right) \tag{15.29}$$

Instead of U_n, given by equation (15.26), we now take RC_n. The periodical payout could either be summed or multiplied. For the arithmetic reverse cliquet this leads to

$$\text{Min} \left(\text{Max} \left(GF, \sum_{n=1}^{N} RC_n \right), GC \right) \tag{15.30}$$

The swing cliquet option

Another version of the basic product is the swing cliquet option. It has payoff:

$$SC_n := \mathrm{Max}(C_{n-1}, \mathrm{Max}(|R_n| - K, 0)) \tag{15.31}$$

The swing cliquet option also has a reversed version. In this case we consider the payoff:

$$RSC_n := \mathrm{Max}(C_{n-1}, \mathrm{Max}(-|R_n| - K, 0)) \tag{15.32}$$

The cliquet option payoffs described above have been used as the basic building blocks of structured equity products.

15.7.4 Results

Since cliquet options are standard examples that show how the volatility skew affects option prices, we deal with these types of options in Chapter 16 in detail and we present results using different numerical schemes to approximate the underlying dynamic. The reader can find the implementation of the different cliquet options on the CD.

15.8   SUMMARY AND CONCLUSIONS

In this chapter we have introduced a Monte Carlo framework that is easy to use and flexible enough to cover many models used in financial engineering. Furthermore, together with our payoff classes within this framework we can deal with many kinds of options such as time-dependency or options involving multiple assets. Variance reduction techniques are implemented to speed up the basic Monte Carlo estimation.

As examples we considered time-dependent options in this chapter. We have documented our results by giving many examples and numerical results.

We verified our results by backtesting the prices obtained by simulation with prices computed by analytical approximation formulae.

15.9   EXERCISES AND PROJECTS

1. (**) Extension of the Asian Option Payoff
   Suppose the market supplies implied volatilities σ_i, $i = 1, 2, ..., n$ for options expiring at time t_n. The price of a geometric Asian option can then be computed from the Black-Scholes formula using the volatility given by

   $$\sigma_{\mathrm{adj}} = \frac{1}{n^2 T} \sum_{i=1}^{n} \sigma_i^2 t_n + 2 \sum_{i=1}^{n-1} (n - i) \sigma_i^2 t_n$$

   Extend the class `AsianOption` to cover this case.
2. (***) Brownian Interpolation
   For continuously monitored Barrier options the barrier may be breached between two consecutive points in the used discretisation. The probability of this event can be approximated by using *Brownian interpolation*.

Suppose we divide the interval $[0, T]$ into n equidistant intervals of length h. To account for this interpolation multiply the payoff by the factor p given by

$$p = \prod_{i=0}^{n-1} p_i = \prod_{i=0}^{n-1} \left(1 - \exp\left(-\frac{2(B - S(t_n))(B - S(t_{n+1}))}{\sigma(S(t_n))^2 h}\right)\right)$$

where $\sigma(S(t_n))$ is the value of the diffusion term at time t_n. This probability is an approximation to the function $1_{\{\max S(t) > B\}}$.

3. (*) Importance Sampling

   Implement *importance sampling* for all kinds of barrier options as described for an *up-and-out* call in section 15.5.3 and Jäckel (2002, chapter 11, section 4).

4. (**) Min and Max Options

   Options involving the minimum or the maximum of an asset can be handled by simulating the running minimum or maximum. To this end, consider the interval $[0, T]$ partitioned into N equidistant intervals of length h, N uniformly distributed random variables $(u_n)_{n=1,\ldots,N}$ and consider first a financial asset S with a discrete path given by

$$S_{n+1} = S_n + \mu_n(S_n)h + \sigma_n(S_n)\sqrt{h}Z_n, n = 1, \ldots, N$$

   We consider the maximum of an interpolating Brownian bridge that we approximate by

$$M_n = \frac{S_{n+1} + S_n + \sqrt{(S_{n+1} - S_n)^2 - 2\sigma_n^2 h \log(u_n)}}{2}, \quad n = 1, \ldots, N$$

   The version for geometric Brownian interpolation is given by

$$\log(M_n) = \frac{\log(S_{n+1}/S_n) + \sqrt{\log(S_{n+1}/S_n)^2 - 2(\sigma_n/S_n)^2 h \log(u_n)}}{2}$$

   and may be better suited for approximation problems.

   Integrate this approximation and the corresponding payoff into the Monte Carlo setup.

16

Affine Stochastic Volatility Models

Nowadays people know the price of everything and the value of nothing.

Oscar Wilde, *The Picture of Dorian Gray*

16.1 INTRODUCTION AND OBJECTIVES

In this chapter we examine affine stochastic volatility models from a simulation point of view. We begin by reviewing two popular models namely the *Heston model* and the *Bates model*. The latter is also known as the stochastic volatility with jumps or *SVJ model*. We call these models affine because the exponent appearing in the *characteristic function*, which we introduce in this chapter, has an affine structure.

Stochastic volatility models have become popular because the observed market logarithmic returns do not obey the normal distribution assumption. Historical data suggests that there are regimes of volatility leading to a skewed distribution. Another phenomenon is the so-called *volatility skew* which contradicts the assumption of the standard model.

After discussing the properties of each model and the stochastic dynamics we proceed by discussing the problems arising when applying a forward discretisation of the underlying process, for example an Euler scheme. This approach leads to unstable and inaccurate results. We discuss what may go wrong using a simple approach and we then improve the implementation by introducing truncated and moment-matched truncated schemes. We give an implementation of a recent approach by Andersen, the *quadratic exponential scheme*, or *QE scheme* for short.

Finally, we benchmark the models using the fully truncated Euler scheme. We consider financial instruments that depend on the model implied volatility skew. We have chosen digital options and cliquet options as already discussed in Chapter 15. Furthermore, we briefly discuss the computation of European prices using Fourier transform methods. For a detailed discussion see Chapter 23. This also serves as a benchmark for the schemes and the algorithms that can be used for calibration of the models to market parameters.

For log returns we observe that there are periods where they change frequently with pronounced high and low peaks. Furthermore, these periods are clustered. This behaviour causes the historical probability distribution to be skewed. Figure 16.1 displays both facts observed for asset returns with the German DAX index as an example.

16.2 THE VOLATILITY SKEW/SMILE

The implied volatilities of quoted European options are not constant and depend both on the strike and the maturity. This phenomenon is referred to as the *market skew* or *smile* (see Figure 16.2). Ignoring it can lead to significant mispricing of options. Digital options as well as cliquet options depend on the (forward) volatility surface. We give examples of such options and apply the simulation schemes introduced in this chapter to include the (forward) skew and smile into the pricing.

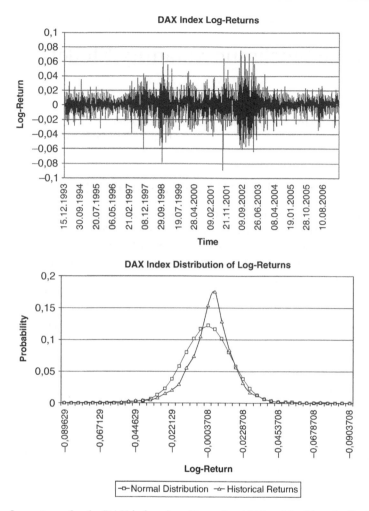

Figure 16.1   Log returns for the DAX index since December 1993 and the historic distribution

One of the simplest ways to incorporate the skew and the smile into pricing and risk management applications is to assign a formula that incorporates the moneyness and the time to maturity. One of the first approaches was the method by Fleming and Whaley (Dumas, Fleming and Whaley, 1998). They assumed

$$\sigma(K, T) = a + bK + cK^2 + dT + eT^2 + fKT \qquad (16.1)$$

for the volatility. The coefficients are estimated such that the observed prices fit the quoted prices from the market. Such models have the drawback that market observed shapes of the volatility structure cannot reasonably be fitted due to the quadratic nature of the function. Another solution is to use the *constant elasticity of variance model* proposed in Cox and Ross (1976). They considered stochastic differential equations of the form

$$dS(t) = \mu S(t)dt + \sigma S(t)^\beta dW(t), \quad \beta \in (0, 1)$$
$$S(0) = S_0$$

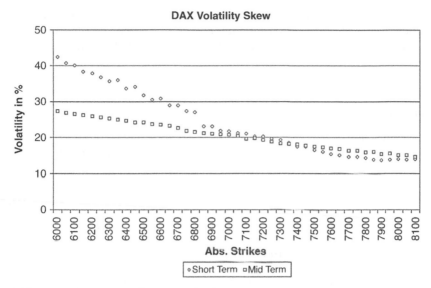

Figure 16.2 Volatility skew for the DAX index from 18.05.2007

The coefficients μ and $\sigma > 0$ have the same meaning as in the usual Black-Scholes framework. The dynamic starts at the spot value S_0. In financial modelling this coefficient adds skew to the model since it introduces a local volatility. The corresponding process is known as a *CEV process*. This process was already discussed in Chapter 3.

16.3   THE HESTON MODEL

The *Heston stochastic volatility model* was introduced in Heston (1993) and we gave an introduction to this model in Chapter 5.

The models considered so far assumed a constant number representing the average volatility over a time period. Figures 16.1 and 16.2 suggest that the volatility also varies over time. If we allow the volatility to be a function of time or even be stochastic we immediately switch to a much more complex model. We have a tradeoff: a more realistic model at the expense of a greater complexity in terms of pricing options. A key feature in modelling is the *time homogeneity*, meaning that the increments $S(t_{n+1}) - S(t_n)$ only depend on the difference $t_{n+1} - t_n$. If the volatility were stochastic the distribution of $S(t_{n+1}) - S(t_n)$ would also depend on the average volatility of that interval and therefore we then have a time inhomogeneous model.

The Heston model, which allows for a stochastic volatility and for tractable numerics, is well known among practitioners and is applied to all kinds of asset classes. The stochastic differential equation is given by

$$dS(t)/S(t) = (r - d)dt + \sqrt{V(t)}dW_1(t) \tag{16.2}$$
$$dV(t) = \kappa(\theta - V(t))dt + \xi\sqrt{V(t)}dW_2(t)$$
$$S(0) = S_0$$
$$V(0) = V_0$$

The parameters r and d denote the riskless rate and the dividend yield. The other parameters κ, θ and ξ represent the mean reversion rate, the long-term variance and the volatility of variance. The driving Brownian motions W_1 and W_2 are correlated and have correlation coefficient ρ.

Characteristic function

The characteristic function θ_{Heston} can be derived in closed form and is useful for computing prices of European options using a Black-Scholes type formula. This evaluation formula is based on

$$\theta_{Heston}(u) \tag{16.3}$$
$$= \exp\Big(iu \log(S(t)) + (r-d)t + \phi\kappa\xi^{-2}((\kappa - \rho\xi iu - \tilde{d})t$$
$$-2\log((1 - ge^{-\tilde{d}t})/(1-g)))$$
$$+V_0^2\xi^{-2}(\kappa - \rho\xi iu - \tilde{d})(1 - e^{-\tilde{d}t})/(1 - ge^{-\tilde{d}t})\Big)$$

with $\tilde{d} = \sqrt{(\rho\xi ui - \kappa)^2 + \xi^2(iu + u^2)}$ and $g = (\kappa - \rho\xi ui - \tilde{d})/(\kappa - \rho\xi ui + \tilde{d})$.

This is the representation leading to stable option prices because discontinuities arising from the complex power and logarithm do not occur here.

Distribution

The distribution of the price of the changes of the underlying $S(t)$ is time-dependent and known in closed form. We will not use the analytic formula; instead, we derive the shape of the distribution from computed European option prices and study the influence for each parameter of the corresponding stochastic differential equation. Figures 16.3, 16.4 and 16.5 illustrate how stochastic volatility affects the distribution. This results in skew for option prices, which is illustrated in Figure 16.6. Also they show the influence of the parameter ρ that is a measure of the dependence of the risk factors driving the underlying, respective volatility. We have chosen the parameters $\kappa = 0.04, \theta = v^2(0) = 0.04, \xi = 0.17$ and $\rho = -0.7$. Here we focused on a time to maturity of one year starting at 100. The interest rate prevailing in the hypothetical market is 5%. For these parameters the model produces a skew structure that is shaped like the one we observe for the DAX index (Figure 16.1).

To produce the figures, we implemented a pricing algorithm for European options in C++ and calculated the partial derivative $\frac{\partial^2 \text{Call}}{\partial K^2}$. Then, we make the algorithms available as an add-in function in Excel, xll, using methods we introduce in section 16.8. For further information on computing option prices and creating functionality using C++, which can be made available into Excel (see also Duffy (2004a) and Joshi (2007)), the reader will find a ready-to-use spreadsheet and all details on the implementation on the CD. For convenience we give the analytical expression for the density:

$$\frac{1}{2\pi} \int_{-\infty}^{+\infty} \exp(iux + F(t, u))du \tag{16.4}$$

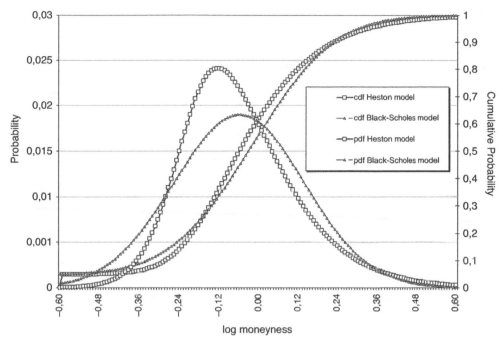

Figure 16.3   Heston model: density and cumulative probability for $\rho > 0$

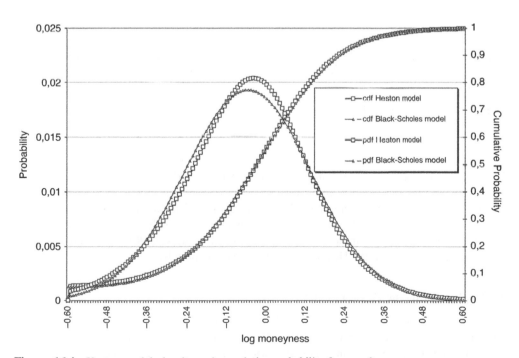

Figure 16.4   Heston model: density and cumulative probability for $\rho = 0$

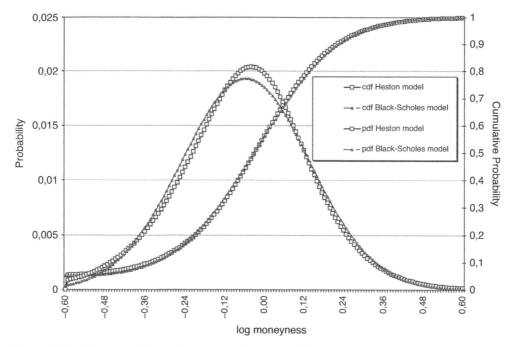

Figure 16.5   Heston model: density and cumulative probability for $\rho < 0$

where

$$F(t, u) = \frac{\kappa\theta}{v^2}\gamma(u)t - \frac{2\kappa\theta}{v^2}\log\left(\cosh\left(\frac{\tilde{d}t}{2}\right) + \frac{\tilde{d}^2 - \gamma(u)^2 + 2\kappa\gamma(u)}{2\kappa\tilde{d}}\sinh\left(\frac{\tilde{d}t}{2}\right)\right)$$

$$\gamma(u) = \kappa + i\rho vu$$

and the notation is the same as below.

Paths

The Heston model is able to fit the mid- and long-term skew. However, we observe that for short-dated options the skew is often very pronounced and the model fit is relatively poor because the model cannot reproduce the corresponding distributions leading to such pronounced skews. To cope with this weakness additional freedom can be achieved by adding jumps to the underlying. A popular model has been introduced in Bates (1996), which combines the features of the Merton and the Heston stochastic volatility models.

16.3.1   Implementing the Heston model

We discuss the difficulties arising by a straightforward implementation of the Heston model using Monte Carlo simulation. First, we apply a simple Euler scheme and observe what can go wrong. Second, we propose a method that is widely applied by practitioners. It is based on a truncated version of the Euler scheme. Finally, the state of the art algorithm, Andersen's *Quadratic Exponential (QE) scheme*, is reviewed and the implementation is discussed.

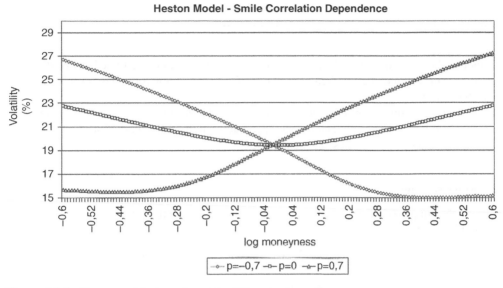

Figure 16.6   Heston model: skew shapes for different values of ρ

We have implemented the Heston model as a standalone class. The interface is

```
class MCHeston : public OneFactorModel
{
public:
    MCHeston();
    MCHeston(double r, double d, double Maturity, double Spot,
             double VInst, double VLong, double MeanRev, double
             VolVol, double Rho);
    virtual ~MCHeston();

    // Get functionality for private data members
    double getdrift() const;
    ...

    // Set functionality for private data members
    void setdrift(const double& Drift);
    ...

private:
    double drift;           // riskless rate r
    double vol;             // volatlity
    double martcorrection;  // martingale correction
    double dividend;        // dividends
    double maturity;        // T
    double spot;            // spot
    double vinst;           // Initial variance
    double vlong;           // Long term variance
    double meanrev;         // mean reversion speed
```

```
    double volvol;          // volatility of variance
    double rho;             // correlation
};
```

This model class can now be used with the schemes such as Euler or Quadratic Exponential. The resulting path will then be supplied to the Monte Carlo evaluation routine as described in Chapter 15 (section 15.2).

The crucial part in implementing an affine stochastic volatility model is to find acceptable discretisation methods for the spot and the variance paths. In the following we suggest some solutions and discuss their strengths and weaknesses.

16.3.2   Euler scheme

We examine the simplest discretisation of the process. Denoting the time step $t_{n+1} - t_n$ by Δ_n, this scheme is given by

$$V_{n+1} = V_n + \kappa(\theta - V_n)\Delta_n + \xi\sqrt{V_n}\sqrt{\Delta_n}Z_n, \quad Z_n \sim \mathcal{N}(0, 1) \tag{16.5}$$

Executing the steps for Monte Carlo simulation we observe that V_n certainly becomes negative since our random number generator will produce samples for which

$$z < -\frac{V_n + \kappa(\theta - V_n \cdot \Delta_n)}{\xi\sqrt{V_n \Delta_n}} \tag{16.6}$$

holds. Then, the term $\sqrt{V_n}$ becomes a complex number and a run-time error occurs.

One way to overcome this problem is to choose very small time steps. This means we decrease the probability for negative V but do not fully rule it out. Also it can be very time consuming to generate a large amount of random numbers and perform all the calculations necessary for constructing a path. However, this strategy does not always work.

16.3.3   Full truncation Euler scheme

To solve the problem addressed in the preceding section, use a truncated version of the Euler scheme. We introduce the truncation operator by $a^+ := \max(a, 0)$. Then the fully truncated Euler scheme is

$$V_{n+1} = V_n + \kappa(\theta - V_n^+)\Delta_n + \xi\sqrt{V_n^+}\sqrt{\Delta_n}Z_n, \quad Z_n \sim \mathcal{N}(0, 1) \tag{16.7}$$

The source code of the simple scheme is easily adapted to this setting.

We have implemented the class `MCEulerFull` which is derived from `OneFactorScheme` as follows:

```
template<class RanGen, class Model>
class MCEulerFull : public OneFactorScheme<RanGen,Model>
{
public:
    MCEulerFull();
    virtual ~MCEulerFull();
```

```
Vector<Vector<double>> calcST(RanGen& rg, Model& model,
                  long Paths, int Factors, long Steps) const;

private:
};
```

Let us start with the truncated Euler scheme and give the main loop implementing the path generation:

```
Vector<Vector<double> >ST(Paths);

// Main loop to generate all the paths
for(long i = minindex_Sims; i<= maxindex_Sims; i++)
{
    // Generate 2 randoms of independent Gaussians
    rg.GenerateVariatesVector(dW1,NormDist);
    rg.GenerateVariatesVector(dW2,NormDist);
    // Create correlated Gaussian the simple way
    dW2 = rho*dW1 + sqrt(1-rho*rho)*dW2;

    Vt = vInst;       // Start at initial variance
    St = S0;          // Start at spot

    // Main loop to generate one path
    for(long j = minindex_TimeSteps; j <=maxindex_TimeSteps; j++)
    {
        // Truncation for Vt to avoid negative values for variance
        Vpos = (Vt <= 0.0 ? 0.0 : Vt);

        // Variance-Path
        Vt += kh*(vLong - Vpos) + ohs*sqrt(Vpos)*dW1[j];
        // Asset-Path exponential version
        St *= 1.0 + rdh + sqrt(Vpos)*hsq*dW2[j];

        // Store the current asset path
        result[j + 1] = St;
    }
    // Store the result for return value
    ST[i] = result;
}

return ST;
```

16.3.4 Andersen's QE scheme

The Euler scheme has serious drawbacks leading to a bias to the real price of the derivative under consideration. Recently, Andersen (2006) has invented a method that combines ease in implementation, speed and accuracy. The key benefit of his result is that we need only to simulate Gaussian numbers and the construction can be split up by first simulating the variance path and then using this path to generate the spot price path. We now give a detailed description of the method and show how to code it in C++.

Discretisation of variance process

The main idea for discretisation of the Heston dynamics for the variance process using Andersen's QE scheme is the observation that for reasonable large values of the variance at the current time step from t_n to t_{n+1}, V_n, the distribution of V_{n+1} can be approximated by a moment-matched random variable M given by

$$M = a(b + Z)^2, \quad a, b \in \mathbb{R}^+, \quad Z \sim \mathcal{N}(0, 1) \tag{16.8}$$

The constants a and b depend on the coefficient of the Heston dynamics as well as the time discretisation and the current value of variance V_n.

For small values of V_n this cannot be used because the moment-matching procedure fails and cannot be applied. In this case Andersen uses the approximation:

$$F_V(x) := \mathbb{P}[V_{n+1} \leq x] = p\delta + (1 - p)(1 - e^{-\beta x}), \quad p, \beta \in \mathbb{R}^+ \tag{16.9}$$

where δ denotes the Dirac measure, that is $\delta(0) = 1$ and $\delta(x) = 0$ if $x \neq 0$. The only thing left is to determine when to apply (16.8) and (16.9) and how to compute the constants a, b, p and β. Sampling from the corresponding distributions is easy because

$$F_V(x) = \mathbb{P}[V_{n+1} \leq x]$$
$$F_V^{-1}(u) = \begin{cases} 0, & 0 \leq u \leq p \\ \beta^{-1} \ln\left(\frac{1-p}{1-u}\right), & p < u \leq 1 \end{cases} \tag{16.10}$$

We include additional material in Chapter 22 where we discuss random number generation.

We are left with the problem of defining a rule for taking the moment-matching scheme or the truncation scheme and computing the constants. To this end, for a given time step denoted by Δ we choose a switching level Ψ_C at which we switch from approximation (16.8) to (16.9). The level is determined by the current mean and variance level. The number we compare to Ψ_C is $\Psi = s^2/m^2$ with

$$m = \theta + (V_n - \theta)\exp(-\kappa\Delta)$$
$$s^2 = \frac{V_n\xi^2\exp(-\kappa\Delta)}{\kappa}(1 - \exp(-\kappa\Delta)) + \frac{\theta\xi^2}{2\kappa}\left(1 - \exp(-\kappa\Delta)^2\right)$$

Whenever $\Psi \leq \Psi_C$ we use moment-matching, otherwise we apply truncation.

Discretisation of spot price process

After having constructed the variance path we discretise the spot price path. If we denote $X(t) := \ln(S(t))$ and $\Delta_n := t_{n+1} - t_n$ one is tempted to use

$$X_{n+1} = X_n + (r - d)\Delta_n - \frac{1}{2}V_n^2 + \sqrt{V_n\Delta_n}Z$$

with $Z \sim \mathcal{N}(0, 1)$ being correlated to the corresponding Gaussian variable used to construct the variance for the time step from t_n to t_{n+1}. However, this results in leaking correlated variables as explained in Andersen (2006). To overcome this difficulty Andersen proposes another discretisation scheme for the asset price process. This focuses on the exact solution:

$$X_{n+1} = X_n + (r - d)\Delta_n$$
$$+ \frac{\rho}{\xi}((V_n + \Delta_n) - V_n - \kappa\theta\Delta_n)$$
$$+ \left(\frac{\kappa\rho}{\xi} - \frac{1}{2}\right)\int_{t_n}^{t_{n+1}} V(u)du + \sqrt{1 - \rho^2}\int_{t_n}^{t_{n+1}} \sqrt{V(u)}dW(u)$$

To use this exact discretisation we need to handle the time-integral of the variance. The exact sampling via Fourier methods is not feasible. Instead we use the approximation

$$\int_{t_n}^{t_{n+1}} V(u)du \approx \Delta_n(\gamma_1 V_n + \gamma_2 V_{n+1})$$

where γ_1 and γ_2 are constants. The constants can be chosen to be $\gamma_1 = \gamma_2 = 0.5$ to obtain a predictor-corrector scheme. More sophisticated methods apply moment matching to get better results.

Using the predictor-corrector approach the spot price process is approximated using

$$X_{n+1} = X_n + K_0 + K_1 V_n + K_2 V_{n+1} + \sqrt{K_3 V_n + K_4 V_{n+1}} \cdot Z \tag{16.11}$$

with the constants K_0 to K_4 given by

$$K_0 = -\frac{\rho\kappa\theta}{\xi}$$
$$K_1 = \gamma_1\Delta_n\left(\frac{\kappa\rho}{\xi} - \frac{1}{2}\right)$$
$$K_2 = \gamma_2\Delta_n\left(\frac{\kappa\rho}{\xi} - \frac{1}{2}\right)$$
$$K_3 = \gamma_1\Delta_n(1 - \rho^2)$$
$$K_4 = \gamma_2\Delta_n(1 - \rho^2)$$

Implementing the QE scheme

The template class implementing the QE scheme within the framework introduced in Chapter 15 is given by

```
template<class RanGen, class Model>
class MCQE : public OneFactorScheme<RanGen,Model>
{
public:
    MCQE();
    MCQE(Model& model, long Paths, long Steps);
    virtual ~MCQE();

    // Function to compute the spot price path
    Vector<Vector<double>> calcST(RanGen& rg, Model& model,
                        long Paths,
                        int Factors, long Steps) const;
    Vector<Vector<double>> calcST2(RanGen& rg, Model& model,
                        long Pths, long Steps) const;
```

```
private:

    // Function to compute the variance path; used by calcST
    Vector<double> calcVPath(double vInst, double vLong,
                             const Vector<double>& UV,
                             const Vector<double>& Coeff) const;

    // Functions to compute the constanst for
    // discretisation given some Stochastic Volatility Model
    Vector<double> St_Constants(double delta, double r, double d,
                            double vInst, double vLong,
                            double kappa, double omega, double rho,
                            double gamma1) const;
    Vector<double> Vt_Constants(double delta, double vLong,
                            double kappa,
                            double omega) const;

    Vector<double> ConstS_PreCalc;
    Vector<double> ConstV_PreCalc;
};
```

We have three private member functions `calcVPath`, `St_Constants` and `Vt_Constants`. Whereas the last two functions are used to determine the constants, `calcVPath` implements the computation of the variance path as described above. The results are used by the function `calcST`. In order to improve the run-time behaviour we initialise the constants in the function `calcST`. We now consider the algorithm to discretise the paths:

```
// Main loop to generate all the paths
for(long j = minindex_Sims; j <= maxindex_Sims; ++j)
{
    // Start at the log spot each time
    lnS = lnS0;

    // Generate the randoms
    rg.GenerateGaussianVector(W);
    rg.GenerateUniformsVector(UV);

    // Compute variance path due to Andersen algorithm and
    // store it in Vt
    Vt = calcVPath(vInst,vLong,UV,ConstV);

    for(long i = minindex_TimeSteps; i <= maxindex_TimeSteps; i++)
    {
        // Path for the asset as described in Andersen
        lnS = lnS + ConstS[1] + ConstS[2]*Vt[i] + ConstS[3]*Vt[i+1]
            + sqrt(ConstS[4]*Vt[i] + ConstS[5]*Vt[i+1])* W[i];
        result[i + 1] = exp(lnS);
    }

    ST[j] = result;
}

return ST;
```

For the path discretisation we assume that the array Vt[] stores the values of the spot variance for one path. The arrays UV1[] and UV2[] store uncorrelated uniformly distributed variates.

Implementing the variance path

In the C++ implementation below we use a vector of doubles to store the coefficients in the vector Coeff used to compute Ψ. The detailed calculations on how to derive the parameters can be found in Andersen (2006). This is all included in the source code below.

Using Andersen's method it is possible to separate the simulation of the variance from the spot process. To this end we have to supply an array of uniformly distributed random numbers UV1[].

```
for(long i = minindex_TimeSteps; i <= maxindex_TimeSteps; i++)
{
    // E[Vt+Delta]
    m = vLong + (Vt[i] - vLong)*Coeff[1];
    // Var[Vt+Delta]
    s2 = Vt[i]*Coeff[1]*Coeff[2]*Coeff[3]
        + 0.5*vLong*Coeff[2]*Coeff[2]*Coeff[3];

    // Quotient psi=Var[Vt+Delta]/E[Vt+Delta]^2
    Psi = s2 / (m*m);

    // Switching Parameter Psi_C
    if (Psi <= Psi_C)
    {
        // V[t+Delta] approximated as noncentral chi-square
        // with one degree of freedom
        c4 = 2.0 / Psi;
        b2 = max(c4 - 1.0 + sqrt(c4*(c4 - 1.0)),0.0);
        a = m / (1.0 + b2);

        GV = (sqrt(b2) + InverseCumulativeNormal(UV[i]));
        Vt[i+1] = a*(GV*GV);                            // step c
    }
    else
    {
        // Approximation Density with Dirac mass and exponential tail
        p = (Psi - 1.0) / (Psi + 1.0);
        beta = (1-p) / m;
        //  eq. (25)
        if (UV[i] <= p)
            Vt[i+1] = 0.0;
        else
            Vt[i+1] = log((1.0 - p) / (1.0 - UV[i])) / beta;
    }
}
return Vt;
```

A refined method to simulate the variance path is discussed in section 16.11.

Implementing the spot price path

We assume that the variance path is stored in the vector Vt and the constants $K_0, K_1, \ldots, K_4$ are stored in $Par[]$. Then the implementation of the scheme in C++ code is

```
for(int i = 1; minindex_TimeSteps < maxindex_TimeSteps; ++i)
{
    normal = InverseCumulativeNormal(Z[i]);
    lnS = lnS + Par[1] + Par[2]*Vt[i] + Par[3]*Vt[i+1]
    +sqrt(Par[4]*Vt[i] + Par[5]*Vt[i+1])*normal;
    Spot.push_back(exp(lnS));
}
```

The vector $Spot$ stores the discrete spot price process. This vector can be supplied to a certain $PayOff$ operator to compute the price of a derivative.

Further improvements

In Andersen (2006) several improvements on the QE scheme are suggested:

- martingale correction;
- refinement for small values of the variance process;
- time-dependent parameters;
- displacement.

It is possible to extend the QE scheme in a straightforward way. We consider only the martingale correction in this section. To this end, we can replace the constant K_0 in equation (16.11), for example for $M < \infty$, by

$$K_0^* = -\log(M) - (K_1 + 0.5K_3)\, V_n \qquad (16.12)$$

The constant M can be computed explicitly and we have in the first case, namely $\Psi \leq \Psi_c$:

$$M = \frac{\exp\left(\frac{Ab^2 a}{1 - 2Aa}\right)}{\sqrt{1 - 2Aa}}, \quad A < 1/2a$$

For the second case it is given by

$$M = p + \frac{\beta(1 - p)}{\beta - A}, \quad A < \beta$$

where

$$A = K_2 + 0.5K_4 = \frac{\rho}{\omega}(1 + \kappa\gamma_2\Delta) - 0.5\gamma_2\Delta\rho^2$$

as outlined above. The martingale correction approach imposes a restriction on the discretisation in terms of the correlation and the volatility of variance. For negative correlation there is no restriction but if $\rho > 0$ then we have to guarantee that

$$\Delta < \frac{2}{\rho\omega}$$

Let $f(\rho, \omega) = \frac{2}{\rho\omega}$ be the upper bound. The function is monotone in ρ and ω, $f(\rho, \omega_1) > f(\rho, \omega_2)$ for $\omega_1 < \omega_2$ for fixed ρ and $f(\rho_1, \omega) > f(\rho_2, \omega)$ for $\rho_1 < \rho_2$ for fixed ω. The value at $\rho = 0.999$ and $\omega = 200\%$ is greater than 1 and we recommend that Δ be less than 1. Therefore, for practical problems this is not a serious restriction.

16.3.5 A biased-free scheme

Broadie and Kaya (2006) introduced a bias free simulation scheme for the Heston dynamics. They describe the algorithm used to derive the biased-free scheme. To obtain the next spot value S_{n+1} given S_n they start by simulating V_{n+1} given V_n. This can be done using sampling from a Gamma distribution as discussed in Chapter 3. The logarithmic spot price $X_{n+1} = \ln(S_{n+1})$ can be written as

$$X_{n+1} = X_n + \frac{\rho}{\xi}(V_{n+1} - V_n - \kappa\theta\Delta_n)$$

$$+ \left(\frac{\kappa\rho}{\xi} - 0.5\right)\int_{t_n}^{t_{n+1}} V(u)du + \sqrt{1 - \rho^2}\int_{t_n}^{t_{n+1}} \sqrt{V(u)}dW(u)$$

Thus, we have to draw a sample conditionally on V_{n+1} and V_n from the random variable

$$\int_{t_n}^{t_{n+1}} V(u)du \tag{16.13}$$

Broadie and Kaya (2006) show that this can be done because the inverse becomes numerically available by computing the characteristic function of the distribution first. This calculation is very time-consuming and complex because it involves Bessel functions. Such special functions are implemented in the Boost library. Therefore, we do not discuss them here. Finally, the method proposed by Andersen (2006) leads to excellent results and should be the method of choice for real life problems in our experience.

16.4   THE BATES/SVJ MODEL

The *Bates model* has become popular for fitting the implied volatilities known as the stochastic volatility jump (SVJ) model or Heston model with jumps (HSVJ). Although there is a reasonable fit to market parameters for the Heston model to the skew of long-term options, there is a poor fit to short-term options. This gap is filled by the Bates model. While preserving the reasonable fit to mid- and long-term options, it provides additional parameters by introducing a jump component to fit the short-term skew. The governing equations for this model are

$$dS(t) = (r - q)S(t)dt + \sqrt{V(t)}S(t)dW_1(t) + jS(t)dJ \tag{16.14}$$
$$S(0) = S_0$$
$$dV(t) = \kappa(\theta - V(t))dt + \xi\sqrt{V(t)}dW_2(t)$$
$$V(0) = V_0$$

where $W_1(t)$ and $W_2(t)$ are correlated Brownian motions with correlation coefficient ρ, which are independent of the jump component J that is a Poisson process with intensity λ. The coefficient j of the jump component is Gaussian with mean μ_J and volatility σ_J.

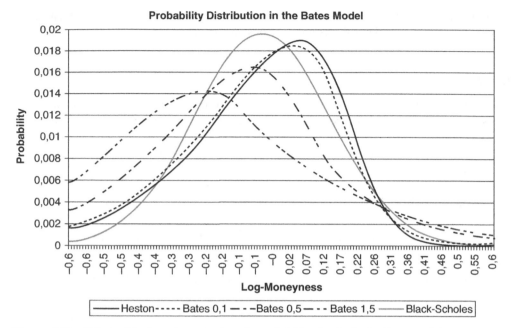

Figure 16.7 Effect of the jump intensity λ on the probability density in the Bates model

Characteristic function

The characteristic function for the Bates model is well known. We give the formula here. We refer to Cont and Tankov (2004) and Schontens (2003). We denote by θ_{Heston} the characteristic function of the Heston model given by equation (16.3), then

$$\theta_{Bates}(u) = \theta_{Heston}\exp(-\lambda\mu_J iut + \lambda t((1+\mu_J)^{iu}\exp(v_J^2(iu/2)(iu-1))-1)) \qquad (16.15)$$

with d and g as defined after equation (16.3). We note that the jump component is independent of the diffusion part.

Distribution

We now use the same techniques that we applied previously to produce Figures 16.3, 16.4 and 16.5. Since we know from the Heston model how stochastic volatility reshapes the probability distribution we study the effect of introducing log normally distributed jumps with a given intensity $\lambda > 0$. Figure 16.7 shows the effect of increasing the jump intensity by keeping the correlation parameter fixed. In our model we have chosen the same parameters as we used for computing the distribution in the Heston model.

Paths

So far there are no new facts concerning the paths. Stochastic volatility suggests that there are volatile and less volatile periods causing small movements whereas the jump part allows for sudden big moves in the underlying.

16.5   IMPLEMENTING THE BATES MODEL

To simulate spot prices using the Bates stochastic volatility model we only have to modify the source code slightly. Since the jumps are independent from the diffusion part and distributed due to the normal distribution, we generate another set of independent random numbers and transform them to fit the distribution. We add the variable J[i] to the spot price path. This vector stores all the jumps. To compute the diffusion component we store the normal variates into the vector N. The source code is

```
class MCJumps
{
public:
    MCJumps();
    MCJumps(double intensity, long Path, double Mue, double Sigma);
    virtual ~MCJumps();

    // generates vector of gaussian jumps
    template<typename RanGen>
    Vector<double> GenerateJumpVector(RanGen& ran)
    {// Generates a vector of jumps

        // The following vectors store the Jumps, Gaussians,
        Poissonians
        Vector<double> J(path),N(path),P(path);
        // Generate the variates
        ran.GenerateGaussianVector(N);          // Gaussian
        ran.GeneratePoissonianVector(P,ji);     // Poissonian

        // compute parameters for the jump height
        double mu = exp(mue + 0.5 * sigma * sigma);

        // Main loop to construct all jumps for the path
        // assumes that J, P and N start with index 1
        for(long i = 1;i <= path;i++)
        {
            // jumps + drift martingale correction
            J[i]= P[i]*mue + sqrt(P[i])*sigma*N[i] - ji * (mu-1.0);
        }
    // Return the jump vector which is used to add to log spot path,
    // resp. mult to exp spot path as well as the drift correction for
    // S(t) exp(-rt) being a martingale
    return J;
    };

private:

    double ji;              // intensity of jumps
    double mue;             // mean of jump height
    double sigma;           // vol of jump height
    long path;              // number of simulated paths
};
```

We use the log spot prices for simulation and we transform the jump component to fit into this setting. To this end we define the variable muehat as the adjusted drift coming from the Ito formula.

If we use the QE scheme we have to modify the for loop that computes the path

```
for(int i = minindex_TimeSteps; i <= maxindex_TimeSteps-1; i++)
{
    // Path for the asset as described in Andersen
    lnS = lnS + ConstS[1] + ConstS[2]*Vt[i] + ConstS[3]*Vt[i+1]
    + sqrt(ConstS[4]*Vt[i] + ConstS[5]*Vt[i+1])*Z[i] + M[i];
    result[i + 1] = exp(lnS);
}
```

16.6   NUMERICAL RESULTS – EUROPEAN OPTIONS

We compare the results obtained in Andersen (2006) with our implementation of the moment-matched fully truncated Euler scheme as well as for the QE scheme. The test cases are for call options with strikes of $K = 70, 100, 140$ starting with a spot price of 100. For the parameters governing the dynamics we use the test data as shown in Table 16.1.

We show our results obtained using five batches of 10 000 paths and grouped by strikes and scenarios. We can compute the true values of the call options corresponding to the test data using an analytic approach. We give only the differences to these prices in the tables. What is striking here is that the QE scheme performs very well even though we only use a small number of steps per year. For the fully-truncated Euler scheme more steps are necessary to achieve a reasonable accuracy. We give a more detailed study in Chapter 26. We display the results in Tables 16.2, 16.3 and 16.4. The first six rows of each table correspond to results using case I, the next six rows correspond to case II and the final six rows to case III. We denote the standard error by SE. The columns QE and $Euler Full$ display the differences to the true price computed using analytic methods.

Furthermore, we compare the results for a simple European call option and increase the number of steps in our simulation. As Table 16.5 shows the quadratic exponential scheme is relatively stable compared to the full truncation Euler scheme. The true price of the option is 5.35434.

We have done the simulation using the following parameter values: Spot = 100.0; Strike = 100.0; $t = 1.0$; $r = 0.03$; $d = 0.01$; $v(0) = 0.04$; $\theta = 0.04$; $\kappa = 0.05$; $\xi = 1.0$; $\rho = -0.9$.

Table 16.1   The examples from Andersen (2006)

	I	II	III
ξ	1	0.9	1
κ	0.5	0.3	1
ρ	−0.9	−0.5	−0.3
T	10	15	5
$V(0)$	4%	4%	9%
θ	4%	4%	9%

Table 16.2   The results for the test cases I to III and Strike = 70

Time steps	QE	SE	Euler full	SE
1	0.0260658	(0.692569)	−3.17729	(0.72654)
2	0.104827	(0.686872)	−1.56152	(0.696159)
4	−0.521861	(0.741056)	−0.646024	(0.707724)
8	−0.0500741	(0.694877)	−0.341575	(0.744465)
16	0.134978	(0.686067)	−0.217834	(0.682599)
32	−0.271988	(0.69747)	0.0539583	(0.759816)
1	−0.013712	(0.604026)	−15.4631	(5.81792)
2	0.191436	(0.72951)	−5.5326	(1.06793)
4	−0.117558	(0.767105)	−2.64978	(0.722577)
8	0.0970971	(0.629013)	−0.618488	(0.664083)
16	0.24357	(0.644605)	−0.453732	(0.650832)
32	0.0400869	(0.655435)	−0.0993747	(0.680933)
1	−2.57027	(0.343113)	−5.44669	(0.437359)
2	−0.710039	(0.33821)	−2.89958	(0.384868)
4	0.0671876	(0.33223)	−1.76769	(0.359305)
8	−0.0609763	(0.329411)	−0.916866	(0.345549)
16	0.0347694	(0.329542)	−0.198728	(0.336398)
32	0.0682706	(0.328482)	−0.103169	(0.331796)

Table 16.3   The results for the test cases I to III and Strike = 100

Time steps	QE	SE	Euler full	SE
1	−0.374736	(0.720747)	−3.1346	(0.664519)
2	−0.294377	(0.623548)	−1.50563	(0.651705)
4	0.395555	(0.618912)	−0.670923	(0.615726)
8	0.026981	(0.632447)	−0.144313	(0.616313)
16	−0.275493	(0.655438)	0.0918095	(0.608449)
32	0.174139	(0.630929)	0.165923	(0.617793)
1	−0.143511	(0.589091)	−11.1086	(1.16727)
2	0.186815	(0.610419)	−6.57239	(1.12636)
4	0.268384	(0.637384)	−3.47485	(0.840676)
8	0.32104	(0.544485)	−1.8266	(0.630903)
16	0.182928	(0.562601)	−1.17867	(0.746872)
32	−0.202173	(0.59224)	−0.31843	(0.662854)
1	−3.18288	(0.242313)	−6.71078	(0.37793)
2	−1.00728	(0.241315)	−3.59383	(0.287549)
4	−0.246419	(0.23826)	−2.14056	(0.267173)
8	0.0541136	(0.236934)	−1.16917	(0.252384)
16	0.109233	(0.235434)	−0.508286	(0.243889)
32	−0.0619711	(0.236469)	−0.247566	(0.239764)

Table 16.4   The results for the test cases I to III and Strike = 140

Time steps	QE	SE	Euler full	SE
1	0.661916	(0.506584)	−2.10914	(0.539989)
2	0.528979	(0.507656)	−0.963987	(0.531909)
4	0.369094	(0.505979)	−0.458552	(0.560981)
8	0.523991	(0.526057)	−0.0132664	(0.510653)
16	0.199435	(0.543208)	0.0122493	(0.524891)
32	0.141944	(0.560985)	0.0561089	(0.513255)
1	0.913916	(0.522433)	−13.6909	(1.45515)
2	0.331859	(0.502261)	−7.17904	(0.779129)
4	−0.0851152	(0.542684)	−3.84472	(0.722973)
8	0.152607	(0.504037)	−1.91764	(0.523398)
16	0.191281	(0.479129)	−0.447289	(0.497827)
32	0.019449	(0.506735)	−0.398837	(0.60342)
1	−0.731797	(0.0951613)	−5.49049	(0.218302)
2	−0.380662	(0.0929648)	−3.01658	(0.155219)
4	−0.116067	(0.0947084)	−1.76993	(0.128394)
8	−0.0162017	(0.0942304)	−0.876531	(0.11219)
16	0.0411328	(0.0947683)	−0.509647	(0.104334)
32	0.0365452	(0.094452)	−0.144093	(0.097492)

16.7   NUMERICAL RESULTS – SKEW-DEPENDENT OPTIONS

We apply the methods of this chapter to path-dependent options. Options depending heavily on the skew are cliquet and digital options as discussed in Chapter 15.

16.7.1   European options – digital options

We elaborate why we use digital options as one reference for illustrating simulations of the stochastic volatility model. The price of a digital option with strike K can be expressed as the limit of a call spread with strikes K and $K + \epsilon$, $\epsilon > 0$. When ϵ tends to 0 this payoff approaches the payoff for a digital option.

This convergence is shown in Figure 16.8. When the implied Black-Scholes volatility denoted by σ_{BS} is a function of the strike price, the price of a digital option can be computed

Table 16.5   Comparing QE and Euler scheme using different time stepping

Time steps	Value QE	Value Euler
4	5.27059 (0.0457068)	8.8577 (0.0902593)
8	5.31423 (0.044418)	7.9062 (0.0743129)
16	5.34294 (0.0439928)	6.95869 (0.0595646)
32	5.35657 (0.042638)	6.20676 (0.0516817)
64	5.27061 (0.0424444)	5.873664 (0.0468555)
128	5.30467 (0.0435436)	5.60464 (0.0449826)

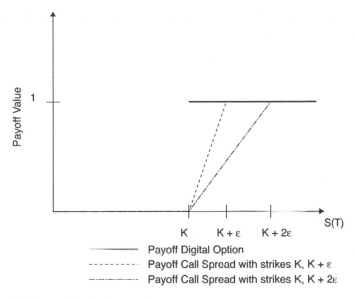

Figure 16.8 Digital payoff and call spreads

as follows (see Gatheral, 2006, p. 104):

$$\text{Digital}(K, T) = -\frac{\partial}{\partial K}\text{Call}(K, T, v_{\text{BS}}(K, T)) \tag{16.16}$$

$$= -\frac{\partial \text{Call}_{\text{BS}}}{\partial K} - \frac{\partial \text{Call}_{\text{BS}}}{\partial v_{BS}}\frac{\partial v_{\text{BS}}}{\partial K} \tag{16.17}$$

For example, using this formula we can study the impact of the volatility skew on pricing digitals. For the numerical example we consider a volatility level of 25% and a skew of 3% per 10%. Then

$$\text{Digital}(1, 1) = \mathcal{N}\left(\frac{-\sigma_{\text{BS}}}{2}\right) - \text{vega} \cdot \text{skew} \approx \mathcal{N}\left(\frac{-\sigma_{\text{BS}}}{2}\right) + 0.12$$

This gives a contribution from the skew of 12% of the price. To this end we will see price differences using models assuming a constant volatility over time and a stochastic volatility model. Table 16.6 gives a numerical example for this test case.

Table 16.6 Pricing a digital using Euler and QE schemes

Volatility of variance	Price QE (SE)
0.5	0.730013 (0.00434455)
0.1	0.827856 (0.00363088)
0.2	0.86577 (0.00321952)

To create our test results we create a new payoff function which is based on the implementation of Chapter 14. The class is given by

```
class PayOff_Digital : public PayOff<double, Vector<double> >
{
public:

    PayOff_Digital();    // Default constructor
    // User constructor
    PayOff_Digital(const SimplePropertySet<string,AnyType*>& pset);

    virtual PayOff<double, Vector<double> >* clone() const;
    virtual double operator()(double Discount, Vector<double>& Spot)
      const;
    virtual double PayOff_Value(double Discount, Vector<double>& Spot,
                                double Strike) const;
    virtual ~PayOff_Digital(){}

    SimplePropertySet<string, AnyType*> PayOff_Digital_Properties;

private:

};
```

We obtain a Monte Carlo price of 0.509782 (0.0049959) using the standard Black-Scholes model and five batches of 10 000 paths for the parameters $r = 3\%$, $d = 1\%$, $T = 1$, $Spot = 100$ and $Strike = 100$. The analytic solution in this case is 0.5096387.

Table 16.6 shows the effect of increasing the influence of the stochastic volatility component by increasing the volatility of variance.

16.7.2 Path-dependent options – cliquet options

We introduced these options in Chapter 15. As an example we consider a locally floored and locally capped cliquet option. Each element has payoff given by

$$\text{Max}\left(\text{Min}\left(R_i, 0\%\right), 10\%\right) \tag{16.18}$$

where R_i is given by equation (15.25). This payoff can be decomposed as follows:

$$\text{Max}\left(\frac{S(t_{n+1})}{S(t_n)}, 0\right) - \text{Max}\left(\frac{S(t_{n+1})}{S(t_n)(1 + x\%)}, 0\right) \tag{16.19}$$

This is a call spread. The calls have different strikes and depend on the difference of the volatility between an option starting at time t_n with strike $S(t_n)$ and $S(t_n) \cdot (1 + x\%)$ expiring at t_{n+1}.

As discussed in Chapter 15 it is easy to incorporate this option into our framework. To test the different numerical schemes and models we only have to supply an STL-vector to the function `Price` of the payoff class. This produces our results. The code for this test can be found on the accompanying CD.

Table 16.7 Pricing a call in Bates model using QE scheme

Jump intensity	Price QE	Time	Analytic price
0.0	6.184526 (0.0145329)	3.651 sec.	6.18535
0.05	6.236656 (0.0159085)	5.813 sec.	6.25175
0.1	6.309792 (0.0172182)	5.803 sec.	6.31821
0.2	6.593279 (0.0194296)	5.850 sec.	6.62973

We vary the jump intensity and we use the Heston model with jumps. The results are summarised in Table 16.7. We have applied the parameters $S(0) = 100.0$, $K = 100.0$, $T = 1.0$, $r = 0.03$, $d = 0.0$, $V(0) = \theta = 0.04$, $\kappa = 0.05$, $\xi = 1.0$ and $\rho = -0.9$.

We have used five batches with 100 000 paths, 12 time steps, jump mean of 1% and jump volatility of 10% to produce the results. We mention that the above time to generate includes the generation of 12 000 000 random numbers, transforming them into normal variates, respectively Poisson distributed variates and calculating the means and standard deviations.

For pricing an arithmetic average cliquet option we have used a local and global floor of 0% and a local cap of 20%. Table 16.8 gives the prices, the standard error and the run-time for different jump intensities.

For generating Table 16.8 we have again applied five batches with 100 000 paths and 12 time steps. The other parameters are the same as for the call option pricing problem.

16.7.3 Results

We now study two types of cliquet options. The first is the usual one and the second is the reverse cliquet option. The payoffs have already been described in Chapter 15, namely equations (15.27) and (15.30). We summarise our findings in Tables 16.9 to 16.14 using the parameter values $S(0) = 100.0$, $K = 100.0$, $T = 1.0$, $r = 0.03$, $d = 0.0$, $V(0) = 0.02$, $\theta = 0.011876$, $\kappa = 1.988937$, $\xi = 0.15$ and $\rho = -0.9$ for the base case. We then vary the parameters as indicated.

16.8 XLL – USING DLL WITHIN MICROSOFT EXCEL

One way to communicate with the Microsoft Excel application is via the COM interface, which we discuss in Chapter 27. Another possibility is to provide new functions by using Microsoft Excel's C Application Protocol Interface or API for short. This way of customising

Table 16.8 Pricing a arithmetic cliquet within Bates model using QE scheme

Jump intensity	Price QE	Time
0.0	0.129962 (0.000420851)	7.25 sec.
0.05	0.130914 (0.000422388)	7.328 sec.
0.1	0.132208 (0.000426606)	7.281 sec.
0.2	0.134641 (0.000430266)	7.344 sec.

Table 16.9 Numerical results for arithmetic cliquet option changing mean reversion and correlation for the Heston model with QE scheme

κ	ρ	(sec.)	QE price (SE)	(sec.)	Euler price (SE)
0.001	−0.9	2.031	0.156131 (0.000597496)	3.25	0.160009 (0.000597307)
0.001	0	2	0.158468 (0.000988489)	3.235	0.15997 (0.000958689)
0.001	0.9	2.015	0.161805 (0.00126515)	3.234	0.160117 (0.00119105)
0.011876	−0.9	2	0.156694 (0.00059701)	3.234	0.15974 (0.000598609)
0.011876	0	2.016	0.15934 (0.000983172)	3.235	0.159773 (0.000955756)
0.011876	0.9	2.016	0.162534 (0.00127331)	3.234	0.159306 (0.00118421)
0.5	−0.9	2.015	0.149957 (0.000535267)	3.234	0.153315 (0.000544823)
0.5	0	2	0.152939 (0.000901358)	3.235	0.153636 (0.000891334)
0.5	0.9	2.016	0.155872 (0.00115664)	3.234	0.153345 (0.00110686)

Table 16.10 Numerical results for arithmetic reverse cliquet option changing mean reversion and correlation for the Heston model with QE scheme

κ	ρ	(sec.)	QE price (SE)	(sec.)	Euler price (SE)
0.001	−0.9	2.016	0.211823 (0.001301)	3.235	0.213884 (0.001254)
0.001	0	2	0.212504 (0.001014)	3.234	0.214338 (0.001026)
0.001	0.9	2.015	0.215673 (0.0006498)	3.25	0.214476 (0.0006987)
0.011876	−0.9	2	0.210952 (0.00129)	3.234	0.213831 (0.001257)
0.011876	0	2	0.213086 (0.0011)	3.235	0.213931 (0.00102)
0.011876	0.9	2.015	0.214806 (0.000648)	3.234	0.214025 (0.0007018)
0.5	−0.9	2.016	0.204131 (0.0011928)	3.234	0.207098 (0.0011719)
0.5	0	2	0.208383 (0.00093709)	3.235	0.208405 (0.00096465)
0.5	0.9	2.016	0.209817 (0.0005922)	3.25	0.207732 (0.0006488)

Table 16.11 Numerical results for simple call option changing mean reversion and correlation for the Heston model with QE scheme

κ	ρ	(sec.)	QE price (SE)	(sec.)	Euler price (SE)
0.001	−0.9	1.843	9.09737 (0.106471)	3.062	9.28424 (0.106993)
0.001	0	1.829	9.99685 (0.0927852)	3.063	10.1186 (0.0935145)
0.001	0.9	1.843	10.6543 (0.0747799)	3.078	10.7243 (0.0774841)
0.011876	−0.9	1.844	9.15635 (0.106527)	3.062	9.3432 (0.107919)
0.011876	0	1.828	10.0022 (0.0920839)	3.063	10.0734 (0.0931741)
0.011876	0.9	1.844	10.6399 (0.0747499)	3.078	10.657 (0.0771962)
0.5	−0.9	1.844	9.06565 (0.102236)	3.063	9.23971 (0.102693)
0.5	0	1.843	9.80916 (0.0898833)	3.078	9.91851 (0.0910149)
0.5	0.9	1.844	10.3651 (0.0739956)	3.062	10.5119 (0.0760904)

Table 16.12 Numerical results for arithmetic cliquet option changing jump intensity and correlation with QE scheme

λ	ρ	sec.	QE price	(SE)
0.05	−0.9	4.875	0.148155	(0.000675145)
0.05	0	4.875	0.15166	(0.00089341)
0.05	0.9	4.86	0.153794	(0.00106087)
0.2	−0.9	4.875	0.176967	(0.0010806)
0.2	0	4.875	0.180457	(0.0012337)
0.2	0.9	4.859	0.182025	(0.00136511)
0.5	−0.9	4.859	0.233275	(0.00159934)
0.5	0	4.859	0.23643	(0.00170526)
0.5	0.9	4.875	0.239405	(0.00179859)

Table 16.13 Numerical results for arithmetic reverse cliquet option changing jump intensity and correlation with QE scheme

λ	ρ	sec.	QE price	SE
0.05	−0.9	4.875	0.194141	(0.00100272)
0.05	0	4.875	0.195828	(0.000792408)
0.05	0.9	4.86	0.198076	(0.000542109)
0.2	−0.9	4.875	0.192568	(0.000988975)
0.2	0	4.859	0.195467	(0.000793299)
0.2	0.9	4.875	0.197581	(0.000545799)
0.5	−0.9	4.875	0.191134	(0.000981629)
0.5	0	4.859	0.194946	(0.000802887)
0.5	0.9	4.875	0.195996	(0.00055315)

Table 16.14 Numerical results for simple call option changing jump intensity and correlation with QE scheme

λ	ρ	sec.	QE price	SE
0.05	−0.9	4.704	8.7526	(0.0927544)
0.05	0	4.703	9.27346	(0.0850966)
0.05	0.9	4.687	9.46051	(0.0744255)
0.2	−0.9	4.703	7.95751	(0.0910535)
0.2	0	4.703	8.38208	(0.084025)
0.2	0.9	4.704	8.70472	(0.0759486)
0.5	−0.9	4.687	6.69793	(0.0879808)
0.5	0	4.703	7.03331	(0.0824504)
0.5	0.9	4.703	7.16768	(0.0756566)

Excel is well understood and has not changed very much up to version 2007. Many people use this API for adding extra functionality to Excel. One can use this interface in its basic form but there are many wrappers available for Excel's API. The framework *XLW* started with the work of Jerome Lécomte. At the time of writing, Mark Joshi distributed version 2.1 and Eric Ehlers in the meantime has released version 3.0. Functions created with XLW are distributed as *xll* files.

16.8.1 What is an xll?

An xll is an extended version of a dll that is designed to work with Microsoft Excel. As dlls, they contain executable code but xlls are not executables themselves. We need an application that calls the executable code.

Excel provides an interface to do so. This interface is the *Function Wizard*. Therefore, a dll having facilities to use this interface is an xll.

16.8.2 XLW – a framework for creating xll

The XLW framework can be seen as an interface builder for C++ functions in order to become usable in Excel. We do not need any knowledge of Excel's C API. This allows us to concentrate on the implementation of models. The distribution then becomes easy using the XLW framework.

The reader may obtain the latest version at XLW (1997).

16.8.3 Developing using XLW

There are two issues in developing add-ins using `XLW`. First, you have to do coding in C++ to implement your functions, which you then use within the Microsoft Excel application. Second, you have to code the interface.

The interface generator

Joshi (2007) has coded the `Interface Generator` examples and extensions. It is a tool to create C++ code which is needed for implementing the Excel interface. We need to supply working C++ functions in terms of the corresponding *.hpp and *.cpp files from which all the information is taken and created as output for a new piece of code suitable for compiling an xll.

The `Interface Generator` uses the basic data types such as `double` or the STL-vector. The next section gives an example of how to extend the data types to be used with the `Interface Generator`. We add the Datasim Classes `Vector<double>` as well as `NumericMatrix<double>` to the library.

Using custom data types

We distinguish between *basic data types* and *extended data types*. Basic data types are standard C++ data types such as `double` or `int`. User-created C++ classes are called extended data types.

We give an example of how to customise your application by adding the classes `Vector<double>` and `NumericMatrix<double>` to be usable within the library and which in particular can be supplied to the `Interface Generator`.

We consider the following files:

- TypeRegistration.cpp;
- MyContainers.h;
- MyContainers.cpp;
- XlfOper.inl;
- XlfOper.h;
- XlfOper.cp.p

We now describe the modifications for each file:

- Since XLW version 2.1, an interface generator is part of the distribution. If we want to use the interface generator we have to register user-defined types such as our class `Numeric-Matrix`. This is all placed into the following function:

```
TypeRegistry::Helper NumMatReg("NumMatDouble", //  new type
"XlfOper", // old type
"AsNumMatrix", // converter name
true, // is a method
true, // takes identifier
"P" // should be empty unless OldType is XlfOper
);
```

and for the `Vector<double>`:

```
TypeRegistry::Helper VectorDoubleReg(
"VectorD", // new type
"XlfOper", // old type
"AsVectorDouble", // converter name
true, // is a method
true, // takes identifier
"R" // should be empty unless OldType is XlfOper
);
```

- In this header file we define the datastructures we want to use in our Excel wrapper. This can for instance be a matrix class. We have chosen the template class `NumericMatrix` to wrap arrays.

```
typedef NumericMatrix<double> NumMatDouble; typedef
Vector<double> VectorD;
```

and

```
double Element(const NumericMatrix<double>& A, unsigned long i ,
unsigned long j);
```

as well as

```
double& ChangingElement(NumericMatrix<double>& A, unsigned long i ,
unsigned long j);
```

- In this file we have placed the implementation of our wrapper. See the code on the CD for details:

```
double Element(const NumericMatrix<double>& A, unsigned long i ,
unsigned long j)
{ return A(i,j); }
```

and

```
double& ChangingElement(NumericMatrix<double>& A, unsigned
long i , unsigned long j)

{ return A(i,j); }
```

- In this file we implement all inline methods for the class XlfOper INLINE:

```
XlfOper::XlfOper(const NumMatDouble& value)
{
    Allocate();
      Set(value);
}
```

and

```
INLINE XlfOper::XlfOper(const VectorD& value)
{
    Allocate();
    Set(value);
}
```

- This is the header file where the implementation of the class XlfOper is defined. This is the interface to communicate with the Excel application.

    We create our own classes if we want to use them with the interface. Therefore, we have to add the following lines to be able to use the interface with our class NumericMatrix:

```
NumMatDouble AsNumMatrix( int* pxlret=0) const;
// ! Converts to a NumericMatrix<double> with error identifier.
NumMatDouble AsNumMatrix( const string& ErrorId,int* pxlret=0)
                         const;
// ! Converts to a Vector<double>
VectorD AsVectorDouble(DoubleVectorConvPolicy policy =
  UniDimensional, int* pxlret = 0) const;
// ! Converts to a Vector<double> with error identifier.
VectorD AsVectorDouble(const string& ErrorId,
DoubleVectorConvPolicy policy = UniDimensional, int * pxlret = 0)
const;
```

- This is corresponding implementation of the interace XlfOper. For details see the file on the CD.

16.9 ANALYTIC SOLUTIONS FOR AFFINE STOCHASTIC VOLATILITY MODELS

We now give an example to show how to use the framework. We apply it to create pricing functions and sensitivities for European options within an affine stochastic volatility framework. We provide a project on the CD.

We take the implementation of the Heston and Bates stochastic volatility models. The implementation is contained in the following files:

- `Heston.h`
- `Heston.cpp`
- `Bates.h`
- `Bates.cpp`

Of course, you should specify the paths for include and source files so that the compiler is able to locate the necessary files to compile the Heston and Bates code.

In this section we want to describe the interface to Excel.

We call our pricing library *StochasticVolatilityLibrary*. This can be done by adding the line:

```
namespace const char* LibraryName = "StochasticVolatilityLibrary";
```

We now specify the registration information. Arguments receive the names to be displayed by the Excel Function manager together with a short comment for each variable.

```
namespace
{
    // The following function appears in Excel's function wizard
    XLRegistration::Arg
    Heston_PriceArgs[]=
    {
        {"Time", "Time to Maturity"},
        {"Strike", "Strike"},
        {"Spot", "Spot"},
        {"Rate", "Interest Rate"},
        {"Dividend", "Dividend"},
        {"CurrentVariance", "Current Variance"},
        {"LongRunVariance", "Long Term Variance"},
        {"Kappa", "Mean Reversion"},
        {"Rho", "Correlation"},
        {"Omega", "Volatility of Variance"},
        {"Method","Quadrature Scheme: 1 -> GaussLegendre,
                                     2 -> GaussLobatto,
                                     3 -> Adaptive GaussLobatto"},
        {"CallPut","1: Call  2: Put"}
    };

    // The following is an explanation of the function
    // appearing in Excel's function wizard
    XLRegistration::XLFunctionRegistrationHelper
```

```
    registerHeston_Price("xlHeston_Price", "Heston_Price",
    "Evaluates European Calls/Puts within a Heston model",
    LibraryName, Heston_PriceArgs, "RRRRRRRRRRRR"
    );
}
```

All the code has been placed into an unnamed `namespace` to avoid any confusion during the linking phase.

The last line needs explanation. It specifies the data types using a code which is

- R for LPXLOPER by reference
- P for LPXLOPER by value
- B for `double`

In the current distribution of XLW only R and P are used.

Next, since the XLW framework uses the C API, we have to provide the function to be exported with the `extern "C"` statement as a C linkage:

```
extern "C"
{
    // Input from Excel used to convert and put into C++ function
    LPXLOPER EXCEL_EXPORT
    xlHeston_Price(LPXLOPER xlTime_, LPXLOPER xlStrike_,
        LPXLOPER xlSpot_,  LPXLOPER xlRate_,   LPXLOPER xlDividend_,
        LPXLOPER xlvInst_, LPXLOPER xlvLong_, LPXLOPER xlKappa_,
        LPXLOPER xlRho_,   LPXLOPER xlOmega_, LPXLOPER xlMethod_,
        LPXLOPER xlCallPut_)
    {
        EXCEL_BEGIN;

        if (XlfExcel::Instance().IsCalledByFuncWiz())
        return XlfOper(true);

        // Transform XlfOper to standard or custom data types
        // used with the function to compute
        XlfOper xlTime(xlTime_);
        double Time(xlTime.AsDouble("Time"));
        XlfOper xlStrike(xlStrike_);
        double Strike(xlStrike.AsDouble("Strike"));
        XlfOper xlSpot(xlSpot_);
        double Spot(xlSpot.AsDouble("Spot"));
        XlfOper xlRate(xlRate_);
        double Rate(xlRate.AsDouble("Rate"));
        XlfOper xlDividend(xlDividend_);
        double Dividend(xlDividend.AsDouble("Dividend"));
        XlfOper xlvInst(xlvInst_);
        double vInst(xlvInst.AsDouble("vInst"));
        XlfOper xlvLong(xlvLong_);
        double vLong(xlvLong.AsDouble("vLong"));
        XlfOper xlKappa(xlKappa_);
        double Kappa(xlKappa.AsDouble("Kappa"));
        XlfOper xlRho(xlRho_);
```

```
        double Rho(xlRho.AsDouble("Rho"));
        XlfOper xlOmega(xlOmega_);
        double Omega(xlOmega.AsDouble("Omega"));
        XlfOper xlMethod(xlMethod_);
        double Methoda(xlMethod.AsDouble("Methoda"));
        int Method(static_cast<int>(Methoda));
        XlfOper xlCallPut(xlCallPut_);
        double CallPuta(xlCallPut.AsDouble("CallPuta"));
        int CallPut(static_cast<int>(CallPuta));

        // Compute the Price using C++ function
        double result(exp(-(Rate-Dividend)*Time)*
                Heston_Price(CallPut,Time,Strike,Spot,Rate,Dividend,
                             vLong,vInst,Kappa,Rho,Omega,Method));
        return XlfOper(result);

    EXCEL_END
    }
}
```

The code starts with the macro EXCEL_BEGIN which uses the class XlfExcel as follows:

```
#define EXCEL_BEGIN XlfExcel::Instance().FreeMemory();\try\{..}
```

EXCEL_BEGIN initialises the library and frees all memory previously allocated by the framework. Then it attempts to execute the commands following the try statement until EXCEL_END. The latter statement is for error handling.

Another macro which is used in the code above is

```
#define EXCEL_EXPORT __declspec(dllexport)
```

This line of code tells the compiler that the function is to be exported.

To start up Excel and use your own spreadsheet for testing purposes and debugging Visual Studio offers a method to attach arguments on the current projects using the project settings. In our example we start Excel and supply the objects *StochasticVol.xll* and *StochasticVol.xls*. After that we choose the settings for debugging and add the path where Excel is located on the machine as well as the arguments.

16.10   SUMMARY AND CONCLUSIONS

We discussed two state of the art stochastic volatility models, namely the Heston and Bates models. After discussing their mathematical properties we gave a detailed description for implementing the models. The methods can then be applied to price all kinds of options on one underlying. We considered simple call options for benchmarking the algorithm as well as options depending on the volatility skew such as digital and cliquet options. Together with the results in Chapter 23 the reader may build up a whole pricing library for exotic equity and index options.

In the second part of this chapter we described how to use the XLW framework to create add-ins to be used with Microsoft Excel. Such add-ins, called xll, are special types of a simple dll. The first step in the development of an xll is to program the function you want to use in C++. In the second step you use the *interface generator* to create the files to your project which can be compiled into an xll.

We have shown all the steps necessary to cope with putting your own functions to work and use proprietary data types within the XLW framework. Finally, we provided a detailed example for computing prices of European call and put options within the stochastic volatility models proposed by Heston and Bates. Such functionality is then the starting point for an application for pricing and calibration.

16.11   EXERCISES AND PROJECTS

1. (****) Improving the QE Scheme
   Implement the improvement on the standard QE scheme as described in this chapter. The details can be found in Andersen (2006) .

   The improvement is for small values of the variance. It involves changing the second case of the switching rule in the QE scheme. Therefore, the algorithm stays the same if $\Psi \leq \Psi_c$ but differs in the case $\Psi > \Psi_c$.

   Suppose you wish to generate the value $\hat{V}(t + \Delta)$ given $\hat{V}(t)$. We consider the second case of the switching rule. To this end we denote the time step by Δ and replace the inverse given in equation (16.10) by first defining the constants:

   $$n = \frac{4\kappa \exp(-\kappa \Delta)}{\omega^2(1 - \exp(-\kappa \Delta))}$$

   $$k = \frac{\exp(-\kappa \Delta)}{4\kappa}(1 - \exp(-\kappa \Delta))$$

   $$d = 4\kappa\theta\omega^2$$

   $$\lambda = \hat{V}(t)\frac{4\kappa \exp(-\kappa \Delta)}{\omega^2(1 - \exp(-\kappa \Delta))}$$

   $$c = \frac{d + 2\lambda}{d + \lambda}$$

   $$q = \frac{d + \lambda}{d + \lambda} - 1$$

Using this set of definitions we compute

$$k_0 = 2\left(\frac{(q + 1)(3q + 4)}{q + 2}\right)^2$$

$$k_1 = q^2\left(\frac{q + 1}{q + 2} - 2\frac{(q + 1)(3q + 4)}{(q + 2)^2}\right) - 4(q + 1)(q + 2)$$

$$k_2 = \frac{2q^2}{(q + 3)(q + 2)^2}$$

And finally

$$y = \frac{-k_1 - \sqrt{k_1^2 - 4k_2k_0}}{2k_2}$$

$$c_1 = (1 - y)(q + 1)(-q)^{-(q+1)}$$

$$\beta = \left(\left(2q + 2 - \frac{c_1}{q+2}(-q)^{q+2}\right) y^{-1} + q\right)^{-1}$$

$$c_2 = y\beta \exp(-\beta q)$$

In the refined version of the algorithm random number generation is realised as follows:

$$H^{-1}(u) = \begin{cases} \dfrac{(q+1)u^{1/(q+q)}}{c_1}, & 0 \le u \le u_c \\[2mm] -\beta^{-1} \log\left(\exp(\beta q) - \frac{u-u_c}{c_2}\right), & u_c < u < 1 \end{cases}$$

with $u_c = \frac{c_1}{q+1}(-q)^{q+1}$

2. (***) Martingale Correction

   Implement the martingale correction method as described in section 16.3.4. Compare the results of the original QE scheme with the martingale corrected version.

3. (**) Options

   Study other volatility-dependent options. A good example is a digital cliquet option. Digital cliquet options with yearly reset pay an amount of money, for example 1 or $S(t_n) - S(t_{n-1})$ if the performance, $\frac{S(t_n)}{S(t_{n-1})}$, is bigger than 1. We therefore consider the payoff $1_{\{S(t_{n+1})>S(t_n)\}}$, respectively $(S(t_{n+1}) - S(t_n)) \cdot 1_{\{S(t_{n+1})>S(t_n)\}}$.

4. (**) Moment-Matched Euler Scheme

   The moment-matched Euler scheme uses the following discretisation of the variance:

$$v_{n+1} = v_n + \kappa(\theta - v_n)\Delta_n + \xi v_n^+ \sqrt{\frac{1 - \exp(-2\kappa\Delta_n)}{2\kappa}} \sqrt{\Delta_n} Z_n \tag{16.20}$$

   Account for the moment-matched version of the Euler scheme by implementing this scheme into the Monte Carlo simulation framework and compare the results to the simple Euler, the fully truncated Euler and the QE scheme.

5. (****) Monte Carlo and XLW

   We have set up several methods for applying the Monte Carlo method. We wish to make the method available in Excel. To this end we use the XLW framework. There are a number of steps to achieve this:

   – Think about the Excel interface. What are the input parameters? Necessary inputs are the numbers of simulations or the seed of the random number generator. Do you wish to make the model or the scheme a parameter?

   – Do you need data structures that must be made available to the XLW framework? If this is the case we have to set them up in the declaration files.

   – Make sure your C++ code compiles. Then, use the *interface generator* to create an interface.

   – Edit the generated file. For example, you may wish to display more information when the user invokes the function using Excel's function manager.

   – The final step is to test the new functionality using your function for Monte Carlo simulation.

6. (***) Boost and XLW

   Take a new class not currently available within the XLW framework: for example, some of the Boost classes for statistical distributions, multi-array or special functions. Make the class known to the XLW framework by following the steps used to handle the `NumericMatrix` class. Use the *interface generator* to create your add-in. You can use the code from the CD corresponding to Chapters 4 and 13. Use the add-in to display convergence tables or compute the prices using different parameter settings.

17

Multi-Asset Options

17.1 INTRODUCTION AND OBJECTIVES

The Monte Carlo method is the method of choice for multi-dimensional problems. For high dimensional problems finite difference methods or trees become unmanageable from a computational point of view. The old rule of thumb 'if the dimension of the underlying problem is greater than 3 then use Monte Carlo' describes the way of thinking.

Financial applications – for example, basket option modelling – may involve many underlying assets. To this end we start this chapter by introducing derivatives depending on more than one underlying. We define spread options and quanto options. Such options are popular, for instance options on equity baskets. We are able to benchmark our implementation since there exist analytic approximation formulae.

The data structure is very important for the implementation of multi-asset models. On the one hand it could be designed to be very flexible, allowing for parameter lists that are initialised at run-time, and on the other hand the data could be hard coded, for example a Vector<double> that stores the volatilities. To combine flexibility with stability we have chosen to model member data as property sets.

We discuss a range of options in detail and we give several examples on how to code them using our instrument hierarchy developed in Chapter 14. Thus, the main objective of this chapter is to introduce types of options involving risk from several risk factors and their implementation in C++. We give numerical results and supply several figures to illustrate characteristics of the option worked out using our Monte Carlo framework.

17.2 MODELLING IN MULTIPLE DIMENSIONS

First, we model multi-asset options in a Black-Scholes framework in order to be able to benchmark our implementation with analytic approximation formulae. We later consider more complex models including stochastic volatilities and stochastic rates.

For the multi-asset Black-Scholes model, we consider d correlated Brownian motions $W_i(t), i = 1, \ldots, d$ for the d underlying assets with spot prices $S_i(t)$ and constant volatilities σ_i, dividend yields d_i and correlations $(\rho_{ij})_{1 \leq i, j \leq d}$. The constant risk-free rate is assumed to be r. In the basic setting the rate is the same for all assets because we assume the assets trade in the same market. Later, when we consider quanto options, the risk-free rate differs since the asset trades in another market. The SDE is given by

$$\begin{cases} dS_i(t) = (r - d_i)S_i(t)dt + \sigma_i S_i(t)dW_i(t), \\ S_i(0) = s_i \end{cases}, \quad 1 \leq i \leq d \tag{17.1}$$

For options on multiple assets there are closed form pricing formulae available and for other option types we can use approximation formulae.

A rule of thumb is to use Monte Carlo valuation for options depending on more than three assets. If we consider path-dependent options it might be the only applicable method.

In order to gain an intuition for the influence of correlation we consider a basket option and a min/max option. For these options we give the modelling in C++ in sections 17.5 and 17.6. The payoff for the first type of option is determined by two risk factors. Increasing the dispersion of the individual assets leads to higher prices since the chance of any asset reaching high values gets bigger. This effect increases with declining correlation. The payoff of a basket option is determined by a weighted sum of the basket components. The influence of dispersion is marginal. The correlation of the assets effects the overall volatility of the basket and thus is one of the main drivers for the price. We mainly observe two impacts of dependencies among the individual assets:

- The influence of correlation on the volatility of a basket option.
- The influence of correlation on the dispersion of individual assets of a basket.

These factors influence the hedging positions in the corresponding options. The reader can use our code to examine the effects and their influence on hedging portfolios respectively.

First, we have to set up a model to support multiple dimensions. For example, we model a multi-dimensional Black-Scholes set-up, (17.1), as

```cpp
class MCBlackScholesMulti : public NFactorModel
{
public:
    MCBlackScholesMulti();
    MCBlackScholesMulti(Vector<double> r, Vector<double> d,
                        Vector<double> sigma, NumericMatrix<double>
                        Corr, double Maturity, Vector<double> Spot);
    virtual  MCBlackScholesMulti();

    // Get functions
    Vector<double> getdrift() const;
    Vector<double> getvol() const;
    NumericMatrix<double> getcorr() const;
    Vector<double> getdividend() const;
    Vector<double> getmartcorrection() const;
    double getmaturity() const;
    Vector<double> getspot() const;
    int getfactors() const;


private:
    Vector<double> drift;        // Vector of Drifts
    Vector<double> vol;          // Vector of Volatilities
    NumericMatrix<double> corr;  // Correlation Matrix
    Vector<double> martcorrection; // Martingale Correction
    Vector<double> dividend;     // Vector of Dividends
    double maturity;             // Maturity
    Vector<double> spot;         // Vector of Spot Prices
    int factors;                 // Number of Factors
};
```

We define the vector for the multiple spots that represent the outcome of the simulation `Vector<NumericMatrix<double> > ST(Path)`. Furthermore, we need an object holding the Gaussians for each simulation step. This is realised by defining the object `Numer-icMatrix<double> W(Factors, Steps)`. Before starting the algorithm we compute constants:

```
// Precalculate the drift and diffusion constants
Vector<double> sigmasigma(sigma.Size());
for(int i =sigma.MinIndex(); i <= sigma.MaxIndex(); i++)
        sigmasigma[i] = sigma[i] * sigma[i];
Vector<double> rdh = (r-d-0.5* sigmasigma)*h;
Vector<double> sdh = sigma * sqrt(h);
```

Then, the algorithm for the multi-dimensional exact solution is given by

```
for(int i = minindex_Sims; i<= maxindex_Sims; i++)
{
    lnSt= S0;
    rg.GenerateCorrelatedGaussian(W,Corr);

    for(int j = minindex_Factors; j <=maxindex_Factors; j++)
    {
        for(int k - minindex_TimeSteps; k <- maxindex_TimeSteps; k++)
        {
            lnSt[j] += rdh[j] + sdh[j] * W(j,k);
            result(j,k+1) = exp(lnSt[j]);
        }
    }
    ST[i] = result;
}
```

We can apply other models and more sophisticated discretisation schemes such as the predictor-corrector method. We discuss other models in Chapter 20. In the following we give a test program to modelling the multi-dimensional case:

```
int main()
{
    // Define the Property Set to use
    SimplePropertySet<string, AnyType*> mc_myset_multi;
    // Used to define the propertyset for the payoff

    static Wrapper<double> Strike = 10.0_;
    static Wrapper<std::string> PayOffType = "call";
    static Wrapper<std::string> Type = "max";

    Vector<double> weights_(5);
    for(long i=weights_.MinIndex(); i<=weights_.MaxIndex(); i++)
        weights_[i] = 1.0;

    static Wrapper<Vector<double>> Weights = weights_;

    mc_myset_multi.add("Strike", &Strike);         // add properties
    mc_myset_multi.add("PayOffType", &PayOffType); // add properties
    mc_myset_multi.add("Weights", &Weights);       // add properties
```

```
mc_myset_multi.add("MinMax",&Type);          // add properties

// Specify the name of payoff used for registration with the
factory string mc_name_multi = "minmax";

// Create a pointer to the payoff for Multi Factor
PayOff<double, NumericMatrix<double> >* minmaxptr =
PayOffFactory<double, NumericMatrix<double> >::
                Instance().CreatePayOff(mc_name_multi,
                mc_myset_multi);

// Define the parameters for your assets and for the option
double Maturity = 2.0;

Vector<double> Spot(5);
Spot[1]=10.0; Spot[2]=10.0; Spot[3]=10.0; Spot[4]=10.0;
Spot[5]=10.0;

Vector<double> r(5);
r[1]=0.03; r[2]=0.03;r[3]=0.03;r[4]=0.03;r[5]=0.03;

Vector<double> d(5);
d[1]=0.0;d[2]=0.0;d[3]=0.0;d[4]=0.0;d[5]=0.0;

Vector<double> sigma(5);
sigma[1]=0.3303; sigma[2]=0.3126; sigma[3]=0.3212;sigma[4]=0.269;
sigma[5]=0.2648;

NumericMatrix<double> corr(5,5);
corr(1,1)=1;        corr(1,2)=0.4417; corr(1,3)=0.4307;
corr(1,4)=0.4366; corr(1,5)=0.4524;
corr(2,1)=0.4417; corr(2,2)=1;        corr(2,3)=0.3549;
corr(2,4)=0.3922; corr(2,5)=0.4051;
corr(3,1)=0.4307; corr(3,2)=0.3549; corr(3,3)=1;
corr(3,4)=0.3586; corr(3,5)=0.3999;
corr(4,1)=0.4366; corr(4,2)=0.3922; corr(4,3)=0.3586;
corr(4,4)=1;        corr(4,5)=0.4713;
corr(5,1)=0.4524; corr(5,2)=0.4051; corr(5,3)=0.3999;
corr(5,4)=0.4713; corr(5,5)=1;


// Define the Timer
DatasimClock myclock;

// Define the model
MCBlackScholesMulti MCBS(r, d, sigma, corr, Maturity, Spot);

// Define the scheme
MCExactGeoBrownianMulti<RandGen<MersenneTwister>,
MCBlackScholesMulti> MCE;
```

```
// Define the Monte Carlo object
MCMonteCarlo<Vector<NumericMatrix<double>>> mc;

// Define the path
Vector<NumericMatrix<double>> mc_path_multi;

// The variable for outputting mean and standard deviation
Vector<double> mcvalue(2);
mcvalue[1] = 0.0; mcvalue[2] = 0.0;

int NoOfBatches = 10;        // Batches
long NoOfPaths = 100;        // Paths per batch
long Timesteps = 1;          // Number of grid points
unsigned long Seed = 123456; // The Seed

RandGen<MersenneTwister> rangen(Seed);

myclock.start();    // Start
// The main Monte Carlo engine
for(int i = 1; i <= NoOfBatches; i++)
{
    mc_path_multi = MCE.calcST(rangen,
                            MCBS,NoOfPaths,5,Timesteps);
    mc.setpath(mc_path_multi);
    mc.mcprice2(1.0,minmaxptr,mcvalue);
}
myclock.stop(); // Stop

// Output
cout << "PV: " << exp(-r[1]*Maturity)*mcvalue[1] / NoOfBatches;
cout << " SE: " << mcvalue[2] / NoOfBatches << endl;
cout << "Time: " << myclock.duration()<< endl;
delete minmaxptr
return 0;
}
```

17.3 IMPLEMENTING PAYOFF CLASSES FOR MULTI-ASSET OPTIONS

We proceed in the same way as we have done for payoffs for European options on a single underlying. We put the necessary information to be used with multi-asset options into the property set.

At this stage we give more details on the usage of property sets, in particular for heterogeneous property sets.

Consider a basket option. At compile-time we do not know the number of underlying assets nor do we know the weights of the assets in the basket. Thus, we provide this data at run-time when we initialise the option. A general PayOff used together with a vector will be initialised at run-time. But that is not what we want here. We use the template class PropertySet with heterogeneous data. Using this setting we provide a Vector<double> weights and we then compute the baskets's value at maturity. Thus, the payoff class does not need any data from the option; it is simply a rule to compute prices at maturity. This is exactly what we want the class `PayOff` to do. We do not want to care about additional member data when we implement a payoff and we therefore place everything in the underlying class `PropertySet`.

The following sections give detailed examples on how to set up multi-asset options and how they fit into the framework.

17.4   SOME MULTI-ASSET OPTIONS

We model several multi-asset options in this chapter and give analytical approximation formulae if applicable. We begin with spread options and quantos. The latter options usually have two underlyings. Problems with more than two underlyings are studied for min/max, basket and mountain range options.

17.4.1   Spread options

Spread options were introduced in Chapter 5. They are a special case of a basket option. The basket consists of two shares S_1 and S_2 and weights $\omega_1 = 1$ and $\omega_2 = -1$. Spread options are a very important class of options. They are used to trade flattening and steepening of the yield curve. For example, we consider swaps where one leg pays coupons corresponding to the difference between the 10 year and the 2 year swap rate, that is $CMS_{10year} - CMS_{2year}$.

Furthermore, these options are very common in foreign exchange and commodities. For example, in the energy market the *crack spread* is a product traded on the New York Mercantile Exchange. It is the spread between heating oil and crude oil futures.

Two special cases of the spread option are the simple call option and the exchange option.

17.4.2   Approximation formulae

Approximation formulae for pricing spread options are given in Bjerksund and Stensland (2006). They state the well-known Kirk approximation formula often used by practitioners. We give details on how to implement it in C++ below. The implementation is based on Haug (2007).

Kirk approximation

The approximative price of the spread option is given by

$$\text{Spreadprice} = (S_2 + K)\left(e^{-rt}S_{Adj}\mathcal{N}(d_1) - K\mathcal{N}(d_2)\right) \tag{17.2}$$

with

$$S_{Adj} = \frac{S_1}{S_2 + K}$$

and corresponding volatility

$$\sigma_{Spread} = \sigma_1^2 + \left(\sigma_2 \frac{S_2}{(S_2 + K)}\right)^2 - 2\rho\sigma_1\sigma_2 \frac{S_2}{(S_2 + K)}$$

with

$$d_1 = \frac{\ln(S_{Adj}) + \frac{\sigma^2}{2}T}{\sigma\sqrt{T}} \text{ and } d_2 = d_1 - \sigma_{Spread}\sqrt{T}$$

The C++ code is:

```
double F1, F2;
F1 = Spot1 * exp(r * Mat);
F2 = Spot2 * exp(r * Mat);

double sigma_kirk = sqrt(sigma1*sigma1-2*F2/(F2+Strike)
                         *rho*sigma1*sigma2
                         + F2*F2/((F2+Strike)*(F2+Strike)) * sigma2 *
                         sigma2);

result = BlackScholesFormula("c", F1/(F2+Strike), Strike, Mat,
                             0, 0 ,sigma_kirk);

if(payofftype == "put")
{
    result = result - (F1-F2-Strike) * exp(-r * Mat);
}
```

We are now in a position to cross-check our Monte Carlo results obtained in a geometric Brownian motion setting with the results produced by the approximate solution 17.2. To this end we have to implement the payoff and register it with the factory. The payoff is represented by the class

```
class PayOff_Spread : public PayOff<double, NumericMatrix<double>>
{
public:

    PayOff_Spread();  // Default constructor
    // User constructor
    PayOff_Spread(const SimplePropertySet<string,AnyType*>& pset);

    virtual PayOff<double, NumericMatrix<double> >* clone() const;
    virtual double operator()(double Discount,
                              NumericMatrix<double>& Spot) const;
    virtual double PayOff_Value(double Discount,
                                NumericMatrix<double>& Spot,
                                double Strike) const;
    virtual  PayOff_Spread(){}

    SimplePropertySet<string, AnyType*> PayOff_Spread_Properties;

private:
    // No private data

};
```

Table 17.1 Numerical results for spread option pricing using Monte Carlo and antithetic sampling

	I	II	III
Type	call	put	call
Spot 1	101.5	101.5	102
Spot 2	100.0	100.0	99
r	3%	3%	3%
σ_1	20%	20%	20%
σ_2	16%	16%	16%
$d\,1$	0%	0%	1%
$d\,2$	0%	0%	2%
ρ	-0.9	-0.9	0.5
Strike	0.5	0.5	1.0
Approx. Price	14.553	13.5382	8.8295
MC Price	14.6128 (0.070453)	13.4482 (0.0644618)	8.8402 (0.0404852)
MC Price (Anti)	14.5451 (0.0496918)	13.5353 (0.0457415)	8.83034 (0.028615)

The following code is for registering the payoff to the unnamed namespace of the file PayoffRegistration.cpp:

```
PayOffConstructor<double, NumericMatrix<double>, PayOff_Spread>
RegisterSpread("spread");
```

Let us state some numerical results for the spread option case. We have applied our framework to pricing spread options using 10 000 paths and with antithetic sampling. The results are summarised in Table 17.1.

Other examples can be studied using our analytical approximation for spread options. The reader may wish to apply other models for the asset price dynamics to price spread options.

17.4.3   Quanto options

Quanto options serve as a good test case because an analytical solution using the Black-Scholes framework is available. Assume a European bank acquires a European call option on a share quoted in a foreign currency, for example in dollars ($). The bank does not want any exposure in $. The premium of the option should be paid in the domestic currency, for example euro (€). The value of the option should furthermore not be exposed to the exchange rate dollar against euro ((FX) $/€). This contract is known as a *Quanto option*. We have the following two factor model:

$$\frac{dS(t)}{S(t)} = r_f dt + \sigma_S dW_1(t) \tag{17.3}$$

$$S(0) = s_0$$

$$\frac{dF(t)}{F(t)} = r_d dt + \sigma_F dW_2(t)$$

$$F(0) = f_0 \tag{17.4}$$

with correlated Brownian motion (W_1, W_2). The drift is determined by r_d (the domestic currency rate) and r_f (the foreign currency rate). The volatility of the exchange rate is denoted by σ_F. The price process starts at the spot s_0 and with an initial exchange rate of f_0. Thus, we simulate two risk factors and then take the payoff:

$$F(T)(S(T) - K) \tag{17.5}$$

The analytical solution to the problem, the so-called *quanto adjustment*, can be directly applied via a Black-Scholes type formula. First, we have to derive the inputs d_1 and d_2 supplied to the cumulative normal distribution function. The C++ code is

```
double d1 = (log(Spot / Strike)
          + (r_f - d - rho * sigma * sigma_fx
          + sigma*sigma / 2.0) * T) / (sigma * sqrt(Mat));
double d2 = d1 - sigma * sqrt(Mat);

if(payofftype == "call")
    result = rate_fx * (Spot * exp((r_f - r_d - d - rho * sigma *
        sigma_fx) * Mat)
    * CumulativeNormal(d1) - Strike * exp(-r_d * Mat) *
        CumulativeNormal(d2));
else
    result = rate_fx * (Strike * exp(-r_d * Mat) *
        CumulativeNormal(-d2) - Spot
    * exp((r_f - r_d - d - rho * sigma * sigma_fx) * Mat) *
        CumulativeNormal(-d1));

return result;
```

17.5   BASKET OPTIONS

Basket options are options where the underlying is a portfolio of assets. We consider a portfolio of d assets $S_i(t), i = 1, \ldots, d$. This portfolio is determined by the weight ω_i of each asset. We denote the price of the portfolio at time t by $B(t)$. Thus, we have

$$B(t) = \sum_{i=1}^{d} \omega_i S_i(T) \tag{17.6}$$

Using the portfolio as the underlying we consider options on this portfolio. The simplest one is a European call option given by the payoff:

$$\max(B(T) - K, 0) = \max\left(\sum_{i=1}^{d} \omega_i S_i(t) - K, 0\right) \tag{17.7}$$

The only thing which changes is that we have to collect a vector of weights from the corresponding property set. To this end we declare a wrapper object, already defined in Chapter 14, as follows:

```
Wrapper<Vector<double> >* result_Vector;
```

This can be used to retrieve the data computed for the present value calculation which is given by

```
double PayOff_Basket::operator()(double Discount,
                                 NumericMatrix<double>& Spot) const
{
    // Defining all the objects necessary for this PayOff
    double strike;
    Vector<double> weights;
    std::string paytype;
    AnyType* anytype;
    Wrapper<double>* result_double;
    Wrapper<std::string>* result_string;
    Wrapper<Vector<double> >* result_Vector;
    double WeightedSpot=0.0;
    double result;

    // Starting to initialise the data
    anytype = PayOff_Basket_Properties.value("Strike");
    result_double = dynamic_cast<Wrapper<double>*> (anytype);
    strike = (*result_double).GetObj();

    anytype = PayOff_Basket_Properties.value("PayOffType");
    result_string = dynamic_cast<Wrapper<std::string>*> (anytype);
    paytype = (*result_string).GetObj();

    anytype = PayOff_Basket_Properties.value("Weights");
    result_Vector = dynamic_cast<Wrapper<Vector<double> >*> (anytype);
    weights = (*result_Vector).GetObj();

    for(int i = Spot.MinRowIndex(); i<= Spot.MaxRowIndex(); i++)
    {
        WeightedSpot += weights[i] * Spot(i,Spot.MaxColumnIndex());
    }
    if(paytype == "call")
        result = max(WeightedSpot- strike,0.0);
    else
        result = max(strike - WeightedSpot, 0.0);

    return result;
}
```

Using the Black-Scholes model we price a simple basket by reducing it to a one factor model and applying the usual pricing formula. This can be done by computing the expectation ($\mathbb{E}[\cdot]$) and the variance ($\mathbb{V}[\cdot]$) by

$$\mathbb{E}\left[\sum_{i=1}^{N} \omega_i\, S_i(t)\right] = \sum_{i=1}^{N} \omega_i\, \mathbb{E}[S_i(t)] \tag{17.8}$$

$$\mathbb{V}\left[\sum_{i=1}^{N} \omega_i\, S_i(t)\right] = \sum_{i,j=1}^{N} \omega_i \omega_j\, \mathrm{Cov}[S_i(t),\, S_j(t)] \tag{17.9}$$

Table 17.2   Pricing a basket option consisting of 20 assets using Monte Carlo simulation and antithetic sampling.

	I	II	III
MC Price	109.25 (1.03318)	268.361 (1.3847)	30.4646 (0.257053)
Runtime	30.67 sec.	30.64 sec.	30.67 sec.
MC Price (Antithetics)	95.924 (0.681204)	243.285(0.931358)	35.7002 (0.195481)
RunTime	37.969	37.844 sec,	37.875 sec.

We have included a 20 factor model on the CD. We restrict the scope to three examples and examine 100 000 paths and a call (I), a put (II) and another call (III) with strikes 1000, 1000 and 600. We keep the other parameters as in the example on the CD. Our results are shown in Table 17.2.

17.6   MIN/MAX OPTIONS

Min/Max options are affected by the correlation structure because the correlation determines the overall volatility of the basket as well as the dispersion within the basket. The dispersion is the tendency of the assets to drift away from each other. Both effects certainly influence the price of the option. Max options are expensive in the sense that the best performing asset determines the payout. In general prices increase if assets are added to the basket (see Figures 17.1, 17.2 and 17.3).

We observe the opposite effect for Min options. The worst performing asset determines the payoff. Prices decrease if assets are added. Another interesting observation is the evolution of the standard error of the simulation for the different options. We consider options with the following payoffs:

$$V_{max}(S_1(T), \ldots, S_d(T), K) = max\left(max_{i=1,\ldots,d} S_i(T) - K, 0\right) \qquad (17.10)$$

$$V_{min}(S_1(T), \ldots, S_d(T), K) = max\left(min_{i=1,\ldots,d} S_i(T) - K, 0\right) \qquad (17.11)$$

The min/max option is an interesting example with a simple payoff and therefore the implementation of the valuation operator ( ) given the spots is straightforward:

```
double PayOff_MinMax::operator()(double Discount,
                          NumericMatrix<double>& Spot) const
{
// Defining all the objects necessary for this PayOff
double strike;
double MinMax;
std::string paytype;
std::string minmax;
AnyType* anytype;
Wrapper<double>* result_double;
Wrapper<std::string>* result_string;
double result;

// Starting to initialise the data
anytype = PayOff_MinMax_Properties.value("Strike");
```

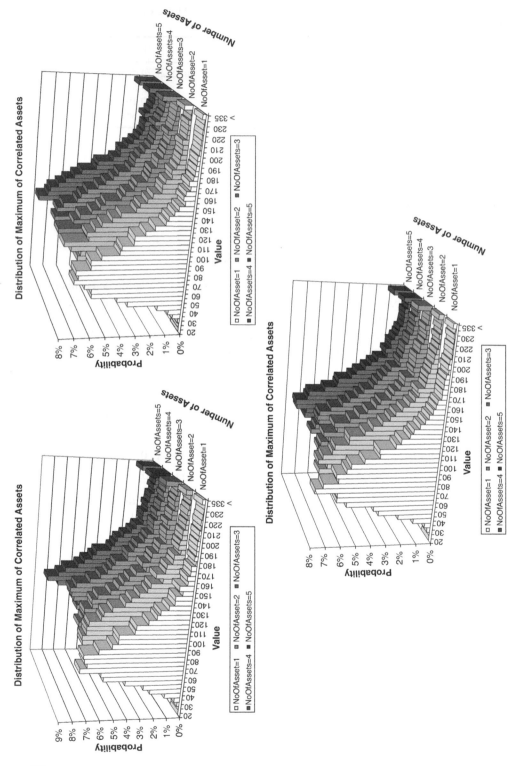

Figure 17.1 Distribution for the maximum for 1 to 5 assets with mainly negative, zero and mainly positive correlation structure

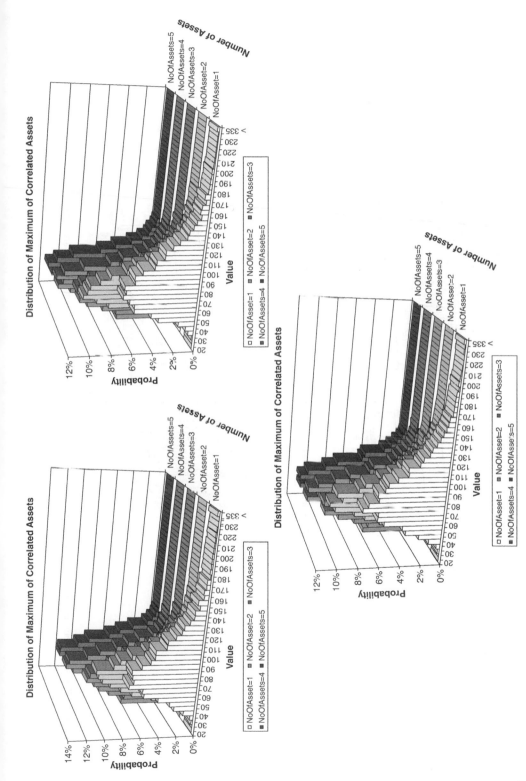

Figure 17.2 Distribution for the minimum for 1 to 5 assets with mainly negative, zero and mainly positive correlation structure

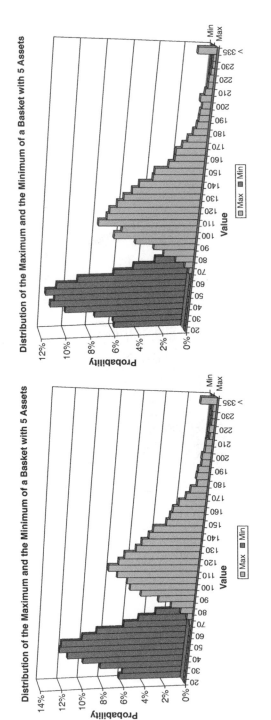

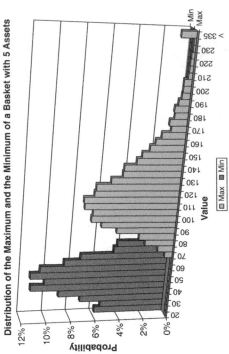

Figure 17.3 Distribution for the minimum and the maximum for 5 assets with mainly negative, zero and mainly positive correlation structure

```
result_double = dynamic_cast<Wrapper<double>*> (anytype);
strike = (*result_double).GetObj();

anytype = PayOff_MinMax_Properties.value("PayOffType");
result_string = dynamic_cast<Wrapper<std::string>*> (anytype);
paytype = (*result_string).GetObj();

anytype = PayOff_MinMax_Properties.value("MinMax");
result_string = dynamic_cast<Wrapper<std::string>*> (anytype);
minmax = (*result_string).GetObj();

MinMax = Spot(Spot.MinRowIndex() ,Spot.MaxColumnIndex());

if(minmax == "min")
for(int i = Spot.MinRowIndex(); i<= Spot.MaxRowIndex(); i++)
MinMax = min(MinMax, Spot(i, Spot.MaxColumnIndex()));
else
for(int i = Spot.MinRowIndex(); i<= Spot.MaxRowIndex(); i++)
MinMax = max(MinMax, Spot(i,Spot.MaxColumnIndex()));

if(paytype == "call")
result = max(MinMax - strike,0.0);
else
result = max(strike - MinMax, 0.0);

return result;
}
```

Baskets show a complex behaviour with respect to correlation. Furthermore, the price depends strongly on the number of underlying assets. Such options can be used to study the effect of correlation on the dispersion and the volatility of the overall contract.

We illustrate this behaviour by considering positively correlated assets, independent assets and negatively correlated assets. Then, we increase the number of factors from one asset to five assets and determine the minimum and the maximum respectively. Figures 17.4 and 17.5 show the corresponding distributions.

For comparison of the distributions for the minimum and maximum we have included Figure 17.3.

We plotted the option values against the standard error based on 5000 paths. The maximum option has a strike of 100. The minimum option has a strike of 50. Both maturities have been chosen to be six years. The riskless rate was assumed to be 3% and the volatilities for the assets are 19.37%, 21.86%, 34.00%, 22.04%, 15.00%, 14.00% and 23.00%.

17.7   MOUNTAIN RANGE OPTIONS

Mountain range options were introduced in 1998. There are many variants of this type of options:

- Altiplano options;
- Atlas options;
- Himalaya options.

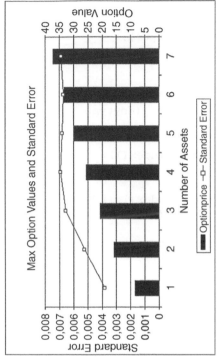

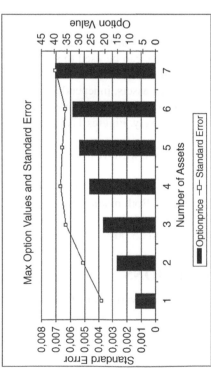

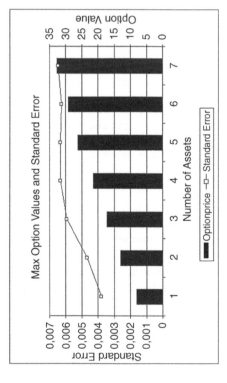

Figure 17.4 Option prices and standard errors for the maximum for 1 to 5 assets with mainly negative, zero and mainly positive correlation structure

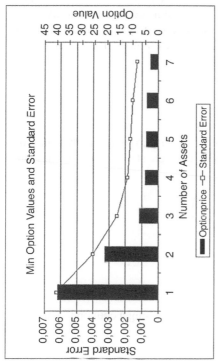

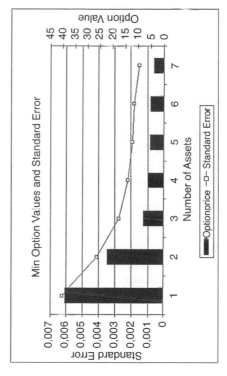

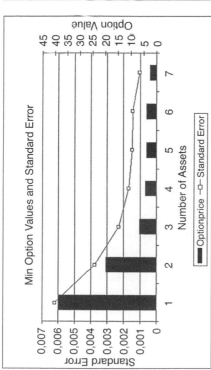

Figure 17.5 Option prices and standard errors for the minimum for 1 to 5 assets with mainly negative, zero and mainly positive correlation structure

These options heavily depend on the co-movement of the basket as well as on the actual paths the assets take. The effects of co-movement on the dispersion and on the volatility come into play simultaneously and therefore we cannot analyse it separately. We cannot hope for analytical solutions even in the multi-dimensional Black-Scholes model let alone stochastic volatility, jump models or stochastic interest rate models.

To perform further analysis we consider a basket of d shares.

Altiplano option

An Altiplano is a path-dependent basket option. It depends on barrier levels that may be breached by one or more of the underlying assets. For a given strike value K they are characterised by the payoff:

$$\delta(t)\text{Max}\left(\sum_{i=1}^{d}\frac{S_i(t)}{S_i(0)} - K\right) \tag{17.12}$$

where

$$\delta(t) = \begin{cases} 1 \; ; \text{Min}_{t_1 \leq t \leq t_2}\left(\frac{S_j(t)}{S_j(0)}\right) \leq \text{Barrier} \\ 0 \; ; \qquad\qquad \text{else} \end{cases}$$

The payoff can be altered by adding more barrier levels and prescribing a coupon if a number of assets close below the given level.

We give the full implementation of the payoff here and the code can be used as a starting point to implement more complex payoffs:

```
class PayOff_Altiplano : public PayOff<Vector<double>,
                                       NumericMatrix<double>& Spot> >
{
    public:
    PayOff_Altiplano();      // Default constructor
    // User constructor
    PayOff_Altiplano(const SimplePropertySet<string,AnyType*>& pset);

    virtual PayOff<Vector<double>, NumericMatrix<double> >* clone()
    const;
    virtual double operator()(Vector<double> Discount,
                         NumericMatrix<double>& Spot) const;
    virtual double PayOff_Value(Vector<double> Discount,
                         NumericMatrix<double> Spot,
                         Vector<double>& Strike) const;
    virtual ~PayOff_Altiplano(){}

    SimplePropertySet<string, AnyType*> PayOff_Altiplano_Properties;

private:
    // No private data

};
```

The evaluation operator for our example is given by

```
double PayOff_Altiplano::operator()(Vector<double> Discount,
                                    NumericMatrix<double>& Spot)
                                    const
{
    // Defining all the objects necessary for this PayOff
    AnyType* anytype;
    Wrapper<std::string>* result_string;
    Wrapper<Vector<double> >* result_Vector;
    Wrapper<int>* result_int;
    Wrapper<double>* result_double;

    // Starting to initialise the data

    // Example for string
    anytype = PayOff_Altiplano_Properties.value("PayOffType");
    result_string = dynamic_cast<Wrapper<std::string>*> (anytype);
    std::string paytype = (*result_string).GetObj();

    // Example for Vector<double>
    anytype = PayOff_Altiplano_Properties.value("Weights");
    result_Vector = dynamic_cast<Wrapper<Vector<double> >*> (anytype);
    Vector<double> weights = (*result_Vector).GetObj();

    // Example for int (barrier1, barrier2)
    anytype = PayOff_Altiplano_Properties.value("barrier1");
    result_int = dynamic_cast<Wrapper<int>*> (anytype);
    int barrier1 = (*result_int).GetObj();

    // Example for double (coupon1, coupon2, level1, level2)
    anytype = PayOff_Altiplano_Properties.value("coupon1");
    result_double = dynamic_cast<Wrapper<double>*> (anytype);
    double coupon1 = (*result_double).GetObj();


    double coupon = 0.0;

    Vector<double> Spots(Spot.MaxColumnIndex()-
                                        Spot.MinColumnIndex()+1);

    for(int i = Spot.minindex_Factors; i<= maxindex_Factors;i++)
    {
        for(int j = minindex_TimeSteps; j <= maxindex_TimeSteps; j++)
        {
            if(Spot(i,j) < level1 * Spots[i])
                barrier1++;
            if(Spot(i,j) < level2 * Spots[i])
                barrier2++;
        }
        if(barrier1 < level1)
            coupon += coupon1 * Discount[i];
        else
```

```
        {
            if(barrier2 < level2)
                coupon += coupon2 * Discount[i];
        }
    }
    return coupon;
}
```

If we examine the implementation, there exists the possibility to add further information (for example, barrier levels) and we realise this functionality by using the property set. Furthermore, the algorithm that computes the coupon for a given path can be modified and extended.

Atlas option

For an Atlas option the d_1 worst performing as well as the d_2 best performing shares are removed from the basket. From the remaining $d - d_1 - d_2$ shares the average performance is calculated to determine the option payoff:

$$\text{Max}\left(\frac{1}{d - d_1 - d_2} \sum_{i=d_1+1}^{d_2} \frac{S_i(T)}{S_i(0)} - K, 0\right) \tag{17.13}$$

The implementation is left as an exercise in section 17.11.

Himalaya option

Himalaya options are combinations of basket options and path-dependent options. Again, our basket consists of d shares. To determine the payoff we fix $N - 1$ future dates, t_n, $n = 1, \ldots, N - 1$. Suppose now we reach date t_1. We calculate the performance of all the shares in the basket by using the formula

$$\text{Pay}(t_1) := \text{Max}_{j=1,\ldots,d}\left(\text{Perf}_{j=1,\ldots,d}(t_1)\right) := \text{Max}_{j=1,\ldots,d}\left(\frac{S_j(t_1)}{S_j(0)}\right)$$

We denoted the performance of the jth asset at time t_n, $\frac{S(t_n)}{S(t_{n-1})} - 1$, by $\text{Perf}_{j,n}$. Suppose the jth share shows the best performance. This share is then removed from the basket. At time t_2 we apply this procedure again. The final payoff will be

$$\sum_{n=1}^{N-1} \text{Pay}(t_n) \tag{17.14}$$

17.8   THE HESTON MODEL IN MULTIPLE DIMENSIONS

In this section we discuss stochastic volatility models in several dimensions. We study the Heston model again. The driving dynamics are given by the stochastic differential equations:

$$dS_i = (r - d)S_i(t)dt + \sqrt{V(t)}S_i(t)dW_i(t) \tag{17.15}$$
$$S_i(0) = s_i$$
$$dV(t) = \kappa(\theta - V(t))dt + \xi\sqrt{V(t)}dW_{i+d}(t)$$
$$V(0) = v_i \tag{17.16}$$

The parameters have the same meaning as those described in Chapter 16 equation (16.2) and the entries of the vector Brownian motion $\underline{W} = (W_1, \ldots, W_{2d})$ are correlated with correlation matrix A given by

$$\begin{pmatrix} A_1 & A_2 \\ {}^t A_2 & A_3 \end{pmatrix}$$

where the matrices are

- correlation structure of the driving Brownian motions corresponding to the asset price processes

$$A_1 = \begin{pmatrix} \rho_{11} & \cdots & \rho_{1d} \\ \vdots & \ddots & \vdots \\ \rho_{d1} & \cdots & \rho_{dd} \end{pmatrix}$$

- correlation structure of the driving Brownian motions corresponding to the asset price processes and the variance processes, called the cross skew

$$A_2 = \begin{pmatrix} \rho_{1,d+1} & \cdots & \rho_{1,2d} \\ \vdots & \ddots & \vdots \\ \rho_{d+1,1} & \cdots & \rho_{2d,1} \end{pmatrix}$$

- correlation structure of the driving Brownian motions corresponding to the variance processes, called the decorrelation

$$A_3 = \begin{pmatrix} \rho_{d+1,d+1} & \cdots & \rho_{d+1,2d} \\ \vdots & \ddots & \vdots \\ \rho_{2d,1} & \cdots & \rho_{2d,2d} \end{pmatrix}$$

17.8.1   Extending the QE scheme

The QE scheme can be generalised to work in multiple dimensions. Suppose we have n assets and variance pairs denoted by (S_i, V_i). The first entry is the asset price and the other its variance. We use the QE scheme for each asset/variance pair but use dependent random variables having correlation corresponding with the matrix A. To obtain the dependent random variables we use the correlation matrix. We place the parameters we have calculated for each pair into a `vector`. The C++ code is given by

```cpp
for(long i = minindex_Factors; i <= maxindex_Factors; i++)
{
    for(long n = minindex_TimeSteps; n <= maxindex_Factors; n++)
    {
        // E[Vt+Delta]
        m = vLong[i] + (Vt(i,n) - vLong[i])*Coeff[i][1];
        // Var[Vt+Delta]
        s2 = Vt(i,n)*Coeff[i][1]*Coeff[i][2]*Coeff[i][3]
                + 0.5*vLong[i]*Coeff[i][2]*Coeff[i][2]*Coeff[i][3];

        // same as for simple Heston model see chapter 16
        if(Psi<=Psi_C)
```

```
    {
        ...
        Vt(i,n+1)  = a*(GV*GV);                    // step c
    }
    else
    {
        ... same as for simple Heston model see chapter 16
        if (CumulativeNormal(Z(i,n)) <= p)
            Vt(i,n+1) = 0.0;
        else
            Vt(i,n+1) = log((1.0 - p) / (1.0 -
                            CumulativeNormal(Z(i,n)))) / beta;
    }
  }
}
```

17.8.2 Spread options

We apply the scheme to a spread option. This example was introduced in Chapter 5 and prices using several discretisation schemes have been derived. We will price this option using the implementation of the multi-dimensional QE scheme. We have run the simulation using the vector (S_1, v_1, S_2, v_2) with the inital values:

```
Spot[1]=100.0; Spot[2]=110.0;
r[1]=0.06; r[2]=0.06;
d[1]=0.04;d[2]=0.04;
VolVol[1]=0.05; VolVol[2]=0.06;
VInst[1] = 0.2*0.2; VInst[2] = 0.3*0.3;
VLong[1]= 0.04; VLong[2]= 0.09;
MeanRev[1]= 1.0; MeanRev[2]= 2.0;
Rho(1,1)=1;        Rho(1,2)=0.2;     Rho(1,3)=0.5;     Rho(1,4)=0.01;
Rho(2,1)=0.2;      Rho(2,2)=1;       Rho(2,3)=0.01;    Rho(2,4)=0.3;
Rho(3,1)=0.5;      Rho(3,2)=0.01;    Rho(3,3)=1;       Rho(3,4)=0.3;
Rho(4,1)=0.01;     Rho(4,2)=0.3;     Rho(4,3)=0.3;     Rho(4,4)=1;
```

This example is taken from Clewlow and Strickland (1998). We study the effect of increasing the number of paths and the time steps per year. The results from applying the multi-dimensional version of the QE scheme are summarised in Tables 17.3 and 17.4.

17.9   EQUITY INTEREST RATE HYBRIDS

In this section we consider another kind of multi-asset problem. We model an equity market where the interest rate r is a stochastic variable. We consider the following model:

$$dr(t) = (\Phi - \alpha r(t))dt + \sigma_r dW_1(t) \tag{17.17}$$

$$r(0) = r_0$$

$$dS(t) = S(t)(r(t) - d)dt + S(t)\sigma_S dW_2(t) \tag{17.18}$$

$$S(0) = s_0$$

Table 17.3 Numerical results for spread options: the time to perform the analysis is based on an Intel T2350 processor with one CPU activated

Paths	Steps p.a.	Price (SE)	(sec.)
10	1	4.02635 (2.032)	0
10	2	4.90515 (2.38677)	0
10	12	6.71823 (3.73695)	0.016
10	24	10.0109 (3.79048)	0
100	1	8.64343 (1.45162)	0
100	2	8.09967 (1.42667)	0.016
100	12	6.91722 (1.30953)	0.015
100	24	6.48949 (1.22354)	0.031
1000	1	6.08798 (0.39827)	0.094
1000	2	7.09937 (0.423476)	0.11
1000	12	7.01116 (0.428315)	0.203
1000	24	6.89594 (0.431652)	0.312
10000	1	6.57314 (0.131295)	1.078
10000	2	6.60054 (0.131158)	1.047
10000	12	6.56593 (0.127962)	2.047
10000	24	6.73524 (0.132697)	3.234

Table 17.4 Numerical results for spread options increasing number of paths by five batches and time steps per year: the time to perform the analysis is based on an Intel T2350 processor with one CPU activated

Paths	Steps p.a.	Price (SE)	(sec.)
10	1	3.75746 (2.09244)	0.015
10	2	6.28102 (3.3309)	0.016
10	12	7.19854 (4.10882)	0
10	24	6.78931 (3.93436)	0.015
100	1	7.07856 (1.28477)	0.047
100	2	6.33845 (1.25473)	0.047
100	12	6.45444 (1.28499)	0.11
100	24	5.76192 (1.1483)	0.156
1000	1	6.43799 (0.4009)	0.437
1000	2	6.53922 (0.401351)	0.5
1000	12	6.36504 (0.404074)	1
1000	24	6.63198 (0.400729)	1.625
10000	1	6.4379 (0.128127)	4.61
10000	2	6.52723 (0.129398)	5.234
10000	12	6.55894 (0.130443)	10.047
10000	24	6.54369 (0.130017)	16.25

with $W_1(t)$ and $W_2(t)$ correlated Brownian motions with correlation coefficient ρ. The parameters Φ, α, d and the volatilities σ_r and σ_S are assumed to be constant. Φ corresponds to the long time rate, α is a measure for the reversion of the rate and σ_r is the volatility.

Let us shortly consider the short rate dynamic given by the SDE for $r(t)$. There is an exact solution given by

$$r(t) = r(s)e^{-\alpha(t-s)} + \frac{\Phi}{\alpha}\left(1 - e^{-\alpha(t-s)}\right) + \sigma_r \int_s^t e^{-\alpha(t-u)}dW_1(u) \qquad (17.19)$$

and according to Brigo and Mercurio (2006) the zero bonds $P(t, T)$ are given by

$$P(t, T) = A(t, T)\exp(-B(t, T)r(t)) \qquad (17.20)$$

with the functions $A(t, T)$ and $B(t, T)$ given by

$$A(t, T) = \exp\left(\left(\frac{\Phi}{\alpha} - \frac{\sigma_r^2}{2\alpha^2}\right)(B(t, T) - T + t) - \frac{\sigma_r^2}{4\alpha}B(t, T)^2\right)$$

$$B(t, T) = \frac{1}{\alpha}\left(1 - e^{-\alpha(T-t)}\right)$$

We follow Overhaus *et al.* (2007). First, we split the short rate process into a stochastic and a deterministic part by considering

$$r(t) = \underbrace{X(t)}_{\text{stochastic}} + \underbrace{\varphi(t)}_{\text{deterministic}} \qquad (17.21)$$

The stochastic part satisfies the stochastic differential equation

$$dX(t) = -\alpha X(t)dt + \sigma_r dW_1(t) \qquad (17.22)$$
$$X(0) = 0$$

The deterministic part $\varphi(t)$ satisfies the differential equation

$$d\varphi(t) = (\Phi(t) - \alpha(t)\varphi(t))dt \qquad (17.23)$$
$$\varphi(0) = r(0)$$

Adding the stochastic processes corresponding to solutions (17.22) and (17.23) satisfies the equation (17.21). In the following we can therefore focus on the solution to the stochastic differential equation (17.22). For the equity component $S(t)$ we simulate the process $\tilde{S}(t)$ implicitly by

$$S(t) = S(0)\exp(\tilde{S}(t))\frac{\exp(-dt)}{P(0, t)} \qquad (17.24)$$

We denote the discount factor implied by the short rate model by $P(0, t)$. The modified dynamic is governed by the stochastic differential equation:

$$d\tilde{S}(t) = \left(r(t) - f(0, t)\frac{\sigma_S^2}{2}\right)dt + \sigma_S dW(t) \qquad (17.25)$$

with $f(t, T) = -\frac{\partial \ln(P(t,T))}{\partial T}$. Then we have

$$X(T) = X(t)\exp(a(T - t)) + \sigma_r \underbrace{\int_t^T \exp(-a(T - s))\,dW_1(s)}_{=:I_1}$$

$$\tilde{S}(T) = \tilde{S}(t) + X(t)\int_t^T \exp(-a(s - t))ds - \frac{1}{2}\sigma_S^2(T - t)$$

$$+ \frac{\sigma_r^2}{2}\left(\int_0^T\left(\int_s^T \exp(-a(u - s))du\right)^2 ds - \int_0^t\left(\int_s^t \exp(-a(u - s))du\right)^2 ds\right)$$

$$+ \underbrace{\sigma_r\int_t^T\int_s^T \exp(-a(u - s))du\,dW_1(s) + \sigma_S(W_2(T) - W_2(t))}_{=:I_2 \qquad\qquad\qquad =:I_3}$$

$$\ln(B(T)) = \ln(B(t)) + \ln(P(0, T)) + X(t)\exp\left(\int_t^T r(s)\right)ds$$

$$+ \underbrace{\sigma_r\int_t^T\int_s^T \exp(-a(u - s))du\,dW_1(s)}_{=:I_2}$$

The above equations involve three stochastic integrals from which we have to simulate random variates. Since each integral is taken with respect to Brownian motion it has a Gaussian distribution. The covariance matrix $(\rho_{ij})_{1\leq i,j\leq 3}$ can be computed using Ito-isometry and the entries $(\rho_{ij})_{i,j=1,2,3}$ are given by

$$\rho_{11} = \sigma_r^2\int_t^T \exp(-2a(T - s))ds,$$

$$\rho_{12} = \sigma_r^2\int_t^T\left(\int_s^T \exp(-a(u - s))du\right)\exp(-a(T - s))ds,$$

$$\rho_{13} = \rho\sigma_r\sigma_S\int_t^T \exp(-a(T - s))ds,$$

$$\rho_{21} = \rho_{12},$$

$$\rho_{22} = \sigma_r^2\int_t^T\left(\int_s^T \exp(-a(u - s))du\right)^2 ds,$$

$$\rho_{23} = \rho\sigma_r\sigma_S\int_t^T\int_s^T \exp(-a(u - s))du\,ds,$$

$$\rho_{31} = \rho_{13},$$

$$\rho_{32} = \rho_{23},$$

$$\rho_{33} = \sigma_S^2(T - t)$$

We denote the corresponding correlation matrix by C:

$$C = \begin{pmatrix} \rho_{11} & \rho_{12} & \rho_{13} \\ \rho_{21} & \rho_{22} & \rho_{23} \\ \rho_{31} & \rho_{32} & \rho_{33} \end{pmatrix} \qquad\qquad (17.26)$$

To carry out the simulation of the random variates, we apply Cholesky decomposition or spectral decomposition to the covariance matrix. Let D denote the decomposition matrix. We have that $^{\ell}DD = \rho I$ and can therefore simulate a vector of correlated normals $\tilde{W}$ using independent normals W by computing the matrix product:

$$\tilde{W} = D \times W$$

The integral expressions to actually compute the covariances can explicitly be computed and they are

$$\int_t^T \int_s^T e^{-\alpha(u-s)}e^{-\alpha(T-s)}duds = \frac{\exp(-a(T-t)-1)^2}{2a^2}$$

$$\int_t^T e^{-\alpha(u-s)}ds = \frac{(1-\exp(-a(T-t)))}{a}$$

$$\int_s^T \int_t^T e^{-\alpha(u-s)} = \frac{-1+\exp(-a(T-t))+a(T-t)-1}{a^2}$$

$$\int_t^T e^{-2\alpha(T-t)}ds = \frac{\exp(2a(T-t))-1}{2a}$$

$$\int_t^T \left(\int_s^T e^{-\alpha(u-s)}du\right)^2 ds = -\frac{3-4\exp(-a(T-t))+\exp(-2a(T-t))-2a(T-t)}{2a^3}$$

In a more general setting, for instance if the parameters Φ, α or σ_r assumed constant are taken to be time-dependent, the integrals have to be evaluated numerically. The latter is the case for most real applications.

17.10   SUMMARY AND CONCLUSIONS

Pricing, hedging and risk management of options on multiple assets demand knowledge of the dependency structure of the assets. This is usually modelled as a correlated Brownian motion. Our framework can be used for simulating multi-dimensional models and various kinds of options on multiple assets.

We have shown how to implement a model with multiple factors and how to set up a numerical scheme in this case. The setup is then applied to a variety of options. We considered spread, quanto and basket options.

For all options we have given approximation formulae used to check the results obtained via Monte Carlo simulation for the Black-Scholes model.

In the last section of this chapter we have discussed how to incorporate a stochastic interest rate into an equity market. We considered the extended Vasicek model for the interest rate and the Black-Scholes framework for the equity. This framework can be extended to other models and to time-dependent parameters. For example, Φ, α and σ_r introduced in section 17.9 are often chosen to be time-dependent functions instead of constants. They can be used to fit the initial term structure of interest rates and quoted option prices.

17.11   EXERCISES AND PROJECTS

1. (**) PayOff Classes
   Create a class `PayOff_Atlas` and `PayOff_Himalaya` to implement the options considered above.

2. (**) Min/Max Options

   Consider a min/max option and study the effect that correlation has on the dispersion. This can, for example, be done by reproducing the results of Tables 17.1, 17.2 and 17.4, 17.5.

3. (*) Spread Options

   Suppose the individual stock prices also obey a stochastic volatility component. Compare your results to the standard Black-Scholes model.

4. (**) Basket Options

   Consider a basket option and study the effect that correlation has on the overall volatility. Use the analytical formula to backtest your solution.

5. (*****) Hybrids

   Simulate an equity with stochastic interest rates using the extended Vasicek model. Take the correlation matrix C, equation (17.26), and implement the integrals arising from the stochastic interest rate r. Since there is a closed form solution in the setting for the hybrid model, check the results against the analytic solution. Using the notation from above we set

   $$V(t, T) = \frac{\sigma_r^2}{a^2} \left[T - t + \frac{2}{a} e^{-a(T-t)} - \frac{1}{2a} e^{-2a(T-t)} - \frac{3}{2a} \right]$$

   $$v^2(t, T) = V(t, T) + \sigma_S^2(T - t) + 2\rho \frac{\sigma_r \sigma_S}{a} \left[T - t - \frac{1 - e^{-a(T-t)}}{a} \right]$$

   Then, the price of a European call option is given by

   $$\begin{aligned} \text{Call} = {} & S(t) e^{-d(T-t)} \mathcal{N} \left(\frac{\ln\left(\frac{S(t)}{KP(t,T)}\right) - d(T - t) + \frac{v^2(t,T)}{2}}{v(t, T)} \right) \\ & - KP(t, T) \mathcal{N} \left(\frac{\ln\left(\frac{S(t)}{KP(t,T)}\right) - d(T - t) - \frac{v^2(t,T)}{2}}{v(t, T)} \right) \end{aligned}$$

   For the put option the formula needs to be modified in an obvious way.

   First, compare your results from Monte Carlo simulation to the analytical results. Second, test the put-call parity for the hybrid model. Finally, compare the effects of the parameters determining the interest rate model on the option price and compare it to the Black-Scholes model where the rate is constant.

6. (**) Correlation Matrix

   Guenther and Kahl (2004) describe a method to compute a valid correlation matrix for stochastic volatility models (including the Heston model). Using this correlation matrix the main Monte Carlo framework can be applied to multi-asset options in a stochastic volatility framework. Implement that model and use it in the general Monte Carlo framework.

18

Advanced Monte Carlo I – Computing Greeks

18.1 INTRODUCTION AND OBJECTIVES

This chapter discusses computing sensitivities (Greeks) for derivatives using Monte Carlo methods. The value of a derivative is given by the expectation of a payoff function h applied to a sample path S. A set of sample paths is used to approximate this expected value. Of course the expectation depends on several model parameters ϕ_i, $i \in \mathbb{N}$. For instance, the current spot price or the current level of volatility affects the price of an option. We indicate this dependence by denoting the sample path by $S(\phi_1, \phi_2, \ldots,)$ or where we consider a single parameter ϕ, we denote the dependence by $S(\phi)$.

The sensitivity we are interested in is the effect of a change of one of the model parameters. Mathematically, this is reflected by the partial derivative with respect to this parameter. The sensitivity or *Greek* with respect to the parameter ϕ is given by

$$\text{Greek}(\phi) := \frac{\partial}{\partial \phi} \mathbb{E}[h(S(\phi))] \tag{18.1}$$

Several methods to apply Monte Carlo simulation to compute the partial derivative (equation (18.1)) have been suggested. Each of the approaches requires additional information which has consequences for the C++ design. We review three methods for computing Greeks in a Monte Carlo framework:

- *Finite Difference Method* (FDM);
- *Pathwise Method* (PWM);
- *Likelihood Ratio Method* (LRM).

We first describe the methods and then show, using design patterns, how to implement these methods in C++. The problem entails either simulating another set of paths or evaluating the paths with a modified payoff. The main building block in this case is again the *Abstract Factory* pattern as discussed in Chapter 9.

Finally, we will summarise the properties of each method and give an overview when it is applicable.

18.2 THE FINITE DIFFERENCE METHOD

The finite difference method approximates the partial derivative given by equation (18.1) by a *difference estimator*. From real analysis it is known that a differentiable function can locally be approximated by a linear function. The finite difference estimator applies this concept to payoffs for financial derivatives.

Let us consider the following setting. We take a payoff function h which may depend on the values of the asset S at N times and on d model parameters:

$$h : \mathbb{R}^N \times \mathbb{R}^d \to \mathbb{R}$$
$$S_1, \ldots, S_N, \phi_1, \ldots, \phi_d \mapsto h(S_{1,\phi_1,\ldots,\phi_d}, \ldots, S_{N,\phi_1,\ldots,\phi_d})$$

To simplify notation we just write $h(S(\phi))$ keeping in mind that this is a shorthand notation. For some $\epsilon > 0$ we approximate Greek(ϕ) from equation (18.1) using the difference estimator:

$$\text{Greek}^{FD}(\phi) := \frac{\mathbb{E}[h(S_{\phi+\epsilon})] - \mathbb{E}[h(S_{\phi-\epsilon})]}{2\epsilon} \tag{18.2}$$

Equation (18.2) is called the *central difference estimator*. We might wish to apply other differences such as the *forward* or the *backward difference* estimator illustrated in Figure 18.1. Let us consider some function f and using the notation from Figure 18.1 we have the following equations for the different estimators:

- central estimator: $\frac{f(c)-f(a)}{c-a}$
- forward estimator: $\frac{f(c)-f(b)}{c-b}$
- backward estimator: $\frac{f(b)-f(a)}{b-a}$

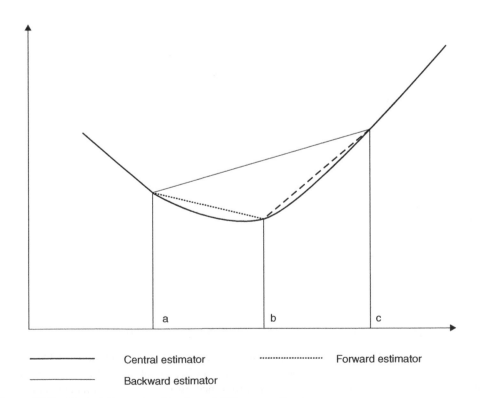

Central estimator   Forward estimator

Backward estimator

Figure 18.1   Central, forward and backward difference estimators

Let us consider a set of simulated paths $S^i(\phi), i = 1, \ldots, N$ depending on the model parameter ϕ and the corresponding Monte Carlo estimator which is given by

$$\widehat{\text{Greek}}^{FD}(\phi) := \frac{1}{N} \sum_{i=1}^{N} \frac{h(S^i(\phi + \epsilon)) - h(S^i(\phi - \epsilon))}{2\epsilon} \tag{18.3}$$

We have used the notation $\widehat{\text{Greek}}^{FD}(\phi)$ to denote the sample estimate of equation (18.2). To apply the finite difference method we do not need any further information on the model, the simulation scheme, the payoff or the nature of the model parameter ϕ. We generate two sets of paths using the disturbed model parameters and compute the finite difference estimator. The Monte Carlo estimator in this case shows a significant dependence on the parameter ϵ. Furthermore, it is not possible to handle discontinuous payoffs. The error for the latter case grows like $O(\epsilon^{-1})$.

If the expectation of the payoff is differentiable with respect to the parameter ϕ, the difference estimator converges if ϵ tends to 0.

It is often necessary to consider the effect of changing two model parameters simultaneously. For example, denoting the spot value by s_0 and the implied volatility by σ, foreign exchange traders are interested in sensitivities given by

$$Vanna = \frac{\partial^2 \mathbb{E}[h(S(s_0, \sigma))]}{\partial s_0 \partial \sigma}$$

or

$$Volga = \frac{\partial^2 \mathbb{E}[h(S(\sigma))]}{\partial \sigma^2}$$

Another example are basket options such as spread options. Such options generally depend on several assets. Therefore, a trader might be interested in the sensitivity of changes in the spot price of asset s_1 and asset s_2 simultaneously. Such sensitivities are called *Cross Gammas* and correspond to partial derivatives of second order:

$$\text{Greek}^{FD}_{\phi_i, \phi_j} = \frac{\partial^2}{\partial \phi_i \partial \phi_j} \mathbb{E}[h(S(\phi_i, \phi_j))] \tag{18.4}$$

Let us consider an m factor model and we wish to disturb the model parameters ϕ_i and ϕ_j by $\epsilon_i > 0$ and $\epsilon_j > 0, i, j = 1, 2, \ldots, m$. Then, the finite difference estimator is given by

$$\text{Greek}^{FD}_{\phi_i, \phi_j} = \frac{1}{4\epsilon_1 \epsilon_2} \Big(\mathbb{E}[h(S(\phi_i + \epsilon_1, \phi_j + \epsilon_2))] - \mathbb{E}[h(S(\phi_i - \epsilon_1, \phi_j + \epsilon_2))]$$
$$- (\mathbb{E}[h(S(\phi_i + \epsilon_1, \phi_j - \epsilon_2))] - \mathbb{E}[h(S(\phi_i - \epsilon_1, \phi_j - \epsilon_2))]) \Big) \tag{18.5}$$

Pitfalls and improvement

A challenge is to determine the parameter $\epsilon > 0$. We need stable results and do not want to run into numerical problems because we have chosen it to be too small or too big. There is, however, no recipe for determining it in practice.

For a discussion on this subject, see for example Jäckel (2005). If V denotes the price of an option Jäckel suggests to set

$$\epsilon = \sqrt{\sqrt{12 \frac{V}{V'''}} \cdot \mathcal{M}_\epsilon}$$

where V''' denotes the third derivative with respect to the underlying parameter and $\mathcal{M}_\epsilon$ is the smallest number which can be represented on your computer. Using C++ you can identify such limits by considering the numeric limits file, `limits.h`, which has already be discussed in Chapter 11, section 11.5.1.

Furthermore, to reduce pricing bias we also suggest using the same random variates for computing both disturbed prices for the central finite difference estimator. Then, both computed prices suffer from the same simulation bias which cancels out by taking the difference.

18.3   THE PATHWISE METHOD

The pathwise method approximates equation (18.1) by an expression involving the derivative of the payoff and the derivative of the simulated path:

$$\text{Greek}^{PW}(\phi) := \mathbb{E}\left[h'(S(\phi)) \frac{\partial}{\partial \phi} S(\phi) \right] \tag{18.6}$$

and the corresponding Monte Carlo estimator is

$$\widehat{\text{Greek}^{PW}}(\phi) := \frac{1}{N} \sum_{i=1}^{N} h'(S(\phi)^i) \cdot \frac{\partial (S(\phi)^i)'}{\partial \phi} \tag{18.7}$$

The pathwise method requires additional knowledge of the model and additional information on the payoff and the parameter ϕ. It leads to an unbiased estimator of the corresponding derivative if the stochastic dynamics and the model fulfil certain mathematical properties specified by the Lebesgue convergence theorem (see Chapter 2 for details). The method is not applicable to discontinuous payoff functions. The pathwise method is based on the following equation to hold:

$$\frac{\partial}{\partial \phi} \mathbb{E}\left[S(\phi) \right] = \mathbb{E}\left[\frac{\partial}{\partial \phi} S(\phi) \right] \tag{18.8}$$

as the relation (18.6) does not hold in general because interchanging the expectation with the differentiation is only possible under certain conditions. The conditions for interchanging both operators are based on Lebesgue's convergence theorem.

How to apply the pathwise method

We consider two examples, namely an exact and an Euler discretised stochastic differential equation of the stochastic differential equation

$$dS(t) = \mu(t, S(t))dt + \sigma(t, S(t))dW(t)$$
$$S(0) = s_0$$

The drift $\mu : \mathbb{R}^+ \times \mathbb{R} \to \mathbb{R}$ and the volatility $\sigma : \mathbb{R}^+ \times \mathbb{R} \to \mathbb{R}^+$ are functions of the time and the asset value. Denoting $\Delta_n := t_{n+1} - t_n$, we have

$$\hat{S}_{n+1} = \hat{S}_n + \mu(t_n, \hat{S}_n)\Delta_n + \sigma(t_n, \hat{S}_n)\sqrt{\Delta_n}Z_{n+1}, \quad Z_{n+1} \sim \mathcal{N}(0, 1) \tag{18.9}$$

and alternatively

$$\hat{S}_{n+1} = \hat{S}_n \exp\left(\mu(t_n, \hat{S}_n)\Delta_n + \sigma(t_n, \hat{S}_n)\sqrt{\Delta_n}Z_{n+1}\right), \quad Z_{n+1} \sim \mathcal{N}(0, 1) \tag{18.10}$$

The asset price and therefore the scheme depend on the model parameter ϕ. For both cases (18.9) and (18.10), the considerations are the same; we only examine equation (18.9). The pathwise derivative with respect to some parameter ϕ, denoted by "'" is

$$\hat{S}'_{n+1} = \hat{S}'_n + \mu'(t_n, \hat{S}_n)\hat{S}'_n \Delta_n + \sigma'(t_n, \hat{S}_n)\hat{S}'_n\sqrt{\Delta_n}Z_{n+1} \tag{18.11}$$

Applying it to all N time steps and taking the sum we find

$$\sum_{i=1}^{N} \frac{\partial h}{\partial \hat{S}_{i\phi}}\left(\hat{S}_{1\phi}, \ldots, \hat{S}_{N\phi}\right)\frac{\partial}{\partial \phi}\hat{S}_i \tag{18.12}$$

with

$$\begin{cases} \dfrac{\partial}{\partial \phi}\hat{S}_{n+1} = \dfrac{\partial}{\partial \phi}\hat{S}_n + \mu'(S_n)\dfrac{\partial}{\partial \phi}\hat{S}_n \Delta_n + \sigma'(S_n)\dfrac{\partial}{\partial \phi}\hat{S}_n\sqrt{\Delta_n}Z_{n+1} \\[2mm] \dfrac{\partial}{\partial \phi}\hat{S}_0 = x \end{cases} \tag{18.13}$$

For example, if we denote the partial derivative with respect to the spot price and abbreviate the partial derivative $\frac{\partial}{\partial s_0}\hat{S}_i$ by $\hat{\Delta}_{S_i}$, we obtain

$$\begin{cases} \hat{\Delta}_{S_{n+1}} = \hat{\Delta}_{S_n} + \mu'(t_n, S_n)\hat{\Delta}_{S_n}\Delta_n + \sigma'(t_n, S_n)\hat{\Delta}_{S_n}\sqrt{\Delta_n}Z_{n+1} \\[2mm] \hat{\Delta}_{S_0} = 0 \end{cases} \tag{18.14}$$

Despite the fact that this method can be applied to a wide range of stochastic dynamics it is computationally expensive because we have to compute the Monte Carlo estimator for each Greek. Therefore, we have to generate random variables and compute the numerical scheme. But if there are no analytic expressions available it might be the only possibility.

As an example, we apply this method to compute the sensitivity with respect to the spot value s_0 for the Black-Scholes model. Coming back to equation 18.9, the drift factor in the Black-Scholes model is $\mu(t, S) = rS(t)$ and the diffusion coefficient is $\sigma(t, S) = \sigma_{BS}S(t)$. Both r and σ_{BS} are positive real numbers.

Since $\sigma'(t_i, S_i) = \frac{\partial}{\partial S_i}\sigma_{BS}S_i = \sigma_{BS}$ and $\mu'(t_i, S_i) = \frac{\partial}{\partial S_i}rS_i = r$ the dynamic in this case is

$$\begin{cases} \hat{\Delta}_{S_{n+1}} = \hat{\Delta}_{S_n} + r\hat{\Delta}_{S_n}\Delta_n + \sigma_{BS}\hat{\Delta}_{S_n}\sqrt{\Delta_n}Z_{n+1} \\[2mm] \Delta_{s_0} = 0 \end{cases} \tag{18.15}$$

For practical purposes it should be possible to pre-compute the differential of the path with respect to a model parameter. The Greeks can then be computed by evaluating a payoff type function for the simulated path.

In fact, for the Black-Scholes model we can use the exact solution instead of the Euler approximation and do not need to evolve the sensitivity through time. Considering equation

(18.10), we see that the following equation holds true:

$$\frac{dV}{ds_0} = \frac{dV}{dS(T)} \frac{dS(T)}{ds_0} \tag{18.16}$$

Using the exact solution, equation (18.10) leads to

$$\frac{dV}{ds_0} = \frac{S(T)}{s_0} 1_{\{S(T)>K\}} \tag{18.17}$$

Therefore, in this case we can compute the pathwise estimator just using another payoff given by equation (18.17). Finally, we give the standard example where the pathwise method cannot be used. We consider a digital option and find

$$0 = \mathbb{E}\left[\frac{dV}{ds_0}\right] \neq \frac{d}{ds_0}\mathbb{E}[V] \tag{18.18}$$

However, we may apply it to a smoothed payoff. Further illustration of this idea is shown by Figures 18.10 and 18.11 later in this chapter. The implementation is left as an exercise in section 18.7.

Let us summarise that in general the pathwise method needs another Monte Carlo simulation but for some models the option only depends on $\frac{S(T)}{s_0}$ which enables us to compute the sensitivity by evaluating another payoff function. Thus, no further simulation is necessary and we can use the same paths we used for pricing the option.

C++ implementation

To implement the pathwise method in C++ we apply the *Abstract Factory* design pattern, as shown in Figure 18.2. First, we proceed as in the case of a general payoff class. Due to

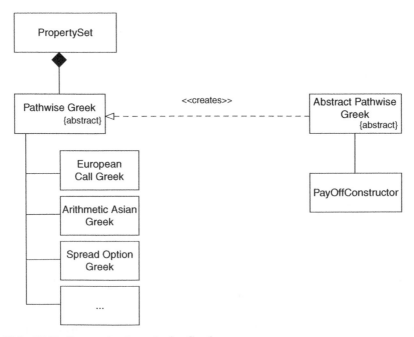

Figure 18.2   UML diagram for the pathwise Greeks

equation (18.6) we have to implement the derivative of the payoff function h. Second, for simple models the process given by equation (18.11) can be explicitly computed. Since then the pathwise estimator is nothing but another payoff function, it can be embedded in a payoff class. For complex models we might need to simulate the process $\hat{\Delta}$, given by (18.15) explicitly. In this case we have to define a model class in C++ and use some numerical scheme to discretise the corresponding dynamics.

Example: Black-Scholes call

We consider the Black-Scholes model. Therefore, $\sigma(S) = \sigma_{BS} \, S$ and $\mu(S) = rS$, $r, \sigma_{BS} > 0$. We already computed the derivative with respect to the spot price s_0. To implement this sensitivity we have to implement another payoff. Therefore, the implementation of the class is essentially the same as for a payoff:

```cpp
class PW_Greeks_Call_Delta : public PayOff<double, double>
{
public:
    PW_Greeks_Call_Delta();
    PW_Greeks_Call_Delta(const SimplePropertySet
                         <string, AnyType*>& pset);
    virtual PayOff<double, double>* clone() const;
    virtual double operator()(double Discount, double Spot) const;
    virtual double PayOff_Value(double Discount, double Spot,
                                double Strike) const;
    virtual  PW_Greeks_Call_Delta()
    SimplePropertySet<string, AnyType*>
      PW_Greeks_Call_Delta_Properties;
private:
    // No private data nor member functions
};
```

The code for calculating the delta is

```cpp
double PW_Greeks_Call_Delta::operator()(double Discount,
                                        double& Spot) const
{
    double strike;
    double startspot;
    std::string paytype;

    if(paytype == "call")
        if(Spot > strike) return Spot / startspot;
        else return 0;
    else
        if(Spot < strike) return - Spot / startspot;
        else return 0.0;
};
```

We now consider the pathwise estimator with respect to the implied volatility σ_{BS}, the vega of the option. It is given by

$$\text{Greek}^{PW}_{\sigma_{BS}} = \exp(-rT)\sigma_{BS}^{-1}\left(\log\left(\frac{S(T)}{s_0}\right) - r + \frac{\sigma_{BS}^2}{2}T\right)S(T)1_{\{S(T)>K\}} \qquad (18.19)$$

Example: Black-Scholes Asian call

The same procedure can be applied to compute estimates for path-dependent options. We show how to adapt the implementation of the `operator ()` to cover arithmetic Asian options. To compute the Greeks with respect to the spot and the implied volatility σ_{BS} we implement the formulae:

$$\text{Greek}^{PW}_{s_0} = \exp(-rT)\frac{\bar{S}(T)}{s_0}1_{\{\bar{S}(T)>K\}} \qquad (18.20)$$

$$\text{Greek}^{PW}_{\sigma_{BS}} = \exp(-rT)\frac{1}{\sigma_{BS}N}\sum_{i=1}^{N}\left(\log\left(\frac{S(t_i)}{s_0}\right) - r + \frac{\sigma_{BS}^2}{2}T\right) \qquad (18.21)$$

$$\cdot\,\bar{S}(T)1_{\{\bar{S}(T)>K\}} \qquad (18.22)$$

To this end we pass parameter values to the `operator ()`. This can be done using the `SimplePropertySet`. For example, we wish to add the volatiliy to a given property set. We use the key 'Volatility' together with a pre-defined variable `vol` which is of type `double`:

```
Property<string,AnyType*> ("Volatility", vol)
```

We can use σ_{BS} to calculate vega which is done as follows:

```
double PW_Greeks_ArithAsian_Vega::operator()(double Discount,
                                    Vector<double>& Spot) const
{
    double strike, startspot, maturity, vol, r;
    long NumberOfSpots;
    double Average = 0.0;
    double vega = 0.0;
    // Declaration of the variables as done for Payoffs...
    for(long i=0; i <= NumberOfSpots-1; ++i)
        Average += Spot[i];
    Average = Average / NumberOfSpots;
    if(paytype == "call")
    {
        if (Average > strike)
        {
            for(size_t j = 1; j <=NumberOfSpots-1; ++j)
                vega += log(Spot[j]/Spot[0]);
            vega *= Average / (vol * double(NumberOfSpots))
                    * (NumberOfSpots -1) * r * vol*vol/2
                    * maturity;
            return vega;
        }
    else
```

```
        return 0.0;
    }
else
    The put case...
};
```

Example: Black-Scholes spread option

An example of an option with payoff depending on more than one underlying is a spread option with strike K. It has payoff $\max(S_2(T) - S_1(T) - K, 0)$. We have considered spread options in Chapters 5 and 17. Since it depends on two assets we have two first order sensitivities with respect to the initial values spot values:

$$\text{Greek}_{S_1(0)}^{PW} = \exp(-rT)\frac{S_2(T)}{S_2(0)}1_{\{S_2(T)-S_1(T)>K\}} \tag{18.23}$$

$$\text{Greek}_{S_2(0)}^{PW} = \exp(-rT)\frac{S_1(T)}{S_1(0)}1_{\{S_2(T)-S_1(T)>K\}} \tag{18.24}$$

We leave the implementation as an exercise for the reader.

18.4   THE LIKELIHOOD RATIO METHOD

The likelihood ratio method is based on *score functions* for a given model. The score function is a function that is multiplied with the payoff of the option such that the Greek can be represented by

$$\text{Greek}^{LR}(\phi) := \mathbb{E}[h(S(\phi))\omega(\phi, S(\phi))] \tag{18.25}$$

$\omega(\cdot, \cdot)$ is the score function. The corresponding Monte Carlo estimator is given by

$$\widehat{\text{Greek}}^{LR}(\phi) := \frac{1}{N}\sum_{i=1}^{N} h(S(\phi)^i)\omega(\phi, S(\phi)^i) \tag{18.26}$$

To apply the likelihood ratio method we need additional information about the model, namely we must have an expression for the score function. The likelihood ratio method (18.26) is an unbiased estimator for the Greek. The likelihood ratio method can be used to compute Greeks for options with discontinuous payoff functions because the derivative of the payoff function is not needed. To see why discontinuous payoffs cause no problems we show how the *integration by parts formula* is applied. The basic idea is to shift the derivative operator from the payoff function to the density of the probability measure which in most cases is sufficiently smooth to apply the derivative operator.

Several authors have studied the likelihood ratio method in a very general setting. It can be seen as an application of the *calculus of variation on path space* or *Malliavin calculus*. The key observation is that by using this calculus, an analogue to the integration by parts formula can be derived and the score function is a *Skorohod integral*, which can be approximated by simulation. In this book we do not cover the theory of Malliavin calculus. We give an introduction to likelihood ratio methods and a finite difference implementation of it. An introduction to Malliavin calculus and the Skorohod integral is given in Nualart (1995).

To introduce the underlying mathematics we give a basic example which only uses the integration by parts formula from ordinary calculus. We work within the Black-Scholes model. Then, the measure of logarithmic returns is normally distributed and the calculations can be carried out explicitly.

We start with the integration by parts. For differentiable functions $f, g : \mathbb{R} \to \mathbb{R}$ the integration by parts formula is the following relationship:

$$f(b)g(b) - f(a)g(a) = \int_a^b f'(s)g(s)ds + \int_a^b f(s)g'(s)ds \tag{18.27}$$

Writing the expectation $\mathbb{E}[h(S(T))]$ as an integral and denoting the density by φ, the expectation can be derived by

$$\mathbb{E}[h(S_T)] = \int h(s)\varphi(\phi, s)ds \tag{18.28}$$

The payoff function h and therefore the density φ depend on model parameters. Let us fix the parameter ϕ (for example, the spot price $\phi = s_0$). Now, to evaluate the Greek with respect to ϕ we consider

$$\mathbb{E}\left[\frac{\partial}{\partial \phi}h(S_T)\right] = \int \underbrace{\frac{\partial}{\partial \phi}h(\phi)(s)}_{f'} \underbrace{\varphi(\phi)(s)}_{g}\, ds$$

With the notation above we can apply the integration by parts rule which leads to

$$\int h(s)\frac{\partial}{\partial \phi}\varphi(\phi, s)ds = \int h(s)\underbrace{\frac{\frac{\partial}{\partial \phi}\varphi(\phi, s)}{\varphi(\phi, s)}}_{=:\omega(\phi,s)}\varphi(\phi)(s)ds$$

The calculation can be seen as an option pricing problem with a new payoff function, which is the initial one multiplied by the *score* $\omega(\phi)$.

Having carried out the calculation of the weights the calculation of the Greek, for instance with respect to the spot price s_0, is straightforward:

$$\mathrm{Greek}_{s_0}^{LR} = \frac{1}{N}\sum_{i=1}^N h_{s_0}(S^i)\omega(s_0, S^i)$$

Let us now give the explicit calculation for the Black-Scholes model. By denoting the logarithmic asset value $X(t) := \ln(S(t))$, the explicit form for the density is given by

$$\varphi_{s_0}(s, X(0)) = \frac{1}{\sigma\sqrt{2\pi}s_0}\exp\left(-\frac{1}{2}\left(\frac{\ln(s) - X(0)}{\sigma}\right)\right)$$

Thus,

$$\frac{\partial_{s_0}\varphi_{s_0}}{\varphi_{s_0}} = \frac{s - X(0)}{\sigma\sqrt{T}}\cdot\partial_{s_0}X(0) = \frac{s - X(0)}{s_0\sigma\sqrt{T}}$$

and the score function is

$$\omega(s_0, s) = \frac{s}{s_0\sigma\sqrt{T}} \tag{18.29}$$

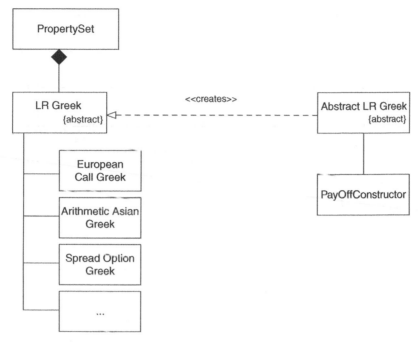

Figure 18.3   UML diagram for the likelihood ratio Greeks

Another property of the likelihood ratio method is that the score function does not depend on the payoff but on the underlying model. Therefore, we can compute the Greek with respect to the spot value for any payoff using the derived score function. This makes it possible to use the *Abstract Factory* design pattern again. The corresponding UML diagram is shown in Figure 18.3.

Let us assume the option has maturity T and the model is the standard Black-Scholes one. To compute the Greeks we multiply the payoff under consideration by the following score functions:

$$\omega(s_0, s) = \frac{s}{s_0 \sigma \sqrt{T}} \tag{18.30}$$

$$\omega(s_0, s_0, s) = \frac{s^2 - s\sigma\sqrt{T} - 1}{s_0^2 \sigma^2 T} \tag{18.31}$$

$$\omega(\sigma_{BS}, s) = \frac{s^2 - 1}{\sigma} - s\sqrt{T} \tag{18.32}$$

The score functions are evaluated at $s = Z_N$ with Z_N being the Gaussian variate used to generate the final value $S(T) = S(t_N)$.

18.4.1   Examples

Let us consider a European call option. Figure 18.4 shows the different approximation methods for the option under consideration. We have chosen the following model parameters: $s_0 = 100$, $K = 101$, $r = 3\%$, $\sigma_{BS} = 25\%$ and $T = 0.75$. We did the same analysis for the second order

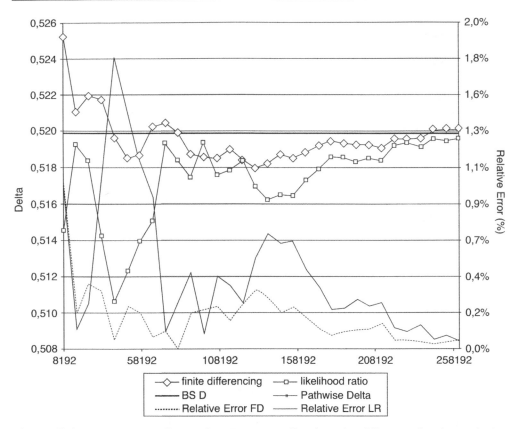

Figure 18.4 Δ-convergence diagram for a European call option using different estimation methods

Greek with respect to the spot, the Γ of the option. The pathwise method cannot be applied since it would correspond to applying it to computing the Greek with respect to the spot for a digital. Figure 18.5 illustrates the results.

Path-dependence and options on multiple assets

We illustrate the possibilities by considering an arithmetic Asian call option and we consider a discrete set of time points $\mathcal{T} = \{0 = t_0 < t_1 < t_2 < \ldots < t_n = T\}$. To simulate the underlying for the given set $\mathcal{T}$ of time points we use the exact solution, which for the Black-Scholes model is

$$S_{i+1} = S_i \exp\left((r - \sigma_{BS}^2/2)\,\Delta_i + \sigma_{BS}\sqrt{\Delta_i}Z_i\right), \quad Z_i \sim \mathcal{N}(0, 1), \quad i = 1, \ldots, N \tag{18.33}$$

This implies that the score functions needed to compute Δ and Γ are the same as for the call and the put option. For computing the vega we have to use the full vector of Gaussian variates used to construct the path:

$$\omega(s_0, Z_1) = \frac{Z_1}{s_0\sigma_{BS}\sqrt{t_1}}, \quad Z_1 \sim N(0, 1) \tag{18.34}$$

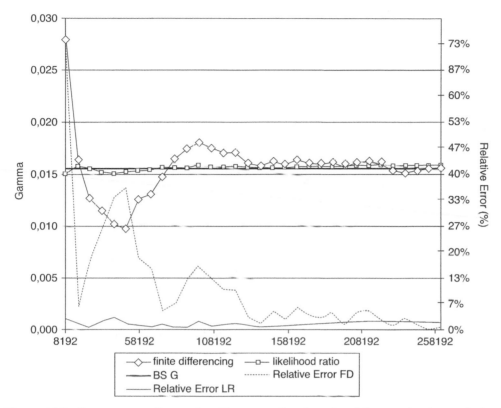

Figure 18.5 Γ-convergence diagram for a European call option using different estimation methods

$$\omega(s_0, s_0, Z_1) = \frac{Z_1^2 - Z_1 \sigma_{BS} \sqrt{t_1} - 1}{s_0^2 \sigma_{BS}^2 t_1}, \, Z_1 \sim N(0, 1) \tag{18.35}$$

$$\omega(s_0, \sigma_{BS}, Z1, \ldots, Z_N) = \sum_{j=1}^{N} \frac{Z_j^2 - 1}{\sigma_{BS}} - Z_N \sqrt{\Delta_{N-1}}, \tag{18.36}$$

$$Z_j \sim \mathcal{N}(0, 1), \quad j = 1, \ldots, N$$

Further applications and new developments are covered in Benhamou (2002), Gobet and Kohatsu Higa (2003), Kohatsu Higa and Montero (2003), Jäckel (2005), Fries and Joshi (2006), Fu (2007), Glasserman and Chen (2007), and Kienitz (2008).

We illustrate the application to estimate the Greeks for a path-dependent option by considering a two year arithmetic Asian call option. We have chosen the model parameters:

$$s_0 = 100, K = 110, \quad r = 3\%, \quad \sigma = 29\%, \quad d = 1\%, \text{ Averaging p.a.} = 12$$

Figure 18.6 summarises the results using the finite difference method as well as the likelihood ratio method.

Again, we applied the likelihood ratio method to compute Γ (see Figure 18.7).

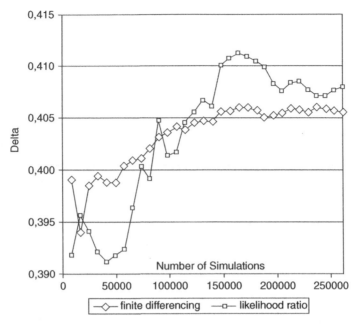

Figure 18.6 Δ-convergence diagram for an arithmetic Asian call option using different estimation methods

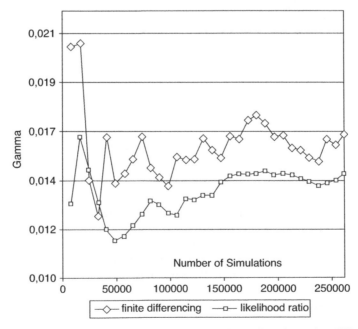

Figure 18.7 Γ-convergence diagram for an arithmetic Asian call option using different estimation methods

Finally, we give an example in a multi-asset setting. We assume a discretisation of a multi-dimensional SDE of the form

$$\hat{S}_i(t_{n+1}) = \hat{S}_i(t_n) \left(1 + \left(r - d_i - \frac{\sigma_i^2}{2} \right) \Delta_n + \sum_{k=1}^{d} a_{ik} \sqrt{\Delta_n} Z_k \right), \ Z_k \sim \mathcal{N}(0, 1)$$

The vector $\underline{Z} = (Z_1, Z_2, \ldots, Z_n)$ is a vector of independent standard Gaussian random variables. $\tilde{A} = (a_{ik}\sqrt{\Delta t})_{ik}$ and the matrix $B = (b_{k,i})_{k,i}$ is given by $B = \tilde{A}^{-1}$. We get the following scores for Δ and cross-Γ:

$$\omega(S_i(0), \underline{Z}) = \frac{\left({}^t\underline{Z}A^{-1} \right)_i}{S_i(0)\sqrt{T}} \tag{18.37}$$

where for a given vector $\underline{V} = (v_1, v_2, \ldots, v_d) \in \mathbb{R}^d$, the notation $(V)_i, i = 1, 2, \ldots, d$ denotes the ith component of the vector $\underline{V}$, that is $(V)_i = v_i$. Denoting by δ_i the Kronecker symbol, the score function for the cross-Γ is given by

$$\omega(S_i(0), S_j(0), \underline{Z}) = \omega(S_i(0), \underline{Z})\omega(S_j(0), \underline{Z}) - \delta_{ij} \frac{\omega(S_i(0), \underline{Z})}{S_j(0)} - \sum_{k=1}^{d} \frac{b_{ki} b_{kj}}{S_i(0)S_j(0)} \tag{18.38}$$

For other score functions in the multi-dimensional setting, see Jäckel (2005).

The likelihood ratio method has been applied to derive Greeks for other models than the Black-Scholes model, for example the Heston model (see Broadie and Kaya, 2006). Other authors have applied the *Malliavin calculus* to obtain score functions for more general models, for example Kohatsu Higa and Montero (2003) or Benhamou (2002).

18.5 LIKELIHOOD RATIO FOR FINITE DIFFERENCES – PROXY SIMULATION

The *Proxy Simulation Scheme* was introduced by Fries and Kampen (2005). We consider two discretisations of the stochastic processes S. The first process, called the target scheme X, is a discretisation of the dynamics under consideration and the second one, called the proxy scheme Y, is a discretisation that is easily computable. We wish to use the transition density. For the corresponding densities φ_X and φ_Y used to compute expectations we require for almost all y that $\varphi_X(y) = 0 \Rightarrow \varphi_Y(y) = 0$. Applying an importance sampling argument we have for the expectation given a payoff function h:

$$\mathbb{E}_{\varphi_S}[h(S)] = \int h(s)\varphi_S(s)ds = \int h(s) \underbrace{\frac{\varphi_S(s)}{\varphi_X(s)}}_{=:\omega} \varphi_X(s) = \mathbb{E}_{\varphi_X}[h(X)\omega]$$

Suppose we wish to compute some sensitivity with respect to a model-parameter ϕ. We simulate the proxy process Y. The sensitivity is then determined as in the likelihood ratio method:

$$\text{Greek}^{Proxy}(\phi) := \mathbb{E}[h(\phi)(S)\omega(\phi)] \tag{18.39}$$

The difference is that we do not compute the likelihood ratio or score function analytically using the proxy scheme. The corresponding Monte Carlo estimator is

$$\frac{1}{N} \sum_{i=1}^{N} h(X) \frac{\omega^i(\phi + \epsilon) - \omega^i(\phi - \epsilon)}{2\epsilon} \tag{18.40}$$

with weight function

$$\omega_{n+1} = \prod_{j=1}^{n} \frac{\pi^X(t_j, Y_j; t_{j+1}, Y_j)}{\pi^Y(t_j, Y_j; t_{j+1}, Y_j)} \tag{18.41}$$

Here π denotes the transition kernel for either the target or the proxy. In practice we take two discretisation schemes:

$$t_{n+1} \to X_{n+1} \quad \text{(Target)} \tag{18.42}$$

$$t_{n+1} \to Y_{n+1} \quad \text{(Proxy)} \tag{18.43}$$

The target scheme is chosen such that it is a reasonable approximation of the dynamics of the process S and that we can compute the transition density of the target scheme.

A crucial observation in this case is that we do not need to sample from the scheme for S but we only need the transition densities to compute the weight function. This enables us to use transition densities that in some cases are readily available, whereas to sample from such densities might be a complex task. In the Monte Carlo simulation computing the weights is easy if we use an Euler or predictor-corrector scheme. In these cases the transition probabilities are (multi)-normal densities and therefore the weights can be computed explicitly.

We have computed the delta and the gamma for a digital option using the proxy method. Figure 18.8 illustrates the convergence of the proxy estimator for the delta.

Figure 18.9 illustrates the convergence of the proxy estimator for the gamma but with a different value for the initial distrubance.

18.6 SUMMARY AND CONCLUSIONS

We have reviewed three important methods to compute Greeks within a Monte Carlo framework and we have also given guidelines on which one to use in a certain application.

Difference estimators are easy to set up but extra simulations are needed and often the bias is large especially if the payoff is discontinuous. The pathwise method is computationally less expensive if it is possible to break it down to evaluating a payoff function. To this end we need the exact solution of the underlying stochastic differential equation. If this is not the case we have to simulate the dynamics of the sensitivity under consideration, which makes the method also computationally expensive. Finally, the likelihood ratio method can be applied to any kind of payoff if the probability density is known and smooth. This is the main drawback since for complex models at least it is not easy to compute the score function. A finite difference version of the likelihood ratio method, the proxy simulation scheme, uses a discretisation to explicitly simulate the score function. This representation is then used to perform the Monte Carlo simulation. This method can be adapted and leads to stable and reasonable results for multi-dimensional and complex models such as stochastic volatility Lévy models.

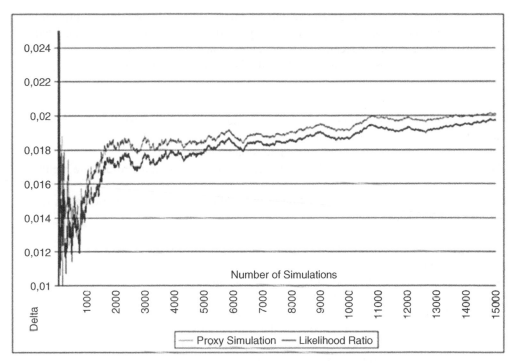

Figure 18.8 Proxy simulation for a (non-discounted) digital payoff with strike 50; $\epsilon = 0.5\%$ of the initial spot price, Δ

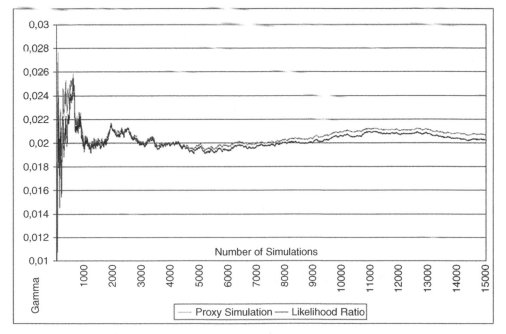

Figure 18.9 Proxy simulation for a (non-discounted) digital payoff with strike 50; $\epsilon = 1\%$ of the initial spot price, Γ

All of the discussed methods have their strengths and weaknesses. We argue that the problem under consideration should be analysed as thoroughly as possible to combine the methods and further apply variance reduction techniques to get efficient and stable estimation.

Let us summarise the pros and cons of each method to compute the Greeks:

- Finite Difference Method:
  - No additional information from the model is needed. We only need the discretisation of the underlying stochastic differential equation.
  - We do not need any further information on the simulation scheme.
  - The method cannot be applied to discontinuous payoffs, therefore the results are highly biased.
  - Computationally burdensome (calculation of two additional Monte Carlo estimators for the central differences).
  - Generic sensitivities.
  - The bias is of order ϵ because the finite difference approximation is of order ϵ.
- Pathwise Method:
  - We do need additional information from the model since we may have to simulate the dynamic of the Greek directly. To this end we need the corresponding partial derivatives for the drift and diffusion coefficients of the stochastic differential equation.
  - We do not need any further information on the simulation scheme.
  - The method cannot be applied to discontinuous payoffs, therefore the results are highly biased and we need to know the partial derivative of the payoff function.
  - Computationally burdensome (calculation of two additional Monte Carlo estimators for the central differences).
  - No generic sensitivities.
  - The estimator is unbiased.
- Likelihood Ratio Method:
  - We need additional information from the model. Especially, we do need the score function which can be computed from the probability density corresponding to the model under consideration.
  - We do not need any further information on the simulation scheme.
  - The method can be applied to discontinuous payoffs.
  - Computationally effective since only multiplication of the score function is involved.
  - No generic sensitivity.
  - The method leads to an unbiased estimator of the Greek.

With the C++ implementation given on the CD the reader can easily adapt the methods to some specific setting.

18.7   EXERCISES AND PROJECTS

1. (**) Pathwise Method

   We have outlined a general procedure to compute Greeks using the pathwise method. To apply it a simulation of another process, (18.15), might be necessary. Use the general framework for modelling this process and test it for the Black-Scholes model.

2. (***) Mollifiers

Consider the mollifier

$$h(x) = \begin{cases} 0 & , \quad |x| \geq 1 \\ \exp\left(-\frac{1}{1-x^2}\right) & , \quad |x| < 1 \end{cases}$$

If we multiply the function h by a constant C we can ensure that $C \int h(y)dy = 1$. We denote the normalised function by $\rho(x) := C^{-1}h(x)$. Given a small real number α consider

$$\rho_\alpha(x) = \frac{\rho(x/\alpha)}{\alpha}$$

Figure 18.10 illustrates the shape of the function for different parameters of α. The function

$$\widetilde{Digital}_\alpha(y) = \int_{-\infty}^{t} \rho_\alpha(y - x)Digital(x)dx$$

can be used to approximate the payoff of a digital option. Apply the finite difference method as well as the pathwise method discussed in this chapter to approximate the payoff and compare it to the results obtained from applying the likelihood ratio method.

Discontinuous payoffs can be approximated using such functions and the technique of convolution. Figure 18.11 illustrates this for approximating the payoff of a digital option.

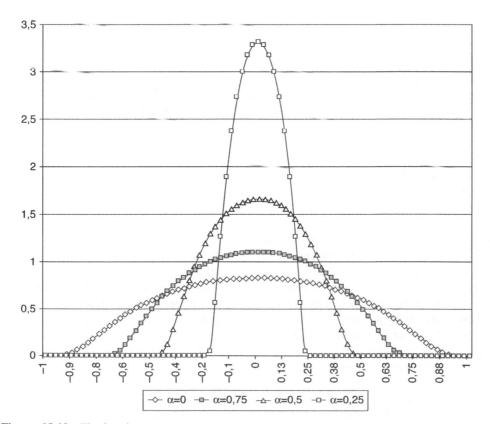

Figure 18.10 The function ρ_α

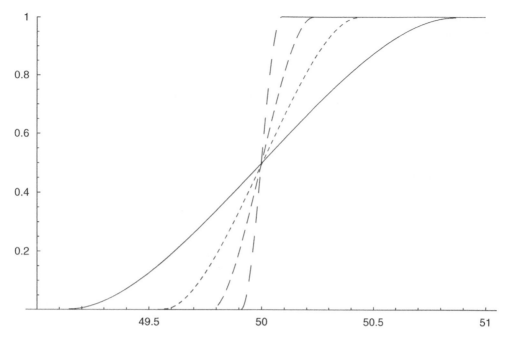

Figure 18.11   Smoothed payoff by applying convolution with ρ_α for a digital payoff with strike 50

3. (**) Digital Option
   Consider the payoff of a digital option with strike K. It is given by $1_{\{S(T)>K\}}$. Consider
   the smoothed payoff using the methods given in exercise 2. Implement a payoff function
   for the smoothed payoff and compute the different estimators for Δ and Γ of this digital
   option.
   Compare the results to the exact solution.
4. (**) Likelihood Ratio
   We stated the formulae for likelihood ratio score functions in multiple dimensions. Use
   formulas (18.37) and (18.38) to implement Greeks for a multi-factor geometric Brownian
   model by coding the corresponding payoff classes.
5. (***) Discontinuous Payoffs
   Consider an option with a discontinuous payoff function. To optimise the calculation we
   can use a hybrid method to compute Greeks. Near the discontinuity we can apply the
   likelihood ratio method and elsewhere we apply the pathwise method.
   Design a class that allows you to combine the pathwise method and the likelihood ratio
   method. This enables you to specify the region in which to apply a certain method. This
   amounts to specifying the discontinuities and selecting ranges around these discontinuities
   where the likelihood ratio method is valid.
   For example consider some payoff function h which has a discontinuity at x_0 (for
   example, a digital around its strike x_0). Take some function $A(x)$ which has the following
   properties:
   – $A(x) = 1, x \in [x_0 - \epsilon_0, x_0 + \epsilon_0]$
   – some interpolation between 0 and 1, $x \in (x_0 - \epsilon_1, x_0 - \epsilon_0) \cup (x_0 + \epsilon_0, x_0 + \epsilon_1)$
   – $A(x) = 0, x \in (-\infty, x_0 - \epsilon_1] \cup [x_0 + \epsilon_1, \infty)$

Then, consider the payoff function

$$h_{\text{new}}(x) = \underbrace{A(x)h(x)}_{I} + \underbrace{(1 - A(x))h(x)}_{II} \tag{18.44}$$

Simulate sample paths and compute two Monte Carlo estimators. One estimator for I and one for II from equation (18.44) with respect to the appropriate method.

6. (****) Proxy Simulation

Consider the proxy simulation. Assume the processes (18.42) and (18.43). Compute the transition densities π^S and π^Y. Use the results to compute the weight function ω in this case.

Hint: the transition probabilities follow a (multi-dimensional) Gaussian distribution.

To approximate the sensitivity with respect to some parameter ϕ compute the estimators:

– Generate paths due to the schemes.
– Compute the weights corresponding to formula (18.41).
– Compute the Monte Carlo estimators with the realisations taken from the proxy scheme (18.43) and compute the scores with respect to the target scheme (18.42):

$$\hat{V} = \frac{1}{N} \sum_{i=1}^{N} h(Y)\omega(\phi + \epsilon), \quad \hat{V} = \frac{1}{N} \sum_{i=1}^{N} h(Y)\omega(\phi - \epsilon)$$

– Compute

$$\frac{\hat{V}(\phi + \epsilon) - \hat{V}(\phi - \epsilon)}{2\epsilon}$$

Advanced Monte Carlo II – Early Exercise

19.1 INTRODUCTION AND OBJECTIVES

Many options, especially options based on interest rates, include early exercise, early termination or callable features. Such features can be seen as further rights for the holder of the option. Such options can be classified as *Bermudan* or *American* options. Bermudan options can be exercised at predetermined times in the future whereas American options can be exercised at any time in the future until maturity. The market participant who is long the contract has to decide at each date whether he exercises the option or not. Therefore, the time to exercise the option is itself a random variable depending on the value of the underlying.

Several methods have been introduced to approximate the price of Bermudan or American options using simulation. Among the methods are state space partitioning (Jin, Tan and Sun, 2007), stochastic mesh methods (Broadie and Glasserman, 2004), stochastic backward equations (Gobet, 2004), Malliavin calculus (Fournie *et al.*, 1999), least squares regression (Longstaff and Schwartz, 2001) or dual methods (Rogers, 2002; Haugh and Kogan, 2001).

We have decided to implement the method introduced in Longstaff and Schwartz (2001) based on *linear least squares regression* and the method considered in Rogers (2002) and Haugh and Kogan (2001). To this end we numerically approximate an optimal stopping problem based on a collection of simulated paths. The method is a combination of simulation and *backward induction*. The chapter is organised as follows. First, we introduce Bermudan and American options and proceed by introducing the optimal stopping problem. After defining the necessary concepts we describe the algorithm based on regression and show how we map the numerical concepts in C++ classes. The algorithm we consider leads to lower bounds on the price of a Bermudan or American option. We suggest improving the results by separating the regression from the pricing. Finally, we discuss several improvements and a method to compute upper bounds.

19.2 DESCRIPTION OF THE PROBLEM

Suppose we have an option with payoff function h. We consider a discrete set of points in the interval $[0, T]$ and denote it by $\mathcal{T}_{Ex} = \{t_0, t_1, \ldots, t_N = T\}$. At each time point t_i, $i = 1, 2, \ldots, N$ we have the opportunity to execute the option. Because we allow exercise at predetermined times in $[0, T]$ we consider a Bermudan option. Pricing an American option can be done by considering many exercise opportunities.

To tackle the problem of pricing a Bermudan option using simulation we formulate the problem in terms of an *optimal stopping problem*. To this end let $(S(t))_{t \in [0,T]}$ be a stochastic process on the filtered probability space $(\Omega, \mathcal{F}, \mathbb{P}, (\mathcal{F}_t)_t)$. A random variable T given by

$$
\begin{aligned}
T : \Omega &\rightarrow [0, T] \\
\omega &\rightarrow T(\omega)
\end{aligned}
$$

is called a stopping time with respect to the filtration $(\mathcal{F}_t)_t$ if it is *adapted* to it, that is $\{T \leq t\} \in \mathcal{F}_t$ for all $t \in [0, T]$.

Let us denote the price of a Bermudan option at time t_n, $t_n \in \mathcal{T}_{\text{Ex}}$, by V_n. The value at t_0, the present value, is given by

$$V(0) = \sup_\tau \mathbb{E}\left[DF(0, \tau)h[S_\tau]\right] \tag{19.1}$$

where we take the sup with respect to all stopping times τ and let $DF(t_1, t_2)$ denote the discount factor for discounting from t_2 to t_1. For the optimal stopping time τ^* corresponding to equation (19.1) we have

$$V(0) = \mathbb{E}\left[DF(0, \tau^*)h[S_{\tau^*}]\right] \tag{19.2}$$

We may think of applying the following stopping rule τ^+ which maximises the discounted option price for each simulated path:

$$\tau^+ = \{\tau | DF(\tau, t)h(S_\tau) \geq DF(s, t)h(S_s); s, \tau \in [t, T]\}$$

Because the random variable τ^+ is not adapted it is not a stopping time and we implicitly use more information at time t than actually available.

In the following we review numerical methods to approximate the optimal stopping time τ^* and discuss how to map these methods to C++ code.

The first method leads to a lower bound for the price of a Bermudan/American option. The second one we review, called the *dual method*, is used to derive an upper bound for the option value.

19.3   PRICING AMERICAN OPTIONS BY REGRESSION

Suppose we have simulated the option on a given mesh:

$$\mathcal{T} = \{t_0, t_1, \ldots, t_{\text{NTime}} = T\}$$

The possibility to exercise the option is given at discrete times $\mathcal{T}_{\text{Ex}} \subset \mathcal{T}$.

The algorithm to compute a lower bound is based on a collection of NSim paths represented by the two-dimensional array $\overline{S} = \left(S_{jk}\right)_{jk}$, $t_k \in \mathcal{T}_{\text{Ex}}$, $j = 1, 2, \ldots$, NSim. S_{jk} is the value of the jth simulated path at time step $t_{\text{Ex}} \in \mathcal{T}$. We start from the values at maturity $S_{N,l}$ and use an induction argument based on regression to work backward until the start date of the option.

To describe the induction we consider the *expected continuation value* at time t_k, $k = 1, 2, \ldots, N$ and denote it by $C_k^E(x)$. It is given as the conditional expectation of the option value at time t_{k+1} prevailing so that the asset price at time t_k is equal to x:

$$C_k^E(x) := \mathbb{E}[h_{t_{k+1}}(S_{k+1})|S_k = x], k \in \mathcal{T} \tag{19.3}$$

The value $C_k^E(x)$ is the value of the option resulting from not exercising it until the next possibility. In contrast to the expected continuation value, we consider the *realised continuation value* at time $t_k \in \mathcal{T}_{\text{Ex}}$ and denote it by $C_k^R(x)$. It is given by

$$C_k^R(x) = \mathbb{E}\left[h(S_{k+1})|S_{k+1} = x\right] \tag{19.4}$$

The realised continuation value is the value of the option evolving the current path into the future and evaluating the payoff with the realised asset price.

We can express the expected continuation value at time t_k in terms of the expected and the realised continuation value as follows:

$$C_k^E(x) = \mathbb{E}\left[C_k^R(S_k), C_{k+1}^E(S_{k+1})|S_k = x\right] \tag{19.5}$$

Let us verify that the continuation value satisfies a *dynamic programming relation*, which further clarifies the backward nature of the problem.

We know the continuation value at maturity

$$C_N^E(x) = 0 \tag{19.6}$$

because there will be no continuation after reaching maturity. For $t_k \in \mathcal{T}_{Ex}$ and using equation (19.5) we can interpret it as a newly issued option starting at t_k. Applying this relation until we reach t_0 the option value is the continuation value at time $t = 0$, which is $C_0^E(S(0))$.

Conversely, for the option values V_k we find

$$V_k(x) = \max(C_k^R(x), C_k^E(x))$$

If the equations (19.6) and (19.5) are satisfied we say a dynamic programming relation holds.

19.4   C++ DESIGN

Before we proceed we discuss the C++ template class AmericanOption.

```
template<class T> class AmericanOption
{
public:
    AmericanOption();
    AmericanOption(const Vector<long>& MC_ExerciseSchedule,
                   VectorFunction<double, double>& MC_Regressors,
                   const Vector<T>& MC_Reg, const Vector<T>&
                   MC_Price);
    virtual ~AmericanOption();

    Vector<double> Price();
    // Calls the regression algorithm
    void Regress();
    // Set Exercise Schedule
    void SetExerciseSchedule(Vector<long>& MC_ExerciseSchedule);
    // Set Discount Factors
    void SetDiscountFactors(Vector<double>& MC_DiscountFactors);
    // Set Regressor Functions
    void SetRegressors(VectorFunction<double, double>&
    MC_Regressors);
    // Paths used for regression
    void SetRegressionPaths(const Vector<T>& MC_Reg);
    // Paths used for pricing
    void SetPricingPaths(const Vector<T>& MC_Price);

private:

    int NumberOfRegressors;                 // Number of functions
                                            // used in regression
```

```
    int NumberOfExerciseDates;            // Number of Exercise
                                             possibilities
    Vector<T> MonteCarloPath_Regression;// implicitly stores number
                                             of regression paths
    Vector<T> MonteCarloPath_Pricing;    // implicitly stores number
                                             of pricing paths
    int NumberOfRegPaths;                // Number of regression
                                             paths
    int NumberOfPricingPaths;            // Number of pricing paths
    VectorFunction<double, double> Regressors;  // RegressorValues
    NumericMatrix<double> OptValues_Current;    // Realised
                                                   continuation
                                                   values
    Vector<double> DiscountFactors;          // The Discount
                                                Factors
    Vector<long> ExerciseSchedule;           // The exercise
                                                schedule
    NumericMatrix<double> RegCoeff;          // The regression
                                                coefficients
    NumericMatrix<double> RegCoeffLater;     // The regression
                                                coefficients
                                             // for regression
                                                later
    // Function to generate the paths
    void Calculate(const Vector<T>& MC_Path, std::string method);

    double OptionPrice_Lower;    // Lower bound
    double OptionPrice_Upper;    // Upper bound
};
```

We have designed the class to be able to consider different sets of paths for applying regression and pricing. This is reflected by the private member data:

- `Vector<T> MonteCarloPath_Regression`
- `Vector<T> MonteCarloPath_Pricing`.

The function `Regress()` is called to perform the regression given the exercise schedule represented by the vector `ExerciseSchedule` and the pricing of the option. The results are then stored in the variables `OptionPrice_Lower` and `OptionPrice_Upper`.

Before we describe the theory and the mathematical concepts we show how the class `AmericanOption` can be applied to price options:

```
int main()
{
    int NumberOfDates=12;        // Number of Columns of Matrix
    int NumberOfAssets=1;        // Number of Rows of Matrix
    int Seed=123456;                  // Seed for Random Generator
    cout << "Seed:";
    cin >> Seed;
    cout << "Seed=" << Seed<<endl;;
    int NumberOfExerciseDates = 11;   // Number exercise dates
    int NumberOfRegressors = 4;    // Number regressors
    int NumberOfRegPaths = 5000;    // Number regression paths
```

```
cout << "Number of Regression Paths";
cin >> NumberOfRegPaths;
cout << "Number of Regression Paths =" << NumberOfRegPaths
     << endl;
int NumberOfPricingPaths = 10000;  // Number of pricing paths
cout << "Number of Pricing Paths";
cin >> NumberOfPricingPaths;
cout << "Number of Pricing Paths =" << NumberOfPricingPaths
      <<endl;
double ScaleFactor = 100.0;    // Scale if numbers too big

double lower = 0.0;
double upper = 100000000.0;

double Spot = 100.0/ScaleFactor;
double dt = 1.0/NumberOfDates;

// Used for regression
Vector<Vector<double> > MC_Org(NumberOfRegPaths);
// Used for pricing
Vector<Vector<double> > MC_Org_Pricing(NumberOfPricingPaths);
// DiscountFactors
Vector<double> DiscountFactors(NumberOfExerciseDates + 1,0);
// ExerciseSchedule
Vector<long> ExerciseSchedule(NumberOfExerciseDates);
// RegressionFunctions
VectorFunction<double, double> myvecfunction(NumberOfRegressors);

// For riskless rate r constant
for(int i = DiscountFactors.MinIndex();
i<=DiscountFactors.MaxIndex();i++)
 DiscountFactors[i] = exp(-r * dt);

for(int i = ExerciseSchedule.MinIndex();
i<=ExerciseSchedule.MaxIndex();i++)
   ExerciseSchedule[i] = i;

// Set the regression functions
const ScalarFunction<double, double, long> myfunction1(Reg1);
const ScalarFunction<double, double, long> myfunction2(Reg2);
const ScalarFunction<double, double, long> myfunction3(Reg3);
const ScalarFunction<double, double, long> myfunction4(Reg4);

myvecfunction.function(1, myfunction1);
myvecfunction.function(2, myfunction2);
myvecfunction.function(3, myfunction3);
myvecfunction.function(4, myfunction4);

Vector<double, long> u01(NumberOfDates);
Vector<double, long> result(NumberOfDates);
```

```
// Init class
AmericanOption<Vector<double> > TestAmerican(ExerciseSchedule,
                                             myvecfunction,
                                             MC_Org,
                                             MC_Org_Pricing);
// Set discount structure
TestAmerican.SetDiscountFactors(DiscountFactors);

double lowerbound = 0.0;
double upperbound = 0.0;

TestAmerican.SetRegressionPaths(MC_Org);        // Set regression
                                                   paths
TestAmerican.SetPricingPaths(MC_Org_Pricing);   // Set pricing
                                                   paths
TestAmerican.Regress();                         // Start regression
Vector<double> out = TestAmerican.Price();      // Call pricing
                                                   func
cout << "Lower: " << ScaleFactor * out[1] << "Upper: "
                  << ScaleFactor * out[2] << endl;
```

We first enter the necessary data by supplying the seed to the random generator, the number of regression and pricing paths. Then, we choose how many basis functions we use and initialise the functions. We create the paths used for regression and pricing. This can be replaced by the methods discussed in the previous chapters.

19.5   LINEAR LEAST SQUARES REGRESSION

We assume that the expected continuation value at time t_k can be approximated using functions ψ_j, $j = 1, 2, \ldots, N_{\text{Reg}}$ such that

$$\hat{C}_k(x) := \sum_{j=1}^{N_{\text{Reg}}} \beta_j \psi_j(x) \tag{19.7}$$

We call the functions ψ_j the *basis functions*. Several functions have been suggested as basis functions. Longstaff and Schwartz (2001) argue for the use of *orthogonal polynomials*, which we discuss in section 23.4.3. In particular they suggest to use Laguerre, Hermite, Jacobi or Legendre polynomials. Another popular choice is to use the polynomials 1, x, x^2, $\ldots$ or variants including the payoff function h.

Since the representation given in equation (19.7) is in general not exact we want to choose the coefficients β_j, $j = 1, 2, \ldots, N_{\text{Reg}}$ such that the squared difference of the continuation value and its approximation is small. The vector $\underline{\beta} =^t (\beta_1, \ldots, \beta_{N_{\text{Reg}}})$ is called the regression coefficient vector and the entries are called the regression coefficients. To this end we consider the vector

$$\underline{E} := \mathbb{E}\left[\left(C_{n-1}^E(S_{n-1}) - \hat{C}_{n-1}(S_{n-1})\right)\right] \tag{19.8}$$

and its squared norm

$$SE_{\underline{E}} = \mathbb{E}\left[\left(C_{n-1}^E(S_{n-1}) - \hat{C}_{n-1}(S_{n-1})\right)^2\right]$$
$$= \mathbb{E}\left[\left(\mathbb{E}\left[V_n(S_n)|S_{n-1}\right] - \hat{C}_{n-1}(S_{n-1})\right)^2\right]$$

Using this representation we can compute the coefficients that minimise the error $\underline{E}$ by differentiating $\underline{E}_i$, $i = 1, 2, \ldots, N_{\text{Reg}}$ with respect to β_i. Then, set the derivative equal to zero and obtain

$$\mathbb{E}\left[\mathbb{E}[V_n(S_n)|S_{n-1}] - \hat{C}_{n-1}(S_{n-1})\psi_j(S_{n-1})\right] = 0 \tag{19.9}$$

Solving equation (19.9) leads to an expression from which we compute β_i:

$$\mathbb{E}\left[V_n(S_n)\psi_j(S_{n-1})\right] = \mathbb{E}\left[\hat{C}_{n-1}(S_{n-1})\psi_j(S_{n-1})\right]$$

$$= \sum_{j=1}^{N_{\text{Reg}}} \mathbb{E}\left[\psi_i(S_{n-1})\psi_j(S_{n-1})\right]\beta_i$$

We can use the sample values $\overline{S}$ to replace the expectation by averages over NSim samples. To this end we approximate by

$$\mathbb{E}\left[\psi_i(S_{n-1})\psi_j(S_{n-1})\right] = \frac{1}{\text{NSim}} \sum_{k-1}^{\text{NSim}} \psi_i(S_{k,n-1})\psi_j(S_{k,n-1}) \tag{19.10}$$

We have computed a matrix $B_{\psi\psi}$ and a vector $\underline{B}_{V\psi}$ given by

$$\left(B_{\psi\psi}\right)_{ij} = \mathbb{E}\left[\psi_i(S_{n-1})\psi_j(S_{n-1})\right]$$
$$\left(\underline{B}_{V\psi}\right)_j = \mathbb{E}\left[V_n(S_n)\psi_j(S_{n-1})\right]$$

Thus, we can now use matrix algebra and find

$$\underline{\beta} = B_{\psi\psi}^{-1}\underline{B}_{V\psi} \tag{19.11}$$

Minimising an error

Let us consider the algorithm for finding the regression coefficients again. To make the method more transparent we show in detail how the regression is done and how we implemented it.

We consider d-dimensional vectors $\underline{X}$ and $\underline{Y}$. We assume that there is a linear dependence of $\underline{Y}$ on $\underline{X}$. The linear dependence is expressed by multiplying the vector $\underline{X}$ with a $d \times d$ matrix R. If the linear dependence is an approximation only we do not reproduce the vector $\underline{Y}$ exactly. Let us denote the error vector by $\underline{\mathcal{E}}$. The relation is now

$$R\underline{X} = \underline{Y} + \underline{\mathcal{E}} \tag{19.12}$$

$$\underline{Y}_i = \sum_{j=1}^{d} R_{ij}\underline{X}_j + \underline{\mathcal{E}}_i \tag{19.13}$$

We aim to minimise the error in the least squares sense. To this end we compute squared error $SE(\underline{X})$ as follows:

$$SE(\underline{X}) = \min {}^t\underline{\mathcal{E}}\underline{\mathcal{E}}$$
$$= \min {}^t(\underline{Y} - R\underline{X})(\underline{Y} - R\underline{X})$$
$$= \min ({}^t\underline{Y}\underline{Y} + {}^t\underline{X}^t RR\underline{X} - 2\underline{X}^t {}^t\underline{X}^t R\underline{Y})$$

The latter representation allows to solve the problem

$$\underline{X} = ({}^t R \times R)^{-1} \times^t R \times \underline{Y} \tag{19.14}$$

We have implemented the necessary matrix algebra to compute the vector $\underline{X}$. Either the *singular value decomposition* or the *Cholesky decomposition* can be used.

Let us consider the implementation of equation (19.14). The solution of the matrix equation is done by applying matrix inversion, transposition and multiplication:

```
Invert(Transpose(RegValues[i]) * RegValues[i])
                       * (Transpose(RegValues[i])
                       * CV_R.Column(i+1));
```

19.5.1   The regression function

In our implementation we have chosen to implement the regression functions 1, x, x^2 and x^3. The C++ code is

```
double Reg1(const double& x)
{
return 1.0;
}

double Reg2(const double& x)
{
return x;
}

double Reg3(const double& x)
{
return x * x;
}

double Reg4(const double& x)
{
return x * x * x;
}
```

The reader can either implement his own regression functions or even create a class hierarchy for testing the pricing problem with several regression functions.

After successfully carrying out the regression we need to consider the decision rule for exercising the option. To this end we consider equation (19.14). We choose to exercise if the current option value is greater than the expected continuation value obtained by matrix multiplication of the values of the regressors and the row vector of the regression coefficient matrix.

We may also apply regression to the next possible exercise time. This method is called *regression later* and refers to this fact. The crucial point when using regression later is that the basis functions have to be martingales. Thus, they have to fulfil the condition:

$$\mathbb{E}[f(S_{k+1})|S_k] = f(S_k), \text{ for all } t_k \in \mathcal{T}_{\text{Ex}}$$

The corresponding continuation values are denoted by $C^{E,+}$ and $C^{R,+}$. To apply regression we assume that the approximated continuation value is a linear combination of martingale basis functions:

$$C_k^{E,+}(x) = \sum_{j=0}^{N_{\text{Reg}}} \beta_j \psi_j(x)$$

Furthermore, the option price at t_k is given by

$$V_{k+1}^+(S_{k+1}) = \sum_{j=0}^{N_{\text{Reg}}} \beta_j \psi_j(S_{k+1})$$

If the underlying process is geometric Brownian motion, possible martingale basis functions are

- $\psi(x) = 1$
- $\psi(x) = x^m \exp\left(-(m(r-d) + m(m-1)\sigma^2/2)(t_k - t_0)\right)$
- $\psi(x) = h(x)$

19.5.2 The exercise decision

To approximate the optimal stopping time we apply the following algorithm:

1. Initialise the vector OptStopRule using the asset values at maturity.
2. Backward induction using the dynamic programming relation for the continuation values:
   (a) Compute cash flows resulting from the payoff under consideration.
   (b) Regress with respect to the given values and regressors.
   (c) Update the optimal stopping time, that is the vector OptStopRule.

Finally, we show the C++ code for performing the regression using regression now as well as regression later:

```
for(long i = NumberOfExerciseDates; i >= 1; i--)
{
// Compute all regressor values and solve the linear equation
if(method == "regress")
{
RegCoeff.Row(i,Invert(Transpose(RegValues[i]) * RegValues[i])
              * (Transpose(RegValues[i]) * CV_R.Column(i+1)));
RegCoeffLater.Row(i,Invert(Transpose(RegValuesLater[i])
              * RegValuesLater[i])
              * (Transpose(RegValuesLater[i] * CV_R.Column(i+1)));
}

// Compute vector of Expected ContinuationValues
double value = 0.0;            // regress now
double valuelater = 0.0;       // regress later

for(long j = 1; j <= NumberOfPaths; j++)
{
value = 0.0;
valuelater = 0.0;
for(long k = 1; k <= NumberOfRegressors; k++) // !
```

```
{
value += RegCoeff(i,k) * RegValues[i](j,k);
valuelater+=RegCoeff(i,k) * RegValuesLater[i](j,k);
}
CV_E(j,i) = value;
CV_E_Later(j,i) = valuelater;
}


        // used for upper bound calculation
Martingale = 0.0;

// Compute realized continuation values
// and if pricing the values of the martingale for upper bounds

for(long j = 1;j<=NumberOfPaths;j++)
{
// Compute realised Continuation Values
if(OptValues_Current(j,i) > CV_E(j,i))
CV_R(j,i) = OptValues_Current(j,i);
else
CV_R(j,i) = DiscountFactors[i] * CV_R(j,i+1);
if(method == "pricing")
{
// Compute the upper bound
Martingale = Martingale + CV_E_Later(j,i) - CV_E(j,i);
U[j] = max(U[j], OptValues_Current(j,i)-Martingale);
}
}
}
```

First, we solve the matrix equation for the regression coefficient. This is done by using the functions `Invert`, `Transpose` and the operator `*`. Then, we use the regression values to compute the expected continuation value which we use for comparison to the current option value to determine whether we exercise or not.

We will discuss the variable `Martingale` and the vector `U` when we discuss the upper bound for the Bermudan price.

Therefore, the V_t are determined by C_t^E and C_t^R.

Using this relation the approximation $\hat{C}_t^E$ for C_t^E gives rise to a stopping time

$$\hat{\tau} = \min\{t \in \{1, \ldots, T\} : h(S(t)) \geq \hat{C}_t^E(S(t))\} \tag{19.15}$$

which is the stopping time we adopt to derive a lower bound on the options price.

19.6   EXAMPLE – STEP BY STEP

To illustrate the abstract setting we give an example for four exercise possibilities and three basis functions. To this end let $\mathcal{T} = \{0, 0.25, 0.5, 0.75, 1\}$ and $\mathcal{T}_{Ex} := \{0.25, 0.5, 0.75, 1\}$. We have sampled the paths $\overline{S}$ at the times 0.25, 0.5, 0.75 and 1.0. The spot value is set to be 100.0 at time 0. The first ten samples are given in Table 19.1.

Table 19.1   The two-dimensional array of simulated trajectories $\overline{S}$

S_0	$S_{0.25}$	$S_{0.5}$	$S_{0.75}$	S_1
100	71.25	56.89	56.96	61.47
100	104.66	86.56	74.42	68
100	87.53	90.7	109.55	96.75
100	93.38	100.68	98.28	89.52
100	122.2	78.89	81.14	92.22
100	79.74	47.95	40.68	43.56
100	88.28	80.86	98.84	86.63
100	71.35	85.3	85.49	67.89
100	94.84	92.83	73.35	100.22
100	100.37	120.14	150.02	105.43
...	...	...	...	...

We take as basis functions the polynomials 1, x and x^2. Using the trajectories of the asset price path we compute the matrix for the regressors values (Table 19.2) used to perform the regression.

We have computed the coefficients using equation (19.14) with R being the 3×10 matrix given in Table 19.2 for each time step and Y being the realised continuation values. The results are given in Table 19.3.

19.7   ANALYSIS OF THE METHOD AND IMPROVEMENTS

To improve the basic method we analyse the errors originating from the regression-based approach.

Since we use simulation based on random experiments we observe that the regression as well as the pricing applied suffer from the usual approximation errors. For one-factor problems, like we consider here, the error from applying an approximation of the expected continuation value using regression is smaller than that of the pricing for the same number of paths. For

Table 19.2   Regressors

0.25			0.5			0.75		
1	x	x^2	1	x	x^2	1	x	x^2
1	67.98	4621.73	1	66.59	4434.91	1	56.96	3245.02
1	94.54	8939.52	1	99.57	9914.67	1	74.42	5539.21
1	87.65	7683.57	1	92.75	8602.74	1	109.55	12003.19
1	103.55	10722.96	1	75.41	5687.44	1	98.28	9660.5
1	125.51	15754.3	1	102.75	10558.77	1	81.14	6584.28
1	80.99	6560.8	1	61.94	3837.57	1	40.68	1655.56
1	85.67	7340.66	1	83.5	6973.81	1	98.84	9769.75
1	88.08	7758.3	1	70.33	4946.71	1	85.49	7309.83
1	94.84	8994.74	1	95.79	9175.76	1	73.35	5380.41
1	104.64	10951.14	1	93.35	8715.12	1	150.02	22506.09
1	123.88	15346.95	1	120.9	14618.49	1	88.24	7787.03
...	...	...	...	...	...	...	...	...

Table 19.3 Regression coefficients
calculated from $\overline{S}$

0.25	0.5	0.75
270.8784	233.7492	115.6569
−4.7114	−4.3703	−1.8007
0.0212	0.0211	0.0069

example, let us consider a put option. The only point where the accuracy matters is the point where the option gets in-the-money, that is around the strike level. Here, the accuracy directly influences the decision of exercising. At all other points the accuracy does not matter.

Thus, if the approximating of the exercise boundary which is done by computing the expected continuation values is slightly biased, the construction of the stopping time is slightly wrong. It is slightly wrong because in the neighbourhood of the true exercise boundary the decision of holding the option or exercising leads to very similar results, but far away a wrong decision leads to very different results. Not exercising a deep in-the-money option leads to losing a lot of money but not exercising a nearly at-the-money option does not.

The approximation of the expected continuation value relies on the choice of basis functions. We observe that the ability to approximate the expected continuation value using a linear combination of the basis functions affects the error vector $\underline{E}$. The better the fit is, the smaller the norm of $\underline{E}$. Therefore, the choice of the basis functions is crucial for this method. Furthermore, this approximation is not linked to the number of paths used to price the early exercise feature of the option. We recommend analysing the payoff and trying to find out which types of basis functions do lead to a good fit. For example, approximating a put option we use not only polynomials but also the payoff itself as a basis function. Figure 19.1 shows the approximation using different basis functions. We used polynomials of different order as well as basis functions including the payoff. We observe that using the payoff together with polynomials leads to reasonable results for fitting the exercise boundary (19.1).

An important error is known as the *foresight bias*. For example, when we constructed the stopping rule τ^+ we used information not fitting the information content reflected by the underlying filtration $(\mathcal{F}_t)_t$. Actually, we used more information than available at a given exercise opportunity. This stopping rule leads to a high foresight biased estimate of the price. First, we could have based the option pricing on the same paths used for regression. But since the option value is based on the regression values it depends on the realised continuation values of the paths. To keep this dependence as small as possible we have chosen to use another set of paths, the pricing paths, to compute the option value. This approach also has practical reasons since the error arising from the pricing is much bigger than that from determining the exercise rule. To this end fewer paths are used for regression than are used for pricing.

19.7.1 Selecting basis functions

We have discussed that the choice of basis function affects the approximation of the exercise boundary. We can reduce the error by choosing appropriate functions. Furthermore, the number of basis functions is also very important. When applying regression each basis function ψ adds another degree of freedom, the corresponding regression coefficient β_ψ. This additional

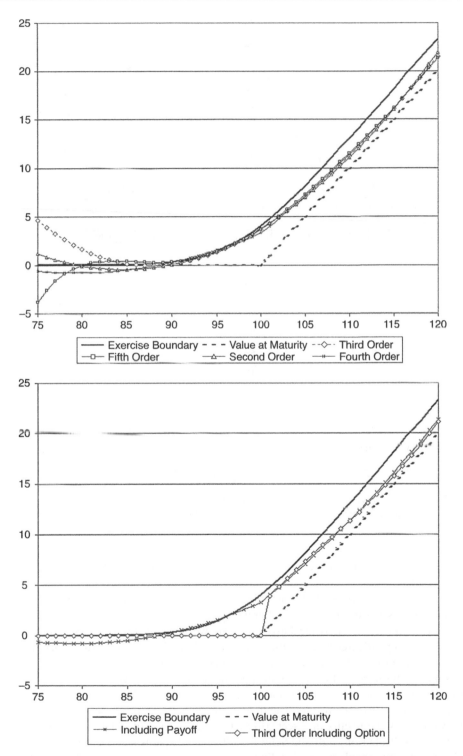

Figure 19.1   Approximating the expected continuation value using different basis functions

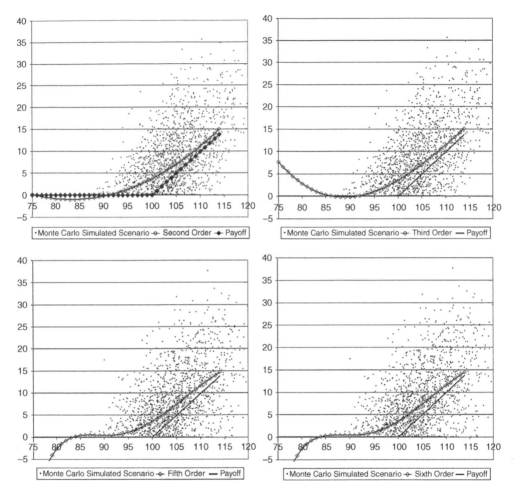

Figure 19.2 Choosing polynomials of different order for regression: the figure shows the realised continuation value and the estimated continuation value obtained using regression

degree of freedom might improve the regression result and therefore the approximation of the exercise boundary.

We can use our framework to study the influence of the choice and the number of basis functions on various kinds of models and different payoffs.

To study the influence of choosing basis functions we have set up a base scenario and choose polynomials up to degree five for fitting the exercise boundary. Then, we have increased, respectively decreased, the volatility and studied the approximation in the new scenario. Figure 19.2 shows the 'performance' of the different approximations in this scenario.

We now use the same setup but change the scenario and consider a lower level of volatility. Figure 19.3 is a summary of the results. The fit looks much better in this case.

Finally, we display the results in a scenario with a higher level of volatility. Figure 19.4 illustrates these results. In Longstaff and Schwartz (2001), only paths leading to in-the-money options (ITM) are used to apply regression. Such options have a positive value. The advantage

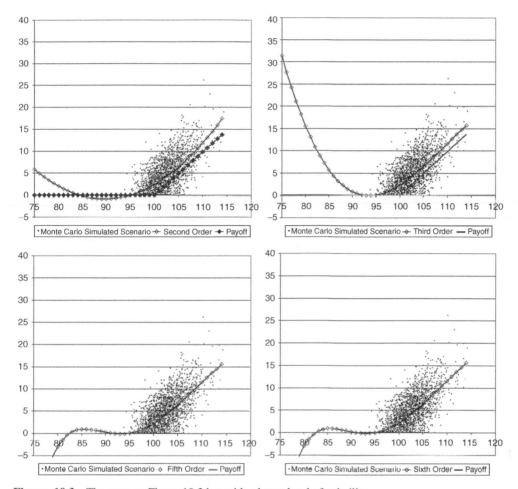

Figure 19.3   The same as Figure 19.2 but with a lower level of volatility

of using ITM only is to gain speed, due to the fact that computing the optimal stopping time is faster, and to reduce the bias.

19.8   UPPER BOUNDS

To conclude this section we review a method to derive upper bounds for the price of Bermudan option. We focus on the *dual method* introduced by Rogers (2002) and Haugh and Kogan (2001).

To compute the present value $V(0)$ for an option with payoff h the key observation is that for a given martingale $(M_t)_t$ we have

$$\mathbb{E}[h_\tau(S_\tau)] = \mathbb{E}[h_\tau(S(\tau)) - M_\tau] \le \mathbb{E}[\max_{k \in T_{\text{Ex}}} h(S_k) - M_k] \qquad (19.16)$$

from which we can deduce

$$\mathbb{E}[h_\tau(S_\tau)] = \inf_M \mathbb{E}[\max_{k \in T_{\text{Ex}}} h(S_k) - M_k] \qquad (19.17)$$

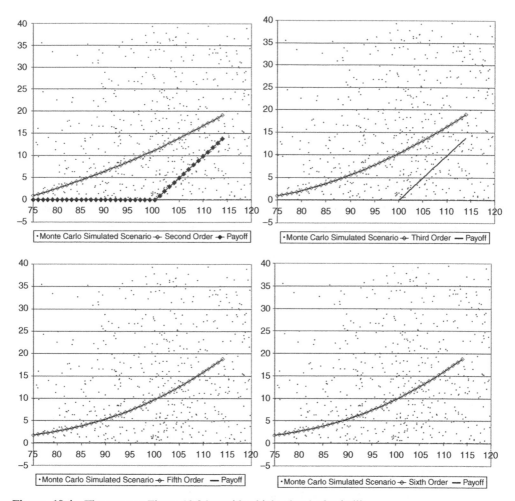

Figure 19.4 The same as Figure 19.2 but with a higher level of volatility

Since this inequality holds for all stopping times τ it holds for the supremum over all stopping times (with equality in fact).

Setting

$$M_k = \sum_{j=1}^{k} U_j, \quad U_j = V(S_k) - \mathbb{E}[V_k(S_k)|S_{k-1}] \tag{19.18}$$

we can compute the payoff as

$$\max_{k \in \mathcal{T}_{\text{Ex}}} h(S_k) - M_k \tag{19.19}$$

To implement the dual method we define the vector

```
Vector<double> U(NumberOfPaths)
```

and initialise it with 0. We then use the regression values at the next exercise opportunity for computing the value `valuelater`. This is only an approximation to a martingale and has already been shown in the code snippet from the beginning. Now, we have to code equation (19.18) to be able to compute the upper bound. In our implementation we have chosen as an approximation for the U_k to expected continuation values. One value is computed using the values of the current time step and one is calculated one time step ahead.

Other possibilities are applying nested simulation to approximate U_k or using martingale basis functions. The following C++ code implements the calculation of the upper bound:

```
Martingale = 0.0;
for(long j = 1;j<=NumberOfPaths;j++)
{
    // Compute realised Continuation Values
    if(OptValues_Current(j,i) > CV_E(j,i))
        CV_R(j,i) = DiscountFactors[i] * OptValues_Current(j,i);
    else
        CV_R(j,i) = DiscountFactors[i] * CV_R(j,i+1);
    if(method == "pricing")
    {
        // Compute the upper bound
        Martingale = Martingale + CV_E_Later(j,i) - CV_E(j,i);
        U[j] = max(U[j], OptValues_Current(j,i)-Martingale);
    }
}
```

19.9   EXAMPLES

We consider an American put option with $S(0) = 36$, $K = 36$, $r = 0.06$, $\sigma = 0.2$ and $T = 1$ and 11 exercise possibilities. Therefore, we can exercise the option every month. Table 19.4 shows the results for applying different numbers of regression and pricing paths and the corresponding estimates for the lower and the upper bound on the option price.

Next we apply our C++ code to the following pricing problems:

1. Call option, Spot = 36.0, Strike = 40.0, $r = 6\%$, $\sigma = 20\%$ and Exercise Dates = 3.
2. Put option, Spot = 36.0, Strike = 40.0, $r = 6\%$, $\sigma = 20\%$ and Exercise Dates = 3.

Table 19.4   Numerical results for computing lower and upper bounds with different numbers of pricing and regression paths and 11 exercise opportunities

Number regression paths	Number pricing paths	Lower (%)	Upper (%)
1000	2000	21.06	30.95
5000	10 000	20.58	22.81
7500	15 000	20.55	21.73
10 000	20 000	20.54	22.75
50 000	100 000	20.41	20.57

Table 19.5 Numerical results for lower and upper bounds for examples 1–4, analytical approximations and the European option prices

Case	Price lower	Price upper	Barone-Adesi & Whaley	Bjersund & Stensland	European
1.	2.1115	2.152	2.1737	2.1737	2.1737
2.	4.3859	5.153	4.4596	4.4628	3.8843
3.	0.6879	0.7178	0.7513	0.7192	0.6731
4.	2.03169	2.22697	2.0920	2.0616	1.8598

3. Put option, Spot = 36.0, Strike = 32.0, $r = 3\%$, $\sigma = 26\%$ and Exercise Dates = 11.
4. Put option, Spot = 36.0, Strike = 36.0, $r = 3\%$, $\sigma = 26\%$ and Exercise Dates = 11.

We consider 5000 paths for regression and 50 000 paths for pricing. Furthermore, we consider a Bermudan option with three exercise opportunities. It is a crude approximation of the price of an American option. Table 19.5 summarises the results. We compare the lower and the upper bounds obtained by simulation to the European prices as well as results from using analytic approximation formulae given in Barone-Adesi and Whaley (1987) and Bjerksund and Stensland (1993).

19.10   SUMMARY AND CONCLUSIONS

In this chapter we described a method for computing the price of an *American* or *Bermudan* option using Monte Carlo simulation. We focused on the Longstaff and Schwarz (2001) approach which is widely used in the financial industry. We discussed each step of the method in detail and showed how to map it to C++ code. We then discussed some improvements and reviewed a method to compute an upper bound. We compared our results to values computed using analytical approximation formulae.

19.11   EXERCISES AND PROJECTS

1. (**) Martingale Basis Functions
   Consider a set of basis functions f_i. A set of martingale basis functions f_i is a set of functions satisfying

$$\mathbb{E}[f(S(t_{i+1}))|S(t_i)] = f(S(t_i))$$

The constants are basis functions because $\mathbb{E}[1|S(t_i)] = 1$.
   Furthermore,

$$f(S(t_i)) = S(t_i)^k \exp(-k(r - d) + k(k - 1)\sigma^2/2)(t_i - t_{i-1} \, i - 1) \qquad (19.20)$$

$$g(S(t_i)) = \exp(-r(t_i - t_{i-1}))\mathbb{E}[f(S(t_i))|S(t_{i-1})] \qquad (19.21)$$

are martingale basis functions.
   Check the martingale property – the fact that $\mathbb{E}[X(S)|X(T)] = X(T)$, $S > T$ – for the above basis functions.

2. (**) Implementation Using Martingale Basis Function

To actually implement the approach using martingale basis functions we cannot use the classes used for defining the regression functions. This is because at run-time we need further information, for example the volatility, the riskless rate or the time interval $t_i - t_{i-1}$. Fortunately, we can use another class we have developed, the

```
ParaDFunction
```

which we also apply to compute analytical prices for stochastic volatility models. Using such functions it is possible to pass a vector of parameters to the function. Thus, we can add all the information we need at run-time! Study the corresponding classes and replace the class we used to implement regressors with the class

```
ParaDFunction
```

Modify the definition of the regressor functions in the above code.

3. (**) Comparison with Analytical Approximation Formulae

There are several analytic approximation formulas available for simple American/Bermudan options. A very well-known one is, for example, the Barone-Adesi and Whaley approximation formula. Check for analytical formulae, implement them in C++ and compare the results with the results obtained by Monte Carlo simulation.

4. (****) Including Other Payoffs

Extend the pricing framework to cover complex options starting with path-dependent options, for example arithmetic Asian options using the framework on the CD. Then, in a second step consult Chapter 14 again and implement a version of the American option pricing routine using the *PayOff Factory*.

5. (*****) Multi-dimensional American Options

We start with a simple spread option on two stocks S_1 and S_2 which has payoff $\max(S_1 - S_2 - K, 0)$. Adjust the framework such that two-dimensional basis functions can be handled. Choose simple basis functions such as $1, x, y, xy, x^2, y^2, x^2y$ or xy^2 for pricing.

Are there any two-dimensional martingale basis functions for the Black-Scholes model?

Analyse the code and search for possibilities to optimise it in terms of speed.

6. (**) Martingale Basis Functions

Assume that the asset price evolves due to a geometric Brownian motion. Show that the following functions are indeed martingales:

- $\psi(x) = 1$
- $\psi(x) = x^m \exp\left(-(m(r - d) + m(m - 1)\sigma^2/2)(t_k - t_0)\right)$
- $\psi(x) = h(x)$

20

Beyond Brownian Motion

The pure and simple truth is rarely pure and never simple.

Oscar Wilde, *The Importance of Being Earnest*

20.1 INTRODUCTION AND OBJECTIVES

In this chapter we consider Lévy processes. We study the class of *Normal Mean Variance Mixture* models which includes the *Normal Inverse Gaussian* (NIG) and *Variance Gamma* (VG) processes.

We give the main properties and show that simulating these processes is possible by subordinating a standard Brownian motion.

We discuss our implementation in C++ and give some examples on how to implement such models. To this end we consider the NIG and VG processes as well as a multi-dimensional version of the NIG model.

20.2 NORMAL MEAN VARIANCE MIXTURE MODELS

Normal mean variance mixture models generalise the multivariate normal distribution in the sense that the mean and the variance are determined by random variables. The idea is to introduce another source of randomness into the covariance matrix and then the mean via a mixing variable. The mixing variable or subordinator W is a non-negative random variable. Some well-known financial models can be expressed and simulated using this setup.

We consider the following setup for a k-dimensional normal and a d-dimensional random variable $\underline{X}$:

$$\underline{X} \sim \underline{\mu} + W\underline{\gamma} + \sqrt{W}\underline{A}\underline{Z} \in \mathbb{R}^d \tag{20.1}$$

with

- $\underline{Z} \sim \mathcal{N}(0, \underline{I}_k)$, Normal with mean vector $\underline{0} =^t (0, \dots, 0)$ and covariance matrix the k-dimensional identity matrix I_k.
- $W \geq 0$ is a positive, scalar valued random variable independent from $\underline{Z}$.
- $\underline{A} \in \mathbb{R}^{d \times k}$ matrix.
- $\underline{\mu}$ and $\underline{\gamma}$ are vectors in $\mathbb{R}^d$.

In this setting the distribution of $\underline{X}|W$ is

$$\underline{X}|W \sim \mathcal{N}(\underline{\mu} + \mathbb{E}[W]\underline{\gamma}, w\underline{A})$$

The expectation and the covariance can be computed in the case of a Gaussian variable:

$$\mathbb{E}[\underline{X}] = \underline{\mu} + \mathbb{E}[W]\underline{\gamma}$$
$$\mathbb{V}[\underline{X}] = \mathbb{E}[W]\underline{A} + \mathbb{V}[W]\underline{\gamma}^t\underline{\gamma}$$

20.2.1   The normal inverse Gaussian model

We consider four parameters μ, δ, α and $\beta \in \mathbb{R}$. We assume that $\delta > 0$ and $0 \leq |\beta| \leq \alpha$. Define $\delta(t) := \delta t$, $\mu(t) := \mu(t)$ and $\gamma := \sqrt{\alpha^2 - \beta^2}$. Then, the probability density of the NIG distribution is given by

$$f^{NIG}_{(x,\alpha,\beta,\delta(t),\mu(t))}(t) = \frac{\alpha}{\pi} \frac{K_1\left(\alpha\delta(t)\sqrt{1 + \left(\frac{x-\mu(t)}{\delta(t)}\right)^2}\right)}{\sqrt{1 + \left(\frac{x-\mu(t)}{\delta(t)}\right)^2}} \exp\left(\delta(t)\left(\gamma + \beta\frac{x-\mu(0)}{\delta(t)}\right)\right)$$

The function K_1 is the modified Bessel function of the second kind given by

$$K_\lambda(z) = \frac{1}{2} \int_0^\infty y^{\lambda-1} \exp\left(-\frac{1}{2}z(y + y^{-1})\right) dy$$

To actually simulate from

$$S(t) = S(0)\exp\left(L(t)\right)$$

with $L(t)$ being an NIG process we have to know the subordinator and how to simulate variates to plug into equation (20.1). In this case the subordinator is a random variable which has the *inverse Gaussian distribution*. A random variable having the inverse Gaussian distribution has density

$$f^{IG}(t) = \frac{\delta(t)}{\sqrt{2\pi}}t^{-3/2}\exp\left(-\frac{1}{2}\frac{\gamma}{t}\left(t - \frac{\delta(t)}{\gamma}\right)^2\right) \tag{20.2}$$

In Chapter 22 we give the method to sample random variates from this distribution.

20.2.2   C++ implementation

We use the implementation of the Monte Carlo engine from Chapter 15. To this end we have to implement a model and the sample path dynamics. From the considerations in section 20.2.1 we have to generate variates both for the normal and the subordinator. The distribution of the subordinator in this case is an inverse Gaussian distribution. Since we have integrated this probability distribution we can use our general framework to generate random variates. We define an object delivering such variates by

```
rg.GenerateVariatesVector(W,SubordinatorDist);
```

`SubordinatorDist` refers to a probability distribution. This probability distribution is defined in the implementation of the model as we can see by considering the class which implements the model:

```
class NIG : public OneFactorModel
{
public:
    NIG();
    NIG(double r, double d, double sigma, double Maturity,
        double Spot, double Alpha, double Beta, double Delta,
        double Mue);
    virtual ~NIG();
```

```
    double getdrift() const;
    double getvol() const;
    double getdividend() const;
    double getjump() const;
    double getmartcorrection() const;
    double getmaturity() const;
    double getspot() const;
    double getalpha() const;
    double getbeta() const;
    double getdelta() const;
    double getmue() const;

    void setsubordinator(double Delta);

    Distribution<double, double>* getsubordinator();

    // Should be private
    IG<double> nigsubordinator;

private:
    double drift;
    double vol;
    double martcorrection;
    double dividend;
    double maturity;
    double spot;
    double alpha;
    double beta;
    double delta;
    double mue;

};
```

We have omitted the member data and the *get functionality* for assessing the values of private member data. The crucial point in the implementation is the distribution of the subordinator. This is used by the scheme to compute the corresponding variates. The scheme is implemented as follows:

```
template<class RanGen, class Model>
class MCNigScheme : public OneFactorScheme<RanGen,Model>
{
public:
    MCNigScheme();
    virtual ~MCNigScheme();

    Vector<Vector<double>> calcST(RanGen& rg,
                                  Model& model,
                                  long Paths,
                                  int Factors,
                                  long Steps) const;
```

```
Vector<Vector<double>> calcST_anti(RanGen& rg,
                                   Model& model,
                                   long Paths,
                                   int Factors,
                                   long Steps) const;

private:
};
```

The main loop in the member function `calcST` generating one asset path is given by the following piece of code:

```
// Precompute some constants used within the scheme
double nudt = (r-d)* deltaT - mue * deltaT + deltaT *
nigmartingalecorrection;

// Define the subordinator
IG<double> subordinator(model.nigsubordinator); // Inverse Gaussian

// Main loop to generate all the paths
for(int i = minindex_Sims; i<= maxindex_Sims ; i++)
{
    // Generate randoms
    rg.GenerateGaussianVector(dW1);                    // Randoms
                                                       // Gaussians
    rg.GenerateVariatesVector(ig,subordinator); // Randoms
                                                       // Subordinator

    // Main loop to generate one path
    for(int j = minindex_TimeSteps; j <=maxindex_TimeSteps; j++)
    {
        // Asset-Path logarithmic version using normal mean
        // mixture with subordinator nig
        nigproc = mue * deltaT + ig[j] * beta + sqrt(ig[j])
        * dW1[j];
        // Store the path into result vector
        result[j] = S0 * exp(nudt + nigproc);
    }
    // Store the result into ST
    ST[i] = result;
}
return ST;
```

We give some typical realisations for the NIG model using the above classes. We have chosen to simulate monthly asset prices. The corresponding paths show significant jumps as illustrated in Figure 20.1.

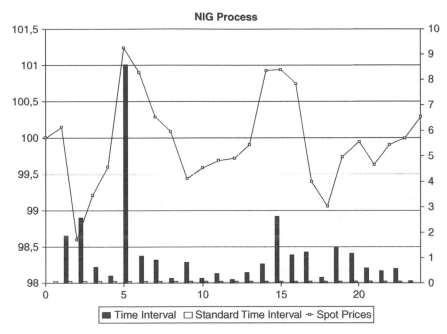

Figure 20.1   A typical path for the NIG process with parameters $\alpha = 1.0$, $\beta = -0.0015$ and $\delta = 0.75$, and monthly stepping

20.2.3   The variance gamma model

A random variable which is distributed with respect a variance gamma distribution has density

$$f^{VG}(t) = \int_0^\infty \frac{1}{\sigma \sqrt{2\pi g}} \exp\left(-\frac{1}{2}\left(\frac{t - \mu g}{\sigma \sqrt{g}}\right)^2\right) \frac{g^{t/\nu - 1}}{\nu^{1/\nu} \exp(-y/\nu) \Gamma(t/\nu)} dg \qquad (20.3)$$

The subordinator in this case is a random variable which is distributed according to a gamma distribution. See Chapter 22, section 22.4.5 for details on the gamma distribution.

20.2.4   Matching underlying assets and martingale dynamics

For option pricing problems the asset price is usually modelled by the (stochastic) exponential of the process chosen to model the returns of the asset. For the geometric Brownian motion the returns are modelled as normally distributed random variables. The spot price process is then given as the exponential of a normal random variable. Because of the stochastic integration rule (Itô calculus) an additional term, $\sigma^2/2$, appears in the formula. This term is also known as the *martingale correction*. This correction ensures that the asset price process is a martingale. For our general model we can compute the martingale correction and add it to the drift. We model the returns of the asset S as normal inverse Gaussian variates and obtain the spot prices by taking the (stochastic) exponential.

If we let the process $L(t)$ be a Lévy process and consider the dynamics of $S(t)\exp(-(r-d)t)$ with

$$S(t) = S(0)\exp((r-d)t + L(t))$$

the process does not in general have the martingale property. We can make it into a martingale by considering

$$S(t) = S(0)\exp((r-d)t + L(t) - \omega t)$$

with $\omega = \mathbb{E}[\exp(L(1))]$. ω is the martingale correction in this case.

With the parameters for the NIG and VG model introduced in this chapter the martingale correction terms are

$$\omega_{NIG} = \mu + \delta\gamma - \delta\sqrt{\alpha^2 - (1+\beta)^2} \qquad (20.4)$$

$$\omega_{VG} = -\frac{1}{\nu}\ln\left(1 - \mu\nu - \frac{\sigma^2\nu}{2}\right) \qquad (20.5)$$

For further details see Ribeiro and Webber (2007) or Schoutens, Simons and Tistaert (2004).

20.3   THE MULTI-DIMENSIONAL CASE

We examined models for stochastic volatility in the last chapter. In particular, we studied a model implementing a random time change of Brownian motion. In the sequel we focus on d-dimensional processes based on a time change of Brownian motion. The most prominent processes arising in this context are the multi-dimensional NIG and the VG processes. We have already described the d-dimensional model, see equation (20.1). The parameters are now vectors and we have to provide a covariance matrix to simulate from a multi-dimensional Gaussian variable.

In Figures 20.2, 20.3 and 20.4 we have simulated paths for a two-dimensional NIG model. Figure 20.2 uses a correlation of 75% between the assets. We assumed independence of the Brownian motions to produce Figure 20.3. The other values have not changed.

20.4   SUMMARY AND CONCLUSIONS

We have considered *Normal Mean Variance Mixture* models. The interpretation as subordinated Brownian motion proved especially helpful for implementation. The only thing needed is the ability to simulate variates from the subordinator. Using the Monte Carlo framework it is also possible to cover stochastic volatility models by interpreting stochastic volatility as a stochastic clock running with respect to some integrated stochastic process such as the variance process considered in the Heston model. To actually apply such processes, a method to obtain market parameters – the calibration of the model – must be set up. Then, the Monte Carlo framework can be used for simulation and pricing.

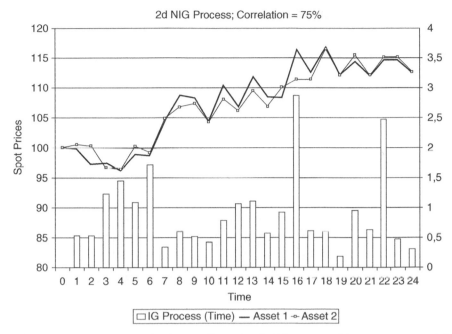

Figure 20.2 Some typical paths for the two-dimensional NIG process with parameters $\alpha = 1.0$, $\beta = 0.2$ and $\delta = 2.0$

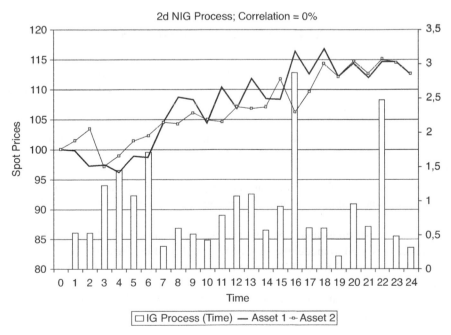

Figure 20.3 A typical path for the two-dimensional NIG process with parameters $\alpha = 1.0$, $\beta = 0.2$ and $\delta = 2.0$

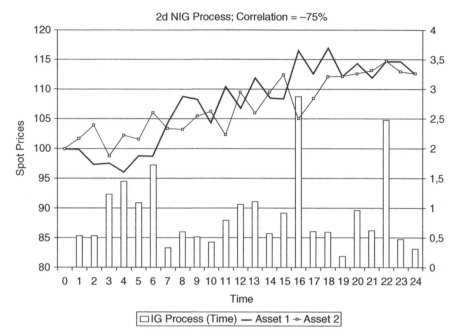

Figure 20.4 A typical path for the two-dimensional NIG process with parameters $\alpha = 1.0$, $\beta = 0.2$ and $\delta = 2.0$

20.5 EXERCISES AND PROJECTS

1. (**) Variance Gamma Model
   Implement the variance gamma model. The implementation can be based on the implementation of the NIG model. Hint: the only things that change are the subordinator distribution and the martingale correction.
2. (**) Mean Variance Mixture
   Integrate mean variance mixture models into the general framework discussed in Chapters 10 and 11.
3. (***) Stochastic Clocks
   To incorporate stochastic volatilty into a normal mean variance mixture model we need to apply a stochastic time change. The sample scheme can be implemented using the following algorithm:
   (a) Simulate the rate of time change process $(y(t))_t = \{y(t), 0 \le t \le T\}$ up to maturity as a CIR process as used to model the stochastic volatility of the Heston model.
   (b) Simulate the integrated time $(Y(t))_t = \{Y(t) = \int_0^t y(s)ds, 0 \le t \le T\}$ up to maturity using (a).
   (c) Simulate the mean variance mixture process $(X(t))_t = \{X(t), 0 \le t \le Y(T)\}$.
   (d) Compute the asset price process using the formula

$$S(t) = S(0)\frac{\exp((r - d)t)}{\mathbb{E}[\exp(X(Y(t))|y(0)]} \exp(X(Y(t)))$$

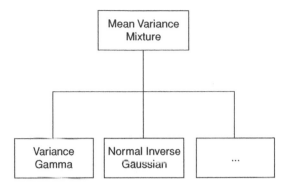

Figure 20.5 The class `MeanVarianceMixture` acts as a base class. The VG and NIG models inherit from the base class. The actual implementation has to be done for each model

The denominator is given by $\varphi_{\text{CIR}}(-i\psi_X(i); t; 1)$ the characteristic function of the CIR model and $\psi(u) = \log(\mathbb{E}[\exp(iuX(1))])$. See Schoutens, Simons and Tistaert (2004) for details.

4. (*) Literature

There are many models that can be set up as subordinated Brownian motion. The simulation library can be extended to cover such models.

5. (**) Inheritance

We can consider a class `MeanVarianceMixtureModels` from which the NIG and the VG models can be derived (see Figure 20.5).

6. (**) Option Pricing

We can take the examples considerd in Chapter 15 and study the pricing of these options within the NIG and the VG model.

Part IV
Supplements

21

C++ Application Optimisation and Performance Improvement

21.1 INTRODUCTION AND OBJECTIVES

In this chapter we introduce a number of techniques that promote the efficiency, reliability and overall applicability of C++ as a programming language for developing finance applications. We concentrate on features to help us produce fast executable code:

- Appropriate use of `virtual` functions.
- Choosing between parametric and subtype polymorphism.
- Classes, inheritance and associated overhead costs.
- RunTime Type Information (RTTI) and dynamic casting.
- Exception handling and associated costs.

We discuss each of these topics in relation to the applications in this book. Another objective in this chapter is to introduce a number of special features from the Boost library (www.boost.org). Although this is not (yet) part of the official C++ language we feel that it is important to discuss it. We have already given an introduction to Boost in Chapter 13. In this chapter, we discuss the following functionality in the library:

- Multi-dimensional arrays.
- Random number generators.
- Boost smart pointers (a fuller discussion was given in Chapter 13).

We hope that this chapter will be of practical value to the reader who wishes to improve the performance of C++ applications.

21.2 MODELLING FUNCTIONS IN C++: CHOICES AND CONSEQUENCES

The ability to model functions in C++ is crucial if we wish to create extendible and efficient applications. In this section we discuss several techniques for modelling functions. When modelling a function in C++, we define the function's *signature*:

- The name of the function.
- The type and number of input parameters of the function.
- The type of the output arguments (the return type) of the function.
- The code that implements the function.

We have touched on some of these issues in Chapter 12.

A function is a mapping from a domain space to a range space. In general, the input and output data can be homogeneous (in which case we use compile-time vectors, for instance) or they can be heterogeneous (in which case we model the data using property maps). The requirements of the problem at hand will determine the most suitable data structure to use. Furthermore, in many cases we model the domain and range as n-dimensional and m-dimensional spaces, respectively. Specialisations correspond to well-known function categories in mathematics:

- C1: Scalar functions ($n = m = 1$).
- C2: Scalar-valued functions (n variable, $m = 1$).
- C3: Vector functions ($n = 1$, m variable).
- C4: Vector-valued functions (n and m variable).

We model these functions using generic programming techniques; both the underlying data and the dimensions of the domain and range spaces are generic. To this end, C++ provides us with the tools that allow us to create customisable code to model functions. We now discuss these issues in the rest of this section.

The reader has a choice: on the one hand easy-to-use solutions where the learning curve is not so steep and on the other hand standard solutions where some more effort is needed to learn and use them in your applications. Our advice is to start on easy problems and then move on to more advanced problems.

21.2.1 Function pointers

Function pointers have their origins in the C language (see Kernighan and Ritchie, 1988) and we have used them by embedding them as member data in classes (see Duffy, 2004a, when solving nonlinear equations, for example). We shall not deal with them here because we assume that the reader knows how to use them. However, an extension of our previous work is that both the input and output parameters of a function can be compile-time vectors. We have used function pointers and vectors in this way when we defined template classes for SDEs. In particular, we model the drift term as a one-dimensional array of function pointers and the diffusion term as a two-dimensional array of function pointers. To this end we wrap the function pointers in a 'transparent' class as follows:

```
template <typename V, int N> struct FunctionWrapper
{ // Models a scalar-valued function

    // Call by value first argument
    V (*f) (V value, const VectorSpace<V,N>& arguments);
};
```

(Incidentally, we shall see that this user-defined 'trick' is not needed when we define *function objects*. These are objects that behave like normal functions.) Having defined the wrapper class we can now model an SDE as follows:

```
template <typename V, int N, int D> class SDE : public SdeThing
{ // Non-linear SDE; N is the number of independent variables and
  // D is the number of Brownian motions

private:

    // INDEXING STARTS AT 0 IN THESE ARRAYS
```

```
FunctionWrapper<V, N> drift[N];// Deterministic drift term
FunctionWrapper<V,N> diffusion[N][D];// Stochastic diffusion

// other data + functions here, see CD for code

public:

// other functions here

// Individual components of drift and diffusion functions
void setDriftComponent (V (*fun) (V value,
        const VectorSpace<V,N>& arguments), int row);

void setDiffusionComponent (V (*fun) (V value,
        const VectorSpace<V,N>& arguments),int row, int column);

// Calculate drift and diffusion functions at a given time value
const VectorSpace<V,N>& calculateDrift (V value,
        const VectorSpace<V,N>& arguments);
const VectorSpace<V,N>& calculateDiffusion (V value,
        const VectorSpace<V,N>& arguments,
        const VectorSpace<V,D>& dW);

// Calculate diffusion using Dynamic Vector<double, long>
const VectorSpace<V,N>& calculateDiffusion (V value,
        const VectorSpace<V,N>& arguments,
        const Vector<V,long>& dW);

const MatrixVectorSpace<V, N, D>& calculateDiffusionMatrix(
        V value, const VectorSpace<V,N>& arguments);

// other functions here

};
#endif
```

We see how the structure has been implemented and we also see that there are member functions for the drift and diffusion terms. The only issue that remains is to show how to use this class. To this end, we define a number of 'real' functions and then assign function pointers to them; for example, the object defining a two-factor SDE is given by

```
const int dim = 2;
const int dim2 = 2;

// Initial condition
VectorSpace<double, dim> input;
input[1] = 2.0;
input[2] = 2.0;

Range<double> range(0.0, 1.0);

SDE<double, dim, dim2> result(range, input);
```

It now remains to define the SDE's drift and diffusion components:

```
// Define the drift terms
result.setDriftComponent(func1, 1);
result.setDriftComponent(func2, 2);

// Define the diffusion matrix
result.setDiffusionComponent(func11, 1, 1);
result.setDiffusionComponent(func22, 2, 2);
result.setDiffusionComponent(func21, 2, 1);
result.setDiffusionComponent(func12, 1, 2);
```

where each of the function arguments in the calls to the SDE's member functions are 'real' functions, for example (the other functions' code can be found on the CD):

```
// Drift function
double func1(double x, const VectorSpace<double,2>& input)
{

        return - 1.0;
}
```

and

```
double func22(double x, const VectorSpace<double,2>& input)
{

        return -(input[2] - input[1]);

}
```

Finally, we can calculate the values of the drift and diffusion functions (notice that these are vector-valued functions) as follows:

```
VectorSpace<double, dim> input2;
input2 [1] = 1.0;
input2 [2] = 3.0;

VectorSpace<double, dim2> dW;
dW[1] = 1.0;
dW[2] = 2.0;

VectorSpace<double, dim> output =
        result.calculateDiffusion(1.0, input2, dW);
print(output);

VectorSpace<double, dim> output2 =
        result.calculateDrift(1.0, input2);
print(output2);
```

We have now shown – by using an example – how to use function pointers in C++ application code.

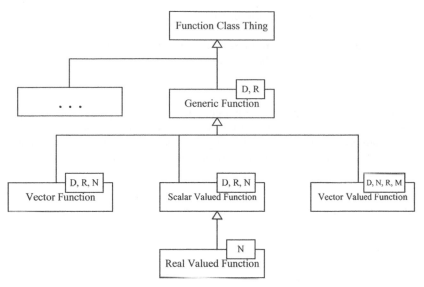

Figure 21.1   Generic function classification

21.2.2   Generic classes that model functions

Another way to model functions is to create a C++ class hierarchy as shown in Figure 21.1. The main types are vector functions (map scalars into vectors), scalar-valued functions (mapping vectors to scalars) and vector-valued functions (functions that map vectors to vectors).

Let us examine some of the code that implements the classes in Figure 21.1. The base class is

```
// Base class for all function categories
class FunctionClassThing
{ // Base class for all function classes
private:

public:
};
```

The above class is empty at the moment. It is also possible to derive your own classes from it. We note that it has no template parameters. The second-level base class represents a generic function mapping a domain space to a range space and is defined by

```
// Mathematical function
template <class D, class R> // D == Domain, R == Range
    class GenericFunction : public FunctionClassThing
{
private:
        R (*f) (const D& d);

protected:
        GenericFunction();
public:
        GenericFunction(R (*myFunction) (const D& d));
```

```
        R evaluate (const D& value);

        // Using STL function object; competitor of evaluate()
        R operator ()(const D& value) const;

};
```

This class encapsulates a function pointer with a generic range and a generic domain; please note that we have two ways of evaluating the function for a given input parameter, one of which is a standard STL technique (overloading the operator ()) whereas the other solution uses evaluate(). The body of these functions consists of 'calling' the function pointer:

```
template <class D, class R>
        R GenericFunction<D,R>::evaluate (const D& value)
{
        return (*f)(value);
}

template <class D, class R>
        R GenericFunction<D,R>::operator ()(const D& value)const
{
        return (*f)(value);
}
```

Having discussed the base classes, we define derived classes in which the domain and range have special structures and where the underlying data elements can be doubles, complex numbers and other types. In order to motivate the code we focus on one class, namely the class of vector functions:

```
// Mapping from Scalar to Array
template <class D, class R, int n>
     class VectorFunction:public GenericFunction<D,VectorSpace<R,n> >
{
public:
     // Constructor
     VectorFunction(VectorSpace<R,n> (*myFunction) (const D& d));

};
```

This class would have more member functions in applications (and possibly member data) but the essential principles are more important at this stage. The code for this class is

```
template <class D, class R, int n>
VectorFunction<D,R,n>::VectorFunction(
            VectorSpace<R,n> (*myFunction) (const D& d))
                : GenericFunction<D, VectorSpace<R,n> > (myFunction)
{

}
```

In this case we use the colon syntax to initialise the private member data of the base class. Finally, we give an example of use. To this end, define a specific function of the correct signature and then use it to initialise an instance of VectorFunction:

```
VectorSpace<double,3> vectorFunc(const double& input)
{
    // Simple example to show use
    VectorSpace<double, 3> result;
    result[1] = input;
    result[2] = input;
    result[3] = input;

    return result;
}
```

We can now use this function as follows:

```
// Vector function
GenericFunction<double, VectorSpace<double,dim> > vf2(vectorFunc);
print (vf2.evaluate(2.0));
cout << "\nfunctor Vector space:\n";
print (vf2(2.0)); cout << endl;
VectorFunction<double, double, dim> svf10(vectorFunc);
print (svf10(2.0)); cout << endl;

VectorFunction<double, double, dim> vf0(vectorFunc);
print (vf0.evaluate(3.1415));
```

We created an earlier version of these function classes and we applied them to approximate the solution of the Black-Scholes equation using the finite difference method (see Duffy, 2004a). This solution used function classes in which the number of input parameters was hard-coded. This solution is not very flexible. Thus, for example we would have needed to define a new class corresponding to each separate space (underlying) dimension. In the current case we have defined a *single* template class that accepts *n*-dimensional vector space objects as input parameters and the code for this class only needs to be written once. This results in reusability and productivity gains.

21.2.3   Function objects in STL

STL supports *function objects* (also known as *functors*). These are objects that behave like functions. In particular, a class will be a function object if it implements the operator '()'. We have seen an example in the previous subsection, namely:

```
template <class D, class R> // D == Domain, R == Range
    class GenericFunction : public FunctionClassThing
{
        //

public:
        //

        R operator ()(const D& value) const;

};
```

Why (and when) should we use function objects? Some reasons are (see Josuttis, 1999)

- Improvement over function pointers: A function object is faster than a function pointer because more details are known at compile-time. Thus, passing function objects as parameters can improve performance.
- A function object has a type: Function objects can have different types even when their signatures are different. It is possible to define two instances (objects) of a function object with each instance having its own state. This behaviour is not possible with function pointers. Furthermore, we can create hierarchies of function objects and it is also possible to use them as a template parameter in a class definition.
- Smart pointers: Function objects do more than just implement the operator ( ) because they may have attributes (member data) and other member functions. Finally, we can initialise function objects at run-time before we use them. This is in contrast to function pointers where there is a possibility that they have not been initialised before calling them.

Some other related functionality that STL offers is

- Predefined function objects.
- Function adapters (for member functions and ordinary functions).
- User-defined function objects for function adapters.

A discussion of these topics is outside the scope of the current book. We have provided several examples of use and these can be found on the CD.

21.2.4   What is polymorphism?

This term means that we can have a single definition to be used with different types of data, specifically different classes. We distinguish between run-time (*subtype*) polymorphism and compile-time (*parametric*) polymorphism. The different kinds of polymorphism are shown in Figure 21.2). First, we have *universal polymorphism* (see Cardelli and Wegner, 1985) whose specialisations are

- *Inclusion polymorphism*: This models subtypes and inheritance. C++ implements this kind of polymorphism using `virtual` functions.

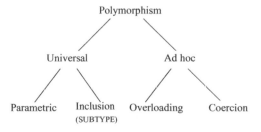

Figure 21.2   Types of polymorphism

- *Parametric polymorphism*: In this case uniformity of type structure is achieved by type parameters. C++ supports this option by using templates.

Ad hoc polymorphism refers to certain properties of monomorphic languages. We say that a language is *monomorphic* if functions and procedures as well as their operands defined in that language have a unique type. *Overloading* allows us to use the same variable name for different functions and the context decides which function is denoted by a particular instance of the name. A *coercion* is a semantic construction that is needed to convert an argument to one that is expected by the function.

It is important to decide whether you wish to define polymorphic functions and if these should be of the subtype or parametric variety. Subtype polymorphism can have a (negative) performance impact in applications.

We give a short discussion on the use of virtual functions in classes and their impact on performance. Let us take an example (this source code is on the CD). We define a virtual function and a non-virtual function in a base class. The derived class overrides the virtual function. We also use a simple clock class to measure elapsed time. The code is given by

```cpp
// testPerformance.cpp
//
// Comparing virtual and non-virtual functions
//

#include "clock.hpp"

struct MyClass
{

    virtual double funcV() { return 1.0; }
    int funcNV() { return 1; }
};

struct Derived : MyClass
{

    double funcV() { return 2.0;}

};

int main()
{

    DatasimClock myClock;

    myClock.start();


    long NSIM = 1000000;      // Number of MC simulations
    long NT = 1500;           // Number of time steps

    long NBig = NSIM * NT;
```

```
MyClass*   myObject = new Derived;
int temp;

myClock.start();
for (long j = 1; j <= NBig; j++)
{
     temp = myObject -> funcNV();
}
myClock.stop();
cout << "Non-virtual: " << myClock.duration() << endl;

myClock.start();
for (long j = 1; j <= NBig; j++)
{
     temp = myObject -> funcV();

}
myClock.stop();
cout << "Virtual: " << myClock.duration() << endl;

delete myObject;

return 0;

}
```

We carried out a number of experiments by running this program in debug and release modes. Furthermore, we used some compiler optimisation techniques but in all cases we can draw the general conclusion: virtual functions are slower than non-virtual functions and the difference in performance can be anywhere in the range [2, 10] depending on the compiler, optimisation levels and other factors. The conclusion is that we should profile our application to see where virtual functions are used (for example, in loops) and what the performance impact is. An alternative might be to use templates and even consider not using virtual functions in the first place.

A particularly important application of virtual functions in C++ can be found in the *Visitor* design pattern (see GOF, 1995) in which two class hierarchies communicate by means of virtual functions. This technique is also called *double dispatch* or *multiple polymorphism*. A safe conclusion is that using virtual functions may have an adverse effect on performance, especially for 'small' functions like 'set' operations. Calling virtual functions in loops is probably not a good idea.

21.3   PERFORMANCE ISSUES IN C++: CLASSIFYING POTENTIAL BOTTLENECKS

In this section we discuss how C++ syntax affects the performance of applications. We determine whether a given feature impairs the response time or throughput in an application. It is also important to examine the corresponding resource usage incurred by a given feature. In general, it is easier and more desirable to improve the efficiency of a well-designed program than maintain a fast but otherwise badly-designed one. Prevention is better than cure. We discuss some tactics that improve program performance and give examples in C++ to show how these work.

21.3.1 Inlining

Inlining is the process of replacing a function call by expanding the body of the function each time it is called. The function call can be eliminated entirely, and this will improve the performance. There are two ways to achieve inlining; first, when creating a class it is not necessary to have separate header and source files; instead, we can place all function declarations and their bodies in one file. This is called *default* or *implicit inlining*. For example, we take the constructor for a class that models persons:

```
class Person
{
public: // Everything public, for convenience only

           // Data
           string nam;                  // Name of person
           DatasimDate dob;             // Date of birth

           DatasimDate createdD;        // Internal, object was created
           DatasimDateTime createdT;    // Internal,object was created

public:
           Person (const string& name, const DatasimDate& DateofBirth)
           {
               nam = name;
               dob = DateofBirth;
               createdD = DatasimDate();       // default, today
               createdT = DatasimDateTime();   // default, today
           }
};
```

The second option is called *explicit inlining*. In this case we use the keyword `inline` in the code file as a hint to the compiler to perform inlining, for example:

```
template <class V>
inline const V& ArrayStructure<V>::Element(size_t index) const
{ // Get element at position

    // Use the subscript operator in derived classes
    return ((*this)[index]);

}
```

In general, we avoid default inlining in production code because it makes code less readable and hence less maintainable in our opinion. Furthermore, default inlining cannot be relied upon for consistent high performance. On the other hand, we have applied explicit inlining to vector and matrix classes from Duffy (2004a) and we have seen performance improvements of up to 25% when compared to code that was not inlined. Inlining is compiler-dependent.

21.3.2 Static and dynamic casting

We avoid the use the static and dynamic casting features in C++ because they can be a sign of a weak design – for example, shaky class hierarchies – but these features are useful for extracting *run-time type information* (RTTI) in a program. The four forms of casting are discussed in Duffy (2006a):

- const cast;
- static cast;
- reinterpret cast;
- dynamic cast.

These syntactic forms are specific to C++ but we can still use the *cast notation* as found in C and C++, for example:

```
int iPi = (int)3.14159;
```

This notation permits explicit type conversion and we note that the first three forms of *type conversion operators* above incur no size or speed penalty versus the equivalent cast notation. Some compilers may even transform the cast notation into one of the type conversion operators when generating code. However, the dynamic cast operator may incur some overhead at run-time if we are using RTTI mechanisms, for example *upcasting* from a derived class pointer to a base class pointer or *downcasting* from a base class pointer to a derived class pointer. It is probably not advisable to use this feature in critical loops in your code.

21.3.3 Preventing unnecessary object construction

This is an important topic and one that can have a considerable (negative) impact on performance. First of all, let us think about the parts of code where objects are created:

- S1: In user-defined constructors and assignment operators.
- S2: In system-generated constructors (for example, default constructors).
- S3: In member functions; using call-by-value input arguments.
- S4: In member functions; return types as value (copy) or as reference.

Scenario S1 is concerned with the initialisation of member data in a class. For example, consider the constructor to create a two-dimensional point:

```
Point::Point(double newx, double newy)
{// Initialize using newx and newy

    // Variables x and y are member data
    x = newx;
    y = newy;
}
```

What is happening here? The answer is that the member data is created and then assigned to the input values. This constitutes two operations. An alternative is to use the *colon syntax* and this entails the member data initialisation, hence avoiding the extra assignment. The modified code now becomes

```
Point::Point(double newx, double newy) : x(newx), y(newy)
{// Initialize using newx and newy

}
```

We note that the colon syntax can only be used with constructors. This syntax can be applied to both built-in types (as in the above example) as well as to user-defined types and the performance benefits in the latter case can be appreciable.

Scenario S2 refers to the fact that the system may generate a default constructor if none has been provided by the programmer. However, we always advise you to define default constructors for each class that you create. This makes your code consistent and standardised.

Scenarios 3 and 4 are concerned with the types and objects used in member functions. Let us first concentrate on scenario 3. We show the different options by using a generic function:

```
func(T t);
func(const T* t);
func(const T& t);
```

The first option is the *call-by-value* mechanism; a temporary copy of the input t argument is made when the function is called. Furthermore, this temporary object is deleted when the function is exited. This overhead may be acceptable for built-in types but not when working with user-defined objects. For this reason, we can choose between the two last alternatives above. We prefer the third option: no temporary object is created and the input argument cannot be modified in the body of the function. This is the style of coding that we employ in this book.

We now discuss scenario 4. The options are

```
T func();
T& func();
const T& func();
```

We take an example; this is a class containing an embedded int. The class interface and code is

```
class X
{
private:

    int val;

public:
    X() { val = 10;}

    // Different functions to return the private data
    int CopyValue() const { return val; } // Copy of state

    // Choice 1
    int& Value()
```

```
    { // Reference is returned

        cout << "Return value non const \n";
        return val;
    }

    // Choice 2
    const int& Value() const
    { // Const reference return

        cout << "Return value const\n";
        return val;
    }


    void print() const
    {
        cout << endl << val << endl;
    }
};
```

A test program to show how to use the class is

```
int main()
{

    X x;
    x.print();

    const int v = x.Value();
    x.print();

    // Return type is ref ==> can use on the left side of assignment
    x.Value() = 12;
    x.print();

    return 0;
}
```

We have employed many of these optimisation techniques in the code in this book and we have distilled the essence of how we did it by using the above representative example. Finally, we can improve the performance by using a number of the object creational patterns as described in GOF (1995). Using them ensures that objects are created only when needed:

- *Singleton*: Create a class that has only one instance; a global access point is provided to allow clients to use this unique object.
- *Prototype*: We create an object as a copy of another, already-created *prototypical object*.
- *Flyweight*: We create an object that is shared among several (other) objects. Thus, the flyweight object is created once and all further access to it is realised using pointers. We normally implement this pattern using boost shared pointers.

- *Builder*: This object is responsible for the lifecycle of other objects in a software system. It initialises and creates objects that are needed in the program and these objects remain in memory until program end (in principle), at which time the builder deletes them.
- *Object Pool*: The ability to reuse and share objects that are expensive to use.

21.3.4   Exception handling

We use the exception handling mechanism sparingly, not because it has an impact on performance as such but because it becomes difficult to understand and maintain code that uses many levels of exception trying, throwing and catching. On the other hand, the mechanism provides a robust way for dealing with errors in a program.

One viewpoint when investigating the efficiency of exception handling is to compare the cost with that incurred by competing error handling techniques, such as

- Using error codes.
- Setting error state indicators (for example, the famous ERRNO).
- Calling error handling functions.

Some advantages of using the exception handling mechanism are (i) it isolates the normal code from the error handling code in a program and (ii) the automatic destruction of stack objects when an exception is thrown ensures that a program is less likely to leak memory resources. We give a list of some sources of overhead when using the exception handling mechanism:

- Data and code associated with *try-blocks* and *catch clauses.*
- Data and code associated with throwing an exception.
- Cleanup of handled exceptions; exceptions that are not rethrown must be destroyed upon exit of the catch clause.
- Exception objects may have nontrivial destructors and constructors.
- Exception handling implies some form of RTTI.

A rule-of-thumb we use is to employ exception handling at the higher layers of an application. For example, we use it when interfacing with Excel to ensure that vectors and matrices have compatible array bounds. A simple example of use in situations where we might have the misfortune of division by zero event is

```
double Divide(double x, double y)
{
        // Precondition: y is not zero
        if (y == 0.0)        // very naive test!
        {

                throw DatasimException(string("\tDivide by zero"),
                string("In function Divide"),
                string("Try with non-zero value"));
        }

        return x/y;
}
```

```
int main()
{
    try
    {
        cout << "Give a number to divide by: " << endl;
        double y; cin >> y;

        cout << Divide(2.0, y);
    }
    catch(DatasimException& e)
    {
        e.print();
        return 0;
    }

    return 0;
}
```

A mature pricing system tends to have more error checking code than actual quant code.

21.3.5   Templates versus inheritance

The object-oriented paradigm is used for developing many kinds of software systems. However, it has been taken to extremes in some cases and we see that this has led to systems that that are difficult to maintain and whose performance is suboptimal. These problems are caused by

- Deep and incorrect inheritance hierarchies. The use of multiple inheritance compounds the problems.
- Using inheritance when the generic approach (templates) is the more natural solution to a given problem.
- Overuse and incorrect use of the `virtual` keyword.
- Touting the object-oriented paradigm as a panacea for all problems when templates are the more correct approach; OOP models ISA (inheritance) relationships while templates model abstract data types and operations on those types. We can emulate templates using OOP and it is possible to emulate OOP using templates, but this is not necessary in this case because C++ supports both paradigms.

We now discuss the impact on performance when using templates and inheritance and when we combine the two paradigms. It is well known that a class or function template generates new code when it is specialised with template parameters. This feature leads to a large amount of code and data. For example, we could carry out an experiment to create instances of specialisations of list<T*> for a specific type T and we could compare the time it takes to create a single instance of list<T*> using different T. Some results suggest that one compiler produced code that was 19 times as large when the two scenarios above were executed. Thus, the use of templates will affect performance to some extent because the size of the executable file is larger than the corresponding file if no templates are used.

21.3.6   Performance and the STL

We have given an introduction to performance issues and STL in Duffy (2006a). In particular, we discussed the efficiency of the algorithms and the related data containers using *complexity analysis* techniques. A major issue concerns the choice of the most appropriate data container for the problem at hand. A general rule is to optimise in space and time. For example, some containers (for example, `vector`) support random-access iterators while others (such as `list`) do not. In short, access is fast in `vector` and slow in `list`.

It is advisable to measure before and after you optimise. One point to bear in mind is that performance depends on issues that are beyond the control of the programmer, for example machine architecture and the kind of compiler used.

21.3.7   Some final tips

We give some hints and guidelines on optimising code:

* Precompute values that do not change. This is important in loops. A particularly important case is when we use iterators in STL:

```
void print(const list<int>& l)
{
    cout << endl << "Size of list is " << l.size() << endl;

    list<int>::const_iterator i;

    const list<int>::const_iterator EndPoint = l.end();
                        // Precomutation

    //for (i = l.begin(); i != l.end(); ++i) OLD, not optimised
    for (i = l.begin(); i != EndPoint; ++i)
    {
        cout << *i << ",";

    }

    cout << endl;
}
```

* Avoid nested lists; you may need to *profile* your application to discover hidden nests.

In Chapters 24 and 25 we shall discuss code optimisation when we introduce *multi-threaded* and *parallel* C++ code.

21.4   TEMPORARY OBJECTS

In the previous section we discussed a number of techniques that improve the performance of C++ applications. In particular, we have shown how to reduce the number of object instantiations. However, C++ can and does create temporary instances of user-defined types (for example, a large matrix) and this process is invisible to the programmer. This phenomenon affects performance. Thus, we first attempt to locate the places in the code where the compiler creates temporary objects and second we propose a number of mitigation techniques to help us avoid unnecessary object creation.

Temporary objects can be created when initialising objects, passing parameters to functions and returning objects from functions. We have already discussed the last two issues. We now focus on the situations where objects are created by the compiler and how to prevent the creation of such objects because temporary objects adversely affect run-time speed and memory footprint. We discuss a number of situations where temporary objects are created:

- An application of operator overloading in which we define code for adding two complex numbers:

```
Complex Complex::operator + (const Complex& c2) const
{ // Add two complex numbers

    Complex result (x + c2.x, y + c2.y);
    return result;
}
```

In this case we create a temporary variable that holds the result; the latter object is then copied into a variable in the calling function. But it is possible to use *return value optimisation* to give the compiler a hint that the process of temporary object creation can be eliminated. To this end, the compiler uses the memory for the function's return value to hold a local object of the same type that would otherwise have to be copied into the return value location. This saves the cost of a copy by using an *anonymous object*:

```
Complex Complex::operator + (const Complex& c2) const
{ // Add two complex numbers

    return Complex(x + c2.x, y + c2.y);
}
```

There may be no discernible differences due to possible new advances in compiler technology.
- Prefix and postfix operators for increment and decrement in loops: The postfix operator expression i++ copies the current value into a temporary object, increments the internal value and then returns the temporary object. On the other hand, the prefix operator expression ++i increments the actual value and then returns a reference to it. The difference in efficiency can be seen when using iterators in STL, for example in the case where we wish to print a set of generic objects:

```
template <class T> void print(const set<T>& mySet, const string&
                                                             name)
```

```
{   // Print the contents of a set. Notice presence of a const
       iterator.

    cout << name << ", size of set is " << mySet.size() << "\n[";

    set<T>::const_iterator i;

    for (i = mySet.begin(); i != mySet.end(); ++i)
    {
                cout << (*i) << ",";

    }

    cout << "]\n";
}
```

- Functions with default values: In this case a function can be created without having to specify its full argument list when it is called, for example:

```
Complex(double real = 0.0, double imag = 0.0);
```

In this case temporary variables/objects are created for each default value. The construction can be expensive and in the cases where the function is called several times (for example, in a loop) it might be advisable to use some other technique. In general, we advise against the use of default values in functions because they introduce *magic numbers* into code.
- Using operators: For types that represent vectors, matrices and other mathematical structures we see opportunities for the compiler to create temporary objects. For example, let us examine the code for multiplying two matrices:

```
// Create matrix with 3 rows, 3 columns, start indices
NumericMatrix<double, int> m(4, 4, 1, 1);

// Matrix multiplication
NumericMatrix<double, int> product = m*m;
```

This is inefficient code for two reasons; first, the matrix m is created before it is actually needed (a constructor is called); second, in the assignment statement a temporary matrix object is created and then it is assigned to the object representing the matrix product. An improvement is

```
NumericMatrix<double, int> product = m;
product *= m;
```

Further performance improvements can be achieved by employing *function objects* and *expression templates* (see Abrahams and Gurtovoy (2005) and Veldhuizen (1995), for example). A discussion of these topics is outside the scope of the current book. A follow-on issue is to decide how to design and implement efficient C++ applications that use vectors and matrices (for example, the applications in this book). Some typical operations are (see Golub and van Loan, 1996):

- Vector scaling.
- Inner product of two vectors.
- Saxpy ('scalar a x plus y').
- Gaxpy ('generalised saxpy').
- Matrix-vector multiplication.
- Matrix multiplication.

These operations should be optimised in order to prevent the creation of temporary objects. One solution to this problem is to define template functions (these are not member functions but global functions that we group into *mechanisms* and namespaces). These functions accept non-const object references for the return type and const references for the other objects. To take an example, the function prototype for the most general matrix multiplication problem above is

```
void MatrixMultiplication (          // A = B * C
        NumericMatrix<double, long>& A,
        const NumericMatrix<double, long>& B,
        const NumericMatrix<double, long>& C,
        double alpha, double beta)
{

    // code here, 2 nested loops
}
```

One final example: the bottlenecks to be optimised when programming the Conjugate Gradient Method (CGM) (Golub and van Loan, 1996) are

- Vector updates (saxpy and gaxpy).
- Inner products of vectors.
- Matrix-vector products.
- Solution of linear systems of equations.

Having efficient routines that implement these steps will improve performance. It becomes even more interesting (and challenging) when we have access to multi-threaded and parallel software libraries.

21.5   SPECIAL FEATURES IN THE BOOST LIBRARY

C++ continues to evolve and STL is part of the official standard.

We now discuss some new developments that are taking place and in particular we give an overview of some special features of the Boost library (www.boost.org), a suite of C++ libraries containing functionality in the form of template classes. Here are some of the libraries in Boost:

- *Multiarray*: Defines a generic interface to multi-dimensional containers.
- *Random numbers*: Contains a number of classes for random number generators and statistical distributions.

- *Property map*: Classes that embody key-value pairs and definition of the corresponding access to these pairs (for example, read and write).
- *Smart pointers*: Objects that store pointers to dynamically allocated memory.

The authors have developed a subset of the functionality contained in these libraries. For example, in Duffy (2004a) and Duffy (2006a) we have implemented a template Property Set class; furthermore, we have created classes for two-dimensional matrices and three-dimensional tensors using nested STL classes.

We give a short description of the functionality in the above Boost libraries. At this stage we avoid dealing with the C++ details on how to use these libraries in an application. We summarise each library as a list of features:

- *Multiarray*:
  - Array classes for *n*-dimensional data.
  - Accessing the elements of array using ( ) and [ ] operators.
  - Creating views of an array having the same or fewer dimensions.
  - Storage ordering of data (C-style, Fortran-style or user-defined).
  - Defining or changing array index (zero is default).
  - Changing an array's shape.
  - Resizing an array (increasing or decreasing the extent of a dimension).
- *Random numbers*:
  - Linear congruential generators.
  - Mersenne Twister generator.
  - Lagged Fibonacci generators.
  - Classes for continuous statistical distributions.
  - Classes for discrete statistical distributions.
- *Property maps*:
  - Key-value pair concept.
  - Readable and writable data.
  - Support for built-in C++ data types.
  - Applicability to Boost Graph Library (BGL).
- *Smart pointers*:
  - Sole ownership to single objects and arrays.
  - Shared ownership of objects and arrays.
  - Shared ownership of objects with embedded reference counting.

The introduction of these features in applications will promote the reliability, maintainability and efficiency of your software.

21.6 BOOST MULTIARRAY LIBRARY

This library consists of several components to model multi-dimensional data containers.

We give a brief overview by giving some examples. First of all, we need to define the include file information:

```
#include "boost/multi_array.hpp"
using namespace boost;
```

We now define a data structure with three underlying dimensions and to this end we create an instance of the container template `multi_array`:

```
// Define structure of tensor
const int dim = 3; // 3d matrix
multi_array<double, dim> tensor;
```

In this case we have called the default constructor but we are really interested in a three-dimensional structure of a certain size; to this end, we modify the size of each dimension in the array as follows:

```
// Define the extents of each separate dimension
const int NT = 3;
const int NSIM = 4;
const int NDIM = 3;
tensor.resize(extents[NT][NSIM][NDIM]);
```

We note that `extents` is a global object that allows us to specify array shape. Having defined the shape of the three-dimensional structure we then construct a three-level loop to initialise its elements:

```
// Define a 3d loop to initialise the data; index is a signed
// integral type for strides and index bases
typedef boost::multi_array<double, dim>::index index;

for (index i = 0; i != NT; ++i)
{
    for (index j = 0; j != NSIM; ++j)
    {
        for (index k = 0; k != NDIM; ++k)
        {
            tensor[i][j][k] = i + j + k;
        }
    }
}
```

It is possible to construct data structures in different ways. Before doing that, we introduce shorthand notation:

```
typedef multi_array<double, dim> Tensor;
```

Now, we can define a tensor by giving its extents in the constructor:

```
Tensor tensor2(extents [NT][NSIM][NDIM]);
```

Alternatively, we can use a collection (called an *extents list*) as a means of initialising a tensor, as follows:

```
// Create a tensor using a Collections, in this case in Boost
array<Tensor::index, 3> extentsList = { { NT, NSIM, NDIM } };
Tensor tensor3 (extentsList);
```

Please see the code on the CD for more examples.

21.7   BOOST RANDOM NUMBER LIBRARY

This library consists of a number of random number generators and classes for statistical distributions.

We first give an overview of the random number generators in this library. The library supports the Mersenne Twister algorithm which is popular in Monte Carlo applications. An example of use is

```cpp
#include <iostream>
#include <boost/random.hpp>

int main()
{
    // Define a mersenne_twister random number generator and
        initialize
    // it with a reproducible seed. The seed is unsigned, otherwise
        the
    // wrong overload may be selected
    boost::mt19937 generator(42u);

    // Define a uniform random number distribution which
    // produces "double" values in interval [0,1)
    boost::uniform_real<> uni_dist(0,1);
    boost::variate_generator<boost::mt19937&,
    boost::uniform_real<> >
        MyRandom(generator, uni_dist);

    // Show 10 random numbers
    for(int i=0; i<10; ++i)
    std::cout << MyRandom() << " ";

    return 0;
}
```

The core concept in this example is the class template `variate_generator` that models a number generator. It joins a random number generator with a distribution. In the above example the object MyRandom is created from a Mersenne Twister generator based on a uniform distribution. We note that the number generator MyRandom is a function object that takes zero arguments. It overloads the operator `()`.

We provide the source code for the above and other examples on the CD. Boost also supports *lagged Fibonacci generators* and these methods are becoming more popular for a number of reasons:

- They are fast.
- They have very long periods.
- They are suitable for use in parallel random number generators.

Before we discuss these methods we give a short overview of 'classical' Fibonacci numbers. These are numbers defined by the recursion

$$F_0 = 0, \quad F_1 = 1$$
$$F_n = F_{n-1} + F_{n-2}, \quad n \geq 2$$

We thus see that this is a finite difference equation with two starting values. The first 29 numbers in the sequence are:

```
0, 1, 1, 2, 3, 5, 8, 13, 21, 34, 55, 89, 144, 233, 377, 610, 987,
1597, 2584, 4181, 6765, 10946, 17711, 28657, 46368, 75025, 121393,
196418, 317811
```

In general, the formula for the nth Fibonacci number is given by

$$F_n = \frac{\rho^{-n} + (-\rho)^{n+2}}{1 + \rho^2}, \quad \rho = \frac{\sqrt{5} - 1}{2}$$

where ρ is the so-called *Golden Mean number*. In the limit when the index n tends to infinity we get the value

$$\lim_{n \to \infty} F_n = \rho^{-n}/(1 + \rho^2)$$

Lagged Fibonacci numbers represent a generalisation of the above recursion formula. The basic recursion is given by

$$X_i = X_{i-p} * X_{i-q}$$

where $p > 0$, $q > 0$ and $p > q$. Furthermore, the operator '$*$' is any arithmetic operation such as multiplication modulo M, addition modulo M, subtraction modulo M and bitwise exclusive *OR* (see Quinn, 2004). Here M is usually some power of 2. The sequence numbers may be integers or floating-point numbers in the case of addition and subtraction. In contrast to linear congruential generators – where we need only one starting value or *seed* – in the current case we need p seeds $X_0, X_1, \ldots, X_{p-1}$. By carefully selecting these seeds in combination with p, q and M we can produce sequences with good random properties and very long periods.

21.8   STL AND BOOST SMART POINTERS: FINAL REMARKS

There are several ways of dealing with pointers in C++. Some important ones are

- 'Raw' C++ pointers.
- STL `auto_ptr()`.
- Boost `shared_ptr()`.

We discuss the two latter options in this section. At the moment of writing there is one standard 'smart' pointer in C++ and this is called `auto_ptr()`. Its use allows us to avoid resource leaks when exceptions are thrown (Josuttis, 1999). The basic idea is simple; we 'wrap' a pointer object whose memory is allocated on the heap in an `auto_ptr` object. Please note that *the relationship between the two objects is one-to-one*, in other words the object is automatically deleted when the `auto_ptr` goes out of scope. This means that the programmer does not have to worry about deleting pointers. Here is a simple example:

```
#include <memory>
#include "Complex.hpp"


int main()
{
    {
        Complex* myComplex = new Complex(1.0, -1.0);
```

```
            using namespace std;
            auto_ptr<Complex> ptr(myComplex);

            // At this stage myComplex is deleted, GOOD!
        }


        return 0;
    }
```

Here we see that the complex number is cleaned up and you can see this by placing a print statement in its destructor. It is important to note that the variable `ptr` has the same interface as an ordinary pointer, for example it can be dereferenced to the object that it points to:

```
    // Now manipulate the object

    // 1. Show coordinates
    double real = ptr -> xVal();
    double imaginary = ptr -> yVal();

    cout << "real part " << real <<
            ", imaginary part " << imaginary << endl;

    // 2. Dereference
    Complex c2 = (*ptr);          // Deep copy
    cout << c2;
```

It is important not to initialise two pointers based on the same object. We note that the copy constructor and assignment operator of these pointers *transfer ownership*, for example:

```
    // Copy constructor and assignment
    auto_ptr<Complex> ptr2(ptr);
    cout << *ptr2;

    auto_ptr<Complex> ptr3 = ptr2;
```

A more extensive discussion of the `auto_ptr` mechanism can be found in Josuttis (1999). We conclude this discussion with some of the shortcomings (or properties) of `auto_prt`:

- It cannot share ownership: the relationship between pointer and object is one-to-one.
- It does not work for arrays.
- It is not a universal mechanism (for example, no support for *reference counting*).

We now turn our attention to smart pointers in Boost and to this end we focus only on `shared_ptr`. This is a smart pointer that uses reference counting and its main use is to share 'handles' to a common object. In general we can have a non-negative number of shared pointers that point to an object. When this number is equal to one and when the shared pointer is destroyed it then automatically deletes the object that it points to. Otherwise it does not delete that object. We take a simple example of using shared pointers:

```
int main()
{
    {
        Complex* myComplex = new Complex(1.0, -1.0);

        using namespace std;
        boost::shared_ptr<Complex> ptr(myComplex);
        boost::shared_ptr<Complex> ptr2(ptr);

        // Now manipulate the object

        // 1. Show coordinates
        double real = ptr2 -> xVal();
        double imaginary = ptr2 -> yVal();

        cout << "real part, ptr2 " << real
             << ", imaginary part " << imaginary << endl;

        // 2. Dereference
        Complex c2 = (*ptr); // Deep copy
        cout << c2;

        boost::shared_ptr<Complex> ptr3(ptr);
        cout << "Pointer 3 " << *ptr3 << endl;

        // At this stage myComplex is deleted, GOOD!
    }


    return 0;
}
```

We provide some more examples on the accompanying CD and a full discussion of smart pointers has been already given in Chapter 13.

21.9   SUMMARY AND CONCLUSIONS

We have discussed a number of issues that improve the performance of C++ applications. In general, we have three phases that we go through when designing and writing code; first, we ensure that the application has been designed properly and that it produces the desired results; that is, the results are accurate. Second, we profile our application by identifying the possible performance bottlenecks. Having done that, we adopt an incremental approach to optimisation of the code by employing the techniques in this chapter.

There is a limit to the amount of optimisation we can perform. Eventually, all attempts may prove fruitless and we then should start to think about multi-threaded and parallel programming models. We discuss these issues in Chapters 24 and 25.

Finally we give a summary of some general tips for improving the performance of your Monte Carlo applications:

- Worry about optimising your code only after it produces accurate results.
- Use efficient data structures to model the data in an application (for example, you can use the appropriate data containers in STL and Boost).
- Avoid memory thrashing: creating and destroying objects willy-nilly.
- Develop or use efficient matrix and vector classes as well as the corresponding mathematical operations.
- Take an incremental approach; optimise, measure and stop when you have reached your target. Make sure your code remains maintainable and understandable.
- Consider using templates instead of inheritance and virtual functions.
- Avoid creating networks of tightly-coupled classes; these monoliths tend to have a negative impact on efficiency.
- Avoid using the assignment operator '=' for vectors and matrices (especially in loops).

We would like to thank Thijs van den Bergh for some initial help with the Boost Random Library.

21.10   EXERCISES, PROJECTS AND GUIDELINES

1. (***) Approximating the Exponential Function exp(-z)
   In numerical analysis it is possible to approximate complex functions by simpler ones. We take the important case of the exponential function and we approximate it by rational functions (these are the quotients of two polynomials) called *Padé approximants* (as discussed in Duffy, 2006a). In general, we approximate exp(-z) by a *rational function* that has the form

$$r(z) = \frac{n(z)}{d(z)}$$

such that $d(z)e^{-z} - n(z) = 0(|z|^{p+q+1})$ as $|z| \to 0$ where $n(z)$ is a polynomial of degree q in z and $d(z)$ is a polynomial of degree p in z.
   Some special cases for specific values of p and q are

$$r(z) = \frac{2 - z}{2 + z} \quad \text{Padé (1, 1)}$$

$$r(z) = \frac{12 - 6z + z^2}{12 + 6z + z^2} \quad \text{Padé (2, 2)}$$

We note that the above relationships hold when z is a complex number. A special case is when complex numbers have zero imaginary parts, that is when they are real numbers.
   The objective of this exercise is to test the *accuracy* and *efficiency* of Padé approximants to exp(-z) for both complex and double precisions numbers. How much faster are these approximations in general when compared to calling the exponential function (there are two numbers in your answer, one for the speedup in the complex case and one for the speedup in the double precision case)?

2. (**) Transformation of Coordinates
   We wish to model transformations between Cartesian and spherical coordinate systems in three dimensions:

$$(x, y, z) \leftrightarrow (r, \theta, \phi)$$

The transformations are given by

$$r = \sqrt{x^2 + y^2 + z^2}$$
$$\theta = \cos^{-1} z/r, \quad 0 \le \theta \le \pi$$
$$\phi = \tan^{-1} y/x$$

and

$$x = r \sin \theta \cos \phi$$
$$y = r \sin \theta \sin \phi$$
$$z = r \cos \theta$$

Write functions to effect these transformations based on the classes in Figure 21.1. Generalise your code to the n-dimensional case:

$$x_1 = r \cos \phi_1$$
$$x_2 = r \sin \phi_1 \cos \phi_2$$
$$x_3 = r \sin \phi_1 \sin \phi_2 \cos \phi_3$$
$$x_{n-1} = r \sin \phi_1 \ldots \sin \phi_{n-2} \cos \phi_{n-1}$$
$$x_n = r \sin \phi_1 \ldots \sin \phi_{n-2} \sin \phi_{n-1}$$

where

$$r = \sqrt{x_1^2 + \ldots + x_n^2}$$

The inverse transformations are given by

$$\tan \phi_{n-1} = \frac{x_n}{x_{n-1}}$$

$$\tan \phi_{n-2} = \frac{\sqrt{x_n^2 + x_{n-1}^2}}{x_{n-2}}$$

$$\vdots$$

$$\tan \phi_1 = \frac{\sqrt{x_n^2 + \ldots + x_2^2}}{x_1}$$

Use function class to model these tranformations.

3. (***) Write a program to compare the relative efficiency of function pointers and function objects. For example, create a class that models SDEs and that uses function objects. Use this new class in a Monte Carlo simulation.

22

Random Number Generation
and Distributions

Anyone who considers arithmetic methods of producing random digits is, of course, in a state of sin.

John von Neumann

22.1 INTRODUCTION AND OBJECTIVES

This chapter discusses a central concept for applying Monte Carlo methods, namely random generation. We develop C++ classes that model pseudo random number generators, distributions and mechanisms in order to combine them to create working C++ code. At the time of writing many random number generation techniques and distributions have been implemented into the Boost library, which we discussed in Chapter 13.

We begin with the mechanism to generate uniform random numbers and then another mechanism to transform a uniform random number into one from a given distribution. To this end we implement a general framework for a random number generator with two custom objects representing a mechanism to create uniform variates and another mechanism to transform uniform variates into variates from a given distribution.

For the mechanisms as well as the distributions we encapsulate essential information in a single class. This is done by implementing a base class from which derived classes inherit.

Clients can instantiate the class to produce the random number generator object by passing previously instantiated random mechanisms and distribution objects. This promotes understandability of the resulting code. Furthermore, the framework can be extended in a flexible way. To sample from a customised distribution the user only has to provide the mechanism for random sampling.

We start by describing some methods for random sampling, namely *congruential* and *shift register generators*. We then consider Sobol numbers which is a popular and effective method to use in quasi Monte Carlo simulation. Then, we proceed by reviewing methods for transforming a uniform random variate into one from a given distribution, and we show how to implement them in C++.

The reader can find more information and several other methods and distributions in Devroye (1986) and Gentle (2003).

22.2 UNIFORM NUMBER GENERATION

The two main methods for generating uniform variates are *pseudo random number generation* and *quasi random number generation*. Using pseudo random numbers one aims to mimic randomness. This is not the case for quasi random numbers. The latter are determined numbers that fulfil certain irregularity criteria.

A reliable pseudo random number generator delivers numbers $U_i \in [0, 1]$, $i = 1, 2, \ldots$, such that

- $U_i, i = 1, \ldots$, are empirically uniformly distributed;
- $U_i, i = 1, \ldots$, are mutually independent.

An effective generator should have these properties but it also should be reliable in the sense that the results are reproducible, computationally efficient and portable.

For quasi random numbers the mutual independence is not valid. The numbers produced by such a generator do not try to mimic randomness and independence by fulfilling the above mentioned properties. Instead, dependence is used to achieve low discrepancy.

22.2.1   Pseudo random number generators

Congruential random number generators

We have implemented the random number generators *Ran0*, *Ran1* and *Ran2*, see also Press *et al.* (2002), which are given on the CD. These generators belong to the class of so-called *congruential random number generators*.

For positive integers a and m such a generator produces uniforms due to the algorithm:

$$X_{i+1} = aX_i \bmod m$$
$$U_{i+1} = X_{i+1}/m$$

The starting value X_0 is known as the *seed* of the generator. It can be shown that a congruential generator returns to its starting value. This means that outcomes of random experiments based on these random numbers are then the same. Such *cycles* or *periods* should be very large in order to get reliable values. In the above setting we achieve a period with maximal length if a^{m-1} is a multiple of m and a^{j-1} is not a multiple of m for all $j = 1, \ldots, m - 2$. Furthermore, we might think of improving the algorithm by considering $(aX_i + c) \bmod m$ for some positive integers with $c < m$ but it has been shown that this does does not improve the properties of the generator very much.

We give the implementation of the congruential generator *Ran2*. It increases the cycle by combining two linear congruential generators:

```
class Ran2
{
    // Ran2 combines two congruential random number generators
    // to achieve a bigger period.
    // Combining two generators breaks up serial correlation
    // The numbers provided for initialisation are from
    // L'Ecuyer Communications of the ACM, vol. 31, pp.742-774, 1988
    // See Glasserman "Monte Carlo Methods in Financial
    // Engineering", pp.50 - 53
public:
    Ran2(long Seed = 1,
         long a1=40014, long a2=40692, long m1=2147483563,
                                       long m2=214783399,
         long q1=53668, long q2=52774, long r1=12211, long r2=3791,
         long ntab = 32, double rnmx = 1.0-3.0e-8);
```

```
    double GetRandomNumber();
    void SetSeed(long Seed);

private:
    mutable long Seed;
    long a1, a2;
    long m1, m2;
    long q1, q2;      // determined using a and m (q = smallest
                         int m / a)
    long r1, r2;      // determined using a and m (r = m mod a)
    long ntab;
    double rnmx;
    mutable std::vector<long> iv;
    int iy;
};
```

This class implements data and member functions for the Ran2 pseudo random generator. The implementation initialises the constants a_1, a_2, m_1 and m_2 with the standard values. The main function here is double GetRandomNumber() that produces a number in the interval (0, 1) on each call. It is advisable to choose the interval (0, 1) since some of the transform methods map the points 0, respectively 1 to $\pm\infty$. This can cause one or both errors at run-time due to the fact that the endpoints of the interval are mapped to infinity. The generator uses two congruential generators and implements a shuffling mechanism to increase its period of returning to the starting value. The code snippet below shows the implementation:

```
double Ran2::GetRandomNumber()
{
        long j, k;
        double output;
        long Seed2 = 123456789;

        if (Seed <= 0 || !iy)
        {
                Seed = (Seed==0 ? 1 : -Seed);
                Seed2 = Seed;
                for(j = ntab + 7; j>=0;j--)
                {
                k = Seed/q1;
                Seed = a1*(Seed-k*q1)-k*r1;
                if(Seed < 0) Seed = Seed + m1;
                if(j < ntab) iv[j]=Seed;
                }
                iy = iv[0];
        }

        // First Congruential Generator
        k=Seed/q1;
        Seed = a1 * (Seed - k * q1) - k * r1;
        if (Seed < 0) Seed += m1;
```

```
// Second Congruential Generator
k = Seed2 / q2;
Seed2= a2 * (Seed2 - k * q2)- k * r2;
if (Seed2 < 0) Seed2 += m2;

j = iy / (1 + (m1 - 1) / 32);
iy = iv[j] - Seed2;
iv[j] = Seed;
if (iy < 1) iy = iy + m1 - 1;
output = 1.0 / double(m1)  * iy;

if (output > rnmx) return rnmx;
else return output;
}
```

For further information the reader may consult Knuth (1997) or Glasserman (2004) and the references therein.

Shift register random generators

The most important example of this class of generators is the *Mersenne Twister*. At the time of writing it is possible to find several updates and extensions of this generator. For example, a 64-bit implementation has been published by Matusumoto. A standard 32-bit version is also part of the Boost library we considered briefly in Chapter 13.

The general idea is to produce a vector of concatenated bits from which we derive integer values and, based on these integers, real numbers in the unit interval $[0, 1]^d$.

Since the full theory makes use of polynomial algebra over Galois fields we will just state some ideas of the mechanism applied in the Mersenne Twister algorithm.

The basic algorithm has grown from ideas originating from the *Generalised Feedback Shift Register* (GFSR) and *Twisted Generalised Feedback Register Generators* (TGFSR).

The name Mersenne Twister stems from the usage of certain positive integers known as *Mersenne primes*.

The main issue in the algorithm is the concept of a *Feedback Shift Register* (FSR). Such generators are of the form:

$$b(n) = c(k - 1)b(n - 1) \oplus c(k - 2)b(n - 2) \oplus \ldots \oplus c(0)b(n - k) \tag{22.1}$$

with $\oplus$ denoting the *xor* operation which is addition modulo 2.

For $k \geq 1$ we introduce operators $H^k b(n) = H^{k-1} b(n + 1)$ and rewrite equation (22.1) and subtract the right-hand side. We then get

$$H^k - c(q - 1)H^{k-1} - \ldots - c(0) = 0 \bmod 2$$

This equation is related to primitive polynomials that we study later when we introduce Sobol numbers.

These generators have been refined by introducing the idea of the GFSR. They are based on primitive polynomials of the form $x^p + x^q + 1$ and a recurrence relation $x(i) = x(i - p) \oplus$

$x(i - q)$ where all the entries are equal to 0 or 1. It can be shown that the maximum period is achieved if the number n is a Mersenne prime, which is a number that can be written as

$$2^n - 1, \text{ for some } n \in \mathbb{N}$$

It has been shown that the generators considered so far heavily depend on the initial seed and have small periods. The class of twisted generalised feedback shift register generators is based on linear recurrence of the form $x(l + n) = x(l + m) \oplus x(l)M$ with M being a matrix with entries 0 or 1.

Finally, the Mersenne Twister is a variant of TGFSR, which provides equidistribution in up to 623 dimensions and has a period of $2^{19937} - 1$. The algorithm generates vectors of *words* of length w representing uniform pseudo random integers between 0 and $2^w - 1$. Dividing by $2^w - 1$, respectively 2^w, leads to a uniform variate. For fixed r the algorithm is based on the recurrence:

$$x(k + n) = x(k + m) \oplus (x(k)^u | x(k + 1)^l)M \qquad (22.2)$$

with $x(k)^u$ denoting the u upper $w - r$ bits of $x(k)$ and $x(k)^l$ the r lower bits. The symbol '|' denotes concatenation. For general references the reader should consult Matsumoto and Nishimura (1998). Our implementation is

```
class MersenneTwister {
public:
    // constructor
    MersenneTwister(unsigned long Seed_ = 4357);

    // get functions
    double GetRandomNumber();
    unsigned long GetSeed();

    // set functions
    // Takes in Seed and then uses SeedInit with this seed
    void SetSeed(unsigned long Seed);
    // init the seed usable for Mersenne Twister main algorithm
    void SeedInit(unsigned long Seed);

private:

    unsigned long Seed;
    long mti;
    std::vector<unsigned long> mt;
    // Static data necessary for Mersenne Twister generator
    unsigned long mag01[2];
    static const unsigned long MT_N = 624;
    static const unsigned long MT_M = 397;
    static const unsigned long MT_D = 227;
    unsigned long MATRIX_A, UPPER_MASK, LOWER_MASK;
    unsigned long TEMPERING_MASK_B;
    unsigned long TEMPERING_MASK_C;
};
```

The main methods are `SeedInit()` and `GetRandomNumber()`. The first one sets up the generator whereas the second generates the next 623 elements in the initial sequence and returns the number divided by $2^w - 1$. In the code one finds the recurrence relation (22.2) such as

```
y = (mt[kk]&UPPER_MASK) | (mt[kk+1]&LOWER_MASK);
```

For more details and the theory behind all the generators, see Tausworthe (1965), Lewis and Payne (1973), Matsumoto and Kurita (1992) and Matsumoto and Nishimura (1998).

The Mersenne Twister generator is fast and gives reliable results. It is certainly worth having it and applying it in Monte Carlo simulation problems.

22.2.2   Quasi random number generators

Quasi random numbers and quasi Monte Carlo simulation have been used by many researchers. References include the papers Acworth, Broadie and Glasserman (1998), Berman (1997) or Boyle, Broadie and Glasserman (1997). Many low discrepancy number sequences underlying such generators have been proposed. Well-known sequences are Halton, Sobol, Faure or Niederreiter sequences; see Halton (1960), Halton and Smith (1964), Sobol (1977), Sobol and Levitan (1976), Faure (1982) and Niederreiter (1988). On the CD we have given the full implementation for generating Halton and Sobol sequences.

22.2.3   Sobol numbers

Sobol numbers are popular in the finance community. Therefore, we give a brief overview of their construction and describe our implementation in some detail. To understand the C++ implementation we begin with the mathematical concepts and basic examples on how to code this kind of quasi random number generator.

Direction numbers

At the heart of Sobol number generation lies the concept of so-called *direction numbers*.

Let *maxbit* denote the maximal number of bits allowed by the compiler. On a 32-bit machine, *maxbit* = 32. For each of the dimensions under consideration we consider *maxbit* numbers $v_i, i = 1, \ldots, maxbit$; one for each bit in its binary representation.

A direction number can be represented either as

$$v_i = 0.v_{i1}v_{i2}\ldots, \tag{22.3}$$

where v_{ij} is the jth bit following the binary point in the expansion of v_i or as

$$v_i = \frac{m_i}{2^i}, \quad i = 1, 2, \ldots, maxbit \tag{22.4}$$

We calculate the nth Sobol number x_n for each dimension using the numbers $v_i, i = 1, \ldots, maxbit$. Since the construction is carried out in the interval $(0, 2^{maxbit} - 1)$ to actually derive a Sobol number in the interval $(0, 1)$ we consider

$$\frac{x_n}{2^{maxbit}} \tag{22.5}$$

The only constraints on the direction numbers are that the i leftmost bits can be nonzero and the ith leftmost bit must be set.

Primitive polynomials

Continuing, we choose a *primitive polynomial* for each dimension. A primitive polynomial P modulo m of degree q is irreducible with respect to m and of order $m^q - 1$, that is it cannot be written as a product of polynomials of lower degree. For the number theoretic background the reader may consult Jäckel (2002). We consider a primitive polynomial P of degree q of the form:

$$P(x) = x^q + a_1 x^{q-1} + \ldots + a_{q-1} x + 1, \quad a \in \{0, 1\} \tag{22.6}$$

The first q initial direction numbers $v_i, i = 1, \ldots, q$ can be chosen arbitrarily within the above mentioned constraints. But the others are determined via a recurrence relation holding for primitive polynomials:

$$v_i = a_1 v_{i-1} \oplus a_2 v_{i-2} \oplus \ldots \oplus a_{q-1} v_{i-q+1} \oplus v_{i-q} \oplus v_{i-q}/2^q, \quad i > q \tag{22.7}$$

where we denoted the XOR operator for bitwise addition by $\oplus$. If two bits are equal the bitwise XOR returns 0 and otherwise 1.

In terms of the m_i the recurrence relation reads

$$m_i = 2a_1 m_{i-1} \oplus 2^2 a_2 m_{i-2} \oplus \ldots \oplus 2^{q-1} a_{q-1} m_{i-q+1} \oplus 2^q m_{i-q} \oplus m_{i-q}, \quad i > q \tag{22.8}$$

Completing the construction

For each new draw we select a *generating integer* $\gamma(n)$ with γ being a bijective function $\gamma : \mathbb{N} \to \mathbb{N}$. In the simplest case we choose $\gamma = id$. Given the generating integer we are able to compute x_n by

$$x_n := \sum_{j=1}^{d} v_j 1_{\{j\text{th bit counting from the right of } \gamma(n) \text{ is set}\}} \tag{22.9}$$

The sum is meant to be in the sense of bitwise *XOR*, using the shorthand notation $\oplus$ introduced in section 22.2.1.

Thus, to generate the actual Sobol number we need to divide by 2^{maxbit}.

As mentioned above, the generating integer could simply be $\gamma(n) = n$ which was originally proposed by Sobol, but other options are also available. One popular choice is $\gamma(n) = G(n)$. With G being a *Gray Code* given by $G(n) := n \oplus [n/2]$.

Example

To illustrate the theory we given an example. To this end let us take the primitive polynomial

$$P(x) = x^3 + x^2 + 1 \tag{22.10}$$

We choose the initial direction numbers as follows:

i	1	2	3
m_i	1	1	5
v_i	0.1	0.01	0.101

where m_i and v_i are linked via $v_i = m_i/2^i$.

The next direction numbers are computed by the recurrence relation (22.7) or (22.8). This gives for m_4 and m_5:

$$
\begin{aligned}
m_4 &= & 10 \oplus 8 \oplus 1 \\
&= & 1010 \oplus 1000 \oplus 01 \\
&= & 3
\end{aligned}
$$

$$
\begin{aligned}
m_5 &= & 6 \oplus 8 \oplus 1 \\
&= & 110 \oplus 1000 \oplus 01 \\
&= & 15
\end{aligned}
$$

Then, to obtain the first numbers of the Sobol sequence $x_{n+1} = x_n \oplus v_c$ we start with $x_0 = 0$. Here c denotes the rightmost zero-bit in the binary representation of n. In the following we denote a number n in binary notation. For example, $n = 100$ means $n = 1 \times 2^2 + 0 \times 2^1 + 0^0 = 4$. Then, the first four Sobol numbers are

$$
\begin{aligned}
x_1 &= & x_0 \oplus v_1 = 0.0 \oplus 0.1 \\
&\stackrel{n=01->c=2}{=} & 0.1(\text{bin}) = 0.5 \\
x_2 &= & x_1 \oplus v_2 = 0.1 \oplus 0.01 \\
&\stackrel{n=10->c=1}{=} & 0.11(\text{bin}) = 0.55 \\
x_3 &= & x_2 \oplus v_1 = 0.11 \oplus 0.1 \\
&\stackrel{n=011->c=3}{=} & 0.01(\text{bin}) = 0.25 \\
x_4 &= & x_3 \oplus v_3 = 0.01 \oplus 0.0011 \\
&\stackrel{n=100->c=1}{=} & 0.111(\text{bin}) = 0.875
\end{aligned}
$$

22.3   THE SOBOL CLASS

To cover all our applications for random number generation we have created a class hierachy (see Figure 22.1) as follows.

Introducing a new name `evenlonger` for `unsigned long long`, we built the class to manage Sobol numbers by using the following definition:

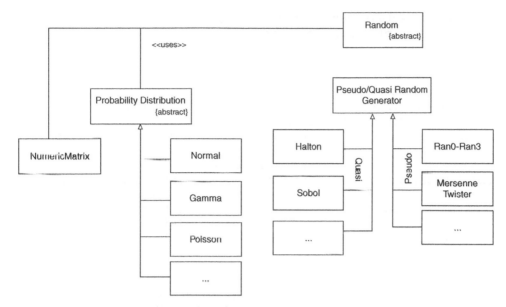

Figure 22.1 Class hierarchy for random number generation

```
class Sobol
{
public:
    Sobol(evenlonger Seed = 1, int DimMax = 1111); // Constructor
    virtual ~Sobol();                               // Destructor

    // computes the place of high bit of n (base 2),
    // i.e. the place of leftmost 1 in dual representation of n
    static int HiBit_2(evenlonger n);
    // computes the place of low bit of n (base 2),
    // i.e. the place of rightmost 1 in dual representation of n
    static int LoBit_2(evenlonger n);
    // computes the degree of a prim. poly.
    static int Degree(evenlonger n);
    // Decodes the prim. poly.
    void Decode(evenlonger n, std::vector<bool>& used);

    void SetSeed(evenlonger Seed);  // Set starting index of
                                    // sequence
    void Initv();                   // Initialize the rest of the
                                    // table v
    // computes the Sobol sequence for dim_num dimensions and
                                                   // index Seed
    void SobolNumbers(unsigned long& Col, unsigned long& Seed);

    evenlonger GetSeed();       // Get current index
    evenlonger GetAtmost();     // Get ATmost
    unsigned long GetDimMax();  // Get the dimensionality of
                                // sequence
```

```
    // Holds the actual vector of Sobol Sequence
    std::vector<double> SobolSequence;

private:

    evenlonger Seed;
    unsigned long DimMax;                  // Max Dimensions = 1111
    mutable std::vector<int> base;         // Basis
    evenlonger Atmost;         // Highest number which can be handled
                                   = 2^62-1
    unsigned int MaxCol;       // HiBit(Atmost)
    NumericMatrix<evenlonger, evenlonger> v; // Initial Direction
                                                numbers
    bool initialized;                       // Set if sequence is
                                               initialized
    static evenlonger poly[1111];           // Polynomials in
                                               binary encoding
};
```

The maximum dimension depends on the chosen direction integers. At the time of writing we have used direction numbers proposed in Joe and Kuo (2008). Direction numbers with reasonable projection properties up to dimension 1111 have been considered.

To use the class `Sobol` we have to specify the numbers of elements we wish to use and the dimensionality. The generated numbers are stored in the vector `SobolSequence`. For example, if we consider Sobol sequences in dimension 3 of length 123, the vector `SobolSequence` is a vector of length 3 and the routine is called 123 times. Of course, we can populate a matrix holding all the Sobol numbers at once. See also the exercises at the end of this chapter.

The following test program shows how to use the Sobol class:

```
// Initialize an object with of type Sobol
 Sobol SobNum(0);

// Input NumberOfDimension and Seed

for ( i = 0; i < l; i++ )
{
    // Call SobolNumbers
    SobNum.SobolNumbers(NumberOfDimensions,Seed); // Compute the
                                                      numbers

    // Print them to console
    for ( j = 0; j < NumberOfDimensions; j++ )
        cout << setw(2) << SobNum.SobolSequence[j] << "   ";
    cout << "/ n";
}
```

22.4 NUMBER GENERATION DUE TO GIVEN DISTRIBUTIONS

Having set up a random number generation mechanism producing uniformly distributed random numbers, the next challenge is to sample from other distributions, for example the Normal distribution or the gamma distribution. Such mechanisms often involve approximations and compromises. The first requirements are accuracy, efficiency and robustness. It implies that the mechanism must lead to the required distribution in reasonable time with reasonable computational effort and it should be applicable to a range of distributions. We have already covered some distributions in Chapter 1 but we describe the full set-up here. For further methods see, for example, Devroye (1986).

22.4.1   Methods for computing variates

A number of methods have been suggested to transform uniform random numbers on the unit interval into random variates of a given distribution. We review two main concepts.

22.4.2   The inverse method

This is the method of choice if it is available. Suppose that we wish to generate variates of a random variable X having cumulative distribution function $F_X = P(X \leq x)$ with inverse

$$F_X^{-1}(u) := \inf\{x : F_X(x) \geq u\} \tag{22.11}$$

then $F_X^{-1}(U) = X$. Thus, if we can compute the function F_X^{-1} we can generate a uniform $u \in [0, 1]$ if we set

$$x := F_X^{-1}(u) \tag{22.12}$$

to compute a sample from the distribution of X.

Hint: if we apply a quasi random number generation mechanism such as Sobol sequences the inverse transform should be the method of choice since it needs only one uniform random variate which is converted. Other methods may need several!

We verify that this method leads to random variates from the desired distribution, as the following calculation shows:

$$\mathbb{P}[X \leq x] = \mathbb{P}[F_X^{-1}(U) \leq x]$$
$$= \mathbb{P}[U \leq F_X(x)]$$
$$= F_X(x)$$

The input variable U can be seen as a random percentile. The inverse F_X^{-1} then maps the random percentile to the corresponding percentile of the probability under consideration.

22.4.3   Acceptance/Rejection and ratio of uniforms

The *Acceptance/Rejection Method* was introduced by John von Neumann and can be applied to a wide range of distributions. Suppose that we wish to sample from a distribution with density f. Assume there exists another probability density g such that

$$f(x) \leq cg(x) \quad \text{for all } x \text{ in the sample space and } c \in \mathbb{R}^+ \tag{22.13}$$

An assumption is that it should be easy and fast to sample from g. Then, we sample X from g and accept it as a variate with probability $\frac{f(X)}{cg(X)}$. Otherwise it is rejected and the procedure is applied as long as the number is accepted.

We prove that this method leads to variates from the desired distribution. Denote by Z conditional on $U \leq f(X)/cg(X)$ obtained from the acceptance-rejection procedure for a given event A. We consider:

$$\mathbb{P}(Z \in A) = c\mathbb{P}(X \in A | U \leq f(X)/cg(X))$$
$$= \frac{\mathbb{P}(X \in A | U \leq f(X)/cg(X))}{\mathbb{P}(U \leq f(X)/cg(X))}$$
$$= c \int_A \frac{f(x)}{cg(x)} g(x) dx$$
$$= \int_A f(x) dx$$

Since we accept with probability $1/c$, c should be near 1 otherwise too many uniforms are needed for one sample of the desired distribution.

A method that is related to the acceptance-rejection method is the *ratio of uniforms method*. To introduce the method let $f \geq 0$ be a density function. Consider a uniformly distributed vector (U_1, U_2) in the two-dimensional region

$$A := \{u = (u_1, u_2) : u_1 \leq \sqrt{f(u_2/u_1)}\}$$

The density of U_2/U_1 is then proportional to f. Let A be contained in a rectangle R.

We apply the following version of acceptance/rejection: generate $U = (U_1, U_2) \in R$ and accept it if $U_1 \leq \sqrt{f(U_2/U_1)}$ otherwise reject it and repeat this procedure until $U_1 \leq \sqrt{f(U_2/U_1)}$. The code is provided on the CD.

22.4.4   C++ implementation

As we have shown so far we need to generate variates due to many different distributions. This section describes the main set-up we use and some distributions that are heavily used in financial modelling. The reader can add custom distribution classes to the library.

We describe how we model a probability distribution. Further material and detailed description of the classes can be found in Duffy (2004a).

We start with the base class `Distribution`.

```
template <class Domain, class Range>
class Distribution
{// Abstract base class for prob dist used for MC
private:
    int NumberOfUniforms;

public:
    //  Constructors
    Distribution();
    Distribution(const Distribution<Domain, Range>& d2);

    ~Distribution();
```

```
Distribution<Domain, Range>& operator =
                        (const Distribution<Domain, Range>& p2);

//  Selector member functions
virtual Range pdf(const Domain& x) const = 0;
virtual Range cdf(const Domain& x) const = 0;
virtual Vector<Domain> icdf(const Vector<Range>& uniforms)
  const = 0;

// Selectors
virtual Range expected() const = 0;
virtual Range variance() const = 0;
virtual Range std() const { return ::sqrt(variance()); }

virtual int GetNoOfU() const = 0;

virtual Distribution<Domain, Range>* clone() const = 0;

};
```

Let us elaborate on the design of this class. The main member functions are pdf, cdf, icdf, expected and variance. The main difference to the probability distribution classes described in Duffy (2004a) is the member function icdf. This function implements the generation of a variate with respect to the underlying distribution. If inversion of the cumulative distribution function can be done efficiently this is the preferable choice. But, for example, to generate gamma distributed random variables we have to apply a version of the acceptance-rejection method (see sections 22.4.2 and 22.4.5).

In general, you can choose between the class from the authors and the corresponding class in the Boost library; see Chapter 13 for a discussion.

22.4.5   Generating normal variates

The normal distribution is the most widely used distribution. Many financial models are based on it. Several methods to generate normal variates have been suggested, for example Box-Muller, Polar-Marsaglia or direct inversion. Some of the methods have been discussed in Chapter 3. Our method of choice is to use the direct inversion method. Stable and accurate approximation algorithms exist to numerically compute the inverse of the cumulative normal distribution. For example, the algorithm in Moro (1995) is a good choice. We have also included the algorithm described in Acklam (2001) on the CD. This algorithm is a state-of-the-art implementation for inverting the cumulative normal distribution.

22.4.6   Generating gamma distributed variates

For generating variates due to a gamma distribution we do not use the inversion of the cumulative distribution function because it is numerically expensive. Here we rely on a version of the acceptance-rejection method. To generate variates for gamma distributed random variables we apply the *ratio-of-uniforms* method. The region from which we sample uniform variates is chosen to be

$$\mathcal{D}_{\text{Gamma}} := \left\{ (u_1, u_2) \in R | 0 \leq \sqrt{(u_2/u_1)^{a-1} \exp(-u_2/u_1)} \right\} \tag{22.14}$$

This set is contained in the rectangle with the lower left (*ll*) and upper-right (*ur*) points

$$ll = (0, ((a-1)/e)^{(a-1)/2}) \text{ and } ur = (0, (a+1)/e^{(a+1)/2}) \tag{22.15}$$

from which we can generate uniform random variables.

Generating gamma variates

For each loop we have to generate two uniform random variates. Therefore, the member data `NumberOfUniforms` in the gamma class has to be set to 2. It can be derived as the other probability distributions from the template class `Distribution<T,T>`:

```
template <class T>
class Gamma : public Distribution<T, T>
{
protected:

    T   r;
    T   a;
    int NumberOfUniforms;

public :
    // Constructors
    Gamma();              // r == 1, a == 1, NumberOfUniforms == 2
    Gamma(const Gamma<T>& distrib2);       // Copy constructor
    Gamma(const T&  alpha, const T&  rr);  // Two parameters

    // Accessing the parameters
    T alpha() const;
    T rcoeff() const;

    T   pdf(const T&  x) const;            // Probability density
    T   cdf(const T& x) const;
    Vector<T> icdf(const Vector<T>& uniforms) const;

    T expected() const; // Expected value
    T variance() const; // Variance

    int GetNoOfU() const;

    // Other functions

    Distribution<T, T>* clone() const { return new Gamma<T> (*this); }

};
```

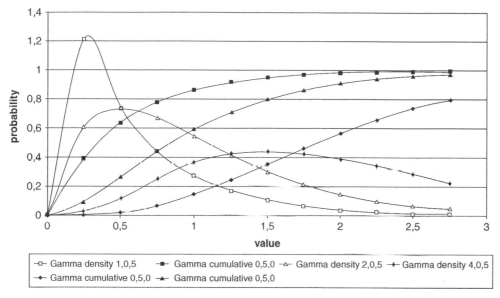

Figure 22.2 Gamma distribution – cumulative and density for changing the first parameter

To generate samples from the gamma distribution we use the method described in Ahrens and Dieter (1974) for $a \leq 1$ and the method explained in Fishman (1996) if $a > 1$. Figures 22.2 and 22.3 display output generated using our classes for various values of the input parameters.

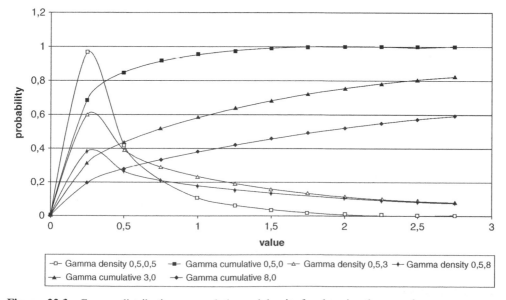

Figure 22.3 Gamma distribution – cumulative and density for changing the second parameter

For the reader's convenience we give the implementation of the algorithm for generating variates.

```
template <class T>
Vector<T> Gamma<T>::icdf(const Vector<T>& uniforms) const
{
    double u1;
    double u2;
    double w1;
    double w2;
    double y;
    double yy;
    double b;
    double c;

    Vector<T> result(2);

    if( a <= 1.0)
    {// This is the Ahrens - Dieter method, see e.g. Glasserman p.127
        b = (a + exp(1.0))/exp(1.0);
        u1 = uniforms[1];
        u2 = uniforms[2];
        y = u1 * b;
        if(y < 1.0)
        {
            yy = pow(y,1/a);
            if(u2 < exp(-yy)) result[2] = 1.0;
        }
        else
        {
            yy = -log((b-y)/a);
            if(u2 < exp(-yy)) result[2] = 1.0;
        }
        result[1] = yy;
    }
    else
    {// This is the GKM1 method, see e.g. Glasserman p. 126
        b = (a - (1.0 / (6.0 * a)))/(a-1);
        u1 = uniforms[1];
        u2 = uniforms[2];
        y = b*u2/u1;
        if(2.0 / (a - 1.0) * u1 - 2.0 / (a - 1.0) - 2.0 + y + 1 /
                                    y <= 0.0) result[2]=1.0;
        else if(2.0 / (a-1) * log(u1) - log(y) + y <= 0.0)
                                    result[2]=1.0;
        result[1]=(a-1.0) * y;
    }
    return r*result;
}
```

For generating gamma variates we could also use inversion but it is more time-consuming than the methods described above. All methods are also implemented in the Boost library as we discussed in Chapter 13. The gamma distribution has already been discussed in Chapter 3.

22.4.7   Generating χ^2-distributed variates

Consider the gamma probability density function:

$$f(y) = \frac{1}{\Gamma(a\beta^a)} y^{a-1} \exp(-y/\beta), \quad y > 0 \tag{22.16}$$

For $\nu \in \mathbb{N}$ we observe that taking $a = \nu/2$ and $\beta = 2$ it is equal to the density of a χ^2-distribution with ν degrees of freedom. This means that if we want to generate χ^2-distributed variates we can simply generate $\Gamma(\nu/2, 2)$-distributed variables.

22.4.8   Generating Poisson distributed variates

Another very important distribution is the *Poisson distribution*. Since the Poisson distribution is a discrete distribution, the implementation has to be adjusted appropriately. In particular, the mechanism for inverting the distribution is a discrete search algorithm. To this end we apply the inverse transform adapted to the discrete setting. However, the algorithm of our random number generator template does not change.

Computing the inverse of a discrete distribution is essentially a sequential search for the smallest number n at which for a given $u \sim U(0, 1)$

$$F(n) \leq u \tag{22.17}$$

holds where F denotes the corresponding distribution function. We do not give the full implementation of the Poisson class but for the member function icdf since it illustrates the inverse method for a discrete distribution:

```
template <class Domain, class Range> Vector<Domain>
Poisson<Domain,Range>::icdf(const Vector<Range>& uniforms) const
{
// inverse cumulative distribution function
    Vector<Domain> result(2);
    double p = exp(-lam);
    double F = p;
    double n = 0.0;
    while(uniforms[1] > F)
    {
        n = n+1;
        p = p * lam / n;
        F = F+p;
    }
    result[1] = n;        // Returns (possible) variate
    result[2] = 1.0;      // Returns 1 = accepted; other = rejected
    return result;
}
```

The `while` statement implements the discrete inversion by searching the value for which the generated uniform is bigger than the value $\exp(-\lambda)$.

22.5   JUMP PROCESSES

In the previous sections we studied stochastic differential equations of the form

$$dS(t) = a(S(t), t)dt + b(S(t), t)dW(t) \tag{22.18}$$

and interpreted the resulting solutions as diffusion processes with drift. The drift in this case can be seen as a trend. A noise represented by W is added to this trend. Both coefficient functions may depend on time as well as on the current level $S(t)$.

Recent models in quantitative finance extend this class of stochastic processes. For example, quantitative analysts wish to cover leptokurtic features of the distribution and smiles. Calculated returns from observed data for equities, funds or credit exhibit behaviour which lead to highly nonhomogeneous models if we work in the above framework of diffusion models. The drift and diffusion coefficients of equation (22.18) would be heavily time-dependent which causes the corresponding models to become very complicated.

An alternative is to include jumps into asset dynamics. This allows us to consider homogeneous models together with a set of other parameters governing the jumps and their distributions. Pure jump models such as *variance gamma* have also been considered in recent work on option pricing.

Jump-diffusion processes are represented by stochastic differential equations of the form

$$dS(t) = a(S(t), t)dt + b(S(t), t)dW(t) + c(S(t), t)dJ(t) \tag{22.19}$$

Here, J is a general Poisson process that is interpreted as the jump part. This part causes discontinuities in the path of the asset value. In the case of (22.18) the equation can be given sense by introducing a stochastic integral with respect to Brownian motion and interpreting dW as the 'differential' of Brownian motion or *White noise process*. The same can be done for the jump part of equation (22.19). In the following sections we consider basic jump processes and explain the rationale of equation (22.19). For a detailed mathematical treatment the interested reader should consult Cont and Tankov (2004).

22.5.1   The Poisson process

A property of the paths corresponding to a diffusion process is that they are continuous. But there are processes with a completely different stochastic movement. In general we distinguish between two kinds of movement. On the one hand it can be a small movement with high probability whereas on the other hand it can be a large movement with low probability. The latter movement is called a *jump*. For a more detailed discussion see Kienitz (2007a).

This stochastic movement can be illustrated by considering a simple example, namely the *Poisson process*. In contrast to diffusion processes it has discontinuous sample paths. It takes values in the positive integers.

To introduce the basic process we consider a sequence of independent exponentially distributed random variables $(\tau_n)_{n \in \mathbb{N}}$ where the probability for each τ_n being equal to $k \in \mathbb{N}$ is given by $\mathbb{P}(\tau_n = k) = (\exp(1)k)^{-1}$. We take the sum $T_n := \sum_{i=1}^{n} \tau_i$ and consider the following mapping:

$$N : \mathbb{R}^+ \times \Omega \to \mathbb{N}; \quad N(t) \mapsto \sum_{n \geq 1} 1_{\{t \geq T_n\}} \qquad (22.20)$$

$(N(t))_{t \in [0,T]}$ is called the Poisson process. This process is also known as a *counting process*. It counts the random times T_n that occur between 0 and t and the modelling assumptions are

- (P1): It starts at zero, $N(0) = 0$.
- (P2): It has stationary, independent increments.
- (P3): The distribution of $N(t)$ is Poisson, i.e. $N(t) \sim \mathcal{P}(t)$.
- (P4): The mapping $t \mapsto N(t)$ is piecewise constant and increases by jumps of size 1.

The sequence $(\tau_n)_n$ models the random times at which jumps occur.

Simulating a Poisson process

We can simulate variates of a pure Poisson process. Suppose we wish to simulate a typical path of a pure Poisson process in the interval $[0, 1]$. We use the variables path_size, dt and lambda to model the number of variates, the time stepping and the intensity of the process. The resulting variates are stored in the Vector<double, long> pure_poisson

```
Vector<double, long> dJ(path_size);      // Stores the Jump component
// Define the Random Number Generator (A)
PseudoRandGen<MersenneTwister> rangenerator_dJ(1234567);

// Init Distribution (B)
Poisson<double, double> PoissonDist(lambda * dt);

// Generate a Vector of Variates due to the given distribution (C)
rangenerator_dJ.GenerateVariatesVector(dJ, PoissonDist);

// Define the path vectors (D)
Vector<double, long> PP(path_size + 1);

// pure Poisson Process (E)
for(int i = dJ.MinIndex(); i <= dJ.MaxIndex(); i++)
{
    cout << "Value at time " << i * dt << ": " << PP[i]  << endl;
    PP[i+1] = PP[i] + dJ[i];
}
```

We now explain each step of the above algorithm.

We initialise a pseudo random number generator (A) which is a mechanism specifying how we generate uniform numbers in the interval $[0, 1]$. The template parameter MersenneTwister defines the C++ class we apply as a number generator. It specifies the method of how to generate uniform variates. The number '1234567' is the seed. It is the starting value given to the random number generator class.

The uniforms have to be transformed into variates from a Poisson distribution. The command (B) is used to initialise the class PoissonDist with intensity parameter $\lambda \cdot dt$. Finally, we use the command (D) to initiate the mechanism of creating all the numbers for building the process $(N(t))_t$ as described by equation (22.20). The final statement (E) prints the values to the console.

22.5.2 Simple generalisations

We may alter the intensity of the exponentially distributed random variables $(\tau_n)_n$ describing the times at which jumps occur. Let us consider $\lambda > 0$ and consider $(\tau_n)_n$ to be exponentially distributed with parameter λ, that is $\mathbb{P}(\tau_n = k) = \exp(-\lambda)\frac{\lambda^k}{k!}$. Proceeding as above the only thing that changes is assumption (P3); the random variable $N(t)$ is now distributed due to $N(t) \sim \mathcal{P}(\lambda t)$. The resulting process is called a Poisson process with intensity λ.

One may be tempted to generalise the above setting by allowing general increasing sequences of random times $(\tau_n)_n$ having any distribution. This leads to general counting processes but the Poisson process plays a special role since it is the only process which fulfils assumption (P2).

22.5.3 Compensation and compounding

The Poisson process does not obey the martingale property because its expected value is λt. Nevertheless, it is easy to make it into a martingale by subtracting its mean at time t. The mean and variance are those of a Poisson distributed random variable and are both equal to λt. This consideration leads to the *compensated Poisson process*, given by $\tilde{N}(t) = N(t) - \lambda t$. Coding can be done by replacing the command creating the counting process by

```
// Define the path vectors
Vector<double, long> CP(path_size + 1);

// Compensated Poisson Process
for(int i = dJ.MinIndex(); i <= dJ.MaxIndex(); i++)
{
    cout << "Value at time " << i * dt << ": " << CP[i]  << endl;
    CP[i+1] = CP[i] + dJ[i] - lambda * dt;
}
```

where again CP is a Vector<double> object.

A *compound Poisson process* with intensity λ and jump size distribution J is a stochastic process given by

$$X(t) = \sum_{i=1}^{N(t)} Y_i(t) \tag{22.21}$$

where $Y_i, i = 1, 2, \ldots$ is a sequence of randoms that are independent and identically distributed and $N(t)$ being a Poisson process independent of $Y_i, i = 1, 2, \ldots$. We have already discussed this topic in Chapter 6.

We observed for Brownian motion that the variance is of order dt. Now the process moves by large jumps each having small probability.

Simulating a compound Poisson process

To give an example of how to code a compound Poisson process we assume that the random variables Y_i are identically distributed due to a normal distribution, $Y_i \sim \mathcal{N}(a, b), i = 1, 2, \ldots$ with constants $a \in \mathbb{R}$ and $b \in \mathbb{R}^+$. Using the same code as above we only need to change the `for` statement to sample from a Compound Poisson process to

```
// Define the path vectors
Vector<double, long> CCP(path_size + 1);
// Compound Poisson Process
for(int i = dJ.MinIndex(); i <= dJ.MaxIndex(); i++)
{
    cout << "Value at time " << i * dt << ": " << CCP[i] << endl;
    if(dJ[i] == 0.0)
        Jump = 0.0;
    else
        Jump = mu_J * dJ[i] + sigma_J * sqrt(dJ[i])* dW1[i];
    CCP[i+1] = CCP[i] + Jump;
}
```

First, we have created the `Vector` dJ as before. If jumps have occurred in the interval $[t_n, t_{n+1}]$ we have to simulate the jump size. Here we assumed them to be normally distributed. The values are stored in the `Vector<double>` denoted by dW1.

Financial applications involve simulating compound Poisson processes where the logarithmic jumps normally distributed are, for instance, the Merton and the Bates models.

If the distribution of the Y_i in equation (22.21) is more complicated we have to simulate dJ[i] random variables Y of this distribution. Our code has to be adapted to that situation by including a `for` statement within the simulation.

22.5.4 Poisson random measures

We interpret the Poisson process as a counting process. The counting measure induced by the process can then be interpreted as the 'derivative' of the process. It counts the jump times T_n. This means that

$$N(t) = \#\{i \geq 1, T_i \in [0, t]\} \tag{22.22}$$

Here, we denote by # the cardinality of a discrete set, in this case the number of is where $T_i \leq t$. With this interpretation as a counting procedure at hand, for an interval A we define a counting measure on the positive real line by

$$J(\omega, A) = \#\{i \geq 1, T_i(\omega) \in A\} \tag{22.23}$$

The measure J is a random measure since it depends on ω. For fixed ω – which we suppressed in the notation of $N(t)$ – we get

$$N(t) = J(\omega, [0, t]) = \int_0^t J(\omega, ds) \tag{22.24}$$

This is the starting point to build a stochastic integral based on jump processes. This will not be discussed any further here and we refer the reader to Cont and Tankov (2004) for a comprehensive and detailed introduction. This is analogous to the derivation of the *White noise* process and we have

$$\frac{d}{dt}N(t) = \sum_{i \geq 1} \delta(T_i(\omega)) \tag{22.25}$$

Here δ denotes the Dirac measure centred in 0, that is

$$\delta(x) = \begin{cases} 1 \text{ if } x = 0 \\ 0 \text{ else} \end{cases}$$

22.5.5 Jump measures

Keeping in mind the example of a Poisson random measure we introduce general *jump measures*. Jump measures are useful when defining a stochastic calculus for general jump processes and this enables us to use the concept of stochastic differential equations for a very general class of stochastic processes.

An informal definition of the jump measure is as follows:

$$J([0, t] \times A) := \left(\begin{array}{c} \text{number of jumps of the process } S(t) \\ \text{occurring in the interval [0,t] with jump size in } A \end{array} \right) \tag{22.26}$$

Security price processes have been introduced as solutions of stochastic differential equations. At every time point t we re-balance our portfolio. Mathematically this *trading strategy* is described as a time-dependent variable ϕ corresponding to the number of shares of the security. The value of the trading strategy is thus

$$\phi(t)S(t), \quad t \in [0, T] \tag{22.27}$$

The cumulative gain of applying this strategy is

$$\int_0^T \phi(t)dS(t) \tag{22.28}$$

The last expression is a stochastic integral which makes sense if the driving force is a Brownian motion. Analogously, a stochastic integral can be introduced for jump processes. In fact the mathematical object of relevance here is the *Random measure*. With the help of that measure the corresponding integral can be defined. Therefore, we continue by describing the security price process by a stochastic differential equation. In the presence of a jump component this equation is given by equation (22.19) where the differential dJ indicates that when computing the integral we refer to the random measure as described above. A detailed discussion is outside the scope of this book; for the theory see Cont and Tankov (2004). However, we give an explicit solution for the *Merton model*. The stochastic differential equation in this case is given by

$$\frac{dS(t)}{S(t)} = (\mu - \lambda \underbrace{\mathbb{E}[Y-1]}_{=k})dt + \sigma dW(t) + dJ(t) \tag{22.29}$$

where J is the associated compound Poisson process with lognormal jumps; that is it has explicit solution

$$S(t) = S(0)\exp\left(\left(\mu - \frac{\sigma^2}{2} - \lambda k\right)t + \sigma W(t)\right)Y(n) \tag{22.30}$$

where $Y(0) = 1$ and $Y(n) = \prod_{i=1}^n Y(i)$.

Simulating a jump diffusion process

To simulate a jump diffusion process we mix the simulation procedure of a diffusion process with that of a compound Poisson process. The resulting C++ code is given by

```
Vector<double, long> dJ(path_size);   // Stores the Jump component
Vector<double, long> dW1(path_size);  // Stores the Brownian component
Vector<double, long> dW2(path_size);  // Stores a Brownian component

// Choose your favourite Random Number Generator
PseudoRandGen<MersenneTwister> rangenerator_dJ(1234567);
PseudoRandGen<MersenneTwister> rangenerator_dW(7766321);

// Init Distributions
Poisson<double, double> PoissonDist(lambda * dt);
NormalD<double,double> NormDist(0.0,1.0);

// Generate a Vector of Variates due to the given distribution
rangenerator_dJ.GenerateVariatesVector(dJ,PoissonDist);
rangenerator_dW.GenerateVariatesVector(dW1,NormDist);
rangenerator_dW.GenerateVariatesVector(dW2,NormDist);

Vector<double, long> JD(path_size+1);
JD[1] = 100.0;


for(int i = dJ.MinIndex(); i <= dJ.MaxIndex(); i++)
{
    cout << "Value at time " << i * dt << ": " << JD[i]  << endl;
    if(dJ[i] == 0)
        Jump = 1.0;
    else
        Jump = exp(mu_J * dJ[i] + sigma_J * sqrt(dJ[i]) * dW1[i]);
        // Accounting for martingale correction then use
        // Jump = exp(mu_J * dJ[i] + sigma_J * sqrt(dJ[i]) * dW1[i])
        //        - lambda * (exp(mu_J+0.5*sigma_J*sigma_J-1.0);
        JD[i+1] = JD[i] * exp((mu - sigma * sigma / 2) * dt
                  + sigma * sqrt(dt) * dW2[i]) * Jump;
}
```

If we examine the code we recognise that we can use the code for the compound Poisson process and add a diffusion term.

22.6   THE RANDOM GENERATOR TEMPLATES

We have already described how to generate uniform variates and how to transform uniforms into variates having a certain distribution. For the first task we could choose from numerous random generators such as congruential random generators including *Ran2* or shift register generators such as *Mersenne Twister*. For the second task we wish to use the inversion method but sometimes this method is not available or is too complex. We then rely on other methods such as acceptance rejection or ratio-of-uniforms methods. Our aim is to place all the methods in one random number generator tool. Thus, we wish to supply a random number generator as well as a distribution and the class should return a vector or a matrix of random numbers due to the given mechanism and distribution. This is realised by the following template class:

```
template <class R, class Domain = double, class Range = double>
class RandGen : public Random { public:

    RandGen(unsigned long Seed=1);          // Constructor
    virtual Random* clone() const;          // Clone

    void SetSeed(unsigned long Seed_);      // Function to set Seed
    unsigned long GetSeed();                // Returns Seed
    void Reset();

    // Random Number Generation
    // Generate a Random Matrices (Uniforms or Variates due to
        Distribution)
    // Method for generating uniforms due to supplied generator
    inline void GenerateUniformsMatrix(NumericMatrix<Range>&
                                                    mvariates);
    // Method for generating variates due to supplied generator and
        distribution
    inline void GenerateVariatesMatrix(NumericMatrix<Range>&
                    mvariates, Distribution<Domain,Range>& dist);

    // Generate a Random Vector (Uniforms or Variates due to
        Distribution)
    inline void GenerateUniformsVector(Vector<Range, long>&
                                                    vvariates);
    inline void GenerateUniformsVec(Vector<double>& vvariates);

    // indirect method, this might be slow
    inline void GenerateVariatesVector(Vector<Range, long>& vvariates,
                                Distribution<Domain,Range>&
                                                        dist);
    // direct method, this is fast
    inline void GenerateGaussianVector(Vector<Range, long>&
                                                    vvariates);
    inline void GeneratePoissonianVector(Vector<Range, long>&
                                vvariates, Range intensity);
    inline void GenerateGammaVariates(Vector<Range, long>& vvariates,
                                                    Range r,
                                                    Range a);
    inline void GenerateIGVariates(Vector<Range, long>& vvariates,
                                                    Range a,
                                                    Range b);

    // Generate a Random Matrix populated with Gaussians
    // Method for generating correlated Gaussian variates
    inline void GenerateCorrelatedGaussian(NumericMatrix<Range>&
```

```
                              variates, NumericMatrix
                                  <Range>& Correlation);


private:

    R MCNumberGen;          // The Random Number Generator
    unsigned long Seed;     // The Seed for the Generator
};
```

We now describe the source code of the class. The mechanism to create uniform variates is implemented as private member data and can be specified at run-time. The object which stores the output can be a `Vector` or a `NumericMatrix` object. There are functions that take such data structures as input. The object storing information on the distribution and how to sample from it can be supplied at run-time and is specified by the functions `GenerateVariatesVector` and `GenerateVariatesMatrix`. The object is a reference to an abstract base class `Distribution<Domain, Range>`.

Also a single uniform number can be obtained by applying the function `GenerateUniform`. Another case that can often be applied is the function to compute a matrix of correlated Gaussian variates. Having defined a correlation matrix `Correlation` the function `GenerateCorrelatedGaussian` can be applied. It returns a `NumericMatrix` of correlated Gaussians. We have shown several examples of how to use the template class for real life applications. The following code snippet shows the mechanism:

```
template <class R, class Domain, class Range>
      inline void RandGen<R,Domain,Range>::
            GenerateCorrelatedGaussian(NumericMatrix<Range>&
                                  variates,
                                  NumericMatrix<Range>&
                                  Correlation)
{
      NormalD<double, double> NormDist(0.0,1.0);
      NumericMatrix<double> Decomposition;
      Decomposition = Correlation.Cholesky();

      unsigned long dim_row = variates.Rows();
      unsigned long dim_col = variates.Columns();
      Vector<double> result(2);
      int NoUniforms;
      // Necessary for Ratio of uniforms and Acceptance-Regectance
         sampling;
      // 1 for InverseCumulativeDistribution
      NoUniforms = NormDist.GetNoOfU();
      Vector<double> uniforms(NoUniforms);

      for (unsigned long i=1; i <= dim_row; i++)
            for (unsigned long j = 1; j <= dim_col; j++)
                  variates(i,j) =
                  InverseCumulativeNormal(MCNumberGen.
                  GetRandomNumber());
      variates = Decomposition * variates;
}
```

The template arguments can be specified to define the random number generator, R, the domain, Domain, and the range, Range, of the distribution. We then initialise a standard normal distribution and compute the Cholesky decomposition to the given correlation matrix, Correlation, and denote them as Decomp. After generating the uniform variates and transforming them into standard Gaussian we multiply the variates with Decomp.

22.7   TESTS FOR RANDOMNESS

Our random number generators should produce independent variates that are uniformly distributed in $[0, 1]^d$. Up to now we did not show how to examine the output of a uniform random number generator to fulfil this property. There are empirical and theoretical methods to test the property of a reasonable random generator.

Empirical tests include *Frequency Test, Serial Test, Collision Test* or *Run Test*. These tests apply statistical methods on generated random numbers. Theoretical approaches are complicated since they examine the generation algorithm of the generator.

There are two popular methods called the χ^2 and the spectral test. For the χ^2 test we divide the interval $[0, 1]$ into k equidistant parts of length $1/k$: k should at least be 2000. Now, we generate variables using our random template mechanism and put them into the corresponding bucket, such that

$$\frac{p-1}{k} \le u \le \frac{p}{k}, \quad p = 1, \dots, k$$

Now, let f_i be the number of variables that have been put into the ith bucket; then

$$\chi^2 = \frac{k}{n} \sum_{i=1}^{k} \left(f_i - \frac{n}{k} \right)^2$$

Low values of χ^2 signify that the uniform distribution is reasonably matched. But as with most statistical tests, there may be exceptions from the general rule.

For the spectral test we create the set of overlapping vectors given by

$$L(s) := \{x_n = (x_n, \dots, x_{n+s-1}), n \ge 0\}$$

The maximal distance between adjacent parallel hyperplanes is measured. The maximum is taken over all parallel hyperplanes that cover all the vectors x_n given above. This method got its name from the first usage by Coveyou and MacPherson (1967) who used Fourier transform methods to analyse the family of linear congruential generators.

22.8   SUMMARY AND CONCLUSIONS

We have described pseudo and quasi random number generation by giving some important examples from each class of generators. We reviewed *Ran2* as a congruential generator and the *Mersenne Twister* algorithm as a representative of a shift register random number generator. We discussed the Sobol sequence from the class of quasi random generators and gave the C++ code.

To illustrate the mechanism of transforming uniform random numbers into those of a given distribution we reviewed the inversion method and the acceptance/rejection method. We described the methods by giving the implementation of several well-known and widely applied distributions:

- normal distribution;
- Poisson distribution;
- Gamma distribution;
- χ^2 distribution.

The section covering the Poisson distribution also gives an account of Poisson processes and processes that are based on simple Poisson processes. We showed how to use such processes to simulate jump diffusion processes. Such process are used in quantitative finance to model fat tails of terminal distributions as well as unpredictable and rare events occurring in the credit market. Examples can be found in Kienitz (2007a), Kienitz (2007b) and Kienitz (2009). Finally, we described the setup that binds the mechanisms together. The random generator template allows us to handle general probability distributions, several methods to generate random numbers and run-time initialisation. For the full implementation see the accompanying CD.

22.9   EXERCISES AND PROJECTS

1. (*) Congruential Generators
   Consider the linear congruential generator considered in section 22.2.1:

$$x(n) = 13x(n - 1) \bmod 31, \quad n \geq 1$$

   Write down the first 20 elements of the generated sequence starting with $x(0) = 15$.
2. (**) Lagged Fibonacci Generators
   Consider a generator of type

$$x(n + 1) = x(n) + x(n - 1) \bmod m$$

Apply the χ^2 test to this generator. The generator is widely known as a *Fibonacci Generator*. Apply the same test to the generator

$$x(n) = x(n - 24) + x(n - 55) \bmod m, \quad n \geq 55$$

and $x(0), \ldots, x(55)$ arbitrary integers which are not all even. Such generators are known as *lagged Fibonacci generators*. Furthermore, use the generators of the Boost library to simulate the stochastic processes considered in this chapter.
3. (*) Congruential Generators
   Consider the two generators

$$x(n) = 3x(n - 1) \bmod 31$$
$$x(n) = 13x(n - 1) \bmod 31$$

Plot the sequence of successive points and analyse how they perform using the spectral test.

4. (**) Probability

    Add some probability distributions, see for example Duffy (2004a). Supply the function `icdf` such that you can use it for Monte Carlo simulation.

5. (**) Sobol Numbers

    Take the class for computing Sobol numbers. Implement a mechanism which allows us to skip n numbers and take $s(1), s(1 + n), \ldots$ as the Sobol sequence. Make the skip a random variable taking values in the set $\{1, \ldots, N\}$ for some positive number N.

6. (***) Sobol numbers

    Take the class `Sobol` for computing Sobol numbers again. Add private member data called `SobolSequenceWhole` of type `NumericMatrix<double, long>` and store the resulting vector from `SobolNumbers` into `SobolSequenceWhole`.

7. (***) Jump Diffusions

    Consider a jump diffusion process where the number of jumps is distributed due to a binomial distribution, $B(n, p)$, and the upward jumps occur with some probability $p \in (0, 1)$ and the downward jumps with probability $q := 1 - p$. The height is distributed according to a gamma distribution with shape parameters α and β.

    To this end the binomial distribution has to be implemented. Then, a mechanism to retrieve the generated random variates must be added. We have illustrated the mechanism for the Poisson distribution; see section 22.5.1.

    We consider N time steps. At each time step generate the number of upward jumps. It is a binomial random variable. Let the realisation be K and determine the upward moves up $\sim \Gamma(K\alpha, \beta)$, then the downward moves $\sim \Gamma((N - K)\alpha, \beta)$ and add the difference $M = \text{up} - \text{down}$ to the diffusion.

8. (***) Combining Two Generators

    A class combining random generators is useful when one wants to combine two (or more) congruential random generators to increase the period of the generator. A template class for such combinations is as follows:

```
template <class RG1, class RG2>
class 2RandGen : private RanGen1, private RanGen2
{
  public:
  2RandGen(long seed1 = 12345, long seed2 = 98765) :
                                        RanGen1(seed1),
                                        RanGen2(seed2) {};

    void SeedInit(long seed1)
    {// Initialise the Seeds
        RanGen1::RandomInit(seed1);
        RanGen2::RandomInit(seed2);
    }

  double GenerateUniform()
  {
    double u = RanGen1::GenerateUniform() + RanGen2::
                            GenerateUniform();
```

```
    if (u >= 1.) u -= 1.;
    return u;
  }

};
```

Code and extend this class and use it with the random number generators *Ran0*, *Ran1* and *Ran2*.

9. (**) Sobol Numbers

   Compute the next five Sobol numbers from the example in Section 22.2.3.

23

Some Mathematical Background

The most powerful single idea in mathematics is the notion of a variable.

K. Dewdney

23.1 INTRODUCTION AND OBJECTIVES

Quantitative finance applications should be built on a solid framework. In our opinion the basic building block is a linear algebra package with a stable implementation of vector and matrix classes together with reliable functions for computing *eigenvalues*, *eigenvectors* and allowing for matrix transforms to solve equations, for example *singular value decomposition*.

In this chapter we consider a matrix class and explain how we set up functions for performing decomposition of matrices, namely *Cholesky* and *spectral decomposition*. We apply the singular value decomposition to price options with early exercise features.

We also introduce functional analytic methods already applied to implement the Longstaff-Schwarz algorithm in Chapter 19 as well as stochastic volatility models in Chapter 16. In particular, we show how to implement integration schemes which are an important part for implementing analytical solutions of affine stochastic volatility models.

23.2 A MATRIX CLASS

Monte Carlo simulation techniques rely on stable and efficient matrix classes and functions. We describe our implementation of a matrix class. For further details see Duffy (2004a), Duffy (2006a) and Chapter 11 of the current book. The template class `NumericMatrix<V,I,S>` implements a matrix. Functions to manipulate matrices are not implemented as member functions but are separated into a different file and are therefore independent from the matrix class.

23.3 MATRIX FUNCTIONS

We have set up some matrix functions that have been applied in Chapters 14 to 20 of this book. These operations contain functions to transform a given matrix or derive parameters from a given matrix. The main functions are Cholesky, spectral and singular value decomposition, *inversion*, eigenvalue and eigenvector computation. We describe the main functions and their implementation in the following sections.

23.3.1 The Cholesky decomposition

Cholesky decomposition is used to simulate multi-dimensional correlated Brownian motion. For a positive integer d, a d-dimensional Gaussian variable is fully determined by the mean and variance vector together with a correlation that is a *positive definite* symmetric $d \times d$ matrix which we call A. This means A has to fulfil

$$A(i, j) = A(j, i), \quad 1 \le i, j \le d \text{ (symmetric)} \tag{23.1}$$

$$\,^t\underline{x}A\underline{x} > 0 \text{ for all vectors } \underline{x} \text{ of size } d \text{ (positive definite)} \tag{23.2}$$

The matrix A is the input to the Cholesky decomposition. The output is a lower triangular matrix L, that is a matrix of the form

$$L = \begin{pmatrix} l_{11} & 0 & 0 & \ldots & 0 \\ l_{12} & l_{22} & 0 & \ldots & 0 \\ \vdots & \vdots & \ddots & \vdots & \vdots \\ l_{1,d-1} & l_{2,d-1} & \ldots & l_{d-1,d-1} & 0 \\ l_{1d} & l_{2d} & \ldots & 0 & l_{dd} \end{pmatrix}$$

such that

$$\,^tLL = A \tag{23.3}$$

The code is given by

```
template <class V, class I, class S>
    NumericMatrix<V,I,S> Cholesky_Decomp(const NumericMatrix<V,I,S>&
                                                          argument)
{
    I Dimension = argument.Rows();
    V sum;
    V value;

    NumericMatrix<V,I,S> CholeskyDecomposition(Dimension, Dimension);

    for(I row = argument.MinRowIndex(); row <= Dimension; row++)
    {
        for(I col = row; col <= Dimension; col++)
        {
            sum = argument(col,row);
            for(I k = argument.MinRowIndex(); k <= row-1;k++)
                sum = sum - CholeskyDecomposition(row,k)
                                *CholeskyDecomposition(col,k);

            if (row == col)
            {
                if (sum <= 0)
                    CholeskyDecomposition(row,row)=0.0;
                else
                    CholeskyDecomposition(row,row)=sqrt(sum);
            }
            else
            {
                value = CholeskyDecomposition(row,row);
                if (value != V(0.0))
                    value = sum / value;
                else
```

```
                    value = V(0.0);
            CholeskyDecomposition(col, row) = value;
            }
        }
    }
    return CholeskyDecomposition;
}
```

The implementation is not the most efficient implementation of the Cholesky decomposition. First, we have to account for practical problems. Whenever we compare numerical values in an algorithm we have to account for rounding problems due to machine precision. Second, the above algorithm can be optimised in terms of performance. It is a straightforward implementation of the mathematical algorithm. We leave both improvements as an exercise (see section 23.7). As an example we take as the input to the Cholesky decomposition the following matrix:

$$A = \begin{pmatrix} 1 & 0.748733508 & 0.888524896 & 0.821526502 \\ 0.748733508 & 1 & 0.726662801 & 0.683150423 \\ 0.888524896 & 0.726662801 & 1 & 0.878266274 \\ 0.821526502 & 0.683150423 & 0.878266274 & 1 \end{pmatrix} \quad (23.4)$$

The output of the Cholesky decomposition is the matrix

$$L = \begin{pmatrix} 1 & 0 & 0 & 0 \\ 0.748733508 & 0.662871129 & 0 & 0 \\ 0.888524896 & 0.092618966 & 0.449383173 & 0 \\ 0.821526502 & 0.102653443 & 0.30889423 & 0.468124804 \end{pmatrix}$$

23.3.2   The spectral decomposition

Often the Cholesky decomposition cannot be applied because the input matrix is not positive definite. There is another way to decompose a matrix and generate correlated normals called *spectral decomposition*. To derive the spectral decomposition of a symmetric $d \times d$ matrix A we consider the n eigenvalue-eigenvector pairs $(\lambda_i, \underline{e}_i)$, $i = 1, \ldots, d$. The spectral decomposition of the matrix A is the matrix C such that

$$A \times C = C \times D, \text{ with } D = \begin{pmatrix} \lambda_1 & 0 & 0 & \ldots & 0 \\ 0 & \lambda_2 & 0 & \ldots & 0 \\ \vdots & \vdots & \ddots & \ddots & \vdots \\ 0 & \ldots & 0 & \ldots & \lambda_n \end{pmatrix} \quad (23.5)$$

The decomposition is particularly useful because it allows us to truncate the negative *spectrum*, which are the negative eigenvalues, and hence obtain a positive semi-definite matrix which approximates the initial correlation matrix in some sense. For details, see Jäckel (2002).

To compute the spectral decomposition of a matrix we need the eigenvalues as well as the eigenvectors of the matrix A. Thus, we have to solve the equation:

$$A\underline{v} = \lambda \underline{v}, \quad \lambda \in \mathbb{R}, \quad \underline{v} \in \mathbb{R}^d \quad (23.6)$$

The spectral decomposition can be applied to any symmetric matrix regardless of whether it is positive definite or not. We implement the decomposition by the following template class:

```
template <class V, class I, class S>
    NumericMatrix<V,I,S> Spectral_Decomp(const NumericMatrix<V,I,S>&
                                                            argument)
{
    // We assume a symmetric matrix as input!
    I Dimension = argument.Rows();

    // Constructor for class for eigenvalues and eigenvector
       calculation
    Eigenvalue<V> eigen(argument);

    // This matrix stores the eigenvectors
    NumericMatrix<V,I,S> Eigenvectors = eigen.getV();
    // This vector stores the eigenvalues
    Vector<V> Eigenvalues = eigen.getRealEigenvalues();

    // Truncate negative eigenvalues and take the squareroot
    for(I i = Eigenvalues.MinIndex(); i<= Eigenvalues.MaxIndex();
                                                            i++)
        if(Eigenvalues[i] < 0.0)
            Eigenvalues[i] = 0.0;
        else
            Eigenvalues[i] = sqrt(Eigenvalues[i]);

    // Create Diagonal Matrix of Eigenvalues
    NumericMatrix<V,I,S> DiagEigen = Vector2Diag(Eigenvalues);

    // Compute norm of each column
    Vector<V,I> Norms(Eigenvectors.Columns());

    Eigenvectors = ConvertStartingIndex(Eigenvectors,I(1),I(1));

    for(I i = Eigenvectors.MinRowIndex(); i <= Eigenvectors.
                                        MaxRowIndex(); i++)
        Norms[i] = Norm(Eigenvectors.Column(i));

    NumericMatrix<V,I,S> NormDiag = Vector2Diag(Norms);

    NumericMatrix<V,I,S> Spectral = Eigenvectors * DiagEigen;

    return Spectral;
}
```

We give two examples of an application of the spectral decomposition. We take as input the symmetric matrix given by equation (23.4). The output of the spectral decomposition is

$$
C = \begin{pmatrix}
-0.148133 & 0.00863866 & 0.246292 & -0.111069 \\
0.290286 & -0.0792683 & 0.0522504 & -0.277455 \\
0.0618291 & -0.515451 & 0.16485 & 0.242996 \\
0.943381 & 0.853201 & 0.953643 & 0.922841
\end{pmatrix}
$$

As another example we refer to Jäckel (2002). The input matrix is given by

$$A = \begin{pmatrix} 1 & 0.9 & 0.7 \\ 0.9 & 1 & 0.4 \\ 0.7 & 0.4 & 1 \end{pmatrix}$$

Its spectral decomposition is

$$C = \begin{pmatrix} -0.131915 & 0.100207 & 0.0538929 \\ -0.0871829 & -0.455364 & 0.633292 \\ 0.98742 & 0.884648 & 0.772034 \end{pmatrix}$$

and therefore the same as in Jäckel (2002).

The following is a short test program for the spectral decomposition as well as for the Cholesky algorithm:

```
int main()
{
    // Define the Matrix M
    NumericMatrix<long double> M(4,4);
    M(1,1) = 1.0; M(1,2) - 0.748734; M(1,3) = 0.888525; M(1,4)
            = 0.821527;
    M(2,1) = 0.748734; M(2,2) = 1.0; M(2,3) = 0.726663; M(2,4)
            = 0.68315;
    M(3,1) = 0.888525; M(3,2) = 0.726663; M(3,3) = 1.0; M(3,4)
            = 0.878266;
    M(4,1) = 0.821527; M(4,2) = 0.68315; M(4,3) = 0.878266; M(4,4)
            = 1.0;

    // Define the Matrix M2
    NumericMatrix<long double> M2(3,3);
    M2(1,1) = 1.0; M2(1,2) = 0.9; M2(1,3) = 0.7;
    M2(2,1) = 0.9; M2(2,2) = 1.0; M2(2,3) = 0.4;
    M2(3,1) = 0.7; M2(3,2) = 0.4; M2(3,3) = 1.0;

    // Derive the Spectral Decomposition of M
    NumericMatrix<long double> Spec = Spectral_Decomp(M);
    printout_mat(Spec);                        // Output
    printout_mat(Spec * Transpose(Spec));      // Output

    // Derive the Cholesky Decomposition of M2
    NumericMatrix<long double> Chol = Cholesky_Decomp(M2);
    printout_mat(Chol);
    printout_mat(Chol * Transpose(Chol));

    return 0;
}
```

Computing eigenvalues and eigenvectors

Since the decomposition algorithms described in the last section used eigenvalues and eigenvectors we discuss our implementation for the computation here. We only compute eigenvalues and eigenvectors for symmetric matrices. The method of choice here is to first compute the *Householder reduction*. The householder algorithm, `tred2()`, reduces a $d \times d$ matrix to tri-diagonal form by applying $d - 2$ orthogonal transformations to the matrix. By orthogonal transformations we mean multiplication with a matrix where all the column vectors are pairwise orthogonal to each other.

After successfully completing this task we compute the eigenvalues and vectors of a tridiagonal matrix using a version of the *QL* algorithm with implicit shifts, `tqr2()`.

For the general case we apply the algorithms `orthes()` and `hqr2()`. For more details on the specific algorithms and the linear algebra involved we refer the reader to Press *et al.* (2002).

Our template class `Eigenvalue` is initialised by supplying a numeric matrix from which we compute the eigenvalues as well as the eigenvectors:

```
template <class Real, class I = long, class S= FullMatrix<Real> >
    class Eigenvalue
{
    I n;            // Only square matrices thus #cols = #rows
    I issymmetric;

    Vector<Real,I> d;           // eigenvalues real part
    Vector<Real,I> e;           // eigenvalues img part
    NumericMatrix<Real,I,S> V;  // All eigenvectors
    NumericMatrix<Real,I,S> H;  // Nonsymmetric Hessenberg form

    Real cdivr, cdivi;

    Vector<Real,I> ort; // for nonsymetric cases

    void tred2();        // Householder reduction to tri-diagonal form
    void tql2();         // Tri-diagonal QL algorithm
    void orthes();       // Non-symmetric reduction to Hessenberg form
    // Scalar division for complex numbers
    void cdiv(Real xr, Real xi, Real yr, Real yi);
    void hqr2 ();        // Hessenberg to Schur form

public:
    Eigenvalue(const NumericMatrix<Real,I,S> &Aorg);    // Constructor
    NumericMatrix<Real,I,S> getV() {    return V;   }// Get
                                                        eigenvectors

    // Get real parts of eigenvalues
    Vector<Real,I> getRealEigenvalues() {   return d;   }
    // Get imag parts of eigenvalues
    Vector<Real,I> getImagEigenvalues() {   return e;   }
    NumericMatrix<Real,I,S> getD(); // Get D
};
```

We have chosen `Vector` and `NumericMatrix` objects to store the eigenvalues and eigenvectors, respectively. As usual we access private member data by implementing get functionality.

The eigenvectors are stored as the rows of a `NumericMatrix`. For the eigenvalues we store the real and the imaginary part (if necessary) separately or use the class `Complex` of Duffy (2004a) or the STL class `complex`. For example, we take as an input the matrix

$$A = \begin{pmatrix} 1 & -0.5 & 0.7 \\ -0.5 & 1 & -0.5 \\ 0.7 & -0.5 & 1 \end{pmatrix}$$

We obtain the eigenvectors (stored as the rows of the matrix)

$$(\underline{e}_1, \underline{e}_2, \underline{e}_3) = \begin{pmatrix} 0.707107 & 0 & -0.707107 \\ -0.372959 & -0.84959 & -0.372959 \\ 0.600751 & -0.527443 & 0.600751 \end{pmatrix}$$

and the eigenvalues $\lambda_1 = 0.3$, $\lambda_2 = 0.561013$ and $\lambda_3 = 2.13899$.

23.3.3   Singular value decomposition

Solving linear regression problems for pricing American options as considered in Chapter 19 involves the inversion of matrices. To this end, for $m, n \in \mathbb{N}$ we take an $m \times n$ matrix A. The rank of the matrix is denoted by r and we have $r \leq m$. The matrix ${}^t A A$ is symmetric. We denote its eigenvalues by

$$\lambda_1 \geq \lambda_2 \geq \ldots \lambda_r > \lambda_{r+1} = \ldots \lambda_m = 0 \tag{23.7}$$

The singular values σ_i of the matrix A are defined to be the eigenvalues of ${}^t A A$. In our setting the singular values are the square roots of the eigenvalues of A, that is $\sigma_i = \sqrt{\lambda_i}$. Applying a standard theorem from linear algebra to the matrix A it can be decomposed into two orthogonal matrices U and V being $m \times n$, respectively $n \times n$, matrices and a diagonal matrix D such that

$$A = U D^t V \tag{23.8}$$

As a reminder: a matrix is orthogonal if its column vectors are pairwise orthogonal. We have integrated this decomposition into the template class SVD. The main body of the class is

```
template <class Real>
    class SVD
{

    NumericMatrix<Real> U, V;
    Vector<Real> s;
    long m, n;


public:
    SVD(const NumericMatrix<Real> &Arg);
    NumericMatrix<Real> getU();
    // Return the right singular vectors
    NumericMatrix<Real> getV();
    // Return the 1-d vector of singular values
    Vector<Real> getSingularValues();
    NumericMatrix<Real> getS();
    // Two norm   (max(S))
    double norm2();
    // Two norm of condition number (max(S)/min(S))
    double cond();
    long rank();
};
```

To compute the singular value decomposition of a matrix with values of type `double` call the constructor `SVD<double> svd(argument)` and get the corresponding matrices by calling the get functionality.

Having the singular value decomposition available we can implement inversion using the following C++ code:

```
template<class V, class I, class S>
    NumericMatrix<V, I, S> Invert(NumericMatrix<V,I,S>& argument)
{
    SVD<V> svd(argument);
    NumericMatrix<V,I,S> resultmatrix(svd.getV()
                        * SimpleInvert(svd.getS())
                        * Transpose(svd.getU()));
    return resultmatrix;
}
```

where the simple inversion is implemented as follows:

```
template<class V, class I, class S>
NumericMatrix<V,I,S> SimpleInvert(NumericMatrix<V,I,S>& argument)
{
NumericMatrix<V,I,S> resultmatrix(argument);

for(I i= argument.MinRowIndex(); i <= argument.MaxRowIndex(); i++)
for(I j = argument.MinColumnIndex(); j <= argument.MaxColumnIndex();
                                                                 j++)
argument(i,j) != V(0.0) ? resultmatrix(i,j) = V(1.0) / argument(i,j)
                                                         : V(0.0);

return resultmatrix;
}
```

Since the singular values are the square roots of the eigenvalues we have another method to derive eigenvectors.

Other useful decomposition techniques exist and are widely applied when dealing with matrices. Among them are *QR*, *QL* and *LU-decomposition*. We do not cover these techniques here because we do not explicitly need them in our analysis. However, the eigenvalue/eigenvector search routine implicitly uses the QL decomposition.

23.4   FUNCTIONAL ANALYSIS

23.4.1   The basics

Functional analysis is the branch of mathematics concerned with the study of function spaces and operators acting on function spaces. It links concepts from topology, analysis and algebra. The roots of functional analysis can be traced back to the early stages of harmonic transforms and variational problems. One of the main objects studied in functional analysis are normed spaces. In the following we consider *Fourier transform* and *Hilbert spaces*. A complementary discussion can be found in Chapters 2 and 3 of this book.

23.4.2   Fourier transform

We give a basic introduction of Fourier transform methods because we think this book is not complete without mentioning them. The method is applied to the pricing of European options in stochastic volatility frameworks such as the Heston model or the Bates model, for instance. Furthermore, it allows the deducing of path properties and distributional properties of stochastic processes; see Lewis (2000), Kienitz (2007a), Kienitz (2007b) and Kienitz (2009).

23.4.3   Hilbert spaces and L_2-basis

Hilbert spaces are used in many mathematical disciplines such as measure and probability theory. Such spaces are complete normed vector spaces of the real or complex numbers obeying an inner product.

Consider a positive integer p and the set of all p-integrable random variables on a given probability space $(\Omega, \mathcal{F}, \mathbb{P})$. We denote this set by

$$\mathcal{L}_p := \mathcal{L}_p(\Omega, \mathcal{F}, \mathbb{P}) :- \{X \text{ random variable} | \mathbb{E}[X^p]| < \infty\}$$

For the set of $\mathbb{P}$ null sets

$$\mathcal{N} := \{X \text{ random variable} | X = 0 \quad \mathbb{P} \text{ almost everywhere}\}$$

we can show that the space of all equivalence classes, $L_p(\Omega) := \mathcal{L}_p(\Omega)/\mathcal{N}$, with respect to the set $\mathcal{N}$, is a *Banach space*, which is a complete space with a norm. In fact it can be shown that $L_2(\Omega)$ is indeed a Hilbert space. In particular the space $L_2(\Omega)$ has some additional structural properties such as an inner product. In the particular case if $f, g \in L_2(\Omega)$ it is given by

$$\langle f, g \rangle_{L_2} := \int_\Omega fg \; d\mathbb{P}$$

We use the concept of a basis. For functions $(g_i)_i$ constituting a basis we have for $f \in L_2(\Omega)$ that it can be written in terms of the basis and the inner product as follows:

$$f = \sum_i \langle f, g_i \rangle g_i$$

Special basis functions are those for which $\langle g_i, g_j \rangle = \delta_{ij}$ where δ_{ij} is the Kronecker symbol. Such a basis is called orthogonal. In our setting we use *orthogonal polynomials* which means that $(g_i)_i$ is an orthogonal basis of polynomial functions. Well-known polynomials are *Legendre*, *Laguerre* or *Hermite* polynomials. We may apply such functions for regression algorithms to price American options as well as for integration problems arising in the valuation of European options for affine stochastic volatility models.

23.4.4   Measures and Fourier transform

We use the definitions from section 23.4.3 to introduce the Fourier transform. To this end let μ be a measure and define the Fourier transform $\hat{\mu}$ of μ by

$$\hat{\mu}(\underline{x}) = \int_{\mathbb{R}^d} \exp(i < \underline{x}, \underline{y} >) d\mu(\underline{y}), \quad i = \sqrt{-1} \tag{23.9}$$

We used the notation $< \underline{x}, \underline{y} > = \sum_{i=1}^{\infty} x_i y_i$. If the measure is defined on $\mathbb{R}^d$ and it has a density $f : \mathbb{R}^d \to \mathbb{R}$ with respect to Lebesgue measure the Fourier transform can equivalently be written as

$$\hat{f}(\underline{x}) = \int_{\mathbb{R}^d} \exp(i < \underline{x}, \underline{y} >) f(\underline{y}) d\underline{y} \tag{23.10}$$

We use the latter version of the Fourier transform.

23.4.5   The characteristic function of a random variable

The *characteristic function* $\hat{\mathbb{P}}_X$ of a random variable $\underline{X}$ is

$$\hat{\mathbb{P}}_X(\underline{x}) := \mathbb{E}_{\mathbb{P}_X}[\exp(i < \underline{x}, X >)] \tag{23.11}$$

The characteristic function is used to derive properties of distributions and path properties of stochastic processes. For details see Kienitz (2007a) or Cont and Tankov (2004).

For instance, let us consider the sum of n independent identically distributed random variables:

$$Y_n := \sum_{i=1}^{n} X_i \tag{23.12}$$

For the characteristic function we have

$$\hat{Y}_n = \prod_{i=1}^{n} \hat{X}_i = \hat{X}_1^n \tag{23.13}$$

The moments of the distribution corresponding to the characteristic function ϕ can be computed by differentiation of ϕ:

$$m_k := \mathbb{E}[X^k] = \frac{1}{i^k} \frac{\partial^k \phi}{\partial z^k}(0) \tag{23.14}$$

23.5   APPLICATIONS TO OPTION PRICING

In this section we review Fourier transform methods to solve option pricing problems. We apply the methods to the Heston model and to the Bates model. The obtained results can be used as benchmark prices to test the Monte Carlo scheme of Chapter 16 for these models.

Prices for European options can be calculated by a Black-Scholes type formula:

$$\delta[e^{-d(T-t)}S \cdot P_1(\delta) - e^{-r(T-t)}K \cdot P_2(\delta)] \tag{23.15}$$

where

$$P_j = \frac{1-\delta}{2} + \delta \cdot \frac{1}{2} + \frac{1}{\pi}\int_0^\infty \mathcal{R}\left[\frac{\phi_j(k)e^{-iky}}{ik}\right]dk \tag{23.16}$$

In the latter expression the characteristic function for the underlying model is needed. For the Heston and Bates stochastic volatility models we have given the expression for the characteristic function in Chapter 16, namely equations (16.3) and (16.15).

Therefore, pricing a European option in such models can be reduced to solving a complex integration problem. The variable δ is determined by the type of the option:

$$\delta = \begin{cases} 1 & \text{Call Option} \\ -1 & \text{Put Option} \end{cases} \tag{23.17}$$

23.5.1   Semi-analytical prices and their C++ implementation

Using the results in Jäckel and Kahl (2006) the integration over the real line can be transformed into one over the unit interval. To this end the authors compute the limit of the integrand for the integration variable approaching 0 and ∞. Then, they apply the transformation, $u(x) = -\log(x)/c$ where c is a suitable constant. The procedure transforms an integral expression of the form

$$\int_0^\infty f(u)du$$

into one of the form

$$\int_0^1 f(u(x))/x\ c\ dx$$

This procedure allows the use of advanced numerical schemes to obtain precise results for the European call and put option prices. To this end we need a reliable implementation of numerical integration routines.

The function implementing the price of a European option in the Heston model, for example, is given by

```
double Heston_Price(int C_or_P, double t, double K, double S,
                                              double r,
               double d, double vLong, double vInst, double kappa,
               double rho, double omega, int method)
{//C_or_P = 1 call, = 0 put
   double X, price;
   X = exp((r-d) * t) * S; // Compute Forward
   vector<double> p1;
//Init parameters vector passed to function
   p1.push_back(K); // Strike
   p1.push_back(X); // Forward
```

```
    pl.push_back(t); // Maturity
    pl.push_back(vLong); // Long Term Variance
    pl.push_back(vInst); // Current Variance
    pl.push_back(kappa); // Mean Reversion
    pl.push_back(rho); // Correlation
    pl.push_back(omega); // Vol of Variance
// Define the integrator as a function depending on parameters
    ParaDFunction<double,double,vector<double> >
                                    func(Comp_Heston_Integrand_JK,pl);
    // Reference to an implemented integration scheme
    IntegratorImp* imp;
    switch(method)
    {
       case 1:
          imp = new GaussLobattoRule;
          break;
       case 2:
          imp = new GaussLegendreRule;
          break;
       default:
          imp = new GaussLobAdaptRule;
    }
    // Domain of integration
    Range<double> rng(0.0, 1.0);
    // Input function, range, scheme, points and error criteria
    NumIntegrator context(func, rng, (*imp), 128, 1E-6);
    if(K == 0)
       price =X;
    else
       price = context.value();    if (C_or_P ==1)
       return price;
    else
       return price + K - X;// Put-Call-Parity
}
```

The integrator uses the function Comp_Heston_Integrand_JK which is a parametric function implemented by the class ParaDFunction. We pass a vector<double> to this function. The vector stores all the model parameters.

For the implementation of the integration mechanism we use the *Bridge* design pattern, which was discussed in Chapter 11, and apply and extend the framework given in Duffy (2004a). The corresponding UML diagram (Figure 23.1) summarises the implementation. In fact we separate the integration class into two parts. One part is invariant and implements the code, which does not change, whereas the second part is the actual implementation of the integration rule, which is different for each scheme. We have full flexibility switching from one scheme to another.

We have implemented the following integration scheme as an example. The full code is on the CD. This code was also used to implement the functions in the Excel worksheet to

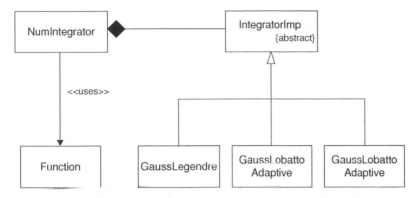

Figure 23.1 UML diagram for integration schemes

illustrate the smile shapes and probability distributions for the Heston model and the Bates model.

The class NumIntegrator delegates all requests from clients to the bridge (Figure 23.1). It uses an object ParaDFunction to encapsulate parametric deterministic functions. The parameters are those of the corresponding stochastic volatility model.

The bridge implementation of the numerical schemes is given by the following code:

- Gauss Legendre Quadrature:

```
class GaussLegendreRule: public IntegratorImp
{
// Simple Gauss Legendre Rule
private:
    // No private data or functions
public:
    virtual double value(const NumIntegrator& f) const;
};.
```

- Gauss Lobatto Quadrature:

```
class GaussLobattoRule: public IntegratorImp
{
// Simple Gauss Lobatto integration rule
private:
    // No private data or functions
public:
    virtual double value(const NumIntegrator& f) const;
};
```

- Adaptive Gauss Lobatto Quadrature; see Gander and Gautschi (2000):

```
class GaussLobAdaptRule: public IntegratorImp
{
// Adaptive Gauss Lobatto integration Rule
```

```
private:
    double adapt(double a, double b, double fa, double fb,
    double is, const NumIntegrator& f) const;
public:
    virtual double value(const NumIntegrator& f) const;
};
```

Using the adaptive version it is possible to include the start and endpoints of the integration domain.

Finally, the C++ implementation using the adapted scheme produces very accurate results.

23.6 SUMMARY AND CONCLUSIONS

We identified transformations that we applied to matrices and we described classes for encapsulating this functionality. We explained our implementation of the following matrix decompositions:

- Cholesky decomposition;
- spectral decomposition;
- singular value decomposition.

The techniques are used to generate correlated random variates, to solve linear equations and to solve linear least squares regression problems. This is due to the fact that such decomposition techniques can be applied to compute the inverse of a given matrix.

We also reviewed basic concepts from functional analysis that we applied to evaluate American options. One of the key tools in quantitative finance is the Fourier transform. It enables us to compute prices for European options in a variety of models. The technique can be used to benchmark the simulation results as well as a basis to derive calibration routines. To this end we have shown how to set up an object-oriented implementation of numerical integration and we have given three implementation methods, namely:

- Gauss Legendre;
- Gauss Lobatto;
- Adaptive Gauss Lobatto.

23.7 EXERCISES AND PROJECTS

1. (***) Decomposition
   The LU-decomposition decomposes a given matrix into the product of two simpler matrices. LU-decomposition can be applied to general full matrices. Duffy (2004a) discusses LU-decomposition for tri-diagonal matrices. Take the algorithm for LU-decomposition and add the code to our framework.
2. (*) Numerical Integration
   The *Tanh-rule* approximates an integral $\int_a^b f(x)dx$ by

$$\int_a^b f(x)dx \approx 2 \tanh\left(\frac{b-a}{2} f\left(\frac{a+b}{2}\right)\right)$$

Use this method to implement another integration scheme using the framework given on the CD.

3. (***) American Options

The pricing of American and Bermudan options relies on the implementation of basis functions. Polynomials constituting an orthogonal basis for the function space L_2 are known as *orthogonal polynomials*. Well-known orthogonal polynomials are the *Legendre* and *Laguerre* ones. The functions are given by the following recurrence relations:

– (Legendre)

$$(j + 1)P_{j+1}(x) = (2j + 1)xP_j(x) - jP_j(x), -1 < x < 1$$
$$P_0(x) = 1$$

– (Laguerre)

$$(j + 1)L_{j+1}(x) = (2j + 1 - x)L_j(x) - jL_{j-1}(x), 0 < x < \infty$$
$$L_0(x) = 1$$

Use the recurrence relation to show

$$P_0(x) = 1; P_1(x) = x; P_2(x) = \frac{1}{2}\left(3x^2 - 1\right); P_3(x) = \frac{1}{2}\left(5x^3 - 3x\right)$$

and

$$L_0(x) = 1; L_1(x) = 1 - x; L_2(x) = \frac{1}{2}\left(x^2 - 4x + 2\right);$$

$$L_3(x) = \frac{1}{6}\left(-x^3 + 9x^2 - 18x + 6\right)$$

Implement the algorithm for computing Legendre and Laguerre polynomials. See also Chapter 19. Replace the basis functions used in Chapter 19 with the orthogonal polynomials from above.

4. (**) FFT

There are a number of other techniques for computing the semi-analytical price of European options for stochastic volatility models. In particular methods using the Fast Fourier Transform (FFT) have been proposed. Use a standard FFT method to compute the integral and check the results using the algorithms on the CD.

5. (***) Exception Handling

We have provided a framework for handling exceptions on the CD. There are several cases and occasions where the code cannot be executed in this case. For example, what happens if the correlation matrix is not positive definite? Try to find out other incidents and use the exception handling framework to catch the exceptions you identified.

6. (***) Loop Optimisation for Cholesky

Optimise the code for the Cholesky decomposition given in section 23.3.1 by the loop optimisation techniques covered in detail in Chapter 24.

24

An Introduction to Multi-threaded and Parallel Programming

24.1 INTRODUCTION AND OBJECTIVES

We introduce a new programming model in this chapter. This is called the *multi-threading* model and it allows us to write software systems whose tasks can be carried out in parallel rather than in a sequential manner as discussed in the earlier chapters of this book. The main reason for writing multi-threaded applications is improved performance and responsiveness. And for applications such as the Monte Carlo method any speed improvement is welcome.

This chapter is an introduction to multi-threaded programming techniques. We introduce the most important concepts that we need to understand in order to write multi-threaded applications in C++. We do not pretend that this is an exhaustive account but it is our hope that the reader will get a feeling for the subject and at some stage should be able to write simple applications using his or her favourite multi-threading library.

The most important thing to learn is the *thread* concept. A thread is a single sequential flow of control within a program. However, a thread is not a program. A thread also has (private) data but it may be able to access other shared data of which it is not necessarily the owner.

The challenge for the software developer is to design a system consisting of several interacting threads in such a way that performance is improved when compared with the corresponding sequential version of the program. We discuss how to achieve this goal and to this end we introduce the important issues of data management, work-sharing models and synchronisation among threads.

Summarising, the goals in this chapter are two-fold; first, to introduce the main ideas and techniques that are needed in order to write multi-threaded applications in C++ and second to motivate how to analyse and design Monte Carlo applications that will subsequently be implemented in C++ in combination with OpenMP.

24.2 SHARED MEMORY MODELS

In this book we are interested in the application of the OpenMP application programming interface (API) to Monte Carlo applications. This library uses a *shared memory model* and it is for this reason that we define what shared memory is.

We are considering the case of a multi-processor system in which each processor has access to all the memory in the system. How this *logical connection* between processors and memory is realized is hardware-dependent. For a detailed discussion of this subject, including applications to numerical analysis and Monte Carlo simulation, see Petersen and Arbenz (2004). We describe the connection in Figure 24.1; each processor has access to any part of the memory. This is in contrast to *distributed memory models* in which each processor has its own private memory. This is shown in Figure 24.2. In this case the processors communicate using message passing. The de-facto standard for this memory model is the Message Passing

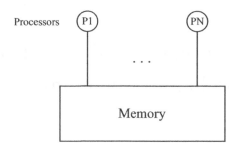

Figure 24.1   Canonical shared memory architecture

Interface (MPI) library (see Gropp, Lusk and Skjellum, 1997). A discussion of this topic is outside the scope of the current book.

It is important to know that memory is hierarchically organised in many shared memory systems. In particular, each processor has a private memory area called the *cache*. We say that a cache is a safe place to hide things. Cache memory is fast, small and expensive (it uses high-speed CMOS (Complementary Metal-Oxide Semiconductor) technology with SRAM (static random access memory) which is faster than DRAM (dynamic random access memory)). It allows the processor to access data and instructions at a high rate. We distinguish between different kinds of cache memory based on their 'distance' from main memory. We speak of *locality of data* and this refers to the assumption that the next data in some computation is close to that last used. There can be many cache levels; in lower levels the cache is smaller and has higher cache access bandwidth.

Closely related to cache memory is the *Translation-Lookaside Buffer* (TLB). Before we discuss it, we note that memory addresses in virtual memory systems are logical addresses and these are mapped to physical addresses; this information is stored in a *page table* which is situated in main memory, the latter being slower than cache memory. In order to improve the performance of applications the TLB cache is used to store the most recently used entries in the page table. A block diagram of a generic duo-core processor with two cache levels is shown in Figure 24.3. An important issue now is to realise that there can be a mismatch between the data stored in the cache and the data stored in main memory. Old data may be in processors and can be used elsewhere; this undesirable state of affairs is called the *memory consistency*

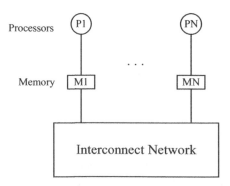

Figure 24.2   Distributed memory model

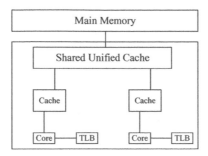

Figure 24.3   Generic duo-core processor

problem. We need a mechanism whereby updates to data in one processor are made known to other processors. Systems that provide this functionality in a transparent way are said to be *cache coherent*.

It is useful to know what cache memory is and how it relates to main memory, especially when we wish to achieve cache coherence in applications using OpenMP. In particular, cache coherence in OpenMP applications is either automatically ensured or is realised by the explicit use of the *flush* construct. In this case this operation makes a thread's temporary view of memory consistent with main memory.

24.3   SEQUENTIAL, CONCURRENT AND PARALLEL PROGRAMMING 101

In general, only one function in a C++ application is active at any given time. In this case we speak of a *serial* or *sequential* program that has a *single thread of control*. Let us take a simple program to show what we mean. The program in question is responsible for getting some data from the console, then creating two vectors of a given size, subsequently calculating the inner product of the vectors and then finally printing the vectors. Since there is one thread of control only one task is active at a given time and furthermore the tasks are executed sequentially. In other words, there is one entry point and one exit point in the program and all tasks are executed in sequential order. The code is almost trivial but it shows the performance bottlenecks associated with sequential programming methods:

```
double InnerProduct(const vector<double>& v1, cons vector<double>&
                                                                v2)
{

    double result = v1[0] * v2[0];

    // Assume sizes of v1 and v2 are equal

    for (int j = 1; j < (int)v1.size(); ++j)
    {
        result += v1[j]*v2[j];
    }

    return result;
```

```
}

void print(const vector<double>& vec)
{

    cout << endl;

    for(int j=0; j < (int)vec.size(); ++j)
    {
        cout << "vec[" << j << "] = " << vec[j] << endl;
    }

    cout << endl;

}

int main()
{

    // Preprocessing: Input
    cout << "Give size of the arrays: ";
    int N; cin >> N;
    cout << "Give value in the first array: ";
    double val1; cin >> val1;
    cout << "Give value in the second array: ";
    double val2; cin >> val2;

    // Step A1: Processing; Data and algorithms
    vector<double> v1(N, val1);
    vector<double> v2(N, val2);

    // Step A2: Calculate the inner product
    double result = InnerProduct(v1, v2); // Sum of products

    // Step A3: Postprocessing: Output
    print(v1);
    print(v2);

    cout << endl << "Inner product is: " << result << endl;

    return 0;

}
```

We can run this program for various values of the vector size; we did some experiments on a PC and achieved a response time of 0.21 seconds for vectors with 10 000 elements and a response time of 2 seconds for vectors with 1 000 000 elements. While a given task is executing the other tasks must wait even though they could be executed independently of the active task. For example, it is possible to find places in the code where it can be run in parallel (that is, by several independent threads):

- Step A1: The creation of vectors v1 and v2 could take place independently of each other.
- Step A2: We would like to partition the loop for the calculation of inner products into independent chunks for processing by separate threads.
- Step A3: We may wish to print the vectors v1 and v2 independently of each other, in which case we could employ two threads.

Based on the above remarks we produce an equivalent multi-threaded program using the OpenMP API. We now discuss how to parallelise each of the above steps using the pragmas (inline commands) in OpenMP. The objective is to motivate its use in C++ code while deferring detailed discussions of the syntax to Chapter 25. For step A1, we use a noniterative work-sharing construct to create the vectors v1 and v2:

```
// Declare vectors
vector<double> v1;
vector<double> v2;

// Processing; Data and algorithms
#pragma omp parallel
{
        #pragma omp sections
        { // Perform the following sequence of tasks in parallel

                #pragma omp section
                {
                    v1 = vector<double>(N, val1);
                }

                #pragma omp section
                {
                    v2 = vector<double>(N, val2);
                }
        }
}

// Implicit barrier: wait until both vectors have been created
```

Having created the vectors we then need to calculate their inner product; the function InnerProduct() has been modified to accommodate *loop-level optimisation*, in other words each thread is allocated a 'chunk' or block of indices:

```
double InnerProduct(const vector<double>& v1, const vector<double>&
                                                                  v2)
{
        double result = v1[0] * v2[0];

        // Assume sizes of v1 and v2 are equal

        // Perform a reduction
        #pragma omp parallel for reduction (+: result)
        for (int j = 1; j < (int)v1.size(); ++j)
        {
            result += v1[j]*v2[j];
```

```
    }

    // implicit barrier here

    return result;
}
```

Notice the presence of the variable `result` which holds the final value of the inner product. Each thread gets a copy of `result` and all thread contributions are added up when the loop completes.

Finally, printing the vectors can be problematic because (i) the order of printing the elements of an individual vector is not guaranteed (threads print their results based on a schedule from the operating system) and (ii) we must ensure that the contents of `ostream` do not get mangled by the different threads. In order to realise these requirements we use the following OpenMP code:

```
void print(const vector<double>& vec)
{

    cout << endl;

    // Define four active threads
    omp_set_num_threads(4);

    // Since we only read the values of vec, the default shared
    // variable access is OK
    #pragma omp parallel for ordered
    for(int j=0; j < (int)vec.size(); ++j)
    {
            #pragma omp ordered
            cout << "vec[" << j << "] = " << vec[j] << endl;
    }

    // implicit barrier here

    cout << endl;
}
```

We have now implemented our original serial code as a simple *multi-threaded program.*

We now discuss the concepts of *concurrent* and *parallel programming.* The former refers to environments in which the tasks in a program can occur in any order. One task can occur before another one whereas other tasks can execute at the same time. Parallel processing, on the other hand, refers to concurrent tasks on different processors. Many libraries – such as Pthreads and OpenMP – specify concurrency. In this book we concentrate on OpenMP and it is possible to write applications for both one-core and multi-processor CPUs. In the former case there is no performance improvement in creating a multi-threaded application (MTA) on a CPU; the performance improvements will be visible when the MTA runs on a CPU with multiple processors. In particular, we shall see that we can include OpenMP *pragmas* (a pragma is similar to a compiler directive) and library function calls in code.

24.4 HOW FAST IS FAST? PERFORMANCE ANALYSIS OF PARALLEL PROGRAMS

In this section we address a number of practical issues when designing and implementing parallel algorithms. Can we make our serial programs run faster (in some sense) by employing multi-core machines and converting and upgrading serial code to multi-threaded and parallel code? Some of the issues that we address and quantify in this section are

- Does a program merit parallelisation? (*Amdahl's law*).
- Evaluate the performance of a parallel program (*Gustafson-Barsis law*).
- What is the principal barrier to improved speedup? (*Karp-Flatt metric*).
- Evaluate the scalability of a parallel program (*Isoefficiency metric*).

The first important measure is the *speedup factor* $\psi(p)$, where p is the number of processors. This indicates how many times faster a parallel program is when compared with its sequential counterpart. The formula is

$$\psi(p) = T(1)/T(p)$$

where $T(p)$ is the total execution time on a system with p hardware or processing elements. We say that the speedup is *perfectly linear* when it is equal to the number of processing elements in the CPU. In general, the operations in a parallel program can be attributed to three sources:

- Computations that must be performed sequentially (the so-called *serial fraction* of the total computation time).
- Computations that can be performed in parallel.
- Parallel overhead (communication operations and redundant computations).

We need some way of estimating these quantities (even approximately).

Amdahl's law calculates the theoretical maximum speedup of an algorithm in a multi-processor CPU. Let f be the fraction of operations in a computation that must be sequentially performed (f has values in the closed interval $[0,1]$). Then the maximum speedup ψ in a multi-processor CPU with p processors is given by

$$\psi \leq \frac{1}{f + (1-f)/p}$$

For example, for an algorithm in which 90% of the computation can be executed in parallel ($f = 0.1$) the speedup with 4 processors is given by

$$\psi \leq \frac{1}{0.1 + (1-0.1)/4} = 3.077$$

On a machine with 8 processors the speedup is 4.7 and on a machine with 16 processors the speedup is 6.67. Finally, on a machine with 100 processors the speedup is 9.17. These are depressing numbers because the speedup is certainly not a linear function of the number of processors. For example, the reader can verify that in the case of an algorithm 95% of which can be parallelised the theoretical maximum speedup is 20, irrespective of the number of processors used.

The *Gustafson-Barsis* law answers the question of how to apply parallelism to increase the performance of an algorithm in a fixed amount of time. For example, we may need to price an option using the Monte Carlo method in a given interval of time and of course adding more processors will hopefully help in this endeavour. Thus, in contrast to Amdahl's law (where time is the output) in this case time is treated as a constant. In particular, let the constant s denote the fraction of the total execution time spent executing serial code in a machine with p processors (this is usually found by *profiling* the algorithm). Then the speedup is given by the formula

$$\psi \leq p + (1 - p)s$$

For example, on a 4-core machine ($p = 4$), if $s = 0.1$ (10% of the time spent executing serial code), then the speedup is given by

$$\psi \leq 4 + (1 - 4) * 0.1 = 4 - 3 * 0.1 = 4 - 0.3 = 3.7$$

The *Karp-Flatt* metric takes the parallel overhead in an application into account when computing speedup. The two previous rules ignore it, thus giving an over-optimistic estimate of speedup. In particular, the Karp-Flatt metric gives an estimate of the *experimentally determined serial fraction e* of the parallel computation:

$$e = \frac{\frac{1}{\psi} - \frac{1}{p}}{1 - \frac{1}{p}}$$

where

$$\psi = \text{speedup}$$
$$p = \text{number of processors}$$

For example, with $p = 4$, $\psi = 3.08$, then

$$e = \frac{4}{3}(0.3246 - 0.25) = 0.10$$

Finally, the *Isoefficiency* metric is related to the *scalability* of a parallel system; it is a measure of its ability to increase the performance as the number of processors increases. To this end, we define the *efficiency $\varepsilon(n, p)$* of a parallel computation of size n on p processors as

$$\varepsilon(n, p) \leq \frac{\sigma(n) + \varphi(n)}{p\sigma(n) + \varphi(n) + p\kappa(n, p)}$$

where

$\sigma(n) = $ serial portion of the computation
$\varphi(n) = $ parallel portion of the computation
$\kappa(n, p) = $ time required for parallel overhead (synchronisation, processor communication and redundant computations)

Define

$$C = \varepsilon(n, p)/(1 - \varepsilon(n, p))$$

and $T_0(n, p)$ to be the total amount of time spent by all processes doing work not done by the sequential algorithm, that is $T_0(n, p) = (p - 1)\sigma(n) + p\kappa(n, p)$.

In order to maintain the same level of efficiency as the number of processors increases, n must be increased so that it satisfies

$$T(n, 1) \geq CT_0(n, p)$$

(see Quinn, 2004).

24.5 AN INTRODUCTION TO PROCESSES AND THREADS

A *process* is a collection of resources that enables the execution of program instructions. Examples of resources are virtual memory, I/O descriptors, run-time stack and signal handlers. It is possible to create a program that consists of a collection of cooperating processes. What is the structure of a process?

- A read-only area for program instructions.
- A read-write area for global data.
- A heap area for memory that we allocate dynamically using the *new* operator or the *malloc* system call.
- A stack where we store the automatic variables of the current procedure.

There are some other resources that define a process but we do not discuss them here. What is important to know is that processes have control over their resources. Processes communicate via IPC (*Inter Process Communication*) mechanisms and they can be seen as *heavyweight* units of execution. Context-switching between processes is expensive. Resource sharing is kept to a minimum.

A *thread*, on the other hand, is a lightweight unit of execution that shares an address space with other threads. In UNIX, a thread is associated with a process and in this case it shares the process' environment. The execution context for a thread is the data address space that contains all variables in a program. This includes both global variables and automatic variables in routines as well as dynamically allocated variables (that is, on the heap). Furthermore, each thread has its own stack within the execution context. Multiple threads invoke their own routines without interfering with the stack frames of other threads. We shall see in Chapter 25 that threads can receive private copies of variables from other threads as well as sharing data with other threads.

24.5.1 The life of a thread

Before a thread can be used, it must be created, for example by using a UNIX *fork* call. The master thread can have one or more child threads. Each thread executes independently of the other threads. With OpenMP we have a similar *fork* mechanism while threads wait on each other using a *join* mechanism. In OpenMP all thread creation and deallocation is taken care of automatically, that is, these activities are not under the control of the programmer.

What is happening in a thread after it has been created and before it no longer exists? A general answer is that it is actually executing or not executing. The latter state may have several causes:

- It is sleeping.
- It is waiting on some other thread.
- It is *blocked*, that is it is waiting on system resources to perform an input or output operation.

An application should make the best possible use of its threads because each thread runs on its own processor and the presence of idle threads is synonymous with resource waste. We shall discuss this issue in greater detail later in this chapter as well as in Chapter 25.

24.5.2   How threads communicate

A multi-threaded application consists of a collection of threads (also known as *units of execution*). Each thread is responsible for some particular task in the application. In order to avoid anarchy we need to address a number of important issues:

- *Synchronisation*: Ensuring that an event in one thread is made known to another thread. This is called *event synchronisation*. This signals the occurrence of an event among multiple threads. Another type of synchronisation is *mutual exclusion* that gives a thread exclusive access to a shared variable or to some other resource for a certain amount of time. This ensures the integrity of the shared variable when multiple threads access and modify it. We place a *lock* on the resource and failure to do this may result in a *race condition*. This unhappy state of affairs occurs when multiple threads share data and at least one of the threads accesses this data without using a defined synchronisation mechanism.
- *Scheduling*: We order the events in a program by imposing some kind of scheduling *policy* on them. In general, there are more concurrent tasks to be executed than there are processors to run them. Then the operating system uses its scheduler to select from its pool of threads. In short, the scheduler synchronises access to the different processors on a CPU.

24.6   WHAT KINDS OF APPLICATIONS ARE SUITABLE FOR MULTI-THREADING?

The main reason for creating a multi-threaded application is performance. Threaded code does not add new functionality to a serial application. Thus, there should be compelling reasons for using parallel programming techniques.

In this section we give an overview of a number of issues that we need to address when developing parallel applications (see Mattson, Sanders and Massingill, 2005 for a more detailed analysis). First, we give a list of criteria that helps us, determine the categories of applications that could benefit from parallel processing. Second, having determined that a given application should be parallelised we discuss how to analyse and design the application with *parallelism in mind*.

24.6.1   Suitable tasks for multi-threading

The ideal situation is when we can design an application that consists of a number of independent tasks in which each task is responsible for its own input, processing and output. In practice, however, tasks are inter-dependent and we must take this into account. We maximise concurrency while we minimise the need for synchronisation. We identify a task that will be a candidate for threading based on the following criteria:

- Its degree of independence from other tasks. Does the task need results or data from other tasks and do other tasks depend on its results? These questions determine the *provide/require* constraints between tasks. An analysis of these questions will lead us to questions (and eventually, answers) concerning task dependencies and resource sharing.
- Does a task spend a long time in a suspended state and is it blocked in potentially long waits? Tasks that consume resources are candidates for threads, for example a typical I/O operation is as expensive as a million integer operations. Thus, if we dedicate a thread for I/O operations then our program will run faster instead of having to wait for I/O operations to complete.
- Calculation-intensive routines. In many applications we may be able to dedicate threads to tasks with time-consuming calculations that are independent of other tasks. Examples of such calculations are array processing, matrix manipulation and random number generation.

24.7 THE MULTI-THREADED APPLICATION LIFECYCLE

Developing multi-threading applications is difficult and a number of techniques have been developed to simplify the process. One approach is described in Mattson, Sanders and Massingill (2005) and we give an overview of the main steps.

24.7.1 Finding concurrency and decomposition patterns

The main goal in this phase is to decompose a problem into components and tasks that execute concurrently. In this case the design elements directly relate to the problem being studied. The two most important decomposition techniques are *task decomposition* and *data decomposition*. The first technique considers the problem to be a stream of instructions that are broken down into tasks that execute concurrently. The second technique concentrates on the data in the problem. The data is broken into independent chunks.

Having found the tasks we then need to group the tasks and analyse the dependencies between them. Finally, after having performed a task or data decomposition we describe how data is shared among the tasks.

24.7.2 Algorithm structure

In this phase we refine the design. To this end, we view this phase as consisting of using well-known *patterns* or *models* that best fit the problem at hand, in much the same way that the GOF and POSA patterns are used for serial programs (see GOF, 1995; POSA, 1996). The most appropriate pattern depends on whether we used *task decomposition* or *data decomposition*.

- *Task parallelism*: Determining how to exploit concurrency in a problem that has been decomposed into a collection of tasks.
- *Divide and conquer*: Applying sequential divide-and-conquer techniques in a parallel environment. We split a program into smaller subprograms.
- *Geometric decomposition*: In this case we organise an algorithm around a data structure that we decompose into concurrently updatable 'chunks'.
- *Recursive data*: How to define concurrent operations on recursive data structures such as trees and graphs.

- *Pipeline*: This is a well-known model that involves performing a calculation based on data flowing through a sequence of stages. This pattern is also known as *Pipes and Filters*.
- *Event-based coordination*: This pattern is useful for applications that have been decomposed into groups of semi-independent tasks that interact in an irregular fashion. All communication is realised using *message-passing*; there are no shared resources. This pattern is suitable for process-control and real-time applications in a distributed memory environment.

24.7.3   Supporting structures, models and patterns

In this phase we translate algorithms and patterns into programs. An important step in this phase is to decide how to represent shared data structures. Some of the low-level patterns are supported in multi-threaded languages and libraries. We shall see some examples in the next chapter when we introduce OpenMP. The most important program structuring patterns are

- *SPMD (Single Program, Multiple Data)*: In this case each unit of execution executes the same (single) program in parallel, but each one gets its own set of data. This will be an important pattern for Monte Carlo applications.
- *Master/Worker*: In this case we have a master thread and one or more child threads. The master is responsible for the initiation of computation and the creation of child threads. It waits until the calculations from individual threads have completed and then shuts down the computation.
- *Loop parallelism*: This pattern translates a serial program that is dominated by a set of computationally intensive loops into a parallel program. This pattern is supported in OpenMP and we discuss it in detail in Chapter 25.
- *Fork/Join*: This pattern is useful in dynamic environments when a given thread *spawns* or *forks* other threads that are terminated or joined at some later stage.
- *Shared data*: This pattern deals with the problem of explicitly managing shared data that is being accessed by a set of concurrent tasks.

24.7.4   Implementation mechanisms

This is the phase in which we address low-level operations and code generation. The major issues are thread lifecycle, thread synchronisation, event ordering and thread communication.

- *Managing units of execution*: An execution unit is a generic term referring to a collection of concurrently executing entities, such as a *process* or a *thread*. Creating, destructing and managing threads (and processes) in a parallel environment are the main issues here. In this book we are mainly interested in OpenMP. It creates and destructs threads on behalf of the developer. This is in contrast to the *Pthreads* library, for example, where the programmer must explicitly use library functions to manage threads. In OpenMP, the number of threads can be controlled by the programmer or left to the operating system to take care of.
- *Synchronisation*: This is to ensure that constraints are enforced on the order of events in a parallel program. In particular, we wish to ensure that the program is correct when shared data is modified by threads, irrespective of the scheduling. An important consideration when using threads is that the threads in a parallel program should have a *consistent* view of memory. There are a number of things that can go wrong. For example, a thread may get a stale value of a variable that was written by another thread, the compiler may optimise the

code, thus leading to subtle errors; furthermore the properties of the memory system may lead to undefined values. In order to resolve this problem we define a *memory fence*; this is a synchronisation event that guarantees that all units of execution get a consistent view of memory. In this way we are assured that writes performed before the fence is reached will be visible as well as reads performed after the fence. In OpenMP, memory fences are implemented using the *flush* statement. In this case cache lines, system buffers and registers are written to memory.

Another synchronisation point is the *barrier*; this is a point in the code that every member of a collection of execution units must reach before any thread can proceed. Finally, a potential problem in parallel programs is that multiple threads may simultaneously attempt to access shared resources, thus leading to a *race condition*. The end-result is that the program will be left in an inconsistent state. One way to resolve this problem is to use a mechanism that ensures that only one thread at a time can access the shared resource. This is called *mutual exclusion*. We shall discuss some specific implementation details on how to avoid race condition in Chapter 25.

- *Communication*: Execution units in a parallel program exchange information. The two extremes are
  - Shared memory environments (all data is shared).
  - Distributed memory environments (few, if any shared resources).

  OpenMP is suitable for shared memory environments while *Message Passing Interface* (MPI) is used in distributed memory environments. MPI uses *message passing* to support data transfer between execution units.

We conclude this chapter by discussing one particular case of *collective communication*. This refers to the case when multiple execution units participate in a single communication event. A special case is the *reduction* and this operation reduces a collection of data items to a single data item by repeatedly combining the data items pairwise with a binary operator. Examples of reductions are

- Sum the elements of a vector.
- Calculate the inner product of two vectors (see the code example in section 24.3).

We have now completed the overview of the analysis and design of parallel programs.

24.8   SOME MODEL ARCHITECTURES

In chapters 0, 8 and 9 we introduced a number of software architectures and patterns for Monte Carlo applications. These applications used the design patterns as described in GOF (1995). In this section we apply the high-level patterns (domain architectures) from Duffy (2004b) to help us in the process of finding suitable decomposition patterns as described in section 24.7.1. As in Chapter 8, we identify three basic models:

- S1: Manufacturing (for example, creating SDE input data), Task 1.
- S2: Resource Allocation (for example, assigning an SDE to a finite difference method), Task 2.
- S3: Management MIS (for example, the Monte Carlo engine), Task 3.

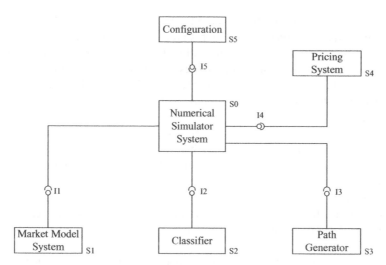

Figure 24.4   Context diagram for path generation

Each of these systems will be a task in the parallel application. Task 2 is a client of Task 1 and Task 3 is a client of Task 2 because in the first case the finite difference schemes use the services of a stochastic differential equation while in the second case the Monte Carlo engine needs path information from the finite difference scheme at each discrete time level.

For each system we have created a context diagram that shows the relationship between the system under discussion (SUD) and each of its external systems. In general, we model each system as a concurrent task that exchanges data with other tasks. To take an example, we examine system S1 above. Its main responsibility is to calculate one path (corresponding to one draw) in a Monte Carlo simulation. It returns a vector to the Monte Carlo engine for further processing. System S1 uses the services of the system that creates the SDE object and it also needs to communicate with a system that produces random numbers. The context diagram is shown in Figure 24.4. This is a generalisation of the models in chapter 0 on the one hand and an elaboration of the general discussion on the software architecture as discussed in section 8.4 on the other hand. We discuss the responsibilities of each system in Figure 24.4 as well as the services it provides and requires (we document these relationships using ball-and-socket notation in the UML language). We use shorthand notation for the names of the systems for convenience:

- S0: Creates a single path in the interval $[0, T]$. It returns a vector of data of the underlying(s) at discrete mesh points (interface I4).
- S4: The client systems (typically a Monte Carlo engine) that use the vector data from system S0. We shall discuss S4 in more detail in section 24.8.1.
- S1: The system that provides an interface I1 (typically for drift and diffusion terms) to S0 so that S0 can calculate these terms at the discrete mesh points. We shall discuss S1 in more detail in section 24.8.2.
- S2: A (small) system that knows which kinds of path generation algorithms should be employed for a given market model. For example, we may wish to find the value at certain

discrete monitoring points in the interval $[0, T]$ or we may need to select an acceptable finite difference solver depending on the type of SDE produced from system S1.

- S3: This is the system where most of the computation in the system takes place, for example mesh generation, random number generation and execution of the discrete algorithms (for example, FDM or Karhunen-Loeve method). It produces the unprocessed vector data that will be eventually used by the Monte Carlo engine S4. It needs to be decomposed into subsystems during detailed design.
- S5: This is a (small) management system for configuring the parameters in system S0. It could be factory or builder system.

We have now described the main tasks in the system. In order to design the system we execute the steps as described in sections 24.7.2 (algorithms) and 24.7.3 (supporting structures). Having done that we then implement the system using C++ and OpenMP. The actual process is a generalisation of the UML models and code that we have discussed in previous chapters. For completeness, we now discuss systems S4 (Pricing System) and S1 (Market Model) and their corresponding context diagrams.

24.8.1   The Monte Carlo engine

The Monte Carlo engine is an MIS system (as discussed in Chapter 8) because it produces high-level decision-support information; it computes us the price of an option or of a portfolio. It may also calculate sensitivities and produce statistical information. The context diagram is shown in Figure 24.5.

- S0: The current system. It coordinates the other systems and delivers decision-support information to client (decision) systems, for example Risk Analysis Systems.
- S1: The system that delivers discrete data pertaining to the underlying assets. We have already discussed this system (see Figure 24.4).

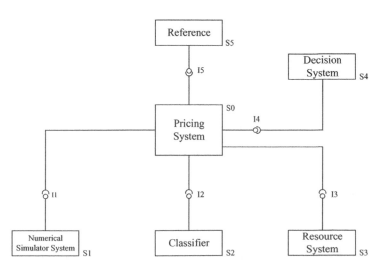

Figure 24.5   Monte Carlo engine

- S2: This system filters the data entering via system S1. We may not need all the incoming data.
- S3: This is the system that aggregates, merges and consolidates data from S1. The result is high-level data that can be reported on. It may use a historical database system.
- S4: The decision-support systems that are recipients of management data from S0. One particular case of S1 is the Excel spreadsheet program.
- S5: A system that contains scheduling or reference information. We are thinking particularly of systems that define option payoffs and contracts.

24.8.2   The market model system

This is essentially a factory or builder system in the sense that it creates a model for the behaviour of the underlying asset. We are in fact constructing the C++ class for the SDE that describes the asset. To this end, the main systems in Figure 24.6 are

- S0: The system under consideration. Its responsibility is to create an SDE instance that is used by system S4 (Numerical Simulator).
- S1: This defines the structure and properties of an asset, a portfolio or some other underlying product. It can be defined in ASCII (for example, using XML syntax) or binary format, for example.
- S2: This system validates and checks the data from system S1 for integrity and syntax. It may contain a library of prototypical SDE instances.
- S3: This system builds the SDE object (which may be quite complex). System S3 may also use the services of a calibration engine that computes the values of the SDE parameters based on market data.
- S4: The system that is described in section 24.8.
- S5: Client management systems.

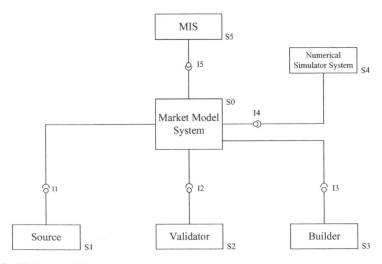

Figure 24.6   Market models

24.8.3   What's next?

Now that we have decomposed the systems into concurrent subsystems as shown in Figures 24.4, 24.5 and 24.6 we then carry out a number of activities before we can use OpenMP:

1. Determine the data exchange/shared data between the different subsystems. For example, in Figure 24.4, the interface I4 contains vector data representing the path for a single simulation while interface I3 in Figure 24.6 returns a reference to a newly-created SDE instance.
2. Determine the algorithms and algorithm structure you will use in each system, as discussed in section 24.7.2. For example, we could employ divide-and-conquer techniques and this approach would bring us close to the system patterns of Chapter 9.
3. Decide on which models and patterns to use to design the systems; we discussed this topic in section 24.7.3.
4. Implementation in C++; this is the subject of Chapter 25.

A discussion of parallel design patterns is given in Mattson, Sanders and Massingill (2005).

24.9   ANALYSING AND DESIGNING LARGE SOFTWARE SYSTEMS: A SUMMARY OF THE STEPS

In this section we give a summary of the steps that we use when analysing and designing large software systems. A full treatment is beyond the scope of this book and the authors will discuss the steps in forthcoming work. Furthermore, the current topics are closely related to software design and software engineering. In general, the analysis steps describe the design at a high level while the design steps describe low-level details that will be implemented in C++.

The analysis steps are

1. System Goal and Core Processing: You should understand what you are trying to solve. In other words, what is the goal/objective of the software system (SUD) and how is this goal realised by a core process? A core process is a series of steps that produces the output of the system based on the system input.
2. Create a context diagram (Figures 24.4 to 24.6 are examples) that shows the SUD and its relationships with systems that it receives services from and the systems that it delivers services to. Determine the inter-system services and interfaces as soon as possible. This will promote *black-box reusability*, by which we mean that we specify the input/output parameters and functions of the SUD.
3. System decomposition of SUD: Since SUD is a large system it is important to decompose it into more specific and dedicated subsystems. To this end, one can use the domain architectures as described in Duffy (2004b). Alternatively, we can use the Whole-Part pattern (as described in POSA (1996) and Chapter 9 of the current book). We determine the responsibilities of each subsystem and its *requires-provides* interfaces with the master SUD and its own 'satellite' systems).
4. What are the viewpoints and requirements of the SUD and its subsystems? In particular, we are interested in the functional and nonfunctional requirements, for example Accuracy,

Efficiency/Performance, Usability, Maintainability and other ISO 9126 product quality characteristics.

5. Document the initial design using UML class and component diagrams. If necessary, create a C++ prototype to determine whether we have found all needed functionality (we call this the *get-it-working* model).

The Design steps are

6. Design each subsystem using POSA and GOF patterns as discussed in Chapters 9 to 12 of the current book.
7. Decide on using object-oriented or generic programming (C++ templates).
8. Program the designs using the authors' codes, STL and Boost (for an overview of Boost, see Chapter 13 and the corresponding code on the CD).

24.10   CONCLUSIONS AND SUMMARY

We have given an introduction to multi-threading programming concepts in this chapter. In particular, we developed enough theory in order to understand how to design and implement multi-threaded applications using C++ and OpenMP, which we discuss in Chapter 25.

24.11   EXERCISES AND PROJECTS

1. (***) Special Cases of Domain Architectures
   We examine Figure 24.4. Answer the following questions:
   (a) Describe how Figure 24.4 is a generalisation of the UML diagram in Figure 0.1 of Chapter 0?
   (b) Determine the interfaces in Figure 24.4 and the data transfer taking place between the components.
   (c) (Project) copy the code from Chapter 0 and adapt it to produce a new serial application in C++ based on the components and interfaces in Figure 24.4.
   (d) After having read Chapter 25 and studied the examples on the CD port the serial code that you created in step (c) above to a parallel program using OpenMP.
2. (*) Speedup
   Find the maximum achievable speedup in a parallel program in which 25% of the operations must be performed sequentially (hint: use Amdahl's law and let the number of processors go to infinity).
3. (**) Data Dependency Graph
   Consider the following computations (or tasks) on the generic components t1 to t8 (that is, they could be numbers, matrices or other computational entities):

```
t1 = DoSomeThing();
t2 = t1 + 4;
t3 = t1 * 8;
t4 = t1 - t3;
t5 = t1 / 2.0;
t6 = t2 * t3;
t7 = t4 - t5;
t8 = t6 * t7;
print(t8);
```

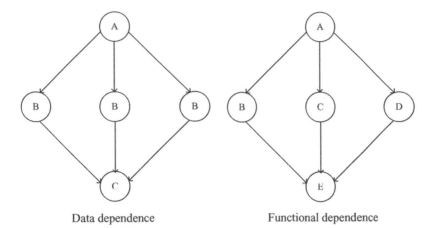

Data dependence   Functional dependence

Figure 24.7   Dependency graph

Create a data or functional dependency graph for this problem by representing tasks of the graph as vertices and edges as dependencies between tasks. It should be possible to visualise the parallel and sequential tasks in this problem. An example of a dependency graph is in Figure 24.7. In the first case we have three tasks concurrently applying task B with different operands while in the second case the different tasks B, C and D are performed concurrently.

4. (***) Data Dependency Graph
   Create a data dependency graph for garden maintenance of a very large garden by a crew of eight gardeners (Quinn, 2004). The tasks are
   − Turn off security system.
   − Mow the lawn.
   − Edge and trim the lawn.
   − Check the sprinkler.
   − Turn on security system.
      In particular, answer the following questions:
   (a) Determine which tasks can be done concurrently and which tasks must be done sequentially.
   (b) Divide the task into subtasks by allocating gardeners to different sections of the garden.
   (c) Think about the scheduling and synchronisation issues; for example, what to do if a gardener has finished work and has nothing to do?

5. (***) Data Dependency Graph for MC
   Apply the techniques of the previous two exercises to create a data dependency graph for the simple Monte Carlo engine in Chapter 0, as depicted in the UML diagram in Figure 0.1.
      Answer the following questions:
   (a) Determine the data flow in this system, from initial input to final product.
   (b) Which tasks can be executed concurrently and which tasks must be executed sequentially?
   (c) Is this problem 'embarrassingly parallel', by which we mean that certain tasks can be executed without any need for synchronisation with other tasks?

An Introduction to OpenMP and its Applications to the Monte Carlo Method

25.1 INTRODUCTION AND OBJECTIVES

In Chapter 24 we gave an introduction to threads and multi-threading programming concepts. This chapter continues the discussion by introducing the OpenMP parallel programming model for shared and distributed shared memory multiprocessors. OpenMP is a collection of compiler directives, library functions and environment variables to specify shared-memory parallelism in C, Fortran and C++.

The main reason for designing and implementing applications using OpenMP is *performance*. How can we employ OpenMP in our applications? The answer is that there are a number of scenarios, the first of which is to use OpenMP's compiler directives, library functions and environment variables to improve the performance of legacy code. In this way we can reduce the response-time of a C++ application in an incremental fashion by adding new performance-enhancing code to the existing sequential code. The second scenario is of relevance when we design an application with parallelism in mind. In other words, we partition a system into a set of loosely-coupled components using process decomposition or data decomposition techniques as introduced in Chapter 24.

In this chapter we discuss OpenMP by giving an overview of its main features, how these features can improve performance and we give some examples of use. Having covered these features we then conclude this chapter by adding OpenMP code to a Monte Carlo framework. We also discuss how we applied OpenMP.

To benefit from this chapter we recommend that you experiment with the code on the CD. We also recommend that you concentrate on the loop-level optimisation techniques in the short term.

25.2 LOOP OPTIMISATION

This section deals with a number of techniques to improve the performance of serial C++ code. In particular, we examine ways to optimise loops:

- Loops in Monte Carlo simulations.
- Loops when working with vectors and matrices.
- Mathematical operations, for example Cholesky decomposition.

Even though we can optimise our code by using multi-core CPUs it is advisable to examine our serial code to see if that can also be optimised. To this end, we focus on loop optimisation. In Chapter 21 we discussed C++ code optimisation in some detail but this section is complementary since we are now interested in loop performance. Having done that we can introduce OpenMP directives into our code. It may even be possible to meet our performance requirements without having to use OpenMP. We now discuss some of the most important loop optimisation techniques.

25.2.1   Loop interchange

This is a technique to improve cache performance when accessing array elements in nested loops. We experience a drop in performance if the contiguously accessed array elements in the loop are from different cache lines. The effectiveness is determined by the cache model used by the underlying hardware and the array layout model used by the compiler. In the case of C++, the elements in a two-dimensional array A are stored consecutively, that is in *row-major order* (that is A[0,0], A[0,1], A[0,3],). Some other languages, for example Fortran, store elements from the same column; we call this *column-major order* (that is A[1,1], A[2,1], A[3,1],). Thus, when we use row-major order indexing in C++, an element and its neighbours are transferred as part of the same cache line.

We take an example of creating a two-dimensional array of complex numbers using heap memory and raw pointers:

```
// A. Run-time matrix
const int NR = 5000;
const int NC = 5000;
// B. Complete HEAP solution (dynamic)
Complex** mat2;
mat2 = new Complex*[NR];
// Define the pointers to the rows
for (int i = 0; i < NR; ++i)
{
        mat2[i] = new Complex[NC];
}
```

The following code is an example of good memory access because the elements of the matrix are accessed row by row:

```
void setValueRowOrder(Complex** cmat, int NRows, int NColumns)
{ // Set all values in matrix to some value

    Complex c(1,1);
    for (int i = 0; i < NRows; ++i)
    {
            for (int j = 0; j < NColumns; ++j)
            {
                    cmat[i][j] = c;
            }
    }
}
```

The following code is an example of bad memory access because elements are accessed column by column and this approach results in poor utilisation of the memory system. We see

performance degradation as the size of the array increases. In other words, the following loop
is not *cache friendly*:

```
void setValueColumnOrder(Complex** cmat, int NRows, int NColumns)
{ // Set all values in matrix to some value

    Complex c(1,1);

    for (int j = 0; j < NColumns; ++j)
    {
        for (int i = 0; i < NRows; ++i)
        {
            cmat[i][j] = c;
        }
    }
}
```

For this particular example, the code based on row-major order performed 15% better than the
code using column-major order. This difference becomes even more pronounced as the size
of the matrix increases. A final remark: it may not be possible to perform loop interchange
without destroying the legality of the code. In this case, the code can produce unexpected and
incorrect output.

We need to make sure that the execution time in a loop is not dominated by the time that is
needed to repeatedly copy data into cache. Loop interchange alleviates these problems. These
conclusions are also valid when using OpenMP.

25.2.2   Loop fission and fusion

Loop fission (or *loop distribution*) breaks a loop into multiple loops where all loops have the
same index range but each loop executes only one part of the original block of code in the
loop. The advantage of this approach is that it can improve the use of cache by isolating a part
of the loop that inhibits full optimisation. We could use fission when the data in a loop does
not fit into cache. An example of use follows:

```
void NonFissioned(vector<Complex>& myComplexArray,
                  vector<Complex>& myComplexArray2)
{
    Complex c(1.0, 1.0);
    for (int j = 0; j < myComplexArray.size(); ++j)
    {
        myComplexArray[j] = c;
        myComplexArray2[j] = myComplexArray[j] + 1.0;
        c = Complex (exp(1.0), exp(1.0));
    }
}
```

The fissioned variant is now given by

```
void Fissioned(vector<Complex>& myComplexArray,
               vector<Complex>& myComplexArray2)
{
    Complex c(1.0, 1.0);
```

```
for (int j = 0; j <  myComplexArray.size(); ++j)
{
       myComplexArray[j] = c;
}
for (int j = 0; j <  myComplexArray.size(); ++j)
{
       myComplexArray2[j] = myComplexArray[j];
}

for (int j = 0; j <  myComplexArray.size(); ++j)
{
       c = Complex (exp(1.0), exp(1.0));
}
}
```

Based on tests, we achieved a 20% performance improvement in some cases by using fission.

Loop fusion (or loop combining) is the opposite of loop fission. In this case we combine two loops if they have the same index range and their bodies do not reference each other's data. Again, the goal is to reduce loop overhead but loop fission may be more efficient in some cases. One reason for using fusion is that in the case of an array that has been initialised in one loop but is then needed in a second loop, it may not be in cache when it is needed. In this case loop fusion may provide some performance improvement.

Here is an example. In this case the array a's cache line may not be in cache when we execute the second loop:

```
for (int j = 0; j < a.size(); ++j)
{
       a[j] = b[j] * 2.0;
}

for (int j = 0; j < a.size(); ++j)
{
       c[j] = a[j] + 2.0;
       x[j] = 2.0 * x[j];
}
```

The fused version of the loop allows the values of a to be reused immediately:

```
for (int j = 0; j < a.size(); ++j)
{
       a[j] = b[j] * 2.0;
       c[j] = a[j] + 2.0;
       x[j] = 2.0 * x[j];
}
```

25.2.3 Loop unrolling

In this case (it is also known as *loop unwinding*) we execute the body of a loop multiple times. This is a technique to reduce the overhead of loop execution. It can help promote cache line utilisation by improving data reuse. In general, loop overhead is high when each iteration has a small number of operations. We take the example of cleaning up memory in a matrix of complex numbers that we discussed in section 25.2.1. The original loop is

```
for (int i = 0; i < NR; ++i)
{
        delete [] mat2[i];
}


delete [] mat2;
```

We now add extra delete statements in the loop and we adjust the increment of the loop index accordingly:

```
for (int i = 0; i < NR; i+= 5)// NR multiple of 10, convenience
{
        delete [] mat2[i];
        delete [] mat2[i+1];
        delete [] mat2[i+2];
        delete [] mat2[i+3];
        delete [] mat2[i+4];
}
delete [] mat2;
```

In general, we can achieve 20% performance improvement using this technique. The optimal offset value (in this case 5) was found by experimentation.

25.2.4   Loop tiling

Loop tiling (also known as *loop blocking*) is a special kind of optimisation technique. It partitions a loop's iteration space into smaller chunks or blocks. This ensures that data in the loop remains in the cache until it is reused. If memory access is bad and if data sizes are large then partitioning a loop into *tiles* may be a useful option. We take the example of transposing a matrix. The non-tiled version is

```
void TransposeNoTiling(Complex** cmat, Complex** ctrans, int N)
{ // Matrix transpose

    for (int i = 0; i < N; ++i)
    {
        for (int j = 0; j < N; ++j)
        {
            ctrans[j][i] = cmat[i][j];
        }
    }
}
```

The tiled version is

```
void TransposeTiling(Complex** cmat, Complex** ctrans, int N)
{ // Matrix transpose, using tiles

    int BLOCK_SIZE = 10; // Experiment with different sizes
    for (int j1 = 0; j1 < N; j1 += BLOCK_SIZE)
```

```
    {
        for (int i = 0; i < N; i++)
        {
            for (int j2 = 0;j2 < std::min(N-j1,BLOCK_SIZE); j2++)
            {
                ctrans[i][j1+j2] = cmat[j1+j2][i];
            }
        }
    }
}
```

In general, loop tiling replaces the original loop by a pair of loops. It may be necessary to experiment to discover the optimal block size (this is the variable BLOCK_SIZE in the above code).

We have now completed our discussion of loop optimisation techniques in serial C++ programs. Optimising compilers may do some of this optimisation, but in general it is important to know how to optimise loops. This hands-on knowledge will be invaluable when we discuss multi-threaded programming in C++.

25.2.5   Serial loop optimisation in Monte Carlo applications

Loop optimisation technques will be needed when we develop applications for the Monte Carlo method. In particular, we are interested in optimsing code that consists of single, double and triple loops:

- Calculating SDE paths using the finite difference method.
- Monte Carlo simulation and averaging of the option price.
- General optimisation related to matrix algebra, for example Cholesky decomposition, Saxpy and Gaxpy operations.
- Optimisation of special functions, for example the exponential function and the gamma function.

Seeing that loops are used in many applications it is important to examine the methods for improving the performance of serial C++ code. We now take some examples related to Monte Carlo applications. The first example is the code for exact path simulation for a one-factor SDE; the essential code (full source code on the CD) entails creating a mesh on the interval, $[0,T]$, generating standard normal variates using the classes that we introduced in Part II of this book and then calculating the exact solution (as in Kloeden, Platen and Schurz, 1997, pages 70, 112):

```
// Exact solution of linear SDE dX = aXdt + bXdw d(a, b are constant)
Vector<double, long> GBMRandomWalk(double X0, double a, double b,
                                                double T, int N)
{ // Kloeden (1997) et al page 112

    // Define a mesh
    Mesher mesh(0.0, T);
    Vector<double, long> x = mesh.xarr(N);// For the Wiener values

    double k = (T - 0.0)/double(N); // Assume interval is [0,T]
```

```
      double sk = sqrt(k);

      double dW; // N(0,1) number

      double c = a - (0.5 * b * b);

      // This will be the vector of random numbers
      Vector<double, long> result(N+1, 1);
      result[result.MinIndex()] = X0;

      // Choose uniform and normal numbers
      Ran0 myRan0;
      myRan0.init(234);
      NormalGenerator* myNormal = new BoxMuller(myRan0);

      double wT = 0.0;
      // Main loop to be optimised
      for (int n = result.MinIndex()+1; n <= result.MaxIndex(); ++n)
      {
          dW = myNormal->getNormal(); // N(0,1) number from generator
          wT += dW * sk;
          result[n] = X0 * ::exp(c*x[n] + b*wT);
      }
      delete myNormal;
      return result;
}
```

If we examine the main loop in this code we see that the body of the loop calculates a normal random number and one value in the resulting path using the exponential function. We have carried out a number of experiments using loop unrolling (slight performance improvement) and loop fission, in which case we generated an array of normal random numbers prior to calculating the exact paths. However, we have seen a degradation in performance when compared with the above code. The conclusion is that further attempts to optimise serial code may end in stalemate.

The second example calculates paths using the finite difference method. The core process is again a loop. An example is the code for path simulation using the explicit Euler method (for example):

```
// VOld is value at level n, VNew is value at level n+1
VOld = initVal;
res[x.MinIndex()] = VOld;
for (long index = x.MinIndex()+1; index <= x.MaxIndex(); ++index)
{
      VNew = VOld  + k * sde.calculateDrift(x[index-1], VOld)
      + sqrk * sde.calculateDiffusion(x[index-1], VOld) * dW[index-1];

      res[index] = VNew;
      VOld = VNew;
}
```

The previous conclusions regarding performance improvement carry over to the current case. We have completed our discussion of optimising serial code. We now introduce multi-threaded code in OpenMP.

25.3   AN OVERVIEW OF OpenMP

OpenMP is a software library consisting of compiler directives (called *pragmas*), library functions and environment variables that developers can use to specify shared-memory parallelism in C. By *shared memory* we mean that all threads share a single address space and they communicate with each other by writing and reading shared variables. The OpenMP Application Programming Interface (API) is portable between various shared memory models. It has been tailored to support programs than run in both parallel and sequential modes. It is especially useful for large array-based applications. The main features are

- Support for parallelisation of loops.
- Work-sharing constructs and the creation of *parallel regions*.
- Synchronisation constructs.
- Sharing and privatisation of data.

We must ask ourselves whether it is always worth trying to parallelise a serial program. To answer this question we first determine the fraction of a program's execution time that is devoted to tasks that must be serially executed (the so-called *serial fraction*). In general, we measure setup, compute and finalisation times; the total time on one processor is given by (see Mattson, Sanders and Messingill, 2005)

$$T_{total}(1) = T_{setup} + T_{compute} + T_{finalisation} \tag{25.1}$$

Given that setup and finalisation phases must execute serially, we can write the formula for the serial fraction as

$$\gamma = \frac{T_{setup} + T_{finalisation}}{T_{total}(1)} \tag{25.2}$$

We now wish to determine what the *speedup* will be when we run an algorithm with P processors. The formula is given by *Amdahl's* law:

$$S(P) = \frac{T_{total}(1)}{(\gamma + \frac{1-\gamma}{P})T_{total}(1)} = \frac{1}{\gamma + \frac{1-\gamma}{P}} \tag{25.3}$$

Thus, this formula gives an upper bound on the attainable speedup whose serial part is a given fraction of the total computing time.

25.4   THREADS IN OpenMP

We introduced threads in Chapter 24. OpenMP supports the functionality of thread libraries (such as *Pthreads*) but in the case of OpenMP the developer does not have to explicitly create and manage threads. Instead, we insert directives or *pragmas* in serial code to signal that the code following the pragma should be multi-threaded. The code reverts to single-threaded mode when it reaches a so-called *barrier*. Figure 25.1 is a visual representation of what we mean; just before point A the code is running in single-threaded mode and at point A we have introduced an OpenMP pragma, at which stage a number of threads will be created, each of

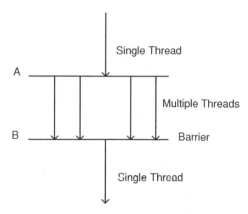

Figure 25.1 Creating multiple threads

which will execute part of the code. This is a *fork-and-join* model. When threads have finished at point B (this is called a *barrier*) we revert to single-threaded mode. The developer does not have to worry about thread lifecycle nor about how the scheduling of tasks is allocated to threads.

Let us take an initial example of how OpenMP manages threads. In this case we calculate the inner products of two STL vectors. The code is as follows:

```
double InnerProduct(const vector<double>& v1, const vector<double>&
                                                                v2)
{
    double result = v1[0] * v2[0];
    // Assume sizes of v1 and v2 are equal
    // Perform a reduction
    #pragma omp parallel for reduction (+: result)     // Point A

    for (int j = 1; j < (int)v1.size(); ++j)
    {
        result += v1[j]*v2[j];
    }
    // implicit barrier here                            // Point B

    return result;
}
```

A barrier directive in OpenMP is a mechanism for synchronising a group of threads within a parallel region. A barrier may be *implicit* (as in the above example), in which case each thread waits for all other threads to arrive at the barrier. Execution continues only when all threads have reached the barrier. We can define an *explicit barrier* as follows: `#pragma omp barrier`.

Returning to the above example, the presence of an OpenMP directive ensures that the master thread forks a number of child threads. Each thread is allocated part of the work to calculate the inner product. Each thread's contribution is added to a global variable `result`. We use a special keyword `reduction` in order to add the individual thread contributions and to avoid race conditions.

The above is a typical example of how to use OpenMP pragmas in serial code. In this way we incrementally improve the performance of an application. In this case, we experience linear speedup (in other words, the code runs roughly twice as fast on a duo-core machine as on a single-core machine) because the individual threads execute on independent pieces of data. Each thread operates on its own block of data. We can define how many threads to use in an application using environment variables and library functions. In the former case we can define the number of threads before compiling the program while in the latter case we can change the number of threads used at run-time.

25.5   LOOP-LEVEL PARALLELISM

Many engineering, scientific and computational finance applications are expressed in the form of loop constructs. In general, loops are needed when we navigate in (hierarchical) data structures such as vectors, matrices, trees and graphs. Improving the performance of applications that rely heavily on loop constructs is a high priority. Given that developers may choose to port their serial programs to OpenMP we now discuss the forces to be reckoned with when we examine the correctness and efficiency of the parallel code:

- *Sequential equivalence*: A given program should produce the same results when executed with one thread or with more than one thread. We apply a series of transformations on the loops to achieve this end. These are called *semantically neutral transformations* if they leave the semantics of the program unchanged. A point to note is that due to round-off errors the results from a serial loop may be different from those in the equivalent parallel loop. For example, adding numbers in a loop will give different answers depending on the order in which they are added, for example if we add the numbers serially or in ascending order. This may be unacceptable and we should then decide not to parallelise the loop.
- *Incremental parallelism*: We parallelise a program by examining one loop at a time, for example. We apply a sequence of incremental transformations and we test sequential equivalence after each increment. In this way we can be assured of correctness and we can measure the performance improvement.
- *Memory utilisation*: In order to achieve good performance it is important to note that the way data is accessed (for example, using indexing operators or by dereferencing) is consistent with the memory model being used.

25.6   DATA SHARING

OpenMP uses a shared memory model in which memory can be accessed by all threads. It is also possible to define memory that is private to a thread. We describe how shared and private data are organised in OpenMP. We concentrate on the lifetime of these forms of data, how they relate to each other, and we describe some of the programming errors that can occur when using them.

Since there are a number of concepts to introduce we have decided to explain them using Figure 25.2 as a visual aid. In this case we have represented memory (consisting of disjoint shared and private parts) as a rectangle. We also have defined two threads t1 and t2 that access this memory. In general, each thread can access shared memory as well as its own private memory but it cannot access the private memory of other threads. The main goal of a multi-threaded program is to improve speedup while at the same time ensuring that it produces

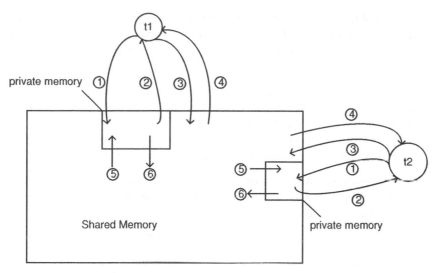

Figure 25.2   Threads and memory access

the same results as the corresponding serial program. We achieve this goal through a number of techniques, one of which is the correct design of data. Returning to Figure 25.2 we see a number of arcs between threads and memory as well as between shared and private memory. The corresponding scenarios are given numbers and we discuss them in general terms:

- 1, 2: Data that is private to a single thread, including its definition and usage.
- 3, 4: Shared data that can be accessed by any thread.
- 5, 6: Copying shared data to private data and vice versa.

We model shared and private memory using variables. In general, it is advisable to explicitly specify whether a variable is shared or private. This promotes the reliability of your code and ensures that the compiler does not assume that a variable is shared when the developer thinks it is a private variable, for example. In the following code, we explicitly define shared variables a and N as well as a private variable b:

```
int N = 1000;
vector<double> a(N);
double b = 0.0;

#pragma omp parallel for shared(a, N), private(b)
for (int j = 0; j < N; ++j)
{
        a[j] = j;
        b = j+1;
}

// Implicit barrier; only 1 master thread at this stage
```

In this case each thread is allocated a block of indices (the index variable j is private by default) and each thread writes elements of the vector a. After the parallel loop has finished, all the new values for a will be in main memory, in which case the master thread can access it. Concerning the variable b, we see that each thread gets a copy of it. Since each thread has its own copy there is no interference between the threads. In general, the values of private variables are undefined on entry to, and on exit from, the above loop. Some remarks concerning the code are

- There is no danger of race conditions in the loop because first, the variable b is private to each thread and it receives a local copy of it and second, each thread updates only a part of the vector a based in its own set of private indices j.
- The value of each thread's copy of the private variable b is uninitialised on entry to the parallel region and the value of b is undefined on exit from the parallel region.

We remain with the above code. We would like to know what actually takes place within the loop. To show what is going on, let us define four threads using an OpenMP library routine to set or modify the number of threads used in execution:

```
omp_set_num_threads(4);        // Number of threads = 4
```

Furthermore, we wish to print some information on the system console and this will be done in the body of the loop. If we do not restrict access to this print statement the threads will mangle the output. We avoid this by defining a so-called *critical section* that ensures that the threads do not attempt to simultaneously update the shared resource (in this case, the console). When a thread encounters a critical construct, it waits until no other thread is executing a critical region with the same name. This tactic avoids the possibility of a race condition:

```
#pragma omp critical(myCS) // This is a named critical section
{ // Ensure multiple threads do not attempt to update the ostream
    cout << "Index: " << j << ", Thread: " << omp_get_thread_num()
        << ", Value: " << b << ", Array value: " << a[j] << endl;
}
```

If the print function had been executed without using the critical construct we would get garbage as output. The disadvantage of a critical section is that it is expensive on system resources and we should provide other constructs.

25.6.1 Ensuring private variable initialisation and finalisation

A possible problem with thread-private variables is that they have undefined initial and terminal values and after the execution of a *parallel for* loop construct the corresponding master thread variable also has an undefined value. This corresponds to scenarios 1 and 2 in Figure 25.2; each thread has its own private memory but it has no influence on shared memory. To resolve this problem, we now discuss scenarios 5 and 6 in which we initialise the private variables and then write them back to the main thread, respectively. First, the *firstprivate* clause is subject to the private clause semantics and it provides a superset of its functionality. However, it ensures that each thread's copy of the variable is initialised. Second, the *lastprivate* clause is used to declare one or more list items to be private in a parallel region and causes the original list to be updated after the end of region.

In short, these two clauses realise scenarios 5 and 6. The form and usage of the two clauses is the same as with the *private* clause. We take a simple example to show how the clauses work. In this case we have a variable d1 that is copied to each thread, a variable d2 that is updated in the body of the loop and which is then copied into the master thread's memory after completion of the loop. We note the presence of the critical section that avoids a race condition:

```
// Using firstprivate and lastprivate for single objects
double d1(2.0), d2(3.0);
N = 10;
#pragma omp parallel for shared(N),
                    firstprivate(d1), lastprivate(d2)
for (int j = 0; j < N; ++j)
{
        #pragma omp critical
        d2 = d1 + j;
}

cout << "Master copy of lastprivate variable d2:" << d2 << endl;
```

Let us take another example of a vector that is initialised outside a parallel loop region and that is modified by the program's threads. Our goal is to use the master's version of the vector after completion of the parallel loop:

```
// Using firstprivate and lastprivate for a vector (N=5)
double initValue = 999.999;
vector<int> myVector(N, initValue);
print(myVector);

#pragma omp parallel for shared(N),
            firstprivate(myVector), lastprivate(myVector)
for (int j = 0; j < N; ++j)
{
        cout << "Maximum number of threads: "
            << omp_get_max_threads() << endl;
        myVector[j] = omp_get_thread_num();
}
print(myVector);
```

In this case, however, the last iteration assigns only some of the elements in the vector, thus leaving the other elements undefined. In this case the vector has the final value [999,999,999,3]. Why is this? Some guidelines and tips are

- A *firstprivate* object must have a publicly defined copy constructor and a *lastprivate* object must have a publicly defined assignment operator, otherwise an error will occur.
- For read-only variables we could choose to make them *shared* instead of *firstprivate*.

25.6.2 Reduction operations

In many applications we may wish to compute some result and store it in a variable. One way is to define a shared variable and restrict access to it by using a critical section; to take an example, we calculate sums and products of the elements of a vector:

```
// Using reduction-like variables
double sum = 0.0;
double product = 1.0;
```

```
N = 4;
vector<double> myVector2(N, 2.0); // All values == 2.0

#pragma omp parallel for shared(N, myVector2, sum, product)

for (int j = 0; j < N; ++j)
{
     #pragma omp critical
     {
       sum += myVector2[j];
       product *= myVector2[j];
     }
}
cout << "Reduction, I: " << sum << ", " << product << endl;
```

There is an easier way; we use a *reduction clause* that explicitly defines reduction variables (for example, sum and product above) and that takes care of all potential race conditions:

```
sum = 0.0;
product = 1.0;
#pragma omp parallel for reduction(+: sum), reduction(*:
                                          product)
for (int j = 0; j < N; ++j)
{
     sum += myVector2[j];
     product *= myVector2[j];
}
cout << "Reduction, II: " << sum << ", " << product << endl;
```

We see that the code is easier to understand than the code in the original version above. We also note that using reductions instead of critical sections results in a tenfold performance improvement.

25.6.3   The *copyin* clause and *threadprivate* directive

The *copyin* clause is used to initialise certain kinds of private variables (called *threadprivate* variables). A *threadprivate* variable is used to identify a global variable in C or C++. The *copyin* clause is used to initialise such variables in threads. Each thread receives its own copy of the variable and its value will be the same as the value in the master thread. An example of use is:

```
// Using copyin and threadprivate
static int Counter = 0;
#pragma omp threadprivate(Counter)
#pragma omp parallel for copyin(Counter), shared(N)
for (int j = 0; j < N; ++j)
{
     #pragma omp critical
         Counter += 1;
}

cout << "Counter: " << Counter << endl;
```

In general, we tend to avoid static objects (because of namespace pollution) but they may be needed when we use scratch space in a thread.

25.6.4   The *flush* directive

This directive is used to identify a synchronisation point in a program. In this case one or more threads need to have a *consistent view* of memory. In Chapter 24 we discussed cache memory and we saw that if a thread updates shared variables then the new values are first written to a register and then back to the local cache. These updates are not always directly visible to other threads. On cache-coherent machines the modification is broadcast to other processors but this process is platform-dependent. OpenMP specifies that all variable updates from cache to main memory occur at *synchronisation points* in the program.

We distinguish between *implicit flush operations* and *explicit flush operations* in code. For example, implicit flush operations occur at the following locations:

- At all explicit and implicit barriers, for example at the end of a parallel region or work-sharing construct. We discuss work-sharing constructs in section 25.7.
- Entry to and exit from critical regions.
- Entry to and exit from lock routines.

A discussion of using the flush operation in code is outside the scope of this book. For a more detailed discussion, see Chandra *et al.* (2001) and Chapman, Jost and van der Pas (2008).

25.7   WORK-SHARING AND PARALLEL REGIONS

We focused on loop-level optimisation in the first part of this chapter. It is relatively easy to deploy this form of parallelism. In this section we are interested in optimising noniterative constructs and this is of particular relevance when we use patterns such as *Whole-Part* and other decomposition techniques. To this end, OpenMP supports the concept of *parallel regions*. A parallel region is an arbitrary block of code that is executed concurrently by multiple threads. This is a form of replicated execution across multiple threads and it is sometimes referred to as SPMD (*Single Program Multiple Data*) style parallelism. Let us take a first example. In this case we have two threads and we print a vector in the body of a loop:

```
omp_set_num_threads(2);      // Number of threads = 2
double initValue = 2.0;
int N = 4;
vector<double> myVector(N, initValue);

// Parallel region; this is not work division across threads
#pragma omp parallel
for (int j = 0; j < N; ++j)
{
        #pragma omp critical
          print(myVector);
}
```

The vector myVector will be printed eight times; this example shows the difference between replicated execution (as seen from the parallel region construct) and the work division across threads (as we have already seen in loop optimisation code).

The use of parallel regions is important when we implement programs that execute exactly the same code segments but with different data. This is useful for the Monte Carlo method, for example where it is possible to create *embarrassingly parallel* applications.

25.7.1   Work-sharing constructs

In some applications we wish to divide work among different threads. As we saw in chapter 24 this can be realised using task decomposition or by data decomposition. In the context of OpenMP this requirement translates to different threads working on different tasks and different threads working on portions of a shared data structure, respectively. For Monte Carlo applications we realise data decomposition using loop-level parallel constructs. For task decomposition (which tend to be noniterative work-sharing constructs) we introduce parallel sections. To this end, the *sections construct* is a general mechanism to perform different tasks independently, for example when executing function calls in parallel. In this construct we define the tasks that should run in parallel, as the following example shows:

```
// Work-sharing construct
#pragma omp parallel
{
        #pragma omp sections
        {
                #pragma omp section
                {
                        funcA();     // Any function!
                }

                #pragma omp section
                {
                        funcB();     // Any function!
                }
        }
}
```

If two or more threads are available, then one thread invokes function funcA() while another thread invokes function funcB(). If only one thread is available then the complete block of code is run sequentially. If more than two threads are available then only two threads will be used and the others will remain idle. An important issue to take into account is that funcA() might be computationally more intensive than funcB(), in which case we speak of a *load imbalance* in the code; we experience performance degradation because one thread may have completed its task while the program has to wait on the other thread to finish. In the above code we cannot make any assumptions about the order in which the functions funcA() and funcB() are executed when there is more than one available thread. To force code to proceed in a certain way we deploy the *ordered* clause. We take the example of printing a vector. Without this clause, elements of the vector a are printed in random order:

```
// Printing ordered and non-ordered
N = 5;
vector<int> a(N);
for (int j = 0; j < N; ++j)
{
        a[j] = j;
```

```
}

#pragma omp parallel for
for (int j = 0; j < N; ++j)
{ // Values will be printed in random order

    cout << endl << a[j] << ",";
}
```

Using the ordered clause we can now print the elements in sequential order:

```
cout << "End of chaos, begin of order\n";
#pragma omp parallel for ordered
for (int j = 0; j < N; ++j)
{ // Values will be printed in random order

    #pragma omp ordered
    cout << endl << a[j] << endl;
}
```

25.7.2   The *nowait* clause

A workshare construct in OpenMP has an implicit barrier at its end. The presence of the barrier may affect performance because processing cannot continue until all threads have reached the barrier. We take an example of initialising two vectors in independent loops; the implicit barriers have been removed and only at the end of the outer workshare construct do we have an implicit barrier. In this case the vectors a and b are computed independently:

```
#pragma omp parallel
{
    #pragma omp for nowait
    for (int j = 0; j < N; ++j)
    {
        a[j] = double(j) * exp(double(j));
    }
    // No implicit barrier here, idle threads can proceed to
       next loop

    #pragma omp for nowait
    for (int j = 0; j < M; ++j)
    {
        b[j] = double(j) * exp(double(j));
    }
    // No implicit barrier here
}
// Implicit barrier here
```

This clause is useful in many technical applications; we wish to independently compute several pieces of data and we wait until they have all been computed, at which stage we can carry out postprocessing activities on them. See exercise 6 in this chapter. One caveat: we should be careful when using *nowait* because barriers are used for a reason, namely avoiding race conditions.

25.8   NESTED LOOP OPTIMISATION

We discuss how OpenMP optimises nested loops. We focus on two-dimensional loops that we use when working with matrices and simulating Monte Carlo paths, for example. We adhere to the coding conventions in section 25.2.1, in particular that the elements of any two-dimensional array are in *row-major order*. So, we now need to answer the important question: how do we optimise a two-dimensional loop with OpenMP? The goal – as always – is to improve performance and avoid data races. Another important issue is *formal equivalence checking*; this process is a part of electronic design automation (EDA), commonly used during the development of digital integrated circuits, to prove formally that two representations of a circuit design exhibit exactly the same behaviour. In our case we wish to ensure that a multi-threaded program produces the same results as its sequential counterpart. This goal may be compromised by the presence of round-off errors.

We take the parallel version of the code in section 25.2.1 that creates the transposed matrix of a complex-valued matrix. We must be careful to determine which part of the code is being parallelised:

```
void TransposeNoTilingOpenMP(Complex** cmat, Complex** ctrans, int N)
{ // Matrix transpose, OpenMP of code in section 25.2.1

    int j;
    #pragma omp parallel private(j)
    for (int i = 0; i < N; ++i)
    {
        for (j = 0; j < N; ++j)
        {
            ctrans[j][i] = cmat[i][j];
        }
    }
}
```

Here we note that the parallel directive is only applicable to the outer loop. This is why we declared the index j of the inner loop to be private.

We conclude this section with the solution of an example that uses matrices and double loops. It is part of a C++ application that approximates a partial differential equation (PDE) using the finite difference method (FDM) (see Duffy, 2006a); in this case we employ the ADE method whereby we sweep in two consecutive directions and compute a matrix of values at each time step (Sauly'ev, 1964; Tannehill, Anderson and Pletcher, 1997):

```
// Set threads to available no of threads/cores
omp_set_num_threads(2);

// start a parallel region
// The important shared variables are (all others are read only)
// current (only written in single section)
// VOld (read-only during calculations; written in single section)
// VNew (each elements written only once, so no conflicts)
// repository (written in single section)
// All other variables are specific for each thread/iteration,
// so marked private.
```

```
#pragma omp parallel \
    default(none) \
    private(xtmp, ytmp, difftmp1, difftmp2, contmp1, contmp2, aW,
          aE, aS, aN, aNE, aNW, aSW, aSE, aC) \
    shared(current, MNew, MOld, repository, \
          index, k, MinC, MaxC, NT, xMesh, yMesh, opt, MinR, MaxR, \
          lambda1, lambda2, beta, gamma, alpha, storeData)

    for (int l=index; l < NT ; l++){ // Each time level is
                                        sequential

    #pragma omp single // single = > only 1 thread at once
    {
          current += k;
          // Discrete BC for level n+1; We use the points of the
          // Compass so that we have 9 points
          DiscreteBC(xMesh, yMesh, current, opt, MNew);
    }
#pragma omp for
for (long j = MinC; j <= MaxC; j++)
    {
          for (long i = MinR; i <= MaxR; i++)
          {
                xtmp = xMesh[i];
                ytmp = yMesh[j];
                difftmp1 = opt.diffusion1(xtmp, ytmp, current);
                difftmp2 = opt.diffusion2(xtmp, ytmp, current);
                contmp1 = opt.convection1(xtmp, ytmp, current);
                contmp2 = opt.convection2(xtmp, ytmp, current);

                // Initialise the coefficients
                aW = lambda1* difftmp1 - beta * contmp1;
                aE = lambda1* difftmp1 + beta * contmp1;
                aS = lambda2* difftmp2 - gamma * contmp2;
                aN = lambda2* difftmp2 + gamma * contmp2;

                aSW = alpha * opt.crossTerm(xtmp, ytmp, current);
                aSE = - aSW;
                aNE = aSW;
                aNW = -aSW;

                aC = 1.0 - 2.0*(lambda1*difftmp1 + lambda2* difftmp2)
                      + k * opt.zeroTerm(xtmp, ytmp, current);

                MNew(i, j) = aW * MOld(i-1,j) + aS * MOld(i,j-1)
                      + aE * MOld(i+1, j) + aN * MOld(i,j+1)
                      + aSW * MOld(i-1,j-1) + aSE * MOld(i+1,j-1)
                      + aNE * MOld(i+1,j+1) + aNW * MOld(i-1,j+1)
                      + aC * MOld(i,j);
          }
    } // end of parallel for
```

```
#pragma omp single
{
    // execute in single thread mode:
    // - global variable index
    // - output into repository of
    // - copy of global variable MOld

    index++;
    if (storeData == true)
    {
        repository[index] = MNew; // Add matrix to tensor
    }
    MOld = MNew;
} // end of single region

} // end of parallel section
```

The notation is the same as used on the CD in Duffy (2006a). The above code can be optimised by using Gaxpy operations instead of using the matrix assignment operators, as we discussed in Chapter 21.

25.9   SCHEDULING IN OpenMP

By definition, the way in which the iterations of a parallel loop are assigned to threads is called the loop's *schedule*. We had not introduced any explicit scheduling into code samples and in these cases we speak of a *default schedule*. This entails distributing work evenly among all threads. In general, it is probably safe to say that the default schedule is close to optimal. However, it is possible to define scheduling policies to improve load balancing. These policies fall into two categories: first, in a *static schedule*, the choice of thread used is a function of the iteration index and the number of threads. Each thread is assigned its indices at the beginning of the loop. In a *dynamic schedule*, the assignment of iterations to threads can vary at run-time, namely from one execution to another. Summarising, the full set of options are

- *Static*: Iterations are divided into chunks of a given size. The chunks are assigned to the threads in a round-robin fashion by using the thread number.
- *Dynamic*: Iterations are assigned to threads as threads request them. A thread requests a chunk of iterations until there are no more chunks to work on.
- *Guided*: This is similar to dynamic scheduling but the size of each successive chunk decreases exponentially
- *Runtime*: If this option is chosen, then the decision of which scheduling type to use is chosen at run-time.

We take an example of a static schedule with a user-defined iteration chunk (the code is a snippet from an MC application that computes a path using the finite difference method):

```
// VNew is a vector; get bounds
int fmin = fdm->VNew.MinIndex();
int fmax = fdm->VNew.MaxIndex();
```

```
// We have rewritten goto into loop to allow
// for OpenMP loop worksharing
index++;
if (fmax-fmin > 10010) exit(0);
VectorSpace<double, N2> mydW[10011];
omp_set_num_threads(2);
// Assume fmax > fmin
#pragma omp parallel for schedule (static, ((fmax-fmin)/2))
for (int loopcnt=index; loopcnt <= maxIndex; loopcnt++)
{
        // calculate all the random number needed
        mydW[loopcnt] =
            RNGMechanisms::createRandomNumbers<double, N2>();
}
for (int loopcnt=index; loopcnt <= maxIndex; loopcnt++)
{
        // Calculate solution at every time level
        fdm->result(mydW[loopcnt], loopcnt);
        for (int i = fmin; i <= fmax; i++)
        {
            res[i][loopcnt] = fdm->VNew[i];
        }
}
index=maxIndex;
```

Our advice is to use user-defined chunks only when all other options fail and you have gained enough experience of OpenMP. Finally, we note that scheduling is only applicable to loops in OpenMP.

25.10   OpenMP FOR THE MONTE CARLO METHOD

We conclude this chapter with a discussion of a Monte Carlo application using OpenMP. We restrict the scope to the application we developed in Chapter 0. The source code uses a *Whole-Part/Mediator* pattern. The whole object mediates between a number of modules for random number generation, calculation of drift and diffusion parameters and the computation of paths using the finite difference method.

We discuss some of the steps that we have taken to implement a multi-threaded MC-based option price. We keep things simple in this section by viewing the problem as consisting of a loop over all simulations or draws. The most important class is the mediator:

```
class BBMediator
{ // This is a (Blackboard mediator)
private:
    FDMTypeDBuilder* bld;    // Creates SDE and FDM object
    double r;                // Interest rate
    double T;

    double (*payoff) (double S);    // PAYOFF FUNCTION

    OneFactorSDE* sde;
    FDMVisitor* fdm;
```

```
public:
        // let the builder create and return new FDMVisitor object
        FDMVisitor* getFDM();

        // Constructor using Builder
        BBMediator(FDMTypeDBuilder& builder, double interest,
                        double expiry, double (*PayOff) (double S));

        // Execute NSIM simulation paths and return vector
        Vector<double, long> MCSim(int NSim);

        // Calculate prices based on terminal values vector
        double price(Vector<double, long>& TerminalValues, int NSim);
};
```

In each iteration of the loop we execute the following operations in sequential order:

- A1: Generate an array dW of standard normal numbers.
- A2: Use dW as the array in the object myfdm that computes the discrete path.
- A3: Calculate the path result; use the *Visitor* pattern on the SDE object sde.
- A4: Extract the last element from result (value of underlying at $t = T$) and place its value in array TerminalValue.

The serial code for these operations is

```
Vector<double, long> BBMediator::MCSim(int NSim)
{
// Loop over each iteration; test is current FDM method is suitable
   for current SDE


     // Create the random numbers
     long N = fdm->getNumberOfSteps();

     setSeed(); // Uses rand()!!

     Vector<double, long > TerminalValue(NSim, 1); // Values at t = T

     Vector<double, long> result(N+1, 1);
     Vector<double, long> dW(N+1, 1);

     // temp
     double sqrT = sqrt(T);

     // A.
     bool fdm_created = false;
     FDMVisitor* myfdm;

     #pragma omp parallel for
             firstprivate(myfdm,fdm_created) num_threads(2)
     for (long i = 1; i <= NSim; ++i)
     { // Calculate a path at each iteration
```

```
                   if (!fdm_created)
                   {
                           myfdm = getFDM();
                           fdm_created=true;
                   }

                   // Step A1
                   Normal(dW);

                   // Step A2
                   myfdm ->SetRandomArray(dW);


                   // Step A3 [Calculate the path by delegation to a visitor]
                   sde -> Accept(*myfdm);
                   result = myfdm->path();

                   // Step A4
                   TerminalValue[i] = result[result.MaxIndex()];

                   // Step A4, conclusion
                   return TerminalValue;
}
```

This phase generates `TerminalValue[NSIM]`, the array of underlying prices at $t = T$. We need this array in the following activities:

- A5: Create a discrete payoff array, still called `TerminalValue`.
- A6: Increment the variable `price`, standard deviation `SD` and standard error `SE`.
- A7: Discount (exponentially) `price`.
- A8: Calculate final values of `SD` and `SE`.

The serial code for these operations is

```
double BBMediator::price(Vector<double, long>& TerminalValue,
                                              int NSim)
{
     double SumCallValue = 0.0;
     double SumCallValueSquared = 0.0;

     // Find value at t = T
     // Return the vectors and calc. payoff vectors + average
     // Discount the value

     //  Step A5: Calculate the payoff function for each asset price
     for (long index = TerminalValue.MinIndex();
             index <= TerminalValue.MaxIndex(); ++index )
     {
             TerminalValue[index] = payoff(TerminalValue[index]);
     }
```

```
//  Step A6: Take the average
double price = TerminalValue[TerminalValue.MinIndex()];
SumCallValue += price;
SumCallValueSquared += price * price;

for (long ii = TerminalValue.MinIndex()+1;
                ii <= TerminalValue.MaxIndex(); ++ii)
{
                price += TerminalValue[ii];
                SumCallValue += price;
                SumCallValueSquared += price * price;
}


// Step A7: Finally, discounting the average price
price *= exp(-r * T);


// Step A8: Postprocessing
double SD = sqrt(SumCallValueSquared-
                SumCallValue*SumCallValue/NSim))
                * exp(-2.0 * r * T)/(NSim -1) ;
double SE = SD/sqrt(double(NSim));

return price;

}
```

The journey from a single-threaded to a multi-threaded application took place in an incremental fashion. We experimented with a number of optimisation techniques (as discussed in Chapter 21 and this chapter), starting with an initial C++ version and ending with the above parallel code. The response times (in seconds) were

- Original code: 99.5.
- Non-parallel optimisation: 17.1 (using the techniques in Chapter 21).
- Sequential loop preparation: 15.2.
- Parallelising MC loop: 8.7.
- Parallel region with ordered scheduling: 36960.
- Parallel loop preparation: 16.3.
- Explicit barriers: 540.
- Ordered sections: 12.9.
- Save redundant data: 12.6.
- Modification of the calling sequences: 4.3.

In the last step we optimise the data flow between the different modules. This improved performance at the expense of possible code understandability and maintainability.

The parallel code for this problem is on the CD.

25.11   CONCLUSIONS AND SUMMARY

We have given an introduction to the OpenMP API for shared memory. It has been accepted by a number of hardware and software vendors and it can be seen as a *de facto standard*. We introduced the main features of the API and we showed how they are used in simple cases. Finally, we have migrated and ported a serial C++ code to one containing OpenMP compiler directives and library function calls. Speedup improvements were reported.

The advent of new and affordable hardware computing environments will help promote the acceptance of parallel programming models in the coming years. In addition, customers are demanding faster application response times. For these reasons we have included two chapters on the multi-threading model and its applications to computational finance. A good way to learn OpenMP is to run the code that we have provided on the CD, namely the simple test cases and Monte Carlo simulator as presented in this chapter. We recommend that you experiment with the different OpenMP clauses and constructs and measure the performance improvements. Then you should be able to apply OpenMP to your own applications.

25.12   EXERCISES AND PROJECTS

1. (*) Amdahl's Law
   Use Amdahl's law (equation (25.3)) to compute the maximum speedup when the number of processors approaches infinity. Why does the law give a pessimistic view of the advantages of extra processors in an application?
2. (*) What Does an Empty Loop Cost?
   Create empty loops (with one, two and three indices). Experiment with different values of the upper index limit in the loops. Calculate the processing time and wall clock time needed for execution.
3. (***) Loop Optimizations
   In this exercise we optimise some of our code in the namespace *ArrayMechanisms*. We have already documented the modules in Duffy (2004a). These modules perform operations on vectors: inner products, averages, minimum and maximum values and other operations that we need in numerical calculations.

   We wish to improve the performance of these operations by first applying the loop optimisation techniques of section 25.2 and then using the library functions in OpenMP. As a first test case, you should concentrate on one function to improve its performance, for example the sum of absolute values of vector:

```
template <typename V, typename I> V sumAbsoluteValues(const
                                          Vector<V,I>& x)
{  // Sum of the absolute values of a vector

    V ans = fabs(x[x.MinIndex()]);

    for (I j = x.MinIndex()+1; j <= x.MaxIndex(); ++j)
    {
        ans += fabs(x[j])
    }

    return ans;
}
```

Answer the following questions:
- Determine whether the techniques in section 25.2 are applicable in the current situation; apply loop unrolling; do you get better performance?
- Optimise the loop using OpenMP and compare the performance improvement with the serial code.

4. (****) Matrix-Vector Multiplication

We use OpenMP to improve the performance of matrix-vector multiplication. We compare solutions based on *task decomposition* and *data decomposition* (as discussed in Chapter 24). The original code based on Duffy (2004a) is

```
template <class V, class I, class S> Vector<V, I>
     NumericMatrix<V, I, S>::operator * (const Vector<V, I>& v)
                                                       const
{
     // Result has same number of rows as m and same start index
         as v
     Vector<V, I> result(Rows(), v.MinIndex());

     V r(0.0); // sum of rows
     for (I i = MinRowIndex(); i <= MaxRowIndex(); i++)
     {
          r = 0.0;
          for (I j = MinColumnIndex(); j<= MaxColumnIndex(); j++)
          {
               r += (*this)(i,j) * v[j];
          }
          result[i] = r;
     }
     return result;
}
```

Optimise this code using OpenMP. In particular, use loop-level optimisation techniques. We can employ task decomposition of the product $V2 = A * V1$, where $V1$ and $V2$ are vectors and A is the matrix, by considering the computation of each element of the product to be a separate task. A data decomposition entails decomposing the product into a set of row blocks (set of adjacent rows).

5. (***) Numerical Integration

In this exercise we investigate developing C++ code to calculate the integrals of real-valued functions in a rectangle (in two dimensions). The function to be integrated (the integrand) may be badly behaved in certain regions of the rectangle. Furthermore, the calculation of the integral should be efficient. To this end, we employ data decomposition techniques and OpenMP to improve speedup. Answer the following questions:
- Implement the algorithm using loop-level optimisation and reduction operations.
- Decompose the rectangle into a fixed number of smaller rectangles (for example, based on the number of available threads). Compute the approximate integral on each sub-rectangle.

- This is an extension of the previous question, except that we associate a specific numerical integration scheme with each sub-rectangle. In this we can customise the integrator that is able to model the integrand in *difficult regions*.
- Compare the relative performance of the solutions to the three previous questions.

6. (***) Calculating Option Sensitivities

We wish to compute option sensitivities using the Monte Carlo method. In particular, we deploy divided differences to calculate the derivatives of the option price with respect to its parameters. In this exercise we concentrate on delta, gamma, vega and theta. We have already provided the divided difference formulae that approximate these sensitivities in Chapter 0.

The objective of this exercise is to design and implement efficient C++ code to compute option sensitivities for the simple plain option problem in Chapter 0. The focus is on getting the algorithmic structure working and optimising performance using loop-level optimisation and OpenMP. On single-processor machines the computing of sensitivities will be extremely time-consuming but since many of the calculations are independent we can assign them to distinct threads. Answer the following questions:

- The output of this program is an array of values representing the computed sensitivities based on input containing option parameters and their perturbations (see Clewlow 1998, page 105 and our Chapter 0):

$$T, \sigma, r, K, S$$
$$\Delta S, \Delta t, \Delta r, \Delta \sigma \text{ (perturbations)}$$

Model the output as a property set and the input as a data structure (call it OptionData) containing the parameters and their perturbations.
- Use the basic module that calculates option price using OptionData as input. Call this function for each sensitivity type. Create a separate function for each sensitivity.
- We now parallelise the code in the previous step. Use the *sections* construct (see section 25.7.1) and compute the sensitivities after the implicit barrier.

A Case Study of Numerical Schemes for the Heston Model

Ever tried. Ever failed. No matter. Try again. Fail again. Fail better.

Samuel Beckett, *Worstward Ho*

26.1 INTRODUCTION AND OBJECTIVES

In this chapter we test the performance and the accuracy of various numerical approximations for the Heston stochastic volatility model. The corresponding SDE can be found in Chapter 16, equation (16.2). We define test scenarios in section 26.2. The scenarios are motivated by popular market products such as *Power Reverse Duals*. In the first section, section 26.2, we describe possible failures of simple numerical schemes when applied to the Heston model. This not only leads to inaccurate results but may crash your simulation. In section 26.3 we apply the following numerical schemes that have been discussed in detail in Chapter 5, including the various formulations of the SDE and the corresponding numerical schemes, namely:

- QE = Quadratic Exponential (Chapter 16);
- SIET = Semi-Implicit Euler Transform;
- SIE = Semi-Implicit Euler;
- EET = Explicit Euler Transform;
- MIL = Milstein;
- SMIL = Semi-Implicit Milstein;
- EE = Explicit Euler;
- PC = Predictor-Corrector;
- EXT = Richardson Extrapolation.

For each scheme we illustrate the results using convergence diagrams and tables. We further emphasise that naively using a sample scheme may lead to wrong estimates of option prices. Finally in section 26.7, we give hints on how to optimise the QE scheme and we discuss extensions such as calibration to market data. Section 26.8 compares the Monte Carlo solution of pricing options within the Heston model to the finite difference method. We compare the performance and the accuracy of both methods on a given set of test problems.

A final remark concerning the finite difference schemes from Chapter 5; first, they are essentially explicit or semi-implicit and the resulting advantage is that we can solve them without having to resort to nonlinear solvers such as Newton-Raphson, for example. Second, the generated mesh is uniform because the mesh size is constant. These two factors reduce the robustness and adaptability of the schemes. As mentioned in Part I of this book, we feel that much more needs to be researched into more accurate and efficient schemes to approximate the solution for SDEs. To this end, exercise 8 in the last section of this chapter discusses the application of a number of schemes that we introduced in Chapter 6 to the Heston model.

26.2   TEST SCENARIOS

For the performance test and the application to path-dependent options we use two common scenarios for model parameters called *Test Case I* and *Test Case II* in foreign exchange and equity markets, respectively. All our results and numerical studies refer to these cases.

We denote the parameters for the Heston model as in Chapter 16. The riskless rate is r, the dividend yield d, the mean reversion κ, the correlation ρ, the long time variance V and the volatility of the variance V. We denote by $S(0)$ and $V(0)$ the spot prices of the asset and the variance respectively.

Test Case I

We consider a European option with strike $K = 123.4$ and maturity $T = 1.0$.

$$r = 0.1$$
$$d = 0.0$$
$$\kappa = 1.98937$$
$$\theta = 0.011876$$
$$\xi = 0.15$$
$$\rho = -0.9$$
$$S(0) = 123.4$$
$$V(0) = 0.02$$

For this test scenario the Feller condition is fulfilled since $\frac{2\kappa\theta}{\xi^2} \geq 1$ (actually it has the value 2.10006739).

Test Case II

We consider a European call option with strike $K = 100.0$ and maturity $T = 10.0$. The other parameters are

$$r = 0.1$$
$$d = 0.0$$
$$\kappa = 0.5$$
$$\theta = 0.04$$
$$\xi = 1.0$$
$$\rho = -0.9$$
$$S(0) = 100.0$$
$$V(0) = 0.04$$

The test case is one for which the Feller condition is not fulfilled since $\frac{2\kappa\theta}{\xi^2} < 1$. We have chosen the scenarios to back-test our results with known cases as discussed in Andersen (2006), for example. Furthermore, the test cases are motivated from current markets, for example an instrument called *Power Reverse Dual*, which is a complex swap product having a funding leg and a structured leg with exotic coupon payments c_i at time t_i with

$$c_i = \max\left(\min\left(\left[\frac{FX(t_i)}{scale}c_f - c_d\right], Caplevel_i\right), Floorlevel_i\right) \qquad (26.1)$$

In this formula, $FX(t)$ is the foreign exchange rate at the given time t and $scale$ denotes a scaling factor, typically the foreign exchange forward rate. The $Caplevel$ is typically infinity whereas the $Floorlevel$ is zero. The *Power Reverse Dual* consists of a portfolio of foreign exchange options. The maturity of such contracts is typically ten years or longer. Noting that $\theta = KTe^{-r_dT}N(d_2) \approx T$ and $v = FX(0)\sqrt{T}e^{-r_fT}n(d_1) \approx \sqrt{T}$ for a call option, we see that the stochastic nature of the interest rate should not be neglected for long dated options.

In some cases the coupon is linked to an equity, for example for Equity-CMS Chameleon structures starting at t_1 and maturity t_2 and having the following payoff:

$$\text{Payoff} = \begin{cases} 100\% + \max\left(\dfrac{S(t_2)}{S(t_1)} - 1, 4CMS_{5Y}\right) & , \quad \text{if not triggered} \\[3mm] \dfrac{S(t_2)}{S(t_1)} & , \quad \text{if triggered} \end{cases} \qquad (26.2)$$

The trigger event is linked to the performance of the equity S; for example, it could be $\frac{S(t_2)}{S(t_1)} > 70\%$.

The volatility of the equity comes in as another risk-factor with further embedded triggers, TARN (*target redemption notes*) or call features, which makes this contract even more complicated and increases the demand on methods and models. We have already shown (section 17.9) how to integrate an interest rate short-rate model and a geometric Brownian motion for the equity process. However, the Power Reverse Dual necessitates more complicated models, see for example Caps (2007).

Since banks often use the Heston model to risk manage smile positions for the individual risk factors it is reasonable to extend the analytic and the Monte Carlo machinery to this setting. Some implementations were not able to cope with such long dated options. The semi-analytic implementation is stable and could cope with long maturities. This is an essential feature when we use it in calibration procedures.

26.3   NUMERICAL APPROXIMATIONS FOR THE HESTON MODEL

We have already discussed the SDE of the Heston stochastic volatility model in Chapter 16. We considered one of the main difficulties, namely negative volatilities, arising using a naive discretisation such as the Explicit Euler scheme. Furthermore, as the volatility can exhibit varying, irregular behaviour, modelling it using a constant is not realistic and may lead to high bias for option prices. Thus, to apply a simple scheme a large number of discretisation steps become necessary resulting in high computational time to achieve accurate results:

```
// Explicit Euler method
VectorSpace<double, 2> EE(const VectorSpace<double, 2>& VOld,
  double WI1, double WI2)
{ // Calculate the solution at time level n+1 in
  // terms of solution at time level n

    result[2] = VOld[2] * (1 - kappa * deltaT)
            + kappa * theta * deltaT
            + (epsilon * sqrt(VOld[2]) * sqrk * WI2);
```

```
        result[1] = VOld[1]*(1.0 + (r - q) * deltaT
                    + sqrt(VOld[2]) * sqrk * WI1);

        return result;
}
```

One possibility in order to avoid negative variance is to adjust the Euler scheme by truncating it.

We have implemented other standard schemes such as Milstein and the QE scheme to approximate the solution of the Heston SDE. We now show how to set up the QE scheme within the general framework for modelling stochastic differential equations.

First, we define several variables in the Heston namespace which we need in the implementation of the scheme:

```
namespace HestonNamespace
{

const int dim = 2;

double r;        // riskless rate
    double q;        // dividend yield
double kappa;    // mean reversion
    double theta;   // long time variance
    double epsilon; // volatility of variance
double rho; // correlation

double IC_S;    // spot asset
double IC_V;    // spot variance

// Variables used in QE scheme - Variance
double Coeff3;

// Variables used in QE scheme - Spot
double gamma1; double gamma2;
double Const1; double Const2; double Const3;
double Const4; double Const5; double Const6;

// Redundant variables
VectorSpace<double, dim> result;
VectorSpace<double, dim> ExtrapolatedResult1, ExtrapolatedResult2;

double deltaT;
double sqrk;

// Explicit Euler method
VectorSpace<double, 2> EE(const VectorSpace<double, 2>& VOld,
                                double WI1, double WI2){..}
// Explicit Milstein method
VectorSpace<double, 2> Milstein(const VectorSpace<double, 2>& VOld,
                                double WI1, double WI2){..}
```

```
// Semi-implicit Euler method Transform
VectorSpace<double, 2> SIETransform(const VectorSpace<double,
                    2>& VOld, double WI1, double WI2){..}

// Semi-implicit Euler method
VectorSpace<double, 2> SIE(const VectorSpace<double,
                    2>& VOld, double WI1, double WI2){..}

// Richardson Extrapolation
VectorSpace<double, 2> Extrapolation(const VectorSpace<double,
                    2>& VOld, double WI1, double WI2){..}

// Implicit Milstein method
VectorSpace<double, 2> ImplicitMilstein(const VectorSpace<double,
                    2>& VOld, double WI1, double WI2){..}

// Semi-implicit Euler method
VectorSpace<double, 2> EETransform(const VectorSpace<double,
                    2>& VOld, double WI1, double WI2){..}

    // Predictor-Corrector
VectorSpace<double, 2> PredictorCorrector(const VectorSpace<double,
                    2>& VOld, double WI1, double WI2){..}

// Quadratic Exponential Scheme
VectorSpace<double, 2> QE(const VectorSpace<double, 2>& VOld,
                    double WI1, double WI2){..}
}
```

In the following we discuss the steps to implement the function:

```
VectorSpace<double, 2> QE(const VectorSpace<double, 2>\& VOld,
double WI1, double WI2)
```

We start by precalculating the variables needed for the scheme:

```
// Variables used in QE scheme - Spot
gamma1 = 0.5;
gamma2 = 1.0 - gamma1;

Const1 = (r-q-rho * kappa * theta / epsilon);
Const2 = gamma1 * (kappa * rho/epsilon - 0.5);
Const3 = gamma2 * (kappa * rho / epsilon - 0.5);
Const4 = gamma1 * (1 - rho * rho);
Const5 = gamma2 * (1 - rho * rho);
Const6 = rho / epsilon;
```

These constants are used for constructing the log spot price process. To generate one path we need two uniformly distributed random numbers WI1 and WI2. We transform these numbers into Gaussian random variates. We generate one path by the following piece of code:

```
for (long index = 1; index <= NT; ++index)
{ // Generate two uniform random numbers

    WI1 = rng.GetRandomNumber();
    WI2 = rng.GetRandomNumber();

    VNew = QE(VOld, WI1, WI2);

    VOld = VNew;
}
```

We generate two uniformly distributed random numbers, WI1 and WI2, using the random number generator rng. Here one can use a proprietary random generator or some quasi random sequence generator as long as it provides the interface GetRandom-Number(). The QE scheme involves a switching mechanism between probability distributions used to approximate the distribution of the variance. We have described the switching mechanism in detail in Chapter 16. The following source code implements the switching:

```
VectorSpace<double, 2> QE(const VectorSpace<double, 2>& VOld,
  double WI1, double WI2)
{ // Calculate the solution at time level n+1 in terms of solution
    at time level n

    // 1.Variance - see Andersen's paper
    double Psi;          // Switching parameter
    double Psi_C = 1.5; // Switching parameter

    // Parameters used in for loop
    double a, b2, p, beta, m, s2, c4;

    // This becomes a Gaussian variate in the for loop
    double GV = 0.0;
    double Coeff1 = exp(-kappa*deltaT);
    double Coeff2 = 1.0 - Coeff1;
    // E[Vt+Delta], eq. (17)
    m = theta + (VOld[2] - theta) * Coeff1;
    // Var[Vt+Delta], eq. (18)
    s2 = VOld[2] * Coeff1 * Coeff2 * Coeff3
        + 0.5 * theta * Coeff2 * Coeff2 * Coeff3;

    Psi = s2 / (m * m);

    // Switching Step
    if (Psi <= Psi_C)
    {
        // V[t+Delta] approximated as noncentral chi-square
        // with one degree of freedom
        c4 = 2.0 / Psi;
        b2 = max(c4 - 1.0 + sqrt(c4*(c4 - 1.0)),0.0);
        a = m / (1.0 + b2);
```

```
        GV = (sqrt(b2) + InverseCumulativeNormal(WI1));

        result[2] = a*(GV*GV);
    }
    else
    {
        // Approx. density with Dirac mass and exponential tail
        p = (Psi - 1.0) / (Psi + 1.0);
        beta = (1-p) / m;

        // eq. (25)
        if (WI1 <= p)
            result[2] = 0.0;
        else
            result[2] = log((1.0 - p) / (1.0 - WI1)) / beta;
    }


    // Spot see Andersen's paper

    result[1] = log(VOld[1]) + Const1 * deltaT + (Const2*deltaT
                + Const6)*VOld[2] + (Const3*deltaT + Const6)*
                                                    result[2]
                + sqrt(Const4*deltaT*VOld[2]
                + Const5*deltaT*result[2])*InverseCumulativeNormal
                                                    (WI2);
    result[1] = exp(result[1]);

    return result;
}
```

Figure 26.1 shows the application of the QE scheme using different values of the steps per year and different numbers of simulated paths. It shows that we get good results, even with

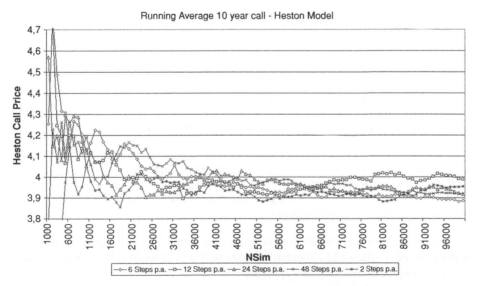

Figure 26.1 Convergence using the QE scheme for a ten year call in the Heston model

only two time steps per year. To use other random number generators such as Mersenne Twister or a congruential random number generator the method should be implemented together with a function to generate uniform random numbers. For our benchmark results we have used the Mersenne Twister and the Park-Miller random generator commonly referred to as the *Ran1*-algorithm.

We initialise the generator for the Mersenne Twister as follows:

```
MersenneTwister mt;
mt.SetSeed(seed);
```

We introduced the C++ class for the Mersenne Twister in Chapter 22.

26.4 TESTING DIFFERENT SCHEMES AND SCENARIOS

We describe the implementation for Monte Carlo evaluation for both path-dependent and path-independent options.

For path-independent options the Monte Carlo evaluation procedure is:

```
for (long i = 1; i <= NSIM; ++i)
{
    VOld[1] = IC_S;
    VOld[2] = IC_V;

    OptionValue = 0.0;
    for (long nt = 1; nt <= NT; ++nt)
    { // Generate two correlation random numbers for all schemes
      // excluding QE where uniforms are needed

        WI1 = mt.GetRandomNumber(); // generate Uniform
        WI2 = mt.GetRandomNumber(); // generate Uniform

        VNew = QE(VOld, WI1, WI2);  // generate path due to scheme

        VOld = VNew;
    }

    OptionValue = PayoffFunction(VNew[1]);
    SumOptionValue += OptionValue;
    SumOptionValueSquared += OptionValue * OptionValue;
}

SumOptionValue = exp(-r * T) * SumOptionValue / NSIM;
double SD = sqrt((SumOptionValueSquared - SumOptionValue*
                            SumOptionValue/NSIM) /NSIM);
double SE = SD/sqrt(double(NSIM));
```

Having simulated a path we evaluate a payoff function called `PayoffFunction` at the final spot price stored in `VNew[1]`. Standard options such as European calls, European puts or digitals can be implemented using this approach.

For the path-dependent options we have to account for values which have to be computed along the path, for example the running maximum $M(t) := \max\{S(u), 0 \le u = t_i \le t$ for some index $i\}$.

```
for (long i = 1; i <= NSIM; ++i)
{
    VOld[1] = IC_S;
    VOld[2] = IC_V;

    OptionValue = 0.0;
    for (long nt = 1; nt <- NT; ++nt)
    { // Generate two correlation random numbers for all schemes
      // excluding QE where uniforms are needed

        WI1 = mt.GetRandomNumber(); // generate Uniform
        WI2 - mt.GetRandomNumber(); // generate Uniform

        VNew = QE(VOld, WI1, WI2);  // generate path due to scheme

        OptionValue += PayoffFunctionLocal(VOld[1], VNew[1], NT);

        VOld = VNew;
    }

    OptionValue = PayoffFunctionGlobal(OptionValue);
    SumOptionValue += OptionValue;
    SumOptionValueSquared += OptionValue * OptionValue;
}

SumOptionValue = exp(-r * T) * SumOptionValue / NSIM;
double SD = sqrt((SumOptionValueSquared - SumOptionValue*
                              SumOptionValue/NSIM) /NSIM);
double SE = SD/sqrt(double(NSIM));
```

For the path-dependent case we have set up two kinds of payoff functions called Payoff-FunctionLocal and PayoffFunctionGlobal respectively. The first function computes the running minimum, maximum or stores the arithmetic average or the performance and the second function implements a payoff on the overall result including the local payoff. We give two examples, namely the corresponding function for valuing a call on the maximum and for an arithmetic Asian option:

```
double PayoffFunctionLocal(double S0, double S1)
{
    return max(S0,S1);
}


double PayoffFunctionLocal(double S0, long Steps)
{
    return S0 / double(Steps);
}
```

and the global payoff function as

```
double PayofFunctionGlobal(double S)
{
    double K = 100.0;
    return max(S-K,0.0);
}
```

Our final example is for a cliquet option. Here the functions are

```
double PayoffFunctionLocal(double S0, double S1, long Steps)
{
    double LocalCap = 0.05;
    double LocalFloor = 0.0;

    return min(max(S1/S0 - 1.0, LocalFloor),LocalCap)/double(Steps);
}

double PayoffFunctionGlobal(double S)
{
    double GlobalCap = 100.0; // In fact GlobalCap = infinity
    double GlobalFloor = 0.0;

    return min(max(S,GlobalFloor),GlobalCap);
}
```

We tested the implementation on two kinds of path-dependent options, namely Asian and cliquet options. First, we use the code to price arithmetic Asian options and second, we use it to price locally floored and globally capped Cliquet options. We generated 100 000 paths for a cliquet option with maturity of one year and resetting quarterly, monthly and half-monthly. Table 26.1 summarises the results for QE, Explicit Euler (EE) and Milstein (MIL) schemes. The errors

```
-1.\#IND,
```

arise due to the fact that the variance for the EE and MIL methods becomes negative if the discretisation is not fine enough. Attempting to compute the square root of this (negative) variance results in a run-time error. The standard deviation needed to compute the next step in

Table 26.1 Comparison of different schemes for 100 000 paths and 4, 12 and 24 time steps per year using the Mersenne Twister and pricing an arithmetic cliquet option

Steps p. a.	Scheme	(sec.)	Value	Standard deviation	Standard error
QE	4	0.2812	0.0241047	0.028918	0.28918
QE	12	0.8531	0.0151876	0.0173526	1.73526
QE	24	1.7032	0.00958591	0.0118796	1.18796
EE	4	0.2953	−1.#IND	−1.#IND	−1.#IND
EE	12	0.6391	−1.#IND	−1.#IND	−1.#IND
EE	24	1.1578	−1.#IND	−1.#IND	−1.#IND
MIL	4	0.2953	−1.#IND	−1.#IND	−1.#IND
MIL	12	0.6391	−1.#IND	−1.#IND	−1.#IND
MIL	24	1.9531	0.0102885	0.0115711	1.15711

Table 26.2 Comparison of different schemes for 10 000 paths and 12 and 24 time steps per year using the Mersenne Twister

	12 steps (sec.)	PV (SE)	Rel. error %	24 steps (sec.)	PV (SE)	Rel. error %
QE	0.078	13.814(0.1242)	0.00324	0.157	13.959(0.1253)	0.00724
SIET	0.062	13.073(0.1253)	0.0567	0.141	13.312(0.1245)	0.03945
SIE	0.062	13.128(0.1249)	0.05277	0.094	13.473(0.125)	0.0279
EET	0.078	12.092(0.1216)	0.12752	0.125	12.941(0.1224)	0.06625
MIL	0.063	13.748(0.1242)	0.00799	0.093	13.542(0.1244)	0.02289
SMIL	0.063	13.872(0.1277)	0.00094	0.094	13.807(0.1259)	0.00378
EE	0.062	11.781(0.1190)	0.14994	0.094	12.855(0.1220)	0.07242
PC	0.062	13.224(0.1262)	0.04584	0.125	13.377(0.1253)	0.03479
EXT	0.172	12.772(0.1210)	0.07842	0.328	13.454(0.1250)	0.02921

the discretisation of the asset can therefore not be computed since it is the square root of the variance. This phenomenon is observed for all schemes except the QE scheme.

We have taken the parameters corresponding to Test Case I as described in section 26.2. For Asian options we consider the averaging on a monthly basis and a weekly basis.

26.5   RESULTS

We state our results in this section by displaying the present values (denoted by PV) and the standard error (denoted by SE) for different values of the number of simulations, the number of steps per year and random number generators.

The key observation is that increasing the number of paths adds more accuracy, meaning that the standard error is reduced. Adding more discretisation steps gives an approvement in the overall pricing error.

Despite the fact that the standard algorithms are not applicable to discretising the Heston stochastic volatility model the results show that the QE scheme is efficient and produces good results. In practical problems the parameters retrieved from quoted option prices or derived using time series analysis often lead to parameter sets which causes problems when standard discretisation schemes are applied. We summarise our results using parameters from Test Case I in Tables 26.2 to 26.9.

Table 26.3 Comparison of different schemes for 100 000 paths and 12 and 24 time steps per year using the Mersenne Twister

	12 steps (sec.)	PV (SE)	Rel. error %	24 steps (sec.)	PV (SE)	Rel. error %
QE	0.797	13.8011(0.0394)	0.00418	1.61	13.8531(0.0395)	0.00043
SIET	0.671	13.1186(0.0398)	0.05343	1.344	13.3026(0.0395)	0.04015
SIE	0.531	13.1687(0.0397)	0.04982	1.063	13.3433(0.0395)	0.03722
EET	0.703	12.0385(0.0384)	0.13136	1.313	12.9188(0.03889)	0.06785
MIL	0.515	13.8376(0.0393)	0.00155	1.031	13.8030(0.0392)	0.00405
SMIL	0.532	13.9752(0.0406)	0.00838	1.062	13.9406(0.0400)	0.00588
EE	0.516	11.9139(0.0380)	0.14036	0.984	12.8524(0.0386)	0.07264
PC	0.625	13.3220(0.0400)	0.03875	1.203	13.3938(0.0396)	0.03357
EXT	1.672	12.9042(0.0387)	0.0689	3.266	13.3724(0.0390)	0.03512

Table 26.4 Comparison of different schemes for 500 000 paths and 12 and 24 time steps per year using the Mersenne Twister

	12 steps (sec.)	PV (SE)	Rel. error %	24 steps (sec.)	PV (SE)	Rel. error %
QE	4.015	13.8068(0.0175)	0.00377	8.016	13.8543(0.0176)	0.00035
SIET	3.406	13.1239(0.0178)	0.05305	6.719	13.3341(0.0177)	0.03788
SIE	2.672	13.1489(0.0177)	0.05124	5.266	13.3623(0.0176)	0.03585
EET	3.515	12.0061(0.0172)	0.1337	6.578	12.9054(0.0174)	0.06881
MIL	2.594	13.7819(0.0175)	0.00557	5.188	13.8357(0.0175)	0.00169
SMIL	2.64	13.9061(0.0181)	0.00339	5.281	13.8853(0.0178)	0.00189
EE	2.641	11.9435(0.0170)	0.13822	4.922	12.8747(0.0172)	0.07103
PC	3.078	13.3157(0.0178)	0.03921	6.031	13.3859(0.0176)	0.03414
EXT	8.375	12.8624(0.0172)	0.07192	16.282	13.3846(0.0174)	0.03424

Table 26.5 Comparison of different schemes for 1 000 000 paths and 12 and 24 time steps per year using the Mersenne Twister

	12 steps (sec.)	PV (SE)	Rel. error %	24 steps (sec.)	PV (SE)	Rel. error %
QE	8.015	13.8538(0.0124)	0.00038	16	13.8720(0.0124)	0.00093
SIET	6.813	13.0865(0.0125)	0.05575	13.406	13.3346(0.0125)	0.03785
SIE	5.359	13.1462(0.0125)	0.05144	10.516	13.3389(0.0124)	0.03753
EET	7.031	11.9946(0.0121)	0.13453	13.125	12.9017(0.0122)	0.06908
MIL	5.203	13.8047(0.0124)	0.00393	10.344	13.7948(0.0124)	0.00464
SMIL	5.297	13.9292(0.0128)	0.00506	10.547	13.8766(0.0126)	0.00126
EE	5.281	11.9558(0.0120)	0.13733	9.844	12.8739(0.0122)	0.07109
PC	6.14	13.3069(0.0126)	0.03984	12.016	13.3845(0.0124)	0.03424
EXT	16.766	12.8884(0.0122)	0.07004	32.578	13.3835(0.0122)	0.03432

Table 26.6 Comparison of different schemes for 10 000 paths and 12 and 24 time steps per year using *Ran1*

	12 steps (sec.)	PV (SE)	Rel. error %	24 steps (sec.)	PV (SE)	Rel. error %
QE	0.078	13.9848(0.1242)	0.00907	0.172	13.8775(0.1245)	0.00133
SIET	0.062	13.1589(0.1256)	0.05052	0.141	13.3848(0.1244)	0.03422
SIE	0.047	13.0995(0.1262)	0.05481	0.109	13.4752(0.1242)	0.0277
EET	0.078	11.9602(0.1207)	0.13701	0.125	12.9631(0.1227)	0.06465
MIL	0.063	13.771(0.1238)	0.00636	0.093	13.5328(0.1235)	0.02354
SMIL	0.063	13.7746(0.1283)	0.0061	0.109	13.9259(0.1256)	0.00482
EE	0.047	11.8961(0.1208)	0.14164	0.094	12.8826(0.1224)	0.07046
PC	0.078	13.2935(0.1258)	0.04081	0.109	13.2885(0.1243)	0.04117
EXT	0.172	12.9103(0.1225)	0.06846	0.344	13.2879(0.1244)	0.04121

Table 26.7 Comparison of different schemes for 100 000 paths and 12 and 24 time steps per year using *Ran1*

	12 steps (sec.)	PV (SE)	Rel. error %	24 steps (sec.)	PV (SE)	Rel. error %
QE	0.812	13.8246(0.0393)	0.00249	1.641	13.843(0.0393)	0.00116
SIET	0.719	13.0893(0.0397)	0.05554	1.359	13.2772(0.0395)	0.04199
SIE	0.547	13.1806(0.0397)	0.04896	1.078	13.3672(0.0393)	0.03549
EET	0.719	11.9778(0.0383)	0.13574	1.344	12.9293(0.0387)	0.06709
MIL	0.531	13.7558(0.0391)	0.00745	1.047	13.8179(0.0391)	0.00297
SMIL	0.547	13.9145(0.0405)	0.004	1.078	13.9052(0.0399)	0.00333
EE	0.547	11.8941(0.0379)	0.14178	1.015	12.8172(0.0386)	0.07518
PC	0.625	13.292(0.0399)	0.04092	1.235	13.3993(0.0394)	0.03318
EXT	1.687	12.8041(0.0386)	0.07612	3.297	13.3435(0.0390)	0.0372

Table 26.8 Comparison of different schemes for 500 000 paths and 12 and 24 time steps per year using *Ran1*

	12 steps (sec.)	PV (SE)	Rel. error %	24 steps (sec.)	PV (SE)	Rel. error %
QE	4.047	13.8329(0.0175)	0.00189	8.109	13.8407(0.0175)	0.00133
SIET	3.469	13.0974(0.0178)	0.05496	6.875	13.2915(0.0176)	0.04096
SIE	2.719	13.1577(0.0177)	0.05061	5.359	13.3429(0.0176)	0.03725
EET	3.563	12.0344(0.0172)	0.13166	6.734	12.9046(0.0173)	0.06887
MIL	2.641	13.768(0.0175)	0.00657	5.281	13.8154(0.0175)	0.00315
SMIL	2.672	13.9057(0.0181)	0.00336	5.344	13.8819(0.0178)	0.00165
EE	2.671	11.9478(0.0170)	0.13791	0.005	12.8974(0.0173)	0.06939
PC	3.141	13.326(0.0178)	0.03847	6.188	13.3815(0.0176)	0.03446
EXT	8.453	12.8807(0.0172)	0.0706	16.422	13.3784(0.0174)	0.03468

Table 26.9 Comparison of different schemes for 1 000 000 paths and 12 and 24 time steps per year using *Ran1*

	12 steps (sec.)	PV (SE)	Rel. error %	24 steps (sec.)	PV (SE)	Rel. error %
QE	8.078	13.844(0.01244)	0.00109	16.14	13.8748(0.0124)	0.00113
SIET	6.922	13.1048(0.0125)	0.05443	13.719	13.3105(0.0124)	0.03958
SIE	5.484	13.1585(0.0125)	0.05055	10.735	13.3682(0.0124)	0.03542
EET	7.187	11.9694(0.0121)	0.13635	13.438	12.9256(0.0122)	0.06736
MIL	5.343	13.7722(0.0124)	0.00627	10.625	13.811(0.0124)	0.00347
SMIL	5.375	13.9281(0.0128)	0.00498	10.657	13.9007(0.0126)	0.003
EE	5.359	11.975(0.0120)	0.13595	10.031	12.8724(0.0122)	0.0712
PC	6.328	13.299(0.0126)	0.04041	12.313	13.3915(0.0125)	0.03374
EXT	16.844	12.8704(0.0122)	0.07134	32.843	13.3648(0.0123)	0.03567

Table 26.10 Numerical results for comparison of the different schemes for different parameters

QE	SIET	SIE	EET	MIL	SMIL	EE	PC	EXT
0.42568	0.52312	0.11652	1.812554	17.15158	0.41466	5.72494	0.57086	19.60892
0.03666	0.88338	0.7513	3.38612	0.56416	0.16384	3.40234	0.24148	1.8913
0.01676	0.75888	0.68576	1.87746	0.07428	0.07268	1.8922	0.5667	0.98388
0.0168	0.5397	0.52568	0.9559	0.0635	0.037	0.98504	0.46266	0.45678
0.01096	0.31356	0.30874	0.46506	0.02006	0.0307	0.47968	0.31542	0.23852
0.02822	0.19826	0.1865	0.22528	0.02074	0.00568	0.21574	0.18756	0.11286
0.00888	0.08992	0.07896	0.09906	0.00744	0.01412	0.1108	0.10282	0.05496

Figure 26.2 illustrates the accuracy of the algorithms for various time steps. The error is determined in absolute terms with respect to the price computed using Fourier transform methods.

26.6 LESSONS LEARNED

During our numerical experiments with the Heston stochastic volatility model we have learned that C++ design can cope with a wide range of numerical schemes to approximate the solution of the corresponding stochastic differential equation.

We have also shown that there is no 'magic' scheme but each financial model has to be analysed in depth and special purpose schemes may have to be designed for the given problem. Simple schemes might be a first try but they have to be used with care since a fine discretisation is necessary to obtain reasonable results.

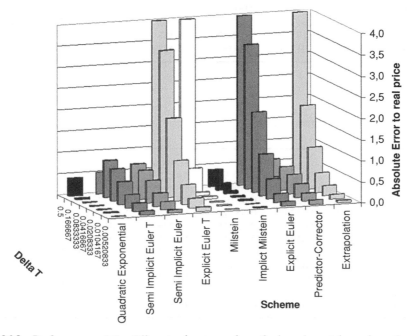

Figure 26.2 Performance of the different schemes; only paths have been taken where the volatility did not become negative

All components contribute to the quality of the simulation. It might be the case that as programmer you have an advanced object-oriented and well-designed software system with a finely-tuned QE scheme for the Heston model in place but use a random number generator such as `rand()` shipping with your C++ compiler. This could lead to unreasonable or even wrong results.

In some situations it is wise to use techniques such as the put-call parity to derive reasonable prices. We simulate the put price using Monte Carlo simulation since its payoff is bounded and we use this result to derive the value of the corresponding call option. This could be the case for a call option where many paths do deliver a value of 0 for the payoff, but on the contrary for the put nearly all paths contribute to the Monte Carlo value which leads to stable option prices in this case.

26.7   EXTENSIONS, CALIBRATION AND MORE

To apply the Heston stochastic volatility model we need to determine the model parameters. There are different ways to calculate these parameters. On the one hand we can use time series of the modelled quantity and compute the parameters using filtering or other statistical methods. On the other hand we can apply a procedure called calibration to match quoted market prices for liquid options. Using the integration formulae to compute prices for European call and put option prices we are able to compute such prices within the Heston model. By defining an error function we can try to minimise the resulting error:

$$\sum_i (\text{Market Price}_i - \text{Model Price}_i)^2 \tag{26.3}$$

On the CD we have included an Excel sheet with a scenario of quoted option prices. In this scenario we have applied a quasi-Newton optimiser as well as a *Differential Evolution* algorithm. The calibrated values are: $V(0) = 0.0938721$, $\theta = 0.07393339$, $\kappa = 3.99866477$, $\epsilon = 0.56567754$ and $\rho = -0.71448381$. After having carried out the calibration there is room for improving the simulation results. The first approach is to take the martingale correction into account and the second approach is to improve the approximation for small values of variance. The workflow for pricing an exotic derivative is as follows:

1. Selecting the instruments (call/put options with maturities and strikes).
2. Calibration to the selected parameters.
3. Price the exotic derivative using Monte Carlo simulation.

In this book we have covered the third topic. Selecting the instruments for calibration entails market knowledge and experience with the option market under consideration. The second step of this workflow leads to implementing some optimisation algorithms suitable for solving the problem under consideration. Some methods are purely analytic methods, for example SQP (Fan, Sarkar and Lasdon, 1988), LFBGS (Nocedal, 1989), Nelder-Mead-Powell (Press *et al.*, 2002); others are based on probabilistic methods, such as Simulated Annealing (Kirkpatrick, Gelatt and Vecchi, 1983) or Differential Evolution (Price, Storn and Lampinen, 2005). The design of a general calibration suite will be discussed elsewhere. It is our opinion that C++ offers all that is needed to succeed in this case. Applying object-oriented design techniques and efficient, reliable algorithms leads to fast and efficient code to carry out the calibration task.

26.8   OTHER NUMERICAL METHODS FOR HESTON

A number of numerical methods to handle option pricing in the Heston model have been proposed. For example, semi-analytical methods such as Fourier transforms and discretisation methods based on approximating the corresponding partial differential equation have been invented. The latter are known as finite difference methods.

These methods lead to excellent results and are very stable because they are able to cope with many markets and in particular long dated options. Furthermore, the methods are fast and can be used in calibration procedures. We have given an example in the last section where we applied our implementation to some option data.

A different approach is to translate the underlying stochastic partial differential equation to a partial differential equation. Finite difference methods can then be applied to solve the partial differential equation. Sheppard has applied this approach to the Heston stochastic volatility model in Sheppard (2007).

Once we have translated the SDE into a PDE we then have to define the corresponding finite difference scheme that approximates the PDE. The Heston PDE is

$$\frac{\partial U}{\partial t} + L_S U + L_V U + \rho \sigma V S \frac{\partial^2 U}{\partial S \partial V} = 0$$

with

$$L_S U = \frac{1}{2} V S^2 \frac{\partial^2 U}{\partial S^2} + r S \frac{\partial U}{\partial S} - r U = 0$$

$$L_v U = \frac{1}{2} \xi V \frac{\partial^2 U}{\partial V^2} + [\kappa (\theta - V) - \lambda (S, V)] = 0$$

where $\lambda()$ denotes the market price of volatility risk, commonly set to 0. The boundary conditions $S \to \infty$, $S \to 0$, $V \to \infty$ and $V \to 0$ have to be defined. These depend on the option under consideration. After having set up the problem a mesh has to be defined and the corresponding finite difference estimation has to be computed. For details see Sheppard (2007) and Duffy (2006a and 2006b). Tables 2.11 and 2.12 give an indication of the performance of a state-of-the-art implemented finite difference method for pricing a call option in the Heston model.

For the integration scheme, applied long dated options are by no means a problem. Alan Lewis pointed out a test of our implementation for long dated options. In his book Lewis (2000)

Table 26.11   Performance of the finite difference method for a long dated call option in the Heston model

Steps spot	Steps variance	Steps time	Time in sec.
200	100	100	7–8
200	100	400	29–32
400	100	100	16–18
200	100	200	15–17

Table 26.12 Monte Carlo prices for only two steps per year for different number of simulated paths

Steps p.a.	NSim	Time in sec.	Call price
2	100000	1.109	3.95488
2	1000000	11.188	3.94531
2	10000000	111.985	3.95537

derives an asymptotic formula for the implied volatility which is given by

$$\sigma_{impl} = \sqrt{\frac{\kappa\theta}{2(1 + \rho^2)\epsilon^2} \left(\sqrt{(2\kappa - \rho\epsilon)^2 + (1 + \rho^2)\epsilon^2} - (2\kappa - \rho\epsilon) \right)}$$

We have tested this for our implementation of the analytic prices and found that our implementation is consistent with this formula. For example, using the parameters for Test Case I yields a value of 0.10892708. Increasing the maturity, first to $T = 300$, leads to 0.10894813 and finally to $T = 1000$, it is 0.10897331. Furthermore, our implementation used for Monte Carlo simulation also suggests this predicted limiting behaviour.

26.9   SUMMARY AND CONCLUSIONS

In this chapter we have tested the accuracy and the performance of several numerical schemes for a financial model. We have concentrated on the Heston model and found that

- The SDE describing the Heston model can be set up into our framework.
- The QE scheme is the best numerical scheme for discretising the dynamics that approximates the Heston SDE. It is also easily set up and integrated into the framework.

The integration of the Payoff functions is left as an exercise to the reader. We have given a hint how to set up Payoffs for path-dependent options here.

After having set up several numerical schemes for approximating the solution, we tested the schemes with regard to performance accuracy and applicability to given markets. The tests indicate that the QE scheme is the most stable and accurate scheme. This allows for fast Monte Carlo implementation on a single processor machine. Furthermore, a Heston model calibrated to market parameters does eventually break the Feller condition. In these cases the QE scheme is the only scheme giving reasonable results. Furthermore, we compared our implementation with the finite difference method. All this suggests that our implementation is fast and accurate.

26.10   EXERCISES AND PROJECTS

1. (*) Payoff Function
   Consider `PayoffFunctions` for the following cases:
   – Arithmetic Asian call;
   – Geometric Asian call;
   – Digital option;
   – Barrier option.
   Use all schemes described in this chaper to price these options. Which scheme performs best?

2. (***) Payoff Functions
   Consider the framework to define Payoffs (Chapter 14). Integrate these classes into the
   main framework of this chapter. Note that there is a difference on how Payoffs have been
   set up in this chapter. Therefore, the classes need to be adapted to supply a whole path
   generated by the discretisation method introduced in the main framework.
3. (***) Martingale Property
   Consult Chapter 16 on stochastic volatility models and the CD with the source code. Adjust
   the QE scheme for the spot price in order to support the martingale property. Implement
   the corresponding correction within the general framework.
4. (*) Accuracy
   Check the call prices produced by the standard QE scheme and obtained using the put-call
   parity. Do the same for the martingale corrected QE scheme.
5. (*) The Bates Model
   Consult Chapter 16 on stochastic volatility models and the CD with the source code to
   implement the Bates stochastic volatility model. This model is in fact the Heston model
   allowing for log-normal jumps in the underlying. To this end in each step a jump together
   with the corresponding drift adjustment has to be added. All the formulas and pieces of
   source code can be found using the above-mentioned sources.
6. (**) Random Number Generators
   Examine the following alternatives for the random number generator using the C++ built
   in function rand():

```
double generateUniformNumber1()
{
    return double(rand()) /double(RAND_MAX);
}
```

```
double generateUniformNumber2()
{
    double factor = 1.0 + double(RAND_MAX);

    return  double(rand()); / factor;
}
```

```
double generateUniformNumber3()
{
    double factor = 1.0 + double(RAND_MAX);

    double uniform = double(rand());

    if (uniform == 0.0)
        uniform = 1.0;
    return  uniform / factor;
}
```

What is the effect of using them together with the inverse transform, for example to generate
normal variates?

7. (*) Richardson Extrapolation

Examine the following piece of code for generating the path due to Richardson Extrapolation and find out in which parts of the implementation there are difficulties or the algorithm does not even implement Richardson's extrapolation method. Correct the parts.

```
// Richardson Extrapolation
VectorSpace<double, 2> Extrapolation(const VectorSpace<double, 2>&
                               VOld, double WI1, double WI2)
{ // Calculate the solution at time level n+1 in
  // terms of solution at time level n

  // Calculate the Euler with NT and 2^NT points
  // and use the magic formula

    result = EE(VOld, WI1, WI2);

    deltaT *= 0.5;
    sqrk = sqrt(deltaT);

    CorrelatedNumbers(WI1, WI2, rho);
    ExtrapolatedResult1 = EE(VOld, WI1, WI2);
    CorrelatedNumbers(WI1, WI2, rho);
    ExtrapolatedResult2 = EE(ExtrapolatedResult1, WI1, WI2);

    result[1] = (2.0 * ExtrapolatedResult2[1]) - result[1];
    result[2] = (2.0 * ExtrapolatedResult2[2]) - result[2];

    deltaT *= 2.0;
    sqrk = sqrt(deltaT);

    return result;
}
```

Check your answers against the QE scheme.

8. (*****) Using Advanced Schemes for the Heston Model

In section 6.7 of Chapter 6 we introduced a number of finite difference schemes that are either not well known or not used to the same extent as the ubiquitous Euler and Milstein methods. These advanced schemes are potentially more powerful than the schemes from Chapter 5. The objective of this exercise (we see it as a project) is to determine whether the schemes in section 6.7 are indeed an improvement. You will apply these schemes to the Heston model (equation (16.2) in Chapter 16). As is known, the main challenge is to ensure that the volatility term does not become negative during the execution of the time-marching schemes. Use the same parameter values as in section 26.2.

Answer the following questions:

(a) Apply the derivative-free Milstein scheme (section 6.7.3) to the Heston model. Compare your results with those in Tables 26.2 to 26.9.

(b) Now, apply the implicit order 1.0 Runge Kutta method (as described in section 6.7.4) to the same problems as in part (a).

(c) Incorporate the schemes in (a) and (b) into the Heston framework by extending the C++ code on the CD.

27

Excel, C++ and Monte Carlo Integration

27.1 INTRODUCTION AND OBJECTIVES

In this chapter we discuss how to integrate our code with Excel. We create applications in which Excel is used as the front-end to Monte Carlo applications. We show how to create the software for user input, output, processing and communication between Excel and C++. We consider this chapter to be important because Excel is a popular application in finance and it is used on a daily basis by quantitative analysts and traders in many banks throughout the world.

There are several techniques that allow us to write C++ applications that interoperate with Excel and we speak of *Excel add-ins* in this context:

- *XLL add-ins*. This is the oldest form of add-in. These add-ins are written in C using the Microsoft XLL application-programming interface. The code is compiled to a dynamic link library (DLL) having the extension .xll. They are useful for the creation of Excel worksheet functions or functions that we call using menus.

   The advantage in this case is that XLL is efficient and it works with all versions of Excel from Excel 95 upwards. To create XLL functionality we use the xlw framework. Using this framework it is easy to create C++ worksheet functions. It generates usable interfaces to transform your already running C++ functions into functions that work within Excel. The framework can be downloaded at xlw.sourceforge.net.
- *COM add-ins*. These were introduced in Excel 2000 and are based on a generic COM (Component Object Model) interface for add-ins. All Office products use this interface as well as the Visual Studio and VBA development environments.

   Some remarks need to be made concerning this kind of add-in. First, having created a COM add-in you must register it in the registry for each host application (for example, Excel or Word) that it supports. This allows the host application to find the add-in. In general terms, the registry is a hierarchical data store that holds many different kinds of data, for example DLLs and their file locations. Second, COM add-ins cannot be used to create Excel worksheet functions, at least not directly. If you wish to do so, then you should call the COM add-in function through an XLA (the VBA way of creating add-ins) add-in worksheet function.
- *Automation add-ins*. This option has been available since the introduction of Excel 2002. It uses COM objects whose public functions are used as worksheet functions. Menus are not supported. An automation add-in is always loaded on demand.

We examine some of the above options in detail. We give a step-by-step account for creating an add-in and we give several examples to show how to create an add-in. In particular, we discuss worksheet functions for library-related functionality as well as complete applications that are started from within Excel.

We provide several complete applications of C++ and Excel interfacing on the CD. This discussion is based on Excel 2003 and Excel 2007, which is where we have tested the software.

27.2   INTEGRATING APPLICATIONS AND EXCEL

In Duffy (2004a) we introduced the topic of Excel and C++ integration. In particular, we traced the steps that are needed in order to create Automation and COM add-ins. In this chapter we extend the presentation by applying the results to the problem of integrating C++ code with the Monte Carlo method. Furthermore, we discuss the foundations of the Active Template Library (ATL). This is Microsoft's software framework for generating C++/COM code. It allows developers to write code without having to know the internals of COM. In fact, it uses macros to generate code stubs that the developer can subsequently change to suit his or her needs. Some of the features that ATL offers are

- Class wrappers for a number of important data types in COM.
- Classes that provide implementations of a number of basic COM interfaces.
- Classes that manage COM servers and server lifecycle management.
- Wizards that generate stub code that the developer can edit to suit the current application needs.

The generated code can be intimidating when first encountered but it becomes easier to understand once we know its intent. This chapter discusses the underlying design of ATL to smoothen the transition to writing ATL-based applications for the Monte Carlo method.

27.3   ATL ARCHITECTURE

In this section we give background information on ATL and how it is used.

27.3.1   Interfaces and data structures

COM objects implement interfaces and they communicate by data exchange. Microsoft has defined standard interfaces that the developer can implement to create applications. Our interest lies in creating Excel-based applications and for this reason we concentrate on a few special interfaces. For the sake of completeness, we mention some of the supported features:

- *Persistence*: The ability to save an object's state or properties to a permanent medium; the interfaces have methods for reading from and writing to a medium. The base interface is called `IPersist` and two derived interfaces are called `IPersistFile` and `IPersistStream` that allow us to interact with disk files and simple streams, respectively. Some applications may wish to load and save data and these interfaces are used for this purpose.
- *Dispatching interfaces using Automation*: Automation allows an application to interact with a COM server using a single standard interface called `IDispatch`. We shall deal with this interface in more detail when we create worksheet functions in Excel. Automation focuses on run-time types.
- `IDTExtensibility2`: This important interface hosts event notifications, for example when add-ins are loaded, unloaded and updated. This interface has a number of methods that we discuss in detail in section 27.3.3. We pay special attention to implementing the methods when we connect to and disconnect from Excel.
- `IUnknown`: This is the interface that all COM objects must implement. It has methods that allow us to determine if a COM object implements a given interface and methods

for reference counting (these two methods ensure that the lifetime of objects are properly managed). As an ATL programmer, you do not have to write the declarations of these methods because this is automatically taken care of by ATL.

- *Connection points*: We know that a COM object implements one or more interfaces. In this sense we say that the object has a number of *provides* interfaces. We now consider the reverse situation, namely the modelling of an object's *requires* interfaces. In this case the connection point mechanism allows an object to expose its capability to call one or more specified interfaces. A connection has two roles; the first role is called the *source* or the *connection point* and the second role is called the *sink* because this is the object that receives the call and hence implements the interface. In general, a given source object may have connections to multiple sink objects. Thus, in UML a sink represents the ball and the source represents the socket in a component diagram.

We now give an introduction to the most important data types and data structures in ATL. It is useful to know what they mean and our main concern lies in defining the data structures associated with an interface's methods, for example its return type and its input and output parameters:

- HRESULT;: Return type of most methods. This is a 32-bit value that is divided into three different fields as shown in Figure 27.1. You only need to know the value of the most significant bit. This bit determines whether the call succeeded (or failed). The possible return codes are (S_ corresponds to success, E_ to failure):
  - E_ABORT: the operation was aborted because of an unspecified error.
  - E_ACCESSDENIED: a general access-denied error.
  - E_FAIL: an unspecified failure has occurred.
  - E_HANDLE: an invalid handle was used.
  - E_INVALIDARG: one or more arguments are invalid.
  - E_NOINTERFACE: the QueryInterface method of the interface IUnknown did not recognise the requested interface. The interface is not supported.
  - E_NOTIMPL: the method is not implemented.
  - E_OUTOFMEMORY: the method failed to allocate memory.
  - E_PENDING: the data necessary to complete the operation is not yet available.
  - E_POINTER: an invalid pointer was used.
  - E_UNEXPECTED: a catastrophic failure occurred.
  - S_FALSE: the method succeeded and returned the boolean value FALSE.
  - S_OK: the method succeeded. If a Boolean return value is expected, the returned value is TRUE.

Figure 27.1 Format of HRESULT

We can check the return type in code by calling the SUCCEEDED and FAILED macros as the following examples show:

```
HRESULT hr = SetStrings ();
if (FAILED (hr))
        return hr;

HRESULT hr2 = pPropBag->Read();
if (SUCCEEDED(hr2))
{
        // code
}
```

It is advisable to use these macros when testing a method's return value instead of comparing the result hr against the raw values; however, it is allowed to use these values as return types in code, for example:

```
HRESULT FinalConstruct()
{
        return S_OK;
}
```

- VARIANT: ATL supports many kinds of data types that can be passed as parameters in methods. Each specific data type has its own discriminator and this allows the marshaller to deal with the data. In C++, it is similar to a void* type. We shall have little use for this data type in this chapter but you may need to know what it is.
- SAFEARRAY: This is a self-describing array type that holds the size and type of each element in it as well as the number of elements and the bounds of the array. This type was created in order to allow arrays of data to be passed between processes. You will see some examples of this type in generated code later but the good news is that you can ignore it. We note that a SAFEARRAY can be copied to a VARIANT.
- *String data types*: Passing strings between processes poses problems in general. The main problem is that strings do not have a predetermined size. The first string type that we are interested in is BSTR, known as basic string or binary string. This is a pointer to a wide character string used by Automation data manipulation functions. In fact, BSTR is a typedef for LPWSTR Automation data. Finally, you may see some examples of strings of type LPSTR in generated code.

27.3.2 The structure of an ATL project and its classes

When developing Automation and COM add-ins we need to create two main classes. The first class is the embodiment of the ATL server and it has the same name as that of the ATL project that contains all relevant code. This class has functions for registering and unregistering the COM object in the Windows registry. The second class is the actual COM object where all the application code resides: in particular, it has functionality for

- Communication with Excel; when connecting to Excel we add a menu item to the Tools menu and when disconnecting from Excel we remove the menu item from the Tools menu, for example.
- ATL generates much of the code that is needed by the COM object.

We now discuss the main code blocks in the above two classes. In section 27.7 we assemble the code in one place. We concentrate on code that we, as developers, modify while we ignore unmodified generated code. The code for registering and unregistering the COM add-in in the Windows registry uses two static member functions developed by the authors. The registration code is

```
STDAPI DllRegisterServer(void)
{

        // Register this COM add-in for Excel
        ComAddinUtils::RegisterCOMAddin("Excel", pszProgID,
            pszFriendlyName, 3);

        // registers object, typelib and all interfaces in typelib
        HRESULT hr = _AtlModule.DllRegisterServer();
            return hr;
}
```

We remark that the add-in can be loaded in different ways (in the above case we load the add-in in the most usual way, namely it is loaded at application startup time, hence the parameter '3'). Other possibilities are

- *Disconnect* (value 0), add-in is not loaded.
- *Connected* (value 1), add-in is loaded.
- *Bootload* (value 2), load add-in on application startup.
- *DemandLoad* (value 8), load add-in only when requested by user.
- *ConnectFirstTime* (value 16), load add-in only once (on next startup).

The code for unregistering the add-in is

```
// DllUnregisterServer - Removes entries from the system registry
STDAPI DllUnregisterServer(void)
{
    // Unregister this COM add-in
    ComAddinUtils::UnRegisterCOMAddin("Excel", pszProgID);

    HRESULT hr = _AtlModule.DllUnregisterServer();
    return hr;
}
```

We mention the notation used in the two above member functions, in particular the use of the shorthand notation:

```
#define STDAPI EXTERN_C HRESULT STDAPICALLTYPE
```

In other words, this defines an API function that returns a HRESULT.

In these cases we define strings for the ProgID (programmable ID) that the registry needs and for a user-friendly name for the add-in that can be seen as one of the entries in the list of add-ins when Excel is running:

```
LPSTR pszProgID = "MyProj.MyComp";
LPSTR pszFriendlyName = "ATL for Chapter 27";
```

We now discuss the application code. The class for this code implements the `IDTExten-sibility2` interface. The project environment generates the stubs for the methods in this interface. We must modify these methods to let them return the value and we modify the code for connecting to and disconnecting from Excel. To this end, we show the definition of this class and its members:

```
#include "ExcelImports.cpp"      // All Excel-related information
#include "ComAddinUtils.hpp"     // Utilities (e.g. registration,
                                 //    conversion, menus and buttons)

class ATL_NO_VTABLE CMyComp :
    public CComObjectRootEx<CComSingleThreadModel>,
    public CComCoClass<CMyComp, &CLSID_MyComp>,
    public IDispatchImpl<IMyComp, &IID_IMyComp, &LIBID_MyProjLib,
        /*wMajor =*/ 1, /*wMinor =*/ 0>,
    public IDispatchImpl<_IDTExtensibility2,
        &_ _uuidof(_IDTExtensibility2),
        &LIBID_AddInDesignerObjects, /* wMajor = */ 1>
private:
    // The Excel instance the add-in communicates with
    Excel::_ApplicationPtr m_xl;

    // The menu item added by the add-in
    Office::_CommandBarButtonPtr m_menuItem;

public:
};
```

Most of this code is generated with the exception of the `private` members, which are defined by the developer. The macro `ATL_NO_VTABLE` wraps some specific code that optimises the C++ code in the application. It is not relevant to our discussion, as long as you have a rough idea of what is going on.

The next step is to define how the COM interfaces in the object can be exposed to clients. To this end, we define the so-called *COM interface* map that is automatically generated and is defined by the macros:

```
    BEGIN_COM_MAP(CMyComp)
        COM_INTERFACE_ENTRY(IMyComp)
        COM_INTERFACE_ENTRY2(IDispatch, IMyComp)    // IMyComp is
                                                    //    user-defined
        COM_INTERFACE_ENTRY(_IDTExtensibility2)
    END_COM_MAP()
```

We must also be able to couple external events (in this application this will be the act of clicking a button in the Tools menu) and in this case we define a *sink map*:

```
    BEGIN_SINK_MAP(CmyComponent)
        SINK_ENTRY_EX(/*nID =*/ 1,
        _ _uuidof(Office::_CommandBarButtonEvents),
        /*dispid*/ 1, OnButtonClick) // Callback function
    END_SINK_MAP()
```

We then need to register the event sink with the menu item. As we shall see, this takes place on connection with Excel by calling the function `DispEventAdvise()` while we unregister the event handler when the add-in is unloaded by calling the function `DispEventUnadvise()`.

The code for the event handler is represented as a method in the COM object:

```cpp
// Handle click event
void __stdcall
CmyComponent::OnButtonClick(Office::_CommandBarButtonPtr Ctrl,
    VARIANT_BOOL * CancelDefault)
{
    m_xl->GetRange("a1:b2")->Value2="Add-In called";
                                        // Simple 101 example
}
```

In this case the body of the code is very simple but it can be replaced by any application code, for example code for Monte Carlo simulation or for the finite difference method. It is advisable to create separate header and code files in the interest of maintainability.

27.3.3 Implementing the methods in IDTExtensibility2

This is the most important interface in the application and it is by means of its methods that we can communicate with Excel. The main events are

- `OnConnection()` occurs whenever an add-in is loaded.
- `OnDisconnection()` occurs whenever an add-in is unloaded.
- `OnAddInsUpdate()` occurs whenever an add-in is loaded or unloaded.
- `OnBeginShutdown()` occurs whenever the host application shuts down while an add-in is running.
- `OnStartupComplete()` occurs whenever an add-in loads, which is set to load when the host application (that is, Excel) starts.

We are interested in the first two methods. First, the method for connection sets the reference to Excel and creates a menu item in the Tools menu. It also registers the event sink with the menu item:

```cpp
STDMETHOD(OnConnection)(LPDISPATCH Application, ext_ConnectMode
            ConnectMode, LPDISPATCH AddInInst, SAFEARRAY * *
                                        custom)
{

    // Store reference to the Excel host application
    // Exit if host application is not excel
    m_xl = Application;
    if (m_xl==NULL)
    {

        return S_OK;
    }

    Office::COMAddInPtr cai=AddInInst;

    if(cai!=NULL)
```

```
     {
          void* id;
          this->QueryInterface(IID_IDispatch, &id);
          cai->put_Object((IDispatch*)id);

          m_menuItem = ComAddinUtils::AddMenuItem(m_xl, cai,
          CComBSTR("Tools"),CComBSTR("My MC ATL"),
          CComBSTR("MCComp"));

          return DispEventAdvise(m_menuItem);     // register the
                                                     event sink

     }


     return S_OK;
}
```

The menu for disconnecting contains code to unregister the event handler when the add-in is unloaded and it removes the menu item from the Tools menu:

```
STDMETHOD(OnDisconnection)(ext_DisconnectMode RemoveMode,
                                  SAFEARRAY * * custom)
{

     if (m_menuItem!=NULL)
     {
          DispEventUnadvise(m_menuItem);     // unregister

          ComAddinUtils::RemoveMenuItem(m_xl, RemoveMode,
               CComBSTR("Tools"),CComBSTR("My MC ATL"));

     }

     return S_OK;
}
```

The other methods have an empty body and return the standard success result code:

```
STDMETHOD(OnAddInsUpdate)(SAFEARRAY * * custom)
{
     return S_OK;
}

STDMETHOD(OnStartupComplete)(SAFEARRAY * * custom)
{
     return S_OK;
}

STDMETHOD(OnBeginShutdown)(SAFEARRAY * * custom)
{
     return S_OK;
}
```

A final remark; STDMETHOD is a macro that wraps the _stdcall calling convention, the virtual specifier and the HRESULT return type.

27.4   CREATING MY FIRST ATL PROJECT: THE STEPS

In this section we enumerate the steps that you take in order to create a COM add-in for Excel. We have already discussed this issue in Duffy (2004a). The same steps are used for the creation of an Automation add-in but in the latter case we do not need to implement the IDTExtensibility2 interface. We use the wizards that the Microsoft IDE delivers and the main challenge is knowing which buttons to press and where to insert your own code in the generated source files (it is also important to know *why* you are doing it):

1. Create an ATL DLL project and give it a name (in the Settings dialog this project should be not attributed). The name of the project determines the names of created source files and the ProgID.
2. Select the project and add an ATL simple object to it (you select the project by navigating to the Solution Explorer, right mouse clicking the project and selecting the Add menu item). Give the ATL simple object a name.
3. (This step is for COM add-in only.) In Class View, add an Implementation Interface called IDTExtensibility2. Code is generated in the header file corresponding to the ATL object; in particular, you should change the return type of the four methods in IDTExtensibility2 to S_OK. (as discussed in section 27.3.3).
4. We now edit the project header file and insert code to register and unregister the add-in:

```
// DllRegisterServer - Adds entries to the system registry
STDAPI DllRegisterServer(void)
{

    // Register this COM add-in for Excel
    ComAddinUtils::RegisterCOMAddin("Excel", pszProgID,
                                    pszFriendlyName, 2);

    // registers object, typelib and all interfaces in typelib
    HRESULT hr = _AtlModule.DllRegisterServer();
    return hr;
}


// DllUnregisterServer - Removes entries from the system registry
STDAPI DllUnregisterServer(void)
{
    // Unregister this COM add-in
    ComAddinUtils::UnRegisterCOMAddin("Excel", pszProgID);
    HRESULT hr = _AtlModule.DllUnregisterServer();
    return hr;
}
```

Furthermore, you need to define two strings in the project header file as follows:

```
    LPSTR pszProgID = "MyProj.MyComp";
    LPSTR pszFriendlyName = "ATL for Chapter 27";
```

Incidentally, our code is default inline for convenience.

5. At this stage you can build the project to check for syntax errors. You can start Excel and you will see your add-in in the list (Tools) but you cannot run it because (i) it is not connected to Excel and (ii) we have not yet defined event sinks and event handlers.
6. We now modify the code for the ATL simple object. In particular, you need to carry out the following steps:
   (a) Define how your object interacts with Excel:

```
private:
// The Excel instance the add-in communicates with
Excel::_ApplicationPtr m_xl;

// The menu item added by the sdd-in
Office::_CommandBarButtonPtr m_menuItem;
```

   (b) Code the connect and disconnect functions. Create a sink map. **Insert your application-specific code in the event handler** (as discussed in the latter half of section 27.3.2)
7. Build the project and you are finished if you have no errors. Start Excel and test your add-in.

We now give some tips and guidelines to help you discover errors and resolve those irritating error messages:

- Make sure you include COMUtil.hpp and COMUtil.cpp in the relevant files and projects (for the project and the ATL simple object) in the Visual Studio project. Make sure that you resolve compiler and linker errors at each stage of the above steps in the project.
- You must import the Excel type libraries for the current version of Excel (see the file ExcelImports.h). In particular software operates with the English version of Excel. If you wish to use it with another language (for example, German) you need to change the following, admittedly hard-coded name Sheet1 to the appropriately-named name in your version of Excel (in the file ExcelDriver.cpp). The source code that uses this hard-coded name is:

```
try
{
    // Initialize COM Runtime Libraries.
    CoInitialize(NULL);

    // Start excel application.
    xl.CreateInstance(L"Excel.Application");
    xl->Workbooks->Add((long) Excel::xlWorksheet);

    // Rename "Sheet1" to "Chart Data".
    Excel::_WorkbookPtr pWorkbook = xl->ActiveWorkbook;
    Excel::_WorksheetPtr pSheet =
        pWorkbook->Worksheets->GetItem("Sheet1");
                                    // Language-dependent!!!
    pSheet->Name = "Chart Data";
}
catch( _com_error & error )
{
    ThrowAsString(error);
}
```

You should change the string 'Sheet1' to the corresponding name in your language.

- Clean the Registry on a regular basis, especially in a development environment.
- In your Project Properties settings, do not use *precompiled headers*.

27.5   CREATING AUTOMATION ADD-INS IN EXCEL

Section 27.3 discussed how to create a COM add-in in Excel. In this section we discuss how
to create an Automation add-in for Excel.

Automation allows a client to communicate with a component. Instead of a component
providing several custom interfaces we note that the component offers those services through
the single standard interface called *IDispatch*. Automation makes it possible for interpretive
languages to access COM components that implement the *IDispatch* interface. Automation
builds on COM. An *Automation server* is a COM component that implements the *IDispatch*
interface and an *Automation controller* is a COM client that communicates with this server
through this interface. In other words, the *IDispatch* interface is the proxy or intermediate
between the controller and server. The requests from the controller are dispatched indirectly
to the server.

Almost all services that COM provides can also be achieved using *IDispatch*. Furthermore,
Automation add-ins are easier to create than COM add-ins.

27.5.1   Automation interfaces

The *IDispatch* interface allows a component to expose any number of methods and properties.
It is an ordinary COM interface and it uses a *vtable* that contains pointers to its methods. The
distinguishing feature, however, is that it has a method called `Invoke` and this method is used
to call other methods. The developer can also specify a *dispatch interface* (or *dispinterface*)
and this specifies those methods that may be invoked. Each method in this interface has a
dispatch identifier (DISPID). This identifier is usually an integer and functions as an index
to some function in the function table. We represent the situation graphically in Figure 27.2.
In fact, this is an array of function pointers. We shall see how to create an add-in based on
the *IDispatch* interface. In particular, we shall use Automation to create worksheet functions

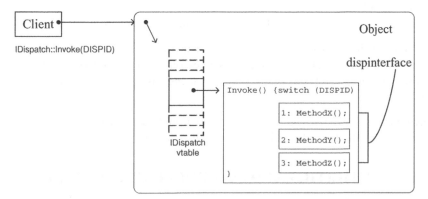

Figure 27.2   Invoking a method in a dispinterface

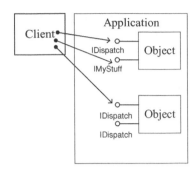

Figure 27.3 Objects that support IDispatch

in Excel. For example, here is an example of generated component code with two simple methods (notice the two DISPID values):

```
interface IComp777 : IDispatch
{
     [id(1), helpstring("method myFunc")] HRESULT myFunc(
             [out,retval] DOUBLE* myArg);
     [id(2), helpstring("method myFunc2")] HRESULT myFunc2(
             [out,retval] LONG* arg);
};
```

There are four methods in *IDispatch*:

- *GetTypeInfo*: If the object has a type library, then this method returns a pointer to the typeinfo object describing the dispinterface. In this way, a client can learn everything about a server, including its methods and associated parameters.
- *GetTypeInfoCount*: This method indicates if an object returns type information at run-time, in other words if the method *GetTypeInfo* will return useful information.
- *GetIDOfNames*: This method allows the client to pass the name of a method (in the form of a string) that is then converted to an integer ID that we subsequently use in *Invoke*.
- *Invoke*: We use this method to invoke the methods in all dispinterfaces.

We note that an object can support multiple *IDispatch* instances as well as ordinary COM interfaces as shown in Figure 27.3.

Using dispinterfaces introduces a number of disadvantages. The main ones are

- Invoking a method using a dispinterface is slower than invoking the same method in a *vtable*.
- The process of packing parameters into variants is time-consuming and impacts performance.
- It takes more time in C++ to program a method using dispinterfaces than to code the equivalent *vtable*.

In order to avoid these drawbacks we create objects that implement *dual interfaces*. In other words, such objects' methods can be called through *IDispatch* and by using *vtable* calls.

27.6   USEFUL UTILITIES AND INTEROPERABILITY PROJECTS

Excel is a popular tool and we can use it in a variety of ways:

- As an input device (by using cells and ranges).

- As an output device (cells, charts).
- As a computational engine.

In this case we are interested in selecting data from Excel, computing some quantities using that data and presenting those results. The kinds of applications that we are interested in are

- Mathematical structures: We created a number of data structures that we use for numerical work, for example vectors, matrices and tensors. Furthermore, we wish to integrate these structures with Excel, for example two-way data exchange with VARIANT and SAFEARRAY.
- Integration with Standard Template Library (STL): We wish to integrate the most important STL containers (such as vector, set and map) with Excel.
- Mechanisms (statistical libraries, interpolation, optimisation): Integration of *Mechanisms* (for vectors, statistics for example) with Automation.
- Solvers (for example, matrix algebra, eigenvalue calculations): Useful building blocks such as linear and nonlinear solvers.
- Applications (PDE, Monte Carlo and other financial applications).

27.7 TEST CASE: A COM ADD-IN AND COMPLETE CODE

We give the most important source code for COM add-ins and Automation add-ins in this section. You can find the complete code on the accompanying CD.

These source files represent the *finished product* as it were and you can compare your code with these to check that you have not forgotten something.

27.7.1 COM add-in

We first discuss the code for the project class. There are two files, namely the .hpp file (which you can ignore because it contains generated code that need not be modified) and the .cpp file that contains code for registration and unregistration:

```
// MyATLProj.cpp : Implementation of DLL Exports.
#include "stdafx.h"
#include "resource.h"
#include "MyATLProj.h"
#include "ComAddinUtils.hpp"

// Developer-supplied strings
LPSTR pszProgID = "MyATLProj.MyATLComp";
LPSTR pszFriendlyName = "Chapter 27 MC book";


class CMyATLProjModule : public CAtlDllModuleT< CMyATLProjModule >
{
public :
     DECLARE_LIBID(LIBID_MyATLProjLib)
     DECLARE_REGISTRY_APPID_RESOURCEID(IDR_MYATLPROJ,
             "{C4CA01E7-957B-46E8-B71F-273228EB4015}")
};

CMyATLProjModule _AtlModule;
```

```
#ifdef _MANAGED
#pragma managed(push, off)
#endif

// DLL Entry Point
extern "C" BOOL WINAPI DllMain(HINSTANCE hInstance, DWORD dwReason,
                                               LPVOID lpReserved)
{
    hInstance;
    return _AtlModule.DllMain(dwReason, lpReserved);
}

#ifdef _MANAGED
#pragma managed(pop)
#endif


// Used to determine whether the DLL can be unloaded by OLE
STDAPI DllCanUnloadNow(void)
{
    return _AtlModule.DllCanUnloadNow();
}


// Returns a class factory to create an object of the requested type
STDAPI DllGetClassObject(REFCLSID rclsid, REFIID riid, LPVOID* ppv)
{
    return _AtlModule.DllGetClassObject(rclsid, riid, ppv);
}


// DllRegisterServer - Adds entries to the system registry
STDAPI DllRegisterServer(void)
{

    // Register this COM add-in for Excel
    ComAddinUtils::RegisterCOMAddin("Excel", pszProgID,
                                    pszFriendlyName, 2);

    // Registers object, typelib and all interfaces in typelib
    HRESULT hr = _AtlModule.DllRegisterServer();
    return hr;
}


// DllUnregisterServer - Removes entries from the system registry
STDAPI DllUnregisterServer(void)
{
    // Unregister this COM add-in
    ComAddinUtils::UnRegisterCOMAddin("Excel", pszProgID);
```

```
        HRESULT hr = _AtlModule.DllUnregisterServer();
        return hr;
}
```

For the ATL simple object, there are two files, namely the .cpp file (which you can ignore because it contains generated code) and the .hpp file that contains code for connecting to and disconnecting from Excel (we shall use default inline code for convenience):

```
// MyATLComp.h : Declaration of the CMyATLComp
#pragma once
#include "resource.h"          // main symbols

#include "MyATLProj.h"

#include "ExcelImports.h"
#include "ComAddinUtils.hpp"
#include "ExcelUtils.hpp"

#if defined(_WIN32_WCE) && !defined(_CE_DCOM) && !defined(_CE_ALLOW_
                                        SINGLE_THREADED_OBJECTS_IN_MTA)
#endif


// CMyATLComp
class ATL_NO_VTABLE CMyATLComp :
        public CComObjectRootEx<CComSingleThreadModel>,
        public CComCoClass<CMyATLComp, &CLSID_MyATLComp>,
        public IDispatchImpl<IMyATLComp, &IID_IMyATLComp,
                &LIBID_MyATLProjLib, /*wMajor =*/ 1, /*wMinor =*/ 0>,
        public IDispatchImpl<_IDTExtensibility2,
                &_ _uuidof(_IDTExtensibility2),
                &LIBID_AddInDesignerObjects,1>
{
public:
        CMyATLComp()
        {
        }

        DECLARE_REGISTRY_RESOURCEID(IDR_MYATLCOMP)


        BEGIN_COM_MAP(CMyATLComp)
                COM_INTERFACE_ENTRY(IMyATLComp)
                COM_INTERFACE_ENTRY2(IDispatch, IMyATLComp)
                COM_INTERFACE_ENTRY(_IDTExtensibility2)
        END_COM_MAP()



        DECLARE_PROTECT_FINAL_CONSTRUCT()

        HRESULT FinalConstruct()
```

```
    {
        return S_OK;
    }

    void FinalRelease()
    {
    }

private:
    // The Excel instance the add-in communicates with
    Excel::_ApplicationPtr m_xl;

    // The menu item added by the add-in
    Office::_CommandBarButtonPtr m_menuItem;

public:
    STDMETHOD(OnConnection)(LPDISPATCH Application,
        ext_ConnectMode ConnectMode,
        LPDISPATCH AddInInst, SAFEARRAY * * custom)
    {

        // Store reference to the Excel host application
        // Exit if host application is not excel
        m_xl = Application;
        if (m_xl==NULL)
        {
            return S_OK;
        }

        Office::COMAddInPtr cai=AddInInst;


        if(cai!=NULL)
        {
            void* id;
            this->QueryInterface(IID_IDispatch, &id);
            cai->put_Object((IDispatch*)id);

            m_menuItem = ComAddinUtils::AddMenuItem(m_xl, cai,
                CComBSTR("Tools"), CComBSTR("My MC ATL2"),
                CComBSTR("MCComp2"));

            return DispEventAdvise(m_menuItem);
        }

        return S_OK;
    }

    STDMETHOD(OnDisconnection)(ext_DisconnectMode RemoveMode,
                                        SAFEARRAY * * custom)
    {
```

```
                if (m_menuItem!=NULL)
                {
                        DispEventUnadvise(m_menuItem);
                        ComAddinUtils::RemoveMenuItem(m_xl, RemoveMode,
                          CComBSTR("Tools"),CComBSTR("My MC ATL2"));

                }

        return S_OK;
        }

        STDMETHOD(OnAddInsUpdate)(SAFEARRAY * * custom)
        {
            return S_OK;
        }

        STDMETHOD(OnStartupComplete)(SAFEARRAY * * custom)
        {
            return S_OK;
        }

        STDMETHOD(OnBeginShutdown)(SAFEARRAY * * custom)
        {
            return S_OK;
        }
};

OBJECT_ENTRY_AUTO(__uuidof(MyATLComp), CMyATLComp)
```

27.7.2   Automation add-in

We have created an add-in whose name contains text (in this case '999') to accentuate the differences between system-generated names and names thought up by the developer. The source file for the project is

```
// AUTO999.cpp : Implementation of DLL Exports.
#include "stdafx.h"
#include "resource.h"
#include "AUTO999.h"


class CAUTO999Module : public CAtlDllModuleT< CAUTO999Module >
{
public :
     DECLARE_LIBID(LIBID_AUTO999Lib)
     DECLARE_REGISTRY_APPID_RESOURCEID(IDR_AUTO999,
     "{11673BE6-472B-42D9-806D-9166EC516F44}")
};
```

```
CAUTO999Module _AtlModule;


#ifdef _MANAGED
#pragma managed(push, off)
#endif

// DLL Entry Point
extern "C" BOOL WINAPI DllMain(HINSTANCE hInstance, DWORD dwReason,
                                                LPVOID lpReserved)
{
    hInstance;
    return _AtlModule.DllMain(dwReason, lpReserved);
}

#ifdef _MANAGED
#pragma managed(pop)
#endif


// Used to determine whether the DLL can be unloaded by OLE
STDAPI DllCanUnloadNow(void)
{
    return _AtlModule.DllCanUnloadNow();
}


// Returns a class factory to create an object of the requested type
STDAPI DllGetClassObject(REFCLSID rclsid, REFIID riid, LPVOID* ppv)
{
    return _AtlModule.DllGetClassObject(rclsid, riid, ppv);
}


// DllRegisterServer - Adds entries to the system registry
STDAPI DllRegisterServer(void)
{
    // registers object, typelib and all interfaces in typelib
    HRESULT hr = _AtlModule.DllRegisterServer();
    return hr;
}


// DllUnregisterServer - Removes entries from the system registry
STDAPI DllUnregisterServer(void)
{
    HRESULT hr = _AtlModule.DllUnregisterServer();
    return hr;
}
```

The source code for the header file for the simple ATL object contains one method in this case (you may define any number of methods in this object). In this case we just return a number but in your case you can add code that is relevant to your application:

```cpp
// Comp999.h : Declaration of the CComp999
#pragma once
#include "resource.h"        // main symbols

#include "AUTO999.h"


#if defined(_WIN32_WCE) && !defined(_CE_DCOM) &&
    !defined(_CE_ALLOW_SINGLE_THREADED_OBJECTS_IN_MTA)
#endif



// CComp999
class ATL_NO_VTABLE CComp999 :
    public CComObjectRootEx<CComSingleThreadModel>,
    public CComCoClass<CComp999, &CLSID_Comp999>,
    public IDispatchImpl<IComp999, &IID_IComp999, &LIBID_AUTO999Lib,
        /*wMajor =*/ 1,
        /*wMinor =*/ 0>
{
public:
    CComp999()
    {
    }

    DECLARE_REGISTRY_RESOURCEID(IDR_COMP999)


    BEGIN_COM_MAP(CComp999)
            COM_INTERFACE_ENTRY(IComp999)
            COM_INTERFACE_ENTRY(IDispatch)
    END_COM_MAP()



    DECLARE_PROTECT_FINAL_CONSTRUCT()

    HRESULT FinalConstruct()
    {
            return S_OK;
    }

    void FinalRelease()
    {
    }
```

```
public:
    STDMETHOD(myPI999)(void);
    STDMETHOD(func999)(DOUBLE* myarg);
};


OBJECT_ENTRY_AUTO(_ _uuidof(Comp999), CComp999)
```

The code file for the ATL simple object is given by

```
// Comp999.cpp : Implementation of CComp999
#include "stdafx.h"
#include "Comp999.h"


// CComp999
STDMETHODIMP CComp999::myPI999(void)
{
    // TODO: Add your implementation code here


    return S_OK;
}

STDMETHODIMP CComp999::func999(DOUBLE* myarg)
{
    // TODO: Add your implementation code here

    *myarg = 1.42;
    return S_OK;
}
```

27.7.3   The utilities class

We have provided a number of useful functions to ease the pain of writing Excel applications in C++. We include the following functionality (which was included in Duffy, 2004a and Duffy, 2006a) for registration/unregistration, for interfacing with Excel and for creating buttons and menu items in the Excel user interface.

The first class has functions for registering and unregistering the component in the Windows registry:

```
#ifndef ComAddinUtils_hpp
#define ComAddinUtils_hpp

#include "atlsafe.h"
#include "atlbase.h"
#include "Excel\ExcelImports.h"

class ComAddinUtils
{
public:
    // Register a COM add-in
```

```
        static HRESULT RegisterCOMAddin(CComBSTR officeApp,
                CComBSTR progID, CComBSTR friendlyName, DWORD
                                        dwStartupContext);

        // Unregister a COM add-in
        static HRESULT UnRegisterCOMAddin(CComBSTR officeApp,
                                        CComBSTR progID);

        // Set a key in the registry
        static BOOL SetKeyAndValue(HKEY hKeyRoot, CComBSTR path,
                        CComBSTR subkey, CComBSTR value);

        // Recursively delete a key in the registry
        static LONG RecursiveDeleteKey(HKEY hKeyParent,
                                        CComBSTR keyChild);
};


#endif ComAddinUtils_hpp
```

The second file contains application-specific functionality:

```
#ifndef ExcelUtils_hpp
#define ExcelUtils_hpp

#include "atlsafe.h"
#include "Excel\ExcelImports.h"

// _IDTExtensibity2 import
#import "C:\Program Files\Common Files\Designer\MSADDNDR.DLL"
    raw_interfaces_only, raw_native_types, no_namespace,
                                named_guids, auto_search

#include "VectorsAndMatrices\Vector.hpp"
#include "VectorsAndMatrices\NumericMatrix.hpp"

class ExcelUtils
{
public:
        // Add menu item to Excel
        static Office::_CommandBarButtonPtr
            AddMenuItem(Excel::_ApplicationPtr xl,
            Office::COMAddInPtr addin, CComBSTR menuName,
                    CComBSTR menuItemCaption, CComBSTR menuItemKey);

        // Remove menu item from Excel
        static void RemoveMenuItem(Excel::_ApplicationPtr xl,
            ext_DisconnectMode removeMode, CComBSTR menuName,
                            CComBSTR menuItemCaption);
        // Convert variant to vector with doubles
```

```
       static Vector<DOUBLE> ExcelRangeToVector(VARIANT* range);

       // Convert Excel range to vector with doubles
       static Vector<DOUBLE> ExcelRangeToVector(Excel::RangePtr
                                                    pRange);

       // Convert variant to STL vector with doubles
       static std::vector<DOUBLE> ExcelRangeToStlVector(VARIANT*
                                                    range);

       // Convert Excel range to STL vector with doubles
       static std::vector<DOUBLE> ExcelRangeToStlVector(Excel::
                                                    RangePtr pRange);

       // Convert variant to numeric matrix with doubles
       static NumericMatrix<DOUBLE> ExcelRangeToNumericMatrix(VARIANT*
                                                    range);

       // Convert Excel range to matrix with doubles
       static NumericMatrix<DOUBLE> ExcelRangeToNumericMatrix(Excel::
                                                    RangePtr pRange);

       // Retrieve a value from an Excel cell
       static int GetIntFromCell(Excel::_WorksheetPtr sheet,
                                                    CComBSTR cell);
       static long GetLongFromCell(Excel::_WorksheetPtr sheet,
                                                    CComBSTR cell);
       static float GetFloatFromCell(Excel::_WorksheetPtr sheet,
                                                    CComBSTR cell);
       static double GetDoubleFromCell(Excel::_WorksheetPtr sheet,
                                                    CComBSTR cell);

       // Put a value in an Excel cell
       static void SetCellValue(Excel::_WorksheetPtr sheet,
                                        CComBSTR cell, int value);
       static void SetCellValue(Excel::_WorksheetPtr sheet,
                                        CComBSTR cell, long value);
       static void SetCellValue(Excel::_WorksheetPtr sheet,
                                        CComBSTR cell, float value);
       static void SetCellValue(Excel::_WorksheetPtr sheet,
                                        CComBSTR cell, double value);
       static void SetCellValue(Excel::_WorksheetPtr sheet, CComBSTR
                                        cell, CComBSTR value);
};


#endif ExcelUtils_hpp
```

You can use these classes in your applications. The complete source code is on the CD.

27.8 SUMMARY AND CONCLUSIONS

We have given a detailed account of how to create C++ applications that interface with Excel and we paid particular attention to COM add-ins and Automation add-ins. The latter add-ins are used for worksheet functions where response time is important, whereas the former add-ins are more suitable for compute-intensive applications.

We described the steps that you need to execute in order to create an add-in and we gave examples of the C++ code that implements them. We have provided several nontrivial examples and applications on the CD.

27.9 EXERCISES AND PROJECTS

1. (***) Curve Fitting and Cubic Splines
   The objective of this exercise is to integrate C++ code for cubic spline interpolation (as developed in Duffy, 2006a) with Excel. We wish to write an Automation add-in to calculate the value of the spline for a specific value of the independent variable. Design the program in Excel based on the following input:
   - An array of x values.
   - An array of y values (these two arrays x,y must have the same size).
   - An x value whose spline value we wish to calculate.
   - An array of x values whose spline values we wish to calculate.
   - The kind of boundary conditions used (Duffy, 2006a; Press *et al.*, 2002).
   The class interface that we need is given by

```
enum CubicSplineBC {SecondDeriv, FirstDeriv};

class CubicSplineInterpolator
{
private:
        // ...
private:
        // Private member functions

public:
    CubicSplineInterpolator(const Vector<double, long> xarr,
                            const Vector<double, long> yarr,
                            CubicSplineBC BCType,
                            double alpha = 0.0,
                            double beta = 0.0);

    // Find the interpolated valued at a value x
    double Solve(double xvar) const;

    // Create the interpolated curve, MEMBER DATA AS ABSCISSAE
    Vector<double, long> Curve() const;
};
```

Test your add-in using examples from your own work. The source code for the CubicSpline is on the CD.

2. (**) My First Automation Add-in

In this exercise we use the exact solution of the Black-Scholes formula for put and call options, including the calculation of call and put prices and the sensitivities such as delta, gamma and theta. Use the full C++ code from the CD.

Answer the following questions:

(a) Design the user interface for this problem, in particular the input and output aspects; you will need to define option parameters (such as expiry and strike price), give them values and determine in which cells they are defined. Furthermore, the output cells contain the put and call option prices.

(b) Create an Automation add-in for the design in part (a). Use STL to hold your data structures.

(c) We now extend the add-in to support calculation of the option sensitivities: delta, gamma and vega. Print these values in Excel.

(d) Compare the solution with the solution if you had to do the exercise in VBA. Do you notice performance improvements and what can you say about code maintainability in these two languages?

3. (*****) COM Add-in

In Chapter 0 we developed a simple Monte Carlo framework to price one-factor plain options. We now wish to integrate this code with Excel using a COM add-in. In this case we wish to use the same data as in exercise 2 (namely, option parameters). The C++ code using the console for input and output was

```cpp
int main()
{
    // Create the basic SDE (Context class)
    double T = 30.0;
    Range<double> range (0.0, T);
    double initialCondition = 100.0;

    // Discrete stuff
    long N = 100;
    cout << "Number of subintervals: ";
    cin >> N;


    // Tell the Builder what kinds of SDE and FDM Types you want
    //SDEType {A, B, C, D};
    //FDMType {Euler, PC, CN, MIL, SIE, IE, DerivFree, FRKIto,
                                                           Fit};
    FDMTypeDBuilder fdmBuilder(FDMTypeDBuilder::D,
                               FDMTypeDBuilder::PC, N, range,
                               initialCondition,drift,
                               diffusion,
                               diffusionDerivative);


    // V2 mediator stuff
    long NSimulations = 50000;
    cout << "Number of simulations: ";
```

```
        cin >> NSimulations;

        double r = 0.08;
        cout << "Starting up the mediator...\n";

        try
        {
            MCTypeDMediator mediator(fdmBuilder, NSimulations, r, T,
                                                myPayOffFunction);

            cout << "Final Price: " << mediator.price() << endl;
    }
        catch(string& exception)
        { // CN, IE or IE cannot be used with NL/NL SDEs

            cout << exception << endl;
            cout << "Press any key to stop\n";
            int yy; cin >> yy;
            exit(1);
        }

        return 0;
}
```

The objective of this exercise is to get the same program running while using Excel as the input/output medium. Use the steps in section 27.4 to guide you.

References

Abrahams, D. and Gurtovoy, A. (2005) *C++ Template Metaprogramming*, Addison-Wesley, Reading, MA.

Abramowitz, M. and Stegun, I.A. (1974) *Handbook of Mathematical Functions: with Formulas, Graphs and Mathematical Tables*, Dover, New York.

Acklam, P.A. (2001) An algorithm for computing the inverse normal cumulative distribution function. home.online.no/~pjacklam/notes/invnorm/ (accessed 25th May).

Acworth, P., Broadie, M. and Glasserman, P. (1998) A comparison of some Monte Carlo and quasi Monte Carlo methods for option pricing, in *Monte Carlo and Quasi Monte Carlo Methods 1996*, edited by P. Hellekalek, F. Larcher, H. Niederreiter and P. Zinterhof, Springer, Berlin, pp. 1–18.

Adams, R.A. (1975) *Sobolev Spaces*, Academic Press, New York.

Ahrens, J.H. and Dieter, U. (1972) Computer Methods for Sampling from the Exponential and Normal Distributions, *Commun. ACM*, **15**(10), 873–882.

Ahrens, J.H. and Dieter, U. (1974) Computer Methods for Sampling from the Gamma, Beta, Poisson, and Binomial Distributions, *Computing*, **12**, 223–246.

Alexandrescu, A. (2001) *Modern C++ Design: Generic Programming and Design Patterns Applied*, Addison-Wesley, Reading, MA.

Andersen, L. (2006) Efficient Simulation of the Heston Stochastic Volatility Model, *preprint*.

Asmussen, S., Glynn, P. and Pitman, J. (1995) Discretization Error in Simulation of One-dimensional Reflecting Brownian Motion, *Annals of Applied Probability*, **38**, 482–493.

Barone-Adesi, G. and Whaley, R.E. (1987) Efficient Analytic Approximation of American Option Values, *Journal of Finance*, **42**(2), 301–320.

Bates, D. S. (1991) The Crash of '87: Was it Expected? The Evidence from Options Markets, *The Journal of Finance*, **XLVI**(3), July, 1009–1044.

Bates, D.S. (1996) Jumps and Stochastic Volatility: Exchange Rate Processes Implicit Deutsche Mark Options, *Review of Financial Studies*, **9**(1), 69–107.

Benhamou, E. (2002) Smart Monte Carlo: Various Tricks Using Malliavin Calculus, *Goldman Sachs Working Paper, EFA*.

Benth, F.E. (2004) *Option Theory with Stochastic Analysis: An Introduction to Mathematical Finance*, Springer, Berlin.

Berman, L. (1997) Accelerating Monte Carlo: Quasirandom Sequences and Variance Reduction, *Journal of Computational Finance*, **1**, 79–95.

Bharucha-Reid, A.T. (1972) *Random Integral Equations*, Academic Press, New York.

Bjerksund, P. and Stensland, P. (1993) American Exchange Options and a Put-Call Transformation: A Note, *Journal of Business Finance and Accounting*, **20**(5), 761–764.

Bjerksund, P. and Stensland, P. (2006) Closed Form Spread Option Valuation, *Technical Report, NHH Norway*.

Black, F. and Scholes, M. (1973) The Pricing of Options and Corporate Liabilities, *Journal of Political Economy*, **81**, 637–654.

Boyle, P., Broadie, M. and Glasserman, P. (1997) Monte Carlo Methods for Security Pricing, *Journal of Economic Dynamics and Control*, **21**, 241–250.

Box, G.E.P. and Muller, M.E. (1958) A Note on the Generation of Random Normal Deviates, *Annals of Mathematical Statistics*, **29**, 610–611.

Brandt, A. (1977) Multi-level Adaptive Solutions to Boundary Value Problems, *Math. Comput.*, **31**, 333–390.

Brigo, D. and Mercurio, F. (2006) *Interest Rate Models – Theory and Practice* (second edition), Springer, Berlin.

Broadie, M. and Glasserman, P. (2004) A Stochastic Mesh Method for Pricing High-dimensional American Options, *Journal of Computational Finance*, **7**(4), 35–72.

Broadie, M. and Kaya, O. (2006) Exact Simulation of Stochastic Volatility and Other Affine Jump Diffusion Processes, *Operations Research,* **54**(2), 217–231.

Bronson, R. (1989) *Theory and Problems of Matrix Operations*, Schaum's Outline Series, McGraw-Hill, New York.

Caps, O. (2007) On the Valuation of Power Reserve Duels and Equity Rates Hybrids, *Mathfinance Conference*, Frankfurt.

Cardelli, L. and Wegner, P. (1985) On Understanding Types, Data Abstractions and Polymorphism, *Computing Surveys*, **17**(4), 471–522.

Carter, M. and van Brunt, B. (2000) *The Lebesgue-Stieltjes Integral*, Springer, New York.

Chapman, B., Jost, G. and van der Pas, R. (2008) *Using OpenMP*, MIT Press, Cambridge, MA.

Chandra, R., Dagnum, L., Kohr, D., Maydan, D., McDonald, J. and Menon, R. (2001) *Parallel Programming in OpenMP*, Morgan Kaufmann, San Francisco, CA.

Cheng, R.C.H. (1977) The Generation of Gamma Variables, *Appl. Stat.*, **26**, 71–75.

Chay, S.C., Fardo, R.D. and Mazumdar, M. (1975) On Using the Box-Muller Transformation with Multiplicative Congruential Pseudo-random Number Generators, *Appl. Statist.*, **24**(1), 132.

Clewlow, L. and Strickland, C. (1998) *Implementing Derivatives Models*, John Wiley & Sons, Inc., New York.

Cont, R. and Tankov, P. (2004) *Financial Modelling with Jump Processes*, Chapman & Hall/CRC Press, Boca Raton, FL.

Coveyou, R. and MacPherson, R.D.R. (1967) Fourier Analysis of Uniform Random Number Generators, *J. Assoc. Comput. Mach. 2*, **14**, 100–199.

Cox, J. (1975) *Notes on Option Pricing I: Constant Elasticity of Variance Diffusion*, Stanford University.

Cox, J.C. and Ross, S.A. (1976) The Valuation of Options for Alternative Stochastic Processes, *Journal of Financial Economics*, **3**, 145–166.

Dahlquist, G. and Björck, Å. (1974) *Numerical Methods*, Prentice-Hall, New Jersey.

Davis, P.J. (1975) *Interpolation and Approximation*, Dover, New York.

Devroye, L. (1986) *Non-Uniform Random Variable Generation*, Springer, New York.

Dos Reis, G. and Stroustrup, B. (2006) Specifying C++ Concepts, *POPL '06*, 11–13 January, Charleston, South Carolina, USA.

Duffy, D.J. (1980) Uniformly Convergent Difference Schemes for Problems with a Small Parameter in the Leading Derivative, Ph.D. thesis, Trinity College, Dublin.

Duffy, D.J. (1995) *From Chaos to Classes*, McGraw-Hill, London.

Duffy, D.J. (2004a) *Financial Instrument Pricing in C++*, John Wiley & Sons, Ltd, Chichester, UK.

Duffy, D.J. (2004b) *Domain Architectures*, John Wiley & Sons, Ltd, Chichester, UK.

Duffy, D.J. (2006a) *Introduction to C++ for Financial Engineers*, John Wiley & Sons, Ltd, Chichester, UK.

Duffy, D.J. (2006b) *Finite Difference Methods in Financial Engineering*, John Wiley & Sons, Ltd, Chichester, UK.

Dumas, B., Fleming, J. and Whaley, R. (1998) Implied Volatility Functions: Empirical Tests, *Journal of Finance*, **53**, 2059–2106.

L'Ecuyer, P., Simard, R., Chen, E.J. and Kelton, W.D. (2002) An object-oriented random-number package with many long streams and substreams, *Operations Research*, **50**, 1073–1075.

Fabozzi, F.J. (1993) *Bond Markets*, Prentice Hall, New Jersey.

Fan, Y., Sarkar, S. and Lasdon, L. (1988) Experiments with Successive Quadratic Programming Algorithms, *J. Optim. Theory Appl.*, **56**, 356–383.

Faure, H. (1982) Discrepance de Suites Associees a un Systeme de Numeration (en dimension s), *Acta Arithmetica*, 337–351.

Fichera, G. (1956) Sullle equazioni differenziali lineari ellittico-paraboliche del secondo ordine, *Atti Accad. Naz. Lincei. Mem. CI. Sci. Fis. Mat. Nat. Sez.*, **I**(8), 5, 1–30; MR 19, 658, 1432.

Fishman, G.S. (1976) Sampling from the Gamma Distribution on a Computer, *Comm. Assoc. Comp. Mach.*, **19**, 407–409.

Fishman, G.S. (1996) *Monte Carlo Concepts, Algorithms and Applications*, Springer, New York.

Flavell, R. (2002) *Swaps and Other Derivatives*, John Wiley & Sons, Ltd, Chichester, UK.

Fournie, E., Lasry, J.M., Lebuchoux, J., Lions, P.L. and Touzi, N. (1999) Applications of Malliavin Calculus to Monte Carlo Methods in Finance, *Finance and Statistics*, **3**(4), 391–412.

Friedman, A. (1976) *Stochastic Differential Equations and Applications*, Dover, New York.

Fries, C. and Joshi, M. (2006) Partial Proxy Simulation Schemes for Generic and Robust Monte Carlo Greeks, www.christian-fries.de (accessed 25th May 2009).

Fries, C. and Kampen, J. (2005) Proxy Simulation Schemes for Generic and Robust Monte Carlo Sensitivities and High Accuracy Drift Approximation (with Applications to the Libor Market Model), *preprint*.

Fu, M. (2007) Variance-gamma and Monte Carlo, in *Implied and Numerical Harmonic Analysis: Advances in Mathematical Finance*, Springer, pp. 21–34.

Gander, W. and Gautschi, W. (2000) Adaptive Quadrature – Revisited, *BIT*, **40**(1), 84–101 (ftp.inf.ethz.ch/pub/publications/tech-reports/3xx/306.ps.gz).

Gatarek, D., Bachert, P. and Maksymuk, R. (2006) *The LIBOR Market Model in Practice*, John Wiley & Sons, Ltd, Chichester, UK.

Gatheral, J. (2006) *The Volatility Service*, John Wiley & Sons, Ltd, Chichester, UK.

Geman, H. (2005) *Commodities and Commodity Derivatives*, John Wiley & Sons, Ltd, Chichester, UK.

Gentle, E.J. (2003) *Random Number Generation and Monte Carlo Methods*, Springer, New York.

Ghanem, R.G. and Spanos, P.D. (1991) *Stochastic Finite Elements: A Spectral Approach*, Springer, New York.

Gikhmann, I.I. and Skorokhod, A.V. (1972) *Stochastic Differential Equations*, Springer, New York.

Glasserman, P. (2004) *Monte Carlo Methods in Financial Engineering*, Springer, New York.

Glasserman, P. and Chen, N. (2007) Additive and Multiplicative Duals for American Price Options, *Finance and Stochastics*, to appear, www2.gsb.columbia.edu/faculty/pglasserman/other/addmultduality.pdf (accessed 25th May 2009).

Gobet, E. (2004) A Repression-based Monte Carlo Method to Solve Backward Stochastic Differential Equations, *Annals of Applied Probability*, **15**(3) 2171–2202.

Gobet, E. and Kohatsu Higa, A. (2003) Computation of Greeks for Barrier and Lookback Options using Malliavin Calculus, *Electronic Communications in Probability*, **8**, 51–62.

GOF (1995) (Gamma, E., Helm, R., Johnson, R., Vlissides, J.) *Design Patterns, Elements of Reusable Object-Oriented Software*, Addison-Wesley, New Jersey.

Goldberg, S. (1986) *Introduction to Difference Equations*, Dover, New York.

Goldman, B., Sosin, H. and Gatto, M.A. (1979) Path-Dependent Options: But at the Low, Sell at the High, *Journal of Finance*, **34**, 1111–1127.

Golub, G. and van Loan, C.F. (1996) *Matrix Computations*, The Johns Hopkins University Press, Baltimore.

Gropp, W., Lusk, E. and Skjellum, A. (1997) *Using MPI Portable Parallel Programming with the Message-Passing Interface*, MIT Press, Cambridge, MA.

Guenther, M. and Kahl, C. (2004) Complete the Correlation Matrix. *SIAM Journal on Matrix Analysis and Applications*, www.math.uni-wuppertal.de/~kahl/publications/CompleteThe Correlation Matrix.pdf.

Haaser, N.B. and Sullivan, J.A. (1991) *Real Analysis*, van Nostrand Reinhold, New York.

Halton, J.H. (1960) On the Efficiency of Certain Quasi-random Sequences of Points in Evaluation and Multi-dimensional Integrals, *Numerische Mathematik*, **2**, 84–90.

Halton, J.H. and Smith, G.B. (1964) Algorithm 247: Radical Inverse Quasi-random Point Sequence, *Communications of the ACM*, **7**, 701–702.

Haug, E.G. (2007) *The Complete Guide to Option Pricing Formulae*, McGraw-Hill, New York.

Haugh, M. and Kogan, L. (2004) Pricing American Options: A Duality Approach, *Operations Research*, **52**(2), 258–270.

Henrici, P. (1962) *Discrete Variable Methods in Ordinary Differential Equations*, John Wiley & Sons, Ltd, Chichester, UK.

Heston, S.L. (1993) A Closed-Form Solution for Options with Stochastic Volatility with Applications to Bond and Currency Options, *The Review of Financial Studies*, **6**(2), 327–343.

Hsu, H. (1997) *Probability, Random Variables and Random Processes*, Schaum's Outline Series, McGraw-Hill, New York.

Hull, J. (2006) *Options, Futures and Other Derivative Securities*, Prentice-Hall, Englewood Cliffs, NJ.

Ince, E.L. (1967) *Integration of Ordinary Differential Equations*, Oliver and Boyd, Edinburgh, UK.

Ito, K. (1944) Stochastic Integral, *Proc. Imperial Acad.*, **20**, 519–524.

Jäckel, P. (2002) *Monte Carlo Methods in Finance*, John Wiley & Sons, Ltd, Chichester, UK.

Jäckel, P. (2005) *More Likely Than Not*, www.jaeckel.org/ (accessed 25th May 2009).

Jäckel, P. and Kahl, C. (2006) Not-so-complex Logarithms in the Heston Model, *Willmott Magazine*; and available at http://www.math.uni-wuppertal.de/~kahl/publications/NotSoComplexLogarithmsInTheHestonModel.pdf (accessed 29th May 2009).

Jin, X., Tan, H.H. and Sun, J. (2007) A State Space Partitioning Method for Pricing High-dimensional American Style Arrays, *Mathematical Finance*, **17**(3), 399–426.

Joer, S. and Kuo, F.Y. (2008) Constructing Sobol Sequences with Better Two-dimensional Projections, *SIAM J. Sci. Compt.*, **30**(5), 2635–2654.

Jöhnk, M.D. (1964) Erzeugungen von Betaversteilten und Gammaverteilten Zuffalszahlen *Metrika*, **8**, 5–15 (in German).

Joshi, M. (2007) *xlw plus: A System for Building xlls Without Pain*, XLW Plus Documentation and University of Melbourne and http://www.nuclearphynance.com/User%20Files/87/xlw.pdf (accessed 29th May 2009).

Josuttis, N. (1999) *The C++ Standard Library*, Addison-Wesley, New Jersey.

Karatsas, I. and Shreve, S.E. (1991) *Brownian Motion and Stochastic Calculus*, Springer, New York.

Karhunen, K. (1947) Über lineare methoden in der wahrscheinlichkeitsrechnung, *Amer. Acad. Sci. Fennicade, Ser. A, I.*, **37**, 3–79.

Karlsson, B. (2006) *Beyond the C++ Standard Library, An Introduction to Boost*, Addison-Wesley, New Jersey.

Kemma, A. and Vorst, A. (1990) A Pricing Method for Options Based on Average Asset Values, *Journal of Banking and Finance*, **14**, 113–129.

Kernighan, B.W. and Ritchie, D. (1988) *The C Programming Language*, Prentice Hall, New Jersey.

Kienitz, J. (2007a) Stochastic Processes in Finance I, *Willmott Magazine*, **29**.

Kienitz, J. (2007b) Stochastic Processes in Finance II, *Willmott Magazine*, **33**.

Kienitz, J. (2008) A Note on Monte Carlo Greeks for Jump Diffusions and Other Lévy Models, http://papers.ssrn.com/sol3/papers.cfm?abstract_id=1253265 (accessed 29th May 2009).

Kienitz, J. (2009) Stochastic Processes in Finance III, *Willmott Magazine* (forthcoming).

Kirkpatrick, S., Gelatt, C.D. and Vecchi, P. (1983) Optimization of Simulated Annealing, *Science*, **220**(4598), 671–680.

Klahr, C.N. (1960) A Monte Carlo Method for the Solution of Elliptic Partial Differential Equations, in *Mathematical Methods for Digital Computers*, edited by A. Ralston and H.S. Wilf, John Wiley & Sons Inc., New York.

Kloeden, P.E. and Platen, E. (1995) *Numerical Solution of Stochastic Differential Equations*, Springer, Berlin.

Kloeden, P.E., Platen, E. and Schurz, H. (1997) Numerical Solution of SDE Through Computer Experiments, Springer, Berlin.

Knuth, D.E. (1997) *The Art of Computer Programming* (third edition), Addison-Wesley, New Jersey.

Kohatsu Higa, A. and Montero, M. (2003) Malliavin Calculus Applied to Finance, *Physica A*, **320**, 548–578.

Kreiss, H.O. (1970) Initial Boundary Value Problems for Hyperbolic Systems, *Comm. Pure Appl. Math.* **23**, 277–298.

Lambert, J.D. (1991) *Numerical Methods for Ordinary Differential Equations*, John Wiley & Sons, Ltd, Chichester, UK.

Landgraaf, P.K. (2007) *PDE Valuation of Interest Rate Derivatives*, Books On Demand.

Lewis, A. (2000) *Option Valuation under Stochastic Volatility*, Finance Press.

Lewis, T.G. and Payne, W.H. (1973) Generalized Feedback Shift Register Pseudorandom Number Algorithm, *Journal of the Association for Computing Machinery*, **20**(3), 456–468.

Liniger, W. and Willoughby, R.A. (1970) Efficient Integration Methods for Stiff Systems of Ordinary Differential Equations, *SIAM J. Numer. Anal.*, **7**, 47–66.

Longstaff, F.A. and Schwartz, E.S. (2001) Valuing American Options by Simulation: A Simple Least-Squares Approach, *The Review of Financial Studies*, **14**(1) 113–147.

Maghsoodi, Y. (1998) Exact Solution and Doubly Efficient Approximations of Jump-diffusion Ito Equations, *Stochastic Analysis and Applications* **16**, 1049–1072.

Matsumoto, M. and Kurita, Y. (1992) Twisted GFSR Generators, *Research Institute of Mathematical Sciences*, Kyoto University.

Matsumoto, M. and Nishimura, T. (1998) Mersenne Twister: A 623-Dimensionally Equidistributed Uniform Pseudo-Random Number Generator, *ACM Transactions on Modeling and Computer Simulations: Special Issue on Uniform Random Number Generation*, **8**(1), 3–30.

Mattson, T.G., Sanders, B.A. and Massingill, B.L. (2005) *Patterns for Parallel Programming*, Addison-Wesley, Reading, MA.

Merton, R. (1973) Theory of Rational Option Pricing, *Bell Journal of Economics and Management Science*, **4**, 141–144.

Merton, R. (1976) Option Pricing when Underlying Stock Returns are Discontinuous, *Journal of Financial Economics*, May, 125–144.

Mikosch, T. (1999) *Elementary Stochastic Calculus*, World Scientific, Singapore.

Moro, B. (1995) The Full Monte, *Risk Magazine*, **8**(2), 57–58.

Morokoff, W.J. (1998) Generating Quasi-Random Paths for Stochastic Processes, *SIAM Review*, **40**(4), 765–788.

Musiela, M. and Rutkowski, M. (2004) *Martingale Methods in Finance* (second edition), Springer, Berlin.

Neave, H.R. (1973) On Using the Box-Muller Transformation with Multiplicative Congruential Pseudo-random Number Generators, *Appl. Statist.*, **22**, 92–97.

Nefcti, S. (1996) *An Introduction to the Mathematics of Financial Derivatives*, Academic Press.

Niederreiter, H. (1998) Low-discrepancy and Low-dispersion Sequences, *Journal of Number Theory*, **30**, 51–70.

Nocedal, J. (1989) Updating Quasi-Newton Matrices with Limited Storage, *Math. Comp.*, **24**, 773–782.

Nualart, D (1995) *Malliavin Calculus and Related Topics*, Springer, New York.

Øksendal, B. (1998) *Stochastic Differential Equations*, Springer, Berlin.

Oleinik, O.A and Radkevič, E.V. (1973) *Second Order Equations with Nonnegative Characteristic Form*, American Mathematical Society, Providence.

Oseledets, V.I. (1968) Multiplicative Ergodic Theorem: Characteristic Lyapunov Exponents of Dynamical Systems, *Trudy MMO*, **19**, 179–210 (in Russian).

Overhaus, M., Bermudez, A., Buehler, H., Ferraris, A., Jordinson, C. and Lamnouar, A. (2007) *Equity Hybrid Derivatives*, Wiley & Sons, Inc., New Jersey.

Paskov, S.H. (1997) *Computing High Dimensional Integrals with Applications to Finance*, Technical Report CUCS-023-94.

Paskov, S.H. and Traub, J.F. (1995) Faster Valuation of Financial Derivatives, *J. Portfolio Management*, **22**, 113–120.

Petersen, W.P. and Arbenz, P. (2004) *Introduction to Parallel Computing, A Practical Guide with Examples in C*, Oxford University Press, Oxford.

Pilipović, D. (2007) *Energy Risk: Valuing and Managing Energy Derivatives* (second edition), McGraw-Hill, New York.

Platen, E. and Shi, L. (2008) *On the Numerical Stability of Simulation Methods for SDEs*, Research paper 234, University of Technology, Sydney.

POSA (1996) (Buschmann, F., Meunier, R., Rohnert, H., Sommerlad, P., Stal, M.) *Pattern-Oriented Software Architecture: A System of Patterns*, John Wiley & Sons, Ltd, Chichester, UK.

Press, W.H., Teukolsky, S.A., Vetterling, W.T. and Flannery, B.P. (2002) *Numerical Recipes in C++* (second edition), Cambridge University Press, Cambridge.

Price, K., Storn, R. and Lampinen, J.A. (2005) *Differential Evolution*, Springer, New York.

Quinn, M.J. (2004) *Parallel Programming in C with MPI and OpenMP*, McGraw-Hill, Boston, MA.

Radovic, I., Sobol, I.M. and Tichy, R.F. (1996) Quasi-Monte Carlo Methods for Numerical Integration: Comparison of Different Low Discrepancy Sequences, *Monte Carlo Methods Appl.*, **2**(1) 1–14.

Rall, L.B. (1969) *Computational Solution of Nonlinear Operator Equations*, John Wiley & Sons, Ltd, Chichester, UK.

Rannacher, R. (1984) Finite Element Solution of Diffusion Problems with Irregular Data, *Numerische Mathematik*, **43**, 309–327.

Reiner, E. and Rubinstein, M. (1992) Exotic Options, *Working Paper*.

Ribeiro, C. and Webber, N. (2007) A Monte Carlo Method for the Normal Inverse Gaussian Option Valuation Model Using an Inverse Gaussian Bridge, www2.warwick.ac.uk/fac/soc/wbs/research/wfri/rsrchcentres/forc/preprintseries/pp_04.133.pdf (accessed 25th May 2009).

Rivlin, T.J. (1969) *An Introduction to the Approximation of Functions*, Dover, New York.

Rogers, L.C.G. (2002) Monte Carlo Valuation of American Options, *Mathematical Finance*, **12**(3), 271–286.

Rubinstein, R.Y. (1981) *Simulation and the Monte Carlo Method*, John Wiley & Sons, Ltd, Chichester, UK.

Rudin, W. (1964) *Principles of Mathematical Analysis*, Interscience, New York.

Rudin, W. (1970) *Real and Complex Analysis*, McGraw-Hill, London.

Saito, Y. and Mitsui, T. (1996) Stability Analysis of Numerical Schemes for Stochastic Differential Equations, *SIAM J. Numer. Anal.*, **33**(6), 2254–2267.

Sauly'ev, V.K. (1964) *Integration of Equations of Parabolic Type by the Method of Nets*, Pergamon Press, Oxford.

Schmitz, K. A. and Shaw, W. T. (2005) Measure Order of Convergence without an Exact Solution, Euler versus Milstein, *Second International Conference of Applied Mathematics*, Plovdiv, Bulgaria

Schoutens, W. (2003) *Levy Process in Finance – Pricing Financial Derivatives*, Wiley Series in Probability and Stochastics, John Wiley & Sons, Ltd, Chichester, UK.

Schoutens, W., Simons, E. and Tistaert, J. (2004) A Perfect Calibration! Now What?, *Wilmott Magazine*, 2.

Schroder, M. (1989) Computing the Constant Elasticity of Variance Option Pricing Formula, *Journal of Finance*, **44**(1), 211–219.

Schrage, L. (1979) A More Portable Fortran Random Number Generator, *ACM Trans. Math. Software*, **5**(2), 132–138.

Sheppard, R. (2007) Pricing Equity Derivatives under Stochastic Volatility: A Partial Differential Equation Approach, MSc thesis, University of the Witswatersrand, Johannesburg, South Africa.

Shreve, S. (2004) *Stochastic Calculus for Finance II: Continuous-Time Models*, Springer, New York.

Skorokhod, A.V. (1982) *Studies in the Theory of Random Processes*, Dover, New York.

Smart, D.R. (1974) *Fixed Point Theorems*, Cambridge University Press, Cambridge.

Sobol, I. (1977) Uniformly Distributed Sequences with Additional Uniform Properties, *USSR Computation Mathematics and Mathematical Physics*, **16**, 236–242.

Sobol, I. and Levitan, Y.L. (1976) The Production of Points Uniformly Distributed in a Multidimensional Cube (in Russian), *Preprint IPM Akad. Nuak SSSR, Moscow*, **40**.

Sobol, I.M. (1994) *A Primer for the Monte Carlo Method*, CRC Press, Boca Raton, FL.

Spiegel, M. (1969) *Theory and Problems of Real Variables*, Schaum's Outline Series, McGraw-Hill, New York.

Stoer, J. and Bulirsch, R. (1980) *Introduction to Numerical Analysis*, Springer, Berlin.

Stroustrup, B. (1997) *The C++ Programming Language* (third edition), Addison-Wesley, Reading, MA.

Tannehill, J.C., Anderson, D.A. and Pletcher, R.H. (1997) *Computational Fluid Mechanics and Heat Transfer* (third edition), Taylor & Francis, Philadelphia, PA.

Tausworthe, R.C. (1965) Random Numbers Generated by Linear Recurrence Modulo Two, *Mathematics of Computation*, **19**, 201–209.

Tavella, D. and Randall, C. (2000) *Pricing Financial Instruments: The Finite Difference Method*, John Wiley & Sons, Ltd, Chichester, UK.

Thomée, V. and Wahlbin (1974) Convergence Rates of Parabolic Difference Schemes for Non-smooth Data, *Math Comp.*, **28**(125), 1–13.

Tolstov, G.P. (1962) *Fourier Series*, Dover, New York.

Tricomi, F.G. (1985) *Integral Equations*, Dover, New York.

Tsokos, C. and Padgett, W.J. (1974) *Random Integral Equations with Applications to Life Sciences and Engineering*, Academic Press.

Turnbull, S.M. and Wakeman, L.M. (1991) A Quick Algorithm for Pricing European Average Options *Journal of Financial and Quantitative Analysis*, **26**, 377–389.

Varga, R. (1962) *Matrix Iterative Analysis*, Prentice Hall, New Jersey.

Veldhuizen, T. (1995) *Using C++ Template Metaprograms*, SIGS Publications Inc, New York.

Voigt, R.G. (editor) (1984) *Spectral Methods for Partial Differential Equations*, SIAM, Philadelphia.

Wang, X. and Fang, K.-T. (2003) The Effective Dimension and Quasi-Monte Carlo Integration, *Journal of Complexity*, **19**, 101–124.

Widder, D.V. (1989) *Advanced Calculus*, Dover, New York.

Wilmott, P., Howison, S. and Dewynne, J. (1995) *The Mathematics of Financial Derivatives*, Cambridge University Press, Cambridge.

Wong, H.Y. and Jing, Z. (2008) An Artificial Boundary Method for American Option Pricing under the CEV Model, *SIAM J. Numerical Analysis*, **46**(4), May, 2183–2209.

Xiu, D. and Karniadakis, G. (2002) The Wiener–Askey Polynomial Chaos for Stochastic Differential Equations, *SIAM Journal on Scientific Computing*, **24**(2), 619–644.

XLW (1997) xlw.sourceforge.net (accessed 29th May 2009).

Index

Printed and bound by CPI Group (UK) Ltd, Croydon, CR0 4YY

27/10/2024

14580374-0004